# The Science of Gun Policy

## A Critical Synthesis of Research Evidence on the Effects of Gun Policies in the United States

A PART OF THE RAND
Gun Policy in AMERICA
INITIATIVE

RAND CORPORATION

For more information on this publication, visit www.rand.org/t/RR2088

Library of Congress Cataloging-in-Publication Data

Names: Rand Corporation, issuing body.
Title: The science of gun policy : a critical synthesis of research evidence on the effects of gun policies in the United States / The RAND Corporation.
Description: Santa Monica, CA : RAND, [2018] | Includes bibliographical references.
Identifiers: LCCN 2017060115| ISBN 9780833098412 (pbk. : alk. paper) | ISBN 9780833098436 (epub) | ISBN 9780833098443 (prc) | ISBN 9780833098429 (ebook pdf)
Subjects: LCSH: Gun control--United States.
Classification: LCC HV7436 .S387 2018 | DDC 363.330973--dc23
LC record available at https://lccn.loc.gov/2017060115

Published by the RAND Corporation, Santa Monica, Calif.

# Gun Policy in America Research Synthesis Project Team

**Project Director**
Andrew R. Morral, Ph.D.

**Research Synthesis Project Leadership**
Rajeev Ramchand, Ph.D.
Rosanna Smart, Ph.D.

**Literature Review Groups**

*Suicides*
Rajeev Ramchand, Ph.D.

*Homicides and Violent Crime*
Carole Roan Gresenz, Ph.D.
John Speed Meyers, M.P.A.
Rouslan I. Karimov, M.P.A.
Lea Xenakis, M.P.A.

*Accidents and Unintentional Injuries*
Eric Apaydin, M.P.P.
Rajeev Ramchand, Ph.D.

*Mass Shootings and Taxation*
Rosanna Smart, Ph.D.

*Officer-Involved Shootings*
Carter C. Price, Ph.D.

*Defensive Gun Use*
Nancy Nicosia, Ph.D.
John Speed Meyers, M.P.A.

*Hunting and Sport Shooting*
Rosanna Smart, Ph.D.
Eric Apaydin, M.P.P.

*Gun Industry*
Carter C. Price, Ph.D.

*Mental Health*
Stephanie Brooks Holliday, Ph.D.

*Public Information Campaigns*
Elizabeth L. Petrun Sayers, Ph.D.

**Policy Descriptions**
Samantha Cherney, J.D.
Rosanna Smart, Ph.D.

**Methodology Review**
Carole Roan Gresenz, Ph.D.
Beth Ann Griffin, Ph.D.
Andrew R. Morral, Ph.D.
Nancy Nicosia, Ph.D.
Rajeev Ramchand, Ph.D.
Terry L. Schell, Ph.D.
Rosanna Smart, Ph.D.

**Effect-Size Calculation**
Brett Ewing, M.S.

**Programming**
Joshua Lawrence Traub, M.S.

# Preface

Effective gun policies in the United States must balance the constitutional right to bear arms and public interest in gun ownership with concerns about public health and safety. However, current efforts to craft legislation related to guns are hampered by a paucity of reliable information about the effects of such policies. To help address this problem, the RAND Corporation launched the Gun Policy in America initiative. Throughout RAND's 70-year history, in multiple projects, in many policy arenas, and on topics that are sensitive and controversial, researchers have conducted analyses, built tools, and developed resources to help policymakers and the public make effective decisions. The primary goal of the Gun Policy in America project is to create resources where policymakers and the general public can access unbiased information that facilitates the development of fair and effective firearm policies.

This report is one of several research products stemming from the initiative. The research described here synthesizes the available scientific evidence on the effects of 13 types of firearm policies on a range of outcomes related to gun ownership. In addition, this report includes essays on several topics that frequently arise in discussions of gun policy.

Other project components include a survey of policy experts that identifies where access to reliable data would be most useful in resolving policy debates, plus an online tool allowing users to explore how different combinations of gun policies are likely to affect a range of outcomes. In another line of effort, RAND conducted simulation studies to evaluate the strengths and weaknesses of different approaches to modeling the effects of gun policies on outcomes, the results of which will be used to develop new estimates of the effects of state firearm policies. Finally, the project includes the development of a longitudinal database of state firearm laws as a resource for other researchers and the public.

The Gun Policy in America initiative did not attempt to evaluate the merits of different values or principles that sometimes drive policy disagreements. Rather, our focus is strictly on the empirical effects of policies on the eight outcomes specified in this report. All of our resources are publicly available on the project website at www.rand.org/gunpolicy.

The work should be of interest to policymakers and other stakeholders considering decisions related to firearm policy. Furthermore, this report may be of interest to the research community and to the general public.

## RAND Ventures

The RAND Corporation is a research organization that develops solutions to public policy challenges to help make communities throughout the world safer and more secure, healthier and more prosperous. RAND is nonprofit, nonpartisan, and committed to the public interest.

RAND Ventures is a vehicle for investing in such policy solutions. Philanthropic contributions support our ability to take the long view, tackle tough and often-controversial topics, and share our findings in innovative and compelling ways. RAND's research findings and recommendations are based on data and evidence and therefore do not necessarily reflect the policy preferences or interests of its clients, donors, or supporters.

Funding for this venture was provided by gifts from RAND supporters and income from operations.

# Contents

# Figures

# Tables

# Summary

The RAND Corporation's Gun Policy in America initiative is a unique attempt to systematically and transparently assess available scientific evidence on the real effects of gun laws and policies. Our goal is to create resources where policymakers and the general public can access unbiased information that informs and enables the development of fair and effective policies. Good gun policies in the United States require consideration of many factors, including the law and constitutional rights, the interests of various stakeholder groups, and information about the likely effects of different policies on a range of outcomes. This report seeks to provide the third factor—objective information about what the scientific literature examining gun policies can tell us about the likely effects of those policies.

This report synthesizes the available scientific evidence on the effects of various gun policies on firearm deaths, violent crime, the gun industry, participation in hunting and sport shooting, and other outcomes.[1] It builds and expands on earlier comprehensive reviews of scientific evidence on gun policy conducted more than a decade ago by the National Research Council (NRC) (see NRC, 2004) and the Community Preventive Services Task Force (see Hahn et al., 2005).

## Methodology

We used Royal Society of Medicine guidelines for conducting systematic reviews of a scientific literature (Khan et al., 2003). We focused on the empirical literature assessing the effects of 13 classes of firearm policies or of the prevalence of firearms on any of eight outcomes, which include both public health outcomes and outcomes of concern to many gun owners. We reviewed scientific reports that have been published since 2003, a date chosen to capture studies conducted since the last major systematic reviews of the science of gun policy were published by NRC (2004) and Hahn et al. (2005).

---

1 Although not all guns are firearms, in this report, we follow conventional use in U.S. policy discussions and treat the terms *gun* and *firearm* as interchangeable.

The 13 classes of gun policies considered in this research are as follows:

1. background checks
2. bans on the sale of assault weapons and high-capacity magazines
3. stand-your-ground laws
4. prohibitions associated with mental illness
5. lost or stolen firearm reporting requirements
6. licensing and permitting requirements
7. firearm sales reporting and recording requirements
8. child-access prevention laws
9. surrender of firearms by prohibited possessors
10. minimum age requirements
11. concealed-carry laws
12. waiting periods
13. gun-free zones.

The eight outcomes considered in this research are

1. suicide
2. violent crime
3. unintentional injuries and deaths
4. mass shootings
5. officer-involved shootings
6. defensive gun use
7. hunting and recreation
8. gun industry.[2]

## Policy Analyses, by Outcome

Building on the earlier reviews (NRC, 2004; Hahn et al., 2005) and using standardized and explicit criteria for determining the strength of evidence that individual studies provide for the effects of gun policies, we produced research syntheses that describe the quality and findings of the best available scientific evidence. Each synthesis defines the class of policies being considered; presents and rates the available evidence; and describes what conclusions, if any, can be drawn about the policy's effects on outcomes.

In many cases, we were unable to identify any research that met our criteria for considering a study as providing minimally persuasive evidence for a policy's effects. Studies were excluded from this review if they offered only correlational evidence for a

[2] The terms in these lists describe broad categories of policies and outcomes that are defined and described in detail in the full report.

possible causal effect of the law, such as showing that states with a specific law had lower firearm suicides at a single point in time than states without the law. Correlations like these can occur for many reasons other than the effects of a single law, so this kind of evidence provides little information about the effects attributable to specific laws. We did not exclude studies on the basis of their findings, only on the basis of their methods for isolating causal effects. For studies that met our inclusion criteria, we summarize key findings and methodological weaknesses, when present, and provide our consensus judgment on the overall strength of the available scientific evidence. We did this by establishing the following relativistic scale describing the strength of available evidence:

1. *No studies.* This designation was made when no studies meeting our inclusion criteria evaluated the policy's effect on the outcome.
2. *Inconclusive evidence.* This designation was made when studies with comparable methodological rigor identified inconsistent evidence for the policy's effect on an outcome or when a single study found only uncertain or suggestive effects.
3. *Limited evidence.* This designation was made when at least one study meeting our inclusion criteria and not otherwise compromised by serious methodological problems reported a significant effect of the policy on the outcome, even if other studies meeting our inclusion criteria identified only uncertain or suggestive evidence for the effect of the policy.
4. *Moderate evidence.* This designation was made when two or more studies found significant effects in the same direction and contradictory evidence was not found in other studies with equivalent or strong methods.
5. *Supportive evidence.* This designation was made when (1) at least three studies found suggestive or significant effects in the same direction using at least two independent data sets or (2) the effect was observed in a rigorous experimental study.

These ratings are meant to describe the relative strengths of evidence available across gun policy research domains, not any rating of our absolute confidence in the reported effects. For instance, when we find *supportive* evidence for the conclusion that child-access prevention laws reduce self-inflicted injuries and deaths, we do not mean to suggest that it is comparable to the evidence available in more-developed fields of social science. That is, in comparison to the evidence that smoking causes cancer, the evidence base in gun policy research is very limited. Nevertheless, we believe that it may be valuable to the public and to policymakers to understand which laws currently have more or less persuasive evidence concerning the effects the laws are likely to produce.

Table S.1 summarizes our judgments for all policy and outcome pairings. Several outcomes show multiple judgments, and these correspond to different characterizations of the specific policy-outcome association. For instance, we identified limited evidence that background checks reduce *total suicides* and moderate evidence that they reduce *firearm suicides.*

**Table S.1**
**Strength of Evidence Across Gun Policies and Outcomes**

| | Background Checks | Bans on the Sale of Assault Weapons and High-Capacity Magazines | Stand-Your-Ground Laws | Prohibitions Associated with Mental Illness | Lost or Stolen Firearm Reporting Requirements | Licensing and Permitting Requirements | Firearm Sales Reporting and Recording Requirements | Child-Access Prevention Laws | Surrender of Firearms by Prohibited Possessors | Minimum Age Requirements | | Concealed-Carry Laws | | Waiting Periods | Gun-Free Zones |
|---|---|---|---|---|---|---|---|---|---|---|---|---|---|---|---|
| | | | | | | | | | | Purchasing | Possessing | Shall Issue | Permitless Carry | | |
| Suicide | | | | | | | | | | | | | | | |
| Total suicides | ↓ L | | I | ↓ L | | I | | ↓ L | | I | I | I | | | |
| Firearm suicides | ↓ M | | I | ↓ L | | I | | ↓ M | | | I | I | | | |
| Firearm suicides among children | | | | | | | | | | ↓ L | | | | | |
| Firearm self-injuries (nonfatal) | | | | | | | | | | | | I | | | |
| Firearm self-injuries (including suicides) | | | | | | | | ↓ S | | | | | | | |
| Violent crime | ↓ L | | | ↓ M | | | | I | I | | | ↑ L | | I | |
| Total homicides | ↓ L | I | ↑ M | ↓ L | | I | | | | I | I | I | | | |
| Firearm homicides | ↓ M, I[a] | I | ↑ L | I | | I | | I | | I | I | I | | | |
| Intimate partner homicides | | | | | | | | | I | | | | | I | |
| Robberies | | | | | | | | | | | | I | | | |
| Assaults | | | | | | | | | | | | I | | | |
| Rapes | | | | | | | | | | | | I | | | |
| Other violent crime | | | I | | | | | | | | | | | | |

**Table S.1—Continued**

| | Background Checks | Bans on the Sale of Assault Weapons and High-Capacity Magazines | Stand-Your-Ground Laws | Prohibitions Associated with Mental Illness | Lost or Stolen Firearm Reporting Requirements | Licensing and Permitting Requirements | Firearm Sales Reporting and Recording Requirements | Child-Access Prevention Laws | Surrender of Firearms by Prohibited Possessors | Minimum Age Requirements | | Concealed-Carry Laws | | Waiting Periods | Gun-Free Zones |
|---|---|---|---|---|---|---|---|---|---|---|---|---|---|---|---|
| | | | | | | | | | | Purchasing | Possessing | Shall Issue | Permitless Carry | | |
| Unintentional injuries and deaths | | | | | | | | | | | | | | | |
| Unintentional firearm deaths | | | | | | | | | | | I | | | | |
| Unintentional firearm injuries and deaths among adults | | | | | | | | ↓ L | | | | | | | |
| Unintentional firearm injuries and deaths among children | | | | | | | | ↓ S | | | | | | | |
| Unintentional firearm injuries among adults | | | | | | | | | | | | ↑ L | | | |
| Unintentional firearm injuries among children | | | | | | | | | | | | I | | | |
| Mass shootings | I | I | | | | I | | I | | I | | I | I | I | |
| Officer-involved shootings | | | | | | | | | | | | | | | |
| Defensive gun use | | | I | | | | | | | | | | | | |
| Hunting and recreation | | | | | | | | | | | | | | | |

**Table S.1—Continued**

| | Background Checks | Bans on the Sale of Assault Weapons and High-Capacity Magazines | Stand-Your-Ground Laws | Prohibitions Associated with Mental Illness | Lost or Stolen Firearm Reporting Requirements | Licensing and Permitting Requirements | Firearm Sales Reporting and Recording Requirements | Child-Access Prevention Laws | Surrender of Firearms by Prohibited Possessors | Minimum Age Requirements | | Concealed-Carry Laws | | Waiting Periods | Gun-Free Zones |
|---|---|---|---|---|---|---|---|---|---|---|---|---|---|---|---|
| | | | | | | | | | | Purchasing | Possessing | Shall Issue | Permitless Carry | | |
| Gun industry | | | | | | | | | | | | | | | |
| Gun ownership | | | | | | | | | | | | I | | | |
| Prices of banned firearms in the short term | | ↑ L | | | | | | | | | | | | | |

NOTE: I = inconclusive; L = limited; M = moderate; S = supportive. When we identified no studies meeting eligibility criteria, cells are blank. ↑ = the policy increases the outcome; ↓ = the policy decreases the outcome.

[a] We concluded that there is moderate evidence that dealer background checks decrease firearm homicides, and there is inconclusive evidence for the effect of private-seller background checks on firearm homicides.

Rather than concerning how strong a policy's effects are, our findings concern the strength of the available scientific evidence examining those effects. Thus, even when the available evidence is limited, the actual effect of the policy may be strong. Presumably, every policy has some effect on a range of outcomes, however small or unintended. Until researchers design studies that can detect these effects, available evidence is likely to remain inconclusive or limited. But this fact should not be confused with the conclusion that the policies themselves have limited effects. They may or may not have the effects they were designed to produce; available scientific research cannot yet answer that question. Moreover, even a policy with a small effect may nevertheless be beneficial to society or worth its costs. For instance, a policy that reduces firearm deaths by just a few percentage points could save more than 1,000 lives per year. This kind of "small" effect might be very difficult to detect with existing study methods but could represent an important contribution to public health and safety.

## Supplementary Essays

The 13 types of policies reviewed in this report and the scope of the systematic review for the research synthesis were selected a priori and represent the central focus of our research synthesis efforts. Nevertheless, in reviewing evidence on these policies, other important themes emerged that the research team believed provided useful context for the policies or that were frequently cited in gun policy debates. Thus, we also researched what rigorous studies reveal about

- the possible mechanisms by which laws may affect outcomes
- how taxes, access to health care, and media campaigns might affect gun violence
- the effectiveness of laws used to target domestic violence
- methodological challenges in defining and estimating the prevalence of mass shootings and defensive gun use
- how suicide, violence, and mass shootings were affected by Australia's implementation of the National Firearms Agreement.

## Conclusions and Recommendations

Of more than 100 combinations of policies and outcomes, we found that surprisingly few were the subject of methodologically rigorous investigation. Notably, research into four of our outcomes was essentially unavailable, with three of these four outcomes—defensive gun use, hunting and recreation, and the gun industry—representing issues of particular concern to gun owners or gun industry stakeholders. Here, we summarize the key conclusions and recommendations that can be drawn from the policy-outcome combinations with the strongest available evidence (conclusions 1 through 8). Thereafter, we draw conclusions and recommendations concerning how to improve evidence on the effects of gun policies (conclusions 9 through 13).

### Conclusions and Recommendations Based on the Existing Evidence Base

Our first set of conclusions and recommendations describes the policy-outcome combinations with the strongest available evidence as identified through our review of the existing literature, as well as recommendations for policy based on this evidence.

**Conclusion 1**. Available evidence supports the conclusion that child-access prevention laws, or safe storage laws, reduce self-inflicted fatal or nonfatal firearm injuries among youth. There is moderate evidence that these laws reduce firearm suicides among youth and limited evidence that the laws reduce total (i.e., firearm and nonfirearm) suicides among youth.

**Conclusion 2**. Available evidence supports the conclusion that child-access prevention laws, or safe storage laws, reduce unintentional firearm injuries or unintentional firearm deaths among children. In addition, there is limited evidence that these laws may reduce unintentional firearm injuries among adults.

> *Recommendation 1.* States without child-access prevention laws should consider adopting them as a strategy to reduce firearm suicides and unintentional firearm injuries and deaths. We note, however, that scientific research cannot, at present, address whether these laws might increase or decrease crime or rates of legal defensive gun use.

> *Recommendation 2.* When considering adopting or refining child-access prevention laws, states should consider making child access to firearms a felony; there is some evidence that felony laws may have the greatest effects on unintentional firearm deaths.

**Conclusion 3**. There is moderate evidence that background checks reduce firearm suicides and firearm homicides, as well as limited evidence that these policies can reduce overall suicide and violent crime rates.

**Conclusion 4**. There is moderate evidence that stand-your-ground laws may increase state homicide rates and limited evidence that the laws increase firearm homicides in particular.

**Conclusion 5**. There is moderate evidence that laws prohibiting the purchase or possession of guns by individuals with some forms of mental illness reduce violent crime, and there is limited evidence that such laws reduce homicides in particular. There is also limited evidence these laws may reduce total suicides and firearm suicides.

> *Recommendation 3.* States that currently do not require a background check investigating all types of mental health histories that lead to federal prohibi-

tions on firearm purchase or possession should consider implementing robust mental illness checks, which appear to reduce rates of gun violence. The most robust procedures involve sharing data on all prohibited possessors with the National Instant Criminal Background Check System.

**Conclusion 6**. There is limited evidence that before implementation of a ban on the sale of assault weapons and high-capacity magazines, there is an increase in the sales and prices of the products that the ban will prohibit.

**Conclusion 7**. There is limited evidence that a minimum age of 21 for purchasing firearms may reduce firearm suicides among youth.

**Conclusion 8**. No studies meeting our inclusion criteria have examined required reporting of lost or stolen firearms, required reporting and recording of firearm sales, or gun-free zones.

#### Conclusions and Recommendations for Improving Gun Policy Research

Based on our review of the existing literature on the effects of firearm policy changes, we offer the following conclusions and recommendations for improving the evidence base on the effects of gun laws.

**Conclusion 9**. The modest growth in knowledge about the effects of gun policy over the past dozen years reflects, in part, the reluctance of the U.S. government to sponsor work in this area at levels comparable to its investment in other areas of public safety and health, such as transportation safety.

> *Recommendation 4*. To improve understanding of the real effects of gun policies, Congress should consider whether to lift current restrictions in appropriations legislation, and the administration should invest in firearm research portfolios at the Centers for Disease Control and Prevention, the National Institutes of Health, and the National Institute of Justice at levels comparable to its current investment in other threats to public safety and health.

> *Recommendation 5*. Given current limitations in the availability of federal support for gun policy research, private foundations should take further steps to help fill this funding gap by supporting efforts to improve and expand data collection and research on gun policies.

**Conclusion 10**. Research examining the effects of gun policies on officer-involved shootings, defensive gun use, hunting and recreation, and the gun industry is virtually nonexistent.

> *Recommendation 6*. To improve understanding of outcomes of critical concern to many in gun policy debates, the U.S. government and private research sponsors should support research examining the effects of gun laws on a wider

set of outcomes, including crime, defensive gun use, hunting and sport shooting, officer-involved shootings, and the gun industry.

**Conclusion 11**. The lack of data on gun ownership and availability and on guns in legal and illegal markets severely limits the quality of existing research.

*Recommendation 7.* To make important advances in understanding the effects of gun laws, the Centers for Disease Control and Prevention or another federal agency should resume collecting voluntarily provided survey data on gun ownership and use.

*Recommendation 8*. To foster a more robust research program on gun policy, Congress should consider whether to eliminate the restrictions it has imposed on the use of gun trace data for research purposes.

**Conclusion 12**. Crime and victimization monitoring systems are incomplete and not yet fulfilling their promise of supporting high-quality gun policy research in the areas we investigated.

*Recommendation 9.* To improve the quality of evidence used to evaluate gun policies, the National Violent Death Reporting System should be expanded to include all states with rigorous quality control standards.

*Recommendation 10.* The Bureau of Justice Statistics should examine the cost and feasibility of expanding its existing programs to generate state-level crime data.

*Recommendation 11.* The Bureau of Justice Statistics should continue to pursue its efforts to generate state-level victimization estimates. The current goal of generating such estimates for 22 states is a reasonable compromise between cost and the public's need for more-detailed information. However, the bureau should continue to expand its development of model-based victimization rates for all states and for a wider set of victimization experiences (including, for instance, crimes involving firearm use by an assailant or victim).

**Conclusion 13**. The methodological quality of research on firearms can be significantly improved.

*Recommendation 12.* As part of the Gun Policy in America initiative, we have published a database containing a subset of state gun laws from 1979 to 2016 (Cherney, Morral, and Schell, 2018). We ask that others with expertise on state gun laws help us improve the database by notifying us of its errors, proposing more-useful categorizations of laws, or submitting information on laws not yet incorporated into the database. With such help, we hope to make the database a resource beneficial to all analysts.

*Recommendation 13.* Researchers, reviewers, academics, and science reporters should expect new analyses of the effects of gun policies to improve on earlier studies by persuasively addressing the methodological limitations of earlier studies, including problems with statistical power, model overfitting, covariate selection, poorly calibrated standard errors, multiple testing, undisclosed state variation in law implementation, unjustified assumptions about the time course of each policy's effects, the use of spline and hybrid effect codings that do not reveal coherent causal effect estimates, and inadequate attention to threats of reciprocal causation and simultaneity bias.

In conclusion, with a few exceptions, there is a surprisingly limited base of rigorous scientific evidence concerning the effects of many commonly discussed gun policies. This does not mean that these policies are ineffective; they might well be quite effective. Instead, it reflects shortcomings in the contributions that scientific study can currently offer to policy debates in these areas. It also reflects, in part, the policies we chose to investigate, all of which have been implemented in some U.S. states and, therefore, have proven to be politically and legally feasible, at least in some states. This decision meant that none of the policies we examined would dramatically increase or decrease the stock of guns or gun ownership rates in ways that would produce more readily detectable effects on public safety, health, and industry outcomes. The United States has a large stock of privately owned guns in circulation—estimated in 2014 to be somewhere between 200 million and 300 million firearms (Cook and Goss, 2014). Laws designed to change who may buy new weapons, what weapons they may buy, or how gun sales occur will predictably have only a small effect on, for example, homicides or participation in sport shooting, which are affected much more by the existing stock of firearms. Although small effects are especially difficult to identify with the statistical methods common in this field, they may be important. Even a 1-percent reduction in homicides corresponds to more than 1,500 fewer deaths over a decade.

By highlighting where scientific evidence is accumulating, we hope to build consensus around a shared set of facts that have been established through a transparent, nonpartisan, and impartial review process. In so doing, we also mean to highlight areas where more and better information could make important contributions to establishing fair and effective gun policies.

## Summary References

Cherney, Samantha, Andrew R. Morral, and Terry L. Schell, *RAND State Firearm Law Database*, Santa Monica, Calif.: RAND Corporation, TL-283-RC, 2018. As of March 2, 2018: https://www.rand.org/pubs/tools/TL283.html

Cook, Philip J., and Kristin A. Goss, *The Gun Debate: What Everyone Needs to Know*, New York: Oxford University Press, 2014.

Hahn, Robert A., Oleg Bilukha, Alex Crosby, Mindy T. Fullilove, Akiva Liberman, Eve Moscicki, Susan Snyder, Farris Tuma, and Peter A. Briss, "Firearms Laws and the Reduction of Violence: A Systematic Review," *American Journal of Preventive Medicine*, Vol. 28, No. 2, 2005, pp. 40–71.

Khan, Khalid S., Regina Kunz, Jos Kleijnen, and Gerd Antes, "Five Steps to Conducting a Systematic Review," *Journal of the Royal Society of Medicine*, Vol. 96, No. 3, 2003, pp. 118–121.

National Research Council, *Firearms and Violence: A Critical Review*, Washington, D.C.: National Academies Press, 2004.

NRC—*See* National Research Council.

# Acknowledgments

We wish to thank many staff and researchers inside and outside RAND who helped us to collect, interpret, and present the research discussed in this report. In particular, we wish to thank our quality assurance reviewers who provided expert and valuable guidance on how to improve earlier versions of this report or sections of it. These reviewers included James Anderson, Deborah Azrael, John Donohue, Susan Gates, Andy Hoehn, and Priscillia Hunt, as well as Jack Riley, whom we wish to especially thank for his encouragement and support of the idea that RAND could make important contributions to the gun policy discourse in the United States. The report also benefited from candid written reviews provided by two reviewers who wished to remain anonymous, one affiliated with a gun rights advocacy organization and one affiliated with a gun violence prevention advocacy organization. Within RAND, we wish to acknowledge the exceptional support we received from our research librarians, Roberta Shanman and Sachi Yagyu; our publication editor, Allison Kerns; and members of RAND's Office of External Affairs, including Lee Floyd, Chandra Garber, Stephan Kistler, Heather McCracken, Lauren Skrabala, Mary Vaiana, and Chara Williams.

## Abbreviations

| | |
|---|---|
| aOR | adjusted odds ratio |
| ARIMA | autoregressive integrated moving average |
| ATF | Bureau of Alcohol, Tobacco, Firearms and Explosives |
| BJS | Bureau of Justice Statistics |
| BRFSS | Behavioral Risk Factor Surveillance Survey |
| CAP | child-access prevention |
| CC | concealed carry |
| CDC | Centers for Disease Control and Prevention |
| CI | confidence interval |
| DGU | defensive gun use |
| FBI | Federal Bureau of Investigation |
| FS/S | proportion of suicides that are firearm suicides |
| GSS | General Social Survey |
| IPH | intimate partner homicide |
| IRR | incidence rate ratio |
| NCVS | National Crime Victimization Survey |
| NFA | (Australian) National Firearms Agreement |
| NIBRS | National Incident-Based Reporting System |
| NICS | National Instant Criminal Background Check System |

| | |
|---|---|
| NIS | Nationwide Inpatient Sample |
| NRC | National Research Council |
| NSDS | National Self Defense Survey |
| NSPOF | National Survey of Private Ownership of Firearms |
| NSSF | National Shooting Sports Foundation |
| NVDRS | National Violent Death Reporting System |
| OR | odds ratio |
| VA | U.S. Department of Veterans Affairs |

PART A

# Introduction and Methods

CHAPTER ONE

# Introduction

Americans are deeply divided on gun policy (Parker et al., 2017). Many Americans cherish the traditions of hunting, sport shooting, and collecting guns and value the security and protection that guns can provide. Many regions rely on hunting as an important driver of the tourism economy (Nelson, 2001; BBC Research & Consulting, 2008; Hodur, Leistritz, and Wolfe, 2008), and the wider gun industry employs hundreds of thousands of Americans, including instructors; shooting range operators; hunting equipment suppliers; and manufacturers, distributors, and retailers of firearms and ammunition. At the same time, many Americans have suffered grievous injuries and lost friends and family members in incidents involving firearms.[1] More than 36,000 Americans die annually from deliberate and unintentional gun injuries, and two-thirds of these deaths are suicides (Centers for Disease Control and Prevention [CDC], 2017a). Another 90,000 Americans per year receive care in a hospital for a nonfatal gun injury (CDC, 2017c).

Few are satisfied with the levels of mortality and injury associated with firearms, but there is passionate disagreement about how policies could be shaped to create a better future. There is a quite limited base of science on which to build sound and effective gun policies. Instead, when the public or members of Congress consider proposals affecting gun policy, they encounter conflicting opinions and inconsistent evidence about the likely effects of new laws. Views on what is factual concerning gun policies, or what the facts imply for decisionmaking, frequently divide along political and partisan lines (Kahan, 2017).

Entrenched disagreements on gun policy are not surprising, given the number and variety of contested and contradictory studies, selective misuse of facts by some on all sides of the debate, and today's hyper-partisan political environment. Moving past such roadblocks will be impossible unless decisionmakers can draw on a common set of facts based on transparent, nonpartisan, and impartial research and analysis. Even when individuals disagree about the objectives of gun policies, empirical evidence can help determine the most likely benefits and harms associated with such policies.

[1] Although not all guns are firearms, in this report, we follow conventional use in U.S. policy discussions and treat the terms *gun* and *firearm* as interchangeable.

## Gun Policy in America

To help fill the gap in impartial research and analysis, the RAND Corporation launched the Gun Policy in America initiative, which is premised on the idea that the real effects of policies can be objectively determined and that establishing these facts will help lead to sound policies. Our goal is to create a resource where policymakers and the general public can access unbiased information that informs and enables the development of fair and effective firearm policies.

This report synthesizes the available scientific data on the effects of various firearm policies on firearm deaths, violent crime, the gun industry, participation in hunting and sport shooting, and other outcomes. It builds and expands on earlier comprehensive reviews of scientific evidence on gun policy conducted more than a decade ago by the National Research Council (2004) and the Community Preventive Services Task Force (see Hahn et al., 2005). This report is one of several research products stemming from RAND's Gun Policy in America initiative (see www.rand.org/gunpolicy).

In the Gun Policy in America initiative, we have made no attempt to evaluate the merits of different values and principles that sometimes drive policy disagreements. We also have not evaluated the legality of any candidate laws or how they may infringe on Second Amendment rights. Instead, our focus is strictly on the empirical effects of policies on the eight outcomes specified in this report. However, all of the policies we investigate have been implemented in multiple states, and many have withstood Supreme Court review; therefore, we have selected policies that have previously been found not to violate the Constitution.

Laws are not the only interventions that have been used to shape how guns are used in the United States, and research is available on the effectiveness of other approaches, such as public information campaigns, safety and training programs, policing interventions, and school and community programs. In this report, however, our focus is on what scientific studies tell us about the probable effects of certain laws.

## Research Focus

The primary focus of this report is our systematic review of 13 broad classes of gun policies that have been implemented in some states and the effects of those policies on eight outcomes. We selected the 13 classes from a larger set of more than 100 gun policies that have been advocated for; proposed; or passed into law by the federal government, states, or municipalities. Specifically, we restricted our attention to policies or laws that have already been implemented in some states so that researchers could examine the effects of each. In addition, we sought policies designed to have a direct effect on our selected outcomes. These policies, the presumed mechanisms whereby they produce intended (and possibly unintended) effects on our selected outcomes, and the various ways that U.S. states have implemented them are discussed in detail in Chapters Three through Fifteen of this report. Although, in many cases, these policies have been implemented by local municipalities rather than states, we have not sought to review implementation at the local level.

The 13 classes of gun policies considered in this research are as follows:

1. background checks
2. bans on the sale of assault weapons and high-capacity magazines
3. stand-your-ground laws
4. prohibitions associated with mental illness
5. lost or stolen firearm reporting requirements
6. licensing and permitting requirements
7. firearm sales reporting and recording requirements
8. child-access prevention laws
9. surrender of firearms by prohibited possessors
10. minimum age requirements
11. concealed-carry laws
12. waiting periods
13. gun-free zones.

When deciding on the outcomes to examine in our research, we first included those related to public health and safety—suicide, violent crime, unintentional injuries and deaths, mass shootings, and officer-involved shootings. These are the outcomes most commonly examined in the research literature we were familiar with. However, we recognized that such outcomes omit many of the benefits of gun ownership that are attractive to gun owners and that may also be affected by laws designed to reduce the gun-related harms to public health and safety. Therefore, we also systematically searched the research literature for studies examining how gun laws affect defensive gun use, hunting and recreation, and the gun industry. Together, these eight outcomes cover many of the areas of concern frequently discussed in debates on gun policy. Here, we provide a short description of each outcome.

### Suicide

Official statistics on suicide in the United States are compiled by the CDC. Recent data, from 2015, indicate that 44,193 suicides occurred that year, for a rate of 13.75 per 100,000 people. Of these, 22,018 (49.8 percent) were firearm suicides (CDC, 2017a). Researchers have often examined the effects of laws on total suicides (i.e., suicide deaths by any means, including those involving a firearm), firearm suicides, nonfirearm suicides, and suicide attempts. From a societal perspective, the most important of these outcomes is total suicide; that is, the goal is to reduce the total number of suicide deaths, regardless of how one goes about attempting to die. In many cases, however, we would expect the effects of gun laws to be more easily observed in rates of firearm suicides, not total suicides. The consensus among public health experts is that reducing firearm suicides in contexts where more-lethal means of attempting suicide are unavailable will result in reductions in the total suicide rate (see, for example, Office of the Surgeon General and National Alliance for Suicide Prevention, 2012; World Health Organization, 2014; for review, see Azrael and Miller, 2016). Nevertheless, it is also clear that some people prevented from attempting suicide with a firearm will substitute another lethal means and successfully end their lives. The rate at which this substitution occurs is not known. Thus, for laws that increase or decrease firearm suicides, the effects on total suicides are likely smaller and harder to detect. For this reason, we examine the effects of policies on both total suicides and firearm suicides.

Suicide rates in the United States have increased 25 percent since 1999 (Curtin, Warner, and Hedegaard, 2016).[2] There is some degree of misclassification of suicide deaths, with some suicides likely classified as unintentional deaths (Kapusta et al., 2011) or overdose deaths (Bohnert et al., 2013). The CDC provides limited nationwide data on suicides for all states. More-expansive data are contained in the National Violent Death Reporting System, also maintained by the CDC, but because that system currently releases information on just a subset of U.S. states, we cannot use this data set to characterize suicides nationally.

Data on suicide attempts generally derive from two sources: hospital admission records and self-reports. In hospital data, suicides are generally categorized as "self-harm" with unspecified intent; although there is a field to code cause of injury, this field is completed inconsistently across states (Coben et al., 2001). In 2014, there were 469,096 self-harm, nonfatal hospital admissions to emergency departments in the United States, 3,320 (less than 1 percent) of which were caused by a firearm (CDC, 2017c). This may be because between 83 and 91 percent of those who attempt suicide with a firearm die, which is a higher rate than some other methods of suicide, such as drowning (66–84 percent) or hanging (61–83 percent) (Azrael and Miller, 2016).

Emergency room data contain only self-harm incidents that resulted in an emergency room visit; as a complementary data source, national data based on self-reports reveal that, in 2015, 1.4 million adults aged 18 or older (0.6 percent) attempted suicide in the past year (Piscopo et al., 2016).

### Violent Crime

The Federal Bureau of Investigation (FBI) defines *violent crime* as including forcible rape, robbery, aggravated assault, and murder or nonnegligent manslaughter. The last category excludes deaths caused by suicide, negligence, or accident, as well as justifiable homicides (such as the killing of a felon by a peace officer in the line of duty) (FBI, 2016d).

---

[2] The 25-percent increase in suicides refers to the age-adjusted rate, although the crude rate and the absolute number of suicides have also increased.

One source of data on violent crime is the FBI's Uniform Crime Reporting program, which relies on voluntary reporting of crimes by city, university/college, county, state, tribal, and federal law enforcement agencies. Data from the program indicate that there were approximately 1.2 million violent crimes in the United States in 2015, including 764,449 aggravated assaults, 327,374 robberies, 124,047 rapes, and 15,696 instances of murder or nonnegligent manslaughter (FBI, 2016d). The overall violent crime rate was 372.6 per 100,000 people, with the highest rate for aggravated assault (237.8 per 100,000), followed by robbery (101.9 per 100,000), rape (38.6 per 100,000) and murder or nonnegligent manslaughter (4.9 per 100,000). Nationwide, firearms were used in 71.5 percent of all instances of murder or nonnegligent manslaughter, 40.8 percent of robberies, and 24.2 percent of aggravated assaults in 2015 (FBI, 2016d).

Death certificate data and emergency department admission data provide additional insights into the prevalence and consequences of violent crime. Based on mortality data, the CDC estimated that there were 17,793 homicides in the United States in 2015, for a rate of 5.54 per 100,000 people; of these, 12,979 (73 percent) were caused by a firearm (CDC, 2017a). Emergency department data show that in 2014 there were more than 1.5 million admissions to hospital emergency departments for assault; of these, 60,470 (3.8 percent) were firearm-related (CDC, 2017c).

### Unintentional Injuries and Deaths

Like suicide, official statistics on unintentional injuries and deaths in the United States are compiled by the CDC. The most recent data, from 2015, indicate that 146,571 fatal unintentional injuries occurred that year, for a rate of 46.50 per 100,000 people (CDC, 2017a). Of these, 489 (less than 1 percent) were caused by a firearm. Some of these fatal unintentional injuries were likely misclassified and were actually suicides or homicides. Nevertheless, the true number of unintentional firearm deaths may be substantially greater than reported in the CDC's vital data. For example, inconsistent classification of child firearm deaths by local coroners may result in 35–45 percent of all unintentional firearm deaths being classified instead as suicides or homicides (Everytown for Gun Safety Support Fund, 2014; Hemenway and Solnick, 2015a). We also include research examining nonfatal unintentional injuries. There were close to 29 million unintentional injury discharges from emergency rooms in 2014, of which 15,928 (less than 1 percent) were caused by a firearm. These reports omit injuries that did not result in an emergency room visit.

### Mass Shootings

Although only a small fraction of annual firearm deaths result from a mass shooting, these events attract enormous public, media, and social media attention in the country, and they frequently prompt discussions about legislative initiatives for how better to prevent gun violence. The U.S. government has never defined *mass shooting*, and there is no single universally accepted definition of the term. The FBI's definition of a *mass murderer* requires at least four casualties, excluding the offender or offenders, in a single incident. Public law (the Investigative Assistance for Violent Crime Act of 2012; Pub. L. 112-265) defines a *mass killing* as a single incident in which three or more people were killed. Alternative definitions include two or more injured victims or four or more people injured or killed, including the shooter. Depending on which data source is referenced, and its definitions, there were seven, 65, 332, or 371 mass shootings in the United States in 2015 (see a discussion of these estimates in Chapter Twenty-Two).

### Officer-Involved Shootings

Police shootings of civilians have triggered fierce debates locally and nationally about when use of lethal force is appropriate and whether it is being used disproportionately against minorities. Although the FBI has tried to collect information on police shootings from around 17,000 local law enforcement agencies, recent efforts by news organizations (such as the *Washington Post* and the *Guardian*) have demonstrated that the FBI's data collection misses many such cases. Whereas the FBI's count typically comes to around 400 killings by police per year, the *Washington Post* documented news stories on 963 individuals shot and killed by law enforcement in 2016, a number that could omit any individuals shot and killed by police about whom no news story was written. The FBI has announced plans to begin a new data collection effort that will reportedly track all incidents in which law enforcement seriously injure or kill citizens (Kindy, 2015).

Because reliable data on police shootings are often available only for individual police departments, prior studies using such data typically present information at the city level. For example, using police reports and other administrative data, Klinger et al. (2016) looked at 230 use-of-force shootings by police officers involving 373 suspects in St. Louis between 2003 and 2012. Similarly, medical records of shooting victims contain information on whether the shooter was a member of the law enforcement community. Using data from New York City's medical examiner, Gill and Pasquale-Styles (2009) looked at law enforcement shootings resulting in a fatality there between 2003 and 2006. The data included 42 cases for the four-year period. Like suicide attempts and unintentional injuries and deaths, this data source misses incidents in which the officer did not injure the suspect or the suspect did not seek medical attention.

### Defensive Gun Use

Defensive gun use has typically been measured in the empirical literature using self-reports on surveys of gun owners, although some studies have used firearm deaths coded as justifiable homicides to investigate subsets of defensive gun use. Although there are some variations, *defensive gun use* has often been defined as incidents that involve (1) protection against humans (i.e., not animals); (2) gun use by civilians (not official use by military, police, or security personnel); (3) contact between persons (not, for instance, carrying a firearm to investigate a suspicious sound when no intruder is encountered); and (4) use of a gun, at least as a visual or verbal threat (not incidents in which a gun may have simply been available for use). Definitions this broad would include defensive use of a gun by criminals during the commission of a crime, as well as use of a gun for personal defense by those who are prohibited by law from being in possession of a weapon (itself a crime). More-restrictive definitions specify that the defensive gun use be performed by the victim of certain crimes or by someone trying to protect the victim. These definitions may miss instances in which crimes were deterred or averted when a firearm was brandished.

Differences in the definitions of defensive gun use, and in the manner of collecting information about it, lead to wide differences in estimates of the annual incidence of defensive gun use. Low estimates (based on the experiences of crime victims) are a little more than 100,000 such incidents per year, and high estimates are 4.7 million per year (Cook and Ludwig, 1996, 1997, 1998; McDowall, Loftin, and Wiersema, 1998). This literature and the challenges of defining and measuring defensive gun use are reviewed in Chapter Twenty-Three.

### Hunting and Recreation

Federal statistics on hunters largely come from the National Survey of Fishing, Hunting, and Wildlife-Associated Recreation Survey, which is conducted every five years as a coordinated effort by the U.S. Fish and Wildlife Service and the U.S. Census Bureau. According to the most recent data, from 2011, approximately 13 million people used firearms for hunting, more than 50 percent of all hunters participated in target shooting, and 22 percent of hunters visited shooting ranges (U.S. Fish and Wildlife Service, U.S. Department of the Interior, and U.S. Department of Commerce, 2012). Estimates from the National Shooting Sports Foundation (NSSF) suggest that approximately 20 million individuals participate in target shooting annually (Southwick Associates, 2013). Data from the General Social Survey suggest that hunting has decreased significantly since 1977, when 31.6 percent of adults lived in households where they, their spouse, or both hunted. In 2014, households with a hunter was down to 15.4 percent (Smith and Son, 2015).

### Gun Industry

Estimates produced by the NSSF suggest that there are 141,000 jobs in the United States involving the manufacture, distribution, or retailing of ammunition, firearms, and hunting supplies and potentially another 150,000 jobs in supplier and ancillary industries connected with the firearm market (NSSF, 2017). According to the U.S. Census Bureau, in 2014, more than 90,000 people were employed in U.S. firms coded as being involved in just the manufacture of firearms, ammunition, or ordnance (North American Industry Classification System [NAICS] codes 332992, 332993, and 332994; U.S. Census Bureau, 2016). The manufacturing industry alone is estimated to generate $16 billion in revenue annually (IBISWorld, 2016). In 2011, hunters spent $3 billion on firearms and $1.2 billion on ammunition (U.S. Fish and Wildlife Service, U.S. Department of the Interior, and U.S. Department of Commerce, 2012). More than 9 million firearms were manufactured in the United States in 2014, nearly triple the number manufactured one decade prior. An additional 3.6 million firearms were imported in 2014, while just more than 420,900 firearms were exported from the United States (Bureau of Alcohol, Tobacco, Firearms and Explosives, 2016b).

As of the end of fiscal year 2015, 139,840 federal firearms licensees had active licenses to sell firearms in the United States. Just more than 46 percent of these licenses were held by dealers or pawnbrokers, 43 percent were held by collectors, about 9 percent were held by manufacturers of ammunition or firearms, and less than 1 percent were held by importers (Bureau of Alcohol, Tobacco, Firearms and Explosives, 2016b).

## Organization of This Report

The report is organized into five parts. Part A introduces the project scope and objectives in Chapter One and the methods used to conduct systematic reviews and syntheses of the literature in Chapter Two. In Part B, we present a research synthesis on each of the 13 state policies selected for review (Chapters Three through Fifteen). Each of these chapters defines the class of policies under review; presents and rates the available evidence; and describes what conclusions, if any, can be drawn about how each policy affects each outcome. Part B includes all of the research syntheses we selected a priori; however, in the course of developing these, several related themes frequently came up in the literature and in policy debates, and we believed that these themes warranted further discussion or review. Therefore, to augment and provide context for Part B's syntheses, Part C presents supplementary essays on what rigorous studies reveal about

- the possible mechanisms by which laws may affect outcomes (Chapters Sixteen and Seventeen on the effects of firearm prevalence on suicide and violent crime)
- how taxes, access to health care, and media campaigns might affect gun violence (Chapters Eighteen through Twenty)
- the effectiveness of laws used to target domestic violence (Chapter Twenty-One)
- methodological challenges in defining and estimating the prevalence of mass shootings and defensive gun use (Chapters Twenty-Two and Twenty-Three)
- how suicide, violent crime, and mass shootings were affected by Australia's implementation of the National Firearms Agreement (Chapter Twenty-Four).

In Part D, we draw general conclusions from the main policy analyses and offer recommendations for how to improve the state of evidence for the effects of state laws. Finally, in an appendix section, Appendix A describes common methodological shortcomings found in the existing scientific literature examining gun policy, and Appendix B describes the source data used to display study effect sizes and rate study methodologies.

## Chapter One References


Azrael, Deborah, and Matthew Miller, "Reducing Suicide Without Affecting Underlying Mental Health: Theoretical Underpinnings and a Review of the Evidence Base Lining the Availability of Lethal Means and Suicide," in Rory C. O'Connor and Jane Pirkis, eds., *The International Handbook of Suicide Prevention*, 2nd ed., Hoboken, N.J.: John Wiley and Sons, 2016.

BBC Research & Consulting, *The Economic Impacts of Hunting, Fishing and Wildlife Watching in Colorado*, Denver, Colo., September 26, 2008. As of October 13, 2017:
https://cpw.state.co.us/Documents/About/Reports/08DOWEconomicImpactReport.pdf

Bohnert, A. S., J. F. McCarthy, R. V. Ignacio, M. A. Ilgen, A. Eisenberg, and F. C. Blow, "Misclassification of Suicide Deaths: Examining the Psychiatric History of Overdose Decedents," *Injury Prevention*, Vol. 19, No. 6, 2013, pp. 326–330.

Bureau of Alcohol, Tobacco, Firearms and Explosives, *Firearms Commerce in the United States: Annual Statistical Update 2016*, Washington, D.C.: U.S. Department of Justice, 2016b.

CDC—*See* Centers for Disease Control and Prevention.

Centers for Disease Control and Prevention, "Fatal Injury Reports, National, Regional, and State 1981–2015," WISQARS database, Atlanta, Ga., 2017a. As of May 8, 2017:
https://webappa.cdc.gov/sasweb/ncipc/mortrate.html

———, "Nonfatal Injury Reports: 2001–2014," WISQARS database, Atlanta, Ga., 2017c. As of January 15, 2017:
https://webappa.cdc.gov/sasweb/ncipc/nfirates2001.html

Coben, J. H., C. A. Steiner, M. Barrett, C. T. Merrill, and D. Adamson, "Completeness of Cause of Injury Coding in Healthcare Administrative Databases in the United States," *Injury Prevention*, Vol. 12, No. 3, 2001, pp. 199–201.

Cook, Philip J., and Jens Ludwig, *Guns in America: Results of a Comprehensive National Survey on Firearms Ownership and Use*, Washington, D.C.: Police Foundation, 1996.

———, *Guns in America: National Survey on Private Ownership and Use of Firearms: Research in Brief*, Rockville, Md.: National Institute of Justice, 1997.

———, "Defensive Gun Uses: New Evidence from a National Survey," *Journal of Quantitative Criminology*, Vol. 14, No. 2, 1998, pp. 111–131.

Curtin, Sally C., Margaret Warner, and Holly Hedegaard, *Suicide Rates for Females and Males by Race and Ethnicity: United States, 1999 and 2014*, Atlanta, Ga.: Centers for Disease Control and Prevention, 2016.

Everytown for Gun Safety Support Fund, *Innocents Lost: A Year of Unintentional Child Gun Deaths*, June 2014. As of May 12, 2017:
https://everytownresearch.org/documents/2015/04/innocents-lost.pdf

FBI—*See* Federal Bureau of Investigation.

Federal Bureau of Investigation, "Crime in the United States 2015: Violent Crime," Washington, D.C.: U.S. Department of Justice, 2016d. As of May 8, 2017:
https://ucr.fbi.gov/crime-in-the-u.s/2015/crime-in-the-u.s.-2015/offenses-known-to-law-enforcement/violent-crime/violentcrimemain_final.pdf

Gill, J. R., and M. Pasquale-Styles, "Firearm Deaths by Law Enforcement," *Journal of Forensic Science*, Vol. 54, No. 1, 2009, pp. 185–188.

Hahn, Robert A., Oleg Bilukha, Alex Crosby, Mindy T. Fullilove, Akiva Liberman, Eve Moscicki, Susan Snyder, Farris Tuma, and Peter A. Briss, "Firearms Laws and the Reduction of Violence: A Systematic Review," *American Journal of Preventive Medicine*, Vol. 28, No. 2, 2005, pp. 40–71.

Hemenway, David, and Sara J. Solnick, "Children and Unintentional Firearm Death," *Injury Epidemiology*, Vol. 2, No. 26, 2015a.

Hodur, Nancy M., F. Larry Leistritz, and Kara L. Wolfe, "Developing the Nature-Based Tourism Sector in Southwestern North Dakota," *Great Plains Research: A Journal of Natural and Social Sciences*, Vol. 18, Spring 2008, pp. 81–92.

IBISWorld, *Guns and Ammunition Manufacturing in the U.S.: Market Research Report,* Los Angeles, Calif., August 2016.

Kahan, Dan M., "On the Sources of Ordinary Science Knowledge and Extraordinary Science Ignorance," in Kathleen Hall Jamieson, Dan Kahan, and Dietram A. Scheufele, eds., *Oxford Handbook of the Science of Science Communication*, Oxford, UK: Oxford University Press, 2017.

Kapusta, N. D., U. S. Tran, I. R. Rockett, D. DeLeo, C. P. Naylor, T. Niederkrotenthaler, M. Voracek, E. Etzersdorfer, and G. Sonneck, "Declining Autopsy Rates and Suicide Misclassification: A Cross-National Analysis of 35 Countries," *Archives of General Psychiatry*, Vol. 68, No. 10, 2011, pp. 1050–1057.

Kindy, Kimberly, "FBI to Sharply Expand System for Tracking Fatal Police Shootings," *Washington Post*, December 8, 2015.

Klinger, D., R. Rosenfeld, D. Isom, and M. Deckard, "Race, Crime, and the Micro-Ecology of Deadly Force," *Criminology and Public Policy,* Vol. 15, No. 1, February 2016, pp. 193–222.

McDowall, D., C. Loftin, and B. Wiersema, "Estimates of the Frequency of Firearm Self Defense from the National Crime Victimization Survey," Albany, N.Y.: State University of New York, School of Criminal Justice, Violence Research Group Discussion Paper 20, 1998 (unpublished).

National Research Council, *Firearms and Violence: A Critical Review*, Washington, D.C.: National Academies Press, 2004.

National Shooting Sports Foundation, *Firearms and Ammunition Industry Economic Impact Report,* Newtown, Conn., 2017. As of October 18, 2017:
https://d3aya7xwz8momx.cloudfront.net/wp-content/uploads/2017/07/EconomicImpactofIndustry2017.pdf

Nelson, Charles M., *Economic Implications of Land Use Patterns for Natural Resource Recreation and Tourism*, Lansing, Mich.: Michigan Land Resource Project, Public Sector Consultants, 2001.

NSSF—*See* National Shooting Sports Foundation.

Office of the Surgeon General and National Action Alliance for Suicide Prevention, *National Strategy for Suicide Prevention: Goals and Objectives for Action: A Report of the U.S. Surgeon General and of the National Action Alliance for Suicide Prevention,* Washington, D.C.: U.S. Department of Health and Human Services, 2012.

Parker, Kim, Juliana Menasce Horowitz, Ruth Igielnik, Baxter Oliphant, and Anna Brown, *America's Complex Relationship with Guns*, Washington, D.C.: Pew Research Center, June 22, 2017. As of August 14, 2017:
http://assets.pewresearch.org/wp-content/uploads/sites/3/2017/06/06151541/Guns-Report-FOR-WEBSITE-PDF-6-21.pdf

Piscopo, Kathryn, Rachel N. Lipari, Jennifer Cooney, and Christie Galsheen, *Suicidal Thoughts and Behavior Among Adults: Results from the 2015 National Survey on Drug Use and Health*, NSDUH Data Review, September 2016. As of May 23, 2017:
https://www.samhsa.gov/data/sites/default/files/NSDUH-DR-FFR3-2015/NSDUH-DR-FFR3-2015.pdf

Public Law 112-265, Investigative Assistance for Violent Crimes Act of 2012, January 14, 2013.

Smith, T. W., and J. Son, *Trends in Gun Ownership in the United States, 1972–2014,* Chicago, Ill.: NORC at the University of Chicago, March 2015. As of March 9, 2017:
http://www.norc.org/PDFs/GSS%20Reports/GSS_Trends%20in%20Gun%20Ownership_US_1972-2014.pdf

Southwick Associates, *Target Shooting in America*, Newtown, Conn.: National Shooting Sports Foundation, 2013.

U.S. Census Bureau, *Number of Firms, Number of Establishments, Employment, and Annual Payroll by Enterprise Employment Size for the United States, All Industries: 2014,* Washington, D.C., December 2016. As of January 15, 2017:
https://www.census.gov/data/tables/2014/econ/susb/2014-susb-annual.html

U.S. Fish and Wildlife Service, U.S. Department of the Interior, and U.S. Department of Commerce, *2011 National Survey of Fishing, Hunting, and Wildlife-Associated Recreation*, Washington, D.C., FH2/11-NAT, 2012.

World Health Organization, *Preventing Suicide: A Global Imperative,* Geneva, 2014. As of May 8, 2017:
http://apps.who.int/iris/bitstream/10665/131056/1/9789241564779_eng.pdf

CHAPTER TWO

# Methods

Our review of evidence concerning the effects of 13 policies on eight outcomes used Royal Society of Medicine (Khan et al., 2003) guidelines for conducting systematic reviews of a scientific literature. Those guidelines consist of a five-step protocol: framing questions for review, identifying relevant literature, assessing the quality of the literature, summarizing the evidence, and interpreting the findings. Our objective was to identify and assess the quality of evidence provided in research that estimated the causal effect of one of the selected gun policies (or the prevalence of firearm ownership) on any of our eight key outcomes.

Before undertaking the review, we knew that we would need to draw on primarily observational studies across a range of disciplines, including economics, psychology, public health, sociology, and criminology. The Royal Society of Medicine approach is suitable in this context because of its flexibility and applicability to social and policy interventions. Other approaches for systematic reviews (e.g., Institute of Medicine, 2011; Higgins and Green, 2011) are designed primarily for reviews specific to health care. We consulted guidelines from the Campbell Collaboration to ensure that our review criteria were based on relevant factors prescribed for reviews of social and policy interventions (e.g., determination of independent findings, statistical procedures; Campbell Collaboration, 2001). However, to more efficiently examine the range of outcomes and interventions we set out to review, and because of the wide range of methods researchers have used to examine these effects, we do not follow the Campbell Collaboration guidelines exactly, as detailed next.

## Selecting Policies

RAND assembled a list of close to 100 distinct gun policies advocated by diverse organizations, including the White House and other U.S. government organizations, advocacy organizations focused on gun policy (such as the National Rifle Association and the Brady Campaign to Prevent Gun Violence), academic organizations focused on gun policy or gun policy research, and professional organizations that had made public recommendations related to gun policy (e.g., the International Association of Chiefs of

Police and the American Bar Association). Our objective was to evaluate state firearm laws because there is considerable variation that could be examined to understand the causal effects of such laws. Moreover, because the laws are applied statewide, observed effects may generalize to new jurisdictions better than the effects of local gun policies or programs that may be more tailored to the unique circumstances giving rise to them. We therefore eliminated policies that chiefly concerned local programs or interventions that are not mandated by state laws (e.g., gun buy-back programs or policing strategies that have been recommended on the basis of favorable research findings). For the same reason, we eliminated policies that either have never been passed into state laws or that have not yet had their intended effects (e.g., laws requiring new handguns to incorporate smart-gun technologies). We excluded policies that we concluded were likely to have only an indirect effect on any of the eight outcomes we were examining (e.g., policies concerning mental health coverage in group health insurance plans; the public availability of Bureau of Alcohol, Tobacco, Firearms and Explosives data on gun traces). We clustered some policy proposals that we regarded as sufficiently similar in concept to be included in the same general class of policies (e.g., policies of repealing the Safe Schools Act and the conceptually similar policy to prohibit gun-free zones).

This process resulted in 13 classes of firearm policies that we subsequently reviewed with multiple representatives of two advocacy organizations (one strongly aligned with enhanced gun regulation, and one strongly aligned with reduced gun regulation). The purpose of these consultations was to establish whether we had identified policies that are important, coherent, and relevant to current gun policy debates. This consultation resulted in substituting two of our original 13 classes of laws. As noted in Chapter One, the final set of policies, defined and explained in Chapters Three through Fifteen, is as follows:

1. background checks
2. bans on the sale of assault weapons and high-capacity magazines
3. stand-your-ground laws
4. prohibitions associated with mental illness
5. lost or stolen firearm reporting requirements
6. licensing and permitting requirements
7. firearm sales reporting and recording requirements
8. child-access prevention laws
9. surrender of firearms by prohibited possessors
10. minimum age requirements
11. concealed-carry laws
12. waiting periods
13. gun-free zones.

These classes of gun policies do not comprehensively account for all—or necessarily the most effective—laws or programs that have been implemented in the United States with the aim of reducing gun violence. For example, our set of policies does not include mandatory minimum sentencing guidelines for crimes with firearms. Further, by restricting our evaluation to state policies, we exclude local interventions (e.g., problem-oriented policing, focused deterrence strategies) that have been found to reduce overall crime in prior meta-analyses (Braga, Papachristos, and Hureau, 2014; Braga and Weisburd, 2012). However, we recognize the potential importance of these other interventions and believe a similar systematic review of their effects on outcomes relevant to the firearm policy debate merits future research.[1]

While Part B of this report evaluates the existing literature on the effects of these 13 classes of firearm policies, Part C includes essays describing scientific research on possible mechanisms by which laws may affect firearm-related outcomes, such as by affecting the prevalence of gun ownership (see Chapters Sixteen and Seventeen).

## Selecting and Reviewing Studies

Our selection and review of the identified literature involved the following steps:

1. Article retrieval: Across all outcomes, we identified a common set of search terms to capture articles relevant to firearm prevalence or firearm policies. We then identified search terms unique for each outcome.
2. Title and abstract review: We conducted separate title and abstract reviews for each outcome using DistillerSR to code criteria used to determine whether the article appeared to meet minimum inclusion criteria (described later).
3. Full-text review: All studies retained after abstract review received full-text review and coding using DistillerSR. The purpose of this review was to identify studies that examined the effects of one or more of our policies on any of our outcomes and that employed methods designed to clarify the causal effects of the policy.
4. Synthesis of evidence: Once we identified the subset of quasi-experimental studies for each outcome and policy,[2] members of the multidisciplinary methodology team met to discuss each study's strengths and limitations. Then, the group discussed each set of studies available for a policy-outcome pair to make a determination about the level of evidence supporting the effect of the policy on each outcome.

---

[1] For a recent review of the evidence on criminal justice interventions to reduce criminal access to firearms, see Braga, 2017.

[2] We identified no experimental studies.

## Article Retrieval

In spring 2016, we queried all databases listed in Table 2.1 for English-language studies. Because the National Research Council (NRC) (2004) and the Community Preventive Services Task Force (Hahn et al., 2005) published comprehensive and high-quality research reviews in 2004 and 2005, we limited our search primarily to research published during or after 2003 (assuming a lag from the time the NRC review was complete and the final report was published). We supplemented this search with a review of all studies reviewed by NRC (2004) and Hahn et al. (2005). Finally, to ensure inclusion of the most-seminal studies, including those that may have been missed by NRC or Hahn et al., we conducted additional searches in the Web of Science and Scopus

**Table 2.1**
**Databases Searched for Studies Examining the Effects of Firearm Policies**

| Database | Details |
|---|---|
| PubMed | National Library of Medicine's database of medical literature. *Not used for gun industry or hunting searches.* |
| PsycINFO | Journal articles, books, reports, and dissertations on psychology and related fields. *Not used for gun industry or hunting searches.* |
| Index to Legal Periodicals | Includes indexing of scholarly articles, symposia, jurisdictional surveys, court decisions, books, and book reviews. |
| Social Science Abstracts | Journal articles and book reviews on anthropology, crime, economics, law, political science, psychology, public administration, and sociology. |
| Web of Science | Includes the Book Citation Index, Science Citation, Social Science Citation, Arts & Humanities Citation Indexes, and Conference Proceedings Citation Indexes for Science, Social Science, and Humanities, which include all cited references from indexed articles. |
| Criminal Justice Abstracts | Abstracts related to criminal justice and criminology; includes current books, book chapters, journal articles, government reports, and dissertations published worldwide. |
| National Criminal Justice Reference Service | Contains summaries of the more than 185,000 criminal justice publications housed in the National Criminal Justice Reference Service Library collection. |
| Sociological Abstracts | Citations and abstracts of sociological literature, including journal articles, books, book chapters, dissertations, and conference papers. |
| EconLit | Journal articles, books, and working papers on economics. |
| Business Source Complete | Business and economics journal articles, country profiles, and industry reports. |
| WorldCat | Catalog of books, web resources, and other material worldwide. |
| Scopus | An abstract and citation database with links to full-text content, covering peer-reviewed research and web sources in scientific, technical, medical, and social science fields, as well as arts and humanities. |
| LawReviews (LexisNexis) | A database of legal reviews. |

databases for any study that had been cited in the literature 70 or more times, regardless of its publication date. Finally, after completing our search, several relevant studies were published in summer and fall 2016. When we became aware of these, we included them in our review.

We conducted separate searches for each of the eight outcomes. The search strings that were applied universally across all outcomes included the following:

- gun or guns or firearm* or handgun* or shotgun* or rifle* or longgun* or machinegun* or pistol* OR automatic weapon OR assault weapon OR semi-automatic weapon OR automatic weapons OR assault weapons OR semi-automatic weapons
  AND
- ownership OR own OR owns OR availab* OR access* OR possess* OR purchas* OR restrict* OR regulat* OR distribut* OR "weapon carrying" OR "weapon-carrying" OR legislation OR legislating OR legislative OR law OR laws OR legal* OR policy OR policies OR "ban" OR "bans" OR "banned."

The outcome-specific search terms included the following:

- suicide AND (suicide* OR self-harm* OR self-injur*); the following were the only terms used for "firearms" for this search: gun or guns or firearm* or handgun* or shotgun* or rifle* or longgun* or machinegun* or pistol*
- violent crime AND homicide* OR murder* OR manslaughter OR "domestic violence" OR "spousal abuse" OR "elder abuse" OR "child abuse" OR "family violence" OR "child maltreatment" OR "spousal maltreatment" OR "elder maltreatment" OR "intimate relationship violence" OR "intimate partner violence" OR "dating violence" OR (violen* AND [crime* OR criminal*]) OR rape OR rapes OR rapist* OR "personal crime" OR "personal crimes" OR robbery OR assault* OR stalk* OR terroris*
- unintentional injuries and deaths AND accident* OR unintentional
- mass shootings AND "mass shooting" OR "mass shootings"
- officer-involved shootings AND "law enforcement" OR police* OR policing
- defensive gun use AND self-defense OR "self defense" OR "personal defense" OR defens* OR self-protect* OR self protect* OR DGU OR SDGU
- hunting and recreation AND hunt OR hunting OR "sport shooting" OR "shooting sports" OR recreation* (The terms "ammunition" and "bullets" were also included in the set containing the terms for "firearms.")
- gun industry AND industr* OR manufactur* OR produc* OR distribut* OR supply OR trade OR price* OR export* OR revenue* OR sales OR employ* OR profit* OR cost OR costs OR costing OR "gun show" OR tax OR taxes OR taxing OR taxation OR payroll OR "federal firearms license."

We used a three-stage study review process and standardized review criteria (described next) to identify all studies with evidence for policy effects meeting minimum evidence standards. When possible, we calculated and graphed standardized effect sizes for reported effects included in our research syntheses (Chapters Three through Fifteen).

In addition to the planned research syntheses analyzing the effects of the 13 policies outlined in Chapter One, we summarized evidence on other topics when members of the research team believed that a topic provided important supplemental evidence or explanatory information (see Chapters Sixteen through Twenty-Four). For instance, we identified a substantial literature examining the effects of firearm prevalence on rates of suicide (Chapter Sixteen) and homicide (Chapter Seventeen). This literature did not evaluate the effects of a specific policy but nevertheless examined a key mechanism by which policies might affect the outcomes. For these discussions, we occasionally augmented the search strategy described earlier, as detailed in the individual chapters.

### Title and Abstract Review

At this stage, we screened studies to determine whether they met our inclusion criteria. In all cases, a study was included if it met the following: *any empirical study that demonstrated a relationship between a firearm-related public policy and the relevant outcome* OR *any empirical study that demonstrated a relationship between firearm ownership and access and a relevant outcome (including proxy measures for gun ownership).*

Studies were excluded if they were case studies, systematic reviews, dissertations, commentaries or conceptual discussions, descriptive studies, studies in which key variables were assumed rather than measured (e.g., a region was assumed to have higher rates of gun ownership), studies that did not concern one of the eight outcomes we selected, studies that did not concern one of the 13 policies we selected (or gun ownership), or studies that duplicated the analyses and results of other included studies.

### Full-Text Review

Next, we used full-text review to ensure that the studies included thus far did not meet any of the exclusion criteria and to exclude studies with no credible claim to having identified a causal effect of policies. In addition to coding all studies on the policy and outcome they examined and on their research design, we coded the country or countries in which the policy effects were evaluated. Because of the United States' unique legal, policy, and gun ownership context, we excluded studies examining the effects of policies on foreign populations. However, in the special-topic discussions (Chapters Sixteen through Twenty-Four), we include analysis of some studies in foreign countries (such as an analysis of the Australian experience with gun regulation) and various foreign studies of the effects of gun prevalence on suicide.

Our research syntheses (Chapters Three through Fifteen) focus exclusively on studies that used research methods designed to identify causal effects among observed associations between policies and outcomes. Specifically, we required, at a minimum, that studies include time-series data and use such data to establish that policies preceded their apparent effects (a requirement for a causal effect) and that studies include a control group or comparison group (to demonstrate that the purported causal effect was not found among those who were not exposed to the policy). Experimental designs provide the gold standard for establishing causal effects, but we identified none in our literature reviews. On a case-by-case basis, we examined studies that made a credible claim to causal inference on the basis of data that did not include a time series. In practice, these discussions determined that some studies using instrumental-variable approaches to isolating causal effects satisfied our minimum standards for inclusion.

We refer to the studies that met our inclusion criteria as *quasi-experimental*. We distinguish these from simple *cross-sectional* studies that may show an association between states with a given policy and some outcome but that have no strategy for ensuring that it is the policy that caused the observed differences across states. For instance, there could be some other factor associated with both state policy differences and outcome differences or there could be reverse causality (that is, differences in the outcome across states could have caused states to adopt different policies). In excluding cross-sectional studies from this review, we have adopted a more stringent standard of evidence for causal effects than has often been used in systematic reviews of gun policy.

Although excluding cross-sectional research eliminates a large number of studies on gun policy, longitudinal data are much better for estimating the causal effect of a policy. Specifically, empirical demonstration of causation generally requires three types of evidence (Mill, 1843):

- The cause and effect regularly co-occur (i.e., association).
- The cause occurs before the effect (i.e., precedence).
- Alternative explanations for the association have been ruled out (i.e., elimination of confounds).

Cross-sectional research is largely limited to demonstrating association. Longitudinal studies that include people or regions that are exposed to a policy and those that are not exposed have the potential to provide all three types of evidence. Such a design can demonstrate that the policy preceded the change in the outcome of interest, and it can rule out a wider range of potential confounds, including historical time trends and the time-invariant characteristics of the jurisdictions in which the policies were implemented (Wooldridge, 2002).

We also excluded studies that offered no insight into the causal effects of individual policies. For instance, we excluded studies that evaluated the effects of an aggregate state score describing the totality of each state's gun policies or studies of the aggregate effects of legislation that included multiple gun policies. In rare cases, we excluded from consideration studies that provided insufficient information about their methodologies to evaluate whether they used a credible approach to isolating a causal effect of policies. In one case (Kalesan et al., 2016), we excluded a study that examined the effects of many of our selected policies on firearm deaths. We did so because of significant methodological problems that we concluded made the findings uninformative, as documented in Schell and Morral (2016). In cases in which authors updated prior published analyses, we generally chose the updated study. However, in one case (Cook and Ludwig, 2003), we present the results from the earlier analysis (Ludwig and Cook, 2000), which was inclusive of more years of data, provided more detail, and included multiple model specifications (although findings were qualitatively the same). The identified studies included individual-level studies (i.e., studies comparing outcomes among people over time) and ecological studies (i.e., studies comparing outcomes in regions over time).

Finally, we excluded studies published prior to 2003 on one policy-outcome pair—concealed-carry laws and violent crime. Our discussion of this topic (see Chapter Thirteen) reviews much of the earlier literature in this area, but we do not count the earlier work in our evidence ratings for several reasons. For starters, this area of gun policy has received the greatest research attention since 2003, and considerable advances have been made in understanding the effects of these laws. In addition, researchers have uncovered serious problems with data sets that were frequently used before 2003. Indeed, Hahn et al. (2005) dismissed all the earlier work that had been done with county-level data (which meant most of the work) on grounds that it was too flawed to rely on for evidence. We do not take that position but do agree with NRC (2004) and Hahn et al. (2005) that the primary conclusion that can be drawn from this earlier literature is that estimates of the effects of concealed-carry laws are highly sensitive to model specification choices, meaning no conclusive evidence can be drawn from the estimates. Because many of the authors engaged in the pre-2003 concealed-carry research continued to publish improved models on improved data sets, we restrict our evidence ratings to just this later work. We do not exclude pre-2003 studies of concealed-carry laws for outcomes other than violent crime, because there are much fewer later studies on which to base evidence ratings for these other outcomes.

Using these inclusion and exclusion criteria, we identified the studies providing the highest-quality evidence of a causal relationship between a policy and an outcome. In judging the quality of studies, we always explicitly considered common methodological shortcomings found in the existing gun policy scientific literature (see Appendix A), especially the following:

- *Models that may have too many estimated parameters for the number of available observations.* We consistently note whenever estimates were based on models with a ratio of less than ten observations per estimated parameter. When the ratio of observations to estimated parameters dropped below five to one and no supplemental evidence of model fit was provided (such as the use of cross-validation or evidence from an analysis of the relative fit of different model specifications), we discount the study's results and do not calculate effect sizes for its estimates.

- *Models making no adjustment to standard errors for the serial correlation regularly found in panel data frequently used in gun policy studies.* We consistently note when studies did not report having made any such adjustment. When a study noted a correction for only heteroscedasticity, we consider that to be evidence of some correction, although this does not generally fully correct bias in the standard errors due to clustering (Aneja, Donohue, and Zhang, 2014).
- *Models for which the dependent variable appears to violate model assumptions, such as linear models of dichotomous outcomes or linear models of rate outcomes (many of which are close to zero).* We consistently note when the data appeared to violate modeling assumptions.
- *Effects with large changes in direction and magnitude across primary model specifications.* We consistently note when a study presented evidence that model results were highly sensitive to different model specifications.
- *Models that identify the effect of policies with too few cases.* We consistently note when the effects of policies were identified on the experiences of a single state or a small number of states. These analyses generally provide less persuasive evidence that observed differences between treated and control cases result from the effects of the policy as opposed to other contemporaneous influences on the outcome.

In Appendix A, we describe other common shortcomings in the existing literature that we do not explicitly discuss in our research syntheses. For instance, in the main chapters of the report, we do not note when papers provided no goodness-of-fit tests or other statistical evidence to justify their covariate selections. Neither do we focus on interpretational difficulties and confusion frequently present in studies using spline or hybrid models to estimate the effects of policies, although we discuss this problem in detail in Appendix A. These problems are so common in this literature that consistently commenting on them as shortcomings would become repetitive and cumbersome.

### Synthesis of Evidence

Members of the research team summarized all available evidence from prioritized studies for each of the 13 policies on each of the eight outcomes. When at least one study met inclusion criteria, a multidisciplinary group of methodologists on the research team discussed each study to identify its strengths and weaknesses. The consensus judgments from these group discussions are summarized in the research syntheses. Then, the group discussed the set of available studies as a whole to make a determination about the level of evidence supporting the effect of the policy on each outcome.

When considering the evidence provided by each analysis in a study, we counted effects with $p$-values greater than 0.20 as providing *uncertain* evidence for the effect of a policy. We use this designation to avoid any suggestion that the failure to find a statistically significant effect means that the policy has no effect. We assume that every policy will have some effect, however small or unintended, so any failure to detect it is a shortcoming of the science, not the policy. When the identified effect has a $p$-value less than 0.05, we refer to it as a *significant effect*. Finally, when the *p*-value is between 0.05 and 0.20, we refer to the effect as *suggestive*.

We include the suggestive category for several reasons. First, the literature we are reviewing is often underpowered. This means that the probability of rejecting the null hypothesis of no effect even when the policy has a true effect is often very low. As we argue in Appendix A, conducting analyses with low statistical power results in an uncomfortably high probability that effects found to be statistically significant at $p < 0.05$ are in the wrong direction and all effects have exaggerated effect sizes (Gelman and Carlin, 2014). If we had restricted our assessment of evidence to just statistically significant effects, we might base our judgments on an unreliable and biased set of estimates while ignoring the cumulative evidence available in studies reporting nonsignificant results. While the selection of $p < 0.20$ as the criterion for rating evidence as suggestive is arbitrary, this threshold corresponds to effects that are meaningfully more likely to be in the observed direction than in the opposite direction. For instance, if we assume that the policy has about as much chance of having a nonzero effect as having no effect, and the power of the test is 0.8, then $p < 0.20$ suggests that there is only a 20-percent probability of incorrectly rejecting the null hypothesis of no effect. For tests that are more weakly powered, as is common in models we review, a *p*-value less than 0.20 will result in false rejection less than half the time so long as the power of the test is above 0.2 (see, for example, Colquhoun, 2014).

In the final step, we rated the overall strength of the evidence in support of each possible effect of the policy. We approached these evidence ratings with the knowledge that research in this area is modest. Compared with the study of the effects of smoking on cancer, for instance, the study of gun policy effects is in its infancy, so it cannot hope to have anything like the strength of evidence that has accrued in many other areas of social science. Nevertheless, we believed that it would be useful to distinguish the gun policy effects that have relatively stronger or weaker evidence, given the limited evidence base currently available. We did this by establishing the following relativistic scale describing the strength of available evidence:

1. *No studies.* This designation was made when no studies meeting our inclusion criteria evaluated the policy's effect on the outcome.
2. *Inconclusive evidence.* This designation was made when studies with comparable methodological rigor identified inconsistent evidence for the policy's effect on an outcome or when a single study found only uncertain or suggestive effects.
3. *Limited evidence.* This designation was made when at least one study meeting our inclusion criteria and not otherwise compromised by serious methodological problems reported a significant effect of the policy on the outcome, even if other studies meeting our inclusion criteria identified only uncertain or suggestive evidence for the effect of the policy.

4. *Moderate evidence.* This designation was made when two or more studies found significant effects in the same direction and contradictory evidence was not found in other studies with equivalent or strong methods.
5. *Supportive evidence.* This designation was made when (1) at least three studies found suggestive or significant effects in the same direction using at least two independent data sets or (2) the effect was observed in a rigorous experimental study. Our requirement that the effect be found in distinct data sets reflects the fact that many gun policy studies use identical or overlapping data sets (e.g., state homicide rates over several years). Chance associations in these data sets are likely to be identified by all who analyze them. Therefore, our supportive evidence category requires that the effect be confirmed in a separate data set.

These rating criteria provided a framework for our assessments of where the weight of evidence currently lies for each of the policies, but they did not eliminate subjectivity from the review process. In particular, the studies we reviewed spanned a wide range of methodological rigor. When we judged a study to be particularly weak, we discounted its evidence in comparison with stronger studies, which sometimes led us to apply lower evidence rating labels than had the study been stronger.

## Effects of the Inclusion and Exclusion Criteria on the Literature Reviewed

Table 2.2 presents the results of the literature search across all eight outcomes. The final column shows the number of studies meeting all inclusion criteria. No studies satisfying our inclusion criteria were found for two of the eight outcomes.

**Table 2.2**
**Number of Studies Selected for Review at Each Stage of the Review Process**

| Outcome | Total Search Results | Included After Title and Abstract Review | Included After Full-Text Review |
|---|---|---|---|
| Suicide | 1,274 | 183 | 11 |
| Violent crime | 2,656 | 373 | 47 |
| Unintentional injuries and deaths | 531 | 27 | 3 |
| Mass shootings | 77 | 11 | 8 |
| Officer-involved shootings | 187 | 34 | 0 |
| Defensive gun use | 1,435 | 115 | 1 |
| Hunting and recreation | 229 | 0 | 0 |
| Gun industry | 3,180 | 19 | 2 |

Of the studies that were published before 2003, all but Duwe, Kovandzic, and Moody (2002) were considered in the earlier reviews (Hahn et al., 2005; NRC, 2004). Table 2.3 lists the 62 studies meeting all inclusion criteria.

**Table 2.3**
**Studies Meeting Inclusion Criteria**

| No. | Study |
|---|---|
| 1 | Aneja, Donohue, and Zhang (2011) |
| 2 | Aneja, Donohue, and Zhang (2014) |
| 3 | Ayres and Donohue (2003a) |
| 4 | Ayres and Donohue (2003b) |
| 5 | Ayres and Donohue (2009a) |
| 6 | Ayres and Donohue (2009b) |
| 7 | Cheng and Hoekstra (2013) |
| 8 | Cook and Ludwig (2003) |
| 9 | Crifasi et al. (2015) |
| 10 | Cummings et al. (1997a) |
| 11 | DeSimone, Markowitz, and Xu (2013) |
| 12 | Donohue (2003) |
| 13 | Donohue (2004) |
| 14 | Duggan (2001) |
| 15 | Duggan, Hjalmarsson, and Jacob (2011) |
| 16 | Durlauf, Navarro, and Rivers (2016) |
| 17 | Duwe, Kovandzic, and Moody (2002) |
| 18 | French and Heagerty (2008) |
| 19 | Gius (2014) |
| 20 | Gius (2015a) |
| 21 | Gius (2015b) |
| 22 | Gius (2015c) |
| 23 | Grambsch (2008) |
| 24 | Helland and Tabarrok (2004) |
| 25 | Hepburn et al. (2006) |
| 26 | Humphreys, Gasparrini, and Wiebe (2017) |
| 27 | Kendall and Tamura (2010) |
| 28 | Koper (2004) |
| 29 | Kovandzic, Marvell, and Vieraitis (2005) |
| 30 | La Valle (2007) |
| 31 | La Valle (2010) |
| 32 | La Valle (2013) |
| 33 | La Valle and Glover (2012) |
| 34 | Lott (2003) |
| 35 | Lott (2010) |
| 36 | Lott and Mustard (1997) |
| 37 | Lott and Whitley (2001) |
| 38 | Lott and Whitley (2003) |
| 39 | Lott and Whitley (2007) |
| 40 | Luca, Deepak, and Poliquin (2016) |
| 41 | Ludwig and Cook (2000) |
| 42 | Maltz and Targonski (2002) |
| 43 | Manski and Pepper (2015) |
| 44 | Martin and Legault (2005) |
| 45 | Moody and Marvell (2008) |
| 46 | Moody and Marvell (2009) |
| 47 | Moody et al. (2014) |
| 48 | Plassman and Whitley (2003) |
| 49 | Raissian (2016) |
| 50 | Roberts (2009) |
| 51 | Rosengart et al. (2005) |
| 52 | Rudolph et al. (2015) |
| 53 | Sen and Panjamapirom (2012) |
| 54 | Strnad (2007) |
| 55 | Swanson et al. (2013) |
| 56 | Swanson et al. (2016) |
| 57 | Vigdor and Mercy (2003) |
| 58 | Vigdor and Mercy (2006) |
| 59 | Webster, Crifasi, and Vernick (2014) |
| 60 | Webster and Starnes (2000) |
| 61 | Webster et al. (2004) |
| 62 | Wright, Wintemute, and Rivara (1999) |
| 63 | Zeoli and Webster (2010) |

In a few cases, some studies published updates to earlier works that expanded the time frame of the analysis, corrected errors, or applied more-advanced statistical methods to a nearly identical data set. In these cases, we do not treat both the earlier and later works as each contributing an equally valid estimate of the effects of a policy. Instead, we treat the latest version of the analysis as superseding the earlier versions, and we focus our reviews on the superseding analysis. In one case, we substituted an earlier study (Ludwig and Cook, 2000) for a later study (Cook and Ludwig, 2003). We did this because the earlier study included a longer data series, used a model with greater statistical power, and provided more-detailed results; in addition, the estimated effects of policies in the two papers were identical for the estimates of interest to us in this review. Table 2.4 lists the superseded studies and their superseding versions.

Table 2.5 describes the policies and outcomes evaluated by each study that was not superseded, and studies are indicated with their corresponding number in Table 2.3. These studies are discussed in detail in subsequent chapters.

**Table 2.4**
**Superseded Studies**

| Superseded | Superseding |
|---|---|
| Aneja, Donohue, and Zhang (2011); Ayres and Donohue (2003a, 2003b, 2009a, 2009b); Donohue (2003, 2004) | Aneja, Donohue, and Zhang (2014) |
| La Valle (2007, 2010) | La Valle (2013), La Valle and Glover (2012) |
| Moody and Marvell (2008, 2009) | Moody et al. (2014) |
| Vigdor and Mercy (2003) | Vigdor and Mercy (2006) |

**Table 2.5**
**Included Studies, by Policy and Outcome**

| Policy | Suicide | Violent Crime | Unintentional Injuries and Deaths | Mass Shootings | Officer-Involved Shootings | Defensive Gun Use | Hunting and Recreation | Gun Industry | Total |
|---|---|---|---|---|---|---|---|---|---|
| Background checks | 15, 41, 53 | 15, 20, 32, 35, 41, 53, 55, 56, 58, 62 | | 40 | | | | | **11** |
| Bans on the sale of assault weapons and high-capacity magazines | | 19, 35 | | 22, 40 | | | | 28 | **5** |
| Stand-your-ground laws | 26 | 7, 26, 59 | | | | 7 | | | **3** |
| Prohibitions associated with mental illness | 53, 56 | 53, 55, 56 | | | | | | | **3** |
| Lost or stolen firearm reporting requirements | | | | | | | | | **0** |
| Licensing and permitting requirements | 9, 61 | 32, 52, 59 | | 40 | | | | | **6** |
| Firearm sales reporting and recording requirements | | | | | | | | | **0** |
| Child-access prevention laws | 10, 11, 21, 37, 61 | 10, 37 | 10, 11, 21, 25, 37, 60, 61 | 34 | | | | | **8** |
| Surrender of firearms by prohibited possessors | | 49, 58, 63 | | | | | | | **3** |
| Minimum age requirements | 21, 51, 61 | 51, 52 | 21 | 40 | | | | | **5** |
| Concealed-carry laws | 11, 51 | 2, 16, 18, 19, 23, 24, 27, 29, 32, 33, 38, 39, 42, 43, 44, 47, 48, 50, 51, 54, 59 | 11, 36 | 17, 34, 40 | | | | 14 | **27** |
| Waiting periods | 41 | 41, 50 | | 34, 40 | | | | | **4** |
| Gun-free zones | | | | | | | | | **0** |
| **Total** | **12** | **37** | **8** | **4** | **0** | **1** | **0** | **2** | **50** |

NOTE: Numbers refer to individual studies; see Table 2.3 to view which study corresponds to which number. Totals along the bottom row do not exactly match those in Table 2.2 because superseded studies are not counted in this table, and other studies were identified after the initial literature search.

## Effect Size Estimates

To compare the magnitude of effects across studies, we calculated and present incidence rate ratios (IRRs) for most of the estimates of policy effects that we considered in reaching our consensus ratings. In rare cases noted in the text, we were unable to calculate IRRs from the information provided in the report. Studies reporting the results from a negative binomial or Poisson regression model are directly reported in our report figures as IRRs with their associated confidence intervals (CIs). Given the low probability of most of our outcomes, odds ratios were interpreted and reported as IRRs with their associated CIs.

Many studies used fixed-effects ordinary linear regression models. In these cases, an average base rate (usually taken from the study's paper itself) of the outcome of interest was determined. We then used the base rate to transform the regression estimate, $\beta$, to an IRR using the following formula:

$$IRR = \frac{(\text{average base rate} + \beta)}{\text{average base rate}}.$$

However, if the linear model used a logged dependent variable, we used the exponentiated estimate as its IRR. CIs for the IRRs derived from the linear regression models were transformed in a similar fashion.

When a study did not report a measure of variation, we performed back calculation from a test statistic to estimate the CIs. For Rudolph et al. (2015), we inferred approximate standard errors from the *p*-value associated with a permutation test presented to demonstrate the likely statistical significance of the reported finding. For Crifasi et al. (2015), we present the IRR and CI for a secondary specification that used a negative binomial model. For several other studies, we note that we could not extrapolate an IRR or its CIs from the data provided in the paper.

Models estimating linear or other trend effects for policies do not have a constant effect size over time. Even if we selected an arbitrary period over which to calculate an effect size, these papers do not provide sufficient information to estimate CIs for such effects. Therefore, we do not calculate or display IRR values that take into account trend effects or effects calculated as the combination of a trend and a step effect (*hybrid models*). Although we report the authors' interpretation of these effects, we do not count them as compelling evidence for the effects of a policy, for reasons discussed in Appendix A.

IRRs are calculated and graphed so that estimates of the effects of policies can be compared on a common metric. We do not use them to construct meta-analytic estimates of policy effects for two reasons. First, most studies we reviewed examining the effect of a policy on a particular outcome used nearly identical data sets, meaning the studies do not offer independent estimates of the effect. Second, there are usually only two or three studies available on which to estimate the effect of the policy, and these studies often differ considerably in their methodological rigor. These limitations in the existing literature led us to pursue a more qualitative evaluation of the conclusions that available studies can support.

## Chapter Two References


Aneja, Abhay, John J. Donohue III, and Alexandria Zhang, "The Impact of Right-to-Carry Laws and the NRC Report: Lessons for the Empirical Evaluation of Law and Policy," *American Law and Economics Review*, Vol. 13, No. 2, 2011, pp. 565–631.

———, *The Impact of Right to Carry Laws and the NRC Report: The Latest Lessons for the Empirical Evaluation of Law and Policy*, Stanford, Calif.: Stanford Law School, Olin Working Paper No. 461, December 1, 2014. As of May 21, 2017:
https://papers.ssrn.com/sol3/papers.cfm?abstract_id=2443681

Ayres, Ian, and John J. Donohue III, "Shooting Down the More Guns, Less Crime Hypothesis," *Stanford Law Review*, Vol. 55, No. 4, 2003a, pp. 1193–1312.

———, "The Latest Misfires in Support of the More Guns, Less Crime Hypothesis," *Stanford Law Review*, Vol. 55, No. 4, 2003b, pp. 1371–1398.

———, "Yet Another Refutation of the More Guns, Less Crime Hypothesis—with Some Help from Moody and Marvell," *Econ Journal Watch*, Vol. 6, No. 1, January 2009a, pp. 35–59.

———, "More Guns, Less Crime Fails Again: The Latest Evidence from 1977–2006," *Econ Journal Watch*, Vol. 6, No. 2, May 2009b, pp. 218–238.

Braga, Anthony A., "Guns and Crime," in F. Parisi, ed., *The Oxford Handbook of Law and Economics*, Vol. 3: *Public Law and Legal Institutions*, New York: Oxford University Press, 2017, pp. 344–369.

Braga, Anthony A., Andrew V. Papachristos, and David M. Hureau, "The Effects of Hot Spots Policing on Crime: An Updated Systematic Review and Meta-Analysis," *Justice Quarterly*, Vol. 31, No. 4, 2014, pp. 633–663.

Braga, Anthony A., and David L. Weisburd, "The Effects of Focused Deterrence Strategies on Crime: A Systematic Review and Meta-Analysis of the Empirical Evidence," *Journal of Research in Crime and Delinquency*, Vol. 49, No. 3, 2012, pp. 323–358.

Campbell Collaboration, *Guidelines for Preparation of Review Protocols*, Version 1.0, Oslo, Norway, January 1, 2001. As of October 13, 2017:
https://www.campbellcollaboration.org/images/pdf/plain-language/C2_Protocols_guidelines_v1.pdf

Cheng, Cheng, and Mark Hoekstra, "Does Strengthening Self-Defense Law Deter Crime or Escalate Violence? Evidence from Expansions to Castle Doctrine," *Journal of Human Resources*, Vol. 48, No. 3, 2013, pp. 821–853.

Colquhoun, D., "An Investigation of the False Discovery Rate and the Misinterpretation of *p*-Values," *Royal Society Open Science*, Vol. 1, No. 3, 2014.

Cook, P. J., and Jens Ludwig, "The Effect of the Brady Act on Gun Violence," in B. Harcourt, ed., *Guns, Crime, and Punishment in America*, New York: New York University Press, 2003, pp. 283–298.

Crifasi, C. K., J. S. Meyers, J. S. Vernick, and D. W. Webster, "Effects of Changes in Permit-to-Purchase Handgun Laws in Connecticut and Missouri on Suicide Rates," *Preventive Medicine*, Vol. 79, 2015, pp. 43–49.

Cummings, P., D. C. Grossman, F. P. Rivara, and T. D. Koepsell, "State Gun Safe Storage Laws and Child Mortality Due to Firearms," *JAMA*, Vol. 278, No. 13, 1997a, pp. 1084–1086.

DeSimone, J., S. Markowitz, and J. Xu, "Child Access Prevention Laws and Nonfatal Gun Injuries," *Southern Economic Journal*, Vol. 80, No. 1, 2013, pp. 5–25.

Donohue, John J., "The Impact of Concealed Carry Laws," in Jens Ludwig and Phillip J. Cook, eds., *Evaluating Gun Policy: Effects on Crime and Violence,* Washington, D.C.: Brookings Institution Press, 2003, pp. 287–341.

———, "Guns, Crime, and the Impact of State Right-to-Carry Laws," *Fordham Law Review,* Vol. 73, No. 2, 2004, pp. 623–652.

Duggan, Mark, "More Guns, More Crime," *Journal of Political Economy,* Vol. 109, No. 5, 2001, pp. 1086–1114.

Duggan, Mark, Randi Hjalmarsson, and Brian A. Jacob, "The Short-Term and Localized Effect of Gun Shows: Evidence from California and Texas," *Review of Economics and Statistics,* Vol. 93, No. 3, 2011, pp. 786–799.

Durlauf, Steven, S. Navarro, and D. A. Rivers, "Model Uncertainty and the Effect of Shall-Issue Right-to-Carry Laws on Crime," *European Economic Review,* Vol. 81, 2016, pp. 32–67.

Duwe, Grant, Tomislav Kovandzic, and Carlisle E. Moody, "The Impact of Right-to-Carry Concealed Firearm Laws on Mass Public Shootings," *Homicide Studies,* Vol. 6, No. 4, 2002, pp. 271–296.

French, B., and P. J. Heagerty, "Analysis of Longitudinal Data to Evaluate a Policy Change," *Statistics in Medicine,* Vol. 27, No. 24, 2008, pp. 5005–5025.

Gelman, Andrew, and John Carlin, "Power Calculations: Assessing Type S (Sign) and Type M (Magnitude) Errors," *Perspectives on Psychological Science,* Vol. 9, No. 6, 2014, pp. 641–651.

Gius, Mark, "An Examination of the Effects of Concealed Weapons Laws and Assault Weapons Bans on State-Level Murder Rates," *Applied Economics Letters,* Vol. 21, No. 4, 2014, pp. 265–267.

———, "The Effects of State and Federal Background Checks on State-Level Gun-Related Murder Rates," *Applied Economics,* Vol. 47, No. 38, 2015a, pp. 4090–4101.

———, "The Impact of Minimum Age and Child Access Prevention Laws on Firearm-Related Youth Suicides and Unintentional Deaths," *Social Science Journal,* Vol. 52, No. 2, 2015b, pp. 168–175.

———, "The Impact of State and Federal Assault Weapons Bans on Public Mass Shootings," *Applied Economics Letters,* Vol. 22, No. 4, 2015c, pp. 281–284.

Grambsch, P., "Regression to the Mean, Murder Rates, and Shall-Issue Laws," *American Statistician,* Vol. 62, No. 4, 2008, pp. 289–295.

Hahn, Robert A., Oleg Bilukha, Alex Crosby, Mindy T. Fullilove, Akiva Liberman, Eve Moscicki, Susan Snyder, Farris Tuma, and Peter A. Briss, "Firearms Laws and the Reduction of Violence: A Systematic Review," *American Journal of Preventive Medicine,* Vol. 28, No. 2, 2005, pp. 40–71.

Helland, E., and A. Tabarrok, "Using Placebo Laws to Test 'More Guns, Less Crime,'" *Advances in Economic Analysis and Policy,* Vol. 4, No. 1, 2004.

Hepburn, L., D. Azrael, M. Miller, and D. Hemenway, "The Effect of Child Access Prevention Laws on Unintentional Child Firearm Fatalities, 1979–2000," *Journal of Trauma-Injury Infection and Critical Care,* Vol. 61, No. 2, 2006, pp. 423–428.

Higgins, Julian P. T., and Sally Green, eds., *Cochrane Handbook for Systematic Reviews of Interventions,* Version 5.1.0, London: Cochrane Collaboration, March 2011. As of October 13, 2017: http://handbook.cochrane.org

Humphreys, David K., Antonio Gasparrini, and Douglas J. Wiebe, "Evaluating the Impact of Florida's 'Stand Your Ground' Self-Defense Law on Homicide and Suicide by Firearm: An Interrupted Time Series Study," *JAMA Internal Medicine,* Vol. 177, No. 1, 2017, pp. 44–50.

Institute of Medicine, *Finding What Works in Health Care: Standards for Systematic Reviews*, Washington, D.C.: National Academies Press, 2011.

Kalesan, Bindu, Matthew E. Mobily, Olivia Keiser, Jeffrey A. Fagan, and Sandro Galea, "Firearm Legislation and Firearm Mortality in the USA: A Cross-Sectional, State-Level Study," *Lancet*, Vol. 387, No. 10030, April 30, 2016, pp. 1847–1855.

Kendall, Todd D., and Robert Tamura, "Unmarried Fertility, Crime, and Social Stigma," *Journal of Law and Economics*, Vol. 53, No. 1, 2010, pp. 185–221.

Khan, Khalid S., Regina Kunz, Jos Kleijnen, and Gerd Antes, "Five Steps to Conducting a Systematic Review," *Journal of the Royal Society of Medicine*, Vol. 96, No. 3, 2003, pp. 118–121.

Koper, Christopher S., *Updated Assessment of the Federal Assault Weapons Ban: Impacts on Gun Markets and Gun Violence 1994–2003*, Washington, D.C.: National Institute of Justice, U.S. Department of Justice, 2004.

Kovandzic, T. V., T. B. Marvell, and L. M. Vieraitis, "The Impact of 'Shall-Issue' Concealed Handgun Laws on Violent Crime Rates—Evidence from Panel Data for Large Urban Cities," *Homicide Studies*, Vol. 9, No. 4, 2005, pp. 292–323.

La Valle, James M., "Rebuilding at Gunpoint: A City-Level Re-Estimation of the Brady Law and RTC Laws in the Wake of Hurricane Katrina," *Criminal Justice Policy Review*, Vol. 18, No. 4, 2007, pp. 451–465.

———, "Re-Estimating Gun-Policy Effects According to a National Science Academy Report: Were Previous Reports of Failure Premature?" *Journal of Crime and Justice*, Vol. 33, No. 1, 2010, pp. 71–95.

———, "'Gun Control' vs. 'Self-Protection': A Case Against the Ideological Divide," *Justice Policy Journal*, Vol. 10, No. 1, 2013, pp. 1–26.

La Valle, James M., and Thomas C. Glover, "Revisiting Licensed Handgun Carrying: Personal Protection or Interpersonal Liability?" *American Journal of Criminal Justice*, Vol. 37, No. 4, 2012, pp. 580–601.

Lott, John R., Jr., *The Bias Against Guns: Why Almost Everything You've Heard About Gun Control Is Wrong*, Washington, D.C.: Regnery Publishing, Inc., 2003.

———, *More Guns, Less Crime: Understanding Crime and Gun-Control Laws*, 3rd ed., Chicago, Ill.: University of Chicago Press, 2010.

Lott, John R., Jr., and D. B. Mustard, "Crime, Deterrence, and Right-to-Carry Concealed Handguns," *Journal of Legal Studies*, Vol. 26, No. 1, 1997, pp. 1–68.

Lott, John R., Jr., and John E. Whitley, "Safe-Storage Gun Laws: Accidental Deaths, Suicides, and Crime," *Journal of Law and Economics*, Vol. 44, No. 2, 2001, pp. 659–689.

———, "Measurement Error in County-Level UCR Data," *Journal of Quantitative Criminology*, Vol. 19, No. 2, June 2003, pp. 185–198.

———, "Abortion and Crime: Unwanted Children and Out-of-Wedlock Births," *Economic Inquiry*, Vol. 45, No. 2, 2007, pp. 304–324.

Luca, Michael, Lahotra Deepak, and Christopher Poliquin, *The Impact of Mass Shootings on Gun Policy*, working paper, Boston, Mass.: Harvard Business School, 2016.

Ludwig, J., and P. J. Cook, "Homicide and Suicide Rates Associated with Implementation of the Brady Handgun Violence Prevention Act," *JAMA*, Vol. 284, No. 5, 2000, pp. 585–591.

Maltz, M. D., and J. Targonski, "A Note on the Use of County-Level UCR Data, *Journal of Quantitative Criminology*, Vol. 18, No. 2, 2002, pp. 297–318.

Manski, Charles F., and John V. Pepper, *How Do Right-to-Carry Laws Affect Crime Rates? Coping with Ambiguity Using Bounded-Variation Assumptions*, Cambridge, Mass.: National Bureau for Economic Research, NBER Working Paper 21701, November 2015.

Martin, Robert A., and Richard L. Legault, "Systematic Measurement Error with State-Level Crime Data: Evidence from the 'More Guns, Less Crime' Debate," *Journal of Research in Crime and Delinquency*, Vol. 42, No. 2, May 2005, pp. 187–210.

Mill, John Stuart, *A System of Logic,* London: Parker, 1843.

Moody, Carlisle E., and Thomas B. Marvell, "The Debate on Shall-Issue Laws," *Econ Journal Watch*, Vol. 5, No. 3, 2008, pp. 269–293.

———, "The Debate on Shall-Issue Laws, Continued," *Econ Journal Watch*, Vol. 6, No. 2, 2009.

Moody, Carlisle E., Thomas B. Marvell, Paul R. Zimmerman, and Fasil Alemante, "The Impact of Right-to-Carry Laws on Crime: An Exercise in Replication," *Review of Economics and Finance*, Vol. 4, 2014, pp. 33–43.

National Research Council, *Firearms and Violence: A Critical Review*, Washington, D.C.: National Academies Press, 2004.

NRC—*See* National Research Council.

Plassmann, F., and J. E. Whitley, "Comments: Confirming More Guns, Less Crime," *Stanford Law Review*, Vol. 55, No. 4, 2003, pp. 1313–1369.

Raissian, Kerri M., "Hold Your Fire: Did the 1996 Federal Gun Control Act Expansion Reduce Domestic Homicides?" *Journal of Policy Analysis and Management*, Vol. 35, No. 1, Winter 2016, pp. 67–93.

Roberts, Darryl W., "Intimate Partner Homicide: Relationships to Alcohol and Firearms," *Journal of Contemporary Criminal Justice*, Vol. 25, No. 1, 2009, pp. 67–88.

Rosengart, M., P. Cummings, A. Nathens, P. Heagerty, R. Maier, and F. Rivara, "An Evaluation of State Firearm Regulations and Homicide and Suicide Death Rates," *Injury Prevention*, Vol. 11, No. 2, 2005, pp. 77–83.

Rudolph, K. E., E. A. Stuart, J. S. Vernick, and D. W. Webster, "Association Between Connecticut's Permit-to-Purchase Handgun Law and Homicides," *American Journal of Public Health*, Vol. 105, No. 8, 2015, pp. E49–E54.

Schell, Terry L., and Andrew R. Morral, *Evaluating Methods and Findings from a Study of State Gun Policies*, Santa Monica, Calif.: RAND Corporation, RR-1642-RC, 2016. As of January 13, 2017: http://www.rand.org/pubs/research_reports/RR1642.html

Sen, B., and A. Panjamapirom, "State Background Checks for Gun Purchase and Firearm Deaths: An Exploratory Study," *Preventive Medicine*, Vol. 55, No. 4, 2012, pp. 346–350.

Strnad, Jeff, "Should Legal Empiricists Go Bayesian?" *American Law and Economics Review*, Vol. 9, No. 1, Spring 2007, pp. 195–303.

Swanson, Jeffrey W., Michele M. Easter, Allison G. Robertson, Marvin S. Swartz, Kelly Alanis-Hirsch, Daniel Moseley, Charles Dion, and John Petrila, "Gun Violence, Mental Illness, and Laws That Prohibit Gun Possession: Evidence from Two Florida Counties," *Health Affairs*, Vol. 35, No. 6, 2016, pp. 1067–1075.

Swanson, J. W., A. G. Robertson, L. K. Frisman, M. A. Norko, H. Lin, M. S. Swartz, and P. J. Cook, "Preventing Gun Violence Involving People with Serious Mental Illness," in D. W. Webster and J. S. Vernick, eds., *Reducing Gun Violence in America: Informing Policy with Evidence and Analysis*, Baltimore, Md.: Johns Hopkins University Press, 2013, pp. 33–51.

Vigdor, E. R., and J. A. Mercy, "Disarming Batterers: The Impact of Domestic Violence Firearms Laws," in Jens Ludwig and Phillip J. Cook, eds., *Evaluating Gun Policy: Effects on Crime and Violence,* Washington, D.C.: Brookings Institution Press, 2003, pp. 157–200.

———, "Do Laws Restricting Access to Firearms by Domestic Violence Offenders Prevent Intimate Partner Homicide?" *Evaluation Review*, Vol. 30, No. 3, 2006, pp. 313–346.

Webster, D., C. K. Crifasi, and J. S. Vernick, "Effects of the Repeal of Missouri's Handgun Purchaser Licensing Law on Homicides," *Journal of Urban Health*, Vol. 91, No. 2, 2014, pp. 293–302.

Webster, D. W., J. S. Vernick, A. M. Zeoli, and J. A. Manganello, "Association Between Youth-Focused Firearm Laws and Youth Suicides," *JAMA*, Vol. 292, No. 5, 2004, pp. 594–601.

Wooldridge, J. M., *Econometric Analysis of Cross Section and Panel Data*, Cambridge, Mass.: MIT Press, 2002.

Wright, M. A., G. J. Wintemute, and F. P. Rivara, "Effectiveness of Denial of Handgun Purchase to Persons Believed to Be at High Risk for Firearm Violence," *American Journal of Public Health*, Vol. 89, No. 1, 1999, pp. 88–90.

Zeoli, A. M., and D. W. Webster, "Effects of Domestic Violence Policies, Alcohol Taxes and Police Staffing Levels on Intimate Partner Homicide in Large U.S. Cities," *Injury Prevention*, Vol. 16, No. 2, 2010, pp. 90–95.

PART B

# Evidence on the Effects of 13 Policies

CHAPTER THREE

# Background Checks

Background checks for gun purchases are designed to prevent access to guns by convicted felons and other prohibited possessors—such as minors, fugitives from justice, those who live in the United States illegally, users of controlled substances, those with certain histories of mental illness, those who have been dishonorably discharged from the military, those who have renounced their U.S. citizenship, those subject to a restraining order, and those convicted of domestic violence offenses (18 U.S.C. 922).

The Brady Handgun Violence Prevention Act (the Brady Act), which went into effect in 1994, imposed federal requirements for background checks on sales by licensed dealers (18 U.S.C. 922) but not for private sales or transfers of firearms (such as gifts). Several states have expanded this federal requirement to mandate that background checks be conducted for all firearm sales and transfers, including those between private parties. Such laws are referred to as *universal background check* laws.

Background check laws prevent firearm purchase or possession by individuals thought to be at high risk of presenting a danger to themselves or others. By restricting the means by which dangerous individuals could otherwise access guns, these laws are designed to reduce gun crime and violence. While compliance is likely to be imperfect, a universal background check may still reduce gun-related homicides or suicides by deterring prohibited possessors from attempting to acquire firearms or by making it harder for them to succeed in doing so. Universal background checks may also reduce illegal gun trafficking. For instance, when analyzing crime guns,[1] Webster, Vernick, and Bulzacchelli (2009) found that fewer of the out-of-state guns originated in states with universal background checks than in states with no background checks for private sales of firearms. The magnitude of the effects of such laws will, in part, be influenced by the level of enforcement and the availability of firearms through alternative markets, such as illegal markets or legal markets in states without background checks for private transactions.

[1] The Bureau of Alcohol, Tobacco, and Firearms (2002, p. A-3) defined *crime gun* as "any firearm that is illegally possessed, used in a crime, or suspected to have been used in a crime. An abandoned firearm may also be categorized as a crime gun if it is suspected it was used in a crime or illegally possessed."

We found no routinely collected data on how individuals obtain guns, but a 2015 national survey of gun owners who obtained a firearm within the previous two years found that 22 percent had purchased, or received as a gift or an inheritance, their most recent firearm without undergoing a background check (Miller, Hepburn, and Azrael, 2017). For firearms purchased through private sources, 50 percent were acquired without a background check (Miller, Hepburn, and Azrael, 2017). Obtaining firearms from private sources is likely substantially more common among prohibited possessors. Indeed, a 2004 survey of state prison inmates found that among those who used a gun, only 10 percent purchased the weapon from a licensed dealer, whereas 70 percent acquired it from a friend, family member, or "street" source, such as an illicit broker (Cook, Parker, and Pollack, 2015). Using the same survey data but restricting the sample to 13 states considered by the authors to have less-restrictive firearm regulations, another study found that among inmates who acquired their gun from a friend, family member, or "street" source, just more than 40 percent had a disqualifying condition (e.g., prior felony conviction, dishonorable discharge, under age 18) that should have prohibited them from obtaining the firearm had they undergone a background check (Vittes, Vernick, and Webster, 2012).

Universal background check policies may do little to limit existing illegal sources of firearms to criminal offenders (Kopel, 2016), and background check policies can, at best, prevent such individuals only from acquiring new firearms, not from maintaining possession of those they owned before becoming a prohibited possessor. However, if the implementation and enforcement of such policies is successful in stemming the flow of new firearms and ammunition to criminal markets, universal background check laws could reduce gun crime by increasing the price of firearms in the secondary markets on which criminals mostly rely (Cook, Molliconi, and Cole, 1995).

The effects of background check policies will hinge on the scope of disqualifications for high-risk individuals and whether these disqualifications correctly target individuals who present greater danger to themselves or others. As of April 2017, the Federal Bureau of Investigation (FBI)'s National Instant Criminal Background Check System (NICS) database currently includes more than 16,500,000 active records on prohibited possessors (FBI, 2017). However, this figure substantially undercounts prohibited possessors because states' reporting is incomplete and the FBI does not maintain records on those prohibited only for being underage. The excess risk of firearm violence attributable to prohibited individuals is unknown, although research has shown that the majority of violent offenders have previous involvement with the criminal justice system (Wright and Wintemute, 2010; Cook, Ludwig, and Braga, 2005; Kleck and Bordua, 1983) and that individuals prohibited from owning a firearm because of mental health problems are at elevated risk of suicide (see Chapter Nineteen).

Although firearms are used relatively rarely in intimate partner violence overall—for example, in fewer than 1 percent of nonfatal intimate partner violence police reports in New York City (Joshi and Sorenson, 2010)—the majority of domestic homicides involve firearms (Cooper and Smith, 2011). In addition, more than two-thirds of these homicides are preceded by a history of assaults (Juodis et al., 2014; Campbell et al., 2003; McFarlane et al., 1999). Furthermore, one study found that of the 116 mass shooting incidents between 2009 and 2016 for which information was available, 44 incidents (34 percent) involved a prohibited possessor (Everytown for Gun Safety Support Fund, 2017b). This share may be much lower for public mass shootings; one analysis reports that the majority of recent public mass shooters purchased at least one of their weapons legally and with a federal background check (Buchanan et al., 2016).

In assessing background check policies, the ideal analyses would estimate effects on outcomes specifically for those populations or individuals whose access to firearms became restricted under the regulations. For instance, to study the impact on suicide of background check laws that disqualify individuals with mental illness, one would like to estimate how, after the law was implemented, suicide rates changed specifically among individuals newly prohibited by the law. Similarly, data on the price of firearms in secondary and illegal markets would be valuable for understanding whether background check laws or their expansion to new populations of prohibited possessors cause access to firearms in secondary markets to become restricted.

However, there are numerous challenges to undertaking this type of analysis, because most data sources available to researchers lack detailed information on the characteristics of criminal offenders or suicide victims beyond age, gender, and race/ethnicity. In some cases (e.g., restraining orders), an individual may be only temporarily prohibited from possessing a firearm, and, in the case of crime outcomes, details on the criminal offender can be known only if the perpetrator is known. (See discussion of data limitations in Chapter Twenty-Five.) Given these challenges, it is unsurprising that most of the articles meeting our inclusion criteria for this policy did not use these types of data. Nevertheless, two studies (Swanson et al., 2013; Swanson et al., 2016) were able to merge administrative records from public health and criminal justice agencies to focus on violent crime outcomes for individuals with disqualifying mental health conditions.

## State Implementation of Background Checks

As of January 1, 2017, 19 states and the District of Columbia have promulgated some universal background check laws (Giffords Law Center to Prevent Gun Violence, undated-f). Eight states and the District of Columbia have comprehensive background check laws that require checks at the point of transfer for all firearms.[2] Even within

---

[2] California, Colorado, Delaware, Nevada, New York, Oregon, Rhode Island, and Washington. See Calif. Penal Code §§28220; Colo. Rev. Stat. § 18-12-112; 11 Del.C. § 1448A; Nev. Rev. Stat. Ann. § 202.254; N.Y.

these states, there are some differences in the laws. For example, California, Colorado, Delaware, Nevada, New York, Washington, and the District of Columbia require that all transfers to individuals (with some minor exceptions) are processed through licensed dealers, who conduct the background checks.[3] Somewhat similarly, Oregon requires all transfers and background checks to be processed through dealers, except that sellers at gun shows may request background checks directly with the Department of State Police.[4] Two more states, Pennsylvania and Maryland, have the same universal background check requirements, but they are applicable only to handguns.[5]

Other states require background checks before law enforcement can issue a permit to purchase. Five states have promulgated such laws for all firearms,[6] while four states have such laws for handguns only.[7] Under these laws, firearms (or handguns in the latter four states) may not be purchased without permits, but the permitting systems and rules differ. For example, in Hawaii, a permit for a handgun must be used within ten days of receipt, and a new permit must be issued for each handgun transfer.[8] In Illinois, however, a permit lasts ten years.[9] Furthermore, some states allow exceptions for those who hold permits to carry or concealed-carry permits, which may have longer durations than the permits to purchase.[10]

---

Gen. Bus. Law §§ 897, 898; O.R.S. § 166.435; R.I. Gen. Laws §§ 11-47-35; Wash. Rev. Code Ann. § 9.41.113; D.C. Code Ann. §§ 7-2502.01, 7-2502.03.

3 Calif. Penal Code §§ 27545, 27875; Colo. Rev. Stat. § 18-12-112; 24 Del.C. § 904A; Nev. Rev. Stat. Ann. § 202.254; N.Y. Gen. Bus. Law § 898; Wash. Rev. Code Ann. § 9.41.113; D.C. Code Ann. § 7-2505.02.

4 O.R.S. §§ 166.435, 166.436.

5 18 Pa. Cons. Stat. Ann. § 6111; Md. Code Ann., Pub. Safety § 5-124. In Pennsylvania, the checks must be processed through a licensed dealer. In Maryland, the seller may go through a dealer or contact the law enforcement agency personally.

6 Connecticut, Hawaii, Illinois, Massachusetts, and New Jersey. See Conn. Gen. Stat. §§ 29-33, 28, 36f, 36g; Hawaii Rev. Stat. Ann. § 134-2; 430 Ill. Comp. Stat. 65/2, 65/4; Mass. Gen. Laws Ch.140 §§ 129B, 129C; N.J. Stat. Ann. § 2C: 58-3.

7 Iowa, Michigan, Nebraska, and North Carolina. See Ia. Code § 724.15; Mich. Comp. Laws § 28.422; Neb. Rev. Stat. Ann. § 69-2404 69-2405; N.C. Gen. Stat. § 14-402, 14-404.

8 Hawaii Rev. Stat. Ann. § 134-2. But note that long-gun permits last for one year and can be used for multiple purchases.

9 430 Ill. Comp. Stat. 65/7.

10 For example, individuals purchasing a firearm in Massachusetts must obtain a firearm identification card, which lasts three years; however, there is an exception for holders of permits to carry, which last up to six years (Mass. Gen. Laws Ch. 140 §§ 122, 129C). In Illinois, there is an exception for holders of concealed-carry permits, but those last only five years (compared with the ten years for the permit to purchase), so the exception does not typically extend the permit period for gun purchases (430 Ill. Comp. Stat. 65/2).

## Effects on Suicide

### Research Synthesis Findings

In 2004, the National Research Council (NRC) identified only four quasi-experimental studies that examine the impact of gun policies on suicide outcomes. One of these four was Ludwig and Cook (2000), which studied the impact of the 1994 Brady Act and found uncertain effects of the policy on total suicides, firearm suicides, and the proportion of adult suicides caused by a firearm. When restricted to suicides among those aged 55 and older, however, there was a statistically significant decrease in firearm suicides of around 6 percent and in the proportion of suicides involving a firearm of 2.2 percent. However, there was an offsetting increase in suicides by other means and thus only suggestive evidence of a statistically significant decrease in total suicides in this age group. A limitation of the Ludwig and Cook (2000) study is that it had an unfavorable ratio of estimated parameters to observations (less than one to six), meaning it could have misleading parameter estimates and confidence intervals (CIs) due to model overfitting.[11]

In another systematic review, Hahn et al. (2005) evaluated the effects of the gun-acquisition prohibitions that background checks enforce. That review identified one other study of suicide, but it was cross-sectional and did not meet our inclusion criteria. Hahn and colleagues concluded that "available evidence is insufficient to determine the effects of firearms acquisition restriction on public health and criminal violence" (p. 51).

Since the NRC (2004) and Hahn et al. (2005) reports, two additional studies provided evidence on the impact of background checks on suicide. Sen and Panjamapirom (2012) assessed how different *types* of background checks conducted by states affected suicides between 1996 and 2005. They noted that the supply of state and local records to the NICS is voluntary and that substantial variation exists in state laws regarding the categories of records included in background checks. The authors characterized variation across states in background check requirements using an index of the comprehensiveness of such checks, as well as individual indicators for whether states check on restraining orders, mental illness, fugitive status, misdemeanors, and other miscellaneous records. Using state-level data from 1996 to 2005, the authors examined the effects of these types of checks and the effects of a state having a pre–Brady Act background check requirement on both firearm and total suicides. Their regression models included state-level covariates, a lagged outcome variable, and fixed effects for year and census subregion.

---

[11] Ludwig and Cook (2000) also tested the effects of background checks specifically (separate from waiting periods, also imposed by the Brady Act) by comparing five of 32 states that were required to implement background checks but that did not experience a change in their waiting periods (either because they already had a waiting period of five days or more when the Brady Act required this nationally or they implemented an instantaneous background check). These analyses had a ratio of estimated parameters to observations of less than five to one, which did not meet our inclusion criteria.

Sen and Panjamapirom (2012) found an effect of the total number of background check categories on firearm suicides (adjusted incidence rate ratio [IRR] = 0.98; 95-percent CI: 0.96, 1.00). Background checks for mental illness were related to lower firearm suicide and total suicide rates. Sen and Panjamapirom's estimates suggest the post-policy firearm suicide rate to be 96 percent of the expected rate had this policy not been in effect and the total suicide rate to be 97 percent of the expected rate. Background checks for fugitive status were also associated with lower firearm suicide and total suicide rates; the estimated effect for checks of fugitive status suggests that these checks lower firearm suicide rates to 95 percent of what they would otherwise be, and they lower total suicide rates to 91 percent of the expected rate. In this case, however, so few states changed this policy during the study time frame that these effects cannot persuasively be attributed to the background check policy as opposed to other factors affecting suicides in the states around the same time their laws changed. Checks for misdemeanor offenses were also associated with a firearm suicide rate just 95 percent of the expected rate without such checks, although the effect on total suicide was uncertain.

One additional study (Duggan, Hjalmarsson, and Jacob, 2011) examined the short-term effect of gun shows on firearm suicides. Absent state legislation to the contrary, gun-show vendors (and other private sellers) that are not federally licensed dealers are not required to conduct background checks on purchasers, which Duggan, Hjalmarsson, and Jacob (2011) referred to as the *gun-show loophole and which is hereafter termed the gun-show exception*. Some states have passed legislation requiring background checks for all buyers at gun shows. Duggan, Hjalmarsson, and Jacob (2011) examined whether there is a differential effect of gun shows on suicides (separating firearm from nonfirearm suicides, but not estimating total suicides) in a state that has a gun-show *exception* (Texas) compared with a state that has no such *exception* (California). Although they found small but suggestive decreases in firearm suicides in the four weeks after gun shows in Texas, effects were uncertain for nonfirearm suicides in Texas and for either outcome in California. However, the study focused only on background check requirements as they relate to gun shows and not on a broader set of background check policies. Moreover, as the authors acknowledged, their focus was on very short-term (four-week) and localized effects. The study had low statistical power, meaning that even if gun-show *exceptions* had meaningful effects on violence or homicide, these might not have been detected using this paper's procedures (see Wintemute et al., 2010). No covariates were included in the model to account for demographic, social, or economic differences between regions that could obscure any differential effects gun shows have in states with and without the *exception*.

Finally, Swanson et al. (2016) evaluated how changes in state reporting of gun-disqualifying mental health records to the NICS affected suicide rates among individuals in Florida with a disqualifying mental health condition relative to individuals diagnosed with serious mental health illness but not prohibited from purchasing a firearm. The authors found no significant difference between suicide rates before and after implementing expanded NICS reporting for the two groups.

Figure 3.1 displays the IRRs and CIs associated with the background check policies examined in these studies. Because Swanson et al. (2013) and Swanson et al. (2016) did not provide effect estimates or test statistics for their findings, we do not include effect sizes for these studies in the figure. Duggan, Hjalmarsson, and Jacob (2011) did not test the effect of interest here and did provide enough information for us to calculate effect estimates or test statistics, so they too are omitted from the figure.

***How to Read Forest Plots***

The forest-plot figures in this report show the standardized effect sizes (or incidence rate ratios [IRRs]) and their 95-percent confidence intervals (CIs) for each outcome, by policy or law, as revealed in the studies examined. (See Chapter Two for details on how we calculated these effect sizes.) An effect size of 1.00 indicates that, after a state passes the law, we would expect the outcome (e.g., suicide or firearm suicide) to be unaffected. That is, the rate of suicide after the law was passed would by 1 times the rate before the law was passed. An effect size of less than 1.00 indicates that the law appears to reduce the outcome. For example, if the effect size for the effect of background checks on suicides were 0.92, we would expect the suicide rate to fall to 0.92 times the rate prior to passage of the background check law. Conversely, an effect size of more than 1.00 indicates that the law appears to increase the outcome by a factor equivalent to the effect size value. When the CIs do not include the value of 1.00, the estimated effect is statistically significant at $p < 0.05$.

Where relevant, we note in the text when individual analyses relied on methods that we thought might produce inaccurate estimates or CIs. IRRs corresponding to analyses for which we expressed such concerns are indicated by blue squares in the forest plots. Green circles indicate IRR estimates about which we raise no specific methodological concern. Information on the source data and methodological ratings is available in Appendix B.

**Figure 3.1**
**Incidence Rate Ratios Associated with the Effect of Background Checks on Suicide**

| Study, by Policy | Outcome Measure | Effect Size (IRR) [95% CI] |
|---|---|---|
| **Check on restraining order** | **Suicide** | |
| Sen & Panjamapirom (2012) | Total | 1.02 [0.98, 1.06] |
| Sen & Panjamapirom (2012) | Firearm | 1.03 [0.98, 1.09] |
| **Check on mental illness** | | |
| Sen & Panjamapirom (2012) | Total | 0.97 [0.95, 0.99] |
| Sen & Panjamapirom (2012) | Firearm | 0.96 [0.92, 0.99] |
| **Check on fugitive status** | | |
| Sen & Panjamapirom (2012) | Total | 0.91 [0.87, 0.95] |
| Sen & Panjamapirom (2012) | Firearm | 0.95 [0.90, 0.99] |
| **Check on misdemeanor** | | |
| Sen & Panjamapirom (2012) | Total | 0.98 [0.95, 1.02] |
| Sen & Panjamapirom (2012) | Firearm | 0.95 [0.92, 1.00] |
| **Check on "other miscellaneous" records** | | |
| Sen & Panjamapirom (2012) | Total | 1.00 [0.97, 1.03] |
| Sen & Panjamapirom (2012) | Firearm | 1.01 [0.97, 1.05] |
| **Index of background check comprehensiveness** | | |
| Sen & Panjamapirom (2012) | Firearm | 0.98 [0.96, 1.00] |
| **Brady act** | | |
| Ludwig & Cook (2000) | Total rate, aged 21+ | 0.98 [0.93, 1.03] |
| Ludwig & Cook (2000) | Total rate, aged 55+ | 0.97 [0.93, 1.01] |
| Ludwig & Cook (2000) | Firearm rate, aged 21+ | 0.98 [0.94, 1.02] |
| Ludwig & Cook (2000) | Firearm rate, aged 55+ | 0.94 [0.90, 0.98] |
| Ludwig & Cook (2000) | Nonfirearm rate, aged 21+ | 1.01 [0.95, 1.08] |
| Ludwig & Cook (2000) | Nonfirearm rate, aged 55+ | 1.03 [0.97, 1.11] |
| Ludwig & Cook (2000) | Committed with firearm, %, aged 21+ | 1.17 [0.87, 1.58] |
| Ludwig & Cook (2000) | Committed with firearm, %, aged 55+ | 0.97 [0.94, 0.99] |

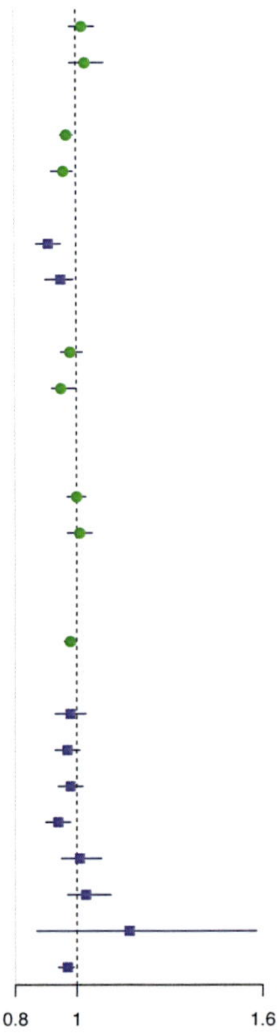


NOTE: IRR values marked with blue squares indicate that methodological concerns are discussed in the text. Green circles indicate that we identified no significant methodological concerns. See Appendix B for details.

## Conclusions

*Total suicides.* We identified two qualifying studies that evaluated the effects of background checks on the total number of suicides using largely independent data sets (one examined state suicide rates from 1990 to 1997, and the other examined state rates from 1996 to 2015). The first concluded that dealer background checks have an uncertain effect on total suicide rates among those aged 21 or older (Ludwig and Cook, 2000). In a secondary analysis, the study found a significant effect that background checks might reduce total suicides in the subgroup of adults aged 55 or older. All of these effects were partially confounded with possible effects of waiting periods that were simultaneously introduced in many states when the Brady Act was implemented. The second study, Sen and Panjamapirom (2012), examined components of background checks, finding significant effects indicating that checks on mental illness and checks on fugitive status reduce total suicide rates. Three other components of background checks (checks on restraining orders, checks on misdemeanor records, and other miscellaneous checks) had only uncertain effects on total suicide rates.

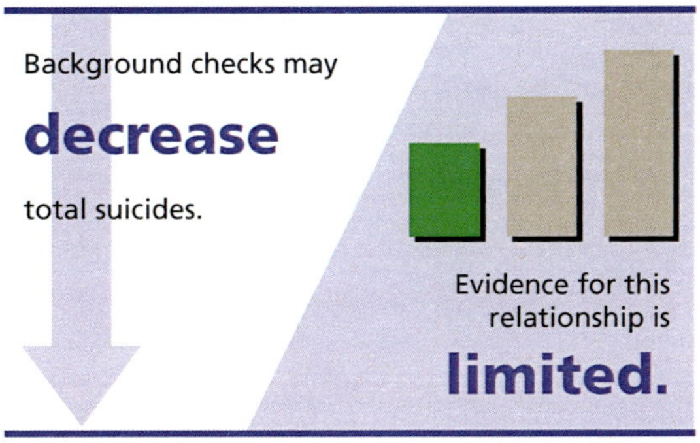


Considering the relative strengths of these studies, we conclude that available research provides *limited evidence that background checks may reduce total suicides.*

*Firearm suicides.* We identified three qualifying studies that evaluated the effects of background checks on firearm suicide rates, including the two studies that examined total suicides. These studies provided two analyses of the total effect of background checks on firearm suicides. Ludwig and Cook (2000) found an uncertain effect of dealer background checks on this outcome among those aged 21 or older, although they reported a statistically significant decrease in firearm suicides associated with background checks for those aged 55 or older. Sen and Panjamapirom (2012) found a statistically significant association between their background check comprehensiveness index and reduced firearm suicides. Across five other reported component analyses, checks on mental illness, fugitive status, and misdemeanors were associated with significant reduction in firearm suicides, whereas checks on restraining orders and other miscellaneous checks had only uncertain effects. Duggan, Hjalmarsson, and Jacob (2011), examining private-seller background checks at gun shows, found that these had uncertain effects.

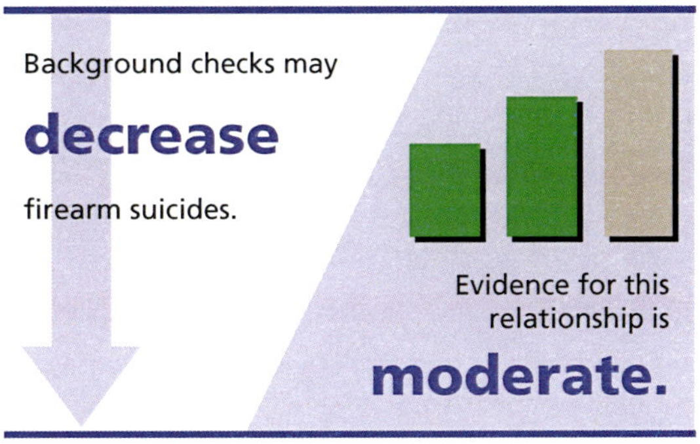


With largely consistent evidence across three studies, and considering the relative strengths of these studies, we conclude that the available studies provide *moderate evidence that background checks reduce firearm suicides.*

## Effects on Violent Crime

### Research Synthesis Findings

Hahn et al. (2005) found insufficient evidence for determining the effectiveness of gun-acquisition restrictions, including background checks, on violent crime. NRC (2004) concluded, "There is not much empirical evidence that assesses whether attempts to reduce criminal access to firearms will reduce gun availability or gun crime." NRC reviewed Ludwig and Cook (2000), which found no difference in homicide rates across states that had laws comparable to those the Brady Act would impose (which initially included both background checks and a waiting period) and states that experienced larger changes in the law when the Brady Act was implemented.[12] The Ludwig and Cook study had an unfavorable ratio of estimated parameters to observations (less than one to six), meaning its parameter estimates and CIs may not be accurate because of model overfitting.

Of studies that examined the relationship between background checks and violent crime, we identified eight that met our inclusion criteria.[13]

Gius (2015a) examined the effect of the federal Brady Act, state-mandated dealer background checks (either a check that was in place before the Brady Act or checks for categories of state-prohibited possessors other than those mandated by the Brady Act), and state-mandated private-seller background checks on gun-related homicides (the paper did not evaluate the effect of these variables on total homicides). The analysis of the federal Brady Act does not meet our criteria for inclusion because although the regression model evaluated whether changes occurred after implementation of the Brady Act, there was no comparison (control) group. State dealer background checks were found to significantly reduce firearm homicides by 20 percent (see Figure 3.2), but the study's design cannot distinguish whether this effect is attributable to a state's implementation of background checks prior to the Brady Act, prohibition of more classes of people from owning guns after the Brady Act was passed, or some combination of the two. Private-seller background checks appeared to increase firearm homi-

---

[12] Ludwig and Cook (2000) also tested the effects of background checks specifically (separate from waiting periods, also imposed by the Brady Act) by comparing five of 32 states that were required to implement background checks but that did not experience a change in their waiting periods (either because they already had a waiting period of five days or more when the Brady Act required this nationally or they implemented an instantaneous background check). These analyses had a ratio of estimated parameters to observations of less than five to one, which did not meet our inclusion criteria. Cook and Ludwig (2003) presents results for a shorter time period but that are qualitatively similar.

[13] We did not consider the findings from two studies because of methodological limitations. Although Ruddell and Mays (2005) had longitudinal data spanning 1999 through 2001 and compared states with various forms of background check systems, the authors created and analyzed a single average homicide rate for each state that spanned this time period. We excluded this study from further consideration because of the resulting cross-sectional nature of the analysis. Likewise, while Sumner, Layde, and Guse (2008) used data from 2002 through 2004, they aggregated the independent and dependent variables over this time period, resulting in a cross-sectional analysis.

cides to levels 131 percent of what would be expected without the policy. Gius (2015a) does not provide information on the variation in state laws over the period evaluated, so the quality of causal effect estimates is uncertain.

La Valle (2013) examined the effect of the existence of a pre–Brady Act state background check law on gun homicides and total homicides (as well as other state policies). Using data from 56 large U.S. cities over 1980–2010, the author found in his preferred models (weighted models with a one-year lag and using control variables that were interpolated over the period, but where the dependent variable was not interpolated) that pre–Brady Act state background check requirements had an uncertain effect on either gun homicides or total homicides.

Sen and Panjamapirom (2012) examined the effects of the *types* of background checks conducted by states on homicides. They noted that the supply of state and local records to the NICS is voluntary and that substantial variation exists in state laws regarding the categories of records included in background checks, such as restraining orders, mental illness, fugitive status, and misdemeanors. The authors characterized variation across states in background check requirements using an index of the comprehensiveness of such checks, as well as individual indicators for whether states check on restraining orders, mental illness, fugitive status, misdemeanors, and other miscellaneous records. Using state-level data from 1996 to 2005, the authors examined the effect of these types of checks on both firearm and total homicides. They found that, compared with background checks that examine only criminal history, background checks that include restraining orders, mental illness, and fugitive status are associated with significantly fewer total homicides and firearm homicides. Background checks that include restraining orders were associated with 13-percent drops in firearm homicide rates and 9-percent drops in overall homicide rates; background checks for mental illness were associated with 7-percent drops in both firearm and overall homicide rates; and background checks for fugitive status were associated with 21-percent and 23-percent reductions in firearm and total homicide rates, respectively (see Figure 3.2). However, so few states changed criminal history background check or fugitive check policies during the study time frame that these effects cannot confidently be attributed to the background check policies as opposed to other factors affecting homicides in the states around the same time their laws changed. Although the authors also included a control for whether a state had a pre–Brady Act background check requirement, the variation in this policy variable was only across states and not over time because the period of analysis was post-Brady only. Thus, the analysis of the effect of pre-Brady background check policy does not meet our criteria for inclusion.

Duggan, Hjalmarsson, and Jacob (2011) examined the localized, short-term effect of gun shows on firearm homicides. Absent state legislation to the contrary, gun-show vendors (and other private sellers) that are not federally licensed dealers are not required to conduct background checks on purchasers, which Duggan, Hjalmarsson, and Jacob (2011) referred to as the *gun-show loophole* and which we call the *gun-show exception*. Some states have legislation requiring background checks for all buyers at gun shows. Duggan, Hjalmarsson, and Jacob (2011) examined whether there is a differential effect of gun shows on violent crime or homicide in a state that has a gun-show *exception* (Texas) compared with a state that has no such *exception* (California). The authors found only uncertain effects of state background check policies on homicides that occur near where gun shows were recently held. However, the study focused only on background check requirements as they relate to gun shows and not on a broader set of background check policies. Moreover, as the authors acknowledged, their focus was on very short-term (four-week) and localized effects. The study had low statistical power, meaning that even if gun-show background check policies had meaningful effects on violence or homicide, these might not have been detected using this paper's procedures (see Wintemute et al., 2010).

Lott (2010) examined how state-required background checks for private sales affect violent crime. Detailed results that include coefficients and test statistics were available for only one specification and for the outcome of homicide (Lott, 2010, Table A6.3). This model indicated an uncertain effect of background checks on homicide rates. This model had an unfavorable ratio of estimated parameters to observations (less than one to ten), meaning the estimated effects and significance values may be inaccurate because of model overfitting.

Swanson et al. (2013) and Swanson et al. (2016) merged administrative records from public health and criminal justice agencies to evaluate how changes in state reporting of gun-disqualifying mental health records to the NICS affected violent crime arrest rates for individuals with a disqualifying mental health condition relative to individuals diagnosed with serious mental health illness but not prohibited from purchasing a firearm. Swanson et al. (2013) obtained data from 2002 to 2009 for individuals in Connecticut who had been hospitalized for schizophrenia, bipolar disorder, or major depressive disorder. The authors estimated changes in violent crime arrest rates for individuals with at least one of the mental health adjudications reported to the NICS before and after Connecticut began reporting mental health records in 2007. The authors found a significant 31-percent decline in the probability of violent crime arrest in their sample of individuals who had a mental health adjudication but no disqualifying criminal record (see Figure 3.2). The authors also estimated the likelihood of violent crime arrest for individuals with at least one voluntary psychiatric hospitalization but no mental health adjudication. Relative to the legally disqualified population, the nondisqualified group had a lower likelihood of violent crime arrest both before and after the NICS reporting change, but the magnitude of the decrease following NICS reporting was smaller than the reduction experienced by the "treated" group with a disqualifying mental health condition. However, neither test statistics nor CIs for this difference were reported.

Swanson et al. (2016) employed analogous methods to analyze the effects of NICS reporting changes in 2007 for two Florida counties using data from 2002 to

2011. The authors similarly found a larger reduction in violent crime arrest rates for individuals with a disqualifying mental health condition compared with individuals with a serious mental health illness that did not legally prohibit firearm acquisition. This difference, a decline of 38 percent (see Figure 3.2), was statistically significant. However, estimates became insignificant when the outcome variable was restricted specifically to violent crimes involving firearms, which could indicate the absence of a causal connection or could be due to measurement error in classifying crimes as involving firearms (Swanson et al., 2016).

Wright, Wintemute, and Rivara (1999) used a retrospective cohort design to assess whether firearm purchase denial based on criminal record background checks affects subsequent criminal activity among a sample of individuals with a prior felony arrest in California. Specifically, the authors examined subsequent arrest rates for a sample of individuals with a prior felony arrest who attempted to purchase a handgun in California in 1997, comparing outcomes for a group of individuals who were able to purchase a handgun successfully because they had a prior felony arrest but no conviction ("purchaser cohort") with a group of individuals who should have been denied purchase because of a felony conviction ("denied cohort"). In individual-level analyses, controlling for number of prior weapons and violent arrest charges, the authors found that the purchaser cohort was significantly more likely to be arrested for a subsequent offense in the three-year follow-up period. Estimates showed that, relative to the denied cohort, the purchaser cohort experienced an increase in the risk of arrest of 5 percent for any offense, 21 percent for gun offenses, and 24 percent for violent offenses (see Figure 3.2). While this study did not specifically examine the effects of background check laws, the findings suggest that enforcing background checks for felony records may reduce violent crime.

Finally, Vigdor and Mercy (2006) examined the effects of restraining order and violent misdemeanor background checks on intimate partner homicides and firearm intimate partner homicides, by comparing states with more-comprehensive or less-comprehensive approaches to performing those checks. The authors found small differences in rates of such homicides between states with high and low capacities for performing such checks, but they did not provide a test of the significance of these differences.

Figure 3.2 displays the IRRs and CIs associated with the background check policies examined in these studies. Duggan, Hjalmarsson, and Jacob (2011); Swanson et al. (2013); and Vigdor and Mercy (2006) did not provide sufficient data for us to calculate IRRs and CIs for the effect size of interest, so these are not displayed in figure. Furthermore, we exclude the estimate of the Brady Act from Gius (2015a) because the estimate does not meet our criteria for inclusion. The Swanson et al. (2016) estimate in the figure is the change from before and after the NICS reporting requirements for legally disqualified individuals relative to the change for nonlegally disqualified individuals.

## Figure 3.2
## Incidence Rate Ratios Associated with the Effect of Background Checks on Violent Crime

| Study, by Policy | Outcome Measure | Effect Size (IRR) [95% CI] |
|---|---|---|
| **State dealer background check** | **Homicide** | |
| Gius (2015a) | Firearm | 0.80 [0.73, 0.87] |
| **State private–seller background check** | | |
| Gius (2015a) | Firearm | 1.31 [1.23, 1.39] |
| Lott (2010) | Homicide | 1.02 [0.98, 1.07] |
| **Check on restraining order** | | |
| Sen & Panjamapirom (2012) | Total | 0.91 [0.85, 0.98] |
| Sen & Panjamapirom (2012) | Firearm | 0.87 [0.79, 0.95] |
| **Check on mental illness** | | |
| Sen & Panjamapirom (2012) | Total | 0.93 [0.86, 0.99] |
| Sen & Panjamapirom (2012) | Firearm | 0.93 [0.87, 1.01] |
| **Check on fugitive status** | | |
| Sen & Panjamapirom (2012) | Total | 0.77 [0.71, 0.84] |
| Sen & Panjamapirom (2012) | Firearm | 0.79 [0.72, 0.88] |
| **Check on misdemeanor** | | |
| Sen & Panjamapirom (2012) | Total | 1.02 [0.95, 1.10] |
| Sen & Panjamapirom (2012) | Firearm | 0.99 [0.90, 1.08] |
| **Check on "other miscellaneous" records** | | |
| Sen & Panjamapirom (2012) | Total | 1.05 [0.98, 1.13] |
| Sen & Panjamapirom (2012) | Firearm | 1.12 [1.03, 1.22] |
| **Index of background check comprehensiveness** | | |
| Sen & Panjamapirom (2012) | Firearm | 0.93 [0.91, 0.96] |
| **Brady law** | | |
| La Valle (2013) | Total | 1.00 [0.89, 1.13] |
| La Valle (2013) | Firearm | 1.02 [0.89, 1.17] |
| Ludwig & Cook (2000) | Total rate, aged 21+ | 0.97 [0.87, 1.08] |
| Ludwig & Cook (2000) | Total rate, aged 55+ | 1.00 [0.90, 1.12] |
| Ludwig & Cook (2000) | Firearm rate, aged 21+ | 0.99 [0.86, 1.13] |
| Ludwig & Cook (2000) | Firearm rate, aged 55+ | 1.07 [0.97, 1.16] |
| Ludwig & Cook (2000) | Nonfirearm rate, aged 21+ | 0.94 [0.87, 1.02] |
| Ludwig & Cook (2000) | Nonfirearm rate, aged 55+ | 0.95 [0.81, 1.12] |
| Ludwig & Cook (2000) | Committed with firearm, %, aged 21+ | 1.02 [0.99, 1.04] |
| Ludwig & Cook (2000) | Committed with firearm, %, aged 55+ | 1.07 [0.98, 1.18] |
| **NICS reporting** | **Violent crime** | |
| Swanson et al. (2016) | Violent crime arrest (legally disqualified after) | 0.62 [0.50, 0.76] |
| **No felony checks** | **Arrests** | |
| Wright, Wintemute & Rivara (1999) | Any offense | 1.05 [1.04, 1.07] |
| Wright, Wintemute & Rivara (1999) | Gun offense | 1.21 [1.08, 1.36] |
| Wright, Wintemute & Rivara (1999) | Violent offense | 1.24 [1.11, 1.39] |

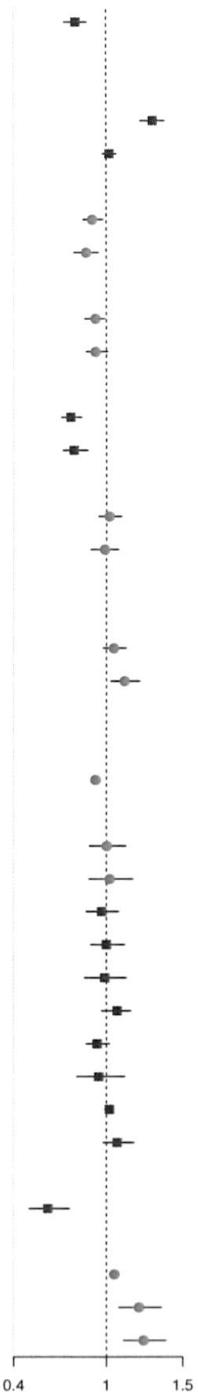


NOTE: IRR values marked with blue squares indicate that methodological concerns are discussed in the text. Green circles indicate that we identified no significant methodological concerns. See Appendix B for details.

## Conclusions

*Homicides and violent crime.* We identified six qualifying studies providing evidence on the effects of background checks, or some component of background checks, on violent crime. Three of these studies provided an overall effect of either dealer background checks or private-seller background checks on total homicide rates, although two of these estimated effects were partially confounded with the effect of waiting periods that were simultaneously introduced in many states when the Brady Act was passed. All three studies found those effects to be uncertain (the analyses of effects on those aged 21 and older in Ludwig and Cook, 2000; the Brady Act effect in La Valle, 2013; and the private-seller background check effect in Lott, 2010). Three background check component analyses identified significant effects indicating that mental illness checks, restraining order checks, or fugitive status checks reduced violent crime specific to homicides (Sen and Panjamapirom, 2012). A fourth component analysis found that mental illness checks significantly reduce violent crime arrests (Swanson et al., 2016). A component analysis of misdemeanor checks found that they had uncertain effects on homicides, while "other miscellaneous checks" had a suggestive effect consistent with increases in homicides (Sen and Panjamapirom, 2012). Finally, a component analysis of background checks targeting firearm purchase by individuals with prior felony convictions (Wright, Wintemute, and Rivara, 1999) found significant effects consistent with a reduction in arrests for firearm and violent crime offenses.

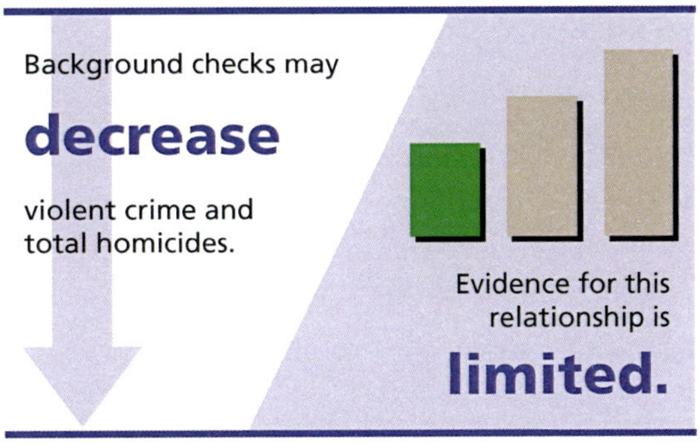


The cumulative evidence is puzzling, as overall effects of background checks appear to be uncertain, but some components of background checks appear to significantly reduce homicides or violent crime. Because the studies examining component effects of background checks generally suffer from fewer noted weaknesses, we conclude that available studies provide *limited evidence that background checks reduce violent crime and total homicide rates.*

*Firearm homicide rates.* We identified four qualifying studies that provided estimates for the effects of background checks, or some component of background checks, on firearm homicide rates. Four studies examined the overall effect of dealer background checks on firearm homicide rates; two used large independent data sets and

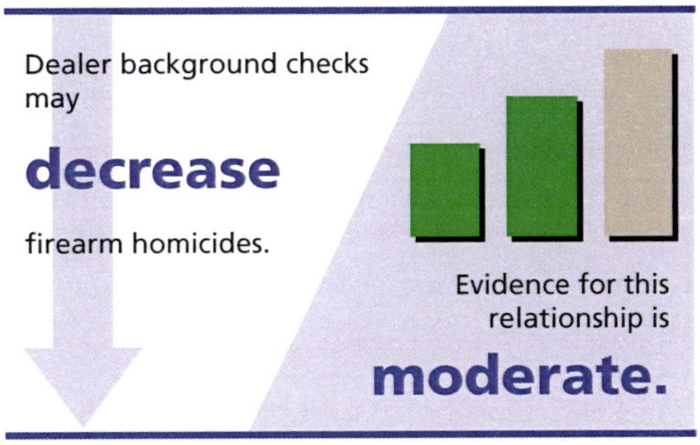

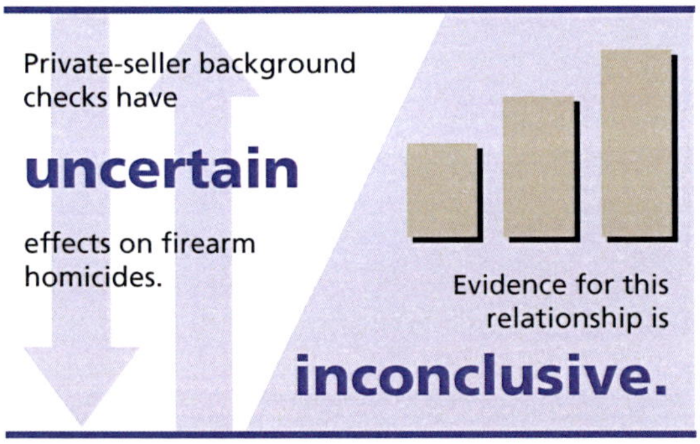


found significant effects indicating that dealer background checks reduce firearm homicides (Gius, 2015a; Sen and Panjamapirom, 2012), and two found uncertain effects (La Valle, 2013; Ludwig and Cook, 2000). One analysis found significant effects consistent with private-seller checks increasing firearm homicides (Gius, 2015a). Component analyses from a single study found significant effects indicating that restraining order and fugitive checks reduce firearm homicides (Sen and Panjamapirom, 2012). The analyses also found that mental illness checks have suggestive effects consistent with a reduction in firearm homicides, uncertain effects for misdemeanor checks, and a significant effect indicating that "miscellaneous checks" increase firearm homicides.

Based on these findings and an assessment of the relative strengths of the studies, we conclude that *available studies provide moderate evidence that dealer background checks may reduce firearm homicides* and *inconclusive evidence for the effect of private-seller background checks on firearm homicides.*

## Effects on Mass Shootings

### Research Synthesis Findings

Neither NRC (2004) nor Hahn et al. (2005) identified research examining the effects of gun policies on mass shootings in the United States. Using a two-way fixed-effects linear probability model, Luca, Deepak, and Poliquin (2016) estimated the effects of background check laws on a binary indicator for whether a mass shooting occurred in a given state-year. The authors included two measures of background check laws: an indicator for whether laws required a background check for all handgun transactions (including private sales) and an indicator for whether laws required a background check for all firearm transactions (including private sales). The authors' regression analysis covered 1989–2014 and included controls for time-invariant state characteristics; national trends; a host of other state-level gun policies; and time-varying state-level demographic, socioeconomic, and political characteristics. Their findings showed an uncertain relationship between background check laws and the probability of at least one mass shooting event occurring (see Figure 3.3). However, assessing the effects of gun policies on mass shootings was not the primary focus of the study, and the authors intended the estimates to serve solely as a robustness check for their main specification (the effects of mass shootings on gun policy). Although the paper provided limited information to use in evaluating the reported statistical models (e.g., on how these policies were coded), it is clear that the analysis used a linear model to predict a dichotomous outcome. Therefore, model assumptions were violated, making CIs unreliable.

Figure 3.3 displays the IRRs and CIs associated with the background check policies examined in Luca, Deepak, and Poliquin (2016).

**Figure 3.3**
**Incidence Rate Ratios Associated with the Effect of Background Checks on Mass Shootings**

| Study, by Policy | Outcome Measure | Effect Size (IRR) [95% CI] |
|---|---|---|
| **Background check** | | |
| **all handgun sales** | **Mass shooting** | |
| Luca, Deepak, & Poliquin (2016) | State-year indicator (no political controls) | 0.07 [0.00, 1.52] |
| Luca, Deepak, & Poliquin (2016) | State-year indicator (political controls) | 0.00 [0.00, 1.57] |
| **Background check** | | |
| **all firearm sales** | | |
| Luca, Deepak, & Poliquin (2016) | State-year indicator (no political controls) | 1.09 [0.00, 3.23] |
| Luca, Deepak, & Poliquin (2016) | State-year indicator (political controls) | 0.73 [0.00, 3.05] |

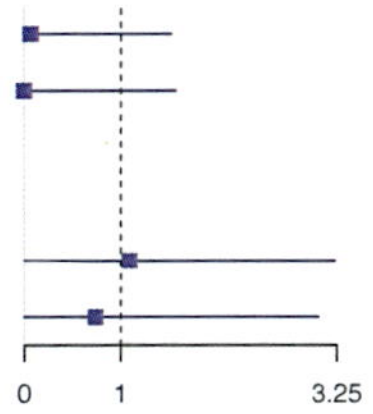


NOTE: IRR values marked with blue squares indicate that methodological concerns are discussed in the text. See Appendix B for details.

## Conclusions

We identified a single qualifying study that estimated the effects of background checks for all handgun sales and for all firearm sales on mass shootings (Luca, Deepak, and Poliquin, 2016). This study found uncertain effects of these universal background check laws on whether at least one mass shooting occurred in a state. Therefore, the available study provides *inconclusive evidence for the effect of background checks on mass shootings.*

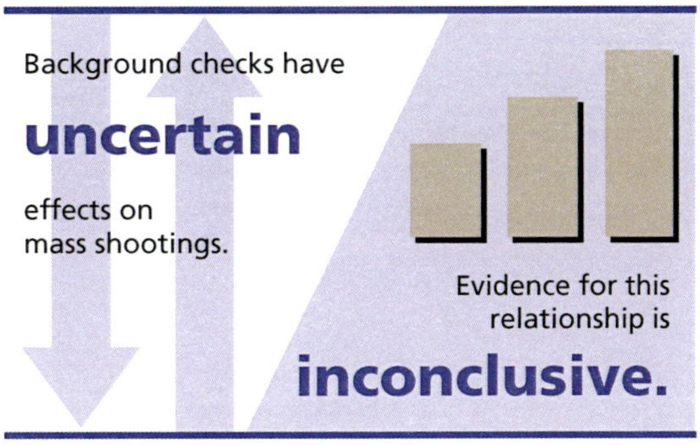

## Outcomes Without Studies Examining the Effects of Background Checks

Neither NRC (2004) nor Hahn et al. (2005) identified any research examining the effects of background check policies on the following outcomes, and we identified no such studies that met our inclusion criteria:

- unintentional injuries and deaths
- officer-involved shootings
- defensive gun use
- hunting and recreation
- gun industry.

## Chapter Three References


Buchanan, Larry, Josh Keller, Richard A. Oppel, Jr., and Daniel Victor, "How They Got Their Guns," *New York Times*, June 12, 2016. As of March 22, 2017: https://www.nytimes.com/interactive/2015/10/03/us/how-mass-shooters-got-their-guns.html?_r=0

Bureau of Alcohol, Tobacco, and Firearms, *Crime Gun Trace Reports (2000): Memphis, Tennessee*, Washington, D.C.: U.S. Department of the Treasury, July 2002.

Campbell, J. C., D. Webster, J. Kozio-McLain, C. Block, D. Campbell, M. A. Curry, F. Gary, N. Glass, J. McFarlane, C. Sachs, P. Sharps, Y. Ulrich, S. A. Wilt, J. Manganello, X. Xu, J. Schollenberger, V. Frye, and K. Laughon, "Risk Factors for Femicide in Abusive Relationships: Results from a Multisite Case Control Study," *American Journal of Public Health*, Vol. 93, No. 7, 2003, pp. 1089–1097.

Cook, Philip J., and Jens Ludwig, "The Effect of the Brady Act on Gun Violence," in B. Harcourt, ed., *Guns, Crime, and Punishment in America*, New York: New York University Press, 2003, pp. 283–298.

Cook, Philip J., J. Ludwig, and A. A. Braga, "Criminal Records of Homicide Offenders," *JAMA*, Vol. 294, No. 5, 2005, pp. 598–601.

Cook, Philip J., Stephanie Molliconi, and Thomas B. Cole, "Regulating Gun Markets," *Journal of Criminal Law and Criminology*, Vol. 86, No. 1, 1995, pp. 59–92.

Cook, Philip J., Susan T. Parker, and Harold A. Pollack, "Sources of Guns to Dangerous People: What We Learn by Asking Them," *Preventive Medicine*, Vol. 79, 2015, pp. 28–36.

Cooper, Alexia, and Erica L. Smith, *Homicide Trends in the United States, 1980–2008*, Washington, D.C.: U.S. Department of Justice, November 2011.

Duggan, Mark, Randi Hjalmarsson, and Brian A. Jacob, "The Short-Term and Localized Effect of Gun Shows: Evidence from California and Texas," *Review of Economics and Statistics*, Vol. 93, No. 3, 2011, pp. 786–799.

Everytown for Gun Safety Support Fund, "Mass Shootings in the United States: 2009–2016," April 11, 2017b. As of May 3, 2017: http://everytownresearch.org/reports/mass-shootings-analysis/

FBI—*See* Federal Bureau of Investigation.

Federal Bureau of Investigation, "Active Records in the NICS Index," April 30, 2017. As of May 8, 2017: https://www.fbi.gov/file-repository/active_records_in_the_nics-index.pdf/view

Giffords Law Center to Prevent Gun Violence, "Universal Background Checks," web page, undated-f. As of October 18, 2017: http://lawcenter.giffords.org/gun-laws/policy-areas/background-checks/universal-background-checks/

Gius, Mark, "The Effects of State and Federal Background Checks on State-Level Gun-Related Murder Rates," *Applied Economics*, Vol. 47, No. 38, 2015a, pp. 4090–4101.

Hahn, Robert A., Oleg Bilukha, Alex Crosby, Mindy T. Fullilove, Akiva Liberman, Eve Moscicki, Susan Snyder, Farris Tuma, and Peter A. Briss, "Firearms Laws and the Reduction of Violence: A Systematic Review," *American Journal of Preventive Medicine*, Vol. 28, No. 2, 2005, pp. 40–71.

Joshi, M., and S. B. Sorenson, "Intimate Partner Violence at the Scene: Incident Characteristics and Implications for Public Health Surveillance," *Evaluation Review*, Vol. 34, No. 2, 2010, pp. 116–136.

Juodis, Marcus, Andrew Starzomski, Stephen Porter, and Michael Woodworth, "A Comparison of Domestic and Non-Domestic Homicides: Further Evidence for Distinct Dynamics and Heterogeneity of Domestic Homicide Perpetrators," *Journal of Family Violence*, Vol. 29, No. 3, 2014, pp. 299–313.

Kleck, G., and D. J. Bordua, "The Factual Foundation for Certain Key Assumptions of Gun Control," *Law and Policy*, Vol. 5, No. 3, 1983, pp. 271–298.

Kopel, D. B., "Background Checks for Firearms Sales and Loans: Law, History, and Policy," *Harvard Journal on Legislation*, Vol. 53, 2016, pp. 303–367.

La Valle, James M., "'Gun Control' vs. 'Self-Protection': A Case Against the Ideological Divide," *Justice Policy Journal*, Vol. 10, No. 1, 2013, pp. 1–26.

Lott, John R., Jr., *More Guns, Less Crime: Understanding Crime and Gun-Control Laws*, 3rd ed., Chicago, Ill.: University of Chicago Press, 2010.

Luca, Michael, Lahotra Deepak, and Christopher Poliquin, *The Impact of Mass Shootings on Gun Policy*, working paper, Boston, Mass.: Harvard Business School, 2016.

Ludwig, J., and P. J. Cook, "Homicide and Suicide Rates Associated with Implementation of the Brady Handgun Violence Prevention Act," *JAMA*, Vol. 284, No. 5, 2000, pp. 585–591.

McFarlane, J., J. C. Campbell, S. Wilt, C. Sachs, Y. Ulrich, and X. Xu, "Stalking and Intimate Partner Femicide," *Homicide Studies*, Vol. 3, 1999, pp. 300–316.

Miller, M., L. Hepburn, and D. Azrael, "Firearm Acquisition Without Background Checks: Results of a National Survey," *Annals of Internal Medicine*, Vol. 166, 2017, pp. 233–239.

National Research Council, *Firearms and Violence: A Critical Review*, Washington, D.C.: National Academies Press, 2004.

NRC—*See* National Research Council.

Ruddell, R., and G. L. Mays, "State Background Checks and Firearms Homicides," *Journal of Criminal Justice*, Vol. 33, No. 2, 2005, pp. 127–136.

Sen, B., and A. Panjamapirom, "State Background Checks for Gun Purchase and Firearm Deaths: An Exploratory Study," *Preventive Medicine*, Vol. 55, No. 4, 2012, pp. 346–350.

Sumner, S. A., P. M. Layde, and C. E. Guse, "Firearm Death Rates and Association with Level of Firearm Purchase Background Check," *American Journal of Preventive Medicine*, Vol. 35, No. 1, 2008, pp. 1–6.

Swanson, Jeffrey W., Michele M. Easter, Allison G. Robertson, Marvin S. Swartz, Kelly Alanis-Hirsch, Daniel Moseley, Charles Dion, and John Petrila, "Gun Violence, Mental Illness, and Laws That Prohibit Gun Possession: Evidence from Two Florida Counties," *Health Affairs*, Vol. 35, No. 6, 2016, pp. 1067–1075.

Swanson, J. W., A. G. Robertson, L. K. Frisman, M. A. Norko, H. Lin, M. S. Swartz, and P. J. Cook, "Preventing Gun Violence Involving People with Serious Mental Illness," in D. W. Webster and J. S. Vernick, eds., *Reducing Gun Violence in America: Informing Policy with Evidence and Analysis*, Baltimore, Md.: Johns Hopkins University Press, 2013, pp. 33–51.

United States Code, Title 18, Section 922, Unlawful Acts.

Vigdor, E. R., and J. A. Mercy, "Do Laws Restricting Access to Firearms by Domestic Violence Offenders Prevent Intimate Partner Homicide?" *Evaluation Review*, Vol. 30, No. 3, 2006, pp. 313–346.

Vittes, K. A., J. S. Vernick, and D. W. Webster, "Legal Status and Source of Offenders' Firearms for States with the Least Stringent Criteria for Gun Ownership," *Injury Prevention*, Vol. 19, No. 1, June 23, 2012, pp. 26–31.

Webster, Daniel W., Jon S. Vernick, and Maria T. Bulzacchelli, "Effects of State-Level Firearm Seller Accountability Policies on Firearm Trafficking," *Journal of Urban Health: Bulletin of the New York Academy of Medicine*, Vol. 86, No. 4, 2009, pp. 525–537.

Wintemute, G. J., D. Hemenway, D. Webster, G. Pierce, and A. A. Braga, "Gun Shows and Gun Violence: Fatally Flawed Study Yields Misleading Results," *American Journal of Public Health*, Vol. 100, No. 10, 2010, pp. 1856–1860.

Wright, M. A., and G. J. Wintemute, "Felonious of Violent Criminal Activity That Prohibits Gun Ownership Among Prior Purchasers of Handguns: Incidence and Risk Factors," *Journal of Trauma and Acute Care Surgery*, Vol. 69, No. 4, 2010, pp. 948–955.

Wright, M. A., G. J. Wintemute, and F. P. Rivara, "Effectiveness of Denial of Handgun Purchase to Persons Believed to Be at High Risk for Firearm Violence," *American Journal of Public Health*, Vol. 89, No. 1, 1999, pp. 88–90.

CHAPTER FOUR

# Bans on the Sale of Assault Weapons and High-Capacity Magazines

The term *assault weapon* is controversial. In state and federal gun laws, it generally refers to specific semiautomatic firearm models that are designed to fire a high volume of ammunition in a controlled way or to firearms that have specified design features, such as folding stocks or pistol grips (Giffords Law Center to Prevent Gun Violence, undated-a).[1] Those in the gun industry refer to many of these firearms as *modern sporting rifles*, contending that *assault rifle* should apply only to automatic weapons used by militaries. Furthermore, they argue that the characteristics used to differentiate banned firearms from nonbanned semiautomatic weapons are cosmetic and do not make them more deadly than similar weapons without those features. In 1994, Congress passed the Violent Crime Control and Law Enforcement Act, which banned "the manufacture of military-style assault weapons, assault weapons with specific combat features, 'copy-cat' models, and certain high-capacity ammunition magazines of more than ten rounds" (U.S. Department of Justice, 1994; see also Pub. L. 103-322). The law included a sunset provision, calling for its repeal after ten years. It was not renewed in 2004, and thus there is not currently a federal assault weapon ban (Plumer, 2012).

Laws banning or restricting assault weapons or high-capacity magazines are primarily intended to reduce firearm-related casualties and fatalities from violent crime—and, more specifically, from mass shooting incidents. The bans could impact firearm-related violence by decreasing the number of shooting incidents, decreasing the number of casualties in a given shooting, and decreasing the case fatality rate. That is, other things being equal, a shooter with an assault weapon or other weapon equipped with a high-capacity magazine can fire more ammunition and hence inflict more casualties in a given length of time than would a shooter using weapons with a lower rate of fire and capacity. In a mass shooting incident, the lower rate of fire should allow for more people to evacuate and for law enforcement or others to intervene. To most precisely

[1] Semiautomatic pistols and rifles, as defined in 27 C.F.R. 478.11, are firearms that use energy expended from the firing cartridge to extract the fired cartridge case and automatically chamber the next round of ammunition but require a pull of the trigger for each shot (Krouse and Richardson, 2015). In contrast, fully automatic weapons (i.e., machine guns) can produce continuous fire by a single trigger function without manual reloading, and their sale and possession has been federally regulated since the National Firearms Act of 1934 (currently codified as amended as 26 U.S.C. 5801 et seq.).

characterize the causal effect of these laws on violent crime or mass shootings, the ideal data would distinguish crime and violence outcomes by whether a designated assault weapon or high-capacity magazine was used. Although limited data on the weapons used in homicides are available through the Federal Bureau of Investigation (FBI)'s Supplementary Homicide Reports and details of the weapons and ammunition used in mass shooting incidents are increasingly being compiled on a case-by-case basis (e.g., by the Stanford University Mass Shootings in America project), none of the articles meeting our inclusion criteria for this policy analyzed crime or violence outcomes by weapon type.

The majority of crimes are not conducted with rifles but with handguns, most of which are not considered assault weapons (although most assault weapon bans also list certain "assault pistols" among the banned firearms). In 2015, 252 of the 9,616 firearm-related murders reported in FBI data involved any type of rifle; the type of firearm used in 2,477 of these murders was not specified (FBI, 2016a). Assuming that no substitution to other types of firearms would occur, the elimination of all rifle homicides would have decreased the number of firearm-related murders by 2.6 percent.

Assault weapons and high-capacity magazines are used disproportionately in mass public shootings and killings of law enforcement officers compared with murders overall. However, these incidents are relatively rare. Data combining 184 mass shooting, spree shooting, and active shooter events from 1982 to 2015 suggest that about 30 percent of incidents involved assault weapons and 37 percent of incidents involved high-capacity magazines (Blau, Gorry, and Wade, 2016). Another analysis that focused on mass shooting events involving four or more fatalities between 2009 and 2016 reported that 15 of these incidents (11 percent) involved an assault weapon or high-capacity magazine, resulting in 155 percent more injuries and 47 percent more fatalities compared with other incidents (Everytown for Gun Safety Support Fund, 2017b). Other research, focused on a small subset of shootings in which multiple victims were targeted, suggests that the rate of fire at mass shootings is not so high that reloading would affect the number of rounds fired (Kleck, 2016). If this finding generalized to all multiple-victim shootings, it would call into question the usefulness of laws banning high-capacity magazines, because the primary objective of such laws is to reduce the number of rounds a shooter can fire before having to reload.

Of the 38 felonious fatal shootings of law enforcement officers in 2015, 18.4 percent involved any type of rifle (FBI, 2016c). Although relatively outdated, estimates from 1994 suggest that between 31 percent and 41 percent of firearms used in murders of police officers involved assault weapons or other guns equipped with high-capacity magazines (Adler et al., 1995).

There is little theoretical basis to suggest that bans of assault weapons and high-capacity magazines would impact rates of suicide or unintentional injury. And although these policies could plausibly impact defensive gun use, the magnitudes of any such effects are likely small. The FBI reported that, in 2015, eight of the 328 firearm-related justifiable homicides by private citizens involved any type of rifle (FBI, 2016b).

Laws banning assault weapons and high-capacity magazines would have direct market effects for the gun industry, including impacts on production, price, and potential spillovers from primary to secondary markets (Koper, 2004). The market effects of restricting the manufacturing and sales of a class of weapons or ammunition will depend on the relative demand for these items, the availability of nonbanned weapons that serve as close substitutes, and the costs of modifying existing weapon types to meet the requirements of the ban, to name a few. A nationwide ban could also impact the industry more broadly by generating market effects for ancillary gun companies that produce or sell certain replacement parts, accessories, or specialized magazines and precision barrels used primarily for sport shooting.

Overall, the effects of these policies will depend largely on the design and implementation of the law. Except for heavily regulated weapons manufactured prior to May 1986, assault weapons capable of automatic fire are not available for sale in the United States. Thus, the specifics of which weapons or weapon features are prohibited by a particular ban are key to understanding the marginal effect of each policy on outcomes of interest. Targeting weapons with close substitutes or features unrelated to the deadliness of the weapon or its likelihood of being used in the perpetration of violence likely limits any potential policy effects on violent crime. Further, most existing state bans (and the federal ban of 1994) influence the flow of only new weapons or magazines and do little to affect the existing stock; the National Shooting Sports Foundation, a trade association for the gun industry, estimates that more than 8.5 million assault rifles were either manufactured in or imported to the United States between the 1990s and 2013 (Chang, 2013).

## State Implementation of Assault Weapon Bans

Seven states and the District of Columbia currently ban assault weapons.[2] Five of the eight jurisdictions list the specific assault weapons banned and prohibit all weapons with specific features; one state bans only the weapons listed, and two states ban only specific features. The laws that list specific banned models are similar state to state, although the lists are not generally identical.

California is an example of a state that has a list of banned assault weapons, both rifles and shotguns, as well as firearms with specific design features. Specifically, it bans "all AK series including, but not limited to, the models identified," and explains

[2] California, Connecticut, Hawaii, Maryland, Massachusetts, New Jersey, New York, and the District of Columbia. See Calif. Penal Code § 30505; Conn. Gen. Stat. § 53-202b; Hawaii Rev. Stat. Ann. § 134-4; Md. Code Ann. § 4-303; Mass. Gen. Laws Ch. 140 § 131M; N.J. Stat. Ann. § 2C:39-1 and 39-5; N.Y. Penal Law § 265.02; D.C. Code Ann. § 7-2502.02.

that the term *series* "includes all other models that are only variations, with minor differences, of those models listed in subdivision (a), regardless of the manufacturer."[3] Furthermore, the state provides a list of features, any one of which renders a firearm an assault weapon and therefore banned.[4] For example, the law states that a "semiautomatic, centerfire rifle that has the capacity to accept a detachable magazine" is an assault weapon if it also contains any of the following features: "(A) a pistol grip that protrudes conspicuously beneath the action of the weapon; (B) a thumbhole stock; (C) a folding or telescoping stock; (D) a grenade launcher or flare launcher; (E) a flash suppressor; (F) a forward pistol grip."[5]

Connecticut's list is similar to California's, but the language is different. For example, in its subsection banning the AK series of weapons, Connecticut's law includes "[a]ny of the following specified semiautomatic centerfire rifles, or copies or duplicates thereof with the capability of any such rifles, that were in production prior to or on April 4, 2013." In addition, like California, Connecticut has a long list of features, any of which render a firearm banned.[6] The District of Columbia's list is shorter and does not include statements that the ban includes similar makes and models to the ones listed. However, the law also bans firearms with specific design features.[7] Maryland and Massachusetts are the other two states that ban by both list and features. Maryland bans weapons that possess any two features from its list.[8] The Massachusetts law, which refers to the now-expired federal law (Pub. L. 103-322), also requires two features to be included.[9]

New Jersey is the only state that includes a list of banned assault weapons but not generic features.[10] Conversely, New York and Hawaii ban a list of only features, not specified models of firearms.[11] However, unlike the other states, Hawaii bans only certain pistols, not rifles.

In addition to definitional differences, the laws are distinct in other ways—notably, their treatment of grandfathered weapons. For example, the District of Columbia does not allow grandfathering of assault weapons (Giffords Law Center to Prevent Gun Violence, undated-a); however, all seven states with assault weapon bans do, but under different regimes. Six of the states require registration of grandfathered assault weap-

---

3 Calif. Penal Code § 30510.

4 Calif. Penal Code § 30515.

5 Calif. Penal Code § 30515.

6 Conn. Gen. Stat. § 53-202a.

7 D.C. Code Ann. § 7-2501.01.

8 Md. Code Ann. § 4-301.

9 Mass. Gen. Laws Ch. 140 § 121.

10 N.J. Stat. Ann. § 2C: 39-1.

11 N.Y. Penal Law § 265.00; Hawaii Rev. Stat. Ann. § 134-1.

ons; in New Jersey, registration allows grandfathered assault weapons to be used only for target shooting.[12]

The same jurisdictions that have banned assault weapons have also banned high-capacity magazines, as has Colorado. Hawaii, which bans only assault pistols, similarly bans only high-capacity magazines for pistols.[13] The rest ban high-capacity magazines for all firearms,[14] although there are differences in definition here too. California, Connecticut, Hawaii, Maryland, Massachusetts, New York, and the District of Columbia ban magazines with a capacity of more than ten rounds.[15] Colorado and New Jersey allow up to 15 rounds.[16]

## Effects on Violent Crime

### Research Synthesis Findings

In their review of available science, Hahn et al. (2005) found insufficient evidence for determining the effectiveness of bans on specific firearms or ammunition on violent crime. In its review, the National Research Council (NRC) (2004) described two studies that examined the effects of the 1994 federal assault weapon ban (Koper and Roth, 2001, 2002). The studies found no short-term (within two years) effect of the ban on gun violence outcomes but a temporary increase in prices of assault weapons in both primary and legal secondary markets.

We identified two studies that evaluated federal and state assault weapon bans and met our criteria. Gius (2014) analyzed state-level data from 1980 through 2009 and controlled for the 1994–2004 federal assault weapon ban and for the existence of state assault weapon bans. The analysis of the federal assault weapon ban does not meet our criteria for inclusion: The author included an indicator for years prior to and after the ban as a control, but there was no comparison (control) group. The author found a suggestive effect consistent with state assault weapon bans decreasing firearm-related homicides (see Figure 4.1). However, the model did not account for serial correlation in panel data, which can result in large biases in standard errors (Aneja, Donohue, Zhang, 2014).

---

12 Calif. Penal Code § 30605; Conn. Gen. Stat. § 53-202c; Hawaii Rev. Stat. Ann. § 134-4; Md. Code Ann. § 4-303; Mass. Gen. Laws Ch. 140 §§ 121, 123, 131, 131M; N.J. Stat. Ann. § 2C: 58-12; N.Y. Penal Law § 265.20.

13 Hawaii Rev. Stat. Ann. § 134-8.

14 Calif. Penal Code §, 32310; Colo. Rev. Stat. § 18-12-302; Conn. Gen. Stat. § 53-202w; Md. Code Ann. § 4-305; Mass. Gen. Laws Ch. 140 § 131M; N.J. Stat. Ann. § 2C: 39-3; N.Y. Penal Law § 265.02; D.C. Code Ann. § 7-2506.01.

15 Calif. Penal Code §§ 16350, 16740; Conn. Gen. Stat. § 53-202w; Hawaii Rev. Stat. Ann. § 134-8; Md. Code Ann. § 4-305; Mass. Gen. Laws Ch. 140 § 121; N.Y. Penal Law § 265.00; D.C. Code Ann. § 7-2506.01.

16 Colo. Rev. Stat. § 18-12-301; N.J. Stat. Ann. § 2C: 39-1.

Lott (2010) examined the effect of assault weapon bans on violent crime. Detailed results that include coefficients and test statistics were available only for the outcome of homicide (Lott, 2010, Table A6.3). This model indicated an uncertain effect of assault weapon bans on homicide rates, but it had an unfavorable ratio of estimated parameters to observations (less than one to ten), meaning the model may have been overfit, and thus its effect estimates and significance levels may be inaccurate.

Figure 4.1 displays the incidence rate ratios (IRRs) and confidence intervals (CIs) associated with the assault weapon ban policies examined in these studies. We exclude the estimate of the federal assault weapon ban from Gius (2014) because the estimate does not meet our criteria for inclusion.

**Figure 4.1**
**Incidence Rate Ratios Associated with the Effect of Assault Weapon Bans on Violent Crime**

| Study, by Policy | Outcome Measure | Effect Size (IRR) [95% CI] |
|---|---|---|
| **Assault weapon ban** | **Homicide** | |
| Lott (2010) | Homicide | 1.00 [0.93, 1.08] |
| **State assault weapon ban** | | |
| Gius (2014) | Firearm | 0.92 [0.81, 1.02] |

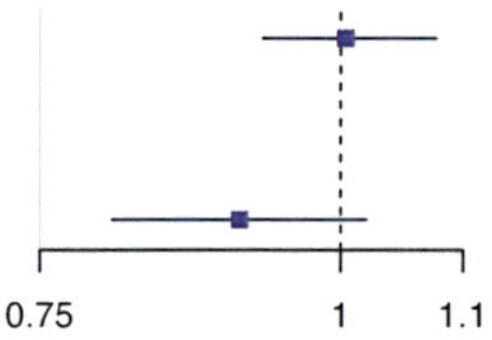


NOTE: IRR values marked with blue squares indicate that methodological concerns are discussed in the text. See Appendix B for details.

## Conclusions

We identified two qualifying studies that estimated the effects of assault weapon bans on different violent crime outcomes. One found uncertain effects of such bans on total homicide rates (Lott, 2010); the other found a suggestive effect consistent with assault weapon bans decreasing firearm homicides (Gius, 2014). Considering the relative strengths of these studies, available evidence is *inconclusive for the effect of assault weapon bans on total homicides and firearm homicides.*

## Effects on Mass Shootings

### Research Synthesis Findings

Neither NRC (2004) nor Hahn et al. (2005) reviewed evidence for the effects of assault weapon bans on mass shootings. Two studies since then met our inclusion criteria. Both used a two-way fixed-effects model, controlling for both state-specific and year-specific effects, to estimate the effects of state or federal assault weapon bans on mass shooting incidents or casualties.[17]

Using a Poisson model and data from 1982 through 2011, Gius (2015c) tested whether state assault weapon bans influence public mass shooting fatalities or public mass shooting injuries, controlling for the federal assault weapon ban and state-level variation in demographic, socioeconomic, and criminal justice characteristics. Although the author found a large and statistically significant association between implementation of the *federal* assault weapon ban and reductions in mass shooting deaths and injuries, the analysis of the federal ban does not meet our criteria for inclusion because the model included an indicator for years prior to and after the federal ban as a control, but there was no comparison group. However, findings showed that *state* assault weapon bans had a statistically significant but smaller effect of reducing mass shooting death rates to 55 percent of what would have been expected without the bans, but uncertain effects on mass shooting injuries (see Figure 4.2). This report provided little detail describing variation in the timing of the state bans in relation to the federal ban, and it is unclear whether the estimated effects were confounded by correlation between the state and federal bans. The model did not account for serial correlation in panel data, which can result in large biases in standard errors (Aneja, Donohue, Zhang, 2014).

Using a linear probability model and data from a later period (1989–2014), Luca, Deepak, and Poliquin (2016) estimated the effects of state assault weapon bans on a binary indicator for whether a mass shooting occurred in a given state-year. In contrast to Gius (2015c), Luca, Deepak, and Poliquin (2016) did not control for the federal assault weapon ban from 1994 through 2004, but they controlled for a host of other state-level gun policies and for state-level demographic, socioeconomic, and political characteristics. Their findings showed uncertain effects of state assault weapon bans on the probability of a mass shooting incident occurring. However, the effects of gun policies on mass shootings were not the primary focus of Luca, Deepak, and Poliquin

[17] The two studies adopted slightly different definitions for *mass shooting* (see Chapter Twenty-Two for further detail on definitional issues). Gius (2015c) focused on *public mass shootings*, which the author defined as incidents resulting in four or more firearm-related fatalities (excluding the offender), where the shooting occurred in a relatively public place, victims were selected indiscriminately, and the shooting was not related to criminal activity. Luca, Deepak, and Poliquin (2016) set the same casualty threshold and also excluded any incident that occurred in connection with criminal activity, but they did not restrict to public settings and excluded all events in which fewer than three of the fatally injured victims were not related to the shooter (e.g., family, romantic partner).

(2016), and the authors intended the estimates to serve solely as a robustness check for their main specification (the effects of mass shootings on gun policy). Although the paper provided limited information to use in evaluating the reported statistical models (e.g., on how these policies were coded), it is clear that the analysis used a linear model to predict a dichotomous outcome. Therefore, model assumptions were violated, making CIs unreliable.

Figure 4.2 displays the IRRs and CIs associated with the assault weapon ban policies examined in these studies. We exclude estimates of the federal assault weapon ban from Gius (2015c) because they do not meet our criteria for inclusion.

**Figure 4.2**
**Incidence Rate Ratios Associated with the Effect of Assault Weapon Bans on Mass Shootings**

| Study, by Policy | Outcome Measure | Effect Size (IRR) [95% CI] |
|---|---|---|
| **Assault weapon ban** | **Mass shooting** | |
| Luca, Deepak, & Poliquin (2016) | State-year indicator (no political controls) | 1.52 [0.60, 2.43] |
| Luca, Deepak, & Poliquin (2016) | State-year indicator (political controls) | 1.56 [0.63, 2.49] |
| **State assault weapon ban** | | |
| Gius (2015c) | Deaths | 0.55 [0.33, 0.92] |
| Gius (2015c) | Injuries | 1.35 [0.81, 2.23] |

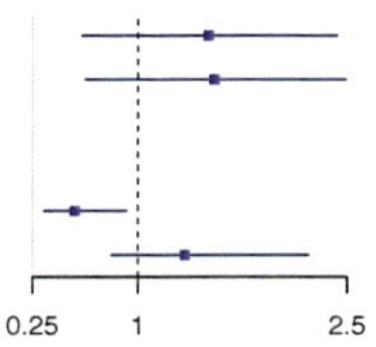


NOTE: IRR values marked with blue squares indicate that methodological concerns are discussed in the text. See Appendix B for details.

## Conclusions

We identified two qualifying studies that estimated the effects of state assault weapon bans on different aspects of mass shootings. Gius (2015c) found that these bans significantly reduce mass shooting deaths but have uncertain effects on injuries resulting from mass shootings. Using a similar data set, Luca, Deepak, and Poliquin (2016) found uncertain effects of state assault weapon bans on the annual incidence of mass shootings. Based on an assessment of these findings and the relative strengths of these studies, we find *inconclusive evidence for the effect of assault weapon bans on mass shootings.*

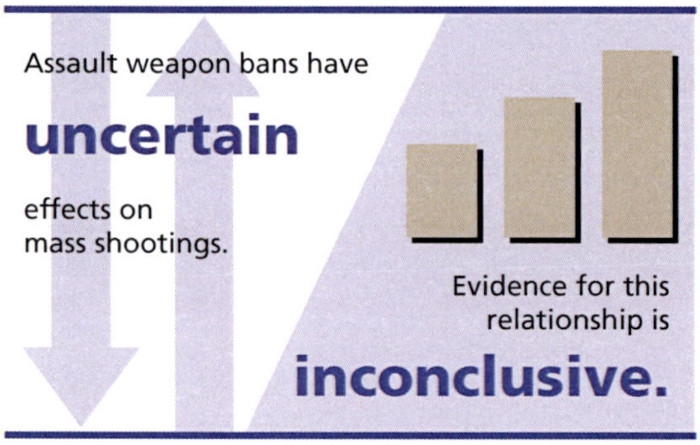

## Effects on the Gun Industry

In its review, NRC (2004) described two studies that examined the effects of the 1994 federal assault weapon ban (Koper and Roth, 2001, 2002). The studies found that the bans were associated with a temporary increase in prices of assault weapons in both primary and legal secondary markets. Hahn et al. (2005) identified no studies on this topic meeting our inclusion criteria.

Since 2003, we identified one study examining the effects of the federal assault weapon ban on prices in secondary markets of assault weapons that were purchased before 1994 and thus not prohibited from being sold under the terms of the federal ban. In an update to the earlier Koper and Roth (2001, 2002) studies, Koper (2004) compared secondary-market prices for firearms banned under the law with prices for similar firearms unaffected by the ban between 1991 and 1999, a period that includes when the federal ban took effect (September 13, 2004). In an analysis of assault pistols covered under the ban, the author reported no significant changes in price before or after the ban. Although the comparison firearms, "Saturday night special" handguns (i.e., inexpensive, small-caliber guns), showed steady declines in price over the same period, the effect of the federal law on these different price trends was not well identified. An analysis of secondary-market prices for banned assault rifles compared with other semiautomatic rifles not covered under the ban found sharp increases in price of the banned rifles in 1994 and 1995, but prices returned to pre-ban levels for the remainder of the study period. In contrast, the price of comparison rifles remained constant over the same time frame.

Koper (2004) also examined manufacturer production of banned and comparison weapons between 1985 and 2001. He found that production of banned assault pistols rose substantially in 1993 and 1994 before the ban took place, but then fell to below pre-ban levels even though several manufacturers were producing modified versions of the banned assault pistols that were not covered by the law. Surprisingly, however, a similar surge and subsequent decline was found for the manufacture of "Saturday night special" handguns, which were not subject to the ban, although these shifts were not as large.

Production of assault rifles also surged immediately prior to the ban but declined to pre-ban levels by 1996. In contrast with assault pistols, a strong demand for semiautomatic rifles modified so as not to be covered by the ban is reflected in a surge of production by the end of the 1990s, and production remained above pre-1993 levels in 2000 and 2001.

### Conclusions

One study provided some evidence that secondary-market prices of assault rifles, but not assault pistols, surged immediately before and in the year after the ban took effect. The ban appeared to affect manufacturer behavior, with production of assault pistols and assault rifles rising in the two or three years prior to the law taking effect. The production of semiautomatic pistols modified so as not to be covered by the ban did not recover to pre-ban levels over the study period, at least for the four manufacturers analyzed. Production of semiautomatic rifles modified so as not to be covered ban did recover to greater than pre-ban levels. Because this is a single study on just one version of an assault weapon ban, we conclude that there is *limited evidence that assault weapon bans led to short-term price increases and had mixed effects on the production of different classes of banned weapons.*

## Outcomes Without Studies Examining the Effects of Assault Weapon Bans

Neither NRC (2004) nor Hahn et al. (2005) identified any research examining the effects of assault weapon bans on the following outcomes, and we identified no such studies that met our inclusion criteria:

- suicide
- unintentional injuries and deaths
- officer-involved shootings
- defensive gun use
- hunting and recreation.

## Chapter Four References


Adler, W. C., F. M. Bielke, D. J. Doi, and J. F. Kennedy, *Cops Under Fire: Law Enforcement Officers Killed with Assault Weapons or Guns with High Capacity*, Washington, D.C.: Handgun Control, Inc., 1995.

Aneja, Abhay, John J. Donohue III, and Alexandria Zhang, *The Impact of Right to Carry Laws and the NRC Report: The Latest Lessons for the Empirical Evaluation of Law and Policy*, Stanford, Calif.: Stanford Law School, Olin Working Paper No. 461, December 1, 2014. As of May 21, 2017: https://papers.ssrn.com/sol3/papers.cfm?abstract_id=2443681

Blau, Benjamin M., Devon H. Gorry, and Chip Wade, "Guns, Laws, and Public Shootings in the United States," *Applied Economics*, Vol. 48, No. 49, 2016, pp. 4732–4746.

Chang, Ailsa, "Why the AR-15 Is More Than Just a Gun," NPR, June 24, 2013. As of June 29, 2017: http://www.npr.org/2013/06/24/194228925/why-the-ar-15-is-more-than-just-a-gun

Code of Federal Regulations, Title 27, Section 478.11, Meaning of Terms.

Everytown for Gun Safety Support Fund, "Mass Shootings in the United States: 2009–2016," April 11, 2017b. As of May 3, 2017:
http://everytownresearch.org/reports/mass-shootings-analysis/

FBI—*See* Federal Bureau of Investigation.

Federal Bureau of Investigation, "Crime in the United States 2015: Expanded Homicide Data Table 8," web page, 2016a. As of May 9, 2017:
https://ucr.fbi.gov/crime-in-the-u.s/2015/crime-in-the-u.s.-2015/tables/expanded_homicide_data_table_8_murder_victims_by_weapon_2011-2015.xls

———, "Crime in the United States 2015: Expanded Homicide Data Table 15," web page, 2016b. As of May 9, 2017:
https://ucr.fbi.gov/crime-in-the-u.s/2015/crime-in-the-u.s.-2015/tables/expanded_homicide_data_table_15_justifiable_homicide_by_weapon_private_citizen_2011-2015.xls

———, "Crime in the United States 2015: Expanded Homicide Data Table 28," web page, 2016c. As of May 9, 2017:
https://ucr.fbi.gov/leoka/2015/tables/table_28_leos_fk_type_of_weapon_2006-2015.xls

Giffords Law Center to Prevent Gun Violence, "Assault Weapons," web page, undated-a. As of October 18, 2017:
http://lawcenter.giffords.org/gun-laws/policy-areas/hardware-ammunition/assault-weapons/

Gius, Mark, "An Examination of the Effects of Concealed Weapons Laws and Assault Weapons Bans on State-Level Murder Rates," *Applied Economics Letters*, Vol. 21, No. 4, 2014, pp. 265–267.

———, "The Impact of State and Federal Assault Weapons Bans on Public Mass Shootings," *Applied Economics Letters*, Vol. 22, No. 4, 2015c, pp. 281–284.

Hahn, Robert A., Oleg Bilukha, Alex Crosby, Mindy T. Fullilove, Akiva Liberman, Eve Moscicki, Susan Snyder, Farris Tuma, and Peter A. Briss, "Firearms Laws and the Reduction of Violence: A Systematic Review," *American Journal of Preventive Medicine*, Vol. 28, No. 2, 2005, pp. 40–71.

Kleck, Gary, "Large-Capacity Magazines and the Casualty Counts in Mass Shootings: The Plausibility of Linkages," *Justice Research and Policy*, Vol. 17, No. 1, 2016, pp. 28–47.

Koper, Christopher S., *Updated Assessment of the Federal Assault Weapons Ban: Impacts on Gun Markets and Gun Violence 1994–2003*, Washington, D.C.: National Institute of Justice, U.S. Department of Justice, 2004.

Koper, Christopher S., and Jeffrey A. Roth, "The Impact of the 1994 Federal Assault Weapon Ban on Gun Violence Outcomes: An Assessment of Multiple Outcome Measures and Some Lessons for Policy Evaluation," *Journal of Quantitative Criminology*, Vol. 17, No. 1, 2001, pp. 33–74.

———, "Impact of the 1994 Federal Assault Weapons Ban on Gun Markets: An Assessment of Short-Term Primary and Secondary Market Effects," *Journal of Quantitative Criminology*, Vol. 18, 2002, pp. 239–266.

Krouse, William J., and Daniel J. Richardson, *Mass Murder with Firearms: Incidents and Victims, 1999–2013*, Washington, D.C.: Congressional Research Service, R44126, 2015.

Lott, John R., Jr., *More Guns, Less Crime: Understanding Crime and Gun-Control Laws*, 3rd ed., Chicago, Ill.: University of Chicago Press, 2010.

Luca, Michael, Lahotra Deepak, and Christopher Poliquin, *The Impact of Mass Shootings on Gun Policy*, working paper, Boston, Mass.: Harvard Business School, 2016.

National Research Council, *Firearms and Violence: A Critical Review*, Washington, D.C.: National Academies Press, 2004.

NRC—*See* National Research Council.

Plumer, Brad, "Everything You Need to Know About the Assault Weapons Ban, in One Post," *Washington Post*, December 17, 2012. As of May 30, 2017:
https://www.washingtonpost.com/news/wonk/wp/2012/12/17/everything-you-need-to-know-about-banning-assault-weapons-in-one-post/

Public Law 103-322, Violent Crime Control and Law Enforcement Act of 1994, 1994.

United States Code, Title 26, Section 5801, Imposition of Tax.

U.S. Department of Justice, "Violent Crime Control and Law Enforcement Act of 1994 Fact Sheet," Washington, D.C., October 24, 1994. As of May 30, 2017:
https://www.ncjrs.gov/txtfiles/billfs.txt

CHAPTER FIVE

# Stand-Your-Ground Laws

Self-defense has long been available as a criminal defense for fatal and nonfatal confrontations. Traditionally, this defense imposes a duty to retreat before using force, if safe retreat is available. Stand-your-ground laws—referred to by some as *shoot-first laws*—remove this duty to retreat in some cases of self-defense. By removing that rule, stand-your-ground laws are intended to reduce barriers for self-defense with the aim of further deterring aggressive or antisocial behavior. Given the availability of self-defense laws for situations in which safe retreat is not possible, stand-your-ground laws primarily apply when an individual could safely retreat from an attack , or when the availability of safe retreat is ambiguous.

By reducing the threshold for the justified use of lethal force for self-protection, stand-your-ground laws should increase defensive gun use and, if a deterrent effect exists, may reduce rates of crime and violence. Specifically, stand-your-ground laws reduce the expected legal costs of defensive gun use by reducing the probability of incurring criminal or civil liability for inflicting fatal or nonfatal injury. The laws, in turn, increase the expected costs of violent criminal behavior, as victims are more likely to respond using deadly force. This mechanism could serve to lower crime rates or could induce criminals to substitute to other types of crime in which they are less likely to encounter armed resistance. In that case, crime rates could remain stable while the composition of crime types (e.g., robbery versus larceny) shifts.

Alternatively, by lowering the legal risks of using deadly force, these laws could encourage the escalation of aggressive encounters, resulting in an overall increase in firearm homicides or injuries. Furthermore, the greater likelihood of facing a citizen willing to use a firearm defensively under these policies could induce criminals to carry firearms more often and thus increase the share of violent or property crimes involving firearms.

To disentangle these mechanisms, the ideal analyses would distinguish between the effects of stand-your-ground laws on criminal violence and the effects on violence committed in self-defense. Data on homicides, violent crime, and property crime are readily available. Methodological weaknesses in collecting data on defensive gun use are well-documented, but several data sources do exist (see Chapter Twenty-Three for further discussion). Ideally, analyses of the effects of stand-your-ground laws on defensive gun use would use data that capture whether the laws affected self-defense rates in the home (where castle-doctrine law already relieves victims of a duty to retreat) or in other areas as allowed under expanded stand-your-ground laws. However, this level of detail on the circumstances surrounding defensive gun use is not readily available from existing data sources, and there may be additional concerns about changes in the reporting of defensive gun use (as opposed to changes in actual prevalence) should estimation rely on self-reported data on gun use for self-protection. One of the two studies we identified that met our inclusion criteria for this policy separately examined total homicides (as well as other crime types) and justifiable homicides using statistics collected through the Federal Bureau of Investigation (FBI)'s Uniform Crime Reporting Program—although, as the authors point out, the program's definition of *justifiable homicide* does not capture certain incidents that would explicitly count as defensive gun use under expanded stand-your-ground laws (Cheng and Hoekstra, 2013).

There is likely to be little effect of stand-your-ground laws on hunting or recreational gun use. However, should these policies encourage more individuals to obtain or carry firearms, we might expect increased gun sales, unintentional injuries and deaths, and suicides outside the home following passage of the law. To assess this possibility, one would ideally like to know whether there are greater increases in gun ownership and carrying following passage of stand-your-ground laws compared with other states, but data on gun ownership have not been collected systematically over time. Only one of the studies we identified that met our criteria evaluated the effects of stand-your-ground laws on these outcomes: Humphreys, Gasparrini, and Wiebe (2017) estimated the impact of such laws on suicide rates as a placebo test (i.e., on the theory that stand-your-ground laws should have no effect on suicides).

## State Implementation of Stand-Your-Ground Laws

Utah passed a stand-your-ground law in 1994, but widespread legislative change did not begin until 2005. That year, Florida adopted such a law, which became the basis for a model law adopted by the American Legislative Exchange Council. In the ensuing decade, an additional 26 states passed similar laws (Giffords Law Center to Prevent Gun Violence, undated-e). It is important to note that different experts use "stand-your-ground" terminology differently. In particular, we include states where castle doctrine is expanded to motor vehicles. Other sources, therefore, count fewer states with stand-your-ground laws (e.g., Everytown for Gun Safety Support Fund, 2013).

Utah's law states, "A person does not have a duty to retreat from the force or threatened force described in Subsection (1) in a place where that person has lawfully entered or remained, except as provided in Subsection (2)(a)(iii)." Subsection 1 says, in part, that force that is likely to cause death or serious injury is justified to "prevent death or serious bodily injury . . . as a result of another person's imminent use of unlawful force, or to prevent the commission of a forcible felony." The exception in (2)(a)(iii) applies to a situation where the individual in question was the aggressor or was "engaged in combat by agreement," unless they have withdrawn from the combat or expressed their intention to do so.[1]

Florida's stand-your-ground law is similar to Utah's. It says that a "person who is attacked in his or her dwelling, residence, or vehicle has no duty to retreat and has the right to stand his or her ground and use or threaten to use force, including deadly force, if he or she uses or threatens to use force in accordance with Sections 776.012(1) or (2) or sections 776.013(1) or (2)."[2] Section 776.012(2) and 776.013(2) both provide that deadly force is justified when "necessary to prevent imminent death or great bodily harm to [oneself] or another or to prevent the imminent commission of a forcible felony."[3]

States that followed Florida generally modeled their laws on those of Florida and Utah,[4] sometimes with distinct features.[5] A few other laws strayed further from the Florida and Utah statutes.[6] For instance, Mississippi's law uses the term *felony* rather than the narrower *forcible felony*.[7] Other states do not include the language that there is no duty to retreat to prevent the commission of a forcible felony, but they do allow individuals to use deadly force to prevent specific, named felonies. In most states, this is quite broad, either listing many types of felonies or describing a class of felonies.[8] In

---

1 Utah Code Ann. § 76-2-402.

2 Florida Stat. Ann. § 776.013.

3 Florida Stat. Ann. §§ 776.012, 776.013.

4 In particular, Georgia, Indiana, Montana, and Oklahoma. See Ga. Code Ann. §§ 16-3-23.1, 16-3-21; Ind. Code Ann. § 35-41-3-2; Mont. Ann. Code §§ 45-3-102, 103, 104, 110; Okla. Stat. Ann. Tit. 21 § 1289.25.

5 Alabama, Alaska, Arizona, Kansas, Kentucky, Louisiana, Michigan, Mississippi, Missouri, Nevada, New Hampshire, North Carolina, North Dakota, Pennsylvania, South Carolina, South Dakota, Tennessee, Texas, and Wisconsin. See Ala. Code § 13A-3-23; Alaska Stat. Ann. § 11.81.335; Ariz. Rev. Stat. Ann. § 13-411; Kan. Stat. Ann. §§ 21-5222, 5223, 5230; Ky. Rev. Stat. Ann. §§ 503.050, 503.055; La. Stat. Ann. § 14:20; Mich. Comp. Laws § 780.972; Miss. Ann. Code § 97-3-15; Mo. Stat. Ann. § 563.031; Nev. Rev. Stat. Ann. § 200.120; N.H. Rev. Stat. Ann. §§ 627:4, 627:7; N.C. Gen. Stat. Ann. §§ 14-51.3, 51.2; N.D. Ann. Code § 12.1-05-07; 18 Pa. Const. Stat. § 505; S.C. Ann. Code §§ 16-11-440, 16-1-60; S.D. Laws § 22-18-4; Tenn. Ann. Code § 39-11-611; Tex. Penal Code § 9.32; Wisc. Stat. Ann. § 939.48.

6 Iowa, Ohio, and West Virginia. See Iowa Code Ann. § 704.1, which states that deadly force may be used even if there is an alternative, if the alternative requires one to retreat from one's dwelling or workplace. Ohio Rev. Code Ann. § 2901.09, which applies to every section in the code that sets forth a criminal offense. W. Va. Ann. Code § 55-7-22, which strays from Florida's and Utah's laws in the section dealing with civil actions, discussing lawsuits brought by intruders or attackers for injuries sustained.

7 Miss. Ann. Code § 97-3-15.

8 For example, Ala. Code § 13-A-3-23 (kidnapping; assault; burglary; robbery; forcible rape; forcible sodomy; "using or about to use physical force against an owner, employee, or other person authorized to be on business property when the business is closed to the public while committing or attempting to commit a crime involving death, serious physical injury, robbery, kidnapping, rape, sodomy, or a crime of a sexual nature involving

some states, the list of felonies is quite limited.[9] Finally, four states limit their laws to defense of self and others in the face of death or serious physical injury, thereby implicitly excluding any other felonies.[10]

West Virginia, which discusses stand-your-ground laws only in the context of civil actions, does not require an individual to retreat if facing risk of death, serious bodily harm, or commission of a felony in his or her own home. However, the law requires the risk of death or serious bodily harm for the stand-your-ground provisions to apply when outside the home.[11] In North Dakota, the stand-your-ground law applies in an individual's home, workplace, or occupied motor home or travel trailer, unless the individual "is assailed by another individual who the individual knows also dwells or works there or who is lawfully in the motor home or travel trailer."[12] Ohio's statute applies only in the person's home, vehicle, or vehicle owned by an immediate family member.[13] In Wisconsin, the law applies in an individual's home, motor vehicle, or place of business.[14] In Iowa and Connecticut, it applies in the home or workplace.[15]

---

a child under the age of 12"; or against someone who "in the process of unlawfully and forcefully entering, or has unlawfully and forcefully entered, a dwelling, residence, business property, or occupied vehicle, or federally licensed nuclear power facility, or is in the process of sabotaging or attempting to sabotage a federally licensed nuclear power facility, or is attempting to remove, or has forcefully removed, a person against his or her will from any dwelling, residence, business property, or occupied vehicle when the person has a legal right to be there, and provided that the person using the deadly physical force knows or has reason to believe that an unlawful and forcible entry or unlawful and forcible act is occurring"); Alaska Stat. Ann. § 11.81.335 (in addition to death and serious physical injury, lists kidnapping, sexual assault, sexual abuse of a minor, and robbery); Ky. Rev. Stat. Ann. § 503.050, 503.055 (503.050 states that an individual may stand his or her ground when at risk of kidnapping or sexual intercourse compelled by force or threat of force, in addition to death, great bodily harm, or felony by force, while 503.055 states that individuals may stand their ground when they or other individuals face only death, great bodily harm, or felony by force); Mo. Stat. Ann. § 563.031 (adds defense of unborn child); and Nev. Rev. Stat. Ann. § 200.120 ("necessary self-defense, or in defense of an occupied habitation, an occupied motor vehicle or a person, against one who manifestly intends or endeavors to commit a crime of violence, or against any person or persons who manifestly intend and endeavor, in a violent, riotous, tumultuous or surreptitious manner, to enter the occupied habitation or occupied motor vehicle, of another for the purpose of assaulting or offering personal violence to any person dwelling or being therein"). See also La. Stat. Ann. § 14:20; N.H. Rev. Stat. Ann. §§ 627:4, 627:7; N.D. Ann. Code § 12.1-05-07; Ohio Rev. Code Ann. § 2901.09; S.C. Ann. Code §§ 16-11-440, 16-1-60; S.D. Laws §§ 22-18-4, 22-18-34, 22-18-35; Tex. Penal Code § 9.32.

[9] Mich. Comp. Laws § 780.972 (sexual assault); N.C. Gen. Stat. Ann. §§ 14-51.3, 51.2 (forcibly entering home, motor vehicle, or workplace or attempting to remove someone from their home, motor vehicle, or workplace); 18 Pa. Cons. Stat. § 505 (kidnapping or sexual intercourse by force or threat).

[10] Iowa, Kansas, Tennessee, and Wisconsin. See Iowa Code Ann. § 704.1; Kan. Stat. Ann. §§ 21-5222, 5223, 5230; Tenn. Ann. Code § 39-11-611; Wisc. Stat. Ann. § 939.48.

[11] W. Va. Ann. Code § 55-7-22.

[12] N.D. Ann. Code § 12.1-05-07.

[13] Ohio Rev. Code Ann. § 2901.09.

[14] Wisc. Stat. Ann. § 939.48.

[15] Iowa Code Ann. § 704.1; Conn. Gen. Stat. Ann. § 53a-20.

Some states exclude specific situations from applying under the stand-your-ground doctrine. In Louisiana, it "shall not apply when the person committing the homicide is engaged, at the time of the homicide, in the acquisition of, the distribution of, or possession of, with intent to distribute a controlled dangerous substance in violation of the provisions of the Uniform Controlled Dangerous Substances Law."[16] Other policies are broader, excluding any situation where the individual is "actively engaged in conduct in furtherance of criminal activity."[17]

## Effects on Suicide

### Research Synthesis Findings

Neither the National Research Council (NRC) (2004) nor Hahn et al. (2005) identified any research examining the effects of stand-your-ground laws on suicide. However, we identified one study that met our criteria (Humphreys, Gasparrini, and Wiebe, 2017), although this study's analysis of the impact of stand-your-ground laws on suicide rates was used as a placebo test (i.e., on the theory that stand-your-ground laws should have no effect on suicides) to support the authors' primary findings of an effect of the laws on homicide rates.[18]

Humphreys, Gasparrini, and Wiebe (2017) examined changes between 1999 and 2014 in Florida's monthly total and firearm suicide rates before and after the introduction of Florida's 2005 stand-your-ground law compared with changes over time in these rates in four of the 27 states without stand-your-ground laws at the beginning of the period (New Jersey, New York, Ohio, and Virginia). The paper reported that these were the only states with consistent monthly homicide data. It did not indicate if suicide data were available on a wider set of control states. The authors found uncertain evidence of an effect of the stand-your-ground law on either total or firearm suicides in Florida; they did find a suggestive reduction in control states' firearm suicide rates after Florida's stand-your-ground law was passed, but no evidence that this effect was different from the uncertain change in Florida. Their model included no covariates to adjust for other sources of differences between Florida and control states in suicide rates over time, potentially obscuring the effects of the stand-your-ground law in Florida.

Figure 5.1 displays the incidence rate ratios (IRRs) and confidence intervals (CIs) associated with the stand-your-ground policies examined in Humphreys, Gasparrini, and Wiebe (2017).

---

[16] La. Stat. Ann. § 14:20.

[17] Nev. Rev. Stat. Ann. § 200.120; Tex. Penal Code § 9.32; Wisc. Stat. Ann. § 939.48.

[18] We identified one additional study that examined the effects of castle-doctrine legislation on the proportion of firearm suicides as a proxy for firearm ownership (Wallace, 2014). However, without simultaneously examining firearm or total suicide rates, this outcome is difficult to interpret as providing a causal effect of stand-your-ground law, so the study did not meet our inclusion criteria.

**Figure 5.1**
**Incidence Rate Ratios Associated with the Effect of Stand-Your-Ground Laws on Suicide**

| Study, by Policy | Outcome Measure | Effect Size (IRR) [95% CI] |
|---|---|---|
| **Stand your ground** | **Suicide** | |
| Humphreys, Gasparrini, & Wiebe (2017) | Total rate, all ages | 0.99 [0.59, 1.67] |
| Humphreys, Gasparrini, & Wiebe (2017) | Firearm rate, all ages | 1.03 [0.93, 1.14] |

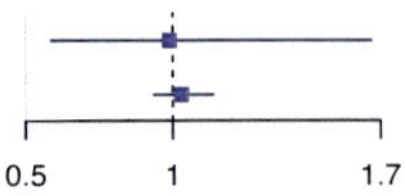


NOTE: IRR values marked with blue squares indicate that methodological concerns are discussed in the text. See Appendix B for details.

### Conclusions

We identified one qualifying study that estimated the effects of stand-your-ground laws on total suicides and firearm suicides. The estimates for these effects in Humphreys, Gasparrini, and Wiebe (2017) suggest that such laws have an uncertain effect on both total suicides and firearm suicides. Therefore, available studies provide *inconclusive evidence for the effect of stand-your-ground laws on total suicides and firearm suicides.*

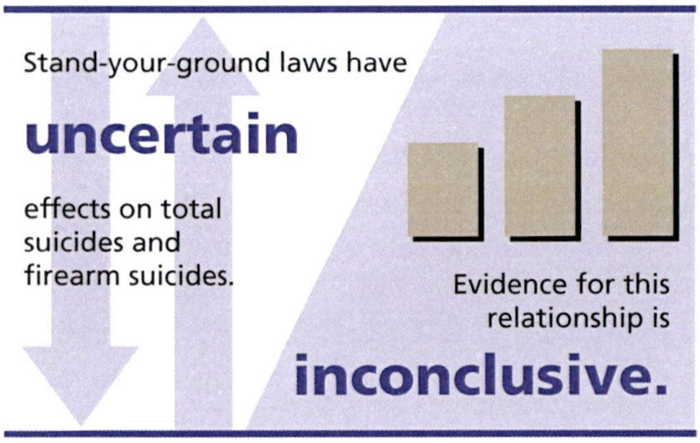


## Effects on Violent Crime

### Research Synthesis Findings

Neither NRC (2004) nor Hahn et al. (2005) identified any research examining the effects of stand-your-ground laws on violent crime.

We identified three studies that met our criteria. Cheng and Hoekstra (2013) exploited state and time variation in the passage of stand-your-ground laws using data from 2000 to 2010 to estimate the laws' effects on homicide rates. The authors defined stand-your-ground laws using a binary variable equal to one for polices that "remove the duty to retreat in some place outside the home" (Cheng and Hoekstra, 2013, p. 825). Controlling for state and year fixed effects, the study explored several model specifications, including additional controls for region-by-year fixed effects, time-varying covariates that account for changes in policing and incarceration rates, and state-specific linear trends. Using negative binomial regression models, they found stand-your-ground laws to be associated with significant increases in homicide rates of 6 to 11 percent, a result that is relatively robust across model specifications. However, given the relatively short time frame studied and large set of controls, the ratio of estimated parameters to observations is less than one to six in specifications that include time-varying covariates, indicating that the model may have been overfit, and thus its estimates and their CIs may be unreliable indicators of the true effect of the law.

Covering a similar period (1999–2010) with state-level data, Webster, Crifasi, and Vernick (2014) analyzed the effects of stand-your-ground laws on age-adjusted homicide rates. Using generalized least-squares regression models, their estimates showed an uncertain association between stand-your-ground laws and homicides rates, firearm homicide rates, and nonfirearm homicide rates. The statistical model used to arrive at these results used a large number of estimated parameters relative to observations (a ratio of about one to eight), meaning the model may have been overfit, and thus its estimates of the laws' effects may not generalize to other implementations of a stand-your-ground law.

Humphreys, Gasparrini, and Wiebe (2017) used segmented quasi-Poisson regression analysis to examine changes between 1999 and 2014 in Florida's monthly homicide rate before and after the introduction of Florida's 2005 stand-your-ground law. They compared these changes in four of the 27 states without stand-your-ground laws at the beginning of the period (New Jersey, New York, Ohio, and Virginia). The paper reported that these were the only states with reliable monthly homicide data. The authors found that the stand-your-ground law increased both total homicides and firearm homicides. Their estimates show that Florida experienced a significant 24-percent increase in total homicides and 32-percent increase in firearm homicides following enactment of the stand-your-ground law in 2005 (see Figure 5.2). The comparison states experienced a statistically insignificant 6-percent increase in total homicides and 8-percent increase in firearm homicides after 2005. The authors' model included no covariates to adjust for other sources of differences between Florida and control states in homicide rates over time, meaning that factors other than the stand-your-ground law cannot be ruled out as the cause of the observed differences between Florida and the control states.

Figure 5.2 displays the IRRs and CIs associated with the stand-your-ground policies examined in these studies.

**Figure 5.2**
**Incidence Rate Ratios Associated with the Effect of Stand-Your-Ground Laws on Violent Crime**

| Study, by Policy | Outcome Measure | Effect Size (IRR) [95% CI] |
|---|---|---|
| **Stand your ground** | **Homicide** | |
| Humphreys, Gasparrini, & Wiebe (2017) | Total rate, all ages | 1.17 [1.07, 1.28] |
| Humphreys, Gasparrini, & Wiebe (2017) | Firearm rate, all ages | 1.22 [1.08, 1.38] |
| Webster, Crifasi, & Vernick (2014) | Total rate | 1.02 [0.96, 1.07] |
| Webster, Crifasi, & Vernick (2014) | Firearm rate | 1.04 [0.97, 1.11] |
| Webster, Crifasi, & Vernick (2014) | Nonfirearm rate | 1.00 [0.92, 1.09] |
| Cheng & Hoekstra (2013) | Homicide rate | 1.10 [1.04, 1.16] |
| | **Violent crime** | |
| Cheng & Hoekstra (2013) | Burglary | 1.02 [0.98, 1.07] |
| Cheng & Hoekstra (2013) | Robbery | 1.03 [0.98, 1.07] |
| Cheng & Hoekstra (2013) | Aggravated assault | 1.04 [0.97, 1.10] |

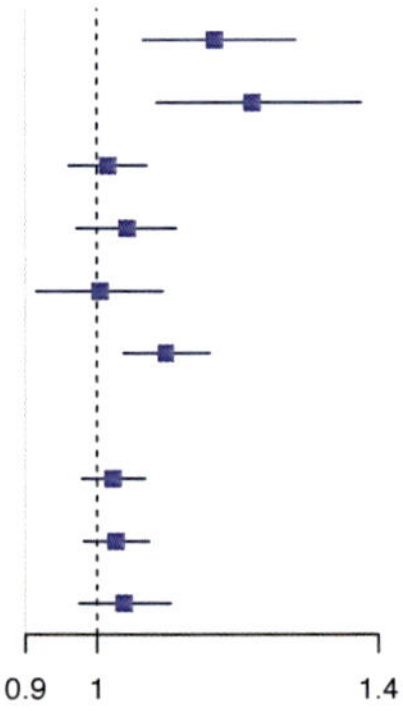


NOTE: IRR values marked with blue squares indicate that methodological concerns are discussed in the text. See Appendix B for details.

## Conclusions

*Homicides and other violent crime.* We identified three qualifying studies that estimated the effects of stand-your-ground laws on total homicides or other violent crimes. Cheng and Hoekstra (2013) found that these laws significantly increase homicide rates, but they have uncertain effects on robbery, aggravated assault, and burglary rates. Webster, Crifasi, and Vernick (2014) found that these laws have an uncertain effect on the total homicide rate. Finally, Humphreys, Gasparrini, and Wiebe (2017) found significant effects consistent with the law increasing total homicides in Florida after its passage. These studies draw on two distinct data sources: FBI crime-rate data from the Uniform Crime Reports system and the Center for Disease Control and Prevention's Fatal Injury Reports.

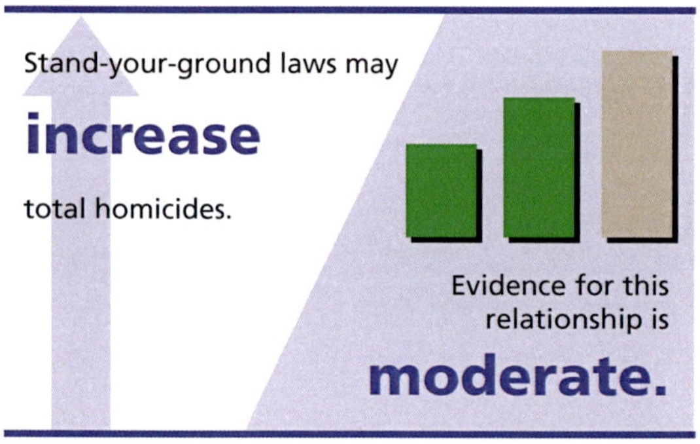


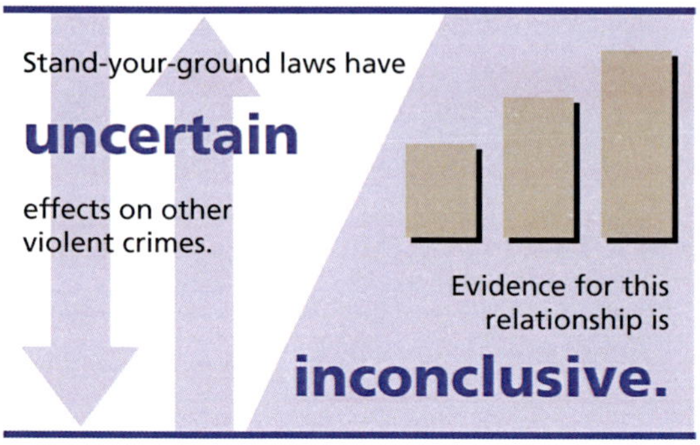


Based on these findings, we conclude that there is *moderate evidence that stand-your-ground laws may*

*increase homicide rates* but *inconclusive evidence for the effect of stand-your ground laws on other types of violent crime.*

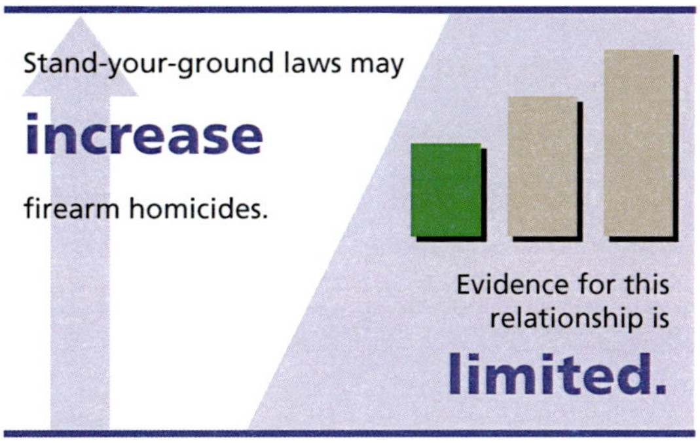


*Firearm homicides.* We identified two qualifying studies that estimated the effects of stand-your-ground laws on firearm homicide rates. Webster, Crifasi, and Vernick (2014) found that these laws have uncertain effects on firearm homicides. Humphreys, Gasparrini, and Wiebe (2017) found a significant effect suggesting that after the law's introduction, it increased firearm homicides in Florida. Based on these findings, we conclude that there is *limited evidence that stand-your-ground laws may increase firearm homicides.*

## Effects on Defensive Gun Use

### Research Synthesis Findings

Neither NRC (2004) nor Hahn et al. (2005) identified any research examining the effects of stand-your-ground laws on defensive gun use. We identified one such study meeting our inclusion criteria.

Cheng and Hoekstra (2013) exploited state-time variation in the passage of stand-your-ground laws using data from 2000 to 2010 to estimate such laws' effects on justifiable homicides committed by private citizens. The authors defined stand-your-ground laws using a binary variable equal to one for polices that "remove the duty to retreat in some place outside the home" (Cheng and Hoekstra, 2013, p. 825), and data on justifiable homicides were collected from the FBI's supplementary homicide data. Under the FBI's classification in this data set, for a homicide to be considered justifiable, the incident must have occurred in conjunction with other offenses (e.g., the fatal shooting of an armed robber by a storeowner during the commission of the robbery), and those other offenses must have been reported. As noted by the authors, justifiable homicides are likely severely underreported in this data source. Controlling for state and year fixed effects, the study explored several model specifications, including additional controls for region-by-year fixed effects, time-varying covariates that account for changes in policing and incarceration rates, and contemporaneous crime rates. Using negative binomial regression models, they found stand-your-ground laws to be associated with increases in justifiable homicide, ranging from an uncertain 28-percent rise to a significant 57-percent rise depending on the model specification. However, given the relatively short time frame studied and large set of controls, the ratio of estimated parameters to observations is less than one to six in specifications that include time-varying covariates, indicating that the model may have been overfit, and thus it may yield estimates that are unreliable indicators of the true causal effect of stand-your-ground laws.

Figure 5.3 displays the IRRs and CIs associated with the stand-your-ground policies examined in Cheng and Hoekstra (2013).

**Figure 5.3**
**Incidence Rate Ratios Associated with the Effect of Stand-Your-Ground Laws on Defensive Gun Use**

| Study, by Policy | Outcome Measure | Effect Size (IRR) [95% CI] |
|---|---|---|
| **Stand your ground laws** | | |
| Cheng & Hoekstra (2013) | Justifiable homicide | 1.33 [0.84, 2.10] |

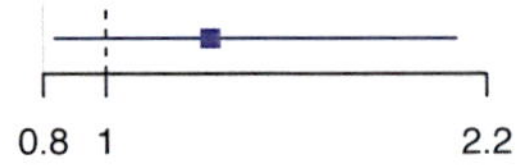


NOTE: IRR values marked with blue squares indicate that methodological concerns are discussed in the text. See Appendix B for details.

## Conclusions

We identified one study that estimated the effects of stand-your-ground laws on justifiable homicides, which is an imperfect measure of the rate of defensive gun use. In their specification that accounts for how justifiable homicides are counted and controls for time-varying state characteristics, Cheng and Hoekstra (2013) found that the effect of the law on this outcome is uncertain. Therefore, we find *inconclusive evidence for the effect of stand-your-ground laws on defensive gun use.*

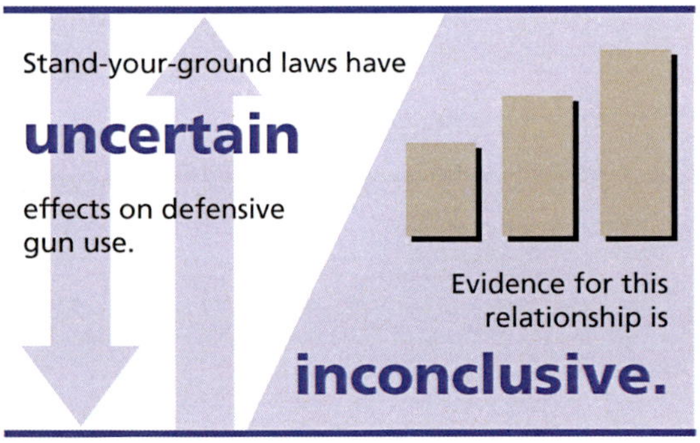


## Outcomes Without Studies Examining the Effects of Stand-Your-Ground Laws

Neither NRC (2004) nor Hahn et al. (2005) identified any research examining the effects of stand-your-ground laws on the following outcomes, and we identified no such studies that met our inclusion criteria:

- unintentional injuries and deaths
- mass shootings
- officer-involved shootings
- hunting and recreation
- gun industry.

## Chapter Five References

Cheng, Cheng, and Mark Hoekstra, "Does Strengthening Self-Defense Law Deter Crime or Escalate Violence? Evidence from Expansions to Castle Doctrine," *Journal of Human Resources*, Vol. 48, No. 3, 2013, pp. 821–853.

Everytown for Gun Safety Support Fund, *Shoot First: "Stand Your Ground" Laws and Their Effect on Violent Crime and the Criminal Justice System*, New York, 2013.

Giffords Law Center to Prevent Gun Violence, "'Stand Your Ground' Laws," web page, undated-e. As of October 18, 2017:
http://lawcenter.giffords.org/gun-laws/policy-areas/guns-in-public/stand-your-ground-laws/

Hahn, Robert A., Oleg Bilukha, Alex Crosby, Mindy T. Fullilove, Akiva Liberman, Eve Moscicki, Susan Snyder, Farris Tuma, and Peter A. Briss, "Firearms Laws and the Reduction of Violence: A Systematic Review," *American Journal of Preventive Medicine*, Vol. 28, No. 2, 2005, pp. 40–71.

Humphreys, David K., Antonio Gasparrini, and Douglas J. Wiebe, "Evaluating the Impact of Florida's 'Stand Your Ground' Self-Defense Law on Homicide and Suicide by Firearm: An Interrupted Time Series Study," *JAMA Internal Medicine*, Vol. 177, No. 1, 2017, pp. 44–50.

National Research Council, *Firearms and Violence: A Critical Review*, Washington, D.C.: National Academies Press, 2004.

NRC—*See* National Research Council.

Wallace, Lacey N., "Castle Doctrine Legislation: Unintended Effects for Gun Ownership?" *Justice Policy Journal*, Vol. 11, No. 2, Fall 2014.

Webster, D., C. K. Crifasi, and J. S. Vernick, "Effects of the Repeal of Missouri's Handgun Purchaser Licensing Law on Homicides," *Journal of Urban Health*, Vol. 91, No. 2, 2014, pp. 293–302.

CHAPTER SIX

# Prohibitions Associated with Mental Illness

Federal law prohibits the possession or purchase of firearms by certain individuals who have been adjudicated as mentally ill (18 U.S.C. 922).[1] The number of people covered by that exclusion is not known. An estimated 44 million adults in the United States have some form of *mental illness*, defined as any "diagnosable mental, behavioral, or emotional disorder, other than a developmental or substance use disorder" (Substance Abuse and Mental Health Services Administration, 2016). Of these adults, approximately 10 million suffer from a "serious mental illness" that results in substantial impairment in carrying out major life activities. Existing laws that prohibit those with mental health conditions from accessing firearms affect a subset of individuals who likely fall into the "serious mental illness" category. Expanding such prohibitions has the potential to affect a much larger subset of individuals who fall within the "any mental illness" category, although broadening the scope of mental health restrictions poses technological, coordination, and legal (i.e., privacy) challenges (Liu et al., 2013).

If individuals with mental illness present a higher violence risk to themselves or others compared with those without mental illness, then restricting their access to firearms should reduce suicides or homicides. The magnitude of these effects will depend primarily on the reliability of the screening process instituted to identify disqualifying mental health conditions, the size of the marginal population affected by the expanded prohibitions, and the likelihood of individuals in that population committing harm to others or to themselves.

Epidemiological evidence suggests that a diagnosis of mental illness alone has little relation to risk of interpersonal violence (Swanson et al., 2015); in particular, studies estimate that between 2 percent and 4 percent of all violent behavior may be attributable to mental illness (Corrigan and Watson, 2005; Swanson, 1994). One study found that among a sample of convicted murderers in Indiana, perpetrators with serious mental illness were significantly less likely to have used a firearm compared with other perpetrators (Matejkowski et al., 2014). A study of 82,000 individuals with mental illness in Florida showed that the arrest rate for violent crimes involving a firearm

[1] The Gun Control Act of 1968 prohibited the sale of firearms to any person who has been "adjudicated as a mental defective or has been committed to any mental institution" (Pub. L. 90-618).

was the same among the study population as the estimated general population rate—approximately 215 arrests per 100,000 people (Swanson et al., 2016). Elevated rates of violence tend to be reported for involuntarily committed patients (Choe, Teplin, and Abram, 2008), but this population is already barred from acquiring firearms through existing federal mental health–related prohibitions. Overall, between 2001 and 2010, less than 5 percent of the 120,000 firearm-related homicides in the United States were committed by individuals diagnosed with a mental illness (Metzl and MacLeish, 2015), suggesting that expanded prohibitions based on mental health status may not have a large effect on firearm crimes.

Although media coverage often links mass shootings with serious mental illness (McGinty et al., 2014), an analysis of 133 mass shooting events between 2009 and 2015 (Everytown for Gun Safety Support Fund, 2017b) reported that in only one incident (0.8 percent) did the perpetrator have a history of mental illness that prohibited purchase of a firearm from a federally licensed dealer; however, formal concerns about the mental health of the perpetrator had been previously expressed for 15 cases (11.3 percent), and informal concerns about the shooter's mental health had been previously expressed for 13 additional cases (9.8 percent). Although public mass shooters are more likely to have a psychotic disorder compared with perpetrators of multiple-victim shootings related to familicide or profit-motivation, the prevalence of severe mental illness among this subgroup is still quite low (Fox and Levin, 2015). Counting less-severe forms of mental illness, Follman, Aronsen, and Pan (2017) found that 50 of the 90 public mass shootings between 1982 and 2017 that were identified by *Mother Jones* magazine involved a shooter with a history of possible mental health problems.

At the same time, research indicates that individuals with mental disorders are more likely to be victims than perpetrators of violence (Desmarais et al., 2014). One study of persons with severe mental illness (in treatment at mental health agencies in Chicago) found that their annual exposure to violent crime victimization was more than four times higher than rates in the general population (Teplin et al., 2005). Another meta-analysis produced similar results, finding the prevalence of violent victimization among individuals with mental illness to be 24 percent (with estimates of the reviewed studies ranging from 7 percent to 63 percent) (Hughes et al., 2012). Extrapolating this estimate to the national population of individuals with serious mental illness in 2015 would suggest that approximately 2.3 million individuals with serious mental illness are victims of violent crime each year; however, this is likely an overestimate because most studies sampled individuals who were receiving inpatient or outpatient treatment for diagnosed psychiatric illnesses or focused on severe mental illnesses (such as schizophrenia) (Hughes et al., 2012). For instance, while the National Crime Victimization Survey (NCVS) does not collect information on mental health directly, NCVS estimates suggest that there are about 780,000 cases annually of violent crime against individuals with cognitive disabilities (defined as serious difficulty in concentrating, remembering, or making decisions because of a physical, mental, or emotional condition) (Harrell, 2017). Therefore, expanding the class of prohibited possessors to include more people with severe mental illness may lead to additional victimization because those people have reduced opportunities for defensive gun use. At the same time, such an expansion may decrease violent crime, mass shootings, and suicides carried out by this population.

Indeed, evidence supports that expanding prohibitions associated with mental illness may have larger effects in reducing rates of firearm suicides. Research has demonstrated a strong link between mental illness and suicide; it is estimated that between 47 percent and 74 percent of suicides are attributed to mental disorders (Li et al., 2011; Cavanagh et al., 2003). A study of 82,000 individuals with mental illness in Florida found that suicide was nearly four times as prevalent among this subpopulation compared with the general population, but firearms were half as likely to be used as a means of suicide; in more than 70 percent of these firearm suicide cases, the individual's mental health condition did not prohibit him or her from obtaining a firearm legally (Swanson et al., 2016).

To assess the effects of expanded mental health–related prohibitions, the ideal data would distinguish outcomes between those who are affected by the expanded prohibitions and those who are not. This type of analysis would necessitate a detailed database containing rich information on the mental health conditions of perpetrators of crime or victims of suicide. Because an individual's medical records are private, it may be particularly difficult to identify firearm-involved crime incidents in which the perpetrator was a prohibited possessor because of mental illness. Given these data challenges, as well as wide variation across states in mental health disqualifiers and inconsistencies in reporting, it is not surprising that we identified no studies meeting our inclusion criteria that estimated the effects of expanded prohibitions associated with mental illness. Nevertheless, three studies reviewed in Chapter Three (on background checks) examined the effect of implementing the Brady Handgun Violence Prevention Act (the Brady Act) checks on certain mentally ill people. Implementation of this law had the effect of expanding the class of mentally ill people who could not purchase a firearm, so we review those studies in this chapter as well.

## State Implementation of Prohibitions Associated with Mental Illness

The District of Columbia and 33 states have laws restricting access to firearms by individuals with mental illness. Although the laws may use different language,[2] many

[2] For example, Alabama prohibits "anyone of unsound mind" from owning, possessing, or controlling a firearm and defines *unsound mind* as anyone

> (1) Found by a court, board, commission, or other lawful authority that, as a result of marked subnormal intelligence, mental illness, incompetency, condition, or disease, is a danger to himself or herself or others or lacks the mental capacity to contract or manage his or her own affairs; . . . [or] (3) Involuntarily committed for a

states have basically adopted the same standards as the federal Brady Act, which went into effect in 1994.[3]

In other cases, states have narrower prohibitions than found in the Brady Act. For example, several states prohibit firearm possession by only those committed to psychiatric institutions, not those adjudicated as mentally incompetent.[4] In some states, such as Missouri, only those adjudicated as mentally incompetent are prohibited.[5] In Michigan and North Carolina, the prohibition applies only to handguns.[6] Oklahoma and Tennessee prohibit only the transfer of firearms to these prohibited individuals, but the laws are silent on whether such individuals may possess a firearm.[7]

In contrast, California, Connecticut, Illinois, Maryland, and the District of Columbia have expanded the Brady Act prohibitions to include individuals who have been voluntarily admitted into psychiatric hospitals.[8] Hawaii has extended the prohibition to those diagnosed with "significant" mental disorders, and California, Connecticut, Illinois, and Maryland have widened the class of prohibited possessors in other ways.[9]

---

> final commitment for inpatient treatment to the Department of Mental Health or a Veterans' Administration hospital by a court after a hearing. (Ala. Code § 13A-11-72)

Alabama also includes individuals who have been "found to be insane, [found to be] not guilty by reason of mental disease or defect, found mentally incompetent to stand trial, or found not guilty by reason of a lack of mental responsibility." The Center to Prevent Gun Violence considers these restrictions separately, and we agree.

3 Alabama, Arkansas, California, Florida, Nevada, New York, Ohio, Oregon, Pennsylvania, Rhode Island, South Carolina, Utah, Virginia, West Virginia, and Wyoming. See Ala. Code § 13A-11-72; Ark. Code Ann. § 5-73-103; Calif. Welf. and Inst. Code §§ 8100, 8103; Fla. Stat. Ann. § 790.065; Nev. Rev. Stat. Ann. § 202.360; N.Y. Penal Law §§ 265.00, 400, N.Y. Mental Hygiene Law § 9.46; Ohio Rev. Code Ann § 2923.13; Ore. Rev. Stat. Ann. §§ 166.250, 426.130; 18 Pa. Cons. Stat. § 6105; R.I. Gen. Laws. § 11-47-6; S.C. Ann. Code § 23-31-1040; Utah Code Ann. § 76-10-503; Va. Ann. Code § 18.2-308.1:2; W. Va. Ann. Code § 61-7-7; Wyo. Stat. Ann. § 6-8-404.

4 Arizona, Connecticut, Delaware, Hawaii, Kansas, Maine, Maryland, Massachusetts, Minnesota, New Jersey, North Dakota, Washington, Wisconsin, and the District of Columbia. See Ariz. Rev. Stat Ann. §§ 13-3101, 13-3102, 36-540; Conn. Gen. Stat. § 53a-217; Del. Code Ann. Tit. 11 § 1448; Hawaii Rev. Stat. Ann. § 134-7; Kan. Stat. Ann. §§ 21-6301, 59-2946; Me. Rev. Stat. Ann. § 393; Md. Ann. Code § 5-133; Mass. Gen. Laws Ann. § 129B; Minn. Stat. Ann. § 624.713; N.J. Stat. Ann. § 2C:39-7; N.D. Cent. Code § 62.1-02-01; Wash. Rev. Code § 941.040; Wisc. Stat. §§ 941.29, 51.20, 54.10; D.C. Ann. Code § 7-2502.03.

5 Mo. Stat. Ann. § 571.070.

6 Mich. Comp. Laws. Ann. § 28.422; N.C. Gen. Stat. Ann. § 140-402. Furthermore, in Michigan, the prohibition applies only to those committed to psychiatric institutions.

7 Okla. Stat. Ann. § 1289.10; Tenn. Code Ann. § 39-17-1316.

8 Calif. Welf. and Inst. Code § 8100 (while voluntarily in treatment for being a threat to themselves or others); Conn. Gen. Stat. Ann. § 53a-217 (admitted within previous six months); 430 Ill. Comp. Stat 65/1.1, 65/8 (admitted within past five years), 405 Ill. Comp. Stat. 5/6-103.1; Md. Ann. Code § 5-133 (admitted for more than 30 consecutive days); D.C. Code Ann. § 7-2502.03 (admitted within past five years).

9 In Hawaii, possession is prohibited by those "diagnosed as having a significant behavioral, emotional, or mental disorder" (Hawaii Rev. Stat. Ann. § 134-7). California has a long list of disqualifiers, including threats

Arizona, Oregon, Pennsylvania, and Virginia have also extended the mental health–related prohibitions to individuals ordered to attend outpatient treatment.[10] New York extended the prohibitions to individuals who were committed for inpatient treatment.[11]

## Effects on Suicide

### Research Synthesis Findings

Neither the National Research Council (NRC) (2004) nor Hahn et al. (2005) identified any research examining the effects of mental health–related prohibitions on suicide. Using state-level data from 1996 to 2005, Sen and Panjamapirom (2012) assessed how different *types* of background checks conducted by states affect suicides. They noted that there is substantial variation in state laws regarding which mental health records must be considered in background checks. The authors characterized variation in whether states can examine relevant mental illness records as part of the background check process. Their regression models included state-level covariates, a lagged outcome variable, and fixed effects for year and census subregion.

Sen and Panjamapirom (2012) found that, compared with states with background checks that investigate only criminal history, checks of mental health records were associated with significantly lower firearm suicide and total suicide rates. Their estimates suggest that after implementing a state check on mental health records, the firearm suicide rate was 96 percent of the expected rate had this policy not been in effect, and the total suicide rate was 97 percent of the expected rate.

Swanson et al. (2016) evaluated how changes in state reporting of gun-disqualifying mental health records to the Federal Bureau of Investigation's National Instant Criminal Background Check System (NICS) database affected suicide rates among individuals in Florida with a disqualifying mental health condition relative to individuals diagnosed with a serious mental health illness but not prohibited from purchasing a firearm. They found no significant difference between suicide rates before and after implementing expanded NICS reporting for the two groups.

---

of physical violence, various lengths of detention, and court-ordered evaluation and counseling (Calif. Welf. and Inst. Code §§ 8100, 8103, 5200-5213). Maryland restricts possession from any person who "suffers from a mental disorder . . . and has a history of violent behavior against the person or another" (Md. Ann. Code § 5-133), and Illinois and Connecticut restrict possession from those who threaten violence or demonstrate threatening behavior (430 Ill. Comp. Stat 65/1.1; Conn. Gen. Stat. Ann. § 53a-217).

[10] Ariz. Rev. Stat §§ 36-540(A)(1), 13-3101(A)(7); Ore. Rev. Stat. §§ 166.250(1)(c)(D), 426.133; 18 Pa. Cons. Stat. § 6105; Va. Code. Ann. § 18.2-308.1:3(A).

[11] N.Y. Penal Law § 400.001(1), N.Y. Ment. Hyg. Law § 9.27.

Figure 6.1 displays the incidence rate ratios (IRRs) and confidence intervals (CIs) associated with the mental health–related prohibition policies examined in Sen and Panjamapirom (2012). Swanson et al. (2016) did not provide effect estimates or test statistics, so we do not include effect sizes for this study in the figure.

**Figure 6.1**
**Incidence Rate Ratios Associated with the Effect of Mental Health–Related Prohibitions on Suicide**

| Study, by Policy | Outcome Measure | Effect Size (IRR) [95% CI] |
|---|---|---|
| **Check on mental illness** | **Suicide** | |
| Sen & Panjamapirom (2012) | Total | 0.97 [0.95, 0.99] |
| Sen & Panjamapirom (2012) | Firearm | 0.96 [0.92, 0.99] |

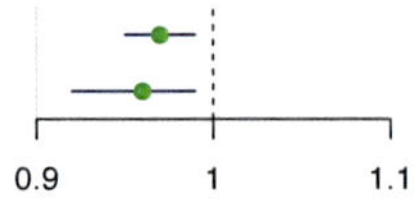


NOTE: IRR values marked with green circles indicate that we identified no significant methodological concerns. See Appendix B for details.

## Conclusions

One study found evidence that when states check mental health records as part of the firearm background check process, their rates of firearm suicide and total suicide are reduced by a few percentage points. This study did not examine the effect of expanding mental health–related prohibitions beyond those in federal law. Instead, it examined how improved compliance with existing federal law concerning mental health checks affects suicide rates. Because improved compliance has the effect of prohibiting gun purchases by some with mental health conditions who would not previously have been prevented from purchasing a weapon, this study provides limited evidence that prohibitions associated with mental illness can reduce total suicides and firearm suicides. A second study reported finding no effect of implementing NICS mental health–related prohibitions on suicide but did not provide detailed results.

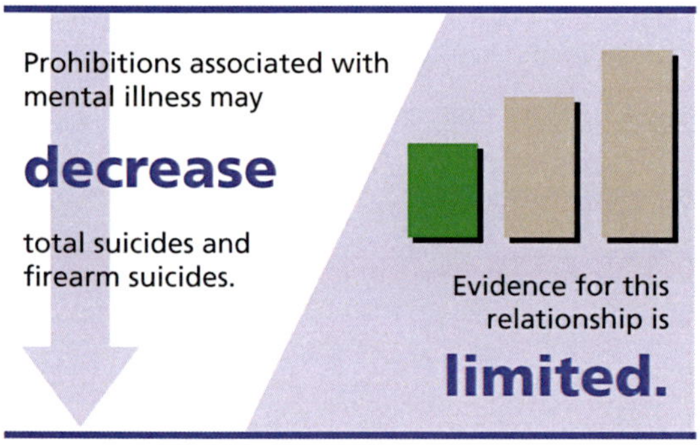


Based on these results, we conclude that there is *limited evidence that some state or federal laws prohibiting those with a mental illness from buying a gun reduce total suicide rates and firearm suicide rates.*

## Effects on Violent Crime

### Research Synthesis Findings

Neither NRC (2004) nor Hahn et al. (2005) identified any research examining the effects of mental health–related prohibitions on suicide. Since 2003, three studies examined the effects of implementing background checks for individuals prohibited from purchasing or possessing firearms because of a mental illness. Using state-level data from 1996 to 2005, Sen and Panjamapirom (2012) assessed how different *types* of background checks conducted by states affect total homicides and firearm homicides. They noted that there is substantial variation in state laws regarding which mental health records must be considered in background checks. The authors characterized variation in whether states can examine relevant mental illness records as part of the background check process. Their regression models included state-level covariates, a lagged outcome variable, and fixed effects for year and census subregion.

Sen and Panjamapirom (2012) found that, compared with background checks that examine only criminal history, background checks that include mental illness records are associated with fewer total homicides and firearm homicides. However, only the reductions for total homicides reached conventional levels of statistical significance, and estimates for firearm homicides were suggestive. The authors found that, after implementation of state background checks that included mental illness records, firearm homicide rates declined to 93 percent of the level that would otherwise be expected (see Figure 6.2).

Swanson et al. (2013, 2016) merged administrative records from public health and criminal justice agencies to evaluate how changes in state reporting of gun-disqualifying mental health records to the NICS database affected violent crime arrest rates for individuals with a disqualifying mental health condition relative to individuals diagnosed with a serious mental health illness but not prohibited from purchasing a firearm. Swanson et al. (2013) obtained data from 2002 to 2009 for individuals in Connecticut who had been hospitalized for schizophrenia, bipolar disorder, or major depressive disorder. The authors estimated changes in violent crime arrests for individuals with at least one of the mental health adjudications reported to the NICS before and after Connecticut began reporting mental health records in 2007. The authors found a 31-percent decline in the probability of violent crime arrest in their sample of individuals who had a mental health adjudication but no disqualifying criminal conviction. For comparison, the authors also estimated the likelihood of violent crime arrest for individuals with at least one voluntary psychiatric hospitalization but no mental health adjudication (i.e., individuals with serious mental health problems who were not prohibited from purchasing firearms). Relative to the legally disqualified population, the nondisqualified group had lower rates of arrest both before and after the NICS reporting change, but the magnitude of the decrease following NICS reporting was smaller than the reduction seen in the "treated" group with a disqualifying condition. However, no statistical tests were provided to demonstrate that the difference was statistically significant.

Using data from 2002 to 2011, Swanson et al. (2016) employed analogous methods to analyze the effects of NICS reporting changes in 2007 for two Florida counties. The authors similarly found a larger reduction in violent crime arrest rates for individuals with a disqualifying mental health condition relative to individuals with a serious mental health illness that did not legally prohibit firearm acquisition. This difference, a relative decline of 38 percent (see Figure 6.2), was statistically significant. However, estimates became insignificant when the outcome variable was restricted specifically to violent crimes involving firearms, which could indicate the absence of a causal connection or could be due to measurement error in classifying crimes as involving firearms (Swanson et al., 2016).

Figure 6.2 displays the IRRs and CIs associated with the mental health–related prohibition policies examined in these studies. Swanson et al. (2013) did not provide enough information for us to calculate IRRs and CIs for the effect size of interest, so we do not include these in the figure. The Swanson et al. (2016) estimate is the change from before and after the NICS reporting requirements for legally disqualified individuals relative to the change for nonlegally disqualified individuals.

**Figure 6.2**
**Incidence Rate Ratios Associated with the Effect of Mental Health–Related Prohibitions on Violent Crime**

| Study, by Policy | Outcome Measure | Effect Size (IRR) [95% CI] |
|---|---|---|
| **Check on mental illness** | **Violent crime** | |
| Sen & Panjamapirom (2012) | Total homicide | 0.93 [0.86, 0.99] |
| Sen & Panjamapirom (2012) | Firearm homicide | 0.93 [0.87, 1.01] |
| **NICS reporting** | | |
| Swanson et al. (2016) | Violent crime arrest (legally disqualified after) | 0.62 [0.50, 0.76] |

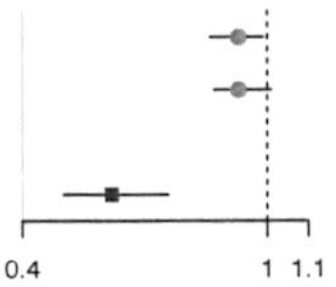


NOTE: IRR values marked with blue squares indicate that methodological concerns are discussed in the text. Green circles indicate that we identified no significant methodological concerns. See Appendix B for details.

**Conclusions**

We identified two qualifying studies that estimated how laws prohibiting gun purchases by those with a mental illness affect violent crime or homicides. Sen and Panjamapirom (2012) found that procedures to enforce state and federal mental health–related prohibitions significantly reduced total homicides. They also found a suggestive effect consistent with these procedures reducing firearm homicides. Swanson et al. (2016) found that enforcement of such federal prohibitions significantly decreased arrests for violent crime offenses in Florida among the targeted population relative to individuals without a disqualifying mental health adjudication.

Based on these results, we conclude that there is *moderate evidence that some state or federal mental health–related prohibitions on gun ownership reduce violent crime generally* and *limited evidence that these prohibitions reduce total homicide rates in particular. Evidence for the effect of these prohibitions on firearm homicides is inconclusive.*

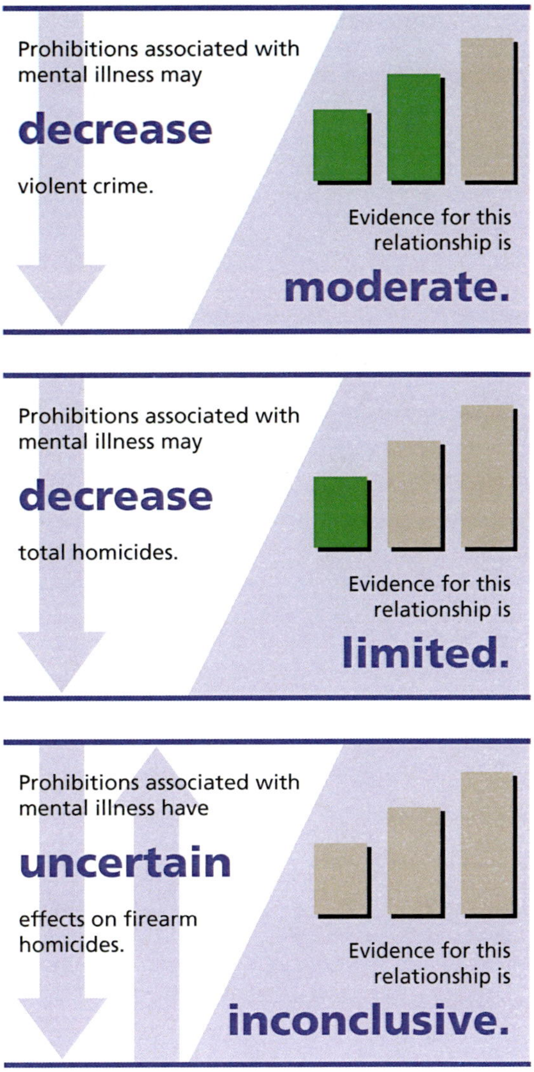

## Outcomes Without Studies Examining the Effects of Prohibitions Associated with Mental Illness

Neither NRC (2004) nor Hahn et al. (2005) identified any research examining the effects of mental health–related prohibitions on the following outcomes, and we identified no such studies that met our inclusion criteria:[12]

- unintentional injuries and deaths
- mass shootings
- officer-involved shootings
- defensive gun use
- hunting and recreation
- gun industry.

---

[12] Sen and Panjamapirom (2012) examined whether state-level mental health records or data were available for conducting background checks, not which mental health–related prohibitions states impose.

## Chapter Six References


Cavanagh, J. T., A. J. Carson, M. Sharpe, and S. M. Lawrie, "Psychological Autopsy Studies of Suicide: A Systematic Review," *Psychological Medicine*, Vol. 33, 2003, pp. 395–405.

Choe, J. Y., L. A. Teplin, and K. M. Abram, "Perpetration of Violence, Violent Victimization, and Severe Mental Illness: Balancing Public Health Outcomes," *Psychiatric Services*, Vol. 59, No. 2, 2008, pp. 153–164.

Corrigan, P. W., and A. C. Watson, "Findings from the National Comorbidity Survey on the Frequency of Violent Behavior in Individuals with Psychiatric Disorders," *Psychiatry Research*, Vol. 136, 2005, pp. 153–162.

Desmarais, S. L., R. A. Van Dorn, K. L. Johnson, K. J. Grimm, K. S. Douglas, and M. S. Swartz, "Community Violence Perpetration and Victimization Among Adults with Mental Illness," *American Journal of Public Health*, Vol. 104, 2014, pp. 2342–2349.

Everytown for Gun Safety Support Fund, "Mass Shootings in the United States: 2009–2016," April 11, 2017b. As of May 3, 2017:
http://everytownresearch.org/reports/mass-shootings-analysis/

Follman, Mark, Gavin Aronsen, and Deanna Pan, "U.S. Mass Shootings, 1982–2017: Data from *Mother Jones*' Investigation," *Mother Jones*, June 14, 2017. As of August 25, 2017:
http://www.motherjones.com/politics/2012/12/mass-shootings-mother-jones-full-data/

Fox, James A., and Jack Levin, *Extreme Killing: Understanding Serial and Mass Murder*, 3rd ed., Thousand Oaks, Calif.: Sage Publications, 2015.

Hahn, Robert A., Oleg Bilukha, Alex Crosby, Mindy T. Fullilove, Akiva Liberman, Eve Moscicki, Susan Snyder, Farris Tuma, and Peter A. Briss, "Firearms Laws and the Reduction of Violence: A Systematic Review," *American Journal of Preventive Medicine*, Vol. 28, No. 2, 2005, pp. 40–71.

Harrell, Erika, *Crime Against Persons with Disabilities, 2009–2015—Statistical Tables*, Washington, D.C.: U.S. Department of Justice, Bureau of Justice Statistics, NCJ 250632, 2017.

Hughes, Karen, Mark A. Bellis, Lisa Jones, Sara Wood, Geoff Bates, Lindsay Eckley, Ellie McCoy, Christopher Mikton, Tom Shakespeare, and Alana Officer, "Prevalence and Risk of Violence Against Adults with Disabilities: A Systematic Review and Meta-Analysis of Observational Studies," *Lancet*, Vol. 379, 2012, pp. 1621–1629.

Li, Z., A. Page, G. Martin, and R. Taylor, "Attributable Risk of Psychiatric and Socio-Economic Factors for Suicide from Individual-Level, Population-Based Studies: A Systematic Review," *Social Science and Medicine*, Vol. 72, No. 4, 2011, pp. 608–616.

Liu, E. C., E. Bagalman, V. S. Chu, and C. S. Redhead, *Submission of Mental Health Records to the NICS and the HIPAA Privacy Rule*, Washington, D.C.: Congressional Research Service, R43040, 2013.

Matejkowski, J., J. Fairfax-Columbo, S. W. Cullen, S. C. Marcus, and P. L. Solomon, "Exploring the Potential of Stricter Gun Restrictions for People with Serious Mental Illness to Reduce Homicide in the United States," *Journal of Forensic Psychiatry and Psychology*, Vol. 25, No. 3, 2014, pp. 362–369.

McGinty, E. E., D. W. Webster, M. Jarlenski, and C. L. Barry, "News Media Framing of Serious Mental Illness and Gun Violence in the United States," *American Journal of Public Health*, Vol. 104, No. 3, 2014, pp. 406–413.

Metzl, J. M., and K. T. MacLeish, "Mental Illness, Mass Shootings, and the Politics of American Firearms," *American Journal of Public Health*, Vol. 105, No. 2, 2015, pp. 240–249.

National Research Council, *Firearms and Violence: A Critical Review*, Washington, D.C.: National Academies Press, 2004.

NRC—*See* National Research Council.

Public Law 90-618, Gun Control Act of 1968, October 22, 1968.

Sen, B., and A. Panjamapirom, "State Background Checks for Gun Purchase and Firearm Deaths: An Exploratory Study," *Preventive Medicine*, Vol. 55, No. 4, 2012, pp. 346–350.

Substance Abuse and Mental Health Services Administration, *Results from the 2013 National Survey on Drug Use and Mental Health: Mental Health Detailed Tables*, Rockville, Md., 2016. As of May 9, 2017:
https://www.samhsa.gov/data/sites/default/files/2013MHDetTabs/NSDUH-MHDetTabs2013.pdf

Swanson, Jeffrey W., "Mental Disorder, Substance Abuse, and Community Violence: An Epidemiological Approach," in J. Monahan and H. Steadman, eds., *Violence and Mental Disorder*, Chicago, Ill.: University of Chicago Press, 1994, pp. 101–136.

Swanson, Jeffrey W., Michele M. Easter, Allison G. Robertson, Marvin S. Swartz, Kelly Alanis-Hirsch, Daniel Moseley, Charles Dion, and John Petrila, "Gun Violence, Mental Illness, and Laws That Prohibit Gun Possession: Evidence from Two Florida Counties," *Health Affairs*, Vol. 35, No. 6, 2016, pp. 1067–1075.

Swanson, J. W., E. E. McGinty, S. Fazel, and V. M. Mays, "Mental Illness and Reduction of Gun Violence and Suicide: Bringing Epidemiologic Research to Policy," *Annals of Epidemiology*, Vol. 25, No. 5, 2015, pp. 366–376.

Teplin, L. A., G. M. McClelland, K. M. Abram, and D. A. Weiner, "Crime Victimization in Adults with Severe Mental Illness: Comparison with the National Crime Victimization Survey," *Archives of General Psychiatry*, Vol. 62, No. 8, 2005, pp. 911–921.

United States Code, Title 18, Section 922, Unlawful Acts.

CHAPTER SEVEN

# Lost or Stolen Firearm Reporting Requirements

Federal law requires licensed firearm dealers to report lost or stolen guns to local authorities or the U.S. Attorney General within 48 hours (18 U.S.C. 923). There is no federal law requiring individuals to report lost or stolen firearms.

In 2015, federally licensed firearm dealers reported 14,800 firearms as lost or stolen (Bureau of Alcohol, Tobacco, Firearms and Explosives [ATF], 2016a). Quantifying the number of firearms lost or stolen from private citizens is more challenging, but based on data from ATF, 173,675 firearms were reported lost or stolen from non–federal firearm licensee entities and private citizens in 2012 (ATF, 2013). Using an alternative data source, another study estimated that about 233,000 guns were stolen annually during household property crimes between 2005 and 2010, and about four out of five firearms stolen were not recovered (Langton, 2012). Data from police departments in 14 American cities suggest that the number of guns reported lost or stolen in 2014 varies from 17 in San Francisco to 364 in Las Vegas (Everytown for Gun Safety Support Fund, 2016). A recent national survey (Hemenway, Azrael, and Miller, 2017) estimates that 2.4 percent of American gun owners had at least one gun stolen in the past five years and that the average number of guns stolen per person was 1.5. The authors use these data to estimate that 380,000 guns were stolen per year.

Laws requiring gun owners to report lost or stolen firearms are intended to help prevent gun trafficking and straw purchases (in which a lawful buyer makes the purchase on the behalf of a prohibited buyer) and to help ensure that prohibited possessors are disarmed. Data collected from ATF trafficking investigations covering 1999 to 2002 showed that 6.6 percent (7,758 of 117,138) of diverted firearms were stolen from a residence or vehicle (Braga et al., 2012).

There are several plausible mechanisms through which these policies might reduce criminal use or trafficking of firearms. First, reporting requirements might encourage private gun owners to take steps that decrease the ease with which their firearms might be lost or stolen. Second, reporting requirements could deter some straw purchasers who are reluctant to report as stolen the guns they have diverted to prohibited possessors but who also fear that failure to report transferred guns as stolen could leave them accountable for explaining how their guns later turned up at crime scenes. Third, timelier reporting of gun losses or thefts may aid law enforcement gun-tracing efforts and increase criminal prosecutions of illegal users or traffickers of stolen firearms, potentially reducing the stock of firearms among prohibited possessors. However, required reporting policies could have the unintended effect of discouraging individuals from reporting lost or stolen weapons in order to avoid legal penalties from failing to report loss or theft within a certain number of days. Thus, to estimate how requirements for reporting lost or stolen firearms affect such outcomes as violent crime, we might first examine to what extent such policies affect gun owners' reporting and storage behavior.

To assess whether required reporting of lost or stolen guns reduces violent crime by disrupting illegal firearm trafficking, causal inference could be strengthened by examining crime gun trace data,[1] as well as changes in homicide or violent crime rates. Specifically, if these laws restrict trafficking operations from in-state sources, one should observe a larger share of crime guns originating from out-of-state sources after law passage, as well as a reduction in guns with a short time-to-crime (Webster and Wintemute, 2015; Braga et al., 2012).[2] However, a series of provisions attached to ATF appropriations (commonly known as the Tiahrt Amendments) has denied most researchers access to firearm trace data since 2003, making it currently infeasible to conduct this type of analysis (Krouse, 2009).

Requiring gun owners to report lost or stolen firearms is unlikely to have measureable effects on such outcomes as suicide, unintentional injuries and death, defensive gun use, or hunting and recreation. If the requirements successfully discouraged straw purchases, it could have a small effect on firearm sales.

## State Implementation of Lost or Stolen Firearm Reporting Requirements

A minority of states require firearm owners to report to law enforcement when their weapons are lost or stolen. California,[3] Connecticut,[4] Delaware,[5] Illinois,[6]

---

1 The Bureau of Alcohol, Tobacco, and Firearms (2002, p. A-3) defined *crime gun* as "any firearm that is illegally possessed, used in a crime, or suspected to have been used in a crime. An abandoned firearm may also be categorized as a crime gun if it is suspected it was used in a crime or illegally possessed."

2 Per Webster and Wintemute (2015), the metric known as *time-to-crime* is the "unusually short interval—ranging from less than 1 year to less than 3 years—between a gun's retail sale and its subsequent recovery by police from criminal suspects or crime scenes . . . . A short [time-to-crime] is considered an indicator of diversion, especially when the criminal possessor is someone different from the purchaser of record."

3 Calif. Penal Code § 25250 (within five days).

4 Conn. Gen. Stat. § 53-202g (report within 72 hours).

5 Del. Code tit. 11 § 1461 (report within seven days).

6 720 Ill. Comp. Stat. 5/24-4.1 (report within 72 hours).

Massachusetts,[7] New Jersey,[8] New York,[9] Ohio,[10] Rhode Island,[11] and the District of Columbia[12] require individuals to report the loss or theft of all firearms. Maryland requires the reporting of loss or theft of handguns and assault weapons,[13] and Michigan requires the reporting of thefts, but not loss, of all firearms.[14]

## Outcomes Without Studies Examining the Effects of Lost or Stolen Firearm Reporting Requirements

Neither the National Research Council (2004) nor Hahn et al. (2005) identified any research examining the relationship between required reporting of lost or stolen firearms and the following outcomes, and we identified no such studies that met our inclusion criteria:

- suicide
- violent crimes
- unintentional injuries and deaths
- mass shootings
- officer-involved shootings
- defensive gun use
- hunting and recreation
- gun industry.

---

7 Mass. Gen. Laws Ch. 140 § 129C.

8 N.J. Stat. Ann. § 2C:58-19 (within 36 hours).

9 N.Y. Penal Law § 400.10 (within 24 hours).

10 Ohio Rev. Code § 923.20.

11 R.I. Gen. Laws § 11-47-48.1 (within 24 hours).

12 D.C. Code Ann. § 7-2502.08.

13 Md. Ann. Code § 5-146 (within 72 hours).

14 Mich. Comp. Laws § 28.430 (within five days).

## Chapter Seven References

ATF—*See* Bureau of Alcohol, Tobacco, Firearms and Explosives.

Braga, Anthony A., Garen J. Wintemute, Glenn L. Pierce, Philip J. Cook, and Greg Ridgeway, "Interpreting the Empirical Evidence on Illegal Gun Market Dynamics," *Journal of Urban Health*, Vol. 89, No. 5, 2012, pp. 779–793.

Bureau of Alcohol, Tobacco, and Firearms, *Crime Gun Trace Reports (2000): Memphis, Tennessee*, Washington, D.C.: U.S. Department of the Treasury, July 2002.

Bureau of Alcohol, Tobacco, Firearms and Explosives, *2012 Summary: Firearms Reported Lost and Stolen*, Washington, D.C.: U.S. Department of Justice, 2013. As of May 9, 2017:
https://www.atf.gov/resource-center/docs/2012-firearms-reported-lost-and-stolenpdf-1/download

———, *FFL Thefts/Losses: January 1, 2015–December 31, 2015*, Washington, D.C.: U.S. Department of Justice, 2016a. As of May 9, 2017:
https://www.atf.gov/firearms/docs/report/2015-summary-firearms-reported-lost-and-stolen/download

Everytown for Gun Safety Support Fund, *Strategies for Reducing Gun Violence in American Cities*, June 2016. As of May 3, 2017:
https://everytownresearch.org/documents/2016/06/
strategies-reducing-gun-violence-american-cities.pdf

Hahn, Robert A., Oleg Bilukha, Alex Crosby, Mindy T. Fullilove, Akiva Liberman, Eve Moscicki, Susan Snyder, Farris Tuma, and Peter A. Briss, "Firearms Laws and the Reduction of Violence: A Systematic Review," *American Journal of Preventive Medicine*, Vol. 28, No. 2, 2005, pp. 40–71.

Hemenway, David, Deborah Azrael, and Matthew Miller, "Whose Guns Are Stolen? The Epidemiology of Gun Theft Victims," *Injury Epidemiology*, Vol. 4, No. 1, 2017, p. 11.

Krouse, W. J., *Gun Control: Statutory Disclosure Limitations on ATF Firearms Trace Data and Multiple Handgun Sales Reports*, Washington, D.C.: Congressional Research Service, 7-5700, 2009.

Langton, L., *Firearms Stolen During Household Burglaries and Other Property Crimes, 2005–2010*, Washington, D.C.: U.S. Department of Justice, Bureau of Justice Statistics, NCJ 239436, 2012.

National Research Council, *Firearms and Violence: A Critical Review*, Washington, D.C.: National Academies Press, 2004.

United States Code, Title 18, Section 923, Licensing.

Webster, D. W., and G. J. Wintemute, "Effects of Policies Designed to Keep Firearms from High-Risk Individuals," *Annual Review of Public Health*, Vol. 36, 2015, pp. 21–37.

CHAPTER EIGHT

# Licensing and Permitting Requirements

Federal law does not require individuals to obtain a license or permit to purchase a firearm. Several states, however, have permit-to-purchase laws that function similarly to universal background check laws. Both seek to ensure that individuals who acquire firearms through private transfers meet the same requirements as those who purchase firearms from federally licensed dealers. State policies that require permits or licenses to be renewed create a mechanism whereby law enforcement routinely confirms that a firearm owner remains eligible to possess or purchase a firearm, and the policies could facilitate firearm removal from owners who become ineligible. Requiring permits to purchase ammunition makes it more difficult for prohibited possessors to use their illicit firearms. Where no such checks occur, prohibited possessors may represent a considerable share of the market for ammunition. For instance, in a two-month period in the City of Los Angeles, prohibited possessors purchased at least 10,500 rounds of ammunition, accounting for about 2.6 percent of all such sales (Tita et al., 2006). The effects of these policies on violent crime and suicide will depend on whether they better identify disqualified firearm purchasers or possessors compared with the status quo, and whether these disqualifications correctly target individuals who are at greater risk of inflicting harm to themselves or others.

As with more-comprehensive background check laws, by restricting access to firearms for individuals presumed to present greater risk of misusing those firearms, licensing and permitting requirements are intended to reduce gun violence. Different designations for the types of conditions that disqualify an individual may generate differential impacts on such outcomes as homicide or mass shootings compared with suicides. Although compliance is likely to be imperfect, licensing and permitting laws may still reduce gun-related homicides or suicides by deterring prohibited possessors from attempting to acquire firearms. The magnitude of these effects will be influenced, in part, by the level of enforcement, the availability of firearms or ammunition through unregulated markets, and the likelihood that an individual who would be disqualified through the permitting process will seek to obtain a firearm through alternative markets.

Unlike background check laws, licensing and permitting regulations often require individuals seeking to purchase or possess a firearm to submit their applications in person at a law enforcement agency and to submit to fingerprinting. There is some evidence that even licensed dealers sometimes fail to require valid identification cards (U.S. General Accounting Office, 2001); thus, these additional procedural requirements may be more effective in limiting prohibited possessors from accessing firearms by preventing fraud or identification inaccuracies. However, licensing systems requiring substantial coordination between local, state, and federal databases and institutions may pose technical and regulatory challenges, and it is unknown how much the additional administrative requirements of licensing and permitting laws will reduce firearm access by prohibited individuals.

State laws that additionally require an individual to pass a safety course or exam to qualify for a license or permit could reduce unintended injuries and deaths, although these effects will depend on whether passing a safety course or exam affects the storage or handling behavior of firearm owners. One 1995 survey found that gun owners who received formal firearm training (where 80 percent of training courses covered proper gun storage) were significantly more likely to store their firearms loaded and unlocked compared with gun owners who had not received formal training; however, the most common source of training for this sample was through the military, which may not produce the same effects as the training available to civilians (Hemenway, Solnick, and Azrael, 1995).

These laws could also plausibly affect defensive or recreational gun use by increasing the costs of obtaining or continuing to possess a firearm. While the monetary costs of acquiring a license or permit typically range between $10 and $100,[1] the total time and energy costs, in addition to concerns about privacy, may dissuade some legal firearm purchasers, in which case the laws could affect sales of new firearms.

To evaluate whether the effects of licensing or permitting requirements on violent crime or suicides operate through more-effective identification of prohibited possessors (as applied to purchase, possession, or both), the ideal analyses would estimate effects on outcomes specifically for those populations that would be prevented from legally acquiring or owning a firearm under the licensing law. For outcome data in which the type of weapon used can be identified, analyses also could exploit state-level variation in the types of guns that require licenses or permits and could estimate effects stratified by the type of weapon used in a violent crime, mass shooting, or suicide.

To assess whether licensing or permitting laws reduce violent crime through disrupting illegal firearm trafficking, causal inference could be strengthened by examining crime gun trace data and changes in homicide rates.[2] Specifically, if permit-to-purchase laws restrict trafficking operations from in-state retailers, one should observe a larger share of crime guns originating from out-of-state sources after law passage

---

1 New York City's license for handgun purchase and possession (which lasts three years) is the most expensive, at $340, not including an additional fingerprint fee (Csere, 2013).

2 The Bureau of Alcohol, Tobacco, and Firearms (2002, p. A-3) defined *crime gun* as "any firearm that is illegally possessed, used in a crime, or suspected to have been used in a crime. An abandoned firearm may also be categorized as a crime gun if it is suspected it was used in a crime or illegally possessed."

and/or a reduction in guns with a short time-to-crime (Webster and Wintemute, 2015; Braga et al., 2012).[3] However, a series of provisions attached to Bureau of Alcohol, Tobacco, Firearms and Explosives appropriations (commonly known as the Tiahrt Amendments) has denied most researchers access to firearm trace data since 2003; therefore, while law enforcement agencies may analyze such data, the information generally has not been available for research purposes (Krouse, 2009).

## State Implementation of Licensing and Permitting Requirements

Nine states have implemented permit-to-purchase regimes for firearms.[4] All such laws require these licenses for most private transactions. Of the nine states, four require permits for all firearms,[5] and five require them for the purchase of handguns only.[6] New York requires a license to own a firearm.[7] Michigan, Massachusetts, and Illinois require both a permit to purchase and a license to own a firearm.[8] Michigan's law, however, applies only to handguns, and it has a broad exemption for individuals who purchase handguns from licensed dealers following a background check.[9] The District of Columbia also requires that individuals obtain a registration certificate to purchase and possess a firearm.[10]

In terms of the requirements that must be met to receive a license to own or permit to purchase a firearm, some states require that applicants pass a safety course or exam,[11] while others do not. Another distinction between states' laws is the duration of

---

[3] Per Webster and Wintemute (2015), the metric known as *time-to-crime* is the "unusually short interval—ranging from less than 1 year to less than 3 years—between a gun's retail sale and its subsequent recovery by police from criminal suspects or crime scenes . . . . A short [time-to-crime] is considered an indicator of diversion, especially when the criminal possessor is someone different from the purchaser of record."

[4] California, Connecticut, Hawaii, Iowa, Maryland, Nebraska, New Jersey, North Carolina, and Rhode Island. Calif. Penal Code § 31610; Conn. Gen. Stat. §§ 29-33, 29-37a; Hawaii Rev. Stat. § 134-2; Iowa Code § 724.15; Md. Public Safety Code § 5-117.1; Neb. Rev. Stat. Ann. § 69-2404; N.J. Stat. Ann. § 2C:58-3; N.C. Gen. Stat. § 14-402; R.I. Gen. Laws § 11-47-35.

[5] Calif. Penal Code § 31615; Conn. Gen. Stat. §§ 29-33, 29-37a; Hawaii Rev. Stat. § 134-2; N.J. Stat. Ann. § 2C:58-3.

[6] Iowa Code § 724.15; Md. Public Safety Code § 5-117.1; Neb. Rev. Stat. Ann. § 69-2404; N.C. Gen. Stat. § 14-402; R.I. Gen. Laws § 11-47-35.

[7] N.Y. Penal Law § 400.00.

[8] Mich. Comp. Laws § 28.422; 430 Ill. Comp. Stat. 65/2; Mass. Gen. Laws Ch. 140 § 129B, 131A, 131E.

[9] Mich. Comp. Laws § 28.422.

[10] D.C. Code Ann. § 7-2502.01.

[11] Calif. Penal Code §§ 31610, 31640; Conn. Gen. Stat. §§ 29-36f, 29-37p; Hawaii Rev. Stat. § 134-2; Md. Public Safety Code § 5-117.1; Mass. Gen. Laws Ch. 140 § 131P; R.I. Gen. Laws § 11-47-35; D.C. Code Ann. § 7-2502.03. The laws in Hawaii, Maryland, and Rhode Island apply to handguns only.

the licenses or permits. A handful of states issue permits to purchase that are valid for a few days or months only.[12] Other states issue permits or licenses that may last years.[13] In New Jersey, firearm identification cards are required for rifles and shotguns and remain valid indefinitely, unless the issuing or other law enforcement agency identifies specific behavior and character disqualifiers—such as being convicted of a crime, being subject to a restraining order, or having a drug dependency; for handguns, purchasers must obtain a permit to purchase, which lasts 90 days.[14] Rhode Island's law does not specify the duration of the permit to purchase.[15]

Another feature that differs among the state permit-to-purchase regimes is whether the permit covers multiple purchases. The laws in Hawaii, New Jersey, and North Carolina require separate permits for each purchase, though with some differences.[16] For example, Hawaii requires a permit for each handgun purchase but allows multiple long-gun purchases under a single permit.

Some of the aforementioned states have also extended their permitting systems to the purchase or ownership of ammunition.[17]

## Effects on Suicide

### Research Synthesis Findings

When the National Research Council (NRC) completed its review in 2004, there was no evidence from quasi-experimental studies on requiring a license or permit to purchase firearms. Similarly, Hahn et al. (2005) concluded that the evidence for how licensing or registration affects any violence outcomes was inconclusive, based on the five cross-sectional studies they examined that would not meet our inclusion criteria.

We identified two U.S.-based longitudinal studies examining the effect of firearm licensing or permitting requirements on suicide. Examining the effects of firearm

---

[12] Hawaii Rev. Stat. § 134-2 (ten days for handguns); Mich. Comp. Laws § 28.422 (30 days for handguns), Mass. Gen. Laws Ch. 140 § 131A (ten days for permit to purchase); N.J. Stat. Ann. § 2C:58-3 (90 days for handguns, may be renewed for another 90 days with good cause).

[13] Mass. Gen. Laws Ch. 140 § 129B (six years for license to own); Calif. Penal Code § 31655 (five years); Conn. Gen. Stat. §§ 29-36h, 29-37r (five years); Hawaii Rev. Stat. § 134-2 (one year for long guns); 430 Ill. Comp. Stat. 65/7 (ten years); Md. Public Safety Code § 5-117.1 (ten years for handguns); Neb. Rev. Stat. Ann. § 69-2407 (three years for handguns); N.Y. Penal Law § 400.00 (five years for handguns); N.C. Gen. Stat. § 14-403 (five years for handguns); D.C. Code Ann. § 7-2502.07a (three years).

[14] N.J. Stat. Ann. § 2C:58-3.

[15] R.I. Gen. Laws § 11-47-35.

[16] Hawaii Rev. Stat. § 134-2; N.J. Stat. Ann. § 2C:58-3; N.C. Gen. Stat. § 14-403 (handguns only).

[17] Connecticut, Illinois, Massachusetts, New Jersey, and the District of Columbia. Conn. Gen. Stat. §§ 29-38n; 430 Ill. Comp. Stat. 65/2; Mass. Gen. Laws Ch. 140 § 129C; N.J. Stat. Ann. § 2C:58-3.3; D.C. Code Ann. § 7-2502.02.

policies on suicides among teens (aged 14–17) and young adults (aged 18–20) between 1976 and 2001, Webster et al. (2004) included an indicator variable for the presence of state permit-to-purchase laws. They used negative binomial models that employed generalized estimating equations and included state-level fixed effects, controls for other firearm policies, and time-varying covariates (including the proportion of suicides by firearm as a proxy of gun prevalence). Using these methods, the authors found a significant effect of permit-to-purchase laws increasing the total suicide rate by 17.7 percent among those aged 18–20, driven by an estimated 22-percent increase in firearm suicides, with an uncertain change in nonfirearm suicides. The authors also found permit-to-purchase laws to be associated with a statistically significant 27-percent increase in *nonfirearm* suicides among those aged 14–17 but to have uncertain associations with firearm or total suicides among this age group. As the authors suggested, this perplexing set of results may be partially attributable to the fact that the effect estimate was based on changes to only three state laws during the study time frame. Therefore, the effect of permit-to-purchase laws is not well identified, and apparent effects may be attributable to other concurrent changes affecting suicide rates.

Using a synthetic control approach, Crifasi et al. (2015) estimated the percentage change in total suicide and firearm suicide in Connecticut before and after the state established a permit-to-purchase law in 1995, as well as before and after the repeal of Missouri's permit-to-purchase law in 2007. This approach enabled the researchers to estimate the likely outcomes had Connecticut and Missouri not enacted these laws, drawing on data from states that looked most similar in the pre-law period but that did not have or enact such policies (for Connecticut) or that had such policies and did not repeal them (for Missouri) during the study period.

Crifasi et al. (2015) found evidence that there was a reduction in firearm suicide rates in Connecticut and its synthetic comparison group after the law, but the reduction was greater in Connecticut. Specifically, Connecticut's firearm suicide rate was 15.4 percent lower than that of its synthetic control during the ten-year post-law period, decreasing from roughly four firearm suicides per 100,000 people the year the law was enacted to around three per 100,000 in the post-law period. The nonfirearm suicide rate remained constant in Connecticut but increased in its synthetic comparison group after the law. However, these findings were tempered by alternative regression model specifications in which Connecticut experienced a statistically significant *increase* in nonfirearm suicides after passage of the law and an uncertain effect on overall suicides.

Missouri's firearm suicide rate was consistently higher than that of its synthetic control, and rates in both the state and its synthetic control increased after the repeal of the law, although Missouri's rate grew more rapidly over the subsequent five years. In the five-year post-repeal period, the suicide rate in Missouri was 16.1 percent higher than in the synthetic control group, increasing from 7.5 firearm suicides per 100,000 people the year the law was repealed to 9.0 per 100,000. Little difference was observed between Missouri's nonfirearm suicide rate and that of its synthetic control over the study period.

Because both the Connecticut and Missouri analyses examined only a single state's experience with either adoption or repeal of the law, the study offers limited evidence that noted differences are due to the change in the law rather than to other contemporaneous influences over each state's suicide rate around the time the law was changed. For instance, in Connecticut, the permit-to-purchase law was implemented along with other rule changes, such as raising the minimum age to purchase handguns and requiring completion of eight hours of gun-safety training. Similarly, Missouri's repeal occurred at the same time it implemented a stand-your-ground law. The study design cannot rule out that these other factors, rather than the permit-to-purchase requirement, were the cause of observed changes. Therefore, the estimates reported in Crifasi et al. (2015) may not be reliable indicators of the direction or magnitude of the true effects of permit-to-purchase laws on suicide.

Figure 8.1 displays the incidence rate ratios (IRRs) and confidence intervals (CIs) associated with the licensing and permitting policies examined in these studies. Because the synthetic control model estimates for nonfirearm suicides in Crifasi et al. (2015) have no CIs, we plot the alternative regression model estimates.

**Figure 8.1**
**Incidence Rate Ratios Associated with the Effect of Licensing and Permitting Requirements on Suicide**

| Study, by Policy | Outcome Measure | Effect Size (IRR) [95% CI] |
|---|---|---|
| **Permit to purchase** | **Suicide** | |
| Webster et al. (2004) | Total, aged 14–17 | 1.06 [0.92, 1.23] |
| Webster et al. (2004) | Total, aged 18–20 | 1.18 [1.04, 1.34] |
| Webster et al. (2004) | Firearm, aged 14–17 | 0.92 [0.76, 1.10] |
| Webster et al. (2004) | Firearm, aged 18–20 | 1.22 [1.04, 1.43] |
| Webster et al. (2004) | Nonfirearm, aged 14–17 | 1.27 [1.00, 1.61] |
| Webster et al. (2004) | Nonfirearm, aged 18–20 | 1.14 [0.93, 1.39] |
| Crifasi et al. (2015) | Total, total population | 1.01 [0.95, 1.08] |
| Crifasi et al. (2015) | Firearm, total population | 0.88 [0.81, 0.96] |
| Crifasi et al. (2015) | Nonfirearm, total population | 1.14 [1.05, 1.24] |
| **Repeal of permit to purchase** | | |
| Crifasi et al. (2015) | Total, total population | 1.03 [0.97, 1.08] |
| Crifasi et al. (2015) | Firearm, total population | 1.02 [0.96, 1.09] |
| Crifasi et al. (2015) | Nonfirearm, total population | 1.03 [0.95, 1.11] |

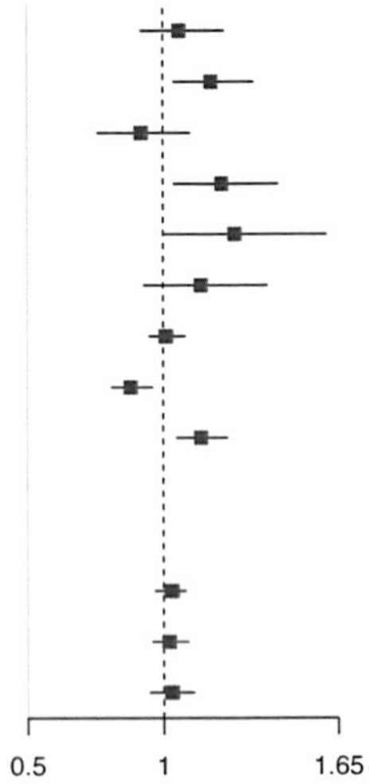


NOTE: IRR values marked with blue squares indicate that methodological concerns are discussed in the text. See Appendix B for details.

### Conclusions

We identified two qualifying studies examining the effects of permit-to-purchase laws on total and firearm suicides. Webster et al. (2004) identified an uncertain effect of these laws on total suicide and firearm suicide rates, as well as a suggestive effect consistent with an increase in nonfirearm suicides, among children aged 14–17. They also identified a significant increase in suicides and firearm suicides among those aged 18–20. Crifasi et al. (2015) identified the effect of implementing a permit-to-purchase law in Connecticut and a separate effect of repealing such a law in Missouri. Both sets of effects suggested that these changes in law had uncertain effects on total suicides. However, implementation of the law significantly reduced firearm suicides in Connecticut, whereas repeal of the law in Missouri had only uncertain effects on firearm suicides.

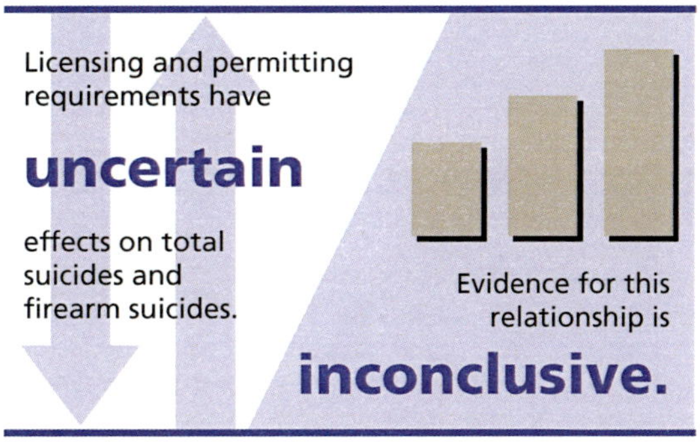


Based on these studies, we find *inconclusive evidence for the effect of licensing and permitting requirements on total suicides and firearm suicides.*

## Effects on Violent Crime

### Research Synthesis Findings

Hahn et al. (2005) found insufficient evidence for determining the effectiveness of firearm registration and licensing on violent crime. NRC (2004) concluded, "There is not much empirical evidence that assesses whether attempts to reduce criminal access to firearms will reduce gun availability or gun crime."

Our synthesis identified two studies that examined permit-to-purchase laws in specific states. Webster, Crifasi, and Vernick (2014) used state-level data from 1999 to 2010 to analyze the effect of Missouri's repeal of a permit-to-purchase law that included a background check requirement even for private sellers and a requirement that background checks be requested at the local sheriff's office. They found a significant increase in total homicides and firearm homicides from the repeal of the law and an uncertain effect on nonfirearm homicides. Specifically, after the repeal, the total homicide rate was 115 percent of the rate expected had the law not been repealed, and the firearm homicide rate was 125 percent of the expected rate (see Figure 8.2). However, because the focus of this study was a single state, the effects associated with the law may be confounded with other changes in the state that affected homicide rates around the same time the law was passed. The statistical model used to arrive at these results used a large number of estimated parameters relative to observations (a ratio of about one to eight), meaning the model may have been overfit, and thus its estimates of the laws' effects and their apparent statistical significance could provide little generalizable information about the true causal effects of the permit-to-purchase law.

Using a synthetic control approach, Rudolph et al. (2015) found a decrease in firearm homicides (and no statistically significant effect on nonfirearm homicides) from the implementation of a permit-to-purchase law in Connecticut that strengthened background check requirements for handguns sold by private sellers and licensed dealers by requiring purchasers to obtain an eligibility certificate in person from the local police department, increasing the minimum age of purchase from 18 to 21, and requiring individuals to complete eight hours of gun-safety training. After these policy changes, the firearm homicide rate was 63 percent of what was expected without such changes. Because only a single state experienced the law in this study, it is not possible to conclude that the changes were a result of the permit-to-purchase portion of the law as opposed to other factors influencing homicides in the state around the same time.

Figure 8.2 displays the IRRs and CIs associated with the licensing and permitting policies examined in these studies.

**Figure 8.2**
**Incidence Rate Ratios Associated with the Effect of Licensing and Permitting Requirements on Violent Crime**

| Study, by Policy | Outcome Measure | Effect Size (IRR) [95% CI] |
|---|---|---|
| **Permit to purchase** | **Homicide** | |
| Rudolph et al. (2015) | Firearm | 0.60 [0.37, 0.97] |
| **Repeal of permit to purchase** | | |
| Webster, Crifasi, & Vernick (2014) | Total | 1.15 [1.10, 1.20] |
| Webster, Crifasi, & Vernick (2014) | Firearm | 1.23 [1.17, 1.29] |
| Webster, Crifasi, & Vernick (2014) | Nonfirearm | 0.96 [0.87, 1.05] |

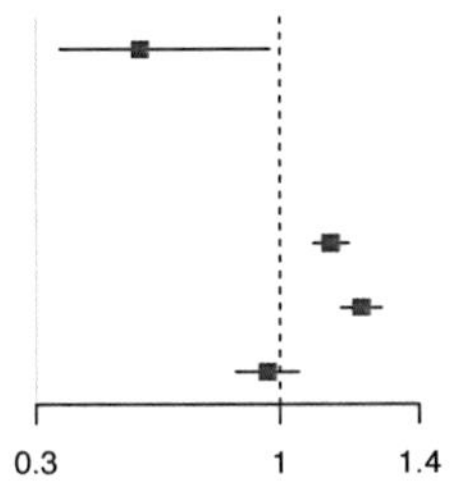


NOTE: IRR values marked with blue squares indicate that methodological concerns are discussed in the text. See Appendix B for details.

### Conclusions

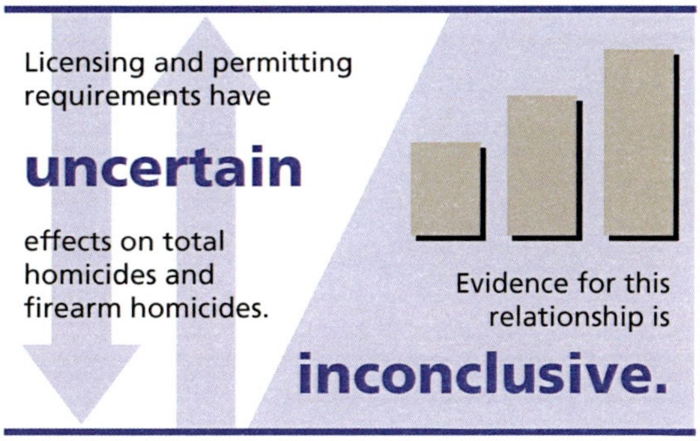


We identified two qualifying studies examining the effects of permit-to-purchase laws on total and firearm homicides. Webster, Crifasi, and Vernick (2014) found that Missouri's repeal of its law resulted in increased total and firearm suicide rates. Rudolph et al. (2015) reported a significant effect consistent with these laws reducing firearm homicide rates, but because a law establishing a minimum age for purchase was passed concurrently in the one state evaluated, they could not attribute this effect solely to permit-to-purchase laws. Based on this evidence and an evaluation of the studies' strengths, we find *inconclusive evidence for the effect of licensing and permitting requirements on total homicides and firearm homicides.*

## Effects on Mass Shootings

### Research Synthesis Findings

Neither NRC (2004) nor Hahn et al. (2005) identified research examining the effects of licensing and permitting requirements on mass shootings in the United States. Our search yielded one such study that met our inclusion criteria. Using a two-way fixed-effects linear probability model, Luca, Deepak, and Poliquin (2016) estimated the effects of state laws requiring permits to purchase a handgun on a binary indicator for whether a mass shooting occurred in a given state-year. The authors' regression analysis covered 1989–2014 and included controls for time-invariant state characteristics; national trends; a host of other state-level gun policies; and time-varying state-level demographic, socioeconomic, and political characteristics. They found uncertain effects of handgun permitting requirements on the probability of a mass shooting event occurring. However, assessing the effects of gun policies on mass shootings was not the primary focus of Luca, Deepak, and Poliquin (2016), and the authors intended the estimates to serve solely as a robustness check for their main specification (the effects of mass shootings on gun policy). Although the paper provided limited information to use in evaluating the reported statistical models (e.g., on how these policies were coded), it is clear that the analysis used a linear model to predict a dichotomous outcome. Therefore, model assumptions were violated, making CIs unreliable.

Figure 8.3 displays the IRRs and CIs associated with the licensing and permitting policies examined in Luca, Deepak, and Poliquin (2016).

**Figure 8.3**
**Incidence Rate Ratios Associated with the Effect of Licensing and Permitting Requirements on Mass Shootings**

| Study, by Policy | Outcome Measure | Effect Size (IRR) [95% CI] |
|---|---|---|
| **Handgun permit system** | **Mass shooting** | |
| Luca, Deepak, & Poliquin (2016) | State-year indicator (no political controls) | 0.92 [0.00, 2.80] |
| Luca, Deepak, & Poliquin (2016) | State-year indicator (political controls) | 1.03 [0.00, 2.94] |

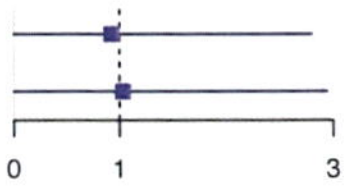


NOTE: IRR values marked with blue squares indicate that methodological concerns are discussed in the text. See Appendix B for details.

### Conclusions

We identified one qualifying study that estimated the effects of licensing and permitting laws on mass shootings (Luca, Deepak, and Poliquin, 2016). This study found uncertain effects of these laws on whether at least one mass shooting occurred in a state. Therefore, available studies provide *inconclusive evidence for the effect of licensing and permitting requirements on mass shootings.*

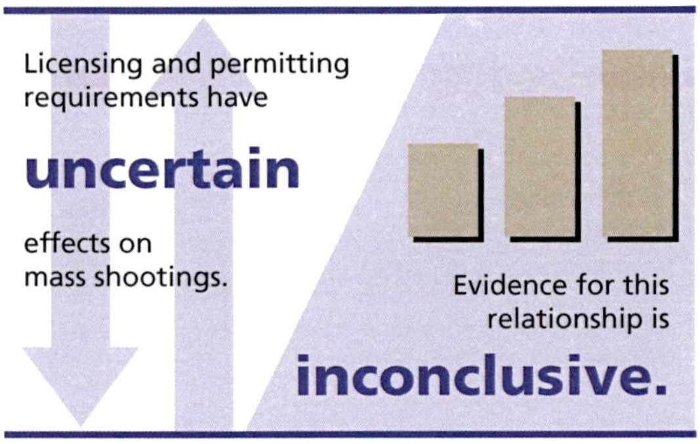


## Outcomes Without Studies Examining the Effects of Licensing and Permitting Requirements

Neither NRC (2004) nor Hahn et al. (2005) identified any research examining the effects of licensing and permitting requirements on the following outcomes, and we identified no such studies that met our inclusion criteria:

- unintentional injuries and deaths
- officer-involved shootings
- defensive gun use
- hunting and recreation
- gun industry.

## Chapter Eight References


Braga, Anthony A., Garen J. Wintemute, Glenn L. Pierce, Philip J. Cook, and Greg Ridgeway, "Interpreting the Empirical Evidence on Illegal Gun Market Dynamics," *Journal of Urban Health*, Vol. 89, No. 5, 2012, pp. 779–793.

Bureau of Alcohol, Tobacco, and Firearms, *Crime Gun Trace Reports (2000): Memphis, Tennessee*, Washington, D.C.: U.S. Department of the Treasury, July 2002.

Crifasi, C. K., J. S. Meyers, J. S. Vernick, and D. W. Webster, "Effects of Changes in Permit-to-Purchase Handgun Laws in Connecticut and Missouri on Suicide Rates," *Preventive Medicine*, Vol. 79, 2015, pp. 43–49.

Csere, M., *State Comparison of Gun Permit Fees*, Hartford, Conn.: Connecticut General Assembly, Office of Legislative Research, OLR Research Report 2013-R-0048, 2013. As of May 24, 2017: https://www.cga.ct.gov/2013/rpt/2013-R-0048.htm

Hahn, Robert A., Oleg Bilukha, Alex Crosby, Mindy T. Fullilove, Akiva Liberman, Eve Moscicki, Susan Snyder, Farris Tuma, and Peter A. Briss, "Firearms Laws and the Reduction of Violence: A Systematic Review," *American Journal of Preventive Medicine*, Vol. 28, No. 2, 2005, pp. 40–71.

Hemenway, David, Sara J. Solnick, and Deborah R. Azrael, "Firearm Training and Storage," *JAMA*, Vol. 273, No. 1, 1995, pp. 46–50.

Krouse, W. J., *Gun Control: Statutory Disclosure Limitations on ATF Firearms Trace Data and Multiple Handgun Sales Reports*, Washington, D.C.: Congressional Research Service, 7-5700, 2009.

Luca, Michael, Lahotra Deepak, and Christopher Poliquin, *The Impact of Mass Shootings on Gun Policy*, working paper, Boston, Mass.: Harvard Business School, 2016.

National Research Council, *Firearms and Violence: A Critical Review*, Washington, D.C.: National Academies Press, 2004.

NRC—*See* National Research Council.

Rudolph, K. E., E. A. Stuart, J. S. Vernick, and D. W. Webster, "Association Between Connecticut's Permit-to-Purchase Handgun Law and Homicides," *American Journal of Public Health*, Vol. 105, No. 8, 2015, pp. E49–E54.

Tita, G. E., A. A. Braga, G. Ridgeway, and G. L. Pierce, "The Criminal Purchase of Firearm Ammunition," *Injury Prevention*, Vol. 12, No. 5, 2006, pp. 308–311.

U.S. General Accounting Office, *Firearms Purchased from Federal Firearm Licensees Using Bogus Identification*, Washington, D.C., GAO-01-427NI, 2001.

Webster, D., C. K. Crifasi, and J. S. Vernick, "Effects of the Repeal of Missouri's Handgun Purchaser Licensing Law on Homicides," *Journal of Urban Health*, Vol. 91, No. 2, 2014, pp. 293–302.

Webster, D. W., J. S. Vernick, A. M. Zeoli, and J. A. Manganello, "Association Between Youth-Focused Firearm Laws and Youth Suicides," *JAMA*, Vol. 292, No. 5, 2004, pp. 594–601.

Webster, D. W., and G. J. Wintemute, "Effects of Policies Designed to Keep Firearms from High-Risk Individuals," *Annual Review of Public Health*, Vol. 36, 2015, pp. 21–37.

CHAPTER NINE

# Firearm Sales Reporting and Recording Requirements

Under federal law, licensed dealers must maintain records of firearm sales indefinitely (18 U.S.C. 923). Although licensed dealers must respond to specific Bureau of Alcohol, Tobacco, Firearms and Explosives (ATF) inquiries about sales of individual guns, federal law does not mandate that dealers report sales; indeed, federal authorities are explicitly prohibited by law from maintaining a database of firearm sales. In addition, there is no federal law requiring recording or reporting of firearm sales by private sellers (Giffords Law Center to Prevent Gun Violence, undated-d).

As with laws requiring the reporting of lost or stolen firearms, laws requiring the recording and reporting of gun sales are designed to facilitate law enforcement traces of weapons used in crimes. Without such laws, tracing crime guns typically identifies where a gun was first legally sold, and to whom.[1] However, secondary markets appear to be the leading source of guns used in crimes (Harlow, 2001). By requiring a record of each subsequent transfer or sale of a firearm after its initial sale by a licensed dealer, ATF and other law enforcement agencies would gain valuable investigative information. Presumably, requiring recordkeeping and reporting of private gun sales could also deter illegal sales.

Furthermore, law enforcement access to sales data could facilitate identification of firearm owners who have become prohibited possessors. For instance, California passed Proposition 63 in 2016, which, among other things, requires courts to search California's centralized records of firearm sales and transfers whenever an individual is convicted of an offense that makes him or her a prohibited possessor. When such individuals are found to have purchased firearms, they will be required to relinquish or dispose of them.[2]

Required recordkeeping and reporting may impose costs to sellers of maintaining compliance, and concerns about privacy may deter some individuals seeking to acquire a firearm for self-protection or recreational gun use, with consequences for gun sales.

---

[1] The Bureau of Alcohol, Tobacco, and Firearms (2002, p. A-3) defined *crime gun* as "any firearm that is illegally possessed, used in a crime, or suspected to have been used in a crime. An abandoned firearm may also be categorized as a crime gun if it is suspected it was used in a crime or illegally possessed."

[2] Calif. Penal Code, Sec. 29810.

Because the principal intended benefit of laws requiring firearm sales to be reported concerns crime investigation, the data most relevant to understanding the effects of such laws would include *firearm crime clearance rates*, or the rates at which law enforcement is successful in identifying suspects in firearm-related crimes, including violent and property crimes, and firearm trafficking crimes. In California and other states that use these records to identify prohibited possessors with weapons, data on firearm-involved crime and violence perpetrated by prohibited possessors would be valuable, but such data are not generally available.

## State Implementation of Firearm Sales Reporting and Recording Requirements

Several states have laws that require firearm sellers (dealers, private sellers, or both) to maintain records of all gun sales, and some have laws that require sellers to report sales information to law enforcement. Twenty jurisdictions require firearm sellers to keep records of at least some firearm sales. Eleven states and the District of Columbia require licensed dealers to maintain records of all firearm sales,[3] and seven states and the District of Columbia require private sellers to do so.[4] Some states require recordkeeping for handgun sales only: Six states have such laws for dealers,[5] and four have them for private sellers.[6] Overall, five jurisdictions require all sellers to record all firearm sales,[7] while the other 15 states with such laws have some lesser combinations of recordkeeping requirements. In terms of recordkeeping by private sellers, some states

---

[3] California, Connecticut, Delaware, Illinois, Maine, Massachusetts, Michigan, New Jersey, Oregon, Pennsylvania, Rhode Island, and the District of Columbia. See Calif. Penal Code § 28100; Conn. Gen. Stat. Ann. § 29-31; Del. Code Ann. tit. 24 § 904; 40 Ill. Comp. 65/3, 720 Ill. Comp. 5/24-4; Me. Rev. Stat. Ann. tit. 15 § 455; Mass. Gen. Laws Ch. 140 § 123; Mich. Comp. Laws §§ 28.422, 28.422a, 750.232; N.J. Stat. Ann. §2C: 58-2, N.J. Admin. Code § 13:54-3.14; Oreg. Rev. Stat. §§ 166.412, 166.434; 18 Pa. Cons. Stat. §§ 6111, 6102; R.I. Gen. Laws §§ 11-47-35, 11-47-35.2; D.C. Code Ann. § 7-2504.

[4] California, Colorado, Connecticut, Delaware, Illinois, New York, Rhode Island, and the District of Columbia. See Calif. Penal Code § 28210; Colo. Rev. Stat. § 18-12-112; Conn. Gen. Stat. Ann. § 29-31; Del. Code Ann. tit. 11 § 1448B, tit. 24 § 904; 40 Ill. Comp. 65/3, 720 Ill. Comp. 5/24-4; N.Y. Gen. Bus. Law § 898; R.I. Gen. Laws §§ 11-47-35, 11-47-35.2, D.C. Code Ann. §§ 7-2505.02, 7-2504.04.

[5] Colorado, Maryland, New York, North Carolina, Vermont, and Washington. See Colo. Rev. Stat. § 12-26-102; Md. Ann. Code §§ 5-120, 5-145; N.Y. Penal Law §§ 265.00, 400,00; N.C. Gen. Stat. § 14-402; Vt. Stat. Ann. tit. 13 § 4006; Wash. Rev. Code § 9.41.110.

[6] Maryland, New Jersey, Michigan, and Pennsylvania. See Md. Ann. Code § 5-120 (private sellers are required to maintain copies of the application, not a sales record); N.J. Stat. Ann. § 2C: 58-3 (private sellers are required to maintain copies of the permit); Mich. Comp. Laws Ann. §§ 28.422, 28.422a, 750.232; 37 Pa. Cons. Stat. § 33.111.

[7] California, Delaware, Illinois, Rhode Island, and the District of Columbia.

require the sellers to maintain the records,[8] and others require licensed dealers to maintain records for private sales.[9]

States differ on how long sales records must be maintained. Some do not specify the required duration,[10] and some require the records be kept for a set number of years or permanently.[11]

Some states recently abolished their recordkeeping requirements. In 2015, for example, Alabama repealed the section of law requiring dealers to maintain detailed handgun sales records. In fact, the state enacted a section stating that, within 180 days of the new law's passage, dealers and law enforcement must destroy any records they created to comply with the repealed law,[12] although gun sellers' federal recordkeeping requirements would remain.

In addition to recordkeeping requirements, 11 states require that sales records be transmitted to a law enforcement agency. Four of the states require records of all sales to be transmitted, including those by licensed dealers and private sellers.[13] Similarly, the District of Columbia's registration requirement gives law enforcement access to all sales records.[14] Five states require dealers and private sellers to report only handgun sales to law enforcement.[15] Washington requires dealers to report only handgun sales.[16]

---

[8] Connecticut, Illinois, Maryland, Michigan, Pennsylvania, and Rhode Island. See Conn. Gen. Stat. Ann. § 29-31; 40 Ill. Comp. 65/3, 720 Ill. Comp. 5/24-4; Md. Ann. Code § 5-120; Mich. Comp. Laws Ann. §§ 28.422, 28.422a, 750.232; 37 Pa. Cons. Stat. § 33.111; R.I. Gen. Laws §§ 11-47-35, 11-47-35.2.

[9] California, Colorado, New York, and the District of Columbia. See Calif. Penal Code § 28210; Colo. Rev. Stat. § 18-12-112; N.Y. Gen. Bus. Law § 898l; D.C. Code Ann. §§ 7-2505.02, 7-2504.04.

[10] For example, Massachusetts, Michigan, New York, and the District of Columbia. See Mass. Gen. Laws Ch. 140 § 123; Mich. Comp. Laws §§ 28.422, 28.422a, 750.232; N.Y. Gen. Bus. Law § 898; D.C. Code Ann. § 7-2504.

[11] For example, three years in Maryland for handguns (Md. Ann. Code § 5-120), five years in Oregon (Oreg. Rev. Stat. § 166.412), six years in Rhode Island (R.I. Gen. Laws §§ 11-47-35, 11-47-35.2), ten years in Illinois (40 Ill. Comp. 65/3), and 20 years in Connecticut and Pennsylvania (Conn. Gen. Stat. Ann. §§ 29-33, 29-37a; 18 Pa. Cons. Stat. § 6111). New Jersey requires records be kept permanently (N.J. Stat. Ann. § 2C: 58-3, N.J. Admin. Code § 13:54-3.14).

[12] 2015 Ala. H.B. 47, amending Ala. Code § 13A-11-79.

[13] California, Connecticut, Hawaii, and Massachusetts. See Calif. Penal Code §§ 1106, 27545 (private sales must be conducted through licensed dealers, who in turn must report); Conn. Gen. Stat. §§ 29-33, 29-37; Hawaii Rev. Stat. § 134-2; Mass. Gen. Laws Ch. 140 §§ 123, 128A.

[14] D.C. Code Ann. §§ 7-2502.08, 22-4510.

[15] Maryland, Michigan, New Jersey, New York, and Pennsylvania. See Md. Ann. Code §§ 5-120, 5-124 (firearm applications for private sales must be reported); Mich. Comp. Laws §§ 28.422, 28.422a; N.J. Stat. Ann. § 2C:58-2; N.Y. Penal Law § 400.00; 18 Pa. Cons. Stat. §§ 6111.

[16] Wash. Rev. Code Ann. §§ 9.41.110.

## Outcomes Without Studies Examining the Effects of Firearm Sales Reporting and Recording Requirements

Neither the National Research Council (2004) nor Hahn et al. (2005) identified any research examining the relationship between firearm sales reporting and recording requirements and the following outcomes, and we identified no such studies that met our inclusion criteria:

- suicide
- violent crime
- unintentional injuries and deaths
- mass shootings
- officer-involved shootings
- defensive gun use
- hunting and recreation
- gun industry.

## Chapter Nine References

Bureau of Alcohol, Tobacco, and Firearms, *Crime Gun Trace Reports (2000): Memphis, Tennessee*, Washington, D.C.: U.S. Department of the Treasury, July 2002.

Giffords Law Center to Prevent Gun Violence, "Maintaining Records of Gun Sales," web page, undated-d. As of October 18, 2017:
http://lawcenter.giffords.org/gun-laws/policy-areas/gun-sales/maintaining-records-of-gun-sales/

Hahn, Robert A., Oleg Bilukha, Alex Crosby, Mindy T. Fullilove, Akiva Liberman, Eve Moscicki, Susan Snyder, Farris Tuma, and Peter A. Briss, "Firearms Laws and the Reduction of Violence: A Systematic Review," *American Journal of Preventive Medicine*, Vol. 28, No. 2, 2005, pp. 40–71.

Harlow, Caroline Wolf, *Survey of Inmates in State and Federal Correctional Facilities: Firearm Use by Offenders*, Washington, D.C.: U.S. Department of Justice, Bureau of Justice Statistics, NCJ 189369, November 2001.

National Research Council, *Firearms and Violence: A Critical Review*, Washington, D.C.: National Academies Press, 2004.

United States Code, Title 18, Section 923, Licensing.

CHAPTER TEN

# Child-Access Prevention Laws

Child-access prevention (CAP) laws allow prosecutors to bring charges against adults who intentionally or carelessly allow children to have unsupervised access to firearms. CAP laws aim to reduce unintentional firearm injuries and deaths, suicides, and violent crime among youths chiefly by reducing children's access to stored guns, although weaker laws targeting only reckless provision of firearms to children are sometimes considered alongside CAP laws.

In 2015, 1,458 children under age 18 were killed by firearms, and of these deaths, 566 (38.8 percent) classified as suicide and 77 (5.3 percent) classified as unintentional (calculated using data from Centers for Disease Control and Prevention [CDC], 2015). Nonfatal gun injuries are considerably more common among this age group, with 7,537 nonfatal firearm injuries reported for children under age 18 in 2014 (calculated using data from CDC, 2013). In 2014, juvenile offenders were known to have been involved in approximately 650 murders nationwide, two-thirds of which involved a firearm (Office of Juvenile Justice and Delinquency Prevention, 2016). Youth between ages 18 and 21 have among the highest rates of violent offending of any age group (Loeber and Stallings, 2011).

While current statistics on the type of firearm or circumstances surrounding these incidents are not readily available, an earlier study examining a subset of states from 2001 to 2002 found that about half of firearm-related suicides among this age group involved a handgun, with the remainder involving a rifle or shotgun (Johnson et al., 2010). Among those suicide decedents in which the method of acquisition of the firearm was recorded, 82 percent used a firearm belonging to a family member, and 64 percent of those guns were stored unlocked. Surveys have found that, among juveniles who have been incarcerated or arrested, the youth offenders acquired their firearms through similar sources as adult offenders, with more than 80 percent citing a friend, family member, or the black market as the source of the weapon (Webster et al., 2002; LaFree and Birbeck, 1998).

Conceptually, the effects of CAP laws may extend beyond those age groups that are directly targeted by the policies. In households where owners abide by CAP laws, because either underage children reside in the household or there are underage visitors, gun locks or gun safes could also serve to restrict access to guns by older members of the household. This limited availability could, in turn, influence suicides, unintentional injuries and deaths, and violent crime among the adult population.

Studies of adolescent and adult suicides have generally found that, relative to comparison groups of individuals who died other ways or living community members, those who died by firearm suicide lived in homes where guns were less securely stored (Conwell et al., 2002; Shenassa et al., 2004; Grossman et al., 2005). These studies suggest to one set of researchers a "dose-response" relationship between firearm accessibility and risk for suicide (Azrael and Miller, 2016). However, the relationship is not seen in all studies. Brent et al. (1991, 1993b) found no differences in storage practices in homes with adolescents who died by suicide and a comparison group of adolescents living in the community. Dahlberg, Ikeda, and Kresnow (2004) found no association between storage practices and firearm suicide (versus suicide by other means).

Studies have generally found no difference in storage practices between adults who have thought about or attempted suicide versus those who have not (Smith, Currier, and Drescher, 2015; Ilgen et al., 2008; Betz et al., 2016; Oslin et al., 2004). This finding, along with the finding that those who die by firearm suicide typically live in homes with less-secure storage of firearms, could suggest that the difference between those who successfully kill themselves with a firearm and those who do not is related more to firearm storage differences than to differences in suicidality (Azrael and Miller, 2016). In the absence of strong causal models, however, alternative explanations remain plausible. If, for instance, those most determined to kill themselves leave weapons unsecured so that they will be available for use when the person is ready to die, it could be that suicide risk determines storage practices rather than that storage practices determine suicide risk.

Since 2003, only one individual-level study provided information on the association between firearm storage practices and unintentional injuries. Grossman et al. (2005) found that cases of unintentional firearm-related injury or death were less likely to occur in households where guns were stored unloaded or locked or where guns and ammunition were stored separately.

CAP laws could decrease gun crime rates by making theft of firearms more difficult. Alternatively, the laws could increase rates of crime victimization and decrease opportunities for legal defensive gun use by delaying gun owners' access to their firearms. Similarly, if firearms in the home deter such crimes as burglaries, safe storage requirements could reduce their deterrent value.

Data on suicides and self-inflicted nonfatal injury stratified by age are readily available, so analyses can directly test whether effects of CAP laws on these outcomes are driven by the relevant age group affected by the policy. For outcomes of violent crime and non-self-inflicted injury, causal analyses could be improved with data that report the age of the shooter. However, as most data sources report only the age of the victim,[1] none of the studies we identified that met our inclusion criteria for this policy used this type of data. In estimating potential spillover effects for other age groups, one would ideally know whether different outcomes are observed after implementation of CAP laws among those households most directly affected by the laws (such as households with children under age 18 or 21) and households less directly affected by the safe storage policies.

For any analysis, estimates of causal effects would be strengthened with data showing how CAP laws actually affected gun storage behaviors, but national longitudinal data on firearm storage patterns do not currently exist.

## State Implementation of Child-Access Prevention Laws

Although there is no comparable federal law, a narrow majority of U.S. jurisdictions have imposed some sort of CAP law. Fourteen states and the District of Columbia have implemented laws concerning negligent storage, across which there is some variation. The strictest laws impose criminal penalties for negligent storage regardless of whether a child accesses any guns. Massachusetts, for instance, imposes criminal liability if a gun is stored where a minor "may have access."[2] Three other jurisdictions hold owners liable when they know or reasonably should know that access is "likely."[3] Four additional states impose criminal liability for negligent storage only where a child gains access to a gun, regardless of whether he or she uses it.[4] Some of these jurisdictions impose liability even when the gun is not loaded.[5]

Seven states impose liability for negligent storage if children publicly carry or use improperly stored firearms, although three of these states hold adults liable only if children's access results in death or serious injury.[6]

---

[1] Exceptions include the Federal Bureau of Investigation's Supplementary Homicide Reports, which contain age of victim and age of offender for murders when such information is known, and the National Violent Death Reporting System, which contains information on the age of the shooter for non-self-inflicted fatal injuries when such information is known for a subset of states.

[2] Mass. Gen. Laws Ch. 140, § 131L.

[3] California, Minnesota, and the District of Columbia. See Calif. Penal Code. § 25100; Minn. Stat. Ann. § 609.666; D.C. Code Ann. § 7-2507.02.

[4] Hawaii, Maryland, New Jersey, and Texas. See Hawaii Rev. Stat. § 707-714.5; Md. Code Ann., Crim. Law § 4-104; N.J. Stat. Ann. 2C: 58-15; Tex. Penal Code Ann. § 46.13.

[5] California, Hawaii, Massachusetts, and the District of Columbia. Calif. Penal Code § 25200 (the child must carry the unloaded gun off the premises for liability to attach); Hawaii Rev. Stat. §§ 707-714; 134-10.5; Mass. Gen. Laws Ch. 140, § 131L; D.C. Code Ann. § 7-2507.02.

[6] The states that require the gun to be used but not necessarily to cause injury or death are Florida, Iowa, New Hampshire, and North Carolina. See Fla. Stat. Ann. § 790.174; Iowa Code Ann. § 724.22; Rev. Stat. Ann. N.H. § 650-C:1; N.C. Gen. Stat. Ann. § 14-315.1. The states that require injury or death are Connecticut, Illinois, and

Many of the states imposing criminal liability for negligent storage allow for exceptions or defenses.[7] The most common is when the gun has been stored in a locked container.[8] Other exceptions or defenses include that the firearm had been rendered inoperable,[9] the person carried the firearm or it was close enough to be easily retrieved,[10] or there was a reasonable expectation that children would not be present where the gun was stored.[11] In addition, some states consider it an exception or defense when children enter a storage area illegally[12] or use the firearm for self-defense.[13] Some states have added other defenses too, such as those that apply to children who have a legal right to use firearms for hunting.[14]

Some states impose criminal liability for intentional, knowing, or reckless provision of firearms to children. These laws are weaker than negligent storage laws. Recklessness requires that the actor was aware of the risks involved in their actions, while negligence only requires that they should have been aware (American Law Institute, 1985). Five states impose penalties under the weaker standard for all firearms,[15]

---

Rhode Island. See Conn. Gen. Stat. Ann. §§ 29-37i, 53-217a; 720 Ill. Comp. Stat. 5/24-9; R.I. Gen. Laws Ann. § 11-47-60.1.

7 In some laws, certain actions are not excluded from the definition of the law, while in other states, they are affirmative defenses.

8 Calif. Penal Code § 25105; Conn. Gen. Stat. Ann. § 29-37i; Fla. Stat. Ann. § 790.174; Hawaii Rev. Stat. § 134-10.5; Iowa Code Ann. § 724.22; N.H. Rev. Stat. Ann. § 650-C:1; N.J. Stat. Ann. 2C: 58-15; R.I. Gen. Laws Ann. § 11-47-60.1; Tex. Penal Code Ann. § 46.13; D.C. Code Ann. § 7-2507.02.

9 Calif. Penal Code § 25105; Fla. Stat. Ann. § 790.174; Iowa Code Ann. § 724.22; N.J. Stat. Ann. 2C: 58-15; N.C. Gen. Stat. Ann. § 14-315.1; R.I. Gen. Laws Ann. § 11-47-60.1; Tex. Penal Code Ann. § 46.13.

10 Calif. Penal Code § 25105; Conn. Gen. Stat. Ann. § 29-37i; Hawaii Rev. Stat. § 134-10.5; N.H. Rev. Stat. Ann. § 650-C:1; R.I. Gen. Laws Ann. § 11-47-60.1; D.C. Code Ann. § 7-2507.02.

11 Calif. Penal Code § 25105; N.H. Rev. Stat. Ann. § 650-C:1; R.I. Gen. Laws Ann. § 11-47-60.1.

12 Calif. Penal Code § 25105; Fla. Stat. Ann. § 790.174; Iowa Code Ann. § 724.22; Hawaii Rev. Stat. § 707-714.5; Minn. Stat Ann. § 609.666; Md. Code Ann., Crim. Law § 4-104; N.H. Rev. Stat. Ann. § 650-C:1; N.J. Stat. Ann. 2C: 58-15; N.C. Gen. Stat. Ann. § 14-315.1; R.I. Gen. Laws Ann. § 11-47-60.1; Tex. Penal Code Ann. § 46.13; D.C. Code Ann. § 7-2507.02.

13 Calif. Penal Code § 25105; R.I. Gen. Laws Ann. § 11-47-60.1; Tex. Penal Code Ann. § 46.13.

14 For example, Maryland's law does not apply if the child has a hunting or firearm certificate (Md. Code Ann., Crim. Law § 4-104). In Texas, it is a defense if the child "was supervised by a person older than 18 years of age and was for hunting, sporting, or other lawful purposes" or is "engaged in an agricultural enterprise" (Tex. Penal Code Ann. § 46.13). In New Hampshire, the law does not apply if the child has completed a firearm safety or hunter safety course (N.H. Rev. Stat. Ann. § 650-C:1).

15 Indiana, Missouri, Nevada, Oklahoma, and Utah. See Ind. Code Ann. § 35-47-10-6; Mo. Stat. Ann. § 571.060; Nev. Rev. Stat. Ann. § 202.300; Okla. Stat. Ann. § 1273; Utah Ann. Code § 76-10-509.6 (applies only to parents and guardians regarding minors who have been convicted or adjudicated of a violent felony).

three for loaded firearms,[16] and five for handguns only.[17] Some of the laws require the weapon to be used by the minor in some way.[18] Exceptions and defenses for reckless provision of firearms to children are similar to those for negligent storage, such as that the firearm was in a locked container[19] or had been rendered inoperable.[20] Other exceptions include that the individual carried the firearm or it was close enough to be easily retrieved,[21] the defendant had no reasonable expectation that a child would have access to the premises,[22] or the child accessed the firearm through unlawful entry.[23] Use of the firearm in hunting, hunter safety, and other sporting events[24] or in self-defense[25] are also exceptions.

In addition to the main distinctions among the CAP laws already discussed, another difference is how they define minors. In the majority of states, it is an offense to provide a firearm to an individual under age 18.[26] In Texas, the age is 17.[27] In seven states, the age is 16,[28] and in another four states, a minor is under age 14.[29]

---

16 Delaware, Virginia, and Wisconsin. See Del. Code Ann. tit. 11 § 603 (applies to parents, guardians, and other people legally charged with care of the minor); Va. Code Ann. § 18.2-56.2; Wisc. Stat. Ann. § 948.55.

17 Colorado, Georgia, Kentucky, Mississippi, and Tennessee. See Colo. Rev. Stat § 18-12-108.7; Ga. Code Ann. § 16-11-101.1; Ky. Rev. Stats Ann. § 527.110; Miss. Ann. Code § 97-37-15 (parents, guardians, custodians); Tenn. Code Ann. § 39-17-1320.

18 Ga. Code Ann. § 16-11-101.1 (must be used in the commission of a felony offense); Tenn. Code Ann. § 39-17-1320 (for liability to attach to parents or guardians, the gun must be used in the commission of a felony).

19 Del. Code Ann. § 603; Nev. Rev. Stat. Ann. § 202.300; Wisc. Stat. Ann. § 948.55.

20 Del. Code Ann. tit. 11 § 603; Wisc. Stat. Ann. § 948.55.

21 Wisc. Stat. Ann. § 948.55.

22 Wisc. Stat. Ann. § 948.55.

23 Nev. Rev. Stat. Ann. § 202.300; Wisc. Stat. Ann. § 948.55.

24 Ind. Ann. Code § 35-47-10-1; Miss. Ann. Code § 97-37-14; Nev. Rev. Stat. Ann. § 202.300 (if accompanied or under the charge of a parent or guardian); Okla. Stat. Ann. § 1273 (with permission of parent or guardian); Tenn. Code Ann. § 39-17-1319.

25 Miss. Ann. Code § 97-37-14; Tenn. Code Ann. § 39-17-1319 (if given permission by a parent or guardian).

26 California, Colorado, Delaware, Georgia, Indiana, Kentucky, Massachusetts, Minnesota, Mississippi, Missouri, Nevada, North Carolina, Oklahoma, Tennessee, Utah, and the District of Columbia. See Calif. Penal Code § 25000; Colo. Rev. Stat § 18-12-108.7; Del. Code Ann. tit. 11 § 603; Ga. Code Ann. § 16-11-101.1; Ind. Code Ann. § 35-47-10-1; Ky. Rev. Stats Ann. § 527.110; Mass. Gen. Laws Ch. 140, § 131L; Minn. Stat. Ann. § 609.666; Miss. Ann. Code § 97-37-15; Mo. Stat. Ann. § 571.060; Nev. Rev. Stat. Ann. § 202.300; N.C. Gen. Stat. Ann. § 14-315.1; Okla. Stat. Ann. § 1273; Tenn. Code Ann. § 39-17-1320; Utah Code Ann. § 76-10-509.6; D.C. Code Ann. § 7-2507.02.

27 Tex. Penal Code Ann. § 46.13.

28 Connecticut, Florida, Hawaii, Maryland, New Hampshire, New Jersey, and Rhode Island. See Conn. Gen. Stat. Ann. § 29-37i; Fla. Stat. Ann. § 790.174; Hawaii Rev. Stat. § 707-714.5; Md. Code Ann., Crim. Law § 4-104; N.H. Rev. Stat. Ann. § 650-C:1; N.J. Stat. Ann. § 2C:58-15; R.I. Gen. Laws Ann. § 11-47-60.1.

29 Illinois, Iowa, Virginia, and Wisconsin. See 720 Ill. Comp. Stat. 5/24-9; Iowa Code Ann. § 724.22; Va. Code Ann. § 18.2-56.2; Wisc. Stat. Ann. § 948.55.

In eight states and the District of Columbia, the act of negligent storage of a firearm is a misdemeanor.[30] In Massachusetts, negligent storage is a felony. In nine states, some additional factor—such as the firearm being used to commit an act of violence, it being a second offense, or the child having committed a prior felony—is required for the act to be a misdemeanor.[31] In eight states, such factors make the negligent storage a felony: In four such jurisdictions, these factors bump the crime from a misdemeanor to a felony,[32] and in the other four, there is no misdemeanor offense, only these felonies.[33] Texas makes clear that regardless of what additional factors are included, the crime is always a misdemeanor offense. Among states with laws that prohibit recklessly or knowingly providing firearms to minors, Mississippi and Tennessee make it a misdemeanor, Missouri and Kentucky make it a felony, and Tennessee makes it a felony for a parent to recklessly or knowingly provide firearms to their children.

## Effects on Suicide

### Research Synthesis Findings

The National Research Council (NRC) (2004) and Hahn et al. (2005) reviewed two quasi-experimental studies providing insight into the impact of CAP laws on suicide. These studies, which applied different statistical models to nearly identical data sets, found somewhat conflicting evidence among those under age 15 (Cummings et al., 1997a; Lott and Whitley, 2001). The model specified by Cummings et al. (1997a) found suggestive effects consistent with a reduction in firearm suicides in a model with limited controls. On the other hand, Lott and Whitley (2001) found uncertain effects in models that employed both state and year fixed effects, states' "shall-issue" or "right-to-carry" laws (see Chapter Thirteen), "one-gun-a-month" purchase rules, states that border one-gun-a-month states, waiting periods, mandatory prison penalties for using guns in the commission of a crime, and more than 36 state-level demographic controls. Combined with the state fixed effects, year fixed effects, and law effects, this model had an unfavorable ratio of estimated parameters to observations (approximately one to eight), suggesting that the model may have been overfit, and thus the estimated effects of these laws and their statistical significance may be poor indicators of their true effects. In addition, the model did not adjust for clustered standard errors. Together, these shortcomings suggest that the model results may not accurately describe the true effects of CAP laws.

---

[30] California, Delaware, Hawaii, Maryland, Minnesota, Nevada, New Jersey, Virginia, and the District of Columbia.

[31] Florida, Illinois, Iowa, New Hampshire, North Carolina, Oklahoma, Rhode Island, Utah, and Wisconsin.

[32] California, Nevada, Utah, and the District of Columbia.

[33] Colorado, Connecticut, Georgia, and Indiana.

Published soon before the NRC report, Webster et al. (2004) examined the effect of CAP laws on suicides among teens (aged 14–17) and young adults (aged 18–20) between 1976 and 2001. In negative binomial models that employed generalized estimating equations and that included state-level fixed effects and other covariates (e.g., the proportion of suicides by firearm as a proxy for gun prevalence), the authors found a significant effect that CAP laws lowered the total suicide rate among those aged 14–17 by 8.3 percent, driven by an estimated 10.8-percent reduction in firearm suicides; in addition, they found uncertain effects on nonfirearm suicides. In this age group, the post-policy firearm suicide rate was 89 percent of the rate expected without the policy, and the total suicide rate was 92 percent of what was expected (see Figure 10.1). There was also an indication that the effect was strongest the first year after the CAP law went into effect. These findings were sensitive to the authors' choices about model specifications: An alternatively specified and worse-fitting model yielded uncertain effects.[34] The authors also found that CAP laws were associated with a reduction in total, firearm, and nonfirearm suicides among those aged 18–20. Relative to what would have been expected without the law, suicide rates in this age group were reduced to 89 percent, 91 percent, and 87 percent for total, firearm, and nonfirearm suicides, respectively. The authors questioned the validity of the causal effect detected for those aged 18–20, suggesting that the significant nonfirearm suicide effects "cast doubt on any causal connection between the laws and lower suicides rates among this group of older youth." They did not, however, suggest that this skepticism should extend to the effects found for the lower age group, although the difference between the reductions in nonfirearm suicide detected for the two age groups was not significantly different. Therefore, for this review, we interpret both models as providing some evidence that CAP laws reduce total and firearm suicide.

Gius (2015b) examined data from 1981 to 2010 and found that CAP laws were associated with a reduction in firearm suicides among those aged 0–19, but he did not examine total or nonfirearm suicides. The author controlled for a variety of state-level sociodemographic characteristics, along with two other laws related to youth firearm access (state minimum age requirements for handgun possession and the federal minimum age requirement for handgun possession enacted in 1994). The effect he reports suggests that the post-policy firearm suicide rate was 89 percent of the rate expected if there were no such laws in place, which matches the estimate by Webster et al. (2004) for those aged 14–17 and is close to their estimate of 92 percent for those aged 18–20.

An additional study (DeSimone, Markowitz, and Xu, 2013) found evidence of an effect of CAP laws on nonfatal self-inflicted gun injuries recorded in the Nationwide Inpatient Sample (NIS). Self-inflicted gun injuries are not all suicide attempts; some

---

[34] Specifically, the primary model (which had better model fit based on Akaike information criterion statistics) included adjusting for national suicide rate trends using two linear trend parameters; the alternative model included year fixed effects.

are unintentional injuries. But case fatality rates for suicide attempts with a firearm are around 82.5 percent (Spicer and Miller, 2000), so a substantial number of self-inflicted firearm injuries are likely the result of suicide attempts. Therefore, DeSimone, Markowitz, and Xu (2013) should be understood to evaluate the effects of CAP laws on nonfatal firearm injuries resulting from a combination of suicide attempts and self-inflicted unintentional injuries. The authors looked at hospital discharges in 11 states between 1988 and 2003 and employed fixed effects for state and year in their statistical models (along with other state- and hospital-level covariates). They found that CAP laws based on negligent storage alone or on both negligent storage and reckless provision were associated with a reduction of 66–69 percent in self-inflicted firearm injuries among those under age 18, although estimates showed an uncertain effect on self-inflicted injuries for those 18 or older. These estimated effects were largely unchanged when considering whether the CAP laws were specified as those more-stringent policies that impose criminal penalties for negligent storage or were more broadly defined to include both negligent storage and reckless provision. This similarity in estimated effects is likely because only two states (Colorado and Wisconsin) in the NIS sample passed reckless provision laws during the study time frame; thus, identification in both specifications was largely driven by changes in state laws regarding negligent storage.

As DeSimone, Markowitz, and Xu (2013) note, however, the data set on which their estimates are made is not strictly longitudinal, and it is not possible to determine the extent to which CAP law effect estimates are estimated cross-sectionally or longitudinally. In addition, cases of firearm self-injury among young people were extremely sparse in the data, with just more than 200 such injuries reported in more than 9,000 hospital observations. Finally, the estimated effect sizes that we calculated from the parameter estimates provided in the paper are improbably large and inconsistent with the effect sizes the authors calculated from the same estimates. For these reasons, we are concerned that the parameter estimates and confidence intervals (CIs) reported in DeSimone, Markowitz, and Xu (2013) may not provide generalizable evidence about the effectiveness of CAP laws.

Figure 10.1 displays the incidence rate ratios (IRRs) and CIs associated with the CAP laws examined in these studies. Lott and Whitley (2001) did not provide sufficient data for us to calculate IRRs and CIs for the effect size of interest, so these are not displayed in figure.

**Figure 10.1**
**Incidence Rate Ratios Associated with the Effect of Child-Access Prevention Laws on Suicide**

| Study, by Policy | Outcome Measure | Effect Size (IRR) [95% CI] |
|---|---|---|
| **State CAP law** | **Suicide** | |
| Cummings et al. (1997a) | Firearm, aged 0–14 | 0.81 [0.66, 1.01] |
| Cummings et al. (1997a) | Nonfirearm, aged 0–14 | 0.95 [0.75, 1.20] |
| Webster et al. (2004) | Total, aged 14–17 | 0.92 [0.86, 0.98] |
| Webster et al. (2004) | Total, aged 18–20 | 0.89 [0.85, 0.93] |
| Webster et al. (2004) | Firearm, aged 14–17 | 0.89 [0.83, 0.96] |
| Webster et al. (2004) | Firearm, aged 18–20 | 0.87 [0.82, 0.92] |
| Webster et al. (2004) | Nonfirearm, aged 14–17 | 1.00 [0.91, 1.10] |
| Webster et al. (2004) | Nonfirearm, aged 18–20 | 0.91 [0.85, 0.98] |
| Gius (2015b) | Firearm, aged 0–19 | 0.89 [0.84, 0.94] |
| **State CAP law, negligent storage (11 states)** | | |
| DeSimone, Markowitz, & Xu (2013) | Firearm, aged 0–17 | 0.31 [0.16, 0.61] |
| DeSimone, Markowitz, & Xu (2013) | Firearm, aged 18+ | 1.00 [0.64, 1.56] |
| **State CAP law, negligent storage or reckless provision (11 states)** | | |
| DeSimone, Markowitz, & Xu (2013) | Firearm, aged 0–17 | 0.35 [0.19, 0.62] |
| DeSimone, Markowitz, & Xu (2013) | Firearm, aged 18+ | 1.17 [0.75, 1.83] |

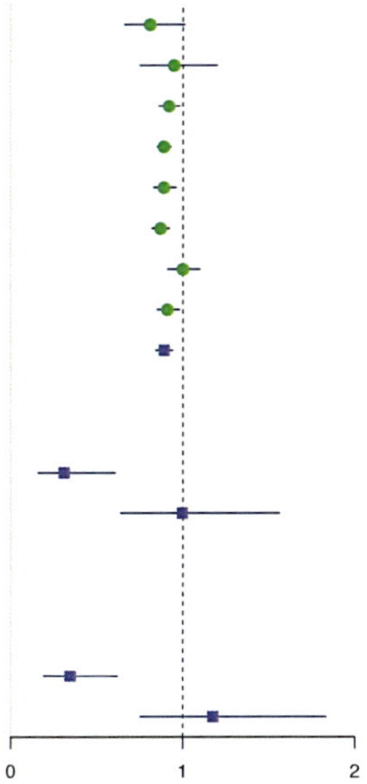


NOTE: IRR values marked with blue squares indicate that methodological concerns are discussed in the text. Green circles indicate that we identified no significant methodological concerns. See Appendix B for details.

## Conclusions

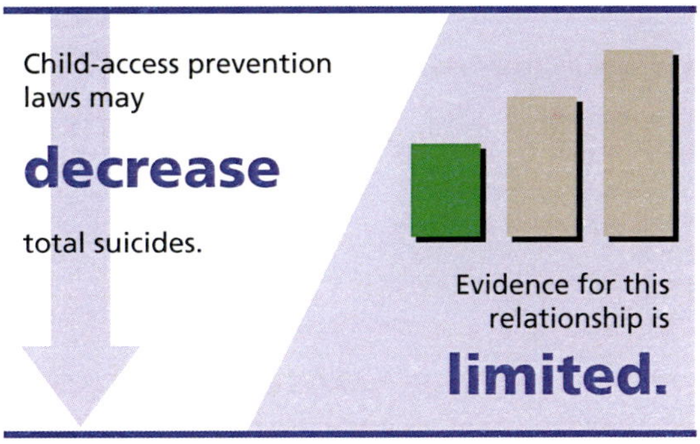


*Total suicides*. We identified one qualifying study that estimated the effect of CAP laws on total suicides in two population groups, those aged 14–17 and those aged 18–20 (Webster et al., 2004). For both groups, significant effects were found consistent with CAP laws reducing total suicides.

We conclude that available research offers *limited evidence that child-access prevention laws reduce total suicides among youth aged 14–20.*

*Firearm suicides and firearm self-injury.* We identified five qualifying studies that estimated the effect of CAP laws on firearm suicide or firearm self-injury. Cummings et al. (1997a) identified a suggestive effect consistent with CAP laws reducing firearm suicides among children 14 or younger. Using a similar data series, Lott and Whitley (2001) identified uncertain effects of CAP laws on those younger than age 15 and among those aged 15–17. Using a longer but overlapping data series, Webster et al. (2004) found significant effects suggesting that CAP laws reduce firearm suicide among those aged 14–17 and those aged 18–20. Gius (2015b) used a later, though partially overlapping, data series and similarly found a significant effect indicating that CAP laws reduce firearm suicides among those aged 19 or younger. Finally, using data on hospitalizations for self-inflicted firearm injuries, DeSimone, Markowitz, and Xu (2013) found significant effects suggesting that CAP laws reduce such injuries among those aged 17 or younger, but they found uncertain effects among adults aged 18 or older.

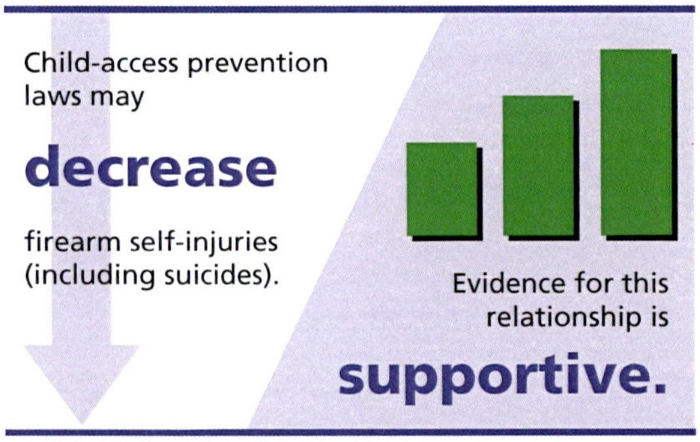


Based on these studies, our assessment of their relative strengths, and the fact that effects are found across multiple data sets, we conclude that *there is supportive evidence that child-access prevention laws reduce all* firearm *self-injuries (including suicide attempts and self-injuries that were not the result of suicide attempts) among young people.* In addition, we find *moderate evidence that CAP laws reduce firearm suicides among this population.*

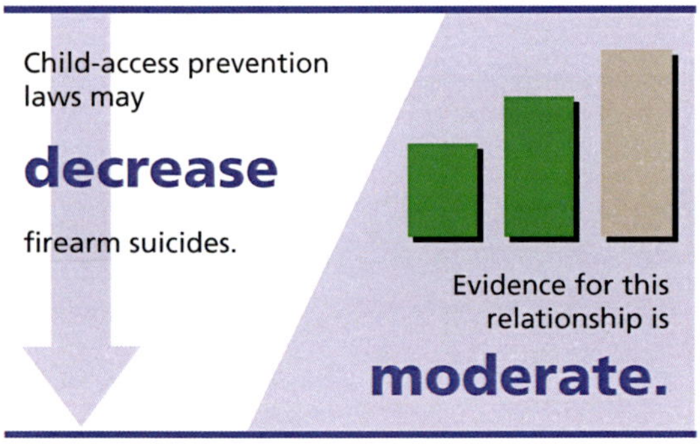


## Effects on Violent Crime

### Research Synthesis Findings

Based on results from the same two quasi-experimental studies (Cummings et al., 1997a; Lott and Whitley, 2001), both NRC (2004) and Hahn et al. (2005) concluded that the evidence of the effects of CAP laws on violent crime was inconclusive. Using a limited set of controls and data spanning 1979 to 1994, Cummings et al. (1997a) found a suggestive relationship between CAP laws and firearm homicides for children aged 15 or younger and uncertain effects for nonfirearm homicides. In contrast, examining an overlapping period from 1977 to 1996, Lott and Whitley (2001) found that CAP laws were significantly related to higher rates of rape (9-percent increase) and robbery (10-percent increase). In additional analyses, estimates showed a suggestive relationship between CAP laws and lower rates of assault, as well as uncertain effects of CAP laws on murder rates. However, the authors' model had an unfavorable ratio of estimated parameters to observations (approximately one to eight), meaning the model may have been overfit, and thus parameter estimates and their CIs may have been invalid. Further, Lott and Whitley (2001) made no adjustment for clustering of standard errors at the state level, which threatens the validity of the significance values estimated from their model. In reviewing the more recent literature, we identified no new studies meeting our inclusion criteria that examined this relationship.

Figure 10.2 displays the IRRs and CIs associated with the CAP laws examined in these studies.

**Figure 10.2**
**Incidence Rate Ratios Associated with the Effect of Child-Access Prevention Laws on Violent Crime**

| Study, by Policy | Outcome Measure | Effect Size (IRR) [95% CI] |
|---|---|---|
| **State CAP law** | **Crime** | |
| Cummings et al. (1997a) | Firearm homicides, aged 0–14 | 0.89 [0.76, 1.05] |
| Cummings et al. (1997a) | Nonfirearm homicides, aged 0–14 | 0.96 [0.86, 1.06] |
| Lott & Whitley (2001) | Murder | 1.04 [0.97, 1.11] |
| Lott & Whitley (2001) | Rape | 1.10 [1.04, 1.16] |
| Lott & Whitley (2001) | Robbery | 1.11 [1.03, 1.20] |
| Lott & Whitley (2001) | Assault | 0.96 [0.91, 1.01] |

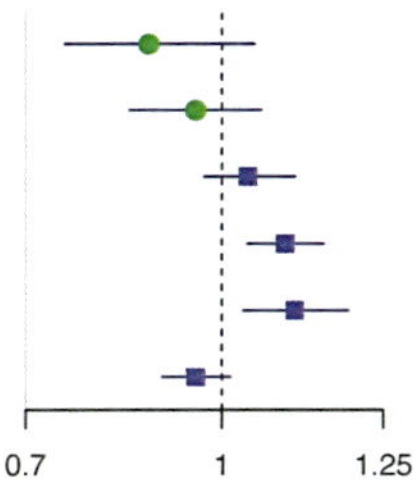


NOTE: IRR values marked with blue squares indicate that methodological concerns are discussed in the text. Green circles indicate that we identified no significant methodological concerns. See Appendix B for details.

## Conclusion

We identified two studies meeting our quality standards that evaluated the effect of CAP laws on any violent crime outcomes. Cummings et al. (1997a) reported a suggestive effect consistent with CAP laws reducing firearm homicide rates among children aged 14 or younger. Lott and Whitley (2001) found that these laws

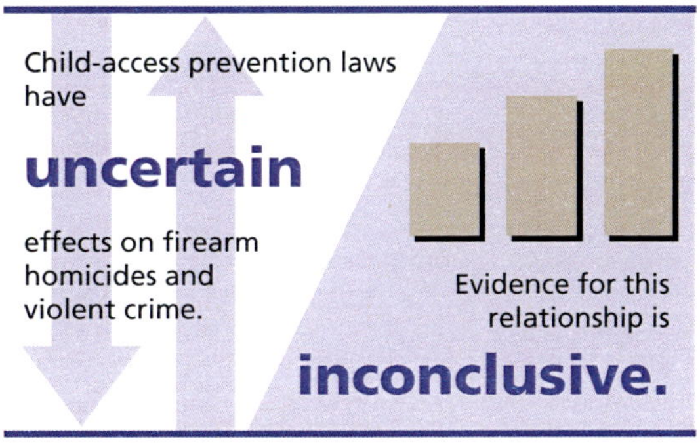

significantly increased rates of robbery and rape. They also reported a suggestive effect consistent with the laws decreasing assault rates. The effect of CAP laws on murder rates was uncertain.

Considering the relative strengths of the two studies, we find *inconclusive evidence for the effect of child-access prevention laws on violent crimes generally and on specific violent crimes, including firearm homicides.*

## Effects on Unintentional Injuries and Deaths

### Research Synthesis Findings

In 2004, NRC reported that "the credibility of existing research [on CAP laws] cannot be assessed." NRC made that conclusion based on three quasi-experimental studies that used overlapping data (Cummings et al., 1997a; Lott and Whitley, 2001; Webster and Starnes, 2000). Hahn et al. (2005) reached virtually the same conclusion after reviewing the same studies. With a limited set of controls, Cummings et al. (1997a) found that CAP laws were associated with a lower risk of unintentional firearm death in children aged 15 or younger (relative risk = 0.77; 95-percent CI: 0.63, 0.94) and suggestive evidence that the laws reduced such deaths in those aged 20–24 as well. In their re-analysis adding three more years of data and more states with CAP laws, Webster and Starnes (2000) also found that CAP laws were associated with a significant decrease in unintentional firearm deaths among those aged 14 or younger. In addition, they showed that this effect was not consistent across all states that have CAP laws. Significant reductions in such deaths were observed in states with felony CAP laws, and in states without felony laws, the effects were uncertain. Indeed, the authors noted that much of the observed effect of CAP laws was attributable to a single state, Florida, without which the overall effect of CAP laws still suggested that they reduce deaths, but the effect was uncertain. On the other hand, Lott and Whitley (2001) found only uncertain effects among youth aged 19 or younger, with some suggestive effects of an increase in unintentional injuries among children aged 5–9. Nevertheless, this model used an unfavorable ratio of estimated parameters to observations (approximately one to eight), meaning the model may have been overfit, and thus parameter estimates and CIs may be invalid; furthermore, no adjustment was made for clustered standard errors, so the standard errors and significance values reported in the paper were unreliable.

Since the NRC (2004) and Hahn et al. (2005) reports, three additional quasi-experimental studies provided new evidence on CAP laws, all of which used state and time fixed-effects models to examine the relationship between state CAP laws and firearm-related unintentional death or injury.

DeSimone, Markowitz, and Xu (2013) performed a fixed-effects analysis on unintentional non-self-inflicted gun injuries using hospital discharge data from the NIS spanning 1988 through 2003. They found that CAP laws based on negligent storage alone or on both negligent storage and reckless provision had uncertain effects on unintentional firearm injuries in children aged 18 or younger in the 11 states that were part of the NIS, but they did find a statistically significant effect of these laws on unintentional firearm deaths among those 18 or older. Specifically, CAP laws that included negligent storage rules only were associated with a decline to 71 percent of the rates expected without implementing such laws; the policies that included both negligent storage and reckless provision rules were associated with a decline to 69 percent of the expected rate. This similarity in estimated effects is likely because only two states (Colorado and Wisconsin) in the NIS sample passed reckless provision laws during the study time frame; thus, identification in both specifications was largely driven by changes in state laws regarding negligent storage. The findings were generally confirmed in a second analysis adding more control states (states without a change in CAP laws over the period); however, in those analyses, safe storage and negligent provision laws were associated with a significant reduction in unintentional injuries for those aged 18 or younger.

As DeSimone, Markowitz, and Xu (2013) note, however, the data set on which their estimates are made is not strictly longitudinal, and it is not possible to determine the extent to which CAP law effect estimates are estimated cross-sectionally or longitudinally. In addition, the estimated effect sizes that we calculated from the parameter estimates provided in the paper are not consistent with the effect sizes the authors calculated from the same estimates. For these reasons, we are concerned that the parameter estimates and CIs reported in DeSimone, Markowitz, and Xu (2013) may not provide generalizable evidence about the effectiveness of CAP laws.

Hepburn et al. (2006) examined the relationship between CAP laws and unintentional firearm deaths from 1979 to 2000 among children aged 14 or younger compared with adults aged 55–74. In their state and time fixed-effects models, CAP laws were significantly associated with fewer unintentional deaths in children 14 or younger (but effects were uncertain among adults aged 55–74). For those 14 or younger, the estimate in Hepburn et al. (2006) suggests that the post-law firearm death rate was 78 percent of what would have been expected without the law. Like the analysis by Webster and Starnes (2000), the reduction was greatest in a model with the subset of states with felony CAP laws, in which rates after the laws were implemented were just 64 percent of the expected rate. In states with misdemeanor CAP laws, the effects were smaller and uncertain; in models excluding California or Florida, the effects were smaller and suggestive for those aged 14 or younger (see Figure 10.3). The authors controlled for firearm availability (using the proportion of suicides that were caused by a firearm as a proxy for availability) and for changes in the coding of causes of death between the ninth and tenth revisions of the International Statistical Classification of Diseases and Related Health Problems (ICD) in 1999. Demographic, social, and economic covariates were not included in this model, meaning that state variation in factors that may correspond with adoption of CAP laws cannot be ruled out as explaining the apparent CAP law effects.

Gius (2015b) also examined the relationship between unintentional firearm deaths among youth and state CAP laws, but in a wider age range (0–19 years) and between 1981 and 2010, which partially overlaps with the period studied by Hepburn et al. (2006). Unlike the earlier studies of similar data sets, this study found uncertain evidence of a reduction in youth unintentional deaths associated with CAP laws. Gius (2015b) controlled for a variety of state-level sociodemographic characteristics, along with two other laws related to youth firearm access (state minimum age requirements for handgun possession and the federal minimum age requirement for handgun possession enacted in 1994). The weighted least-squares statistical model used in this study may not be appropriate for the rate outcome, with low values or zero in many state-year observations. The model's lower bound at zero may result in violations of its assumptions and can yield biased and incorrect parameter estimates and CIs (Freedman, 2006).

Figure 10.3 displays the IRRs and CIs associated with the CAP laws examined in these studies. Lott and Whitley (2001) did not provide enough information for us to calculate IRRs and CIs for the effect size of interest, so we do not include these in the figure.

#### Conclusions

We identified six qualifying studies of the effect of CAP laws on unintentional firearm injuries or deaths. Cummings et al. (1997a) found a significant effect consistent with these laws reducing unintentional firearm deaths among children aged 14 or younger, uncertain effects on unintentional injuries for those aged 15–19, and a suggestive effect consistent with CAP laws reducing unintentional firearm injuries among those aged 20–24. Across four age groups, Lott and Whitley (2001) used an overlapping data set but found three uncertain effects and one suggestive effect consistent with CAP laws increasing unintentional firearm deaths among children aged 5–9.

Using a data set that was extended by one year beyond Lott and Whitley's, Webster and Starnes (2000) found a significant effect suggesting that CAP laws reduce such deaths in children aged 14 or younger. In subgroup analyses, they found that this effect remains strong when examining just those states with felony CAP laws, but the effect was uncertain in states with misdemeanor CAP laws. Hepburn et al. (2006) used a similar data set extended by three years and produced a pattern of findings identical to those of Webster and Starnes (2000). Finally, Gius (2015b) added a decade of data to that studied by Hepburn et al. (2006)

## Figure 10.3
## Incidence Rate Ratios Associated with the Effect of Child-Access Prevention Laws on Unintentional Firearm Injuries and Deaths

| Study, by Policy | Outcome Measure | Effect Size (IRR) [95% CI] |
|---|---|---|
| **State CAP law** | **Unintentional Injuries** | |
| Cummings et al. (1997a) | Firearm deaths, aged 0–14 | 0.77 [0.63, 0.94] |
| Cummings et al. (1997a) | Firearm deaths, aged 15–19 | 0.91 [0.77, 1.08] |
| Cummings et al. (1997a) | Firearm deaths, aged 20–24 | 0.84 [0.68, 1.03] |
| Webster & Starnes (2000) | Firearm deaths, aged 0–14 | 0.83 [0.71, 0.97] |
| Hepburn et al. (2006) | Firearm deaths, aged 0–14 | 0.78 [0.61, 0.99] |
| Hepburn et al. (2006) | Firearm deaths, aged 55–74 | 0.88 [0.63, 1.22] |
| Gius (2015b) | Firearm deaths, aged 0–19 | 0.96 [0.86, 1.06] |
| **State CAP law, negligent storage (11 states)** | | |
| DeSimone, Markowitz, & Xu (2013) | Firearm injuries, aged 0–17 | 0.76 [0.53, 1.09] |
| DeSimone, Markowitz, & Xu (2013) | Firearm injuries, aged 18+ | 0.71 [0.54, 0.94] |
| **State CAP law, negligent storage or reckless provision (11 states)** | | |
| DeSimone, Markowitz, & Xu (2013) | Firearm injuries, aged 0–17 | 0.83 [0.61, 1.12] |
| DeSimone, Markowitz, & Xu (2013) | Firearm injuries, aged 18+ | 0.75 [0.59, 0.96] |
| **Florida CAP law** | | |
| Webster & Starnes (2000) | Firearm deaths, aged 0–14 | 0.49 [0.25, 0.69] |
| **Non-Florida state CAP law** | | |
| Webster & Starnes (2000) | Firearm deaths, aged 0–14 | 0.95 [0.80, 1.12] |
| **CAP laws without Fla.** | | |
| Hepburn et al. (2006) | Firearm deaths, aged 0–14 | 0.86 [0.72, 1.03] |
| Hepburn et al. (2006) | Firearm deaths, aged 55–74 | 0.87 [0.61, 1.28] |
| **CAP laws without Calif.** | | |
| Hepburn et al. (2006) | Firearm deaths, aged 0–14 | 0.77 [0.56, 1.06] |
| Hepburn et al. (2006) | Firearm deaths, aged 55–74 | 0.86 [0.45, 1.27] |
| **Felony CAP law** | | |
| Webster & Starnes (2000) | Firearm deaths, aged 0–14 | 0.69 [0.56, 0.85] |
| Hepburn et al. (2006) | Firearm deaths, aged 0–14 | 0.64 [0.46, 0.89] |
| Hepburn et al. (2006) | Firearm deaths, aged 55–74 | 0.90 [0.72, 1.12] |
| **Misdemeanor CAP law** | | |
| Webster & Starnes (2000) | Firearm deaths, aged 0–14 | 1.00 [0.81, 1.22] |
| Hepburn et al. (2006) | Firearm deaths, aged 0–14 | 0.93 [0.76, 1.13] |
| Hepburn et al. (2006) | Firearm deaths, aged 55–74 | 0.88 [0.54, 1.44] |

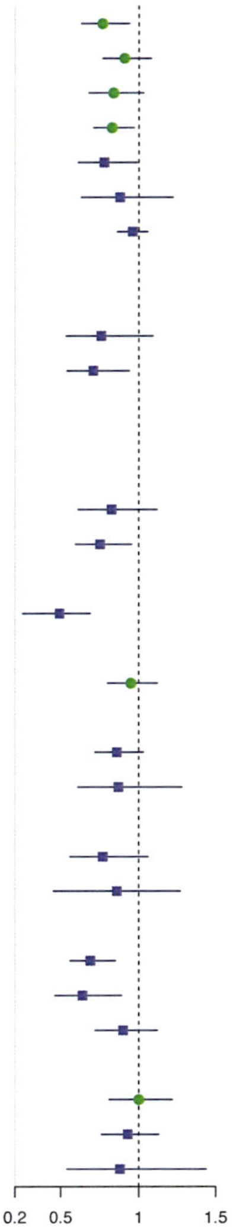


NOTE: IRR values marked with blue squares indicate that methodological concerns are discussed in the text. Green circles indicate that we identified no significant methodological concerns. See Appendix B for details.

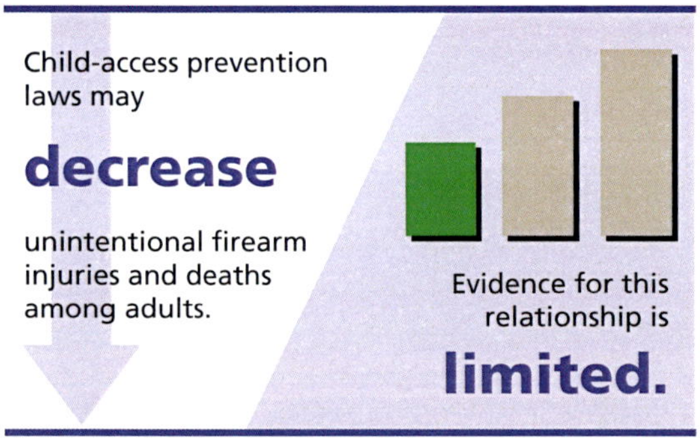


and found uncertain effects of CAP laws on unintentional firearm injuries among those aged 19 or younger.

Using a separate data series, DeSimone, Markowitz, and Xu (2013) found that CAP laws significantly reduced unintentional firearm injuries among those aged 17 or younger and among those 18 or older.

Considering the relative strengths of these studies and the two distinct data sets used in them, we conclude that there is *supportive evidence that child-access prevention laws reduce unintentional firearm injuries and deaths among children*. Although much more limited in number, the studies that have examined effects on young adults or adults provide *limited evidence that these laws may reduce unintentional firearm injuries and deaths among adults as well.*

## Effects on Mass Shootings

### Research Synthesis Findings

Neither NRC (2004) nor Hahn et al. (2005) identified research examining the effects of CAP laws on mass shootings in the United States. Our search yielded one such study that met our inclusion criteria. Using a Poisson specification, Lott (2003) estimated how state laws requiring that guns be safely stored affect fatalities, injuries, and the incidence of *multiple-victim public shootings*, which the author defined as events unrelated to other criminal activity in which two or more people were killed or wounded in a public location. The analysis covered 1977 to 1997, and regression models included controls for state and year fixed effects, other state firearm policies, and a broad range of state-level socioeconomic and demographic characteristics. The findings showed uncertain effects of safe storage laws on total casualties from multiple-victim public shootings and on total number of multiple-victim public shooting incidents. However, these models had an unfavorable ratio of estimated parameters to observations (approximately one to eight), suggesting that the model may have been overfit, and thus the estimated effects of these laws may be poor indicators of their true effects. In addition, the model did not adjust for clustered standard errors. Together, these shortcomings suggest that the model results may not accurately describe the true effects of safe storage laws.

Figure 10.4 displays the IRRs and CIs associated with the CAP laws examined in these studies.

**Figure 10.4**
**Incidence Rate Ratios Associated with the Effect of Child-Access Prevention Laws on Mass Shootings**

| Study, by Policy | Outcome Measure | Effect Size (IRR) [95% CI] |
|---|---|---|
| **Safe storage laws** | **Mass shooting** | |
| Lott (2003) | Total deaths and injuries | 1.07 [0.79, 1.46] |
| Lott (2003) | Number of shooting incidents | 0.83 [0.45, 1.50] |

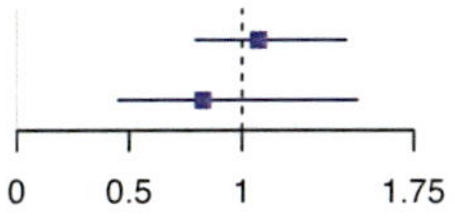


NOTE: IRR values marked with blue squares indicate that methodological concerns are discussed in the text. See Appendix B for details.

### Conclusions

We identified one qualifying study of the effect of CAP laws on mass shootings. Lott (2003) found uncertain effects for these laws on mass shooting casualties and mass shooting incidents. Therefore, we find *inconclusive evidence for the effect of child-access prevention laws on mass shootings.*

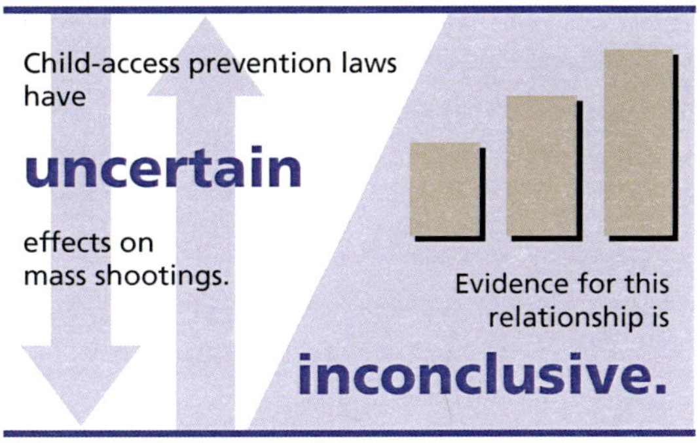


## Outcomes Without Studies Examining the Effects of Child-Access Prevention Laws

Neither NRC (2004) nor Hahn et al. (2005) identified any research examining the relationship between CAP laws and the following outcomes, and we identified no such studies that met our inclusion criteria:

- officer-involved shootings
- defensive gun use
- hunting and recreation
- gun industry.

## Chapter Ten References


American Law Institute, Model Penal Code, Section 2.02 cmt.at 238, 1985.

Azrael, Deborah, and Matthew Miller, "Reducing Suicide Without Affecting Underlying Mental Health: Theoretical Underpinnings and a Review of the Evidence Base Lining the Availability of Lethal Means and Suicide," in Rory C. O'Connor and Jane Pirkis, eds., *The International Handbook of Suicide Prevention*, 2nd ed., Hoboken, N.J.: John Wiley and Sons, 2016.

Betz, M. E., M. Miller, C. Barber, B. Beaty, I. Miller, C. A. Camargo, Jr., and E. D. Boudreaux, "Lethal Means Access and Assessment Among Suicidal Emergency Department Patients," *Depression and Anxiety*, Vol. 33, No. 6, 2016, pp. 502–511.

Brent, D. A., J. A. Perper, C. J. Allman, G. M. Moritz, M. E. Wartella, and J. P. Zelenak, "The Presence and Accessibility of Firearms in the Homes of Adolescent Suicides: A Case-Control Study," *JAMA*, Vol. 266, No. 21, 1991, pp. 2989–2995.

Brent, D. A., J. A. Perper, G. Moritz, M. Baugher, J. Schweers, and C. Roth, "Firearms and Adolescent Suicide—A Community Case-Control Study," *American Journal of Diseases of Children*, Vol. 147, No. 10, 1993b, pp. 1066–1071.

CDC—*See* Centers for Disease Control and Prevention.

Centers for Disease Control and Prevention, "Nonfatal Injury Reports, 2001–2014," WISQARS database, Atlanta, Ga., March 28, 2013. As of March 9, 2017:
https://webappa.cdc.gov/sasweb/ncipc/nfirates2001.html

———, "Fatal Injury Reports, National and Regional, 1999–2015," WISQARS database, Atlanta, Ga., June 24, 2015. As of March 23, 2017:
https://webappa.cdc.gov/sasweb/ncipc/mortrate10_us.html

Conwell, Y., P. R. Duberstein, K. Connor, S. Eberly, C. Cox, and E. D. Caine, "Access to Firearms and Risk for Suicide in Middle-Aged and Older Adults," *American Journal of Geriatric Psychiatry*, Vol. 10, No. 4, 2002, pp. 407–416.

Cummings, P., D. C. Grossman, F. P. Rivara, and T. D. Koepsell, "State Gun Safe Storage Laws and Child Mortality Due to Firearms," *JAMA,* Vol. 278, No. 13, 1997a, pp. 1084–1086.

Dahlberg, L. L., R. M. Ikeda, and M. J. Kresnow, "Guns in the Home and Risk of a Violent Death in the Home: Findings from a National Study," *American Journal of Epidemiology*, Vol. 160, No. 10, 2004, pp. 929–936.

DeSimone, J., S. Markowitz, and J. Xu, "Child Access Prevention Laws and Nonfatal Gun Injuries," *Southern Economic Journal*, Vol. 80, No. 1, 2013, pp. 5–25.

Freedman, David A., "On the So-Called 'Huber Sandwich Estimator' and 'Robust Standard Errors,'" *American Statistician*, Vol. 60, No. 4, 2006, pp. 299–302.

Gius, Mark, "The Impact of Minimum Age and Child Access Prevention Laws on Firearm-Related Youth Suicides and Unintentional Deaths," *Social Science Journal*, Vol. 52, No. 2, 2015b, pp. 168–175.

Grossman, D. C., B. A. Mueller, C. Riedy, M. D. Dowd, A. Villaveces, J. Prodzinski, J. Nakagawara, J. Howard, N. Thiersch, and R. Harruff, "Gun Storage Practices and Risk of Youth Suicide and Unintentional Firearm Injuries," *JAMA*, Vol. 293, No. 6, 2005, pp. 707–714.

Hahn, Robert A., Oleg Bilukha, Alex Crosby, Mindy T. Fullilove, Akiva Liberman, Eve Moscicki, Susan Snyder, Farris Tuma, and Peter A. Briss, "Firearms Laws and the Reduction of Violence: A Systematic Review," *American Journal of Preventive Medicine*, Vol. 28, No. 2, 2005, pp. 40–71.

Hepburn, L., D. Azrael, M. Miller, and D. Hemenway, "The Effect of Child Access Prevention Laws on Unintentional Child Firearm Fatalities, 1979–2000," *Journal of Trauma-Injury Infection and Critical Care*, Vol. 61, No. 2, 2006, pp. 423–428.

Ilgen, M. A., K. Zivin, R. J. McCammon, and M. Valenstein, "Mental Illness, Previous Suicidality, and Access to Guns in the United States," *Psychiatric Services*, Vol. 59, No. 2, 2008, pp. 198–200.

Johnson, R. M., C. Barber, D. Azrael, D. E. Clark, and D. Hemenway, "Who Are the Owners of Firearms Used in Adolescent Suicides?" *Suicide and Life-Threatening Behavior*, Vol. 40, No. 6, 2010, pp. 609–611.

LaFree, G., and C. Birbeck, *Controlling New Mexico Juveniles' Possession of Firearms,* Albuquerque, N.M.: New Mexico Criminal Justice Statistical Analysis Center, Working Paper 27, 1998. As of May 9, 2017:
http://nmsc.unm.edu/reports/1998/JuvFirearmPossession.pdf

Loeber, R., and R. Stallings, "Modeling the Impact of Interventions on Local Indicators of Offending, Victimization, and Incarceration," in R. Loeber and D. P. Farrington, eds., *Young Homicide Offenders and Victims: Risk Factors, Prediction, and Prevention from Childhood*, New York: Springer, 2011, pp. 137–152.

Lott, John R., Jr., *The Bias Against Guns: Why Almost Everything You've Heard About Gun Control Is Wrong*, Washington, D.C.: Regnery Publishing, Inc., 2003.

Lott, John R., Jr., and John E. Whitley, "Safe-Storage Gun Laws: Accidental Deaths, Suicides, and Crime," *Journal of Law and Economics*, Vol. 44, No. 2, 2001, pp. 659–689.

National Research Council, *Firearms and Violence: A Critical Review*, Washington, D.C.: National Academies Press, 2004.

NRC—*See* National Research Council.

Office of Juvenile Justice and Delinquency Prevention, *OJJDP Statistical Briefing Book*, Washington, D.C.: U.S. Department of Justice, May 25, 2016. As of May 9, 2017:
https://www.ojjdp.gov/ojstatbb/

Oslin, D. W., C. Zubritsky, G. Brown, M. Mullahy, A. Puliafico, and T. Ten Have, "Managing Suicide Risk in Late Life: Access to Firearms as a Public Health Risk," *American Journal of Geriatric Psychiatry*, Vol. 12, No. 1, 2004, pp. 30–36.

Shenassa, E. D., M. L. Rogers, K. L. Spalding, and M. B. Roberts, "Safer Storage of Firearms at Home and Risk of Suicide: A Study of Protective Factors in a Nationally Representative Sample," *Journal of Epidemiology and Community Health*, Vol. 58, No. 10, 2004, pp. 841–848.

Smith, P. N., J. Currier, and K. Drescher, "Firearm Ownership in Veterans Entering Residential PTSD Treatment: Associations with Suicide Ideation, Attempts, and Combat Exposure," *Psychiatry Research*, Vol. 229, No. 1–2, 2015, pp. 220–224.

Spicer, R. S., and T. R. Miller, "Suicide Acts in 8 States: Incidence and Case Fatality Rates by Demographics and Method," *American Journal of Public Health*, Vol. 90, No. 12, 2000, pp. 1885–1891.

Webster, D. W., L. H. Freed, S. Frattaroli, and M. H. Wilson, "How Delinquent Youths Acquire Guns: Initial Versus Most Recent Gun Acquisitions," *Journal of Urban Health*, Vol. 79, No. 1, 2002, pp. 60–69.

Webster, Daniel W., and Marc Starnes, "Reexamining the Association Between Child Access Prevention Gun Laws and Unintentional Shooting Deaths of Children," *Pediatrics*, Vol. 106, No. 6, 2000, pp. 1466–1469.

Webster, D. W., J. S. Vernick, A. M. Zeoli, and J. A. Manganello, "Association Between Youth-Focused Firearm Laws and Youth Suicides," *JAMA*, Vol. 292, No. 5, 2004, pp. 594–601.

CHAPTER ELEVEN

# Surrender of Firearms by Prohibited Possessors

Federal law bans the sale of firearms to prohibited possessors, which include minors, illegal immigrants, convicted felons, fugitives from justice, users of controlled substances, those with adjudicated mental illnesses or involuntarily committed to mental institutions, those who have been dishonorably discharged from the military, those who have renounced their U.S. citizenship, those subject to restraining orders, and those convicted of domestic violence offenses (18 U.S.C. 922). However, there is no procedure under federal law for the *removal* of firearms from these same classes of prohibited possessors or for checking to see whether they have firearms at the time they become prohibited possessors.

While background checks and permit-to-purchase laws aim to prevent the purchase of firearms by prohibited individuals, laws requiring certain prohibited possessors to surrender firearms are designed to ensure that firearm owners relinquish their weapons once they are identified as belonging to a class of prohibited possessors. Through this mechanism, these laws should reduce rates of suicide or gun violence in this population, which is assumed to be at elevated risk. For instance, as discussed in Chapter Twenty-One, there is evidence that domestic violence offenders present an especially elevated risk of violence to their partners. For this reason, many state firearm-surrender laws focus on domestic violence offenders at the time they are convicted of such crimes.

To assess the impact of these policies, the ideal analyses would estimate effects on outcomes specifically for those populations required to surrender their firearms under the regulations. For instance, to study the impact on gun violence of laws requiring the removal or surrender of firearms by persons convicted of a domestic violence misdemeanor, one would like to estimate how violent crime rates changed after the law for this subgroup of the population relative to others not directly affected by the law. Further, because these laws will be effective only to the extent that they are enforced, causal inference could be strengthened with information on the number of firearms that were surrendered or the proportion of prohibited possessors that have been disarmed.

## State Implementation of Firearm-Surrender Laws

Although most state laws allow law enforcement to remove the guns they discover in the possession of a prohibited person, fewer have laws that specify any mechanism for such individuals to surrender their firearms on their own (Giffords Law Center to Prevent Gun Violence, undated-b).

Eight states have laws requiring the surrender of firearms by certain prohibited possessors.[1] These states define a range of procedures for prohibited possessors to dispose of their firearms and time frames for doing so, and, in some cases, the laws stipulate roles for judicial officers or law enforcement to ensure that firearms are surrendered or confiscated. In addition, 13 states require the surrender of firearms pursuant to orders of protection to last for the duration of the order.[2]

---

1 California, Connecticut, Hawaii, Illinois, Massachusetts, New York, Pennsylvania, and Wisconsin. See

- Calif. Penal Code § 29810. The court shall provide the notifying defendant of prohibition against firearm possession and provide a form for facilitating the transfer of firearms. The form, which notes that the prohibition is effective immediately, allows the individual to designate another to have power of attorney for the purpose of disposing of or transferring the firearms (California Department of Justice, 2015). The power of attorney lasts for 30 days. The individual may also transfer possession to a licensed dealer for storage. See also Calif. Fam. Code § 6389. The individual shall surrender firearms for the period of the protective order.
- Conn. Gen. Stat. Ann. § 29036k. The individual has two business days to surrender firearms to the state or transfer them to an eligible individual. If surrendered, the individual has one year to transfer firearms to an eligible individual.
- Hawaii Rev. Stat. Ann. § 134-7.3. The individual has 30 days to dispose of or surrender firearms to law enforcement. If not surrendered, law enforcement may seize the firearms. See also Hawaii Rev. Stat. Ann. § 134-7(f). The individual must surrender firearms following any restraining order issued by a court.
- 430 Ill. Comp. Stat. 65/9.5. The individual must surrender his or her firearm owner's identification card; submit a firearm disposition record; and, within 48 hours, place firearms in the location of or with the person reported on the disposition record.
- Mass. Gen. Laws Ch. 140 § 129B, 129D. Upon revocation of firearm identification card, the individual must surrender all firearms "without delay." The individual then has one year to transfer firearms to a licensed dealer or permitted possessor.
- N.Y. Crim. Proc. Law §§ 330.20; 380.96 N.Y. Penal Law § 400.05. A judge shall order revocation of an individual's firearm license and demand the surrender of firearms. The individual has one year to transfer or sell firearms to a licensed dealer or to himself or herself (pursuant to obtaining a valid license).
- 18 Pa. Cons. Stat. Ann. § 6105. The individual has 60 days to sell or transfer firearms to an eligible individual outside his or her household.
- Wisc. Stat. Ann. §§ 51.20, 51.45, 54.10, 55.12. If the court determines that an individual is a prohibited possessor under federal law, the court shall order the seizure of his or her firearms. See also Wisc. Stat. Ann. § 813.12. The individual must surrender firearms following a court-issued injunction after domestic abuse.

2 California, Colorado, Hawaii, Iowa, Maryland, Massachusetts, Minnesota, New Hampshire, New York, North Carolina, Pennsylvania, Tennessee, and Washington. See Calif. Fam. Code § 6389; Colo. Rev. Stat. § 13-14-105.5; Hawaii Rev. Stat. Ann. § 134-7(f); Iowa Code § 724.26(4); Md. Code, Fam. Law § 4-506; Mass. Gen. Laws Ch. 209A §3B; Minn. Stat. § 518B.01, subd. 6(g); N.H. Rev. Stat. Ann. § 173-B:5; N.Y. Fam. Ct. Act § 842-a; N.C. Gen. Stat. Ann. § 50B-3.1; 23 Pa. Cons. Stat. Ann. § 6108; Tenn. Code Ann. § 36-3-625(a); Rev. Code. Wash. Ann. § 9.410.800.

In addition to the states that require surrender by every prohibited possessor, four states require individuals convicted of domestic violence misdemeanors to surrender their firearms.[3]

## Effects on Violent Crime

### Research Synthesis Findings

Neither the National Research Council (NRC) (2004) nor Hahn et al. (2005) reports specifically reviewed policies that provide a mechanism for removing firearms from prohibited possessors. The NRC panel did conclude, "There is not much empirical evidence that assesses whether attempts to reduce criminal access to firearms will reduce gun availability or gun crime." However, three studies published since then provide some evidence on the effects of these laws. Vigdor and Mercy (2006) examined how intimate partner homicide is affected by laws that allow law enforcement officers to confiscate firearms at the scene of alleged domestic violence incidents. (The authors also analyzed the effects of laws that prohibit people under a domestic violence restraining order from purchasing or possessing a gun and that prohibit people who have been convicted of a misdemeanor domestic violence offense from possessing a gun.) Their state-level analysis of intimate partner homicide rates from 1982 to 2002 found no overall effect of confiscation policies. Secondary analyses of the effects of these laws on other crimes found uncertain effects on stranger homicides, rapes, robberies, and motor vehicle thefts but significant effects suggesting that confiscation laws may increase assaults and burglaries. The authors note that the effects of confiscation laws will depend, to a large extent, on how rigorously they are implemented and enforced and suggest that future research should examine associations between crime reduction and implementation differences.

Zeoli and Webster (2010) examined the effects of policies designed to restrict access to weapons by those with domestic violence–related restraining orders or those convicted of misdemeanors. Among the policies they examined were state laws allowing police to confiscate firearms from a domestic violence incident (they simultaneously examined state laws that allow police to make warrantless arrests for domestic violence restraining order violations and that mandate arrest for domestic violence restraining order violations). They analyzed data from 46 cities between 1979 and 2003 and found no evidence that laws that allow police to confiscate firearms from a domestic violence incident affected rates of intimate partner homicide. However, they

---

[3] Illinois, Iowa, Minnesota, and Tennessee. See 730 Ill. Comp. Stat. 5/5-6-3; Iowa Code Ann. § 724.26 (court shall order the convicted individual to sell or transfer firearms; if not possible, court shall store firearms until a qualified transferee is identified or possession allowed); Minn. Stat. Ann. § 2242 (court shall order the convicted individual to transfer firearms to the state, a licensed dealer, or an eligible third party within three days; the transfer may be temporary or permanent); Tenn. Code Ann. § 39-13-111.

did find a significant reduction in intimate partner homicides from laws that restrict access to firearms for domestic violence–related restraining orders and laws that allow police to arrest restraining order violators without a warrant.

A final study also worth noting examined the 1996 Lautenberg Amendment, which was designed to extend prohibited-possessor status to those convicted of misdemeanor domestic violence offenses. The law also stipulated a mechanism for checking the firearm ownership of newly prohibited possessors and requiring that they surrender all firearms. Raissian (2016) identified the effect of the federal law by exploiting states' variation in assault statues, which, because of imprecise language in the Lautenberg Amendment, affected whether the new federal prohibitions applied to domestic violence misdemeanants. In 2009, the U.S. Supreme Court corrected the ambiguity in *United States v. Hayes*. Raissian (2016) found that intimate partner homicides and other family homicides declined when domestic violence misdemeanants were prohibited from possessing firearms and required to surrender any in their possession. However, because this study evaluates a policy change that simultaneously required firearm surrender and expanded the prohibited class, it does not isolate the specific effect of surrender, so we do not include this study as evidence for the effect of surrender per se.

Figure 11.1 displays the incidence rate ratios (IRRs) and confidence intervals (CIs) associated with the firearm-surrender laws examined in these studies.

**Figure 11.1**
**Incidence Rate Ratios Associated with the Effect of Firearm-Surrender Laws on Violent Crime**

| Study, by Policy | Outcome Measure | Effect Size (IRR) [95% CI] |
|---|---|---|
| **State confiscation law** | **Intimate partner homicide (IPH)** | |
| Vigdor & Mercy (2006) | Total IPH | 0.95 [0.87, 1.04] |
| Vigdor & Mercy (2006) | Firearm IPH | 0.94 [0.83, 1.07] |
| Vigdor & Mercy (2006) | Female IPH | 0.98 [0.89, 1.09] |
| Vigdor & Mercy (2006) | Female firearm IPH | 0.96 [0.82, 1.11] |
| Zeoli & Webster (2010) | Total IPH | 1.10 [0.92, 1.31] |
| Zeoli & Webster (2010) | Firearm IPH | 1.19 [0.97, 1.46] |
| Raissian (2016) | Total firearm IPH rate | 0.89 [0.78, 0.99] |
| Raissian (2016) | Female firearm IPH rate | 0.83 [0.72, 0.94] |
| Raissian (2016) | Male firearm IPH rate | 1.01 [0.85, 1.18] |

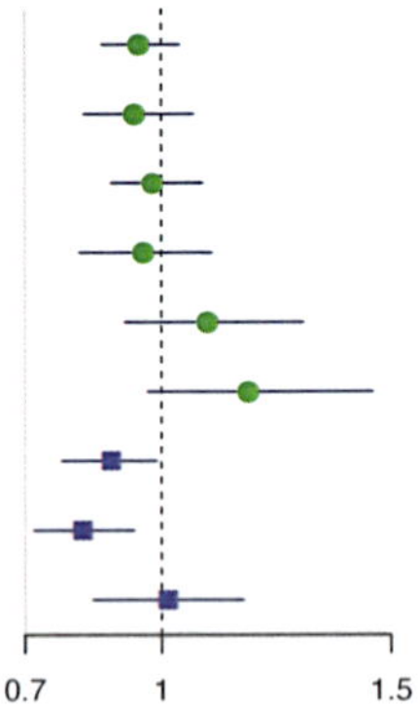


NOTE: IRR values marked with blue squares indicate that methodological concerns are discussed in the text. Green circles indicate that we identified no significant methodological concerns. See Appendix B for details. IPH = intimate partner homicide.

### Conclusions

We identified two qualifying studies that examined the effect on any violent crimes of laws requiring prohibited possessors to surrender firearms. Vigdor and Mercy (2006) found such laws to have uncertain effects on total intimate partner homicides committed with firearms. Similarly, they found only uncertain effects of these laws on intimate partner homicides committed by any means, as well as uncertain effects for firearm intimate partner homicides of women. Zeoli and Webster (2010) also found the effects of surrender laws on intimate partner homicides and firearm intimate partner homicides to be uncertain. Additional analyses by Vigdor and Mercy (2006) that focused on other types of violent crime found significant effects of confiscation laws indicating that they increase assaults and burglaries, but they found uncertain effects of these laws on stranger homicides, rapes, and robberies.

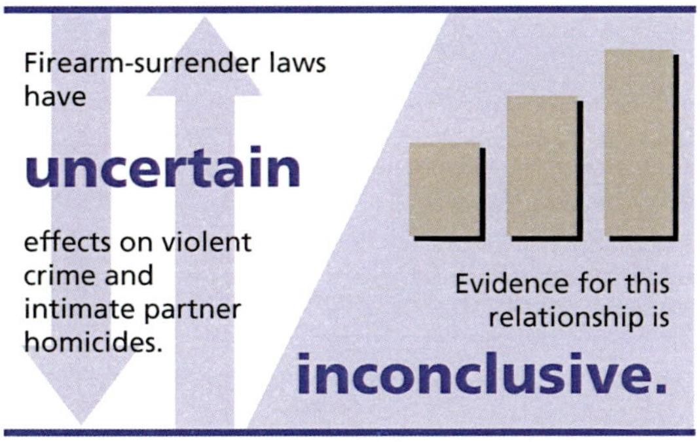


Based on the results of these studies, we find *inconclusive evidence for how laws requiring prohibited possessors to surrender firearms affect violent crime generally and intimate partner homicides in particular.*

## Outcomes Without Studies Examining the Effects of Firearm-Surrender Laws

Neither NRC (2004) nor Hahn et al. (2005) identified any research examining the relationship between the surrender of firearms by prohibited possessors and the following outcomes, and we identified no such studies that met our inclusion criteria:

- suicide
- unintentional injuries and deaths
- mass shootings
- officer-involved shootings
- defensive gun use
- hunting and recreation
- gun industry.

## Chapter Eleven References

California Department of Justice, "General Notice of Firearm Prohibition and Power of Attorney for Firearms Relinquishment, Sale, or Transfer for Storage," BOF 110, October 2015. As of June 29, 2017:
https://www.oag.ca.gov/sites/all/files/agweb/pdfs/firearms/forms/poafirearmsdecl.pdf

Giffords Law Center to Prevent Gun Violence, "Categories of Prohibited People," web page, undated-b. As of October 18, 2017:
http://lawcenter.giffords.org/gun-laws/policy-areas/who-can-have-a-gun/categories-of-prohibited-people/

Hahn, Robert A., Oleg Bilukha, Alex Crosby, Mindy T. Fullilove, Akiva Liberman, Eve Moscicki, Susan Snyder, Farris Tuma, and Peter A. Briss, "Firearms Laws and the Reduction of Violence: A Systematic Review," *American Journal of Preventive Medicine*, Vol. 28, No. 2, 2005, pp. 40–71.

National Research Council, *Firearms and Violence: A Critical Review*, Washington, D.C.: National Academies Press, 2004.

NRC—*See* National Research Council.

Raissian, Kerri M., "Hold Your Fire: Did the 1996 Federal Gun Control Act Expansion Reduce Domestic Homicides?" *Journal of Policy Analysis and Management*, Vol. 35, No. 1, Winter 2016, pp. 67–93.

United States Code, Title 18, Section 922, Unlawful Acts.

Vigdor, E. R., and J. A. Mercy, "Do Laws Restricting Access to Firearms by Domestic Violence Offenders Prevent Intimate Partner Homicide?" *Evaluation Review*, Vol. 30, 2006, pp. 313–346.

Zeoli, A. M., and D. W. Webster, "Effects of Domestic Violence Policies, Alcohol Taxes and Police Staffing Levels on Intimate Partner Homicide in Large U.S. Cities," *Injury Prevention*, Vol. 16, No. 2, 2010, pp. 90–95.

CHAPTER TWELVE

# Minimum Age Requirements

Under federal law, licensed dealers cannot sell or deliver handguns to individuals under age 21 or long guns to those under age 18. Unlicensed individuals cannot sell, transfer, or deliver handguns to individuals under age 18. With some exceptions, federal law prohibits individuals under age 18 from possessing handguns, but it does not place age restrictions on the possession of long guns (18 U.S.C. 922).

Laws requiring a minimum age for purchase aim to make it more difficult for underage individuals to acquire a handgun through formal channels, while laws requiring a minimum age of possession are intended to make it more difficult or risky for an underage individual to carry firearms in public. Thus, although the mechanisms by which these laws influence youth access differ, both are designed to limit the availability of firearms to young people—and therefore reduce the gun violence and unintentional shootings they commit.

Firearm homicides and violent crimes disproportionately involve individuals under age 21, both as perpetrators and as victims. Indeed, in 2012, arrest rates for violent crimes peaked at age 18 (Office of Juvenile Justice and Delinquency Prevention, 2016). Of the 7,152 firearm homicides committed in 2014 for which the age of the offender was known, 47.2 percent were perpetrated by individuals aged 12–24 (Puzzanchera, Chamberlin, and Kang, 2017), although this group represents only 17.7 percent of the general U.S. population (U.S. Census Bureau, 2017). By influencing the possession of guns among youth, minimum age laws could thus reduce rates of firearm crime perpetrated by juveniles. However, youth are similarly at high risk of victimization. Of all deaths among those aged 16–21, 16.5 percent are homicides, which is greater than the homicide rates for the next-highest risk ages (13.3 percent for those aged 22–27; 8.8 percent for those aged 28–33) (Centers for Disease Control and Prevention [CDC], 2017b). In theory, therefore, stricter age limits on purchasing or possessing a firearm could reduce the incidence of defensive gun use by youth and potentially increase perpetration of violence against younger populations if offenders believe that the likelihood of encountering armed resistance is lower (Marvell, 2001).

Conceptually, by restricting youth access, minimum age restrictions could also reduce rates of firearm suicide or unintentional shootings by the affected age group. Research suggests that the association between firearm availability and suicide is strongest among adolescents and young adults (Birckmayer and Hemenway, 2001; Miller and Hemenway, 1999). In 2015, there were 3,111 suicide deaths among individuals aged 16–21, 43.6 percent of which involved a firearm (calculated using data from CDC, 2015). Evidence indicates that 50 percent to 60 percent of all firearm suicides by youth under age 21 involve a handgun, suggesting that minimum age laws that cover all firearms may have larger effects on suicide rates compared with laws focused on handguns alone (Johnson et al., 2010; Wright, Wintemute, and Claire, 2008; Shah et al., 2000; Grossman, Reay, and Baker, 1999).

The effects of laws requiring a minimum purchase age will depend largely on how youth acquire firearms. Much of the existing evidence on sources of guns to youth comes from surveys of juvenile offenders or high-risk adolescents and suggests that purchases from retailers are relatively rare among adolescents involved with criminal activity. Among juveniles who have been incarcerated or arrested, surveys have found that youth offenders acquire their firearms through similar sources as adult offenders, with more than 80 percent citing a friend, a family member, or the black market as the means by which they acquired their weapon (Webster et al., 2002; LaFree and Birbeck, 1998). This finding indicates that minimum age laws may be effective at limiting youth access through legitimate retail sources. An early study of firearms used by students in school-associated firearm deaths (both suicide and homicide) between 1992 and 1999 similarly found that only 9.6 percent of the firearms used in homicide events and none of the firearms used in suicide events were purchased legally (CDC, 2001). Still, in a 1996 national survey of male high school students, 50 percent of respondents reported that they would have little or no trouble obtaining a gun (Sheley and Wright, 1998). In a 1996 national study of students in grades 8 through 12, 21 percent of respondents reported having easy access to guns at home, and the types of firearms available were evenly distributed among handguns, rifles, and shotguns (Ruback, Shaffer, and Clark, 2011).

The effects of laws requiring a minimum age of possession will depend on the expected costs youth perceive to be associated with violating such laws, which will likely be influenced by state legal penalties and the level of enforcement efforts devoted to enforcing the prohibition (Marvell, 2001). Semi-structured interviews with incarcerated adolescent males in 1998 found fear of arrest and incarceration as the most commonly reported reasons for choosing not to acquire or carry a gun (Freed et al., 2001). Still, in 2015, 5.3 percent of high school students reported carrying a gun (Kann et al., 2016). Given the relative importance of the home and family members as a source of guns to juveniles, the most-significant effects of minimum age of possession policies may occur if they create a disincentive for older individuals to keep guns at home or to allow guns in the home to be easily accessed (Marvell, 2001).

Much of the conversation about minimum age restrictions revolves around handguns rather than long guns. This is because handguns are more frequently used than long guns in firearm suicides and violent crime, so, in theory, raising the minimum age for such weapons could decrease violence without impacting lawful activities, such as hunting (Tritch, 2014). More-restrictive minimum age laws could plausibly impact the gun industry by reducing the size of the consumer population and decreasing the ownership and use of guns by youth for hunting or recreational purposes. Overall, hunting participation in the United States has declined dramatically over the past decades, and although data on youth recreational firearm use are limited (Vittes and Sorenson, 2005), estimates from 2006 showed 1.7 million youth hunters aged 6–15 (Families Afield, 2010). Further, the vast majority of adult hunters initiate hunting activities before age 20, and those who have not learned to hunt by age 20 have a very low likelihood of participating in hunting activities as an adult (Duda and Young, 1993). Should minimum age laws reduce initiation of firearm use for hunting or recreational purposes, there could be longer-term effects on these outcomes.

Data on suicides and self-inflicted nonfatal injury stratified by age are readily available; thus, analyses can directly test whether effects of minimum age laws on these outcomes are driven by the relevant age group affected by the policy. For outcomes of violent crime and non-self-inflicted injury, causal analyses could be improved with data that reported the age of the shooter. However, as most data sources report only the age of the victim,[1] none of the studies we identified that met our inclusion criteria for this policy used this type of data. Methodological approaches could also leverage state variation in the types of guns restricted under the minimum age laws for outcome data that have information on the type of firearm involved. For any analysis, estimates of causal effects would be strengthened with data showing how minimum age laws affected gun purchase or carrying behavior by youth of the affected age group. While some national surveys (e.g., the Youth Behavioral Risk Surveillance System, National Survey of Drug Use and Health, National Longitudinal Study of Adolescent to Adult Health) ask youth about gun ownership or carrying behaviors, their samples are often limited to high school students, focused on handguns, or available for a limited set of years.

## State Implementation of Minimum Age Requirements

States have adopted a range of minimum age requirements that are, in some cases, higher or lower than the federal minimums. For instance, nine states and the District of Columbia restrict all handgun sales to individuals aged 21 or older and long gun sales to individuals aged 18 or older. In effect, this raises the minimum age restrictions above those set by federal law in two ways: The age to purchase handguns through pri-

---

[1] Exceptions include the Federal Bureau of Investigation's Supplementary Homicide Reports, which contain age of victim and age of offender for murders when such information is known, and the National Violent Death Reporting System, which contains information on the age of the shooter for non-self-inflicted fatal injuries when such information is known for a subset of states.

vate sales is raised from 18 to 21, and a minimum age for private sales of long guns is set to 18.[2] Two states, Hawaii and Illinois, restrict sales for all firearms to those aged 21 or older.[3] This imposes more-restrictive age limits than federal law on all sales other than handgun sales by dealers. Other states set minimums below the federal limits. For instance, Vermont imposes a minimum age of 16 for all sales, and Maine imposes a minimum age of 18 for handgun sales and 16 for long gun sales.[4] In practice, these affect only long gun sales from nondealers, because minimum age requirements for all other sales would be governed by the more-restrictive federal laws.

As mentioned, federal law places no minimum on the age of possession of long guns (18 U.S.C. 922), but several states have imposed such minimums. For instance, 14 states restrict possession of long guns to those aged 18 or older,[5] and Illinois and the District of Columbia restrict long gun possession to those aged 21 or older.[6] The minimum age for possession of a long gun in Alaska, Minnesota, and New York is 16,[7] and it is 14 in Montana.[8]

## Effects on Suicide

### Research Synthesis Findings

In 2004, the National Research Council (NRC) identified four quasi-experimental studies of gun policy effects on suicide outcomes, none of which examined minimum age restrictions. Hahn et al. (2005) identified one cross-sectional study of the associa-

---

2 California, Connecticut, Delaware, Iowa, Maryland, Massachusetts, New Jersey, Ohio, Rhode Island, and the District of Columbia. See Calif. Penal Code § 27505; Conn. Gen. Stat. Ann. §§ 29-34, 29-37a; Del. Code tit. 24 § 901, 903, tit. 11 § 1445; Iowa Code Ann. § 724.22; Md. Code Ann., Pub. Safety §§ 5-101, 5-134; Mass. Gen. Laws Ch. 140 §§ 121, 130; N.J. Stat. Ann. § 2C:39-10; Ohio Rev. Code Ann. § 2923.21; R.I. Gen. Laws §§ 11-47-30, 11-47-35; D.C. Code Ann. §§ 7-2507.07, 22-4507.

3 Hawaii Rev. Stat. Ann. § 134-2; Ill. Comp. Stat. 65/3, 65/4. Although Hawaii's law is silent about sales, the state issues permits to acquire to those aged 21 or older, and permits are required for purchases. Illinois requires a firearm owner's identification card for transfer, and the card is issued only to those aged 21 or older. However, 720 Ill. Comp. Stat. 5/24-3.1 prohibits sales of handguns to those under age 18.

4 Vt. Stat. Ann. tit. 13, § 4007; Me. Rev. Stat. Ann. tit. 17-A §§ 554-A, 554-B.

5 Florida, Idaho, Indiana, Iowa, Michigan, Nevada, New Jersey, Oklahoma, Oregon, Pennsylvania, Rhode Island, Utah, Washington, and Wisconsin. See Fla. Stat. Ann. § 790.22; Idaho Code Ann. § 18-3302E; Ind. Ann. Code § 35-47-10-5; Iowa Code Ann. § 724.22; Mich. Comp. Laws Ann. § 750.234f; Nev. Rev. Stat. Ann. § 202.300; N.J. Stat Ann. § 2C:58-6.1; Okla. Stat. Ann. §§ 1272, 1273; Ore. Rev. Stat. Ann. § 166.250; Pa. Cons. Stat. § 6110.1; R.I. Gen. Laws Ann. § 11-47-33; Utah Code Ann. § 76-10-509; Wash. Rev. Code Ann. § 9.41.040; Wisc. Stat. § 948.60.

6 Ill. Comp. Stat. Ann. 65/4 (regulates the firearm owners identification card); D.C. Code Ann. § 7-2502.03.

7 Alaska Stat. § 11.61.220; Minn. Stat. § 97B.021 (but individuals aged 14 or 15 and with firearm safety certificates may possess long guns); N.Y. Penal Code § 265.05.

8 Mont. Code Ann. § 45-8-344.

tion between minor age and suicide (Kleck and Patterson, 1993), a study that does not meet our inclusion criteria. Since then, three longitudinal studies provided evidence on the impact of minimum age requirements on suicide.

Using data from 1976 to 2001, Webster et al. (2004) examined the effect of state-level changes in minimum purchase and possession age laws on suicide rates among those aged 14–17 and 18–20. The authors used negative binomial regression models that employed generalized estimating equations and that included state fixed effects and other covariates. They found uncertain effects of the laws on suicide rates among those aged 14–17. However, states that increased the minimum purchase age to 21 saw a statistically significant decrease in firearm suicides among those aged 18–20, but the authors found uncertain effects of the laws on total or nonfirearm suicides. They found that the three states that increased the age of handgun possession to 21 experienced a statistically significant increase in total suicides among those aged 18–20, accounted for, in part, by a suggestive increase in firearm suicides in this group. The authors suggested that this result was weakly estimated, having been based on just three states, two of which implemented their laws in the final years of the study period, meaning there was little time over which to observe changes in state suicide rates attributable to the law. These limitations raise valid questions about whether the observed effects are attributable to raising the age of possession of handguns to 21 or to other factors affecting these states' suicide rates. Finally, the authors examined the effect of federal minimum age of possession and purchase of handguns among states that previously had lower minimum age laws compared with those for which the federal law did not raise the minimum ages. These analyses identified a suggestive increase in total suicides among those aged 14–17 from raising the federal minimum possession age but only uncertain effects for other outcomes associated with raising the minimum age to purchase handguns among this age group.

Gius (2015b) examined how both state-specific laws for minimum age for firearm possession and federal laws for minimum age for handgun possession implemented in 1994 affected suicides by those aged 19 or younger. This analysis controlled for several state-level sociodemographic characteristics and enactment of child-access prevention laws between 1981 and 2010. Its results suggest that state-level minimum age restrictions had uncertain effects on suicide. The weighted least-squares statistical model is not likely to produce reliable estimates for the nonlinear outcome of suicide rates, meaning the model's estimates and their standard errors may be unreliable (Freedman, 2006). The study's estimate for the federal minimum age law for handgun possession passed in 1994 did not meet our inclusion criteria, because, as specified in this model, there was no comparison group that did not get the identical intervention in 1994.

Rosengart et al. (2005) used a similar approach to model the effects of state laws between 1979 and 1998, when "seven states adopted and two states repealed a law restricting the minimum age for the *private purchase* of a handgun to 21 years, [and] five states adopted laws restricting the minimum age for the *private possession* of a handgun to 21 years" (emphasis added). In these models controlling for state fixed effects, time trends, state-level variation in poverty and demographic factors, and two other firearm laws[9] (but not the federal 1994 law imposing a minimum age requirement for handgun possession), they found mostly uncertain effects of these laws on the firearm suicide rate. However, they did find suggestive effects consistent with minimum possession age laws increasing the total suicide rate among those under age 20, as well as minimum purchase age laws increasing total suicides among those aged 20 or older. These models had limited information to use in identifying causal effects of these laws because relatively few states changed one or both laws over the study period; in addition, every state but one that raised its minimum age for possession did so the same year it implemented a minimum purchase law, making the effects of these laws confounded. Moreover, the statistical model had an unfavorable ratio of covariates to observations (less than one to eight), meaning the model may have been overfit, resulting in estimates and confidence intervals (CIs) that are unreliable indicators of the true causal effects of the laws.

Figure 12.1 displays the incidence rate ratios (IRRs) and CIs associated with the minimum age requirements examined in these studies. We do not present estimates of the federal minimum possession age from Gius (2015b) because they do not meet our criteria for inclusion. Estimates of the federal minimum purchase age and minimum possession age laws from Webster et al. (2004) are included because, although details of the model are not specified, it appears to satisfy our inclusion criteria based on the authors' following statement: "The federal law establishing a minimum legal age for handgun purchase and possession was assumed to affect only states that, prior to the federal law, either had no minimum-age law of this type or had a law that established a minimum legal age younger than 18 years."

**Conclusions**

We identified two qualifying studies that examined how suicide rates were affected by laws requiring a minimum purchase age and three that examined how they were affected by laws requiring a minimum possession age.

*Minimum age requirements for purchasing a firearm.* Webster et al. (2004) found uncertain effects for minimum purchase age laws (with restrictions from ages 16 to 21) on suicides among those aged 14–17 and those 18–20. They also found uncertain effects for firearm suicides among the younger age group but a significant effect consistent with these laws reducing firearm suicides among the older group. When re-estimating these effects only for states that set age 21 as the minimum for purchasing a firearm, the authors again found uncertain effects on total suicide rates for the older

[9] The other laws modeled simultaneously were "one-gun-a-month" laws; "shall-issue" laws, otherwise known as right-to-carry laws, which guarantee the right to a concealed-carry permit for all citizens who are not prohibited from possessing a firearm (see Chapter Thirteen); and "junk-gun" laws, which ban the sale of certain cheaply constructed handguns.

**Figure 12.1**
**Incidence Rate Ratios Associated with the Effect of Minimum Age Requirements on Suicide**

| Study, by Policy | Outcome Measure | Effect Size (IRR) [95% CI] |
|---|---|---|
| **State minimum purchase age** | **Suicide** | |
| Webster et al. (2004) | Total, aged 14–17 | 1.04 [0.90, 1.21] |
| Webster et al. (2004) | Total, aged 18–20 | 0.97 [0.91, 1.05] |
| Webster et al. (2004) | Firearm, aged 14–17 | 1.04 [0.87, 1.16] |
| Webster et al. (2004) | Firearm, aged 18–20 | 0.91 [0.83, 1.00] |
| Webster et al. (2004) | Nonfirearm, aged 14–17 | 1.05 [0.85, 1.31] |
| Webster et al. (2004) | Nonfirearm, aged 18–20 | 1.05 [0.94, 1.17] |
| **State minimum purchase age of 21** | | |
| Rosengart et al. (2005) | Total | 1.02 [0.98, 1.07] |
| Rosengart et al. (2005) | Total, aged 0–19 | 1.10 [0.94, 1.29] |
| Rosengart et al. (2005) | Total, aged 20+ | 1.04 [0.99, 1.10] |
| Rosengart et al. (2005) | Firearm | 1.00 [0.94, 1.06] |
| Rosengart et al. (2005) | Firearm, aged 0–19 | 0.94 [0.80, 1.06] |
| Rosengart et al. (2005) | Firearm, aged 20+ | 1.02 [0.96, 1.08] |
| **State minimum possession age** | | |
| Webster et al. (2004) | Total, aged 14–17 | 0.97 [0.90, 1.05] |
| Webster et al. (2004) | Total, aged 18–20 | 1.13 [1.01, 1.27] |
| Webster et al. (2004) | Firearm, aged 14–17 | 1.02 [0.92, 1.12] |
| Webster et al. (2004) | Firearm, aged 18–20 | 1.14 [0.98, 1.34] |
| Webster et al. (2004) | Nonfirearm, aged 14–17 | 0.93 [0.82, 1.05] |
| Webster et al. (2004) | Nonfirearm, aged 18–20 | 1.07 [0.90, 1.27] |
| Gius (2015b) | Firearm death, aged 0–19 | 0.98 [0.93, 1.02] |
| **State minimum possession age of 21** | | |
| Rosengart et al. (2005) | Total | 1.03 [0.96, 1.11] |
| Rosengart et al. (2005) | Total, aged 0–19 | 1.15 [0.93, 1.42] |
| Rosengart et al. (2005) | Total, aged 20+ | 1.04 [0.95, 1.13] |
| Rosengart et al. (2005) | Firearm | 0.99 [0.88, 1.13] |
| Rosengart et al. (2005) | Firearm, aged 0–19 | 0.93 [0.77, 1.12] |
| Rosengart et al. (2005) | Firearm, aged 20+ | 0.99 [0.88, 1.13] |
| **Federal minimum purchase age** | | |
| Webster et al. (2004) | Total, aged 14–17 | 1.02 [0.91, 1.14] |
| Webster et al. (2004) | Firearm, aged 14–17 | 1.00 [0.87, 1.16] |
| Webster et al. (2004) | Nonfirearm, aged 14–17 | 1.08 [0.91, 1.28] |
| **Federal minimum possession age** | | |
| Webster et al. (2004) | Total, aged 14–17 | 0.98 [0.90, 1.08] |
| Webster et al. (2004) | Firearm, aged 14–17 | 0.99 [0.89, 1.09] |
| Webster et al. (2004) | Nonfirearm, aged 14–17 | 1.12 [0.99, 1.26] |

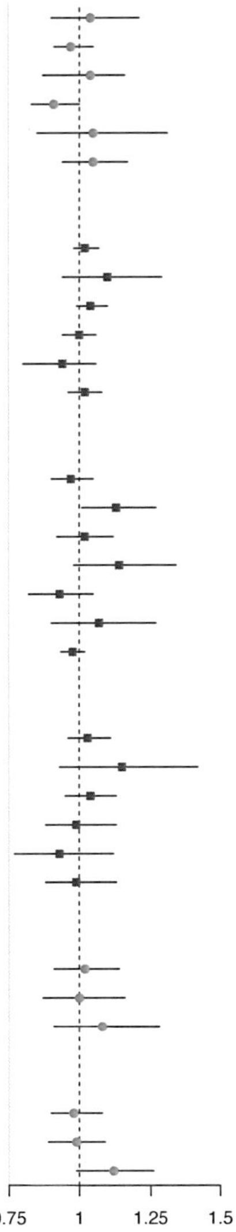


NOTE: IRR values marked with blue squares indicate that methodological concerns are discussed in the text. Green circles indicate that we identified no significant methodological concerns. See Appendix B for details.

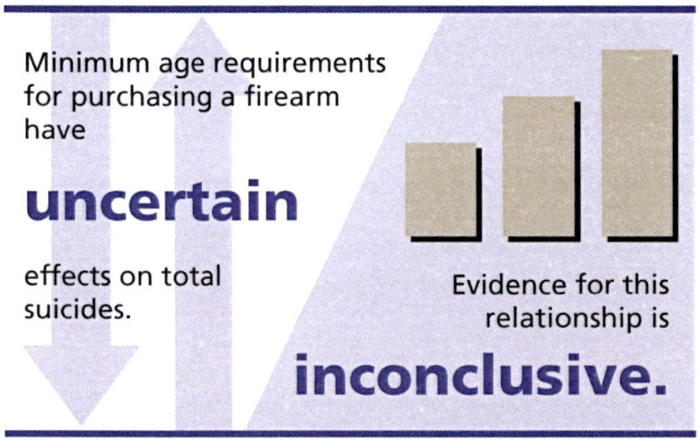

age group and a significant effect indicating such laws reduce firearm suicides among those aged 18–20. Using overlapping, but shorter, time-series data, Rosengart et al. (2005) found the effects of laws requiring a minimum age of 21 to purchase to have uncertain effects on suicides and firearm suicides for all age groups, except for a suggestive effect consistent with these laws increasing total suicides among adults aged 20 or older.

Based on these findings and an assessment of the relative strengths of these studies, we find *inconclusive evidence for how minimum age requirements for purchasing a firearm affect total suicides*. Studies of the effect of laws setting 21 as the minimum age of firearm purchase provide *limited evidence that such laws may reduce firearm suicides among some people aged 20 or younger.*

*Minimum age requirements for possessing a firearm*. Webster et al. (2004) found uncertain effects of minimum possession age laws (with restrictions from ages 14 to 21) on suicides and firearm suicides among those aged 14–17. However, they found that these laws significantly increase suicide rates among those aged 18–20 and a suggestive effect consistent with increases in firearm suicide rates among this group. For laws requiring a minimum handgun possession age of 21, Rosengart et al. (2005) found uncertain effects on suicides overall and among those aged 20 or older, as well as a suggestive effect consistent with these laws increasing suicides among those under age 20. All effects of these laws on firearm suicides, however, were uncertain. Gius (2015b) found only uncertain effects of state minimum age of possession laws on firearm suicides among those aged 19 or younger.

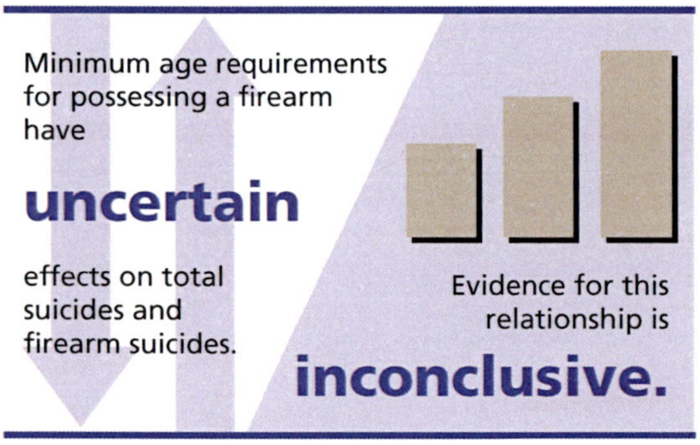


Based on these findings and an assessment of study strengths, we find *inconclusive evidence for how minimum age requirements for possessing a firearm affect suicides and firearm suicides.*

## Effects on Violent Crime

### Research Synthesis Findings

NRC (2004) did not review evidence on the effects of minimum age requirements, and Hahn et al. (2005) identified no research on this topic meeting our inclusion criteria. We identified two studies since 2003 that met our criteria. Rosengart et al. (2005) analyzed state-level data from 1979 to 1998 and examined the effects on violent crime of four types of state laws:

1. restricting handgun purchase to those aged 21 or older
2. restricting private handgun possession to those aged 21 or older
3. limiting the frequency of gun purchases to one gun per 30 days
4. prohibiting the sale of "junk" (cheaply constructed) guns.

The authors controlled for whether a state had a shall-issue (otherwise known as right-to-carry) provision; these results are described in more detail in Chapter Thirteen. The authors found uncertain effects of both types of minimum age laws on total homicide and firearm homicide rates. These models had limited information to use in identifying causal effects of these laws because relatively few states changed one or both laws over the study period; in addition, every state but one that raised its minimum age for possession did so the same year it implemented a minimum purchase age law, making the effects of these laws confounded. Moreover, the statistical model had an unfavorable ratio of covariates to observations (less than one to eight), meaning the model may have been overfit, resulting in estimates and CIs that are unreliable indicators of the true causal effects of the laws.

Rudolph et al. (2015) found a significant effect for a decrease in firearm homicides (and an uncertain effect for nonfirearm homicides) associated with the implementation of a law in Connecticut that established a requirement to have a permit to purchase a firearm and increased the minimum age of handgun purchase from age 18 to age 21. The firearm homicide rate after passage of both provisions was found to be 63 percent of what would have been expected without them. However, because the law included both policies simultaneously, the effect attributable specifically to the minimum age law cannot be identified. In addition, because only one state in the analysis experienced the law change, the effects of the law are not well identified. The observed reduction in firearm homicides could be due to the law or to other events occurring in Connecticut around the same time the law passed.

Figure 12.2 displays the IRRs and CIs associated with the minimum age requirements examined in these studies.

**Figure 12.2**
**Incidence Rate Ratios Associated with the Effect of Minimum Age Requirements on Violent Crime**

| Study, by Policy | Outcome Measure | Effect Size (IRR) [95% CI] |
|---|---|---|
| **State minimum purchase age of 21** | **Homicide** | |
| Rosengart et al. (2005) | Total | 1.00 [0.94, 1.05] |
| Rosengart et al. (2005) | Total, aged 0–19 | 0.92 [0.81, 1.05] |
| Rosengart et al. (2005) | Total, aged 20+ | 1.01 [0.95, 1.06] |
| Rosengart et al. (2005) | Firearm | 0.98 [0.91, 1.06] |
| Rosengart et al. (2005) | Firearm, aged 0–19 | 0.92 [0.80, 1.06] |
| Rosengart et al. (2005) | Firearm, aged 20+ | 0.99 [0.93, 1.06] |
| **State minimum possession age of 21** | | |
| Rosengart et al. (2005) | Total | 1.02 [0.89, 1.18] |
| Rosengart et al. (2005) | Total, aged 0–19 | 0.98 [0.79, 1.20] |
| Rosengart et al. (2005) | Total, aged 20+ | 1.03 [0.88, 1.20] |
| Rosengart et al. (2005) | Firearm | 1.06 [0.88, 1.27] |
| Rosengart et al. (2005) | Firearm, aged 0–19 | 0.91 [0.72, 1.15] |
| Rosengart et al. (2005) | Firearm, aged 20+ | 1.08 [0.89, 1.31] |
| **Permit to purchase + state minimum purchase age of 21** | | |
| Rudolph et al. (2015) | Firearm | 0.60 [0.37, 0.97] |

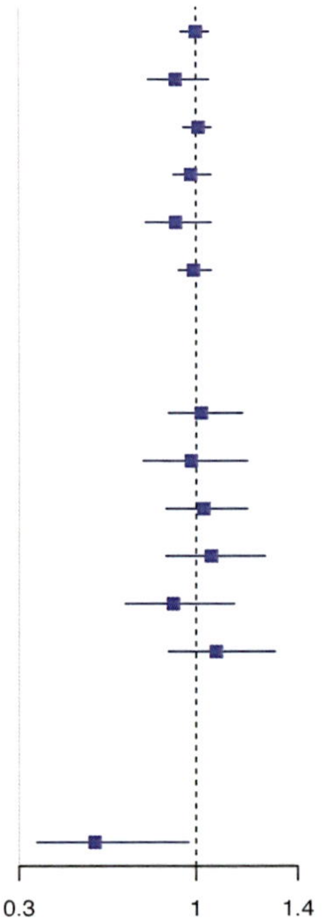


NOTE: IRR values marked with blue squares indicate that methodological concerns are discussed in the text. See Appendix B for details.

## Conclusions

We identified two qualifying studies that examined the effect of minimum age requirements for purchasing or possessing a firearm on total or firearm homicide rates.

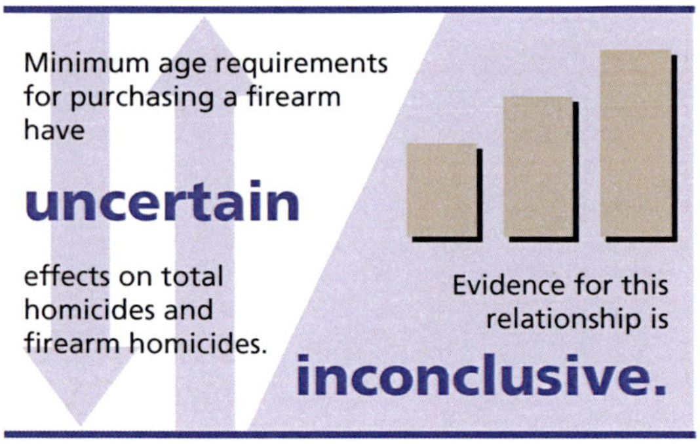


*Minimum age requirements for purchasing a firearm.* Rosengart et al. (2005) found uncertain effects of laws making 21 the minimum age to purchase handguns on homicide rates and firearm homicide rates among all age groups. Rudolph et al. (2015) reported a significant effect consistent with minimum age requirements reducing firearm homicide rates, but they could not attribute this effect solely to a minimum purchase age policy because a permit-to-purchase provision was passed concurrently in the one state evaluated. On the basis of these results, and in consideration of the relative strengths of these studies, we find *inconclusive evidence for how minimum age requirements for purchasing a firearm affect total and firearm homicides.*

*Minimum age requirements for possessing a firearm.* Estimates by Rosengart et al. (2005) for the effect of laws making 21 the minimum age for possession of handguns on total and firearm homicides were uncertain for all age groups examined. Therefore, we find *inconclusive evidence for how minimum age requirements for possessing a firearm affect total and firearm homicides.*

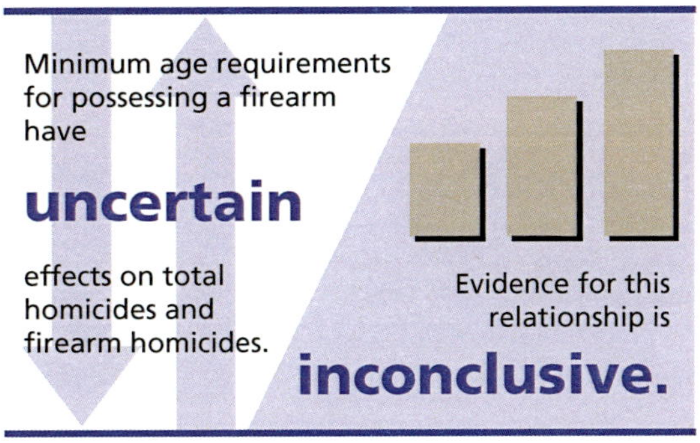


## Effects on Unintentional Injuries and Deaths

### Research Synthesis Findings

Neither NRC (2004) nor Hahn et al. (2005) identified any research examining the effects of minimum age requirements on unintentional injuries and deaths. One longitudinal study since then examined this relationship. Using data from 1981 to 2010, Gius (2015b) examined the effect of the 1994 federal law establishing a minimum age for handgun possession, as well as other state-specific minimum age requirements for handguns. This model controlled for time and state fixed effects, state-level sociodemographic characteristics, and state-level child-access prevention laws. The authors found that state-level minimum age requirements had uncertain effects on unintentional deaths. The weighted least-squares statistical model used in this study may not have been appropriate for the rate outcome, with many values close to zero in state-year observations. The model's lower bound at zero may result in violations of its assumptions and can yield biased and incorrect parameter estimates and CIs.

Figure 12.3 displays the IRR and CI associated with the minimum age requirements examined in Gius (2015b). The analysis of the federal minimum age of possession law in this study did not meet our inclusion criteria, because, as specified in this model, it appeared that there was no comparison group that did not get the identical intervention in 1994. Therefore, this effect is not included in Figure 12.3.

**Figure 12.3**
**Incidence Rate Ratios Associated with the Effect of Minimum Age Requirements on Unintentional Injuries and Deaths**

| Study, by Policy | Outcome Measure | Effect Size (IRR) [95% CI] |
|---|---|---|
| **State minimum possession age** | **Unintentional injuries** | |
| Gius (2015b) | Firearm death, aged 0–19 | 0.93 [0.84, 1.02] |

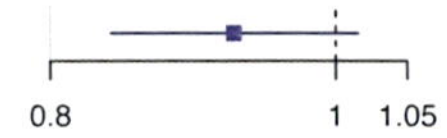


NOTE: IRR values marked with blue squares indicate that methodological concerns are discussed in the text. See Appendix B for details.

### Conclusions

We identified one qualifying study examining the effect of laws requiring either minimum age to purchase or minimum age to possess a firearm. Gius (2015b) found a suggestive effect consistent with minimum possession age laws decreasing unintentional firearm deaths among those aged 19 or younger. Therefore, we conclude that *there is inconclusive evidence that minimum age requirements for possessing a firearm may reduce unintentional firearm deaths among those aged 19 or younger.*

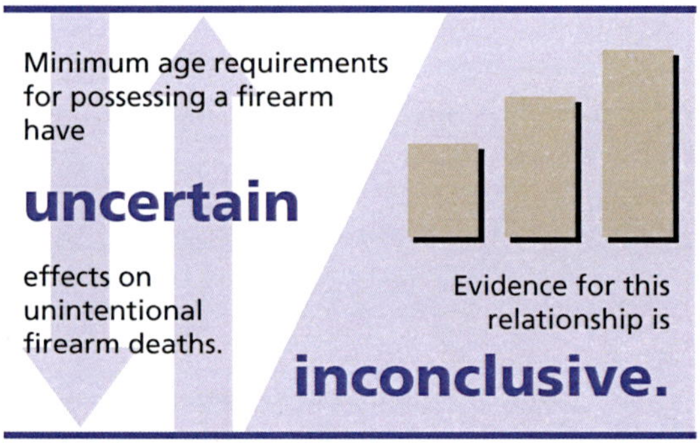


## Effects on Mass Shootings

### Research Synthesis Findings

NRC (2004) did not identify any research examining the effects of minimum age requirements on mass shootings. Hahn et al. (2005) identified one study, but it did not satisfy our inclusion criteria. Our own search yielded one study. Using a two-way fixed-effects linear probability model, Luca, Deepak, and Poliquin (2016) estimated the effects of minimum age requirements on a binary indicator for whether a mass shooting occurred in a given state-year. The authors included two measures of minimum age requirements: (1) an indicator variable for whether laws prevent vendors from selling handguns to those under age 18 or prevent those under age 18 from purchasing handguns and (2) an analogous indicator variable for laws that set the minimum age at 21. The authors' analysis covered 1989–2014 and included controls for time-invariant state characteristics, national trends, and a host of other state-level gun policies, as well as time-varying state-level demographic, socioeconomic, and political characteristics. They found uncertain effects of laws setting 18 as the minimum age of purchase on the probability of a mass shooting event occurring, but they found a suggestive effect consistent with laws setting 21 as the minimum age of purchase reducing the likelihood of a mass shooting occurrence. However, it should be noted that assessing the effects of gun policies on mass shootings was not the primary focus of Luca, Deepak, and Poliquin (2016), and the authors intended the estimates to serve solely as a robustness check for their main specification (the effects of mass shootings on gun policy). Although the paper provided limited information to use in evaluating the reported statistical models (e.g., on how these policies were coded), it is clear that the analysis used a linear model to predict a dichotomous outcome. Therefore, model assumptions were violated, making model estimates and CIs unreliable.

Figure 12.4 displays the IRRs and CIs associated with the minimum age requirements examined in Luca, Deepak, and Poliquin (2016).

**Figure 12.4**
**Incidence Rate Ratios Associated with the Effect of Minimum Age Requirements on Mass Shootings**

| Study, by Policy | Outcome Measure | Effect Size (IRR) [95% CI] |
|---|---|---|
| **State minimum purchase age of 18** | **Mass shooting** | |
| Luca, Deepak, & Poliquin (2016) | State-year indicator (no political controls) | 1.06 [0.65, 1.47] |
| Luca, Deepak, & Poliquin (2016) | State-year indicator (political controls) | 1.08 [0.66, 1.51] |
| **State minimum purchase age of 21** | | |
| Luca, Deepak, & Poliquin (2016) | State-year indicator (no political controls) | 0.51 [0.00, 1.34] |
| Luca, Deepak, & Poliquin (2016) | State-year indicator (political controls) | 0.38 [0.00, 1.21] |

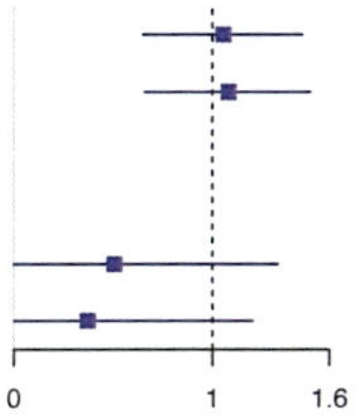


NOTE: IRR values marked with blue squares indicate that methodological concerns are discussed in the text. See Appendix B for details.

## Conclusions

We identified one qualifying study examining how minimum age requirements for purchasing a firearm affect the incidence of mass shootings. Luca, Deepak, and Poliquin (2016) found that laws setting age 18 as the minimum age to purchase a firearm had uncertain effects on mass shooting incidence, but they found a suggestive effect consistent with such laws reducing the incidence of mass shootings when the minimum purchase age is 21. On the basis of this study, *we find inconclusive evidence for how minimum age requirements for purchasing a firearm affect mass shootings.*

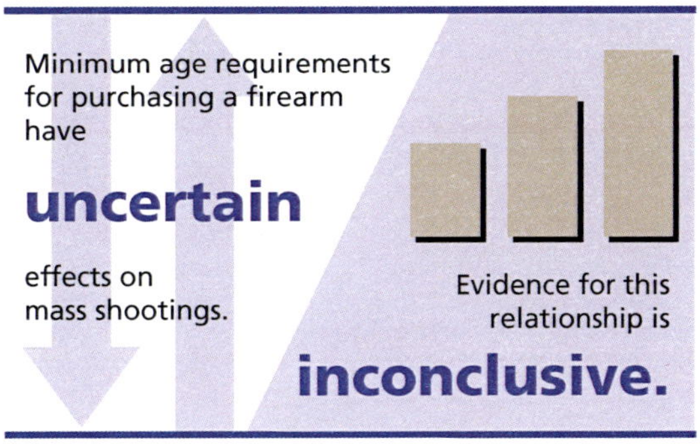

## Outcomes Without Studies Examining the Effects of Minimum Age Requirements

Neither NRC (2004) nor Hahn et al. (2005) identified any research examining the effects of minimum age requirements on the following outcomes, and we identified no such studies that met our inclusion criteria:

- officer-involved shootings
- defensive gun use
- hunting and recreation
- gun industry.

## Chapter Twelve References


Birckmayer, J., and D. Hemenway, "Suicide and Firearm Prevalence: Are Youth Disproportionately Affected?" *Suicide and Life-Threatening Behavior*, Vol. 31, No. 3, 2001, pp. 303–310.

CDC—*See* Centers for Disease Control and Prevention.

Centers for Disease Control and Prevention, "Source of Firearms Used by Students in School-Associated Violent Deaths—United States, 1992–1999," *Morbidity and Mortality Weekly Report*, Vol. 50, No. 31, 2001, pp. 657–660.

———, "Fatal Injury Reports, National and Regional, 1999–2015," WISQARS database, Atlanta, Ga., June 24, 2015. As of March 23, 2017:
https://webappa.cdc.gov/sasweb/ncipc/mortrate10_us.html

———, "Leading Causes of Death Reports, National and Regional, 1999–2015," WISQARS database, Atlanta, Ga., 2017b. As of May 10, 2017:
https://webappa.cdc.gov/sasweb/ncipc/leadcaus10_us.html

Duda, M. D., and K. C. Young, *Factors Related to Hunting and Fishing Participation in the United States*, Harrisonburg, Va.: Responsive Management, report for the U.S. Fish and Wildlife Service, Grant # 14-48-0009-92-1252, 1993.

Families Afield, *An Initiative for the Future of Hunting*, 2010. As of March 23, 2017:
http://www.familiesafield.org/pdf/FamiliesAfield_Report.pdf

Freed, L. H., D. W. Webster, J. J. Longwell, J. Carrese, and M. H. Wilson, "Factors Preventing Gun Acquisition and Carrying Among Incarcerated Adolescent Males," *JAMA Pediatrics*, Vol. 155, 2001, pp. 335–341.

Freedman, David A., "On the So-Called 'Huber Sandwich Estimator' and 'Robust Standard Errors,'" *American Statistician*, Vol. 60, No. 4, 2006, pp. 299–302.

Gius, Mark, "The Impact of Minimum Age and Child Access Prevention Laws on Firearm-Related Youth Suicides and Unintentional Deaths," *Social Science Journal*, Vol. 52, No. 2, 2015b, pp. 168–175.

Grossman, D. C., D. T. Reay, and S. A. Baker, "Self-Inflicted and Unintentional Firearm Injuries Among Children and Adolescents," *JAMA Pediatrics*, Vol. 153, No. 8, 1999, pp. 875–878.

Hahn, Robert A., Oleg Bilukha, Alex Crosby, Mindy T. Fullilove, Akiva Liberman, Eve Moscicki, Susan Snyder, Farris Tuma, and Peter A. Briss, "Firearms Laws and the Reduction of Violence: A Systematic Review," *American Journal of Preventive Medicine*, Vol. 28, No. 2, 2005, pp. 40–71.

Johnson, R. M., C. Barber, D. Azrael, D. E. Clark, and D. Hemenway, "Who Are the Owners of Firearms Used in Adolescent Suicides?" *Suicide and Life-Threatening Behavior*, Vol. 40, No. 6, 2010, pp. 609–611.

Kann, L., T. McManus, W. A. Harris, S. L. Shanklin, K. H. Flint, J. Hawkins, B. Queen, R. Lowry, E. O. Olsen, D. Chyen, L. Whittle, J. Thornton, C. Lim, Y. Yamakawa, N. Brener, and S. Zaza, "Youth Risk Behavior Surveillance—United States, 2015," *Morbidity and Mortality Weekly Report*, Vol. 65, No. 6, 2016, pp. 1–174.

Kleck, G., and E. B. Patterson, "The Impact of Gun Control and Gun Ownership Levels on Violence Rates," *Journal of Quantitative Criminology*, Vol. 9, No. 3, 1993, pp. 249–287.

LaFree, G., and C. Birbeck, *Controlling New Mexico Juveniles' Possession of Firearms*, Albuquerque, N.M.: New Mexico Criminal Justice Statistical Analysis Center, Working Paper 27, 1998. As of May 10, 2017:
http://nmsc.unm.edu/reports/1998/JuvFirearmPossession.pdf

Luca, Michael, Lahotra Deepak, and Christopher Poliquin, *The Impact of Mass Shootings on Gun Policy,* working paper, Boston, Mass.: Harvard Business School, 2016.

Marvell, T. B., "The Impact of Banning Juvenile Gun Possession," *Journal of Law and Economics,* Vol. 44, 2001, pp. 691–713.

Miller, M., and D. Hemenway, "The Relationship Between Firearms and Suicide: A Review of the Literature," *Aggression and Violent Behavior*, Vol. 4, No. 1, 1999, pp. 59–75.

National Research Council, *Firearms and Violence: A Critical Review*, Washington, D.C.: National Academies Press, 2004.

NRC—*See* National Research Council.

Office of Juvenile Justice and Delinquency Prevention, *OJJDP Statistical Briefing Book,* Washington, D.C.: U.S. Department of Justice, May 25, 2016. As of May 10, 2017:
https://www.ojjdp.gov/ojstatbb/

Puzzanchera, C., G. Chamberlin, and W. Kang, "Easy Access to the FBI's Supplementary Homicide Reports: 1980–2014," 2017. As of March 22, 2017:
http://www.ojjdp.gov/ojstatbb/ezashr/

Rosengart, M., P. Cummings, A. Nathens, P. Heagerty, R. Maier, and F. Rivara, "An Evaluation of State Firearm Regulations and Homicide and Suicide Death Rates," *Injury Prevention*, Vol. 11, No. 2, 2005, pp. 77–83.

Ruback, R. B., J. N. Shaffer, and V. A. Clark, "Easy Access to Firearms: Juveniles' Risks for Violent Offender and Violent Victimization," *Journal of Interpersonal Violence*, Vol. 26, No. 10, 2011, pp. 2111–2138.

Rudolph, K. E., E. A. Stuart, J. S. Vernick, and D. W. Webster, "Association Between Connecticut's Permit-to-Purchase Handgun Law and Homicides," *American Journal of Public Health*, Vol. 105, No. 8, 2015, pp. E49–E54.

Shah, S., R. E. Hoffman, L. Wake, and W. M. Marine, "Adolescent Suicide and Household Access to Firearms in Colorado: Results of a Case-Control Study," *Journal of Adolescent Health*, Vol. 26, No. 3, 2000, pp. 157–163.

Sheley, J. F., and J. D. Wright, *High School Youths, Weapons, and Violence: A National Survey*, Washington, D.C.: U.S. Department of Justice, National Institute of Justice, 1998.

Tritch, Teresa, "Keep Handguns Away from Teenagers," *New York Times*, May 30, 2014. As of June 29, 2017:
http://takingnote.blogs.nytimes.com/2014/05/30/keep-handguns-away-from-teenagers/

United States Code, Title 18, Section 922, Unlawful Acts.

U.S. Census Bureau, "U.S. and World Population Clock," 2017. As of March 22, 2017:
https://www.census.gov/popclock/

Vittes, K. A., and S. B. Sorenson, "Recreational Gun Use by California Adolescents," *Health Education and Behavior*, Vol. 32, No. 6, 2005, pp. 751–766.

Webster, D. W., L. H. Freed, S. Frattaroli, and M. H. Wilson, "How Delinquent Youths Acquire Guns: Initial Versus Most Recent Gun Acquisitions," *Journal of Urban Health*, Vol. 79, No. 1, 2002, pp. 60–69.

Webster, D. W., J. S. Vernick, A. M. Zeoli, and J. A. Manganello, "Association Between Youth-Focused Firearm Laws and Youth Suicides," *JAMA*, Vol. 292, No. 5, 2004, pp. 594–601.

Wright, M. A., G. J. Wintemute, and B. E. Claire, "Gun Suicide by Young People in California: Descriptive Epidemiology and Gun Ownership," *Journal of Adolescent Health*, Vol. 43, No. 6, 2008, pp. 619–622.

CHAPTER THIRTEEN

# Concealed-Carry Laws

Apart from specifying classes of people who are prohibited from possessing any type of firearm, federal law imposes no restrictions on who may carry a concealed weapon in public, although it specifically grants concealed-carry rights to active and retired law enforcement officers (18 U.S.C. 926). State laws typically specify who may carry concealed weapons and the procedures those people must follow when they wish to exercise this right.

Most states once prohibited the concealed carrying of guns in public, although none does so now. Over the past several decades, many states have relaxed restrictions on concealed handguns. Several states allow individuals to carry concealed weapons without a permit (referred to as *permitless carry*), but most require gun owners to obtain a permit to carry a concealed handgun. Some states have shifted from laws that restrict concealed-carry permits to those who can demonstrate a legitimate need to carry a weapon or that give law enforcement some discretion in issuing concealed-carry permits (referred to as *may-issue* laws) to laws that guarantee the right to a concealed-carry permit for all citizens who are not prohibited from possessing a handgun (referred to as *shall-issue* or *right-to-carry* laws). The key difference among these law categories is that permitless-carry laws do not require individuals to obtain a permit or license before they can carry a concealed weapon, whereas may-issue and shall-issue laws set forth conditions by which such permits may be granted.

There are several ways that concealed-carry laws could affect gun violence and considerable disagreement about which are most likely. Permitless-carry and shall-issue laws that make it easier for citizens to carry concealed weapons could increase the number of people carrying guns. The increased prevalence of concealed weapons could lead to increased crime and violence if disagreements, perceived threats, and conflicts are more likely to result in casualties when a handgun is readily available. Alternatively, concealed-carry laws could lead to reductions in the prevalence or severity of violent crime and mass shootings either because the prospect of encountering an armed victim serves as a deterrent or because victims will more frequently be able to use a gun to defend themselves (Fortunato, 2015).

Whether those who carry concealed weapons pose an elevated or reduced risk of crime or violence is the subject of debate (Violence Policy Center, 2017; Lott, Whitley, and Riley, 2016). A comparison of criminal conviction rates among holders and non-holders of concealed handgun licenses in Texas found that license holders were less likely to be convicted of crimes, but the license holders' convictions were significantly more likely to involve deadly conduct and intentional killings (Phillips et al., 2013). The likelihood of encountering an armed victim may further lead to increased gun violence by inducing more criminals to carry and use firearms. Alternatively, these laws may result in substitution by criminals to other types of crime, such as larceny, where the probability of encountering armed resistance is lower (Kovandzic and Marvell, 2003).

Each hypothesized effect of relaxed restrictions on concealed carrying produces an effect by increasing the proportion of the population or some subpopulation that is armed. However, data on the prevalence of concealed carrying are not generally available. Indeed, data on the number of persons with carry permits are not readily available for many states. One estimate suggests that the number of concealed-carry permit holders in the United States exceeded 14.5 million in 2016, with substantial variation across states depending on the permit fees in place, duration that the law has been in effect, and whether the law allows local authorities discretion in issuing permits (i.e., may issue versus shall issue) (Lott, Whitley, and Riley, 2016).

We identified only one study that analyzed how changes in the number of concealed-carry permits related to changes in various types of violent crime (Kovandzic and Marvell, 2003). The authors analyzed data from 58 Florida counties spanning 1980–2000, providing coverage of the period before and after the passage of Florida's shall-issue law in 1987. While this study did not analyze the effect of the shall-issue policy change, it did examine how changes in the number of concealed-carry permits over time and across counties corresponded with changes in various types of violent crime. The authors found uncertain effects of changes in per capita concealed-carry permit rates on violent crime.

There is likely to be little effect of concealed-carry laws on hunting or recreational gun use. However, shall-issue policies may encourage more individuals to obtain firearms, thereby increasing handgun sales (Steidley, 2016). To assess these or any other effects of concealed-carry laws, one would ideally like to know whether there are greater increases in gun ownership and carrying in states following passage of shall-issue or permitless-carry laws compared with states that have more-restrictive laws, but such data have not been collected systematically over time. The direct effects of increased concealed carrying by private citizens on suicides, unintentional injuries and deaths, and defensive gun use should be strongest for incidents involving handguns and that occur outside the home (where the laws apply). Similarly, for violent crime, one would expect concealed-carry laws to have greater effects (either negative or positive depending on the role of deterrence) on assaults or homicides occurring in public venues compared with those occurring within the home. Should the effects of concealed-carry laws be driven primarily by expanding the prevalence of gun ownership, then their effects could extend to both private and public areas for such outcomes as suicides, firearm homicides, and unintentional injuries and deaths.

## State Implementation of Concealed-Carry Laws

Prior to the Civil War, most states lacked legislation on the legality of carrying concealed weapons. Those states with laws prohibited the practice. Following World War II, most states adopted discretionary may-issue permit laws (Cramer and Kopel, 2005). In the 1980s, 1990s, and early 2000s, a majority of states transitioned to shall-issue laws (Grossman and Lee, 2008). Since 2003, a handful of states have eliminated the permit requirement altogether, allowing permitless carry.

As of the end of 2016, eight states allowed people to carry concealed weapons without first receiving a permit; that includes Vermont, which has never required a permit for concealed carry.[1] Mississippi allows concealed carry without a permit if the handgun is kept "in a sheath, belt holster or shoulder holster or in a purse, handbag, satchel, other similar bag or briefcase or fully enclosed case."[2] In addition, Missouri passed a permitless-carry law that went into effect on January 1, 2017.[3]

Thirty-two states have shall-issue laws, under which law enforcement agencies have no, or very limited, discretion to deny concealed-carry permits to citizens who are otherwise permitted to possess handguns.[4] Eight states have may-issue laws, in which law enforcement has significant discretionary authority to deny permits.[5]

Many states have reciprocity clauses in their concealed-carry permit laws, meaning that they recognize the concealed-carry permits issued by some but not necessarily all other states (United States Concealed Carry Association, 2013). Often, states honor

---

[1] Alaska, Arizona, Idaho, Kansas, Maine, Vermont, West Virginia, and Wyoming. See Alaska Stat. § 11.61.220; Ariz. Rev. Stat. § 13-3112; Idaho Code Ann. § 18-3302 (applies only outside cities); Kan. Stat. Ann §§ 21-6301, 21-6302; Me. Rev. Stat. Ann. § 2001-A; Vt. Stat. Ann. tit. 13, §§ 4004, 4016 (concerning the only two places one cannot carry a concealed weapon in Vermont); W. Va. Ann. Code § 61-7-3; Wyo. Stat. Ann. § 6-8-104.

[2] Miss. Ann. Code § 45-9-101.

[3] Mo. Senate Bill No. 656.

[4] Alabama, Arkansas, Colorado, Connecticut, Florida, Georgia, Illinois, Indiana, Iowa, Kentucky, Louisiana, Michigan, Minnesota, Montana, Nebraska, Nevada, New Hampshire, New Mexico, North Carolina, North Dakota, Ohio, Oklahoma, Oregon, Pennsylvania, South Carolina, South Dakota, Tennessee, Texas, Utah, Virginia, Washington, and Wisconsin. Ala. Code § 13A-11-75; Ark. Code Ann. § 5-73-309; Colo. Rev. Stat. Ann. § 18-12-203; Conn. Gen. Stat. § 29-28(b); Fla. Stat. Ann. § 790.06; Ga. Code Ann. § 16-11-129; 430 Ill. Comp. Stat. 66/4; Ind. Ann. Code §§ 35-47-2-1, 35-47-2-3; Iowa Code Ann. §§ 724.7, 724.11; Ky. Rev. Stat. Ann. § 237.110; La. Stat. Ann. § 1379.1.1; Mich. Comp. Laws Ann. § 28.425a; Minn. Stat. Ann. § 624.714; Mont. Code Ann. § 45-8-321; Neb. Rev. Stat. § 69-2430; Nev. Rev. Stat. Ann. § 202.3657; N.H. Rev. Stat. Ann. § 159:6; N.M. Stat. Ann. § 29-19-4; N.C. Gen. Stat. § 14-415.11; N.D. Cent. Code § 62.1-04-03; Ohio Rev. Code Ann. § 2923.125; Okla. Stat. Ann. § 1290.5; Ore. Rev. Stat. Ann. § 166.291; 18 Pa. Cons. Stat. § 6109; S.C. Code § 23-31-215; S.D. Codified Laws § 23-7-7; Tenn. Code Ann. § 39-17-1351; Tex. Code Ann. § 411.177; Utah Code Ann. § 53-5-704, Va. Ann. Code § 18.2-308.04; Wash. Rev. Code § 9.41.070; Wisc. Stat. Ann. § 175.60.

[5] California, Delaware, Hawaii, Maryland, Massachusetts, New Jersey, New York, and Rhode Island. See Calif. Penal Code § 26150; Del. Code Tit. 11 § 1441, 1442; Hawaii Rev. Stat. Ann. § 134-9; Md. Code Ann., Pub. Safety §§ 5-301–5-314; Mass. Gen. Laws Ch. 140, § 131; N.J. Stat. Ann. § 2C:58-4; N.Y. Penal Law § 400.00(2)(f); R.I. Gen. Laws § 11-47-11.

permits only from other states with laws similar to their own. There are some states, however, that recognize concealed-carry permits from states with less-restrictive laws. For instance, Delaware has a may-issue law but recognizes the concealed-carry permits from several states with shall-issue laws (USA Carry, 2017).

## Effects on Suicide

### Research Synthesis Findings

In 2004, the National Research Council (NRC) identified only four quasi-experimental studies examining the effects of gun policy on suicide outcomes, none of which examined the effect of concealed-carry laws. Hahn et al. (2005) identified two studies of the effects of shall-issue laws on suicide but concluded that the evidence those studies could provide was inconclusive. Since then, there have been no studies examining the effects of permitless-carry laws on suicide, and two quasi-experimental studies have examined the effect of concealed-carry laws on suicide. Using data from 1979 to 1998, Rosengart et al. (2005) modeled the effect of shall-issue laws on suicide mortality across states. In these models—which controlled for state fixed effects, time trends, state-level variation in poverty and demographic factors, and four other firearm laws—the authors found uncertain effects between shall-issue laws and either total suicide or firearm suicide rates (see Figure 13.1). Nevertheless, the statistical model had an unfavorable ratio of covariates to observations (less than one to eight), meaning the model may have been overfit, resulting in estimates and confidence intervals (CIs) that are unreliable indicators of the true causal effects of the laws.

DeSimone, Markowitz, and Xu (2013) also performed a fixed-effects analysis and examined the effects of shall-issue laws on self-inflicted nonfatal gun injuries using hospital discharge data from the National Inpatient Sample spanning 1988 to 2003. The authors did not find that shall-issue laws were significantly associated with self-inflicted firearm injuries for children under age 18 in the 11 states that were part of the sample, but they did find a statistically significant effect of these laws on self-inflicted firearm injuries among those aged 18 or older. Specifically, their estimate suggests that after implementation of the law, suicides were more than double what would have been expected without the law (see Figure 13.1), which would be extraordinary if true. However, the estimated effects of shall-issue laws in this study were based primarily on implementation in one state that changed its law during the study time frame (Arizona); thus, the study offers little evidence that the observed effects are due to the change in the law rather than to other factors affecting the state's suicide rate that occurred around the same time the law was changed. Moreover, as DeSimone, Markowitz, and Xu (2013) note, the data set on which their estimates are made is not strictly longitudinal, and it is not possible to determine the extent to which child-access prevention law effect estimates are estimated cross-sectionally or longitudinally.

Figure 13.1 displays the incidence rate ratios (IRRs) and CIs associated with the concealed-carry laws examined in these studies.

**Figure 13.1**
**Incidence Rate Ratios Associated with the Effect of Concealed-Carry Laws on Suicide**

| Study, by Policy | Outcome Measure | Effect Size (IRR) [95% CI] |
|---|---|---|
| **Shall-issue laws** | **Suicide** | |
| Rosengart et al. (2005) | Total | 0.98 [0.96, 1.01] |
| Rosengart et al. (2005) | Firearm | 1.00 [0.97, 1.02] |
| DeSimone, Markowitz, & Xu (2013) | Self-inflicted firearm injuries, aged 0–17 | 1.94 [0.45, 8.38] |
| DeSimone, Markowitz, & Xu (2013) | Self-inflicted firearm injuries, aged 18+ | 2.10 [1.53, 2.89] |

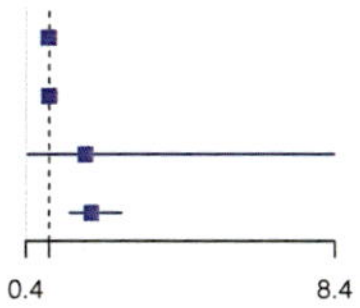


NOTE: IRR values marked with blue squares indicate that methodological concerns are discussed in the text. See Appendix B for details.

## Conclusions

We identified two qualifying studies examining the effects of shall-issue concealed-carry laws on suicide rates or firearm self-injury rates. Ronsegart et al. (2005) found uncertain effects of shall-issue laws on suicides and firearm suicides. DeSimone, Markowitz, and Xu (2013) found the effect of shall-issue laws on firearm self-injuries among those aged 17 or younger to be uncertain. Among all adults aged 18 or older, they found a significant effect indicating that shall-issue laws may increase firearm self-injury.

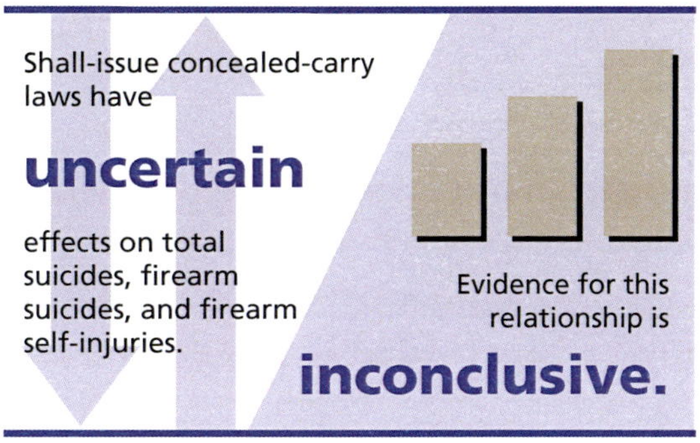


Based on these studies and an assessment of their relative strengths, *we find inconclusive evidence for the effect of shall-issue concealed-carry laws on total suicides, firearm suicides, and firearm self-injuries.*

## Effects on Violent Crime

### Research Synthesis Findings

In its review of existing studies examining shall-issue laws, Hahn et al. (2005) found insufficient evidence for determining the effect of such laws on violent crime. NRC (2004) reviewed much of the same literature and reanalyzed data that were common to many of these analyses: a panel data set originally spanning 1977–1992, then expanded through 2000. These data were originally analyzed in Lott and Mustard (1997) and used again by Lott (2000) in revised analyses. Lott (2000) found that shall-issue laws decreased homicides, rapes, and assaults. Other researchers (e.g., Duggan, 2001; Ayres and Donohue, 2003a, 2003b) and NRC reanalyzed the same data but found different results, as well as significant sensitivity of results to specification. With one member dissenting, the NRC (2004) panel concluded,

> Some studies find that right-to-carry laws reduce violent crime, others find that the effects are negligible, and still others find that such laws increase violent crime. The committee concludes that it is not possible to reach any scientifically supported conclusion because of (a) the sensitivity of the empirical results to seemingly minor changes in model specification, (b) a lack of robustness of the results to the inclusion of more recent years of data (during which there were many more law changes than in the earlier period), and (c) the statistical imprecision of the results. The evidence to date does not adequately indicate either the sign or the magnitude of a causal link between the passage of right-to-carry laws and crime rates. Furthermore, this uncertainty is not likely to be resolved with the existing data and methods. If further headway is to be made, in the committee's judgment, new analytical approaches and data are needed.

Among the studies since 2003 meeting our inclusion criteria, all examined shall-issue laws; none examined permitless-carry laws. Two studies were included in the NRC review (Helland and Tabarrok, 2004; Plassman and Whitley, 2003). Their findings were subsumed into the overarching NRC finding as described earlier. Among studies from the period after the NRC review, several built on and extended analyses of the county-level panel data used in previous studies. These include Roberts (2009); Moody et al. (2014); Aneja, Donohue, and Zhang (2014); and Durlauf, Navarro, and Rivers (2016). Other studies relied on state-level data, either in addition to or instead of county-level analyses. These studies include Aneja, Donohue, and Zhang (2014); Lott (2010); Rosengart et al. (2005); Grambsch (2008); Webster, Crifasi, and Vernick, (2014); and Gius (2014). Several studies used city-level data, including Kovandzic, Marvell, and Vieraitis (2005); La Valle and Glover (2012); and La Valle (2013). We first describe studies that primarily focused on county-level data. We then turn to studies that focused on state-level data, then studies that employed city-level data.

### County-Level Studies

Many of the earliest studies examining the effects of shall-issue laws relied on county-level data, usually county-level data constructed for the Lott and Mustard (1997) report. Subsequent evaluations identified problems with the data for estimating the effects of laws. These problems included:

- Lott and Mustard's data set used county population values that did not correspond to the crime statistics available for counties, especially those with weak reporting of crime statistics (Maltz and Targonski, 2002).
- Large numbers of counties must be dropped from analyses using, for instance, murder rates as a covariate because the counties reported no murders (Ayres and Donohue, 2003a).
- There were errors in the classification of shall-issue states that were only later corrected in this data set.

Lott and Whitley (2003) discounted these concerns, describing them as typical of the types of measurement error commonly encountered in statistical analyses. Moreover, they suggested that even when county-level data were restricted to just those with comparatively low underreporting (where many of the noted problems would have less of an effect), they still observed trends consistent with the view that shall-issue laws reduce crime. NRC (2004) and Hahn et al. (2005), however, disagreed with this claim.

Ayres and Donohue (2009a, 2009b), noting some of the weaknesses of the county-level analyses, reported that some of the significant effects from Lott and Mustard (1997) and Lott (2000) were no longer significant after correcting coding errors. Moreover, Ayres and Donohue (2009a, 2009b) argued that Lott's spline and dummy specifications of the effects of laws were unduly influenced by states that implemented the laws earlier and thus had longer post-implementation periods affecting the estimates. Instead, using county panel data from 1977 to 1997 and a hybrid model that estimated the joint effect that the laws could be shown to have on the levels and trends observed for several crimes, the authors concluded that shall-issue laws were associated with increases in all crime types (with the exception of rape, for which evidence was mixed) in the five years after the laws were passed.

Roberts (2009) analyzed the effect of shall-issue laws on intimate partner homicide rates using county-level data spanning 1985–2004. The author found that (the more-restrictive) may-issue laws significantly increased intimate partner total homicides by 71 percent compared with shall-issue laws, but may-issue (compared to shall-issue) laws had an uncertain effect on intimate partner firearm homicides. The author also found uncertain effects of concealed-carry bans compared with shall-issue laws on either overall or firearm-related intimate partner homicides. However, neither analysis clustered standard errors at the state level, so serial correlation that was unaccounted for in the panel data could have resulted in biased standard errors and CIs.

More recently, Aneja, Donohue, and Zhang (2014) analyzed the county-level data set used in NRC (2004), extended through 2006, and state-level data through 2010. The authors corrected the NRC analyses for several errors that they identified, including data-coding errors related to the timing of shall-issue legislation, an endogenous control variable (arrest rate), and a failure to cluster standard errors at the state level. The authors argued that NRC (2004) was incorrect in its decision not to cluster the standard errors of the county-level analyses at the state level and showed that CIs were badly misestimated when clustering was not accounted for. In their preferred county-level specification including state trend effects, they found no statistically significant effects of shall-issue laws on either the level or trend of any of seven crime rates, and they found only one suggestive effect across the 14 effects they tested.

Moody et al. (2014), responding to an earlier version of the Aneja, Donohue, and Zhang (2014) paper, reestimated their models after adding many more demographic control variables, robbery and assault rates, and a lagged outcome as a predictor meant to capture unmeasured state differences associated with crime rates. Moody et al. (2014) offered statistical tests suggesting that the model with added covariates predicted the data significantly better, which the authors interpreted as evidence that estimates in Aneja, Donohue, and Zhang (2014) suffered from omitted-variable biases. The revised hybrid model results in Moody et al. (2014) suggested that shall-issue laws significantly reduced the trends in rape and murder rates. They found no significant association between shall-issue laws and either assault or robbery. The fact that their model predicted a given outcome better than the Aneja, Donohue, and Zhang (2014) model is not sufficient to demonstrate the claim that the latter's model suffered from omitted variable bias, nor that the model preferred by Moody et al. (2014) offered a less biased estimate. An overfit model can predict the data exceptionally well while producing biased and unreliable coefficient estimates.

Using county-level panel data spanning 1979–2000, Durlauf, Navarro, and Rivers (2016) examined the sensitivity of analyses that estimate the relationship between shall-issue laws and violent crime. They reported that use of population weights may lead to inefficient estimates and upward biases in estimates of the effect of shall-issue laws on crime. In addition, they found that hybrid or spline models are preferred to dummy models and that models that allow for heterogeneity in the effect of laws (including effects that vary with region, the level of gun prevalence, and the level of urbanization in an area) outperform models that do not allow for variation in effects. For the spline model specifications that the authors assessed to perform best for the outcome of violent crime, they estimated that shall-issue laws increase violent crime in the first year after law passage and that violent crime continues to increase in subsequent years. The authors concluded that, overall, there was substantial variation in the estimated effects for each model across the model space analyzed and, thus, there was little evidence that shall-issue laws generate either an increase or a decrease in crime on average.

**State-Level Studies**

Rosengart et al. (2005) examined the effect of several state gun laws, including shall-issue laws, on firearm homicides and total homicides using state-level data. One limitation was that the data covered only 1979–1998, and other studies have shown the sensitivity of results to shorter periods, partly because shorter periods include observation of fewer states that have adopted shall-issue laws. The policy variable was specified as a dummy variable (indicating that a shall-issue law was or was not in place). The authors found suggestive effects that shall-issue laws increased firearm and total homicide rates. French and Heagerty (2008) tested the sensitivity of these results and similarly concluded that shall-issue laws had a suggestive effect consistent with the laws increasing firearm-related homicide rates, although estimates varied across specifications. However, the Rosengart et al. (2005) paper, and presumably the French and Heagerty (2008) paper, also had an unfavorable ratio of model covariates to observations (less than one to eight), suggesting that the model may have been overfit, and thus its estimates and their CIs may be unreliable.

Martin and Legault (2005) demonstrated that Lott (2000) used incorrect state crime rate estimates that differed substantially from official Federal Bureau of Investigation (FBI) state estimates. They replicated Lott (2000)'s model despite misgivings about its specification to demonstrate that the effects Lott reported were sensitive to this measurement error. In their replication exercise using state-level crime data from the FBI's Uniform Crime Reports spanning 1977–1992, Martin and Legault (2005)'s estimates showed that shall-issue laws significantly reduced total violent crime and, specifically, aggravated assault. They found only suggestive effects that the laws reduced rates of robbery and murder, and uncertain effects on rape (see Figure 13.2). However, as with Lott (2000), their models did not statistically adjust for serial correlation in the panel data, and the model's ratio of estimated parameters to observations was less than one to ten, meaning the model may have been overfit, and thus its parameter estimates and their CIs may be unreliable.

Grambsch (2008) conducted a state-level analysis of (total) murder rates (relative to the U.S. murder rate) from 1976 to 2001 using the 25 states that passed shall-issue laws between 1981 and 1996. She found a selection effect among states adopting shall-issue laws—namely, that states that passed shall-issue laws in this period experienced an increasing trend in murder rates prior to adoption relative to other states. Her estimates showed that, after controlling for regression to the mean, there was either an uncertain effect or a significant positive effect of shall-issue laws on relative murder rates (i.e., shall-issue laws increased murder rates) depending on the model used.

Two studies that focused on assessing the relationship between unmarried fertility or abortions and violent crime included shall-issue laws as a covariate in their models (Kendall and Tamura, 2010; Lott and Whitley, 2007). Analyzing data from 1976 to 1998 and using a Poisson model that controlled for state and year fixed effects, state-specific linear trends, and time-varying state covariates, Lott and Whitley (2007) found suggestive or significant effects (depending on specification) indicating that murder rates fell approximately 1 percent faster after the adoption of shall-issue laws relative to states without such policies. Employing a different model specification over a longer period (1957–2002), Kendall and Tamura (2010) estimated that shall-issue laws had a suggestive but small association with reduced rates of murder and uncertain relationships with rape, robbery, and assault.

Using a panel of state data, Lott (2010) provided an update of his earlier analyses examining the effect of shall-issue laws on violent crime. His preferred specification included a set of dummy variables that indicated different time intervals before and after shall-issue legislation was in effect for states that passed such legislation. Many of Lott's modeling results were presented as figures and did not indicate statistical significance. Detailed results were provided only for an analysis of homicide rates. These included information on the statistical significance of each coefficient in the model but not for a test comparing post-implementation time intervals with pre-implementation time intervals. Lott interpreted the pattern of effects as demonstrating that homicides declined significantly after implementation of shall-issue laws, but he did not provide test statistics or sufficient description to clarify what specific effect was observed. The author also included coefficients and their statistical significance from dummy and spline models similar to those from his earlier work, but he did not include standard errors or test statistics. All of the preferred models appear to have a ratio of estimated parameters to observations that is less than one to ten, meaning the model may have been overfit, and thus the reported estimates and their CIs may be unreliable.

Webster, Crifasi, and Vernick (2014) analyzed state-level data from 1999 to 2010, using generalized least-squares regression models to estimate the effect of shall-issue laws on age-adjusted homicide rates. They found suggestive effects indicating an association between the implementation of shall-issue laws and a 10-percent increase in rates of nonfirearm homicide, a 6-percent increase in rates of total homicide, and an 11-percent increase in rates of murder and nonnegligent manslaughter. However, their estimates showed an uncertain association between shall-issue laws and firearm homicide rates. The statistical model used to arrive at these results used a large number of estimated parameters relative to observations (a ratio of about one to eight), meaning the model may have been overfit, and thus its estimates and their apparent statistical significance could provide little generalizable information about the true causal effects of shall-issue laws. In addition, the assumptions of least-squares regression models are typically violated when modeling rate data for which many observations have values close to zero. This too could cause this model's estimates to be unreliable.

Gius (2014) examined the effect of shall-issue laws on gun-related murder rates using state-level data from 1980 to 2009. He found that states with may-issue or more-restrictive policies had higher gun-related murder rates than shall-issue states. Relative to states with shall-issue laws, states with more-restrictive firearm-carry policies had rates of firearm homicide that were 11 percent higher (see Figure 13.2). However, this model did not statistically adjust for the known serial correlation in this panel data, which has been shown to result in misleadingly small standard errors (Aneja, Donohue, and Zhang, 2014). For this reason, the apparently significant effect observed in this study could be invalid.

Using their preferred specification with state-level data from 1979 to 2010 and a dummy, spline, or hybrid specification of shall-issue laws without state trends, Aneja, Donohue, and Zhang (2014) found suggestive evidence that shall-issue laws increase assault by 8 percent (see Figure 13.2). In the dummy specification, shall-issue laws significantly increased rape by 12 percent, although estimates of this effect from the spline model were uncertain. The authors also found suggestive evidence that shall-issue laws increased rates of robbery, although estimates again became uncertain in other specifications. Effects of shall-issue laws on murder rates were uncertain. The authors tested the sensitivity of their results to less-parsimonious (including the Lott and Mustard [1997] specification) and more-parsimonious demographic specifications; the inclusion of state-specific time trends; the inclusion or exclusion of years that were likely to be influenced by the crack cocaine epidemic, which affected crime rates; and the specification of the policy variable (dummy, spline, hybrid). The authors noted that their results, which showed that the significance and sign of estimated effects varied substantially depending on the specification employed, underscored the sensitivity of gun-crime modeling estimates to modeling decisions.

Responding to an earlier version of the Aneja, Donohue, and Zhang (2014) paper, Moody et al. (2014) critiqued the decision to treat models without state-specific trends as the preferred ones. Thus, Moody et al. (2014) reestimated the hybrid models in Aneja, Donohue, and Zhang (2014) and incorporated the state-specific trends and their additional covariates into the corresponding county-level analyses. In doing so, the authors found, as they had with their county-level analyses, that their specification improved model fit over that of Aneja, Donohue, and Zhang (2014). These hybrid models found that shall-issue laws significantly increased assault rate trends and increased robbery rate levels, but they also significantly reduced murder rate trends. As noted earlier, Moody et al. (2014) did not demonstrate either that their model estimates were less biased than those in Aneja, Donohue, and Zhang (2014) or that the latter's model suffered from omitted variable biases. Furthermore, the state-level analyses of Moody et al. (2014) used a statistical model with a large number of estimated parameters relative to observations (close to one to five), meaning the model may have been overfit, and thus the estimates and inferential statistics may provide little generalizable information about the true causal effects of shall-issue laws.

### City-Level Studies

Kovandzic, Marvell, and Vieraitis (2005) examined the effect of shall-issue laws on violent crime (homicide, robbery, assault, and rape) using panel data from 1980 to 2000 for 189 large U.S. cities. The authors clustered the standard errors at the state level, addressed coding errors in previous research, allowed for a time trend in the effect of shall-issue laws, allowed for city-specific time trends, and conducted analyses that allowed for heterogeneity in the effect of shall-issue laws across states. In their analysis that estimated the average effect of shall-issue laws for all included cities using a dummy model specification, Kovandzic, Marvell, and Vieraitis (2005) found uncertain effects for all of the violent crime outcomes analyzed. These findings were largely consistent when they instead modeled the effects of shall-issue laws as a trend variable, except that their preferred spline models showed effects consistent with shall-issue laws increasing assault rates (a significant effect) and increasing rape rates (a suggestive effect). Their estimates for the effect on assault suggest that shall-issue laws are associated with a 10-percent increase in aggravated assault rates after five years. In examining state-specific effects with their spline models, the authors further found that there were more states where shall-issue laws led to statistically significant increases in crime compared with decreases. However, this study had an unfavorable ratio of model covariates to observations (less than one to ten), meaning the model may have been overfit, and thus its estimates and CIs may be unreliable indicators of the true effects of the laws.

La Valle (2013) analyzed data from 56 cities spanning 1980–2010. The author noted that the analyses "include statistical corrections for variation in sample unit independence," but he did not explicitly mention clustering the standard errors at the state level. La Valle (2013) used a dummy variable specification for the shall-issue law. In his preferred specification (using interpolated control variables for inter-censal years, population weighted analysis, and a one-year lagged outcome as a covariate), he found that shall-issue laws significantly reduced gun homicides by 15 percent and total homicides by 13 percent (see Figure 13.2). Results were sensitive to specification, however, and other authors (e.g., Kovandzic, Marvell, and Vieraitis, 2005; Durlauf, Navarro, and Rivers, 2016) have expressed concern that weighting gives undue influence to localities with large populations and worsens, rather than improves, standard error estimation. In unweighted analyses using inter-censal years, La Valle (2013) found that shall-issue laws reduced gun homicides but not total homicides. In La Valle and Glover (2012), which used similar data (panel data on 57 cities from 1980 to 2006) and a similar approach, the authors included separate indicators for may-issue and shall-issue states. In the authors' preferred analysis (with interpolated data for controls for inter-censal years and weighting), shall-issue laws were associated with a significant 23-percent increase in the homicide rate, and may-issue laws were associated with a significant 19-percent decrease in the homicide rate (compared with cities that did not clearly have either a may-issue or shall-issue law). Similarly, shall-issue laws were associated with a significant 32-percent increase in the firearm homicide rate, while may-issue laws were associated with a significant 33-percent reduction in the firearm homicide rate. (No estimates for unweighted data with inter-censal years were provided.) The diametric findings from these two studies further highlight the sensitivity of results to model specification, as well as to how shall-issue laws are classified.

**Other Studies**

Manski and Pepper (2015) investigated the sensitivity of shall-issue effect estimates to a range of assumptions by comparing property and violent crime rates in two states under progressively less-restrictive assumptions about how the laws' effects may vary over time or between states. This study compared outcomes in just two states, meaning causal effects were not well identified. Moreover, it treated Virginia's shall-issue law as having been implemented in 1989, when we believe the correct date is 1995. For these reasons, we do not review this paper's results. Applying Bayesian model comparison techniques, Strnad (2007) reanalyzed Donohue (2004) models of the effects of shall-issue laws. In contrast to the approach of Donohue (2004) and many others, Strnad (2007) did not assess the evidence for or against shall-issue laws in terms of how frequently estimates of the effect were statistically significant or were found to have positive (as opposed to negative) estimated effects under different model specifications. Instead, he used model comparison techniques to establish which models fit the data best and to evaluate whether evidence favored models with or without shall-issue effects. He concluded that Donohue (2004)'s models provided much stronger support for a conclusion that shall-issue laws had little or no effect on most outcomes than Donohue (2004) concluded after examining patterns in the direction and significance levels of these effects.

Figure 13.2 displays the IRRs and CIs associated with the concealed-carry laws examined in the studies published after the NRC (2004) review. In this figure, we highlight effect estimates based only on dummy-coded models, for reasons discussed in Chapter Two and Appendix A. Lott (2010) did not provide enough information for us to calculate IRRs and CIs for the effect size of interest, so we do not include these in the figure. In addition, the estimates in Durlauf, Navarro, and Rivers (2016) were available only for the spline specification; Kovandzic, Marvell, and Vieraitis (2005) preferred their own spline model; Moody and Marvell (2009) and Moody et al. (2014) offered only a hybrid model; and Manski and Pepper (2015) and Strnad (2007) did not seek to produce a preferred estimate of the effect of shall-issue laws. Therefore, we do not include estimates from these studies in Figure 13.2.

## Figure 13.2
## Incidence Rate Ratios Associated with the Effect of Concealed-Carry Laws on Violent Crime

| Study, by Policy | Outcome Measure | Effect Size (IRR) [95% CI] |
|---|---|---|
| **Shall issue (vs. may** | **Crime** | |
| **issue or no issue)** | **Homicide** | |
| Martin & Legault (2005) | Murder rate | 0.95 [0.90, 1.01] |
| Rosengart et al. (2005) | Total homicides | 1.07 [0.98, 1.17] |
| Rosengart et al. (2005) | Firearm homicides | 1.11 [0.99, 1.24] |
| Grambsch (2008) | Murder rate (random effects model) | 1.01 [0.98, 1.03] |
| Grambsch (2008) | Murder rate (fixed effects model) | 1.06 [1.03, 1.09] |
| French & Heagerty (2008) | Firearm homicides | 1.10 [0.99, 1.22] |
| Kendall & Tamura (2010) | Murder rate | 1.00 [0.99, 1.00] |
| Aneja, Donohue, & Zhang (2014) | Murder | 1.03 [0.91, 1.17] |
| Webster, Crifasi, & Vernick (2014) | Total homicides | 1.06 [0.99, 1.14] |
| Webster, Crifasi, & Vernick (2014) | Firearm homicides | 1.06 [0.96, 1.17] |
| Webster, Crifasi, & Vernick (2014) | Nonfirearm homicides | 1.10 [0.99, 1.22] |
| Webster, Crifasi, & Vernick (2014) | Murder and non–negligent manslaughter | 1.11 [0.95, 1.26] |
| | **Rape** | |
| Martin & Legault (2005) | Rape rate | 0.98 [0.94, 1.03] |
| Kendall & Tamura (2010) | Rape rate | 1.00 [0.99, 1.00] |
| Aneja, Donohue, & Zhang (2014) | Rape | 1.12 [1.00, 1.26] |
| | **Robbery** | |
| Martin & Legault (2005) | Robbery rate | 0.96 [0.91, 1.02] |
| Kendall & Tamura (2010) | Robbery rate | 1.00 [1.00, 1.00] |
| Aneja, Donohue, & Zhang (2014) | Robbery | 1.15 [0.98, 1.34] |
| | **Assault** | |
| Martin & Legault (2005) | Aggravated assault | 0.93 [0.89, 0.98] |
| Kendall & Tamura (2010) | Assault rate | 1.00 [1.00, 1.00] |
| Aneja, Donohue, & Zhang (2014) | Assault | 1.08 [0.99, 1.18] |
| | **Violent crime** | |
| Martin & Legault (2005) | Violent crime | 0.94 [0.91, 0.98] |
| **May issue (vs. shall issue)** | **Homicide** | |
| Roberts (2009) | Total intimate partner homicides | 1.71 [1.29, 2.14] |
| Roberts (2009) | Firearm intimate partner homicides | 1.12 [0.87, 1.37] |
| **No concealed carry** | | |
| **(vs. shall issue)** | **Homicide** | |
| Roberts (2009) | Total intimate partner homicides | 0.96 [0.55, 1.38] |
| Roberts (2009) | Firearm intimate partner homicides | 0.86 [0.49, 1.23] |
| **Shall issue or may issue** | | |
| **(vs. no concealed carry)** | **Homicide** | |
| La Valle (2013) | Total homicides | 0.87 [0.77, 0.98] |
| La Valle (2013) | Firearm homicides | 0.85 [0.73, 0.98] |
| Gius (2014) | Firearm homicides | 1.11 [1.05, 1.16] |
| **Shall issue (vs. no issue)** | **Homicide** | |
| La Valle & Glover (2012) | Total homicides | 1.23 [1.05, 1.44] |
| La Valle & Glover (2012) | Firearm homicides | 1.32 [1.14, 1.52] |
| **May issue (vs. no issue)** | **Homicide** | |
| La Valle & Glover (2012) | Total homicides | 0.81 [0.71, 0.92] |
| La Valle & Glover (2012) | Firearm homicides | 0.77 [0.66, 0.90] |

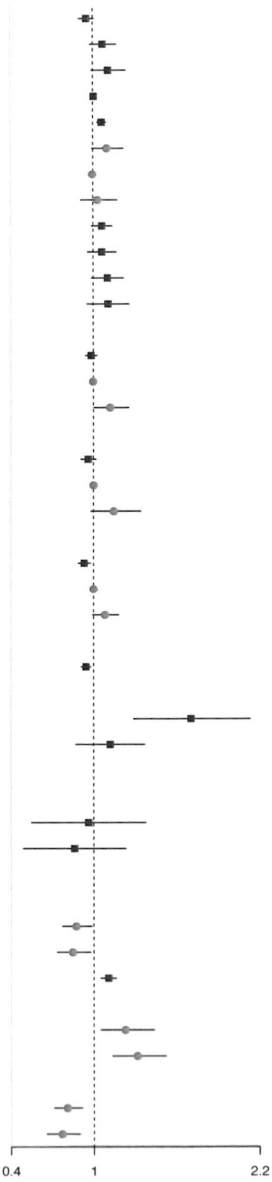


NOTE: IRR values marked with blue squares indicate that methodological concerns are discussed in the text. Green circles indicate that we identified no significant methodological concerns. See Appendix B for details.

## Conclusions

We focused our review on studies examining the effects of concealed-carry laws on violent crime outcomes since NRC (2004) and Hahn et al. (2005) found that estimates of such effects were too sensitive to reasonable differences in methods to draw conclusions about the direction or magnitude of the laws' effects. Because so much more study has been done of this relationship than of any other gun policy and outcome, there is a much richer evidence base to draw on, including studies raising serious methodological concerns and several that did not raise as many concerns among our methodology review team. Therefore, to focus this review on the best available evidence, we draw our conclusions in this section based just on those seven studies that did not raise serious methodological concerns.

*Total homicides.* Five of the seven studies examined the effects of shall-issue laws on total homicides. Two studies found only uncertain effects of these laws (Aneja, Donohue, and Zhang, 2014; Kendall and Tamura, 2010); Moody et al. (2014) found that shall-issue laws cause a downward trend in homicides; La Valle and Glover (2012) found that shall-issue laws increased homicides significantly relative to having no law for the legal carriage of a concealed firearm (*no-issue laws*); and La Valle (2013) found that shall-issue or may-issue laws reduce total homicides relative to no-issue laws. This result cannot be used to distinguish the effect of shall-issue laws per se, but it suggests that either shall-issue, may-issue, or both contribute to reducing total homicides. Because comparable studies reach inconsistent results, we conclude that the best available studies provide *inconclusive evidence for the effect of shall-issue laws on homicides.*

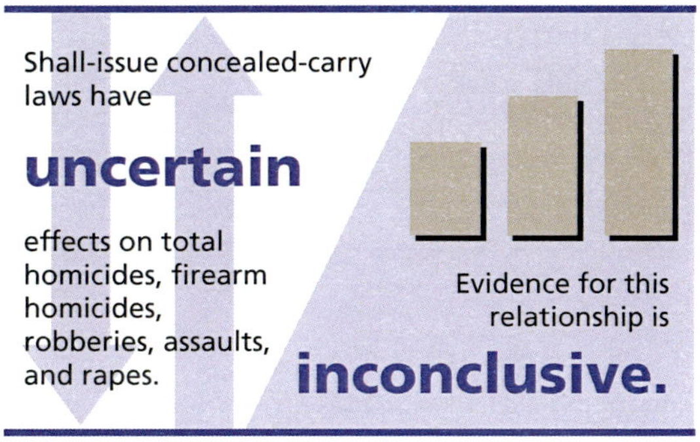


*Firearm homicides.* Three of the seven studies examined the effects of shall-issue laws on firearm homicides. Among these, there was one suggestive (French and Heagerty, 2008) and one significant (La Valle and Glover, 2012) effect, suggesting that these laws increase firearm homicides. La Valle (2013) found that shall-issue or may-issue laws cause decreases in firearm homicide rates relative to no-issue laws. This result cannot be used to distinguish the effect of shall-issue laws per se, but it suggests that either shall-issue, may-issue, or both contribute to reducing firearm homicides. With seemingly conflicting evidence, we conclude that the best available studies provide *inconclusive evidence for the effect of shall-issue laws on firearm homicides.*

*Robberies.* Aneja, Donohue, and Zhang (2014) found a suggestive effect that shall-issue laws may increase robbery rates. Moody et al. (2014) and Kendall and Tamura (2010) found only uncertain effects of shall-issue laws on robberies. Therefore, we conclude that the best available studies provide *inconclusive evidence for the effect of shall-issue laws on robberies.*

*Assaults.* Aneja, Donohue, and Zhang (2014) found a suggestive effect that shall-issue laws may increase assault rates. Moody et al. (2014) and Kendall and Tamura (2010) found only uncertain effects of shall-issue laws on assault. Therefore, we conclude that the best available studies provide *inconclusive evidence for the effect of shall-issue laws on assaults.*

*Rapes.* Aneja, Donohue, and Zhang (2014) found that shall-issue laws significantly increase rates of rape. Moody et al. (2014) found that shall-issue laws produce a significant downward trend on rates of rape. Kendall and Tamura (2010) found only uncertain evidence of an association between shall-issue laws and rape. Therefore, we conclude that the best available studies provide *inconclusive evidence for the effect of shall-issue laws on rapes.*

*Violent crime.* One study—Durlauf, Navarro, and Rivers (2016)—aggregated all violent crimes into a single category and found that shall-issue laws significantly increase violent crime rates. Because evidence for the effect of shall-issue laws on each component of violent crime is inconclusive, it could be argued that this single study of the effect of these laws on all violent crimes should not suffice to suggest that there is more than inconclusive evidence for such an effect. However, because analyses on all violent crimes may have greater power to detect any such effects, and because our scoring criteria indicate it, we conclude that there is *limited evidence that shall-issue laws may increase violent crime.*

## Effects on Unintentional Injuries and Deaths

### Research Synthesis Findings

NRC (2004) and Hahn et al. (2005) identified one quasi-experimental study examining the effect of shall-issue concealed-carry laws on unintentional injuries and deaths. Both reviews concluded that the effect of such laws could not be determined. Lott and Mustard (1997) examined county-level data on unintentional handgun deaths from national Mortality Detail Records data spanning 1982 to 1991 in counties with and without shall-issue concealed-carry laws. In an ordinary-least-squares regression controlling for arrest rates, population density, and socioeconomic characteristics, shall-issue laws had uncertain effects on unintentional handgun deaths and suggestive effects consistent with increasing unintentional nonhandgun deaths (see Figure 13.3). However, the authors noted that with only 156 unintentional handgun deaths in counties with more than 100,000 people in 1988, most of the observations in the data set were zeros. They re-analyzed the data using Tobit regression to account for this low number of unintentional deaths but still found uncertain effects, cautioning that, because of computing limitations of the time, they were unable to include covariates other than state dummies in these regressions.

Although Lott and Mustard's 1997 study has been reanalyzed, including by the NRC review panel, the focus of most subsequent work has been on the violence and other crime outcomes they examined, not on unintentional deaths (see the previous section on the effects on violent crime).

We identified only one additional study meeting our inclusion criteria that examined the effect of shall-issue laws on unintentional injuries (no studies identified the relationship between permitless-carry laws and this outcome). DeSimone, Markowitz, and Xu (2013) performed a fixed-effects analysis to examine the effect of shall-issue laws on unintentional firearm injuries using hospital discharge data from the National Inpatient Sample spanning 1988 to 2003. In the 11 states that were part of the sample, the authors found a suggestive effect consistent with shall-issue laws increasing unintentional firearm injuries for children under age 18 and a statistically significant effect of these laws increasing self-inflicted firearm injuries among those 18 or older. Specifically, the estimate suggests that, after implementation of the law, unintentional firearm injuries among those aged 18 or older were more than twice as frequent as would be expected without the law, which would be extraordinary if true. However, the estimated effects of shall-issue laws in this study were based primarily on one state that changed its law during the study time frame (Arizona); thus, the study offers little evidence that the observed effects are due to the change in the law rather than to other factors affecting the state's unintentional injury rate that occurred around the same time the law was changed. Moreover, as DeSimone, Markowitz, and Xu (2013) note, the data set on which their estimates are made is not strictly longitudinal, and it is not possible to determine the extent to which child-access prevention law effect estimates are estimated cross-sectionally or longitudinally.

Figure 13.3 displays the IRRs and CIs associated with the concealed-carry laws examined in these studies.

**Figure 13.3**
**Incidence Rate Ratios Associated with the Effect of Concealed-Carry Laws on Unintentional Injuries and Deaths**

| Study, by Policy | Outcome Measure | Effect Size (IRR) [95% CI] |
|---|---|---|
| **Shall-issue laws** | **Unintentional injuries** | |
| Lott & Mustard (1997) | Handgun death | 1.03 [0.39, 1.68] |
| Lott & Mustard (1997) | Nonhandgun death | 1.08 [0.99, 1.18] |
| DeSimone, Markowitz, & Xu (2013) | Firearm injuries, aged 0–17 | 1.70 [0.83, 3.47] |
| DeSimone, Markowitz, & Xu (2013) | Firearm injuries, aged 18+ | 2.28 [1.57, 3.31] |

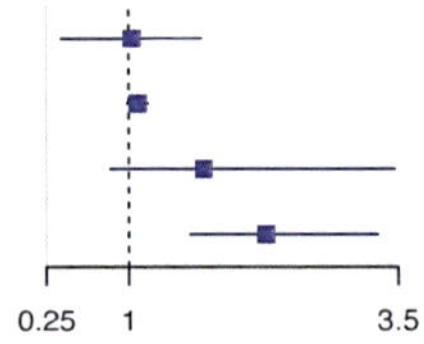


NOTE: IRR values marked with blue squares indicate that methodological concerns are discussed in the text. See Appendix B for details.

## Conclusions

We identified two qualifying studies that examined the effect of shall-issue laws on unintentional firearm deaths. Lott and Mustard (1997) found that shall-issue laws had an uncertain relationship with unintentional handgun deaths and a suggestive relationship with increased nonhandgun unintentional deaths. DeSimone, Markowitz, and Xu (2013) found a significant effect indicating that these laws increase unintentional injury rates among adults aged 18 or older and a suggestive effect in the same direction among youth aged 17 or younger.

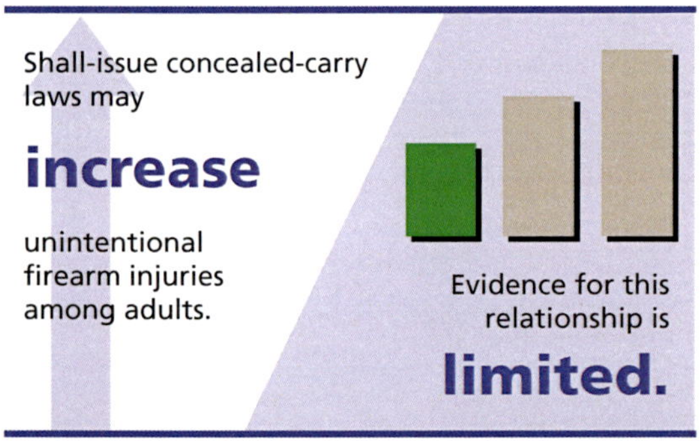


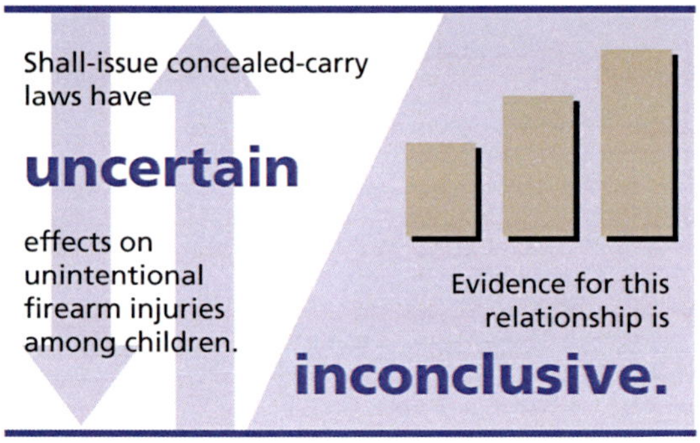


Based on these studies and an assessment of their relative strengths, we conclude that there is *limited evidence that shall-issue concealed-carry laws may increase unintentional firearm injuries among adults* and *inconclusive evidence for the effect of these laws on such injuries among children.*

## Effects on Mass Shootings

### Research Synthesis Findings

Neither NRC (2004) nor Hahn et al. (2005) identified research examining the effects of concealed-carry laws on mass shootings in the United States. Our search of studies since 2003 that met our inclusion criteria yielded one on permitless carry and three on shall-issue laws.

The three studies that examined the effects of shall-issue laws on mass shootings employed a difference-in-differences methodological design, exploiting state variation in the timing of law enactment to identify the causal effect of these policies on mass shooting incidents.[6]

Using a Poisson specification, Lott (2003) estimated the effect of shall-issue laws on fatalities, injuries, and the incidence of multiple-victim public shootings. The analysis covered 1977 to 1997, and regression models included controls for state and year fixed effects, other state firearm policies, and a broad range of state-level socioeconomic and demographic characteristics. Results showed that shall-issue laws were significantly associated with reductions in total casualties from multiple-victim public shootings and in the total number of multiple-victim public shooting incidents. However, these models had an unfavorable ratio of estimated parameters to observations (approximately one to eight), suggesting that the model may have been overfit, and thus the estimated effects of these laws may be poor indicators of their true effects. In addition, the model did not adjust for clustered standard errors. Together, these shortcomings suggest that the model results may not accurately describe the true effects of shall-issue laws.

Duwe, Kovandzic, and Moody (2002) used a fixed-effects negative binomial model—controlling for national time trends, state-level variation in socioeconomic and demographic factors, and state-level criminal justice characteristics (e.g., prison population)—to estimate the effect of these laws on the number of mass public shooting incidents, fatalities from mass public shootings, and injuries from mass public shooting injuries between 1976 and 1999. In their model, shall-issue laws were represented using two separate measures. A step dummy variable that takes a value of 1 the year after the law went into effect (0 otherwise) captured the immediate impact of the law, while a time trend variable captured dynamic effects of the policy. The authors

---

[6] These studies adopted different definitions for *mass shooting* (see Chapter Twenty-Two for further detail on definitional issues). Lott (2003) examined multiple-victim public shootings, which the author defined as events unrelated to other criminal activity in which two or more people were killed or wounded in a public location. Duwe, Kovandzic, and Moody (2002) focused on *mass public shootings*, which the authors defined as incidents resulting in four or more firearm-related fatalities (excluding the offender), where both the victims and offender(s) were not engaged in criminal activities. Luca, Deepak, and Poliquin (2016) set the same casualty threshold as Duwe, Kovandzic, and Moody (2002) but excluded any incident that occurred in connection with criminal activity or in which fewer than three of the fatally injured victims were not related (e.g., family, romantic partner) to the shooter.

estimated several alternative models, including Poisson fixed-effects models and two dynamic fixed-effects negative binomial models, as specification checks. The findings showed uncertain effects (i.e., no statistically significant evidence) for a relationship between the laws and public mass shooting outcomes (see Figure 13.4). The preferred specification had an unfavorable ratio of estimated parameters to observations (less than one to ten), meaning the model may have been overfit, and thus the estimated effects of these laws may be poor indicators of their true effects.

Examining a partially overlapping but later period (1989–2014), Luca, Deepak, and Poliquin (2016) used a linear probability model to estimate the impact of shall-issue concealed-carry laws on a binary indicator for whether a mass shooting occurred in a given state-year. Controlling for time-invariant state characteristics, national trends, and a host of other state-level gun policies, as well as time-varying state-level demographic, socioeconomic, and political characteristics, the authors found a small and uncertain effect of shall-issue laws and a large but statistically insignificant positive effect of permitless-carry laws on the probability of a mass shooting event occurring. However, assessing the effects of gun policies on mass shootings was not the primary focus of this paper, and the authors intended the estimates to serve solely as a robustness check for their main specification (the effects of mass shootings on gun policy). Although the paper provided limited information to use in evaluating the reported statistical models (e.g., on how these policies were coded), it is clear that the analysis used a linear model to predict a dichotomous outcome. Therefore, model assumptions were violated, making CIs unreliable.

Figure 13.4 displays the IRRs and CIs associated with the concealed-carry laws examined in these studies. Estimates from Duwe, Kovandzic, and Moody (2002) are not included in this figure because their approach yielded effect sizes that vary with time.

**Figure 13.4**
**Incidence Rate Ratios Associated with the Effect of Concealed-Carry Laws on Mass Shootings**

| Study, by Policy | Outcome Measure | Effect Size (IRR) [95% CI] |
|---|---|---|
| **Permitless carry** | **Mass shooting** | |
| Luca, Deepak, & Poliquin (2016) | State–year indicator (no political controls) | 2.27 [0.00, 5.24] |
| Luca, Deepak, & Poliquin (2016) | State–year indicator (political controls) | 2.73 [0.00, 5.66] |
| **Shall issue laws** | | |
| Lott (2003) | Total deaths and injuries | 0.22 [0.16, 0.29] |
| Lott (2003) | Number of shooting incidents | 0.33 [0.19, 0.58] |
| Luca, Deepak, & Poliquin (2016) | State–year indicator (no political controls) | 0.91 [0.27, 1.55] |
| Luca, Deepak, & Poliquin (2016) | State–year indicator (political controls) | 0.92 [0.30, 1.55] |

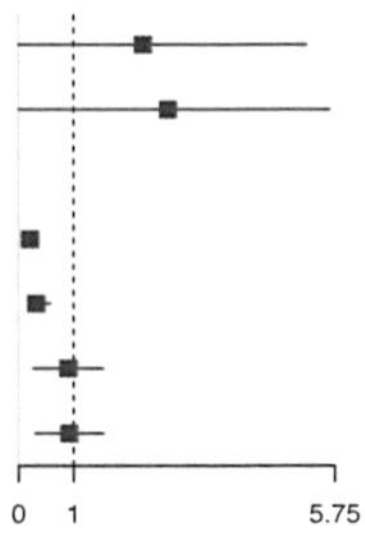


NOTE: IRR values marked with blue squares indicate that methodological concerns are discussed in the text. See Appendix B for details.

### Conclusions

*Permitless-carry laws.* We identified one qualifying study that examined the effects of permitless-carry laws on the incidence of mass shootings. Luca, Deepak, and Poliquin (2016) found that such laws had uncertain effects on the likelihood that at least one mass shooting event occurred in a given state. On the basis of this study, we find *inconclusive evidence for the effect of permitless-carry laws on mass shootings.*

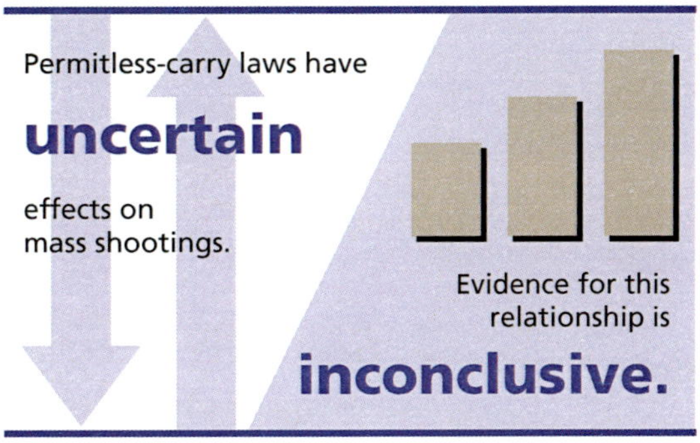


*Shall-issue concealed-carry laws.* We identified three qualifying studies that examined the effect of shall-issue laws on mass shooting outcomes. Lott (2003) found that shall-issue laws were associated with significant reductions in multiple-victim shooting incidence and the number of deaths or injuries resulting from multiple-victim shootings. Duwe, Kovandzic, and Moody (2002) and Luca, Deepak, and Poliquin (2016) found uncertain effects of shall-issue laws on mass shooting outcomes (e.g., incidence, injuries, and fatalities). Based on these studies and an assessment of their relative strengths, we find *inconclusive evidence for the effect of shall-issue laws on mass shootings.*

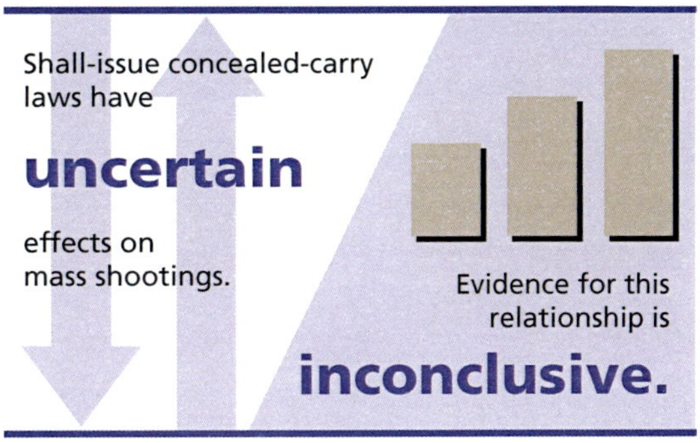


## Effects on the Gun Industry

### Research Synthesis Findings

Neither NRC (2004) nor Hahn et al. (2005) identified research examining the effects of concealed-carry laws on the gun industry. We identified one such study meeting our inclusion criteria. Duggan (2001) examined the effect of shall-issue laws on changes in gun ownership, using state-level subscription rates to *Guns & Ammo* magazine as a proxy for gun ownership. This study identified uncertain effects of these laws on gun ownership. However, the model also had an unfavorable ratio of explanatory variables to observations (approximately one to five) and provided no information about the quality of the model fit. This raises the possibility that the model was overfit, and thus the estimates may be unreliable indicators of the generalizable effect of shall-issue laws on gun ownership.

Figure 13.5 displays the IRR and CI associated with the concealed-carry laws examined in Duggan (2001).

**Figure 13.5**
**Incidence Rate Ratios Associated with the Effect of Concealed-Carry Laws on Gun Ownership**

| Study, by Policy | Outcome Measure | Effect Size (IRR) [95% CI] |
|---|---|---|
| **Shall issue laws** | | |
| Duggan (2001) | Gun ownership | 1.00 [0.98, 1.02] |

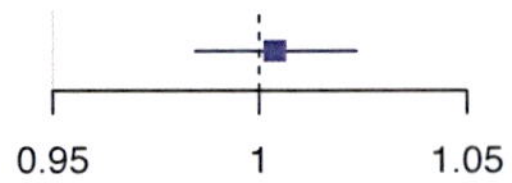


NOTE: IRR values marked with blue squares indicate that methodological concerns are discussed in the text. See Appendix B for details.

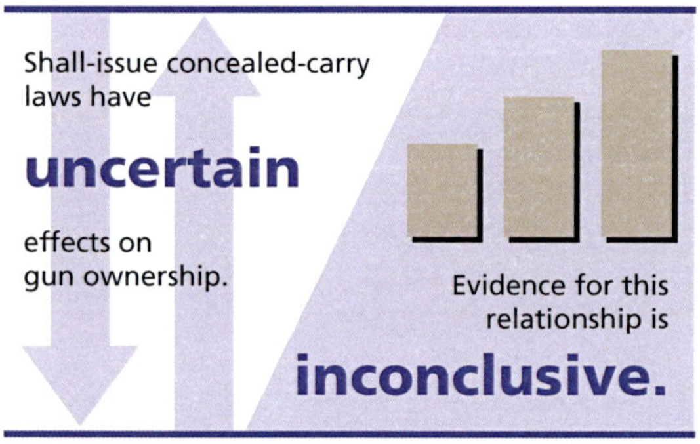


### Conclusions

The single study we identified (Duggan, 2001) found an uncertain effect of shall-issue concealed-carry laws on gun ownership. Therefore, we find *inconclusive evidence for the effect of these laws on gun ownership.*

## Outcomes Without Studies Examining the Effects of Concealed-Carry Laws

Neither NRC (2004) nor Hahn et al. (2005) identified any research examining the effects of concealed-carry laws on the following outcomes, and we identified no such studies that met our inclusion criteria:

- officer-involved shootings
- defensive gun use
- hunting and recreation.

Several of the studies reviewed here drew inferences about how concealed-carry laws influenced the deterrence and defensive benefits of guns, but none we identified directly examined the laws' effects on defensive gun use.

## Chapter Thirteen References

Aneja, Abhay, John J. Donohue III, and Alexandria Zhang, *The Impact of Right to Carry Laws and the NRC Report: Lessons for the Empirical Evaluation of Law and Policy*, Stanford, Calif.: Stanford Law School, Olin Working Paper No. 461, December 1, 2014. As of May 21, 2017: https://papers.ssrn.com/sol3/papers.cfm?abstract_id=2443681

Ayres, Ian, and John J. Donohue III, "Shooting Down the More Guns, Less Crime Hypothesis," *Stanford Law Review*, Vol. 55, No. 4, 2003a, pp. 1193–1312.

———, "The Latest Misfires in Support of the More Guns, Less Crime Hypothesis," *Stanford Law Review*, Vol. 55, No. 4, 2003b, pp. 1371–1398.

———, "Yet Another Refutation of the More Guns, Less Crime Hypothesis—with Some Help from Moody and Marvell," *Econ Journal Watch*, Vol. 6, No. 1, January 2009a, pp. 35–59.

———, "More Guns, Less Crime Fails Again: The Latest Evidence from 1977–2006," *Econ Journal Watch*, Vol. 6, No. 2, May 2009b, pp. 218–238.

Cramer, Clayton E., and David B. Kopel, "'Shall Issue': The New Wave of Concealed Handgun Permit Laws," *Tennessee Law Review*, Vol. 62, No. 3, 2005, pp. 679–757.

DeSimone, J., S. Markowitz, and J. Xu, "Child Access Prevention Laws and Nonfatal Gun Injuries," *Southern Economic Journal*, Vol. 80, No. 1, 2013, pp. 5–25.

Donohue, John J., "Guns, Crime, and the Impact of State Right-to-Carry Laws," *Fordham Law Review*, Vol. 73, No. 2, 2004, pp. 623–652.

Duggan, Mark, "More Guns, More Crime," *Journal of Political Economy*, Vol. 109, No. 5, 2001, pp. 1086–1114.

Durlauf, Steven, S. Navarro, and D. A. Rivers, "Model Uncertainty and the Effect of Shall-Issue Right-to-Carry Laws on Crime," *European Economic Review*, Vol. 81, 2016, pp. 32–67.

Duwe, Grant, Tomislav Kovandzic, and Carlisle E. Moody, "The Impact of Right-to-Carry Concealed Firearm Laws on Mass Public Shootings," *Homicide Studies*, Vol. 6, No. 4, 2002, pp. 271–296.

Fortunato, David, "Can Easing Concealed Carry Deter Crime?" *Social Science Quarterly*, Vol. 96, No. 4, December 2015, pp. 1071–1085.

French, B., and P. J. Heagerty, "Analysis of Longitudinal Data to Evaluate a Policy Change," *Statistics in Medicine*, Vol. 27, No. 24, 2008, pp. 5005–5025.

Gius, Mark, "An Examination of the Effects of Concealed Weapons Laws and Assault Weapons Bans on State-Level Murder Rates," *Applied Economics Letters*, Vol. 21, No. 4, 2014, pp. 265–267.

Grambsch, P., "Regression to the Mean, Murder Rates, and Shall-Issue Laws," *American Statistician*, Vol. 62, No. 4, 2008, pp. 289–295.

Grossman, Richard S., and Stephen A. Lee, "May Issue Versus Shall Issue: Explaining the Pattern of Concealed-Carry Handgun Laws, 1960–2001," *Contemporary Economic Policy*, Vol. 26, No. 2, 2008, pp. 198–206.

Hahn, Robert A., Oleg Bilukha, Alex Crosby, Mindy T. Fullilove, Akiva Liberman, Eve Moscicki, Susan Snyder, Farris Tuma, and Peter A. Briss, "Firearms Laws and the Reduction of Violence: A Systematic Review," *American Journal of Preventive Medicine*, Vol. 28, No. 2, 2005, pp. 40–71.

Helland, E., and A. Tabarrok, "Using Placebo Laws to Test 'More Guns, Less Crime,'" *Advances in Economic Analysis and Policy*, Vol. 4, No. 1, 2004.

Kendall, Todd D., and Robert Tamura, "Unmarried Fertility, Crime, and Social Stigma," *Journal of Law and Economics*, Vol. 53, No. 1, 2010, pp. 185–221.

Kovandzic, Tomislav V., and Thomas B. Marvell, "Right-to-Carry Concealed Handguns and Violent Crime: Crime Control Through Gun Control?" *Criminology and Public Policy*, Vol. 2, No. 3, 2003, pp. 363–396.

Kovandzic, T. V., T. B. Marvell, and L. M. Vieraitis, "The Impact of 'Shall-Issue' Concealed Handgun Laws on Violent Crime Rates—Evidence from Panel Data for Large Urban Cities," *Homicide Studies*, Vol. 9, No. 4, 2005, pp. 292–323.

La Valle, James M., "'Gun Control' vs. 'Self-Protection': A Case Against the Ideological Divide," *Justice Policy Journal*, Vol. 10, No. 1, 2013, pp. 1–26.

La Valle, James M., and Thomas C. Glover, "Revisiting Licensed Handgun Carrying: Personal Protection or Interpersonal Liability?" *American Journal of Criminal Justice*, Vol. 37, No. 4, 2012, pp. 580–601.

Lott, John R., Jr., *More Guns, Less Crime: Understanding Crime and Gun-Control Laws,* Chicago, Ill.: University of Chicago Press, 2000.

———, *The Bias Against Guns: Why Almost Everything You've Heard About Gun Control Is Wrong,* Washington, D.C.: Regnery Publishing, Inc., 2003.

———, *More Guns, Less Crime: Understanding Crime and Gun-Control Laws,* 3rd ed., Chicago, Ill.: University of Chicago Press, 2010.

Lott, J. R., and D. B. Mustard, "Crime, Deterrence, and Right-to-Carry Concealed Handguns," *Journal of Legal Studies*, Vol. 26, No. 1, 1997, pp. 1–68.

Lott John R., Jr., and John E. Whitley, "Measurement Error in County-Level UCR Data," *Journal of Quantitative Criminology*, Vol. 19, No. 2, June 2003, pp. 185–198.

———, "Abortion and Crime: Unwanted Children and Out-of-Wedlock Births," *Economic Inquiry*, Vol. 45, No. 2, 2007, pp. 304–324.

Lott, John R., Jr., John E. Whitley, and Rebekah C. Riley, *Concealed Carry Permit Holders Across the United States*, Crime Prevention Research Center, 2016.

Luca, Michael, Lahotra Deepak, and Christopher Poliquin, *The Impact of Mass Shootings on Gun Policy,* working paper, Boston, Mass.: Harvard Business School, 2016.

Maltz, M. D., and J. Targonski, "A Note on the Use of County-Level UCR Data, *Journal of Quantitative Criminology*, Vol. 18, No. 2, 2002, pp. 297–318.

Manski, Charles F., and John V. Pepper, *How Do Right-to-Carry Laws Affect Crime Rates? Coping with Ambiguity Using Bounded-Variation Assumptions*, Cambridge, Mass.: National Bureau for Economic Research, NBER Working Paper 21701, November 2015.

Martin, Robert A., Jr., and Richard L. Legault, "Systematic Measurement Error with State-Level Crime Data: Evidence from the 'More Guns Less Crime' Debate," *Journal of Research in Crime and Delinquency*, Vol. 42, No. 2, May 2005, pp. 187–210.

Moody, Carlisle E., and Thomas B. Marvell, "The Debate on Shall Issue Laws, Continued," *Econ Journal Watch*, Vol. 6, No. 2, 2009.

Moody, Carlisle E., Thomas B. Marvell, Paul R. Zimmerman, and Fasil Alemante, "The Impact of Right-to-Carry Laws on Crime: An Exercise in Replication," *Review of Economics and Finance*, Vol. 4, 2014, pp. 33–43.

National Research Council, *Firearms and Violence: A Critical Review*, Washington, D.C.: National Academies Press, 2004.

NRC—*See* National Research Council.

Phillips, C. D., O. Nwaiwu, D. K. McMaughan Moudouni, R. Edwards, and S. Lin, "When Concealed Handgun Licensees Break Bad: Criminal Convictions of Concealed Handgun Licensees in Texas, 2001–2009," *American Journal of Public Health*, Vol. 103, No. 1, 2013, pp. 86–91.

Plassmann, F., and J. E. Whitley, "Comments: Confirming More Guns, Less Crime," *Stanford Law Review*, Vol. 55, No. 4, 2003, pp. 1313–1369.

Roberts, Darryl W., "Intimate Partner Homicide: Relationships to Alcohol and Firearms," *Journal of Contemporary Criminal Justice*, Vol. 25, No. 1, 2009, pp. 67–88.

Rosengart, M., P. Cummings, A. Nathens, P. Heagerty, R. Maier, and F. Rivara, "An Evaluation of State Firearm Regulations and Homicide and Suicide Death Rates," *Injury Prevention*, Vol. 11, No. 2, 2005, pp. 77–83.

Steidley, Trent Taylor, *Movements, Malefactions, and Munitions: Determinants and Effects of Concealed Carry Laws in the United States*, dissertation, Columbus, Ohio: Ohio State University, 2016. As of May 12, 2017:
http://rave.ohiolink.edu/etdc/view?acc_num=osu1466007307

Strnad, Jeff, "Should Legal Empiricism Go Bayesian?" *American Law and Economics Review*, Vol. 9, No. 1, Spring 2007, pp. 195–304.

United States Code, Title 18, Section 926, Rules and Regulations.

United States Concealed Carry Association, "Traveling? Know Concealed Carry Permit Info by State," West Bend, Wisc., August 7, 2013. As of June 29, 2017:
https://www.usconcealedcarry.com/traveling-ccw-permit/

USA Carry, "Concealed Carry Permit Reciprocity Maps," web page, April 20, 2017. As of June 29, 2017:
http://www.usacarry.com/concealed_carry_permit_reciprocity_maps.html

Violence Policy Center, "Concealed Carry Killers," web page, 2017. As of March 23, 2017:
http://concealedcarrykillers.org/

Webster, D., C. K. Crifasi, and J. S. Vernick, "Effects of the Repeal of Missouri's Handgun Purchaser Licensing Law on Homicides," *Journal of Urban Health*, Vol. 91, No. 2, 2014, pp. 293–302.

CHAPTER FOURTEEN

# Waiting Periods

The Brady Handgun Violence Prevention Act (the Brady Act), which went into effect in 1994, imposed a five-day waiting period for handguns purchased from licensed dealers in states with unsatisfactory procedures for conducting background checks. However, this requirement lasted only until 1998, when the National Instant Criminal Background Check System (NICS) became available. Since then, all firearm purchases have required NICS background checks, which normally take no more than a few minutes to complete. Nevertheless, in approximately 10 percent of background checks, the NICS check requires supplementary reviews (Criminal Justice Information Services Division, 2014), and federal law allows the Federal Bureau of Investigation (FBI) up to three days to complete these (18 U.S.C. 922). After three days, the dealer may, but is not required to, transfer possession of a firearm to its purchaser even without completion of the background check. By giving the FBI three days to complete the checks before allowing someone to take possession of a new firearm, the federal law can introduce delays comparable to a waiting period, although most buyers experience no such delay.

Waiting-period laws are intended to reduce suicide, violent crime, and mass shootings in several ways. First, waiting periods are primarily designed to disrupt impulsive acts of violence and self-harm, giving angry or distraught buyers time to "cool off" or gain perspective. While it is plausible that this cooling-off period could reduce impulsive interpersonal gun violence, some evidence exists for the potential effects of this mechanism in reducing suicides. Many suicidal acts are impulsive, with a short time between ideation (thinking about suicide) and attempt (Miller, Azrael, and Barber, 2012; Simon et al., 2002). Suicidal crises are often short-lived and characterized by ambivalence (Daigle, 2005; Glatt, 1987). Delaying access to firearms for individuals in these circumstances can reduce suicide attempts (see Chapter Sixteen, on the relationship between firearm prevalence and suicide). Even if many distraught suicide attempters would seek alternative means of killing themselves, waiting periods may still reduce total rates of suicide because of the high case-fatality ratio of firearms compared with other methods (Anestis, 2016; Vyrostek, Annest, and Ryan, 2004).

Still, for some individuals, waiting periods may serve only to delay suicides rather than prevent them. Evidence from a cohort of handgun purchasers in California found that, while almost no firearm suicides were committed by this population during the 15-day waiting period, the most elevated relative risk of firearm suicide (compared with the general population) occurred in the first week after receipt of the weapon and remained highly elevated over the first month of purchase (Wintemute et al., 1999). Moreover, most firearms are purchased by individuals who already own a firearm. Azrael et al. (2017) found that, on average, gun owners had close to five firearms each, and a large majority (62 percent) purchased their most recent weapon from a gun dealer. For those who already own guns, a waiting period may have little or no effect on suicide risk. However, a cooling-off period could still yield some violence reduction benefits by deferring the acquisition of, for instance, more or more-lethal weapons, although such benefits are likely more limited for this group.

Second, waiting periods may provide law enforcement with opportunities to investigate possible straw purchases (in which a lawful buyer makes the purchase on the behalf of a prohibited buyer) under the theory that it is less difficult to intercept a weapon prior to delivery. To assess whether waiting periods disrupt illegal firearm trafficking or transfers through this mechanism, causal inference could be strengthened by examining crime gun trace data in addition to changes in homicide or violent crime rates.[1] Specifically, if these laws restrict straw purchasing from in-state retailers, one should observe a larger share of crime guns originating from out-of-state sources after law passage and/or a reduction in guns with a short time-to-crime (Webster and Wintemute, 2015; Braga et al., 2012).[2] However, a series of provisions attached to Bureau of Alcohol, Tobacco, Firearms and Explosives (ATF) appropriations (commonly known as the Tiahrt Amendments) has denied most researchers access to firearm trace data since 2003, making it currently infeasible to conduct this type of analysis (Krouse, 2009).

Third, waiting periods provide law enforcement agencies with additional time to complete background checks that sometimes cannot be completed within the three-day window provided by the federal law. In 2014, for instance, 2,511 firearms were transferred from federally licensed firearm dealers to prohibited persons as a result of delays in NICS background checks that exceeded three business days (Criminal Justice Information Services Division, 2015). An additional 1 percent of all background checks, or about 230,000, could not be completed within 88 days and were thus purged from the NICS review system by law without a determination about whether the buyer was a prohibited possessor (Office of the Inspector General, U.S. Department of Justice, 2016). When a buyer is determined to have been a prohibited possessor and has

---

[1] The Bureau of Alcohol, Tobacco, and Firearms (2002, p. A-3) defined *crime gun* as "any firearm that is illegally possessed, used in a crime, or suspected to have been used in a crime. An abandoned firearm may also be categorized as a crime gun if it is suspected it was used in a crime or illegally possessed."

[2] Per Webster and Wintemute (2015), the metric known as *time-to-crime* is the "unusually short interval—ranging from less than 1 year to less than 3 years—between a gun's retail sale and its subsequent recovery by police from criminal suspects or crime scenes . . . . A short [time-to-crime] is considered an indicator of diversion, especially when the criminal possessor is someone different from the purchaser of record."

taken possession of a firearm, the NICS alerts ATF, which in the vast majority of cases (e.g., 116 of the 125 examined by the Office of the Inspector General, U.S. Department of Justice, 2016) is successful in recovering the weapon.

Waiting periods provide additional time that can facilitate a more thorough check before buyers take possession of a new weapon, thereby increasing the effectiveness of background check laws in limiting firearm access by prohibited possessors who are considered to present elevated risk of violence. As discussed in Chapter Three, the majority of prohibited possessors who perpetrate gun violence acquire their firearms from social acquaintances or the black market; thus, a large portion of violent gun crime is unlikely to be affected through this mechanism. In addition, it is unclear whether extending the time to complete background checks would reduce mass shootings. An analysis of the sources of firearms used in a sample of 16 mass shootings between 2009 and 2016 found one instance (6.3 percent) in which the shooter acquired a firearm used in the assault because the background check could not be completed in three business days (Buchanan et al., 2016). One additional instance involved an administrative error that resulted in a failure to trigger an automatic rejection and delayed completion of the background check within the requisite three-day period (Buchanan et al., 2016). However, the small sample of mass shooting cases explored in this analysis makes generalizations about the association of waiting periods and mass shooting incidents unwarranted.

Waiting-period laws may have the unintended consequence of delaying needed self-protection, although little empirical evidence exists to assess how often this may occur. The waiting periods may inconvenience some hunters or sport shooters who would otherwise benefit from more quickly obtaining a new firearm and, by extension, could reduce gun sales. Moreover, the laws may discourage some gun sales because they can require buyers to make two trips to the dealer, which delays the satisfaction of taking possession of the weapon.

Ideally, the effects of waiting periods would be studied among those populations most directly affected by the presumed mechanisms of their effect. In particular, it would be valuable to examine the effects of waiting periods on suicide and violence among those who do not already own a gun. However, this information is not available in the large data sets typically used to analyze the effects of gun policy (although there are some data on the time frame between purchase of a firearm and suicide risk; see Chapter Sixteen). Similarly, understanding the effect of waiting periods on the gun industry would be straightforward if sales data were available at state or local levels.

Analyses could also exploit the types of firearms for which waiting periods are required, as well as the duration of the waiting period. The importance of accounting for such policy heterogeneity will depend on the extent to which different types of firearms are substitutes and the marginal effect of requiring an additional day or days of delay before transfer can occur. State waiting-period laws applying to only a subset of firearms (e.g., handguns) should primarily affect outcomes involving those firearms, although one might expect to observe substitution toward other firearms excluded from waiting-period requirements. With respect to the waiting-period length, should the urge to commit suicide subside within one day, waiting periods of 48 hours or two weeks should generate similar effects, but if suicidal impulses persist for one week, different waiting period lengths may generate heterogeneous effects (Lewiecki and Miller, 2013).

## State Implementation of Waiting Periods

A few jurisdictions impose a waiting period to purchase a firearm (Giffords Law Center to Prevent Gun Violence, undated-g). For example, California and the District of Columbia require a ten-day waiting period before buyers take possession of a new firearm.[3] In Hawaii, buyers must wait 14 days to receive a permit to purchase a firearm.[4] Other states impose waiting periods only for handguns or only for handguns and assault rifles.

## Effects on Suicide

### Research Synthesis Findings

The Hahn et al. (2005) review identified six studies that examined the effects of waiting periods on suicides, but the authors found that the evidence was inconclusive. And according to the National Research Council (NRC) (2004, p. 184), "While suicide has rarely been the basis for public support of specific gun laws, suicide prevention may be the unintended by-product of such laws." Although NRC did not make any conclusions about specific gun policies, the report stated, "Some gun control policies may reduce the number of gun suicides, but they have not yet been shown to reduce the overall risk of suicide in any population." On waiting-period policies, NRC concluded, "The risk of suicide is highest immediately after purchase of a handgun, suggesting that some firearms are specifically purchased for the purpose of committing suicide."[5]

Cook and Ludwig (2003) provides results similar to the authors' earlier paper (Ludwig and Cook, 2000). Because the earlier paper included a larger data set spanning a wider time frame, we focus on its analyses, although the results reported in the two papers are comparable. Both papers examined changes in suicide rates before and

---

[3] Calif. Penal Code §§ 26815, 27540, 27545 (the waiting period applies to dealers, but, in California, all sales must be processed through a dealer); D.C. Code Ann. §§ 22-4508.

[4] Hawaii Rev. Stat. Ann. § 134-2. A separate permit is required for each handgun purchase, and the permit expires after ten days; long-gun permits are valid for one year.

[5] This finding derives from studies that have estimated suicide risk after purchase of firearms, described in more detail in Chapters Sixteen and Seventeen.

after the implementation of the Brady Act in 1994, which initially imposed waiting periods and background checks for purchases from licensed firearm dealers. When the Brady Act was implemented, 18 states and the District of Columbia already had background checks, 27 states were required to implement background checks and waiting periods, and five states were required to implement only background checks (because they already had waiting periods or had an instant background check procedure that satisfied the Brady requirements). Ludwig and Cook (2000) sought to identify the effects of waiting periods by comparing reductions in suicide rates found in the states that did and did not implement waiting periods. They found that, when compared with the 18 unaffected states (plus the District of Columbia), the states implementing and those not implementing waiting periods saw uncertain reductions in suicide and firearm suicide rates. A subgroup analysis found a significant 9-percent reduction in firearm suicide rates among older victims in states that introduced waiting periods, whereas the reductions in states that did not have to introduce waiting periods were smaller and uncertain. The paper did not demonstrate that the difference between these rate reductions was statistically significant. In addition, the analyses of states that were not required to implement waiting periods had a ratio of estimated parameters to observations of less than one to three, and the study provided no additional evidence to demonstrate model fit. Therefore, in accordance with our review methodology, we discount the evidence provided by this analysis because of the possibility the model was overfit, and thus the estimated effects and their confidence intervals (CIs) may be unreliable indicators of the true causal effects of the laws.

#### Conclusions

We identified no qualifying studies that estimated the effects of waiting periods on suicides.

## Effects on Violent Crime

#### Research Synthesis Findings

In their review of existing science, Hahn et al. (2005) found insufficient evidence for determining the effectiveness of waiting periods on violent crime. In its review, NRC (2004) profiled a study by Ludwig and Cook (2000)—a version of which was published in our review period (Cook and Ludwig, 2003)—that examined changes in homicide rates before and after implementation of the Brady Act in 1994. The authors sought to identify the effects of waiting periods by comparing reductions in homicide rates in states that had to implement waiting periods in 1994 with reductions in states that did not. Ludwig and Cook (2000) found that, compared with the 18 unaffected states (plus the District of Columbia), states implementing waiting periods saw nonsignificant drops in homicide and nonfirearm homicide rates, whereas the five states that were not required to implement waiting periods saw nonsignificant increases in homicide and firearm homicide rates. However, the paper did not report whether these effects differed by a statistically significant amount. In addition, the analyses of states that were not required to implement waiting periods had a ratio of estimated parameters to observations of less than one to three, and the paper provided no additional evidence to demonstrate model fit. Therefore, in accordance with our review methodology, we discount the evidence provided by this analysis because of the possibility the model was overfit, and thus the estimated effects and their CIs may be unreliable indicators of the true causal effects of the laws.

We identified one study that specifically examined the effect of waiting periods on violent crime. Roberts (2009) separately analyzed the effects of waiting-period length (none, 24 hours, between two and seven days, and more than seven days) and shall-issue laws on intimate partner homicides (using county-level data from 1985 to 2004). The author found that a waiting period of between two and seven days significantly lowered intimate partner homicide rates compared with no waiting period, but longer (more than seven days) or shorter (24-hour) waiting periods (compared with no waiting period) had only suggestive effects on reducing total intimate partner homicides. The author also reported that a waiting period of between two and seven days significantly reduced firearm-related intimate partner homicides (compared with no waiting period), but a waiting period longer than seven days significantly increased intimate partner firearm homicides (compared with no waiting period). However, these analyses did not cluster standard errors at the state level, so serial correlation that was unaccounted for in the panel data could have resulted in biased standard errors and CIs. In addition, the analysis examined alternative specifications, such as spline or hybrid models, for the effects of shall-issue laws.

Figure 14.1 displays the incidence rate ratios (IRRs) and CIs associated with the waiting-period policies examined in these studies (except for Ludwig and Cook [2000] and Cook and Ludwig [2003] for the reasons stated earlier). Our standardized effects suggest that after a 24-hour waiting period went into effect, the intimate partner firearm homicide rate was 58 percent of what would have been expected without the policy, and the intimate partner total homicide rate was 56 percent of what would have been expected without the policy. Further, when the waiting period of between two and seven days went into effect, the intimate partner firearm homicide rate and total homicide rate were 72 percent and 42 percent, respectively, of what would have been expected without the policy. Oddly, waiting periods of longer than seven days were

**Figure 14.1**
**Incidence Rate Ratios Associated with the Effect of Waiting Periods on Violent Crime**

| Study, by Policy | Outcome Measure | Effect Size (IRR) [95% CI] |
|---|---|---|
| **24-Hour waiting period** | **Homicide** | |
| Roberts (2009) | Total intimate partner | 0.56 [0.21, 0.91] |
| Roberts (2009) | Firearm intimate partner | 0.58 [0.23, 0.92] |
| **2–7 Day waiting period** | | |
| Roberts (2009) | Total intimate partner | 0.47 [0.37, 0.57] |
| Roberts (2009) | Firearm intimate partner | 0.72 [0.57, 0.87] |
| **>1 Week waiting period** | | |
| Roberts (2009) | Total intimate partner | 0.74 [0.47, 1.02] |
| Roberts (2009) | Firearm intimate partner | 1.56 [1.01, 2.11] |

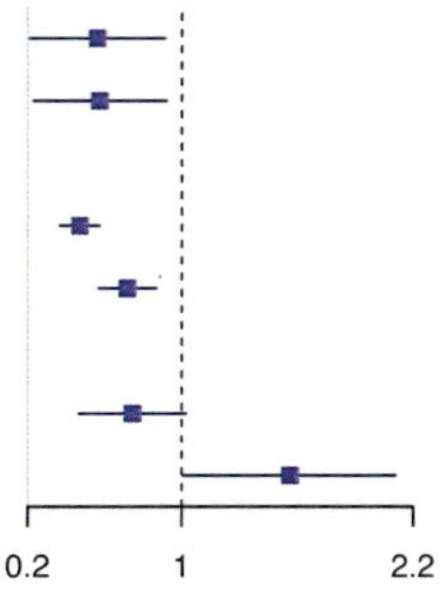


NOTE: IRR values marked with blue squares indicate that methodological concerns are discussed in the text. See Appendix B for details.

estimated to decrease total intimate partner homicide rates by 36 percent but increase firearm intimate partner homicide rates by 56 percent.

## Conclusions

We identified one qualifying study that examined the effects of waiting periods on homicide rates. Specifically, Roberts (2009) found that a waiting period of between two and seven days was significantly associated with reduced intimate partner homicides generally and those committed with firearms in particular. He found only a suggestive effect for 24-hour waiting periods reducing total and firearm-involved intimate partner homicides. He found suggestive effects for waiting periods of more than seven days reducing intimate partner homicides. However, he also found that these longer waiting periods were significantly associated with increases in intimate partner homicides in which a firearm was the murder weapon. Based on this one study and an assessment of its strengths, we find *inconclusive evidence for the effect of waiting periods on violent crime generally or intimate partner homicides in particular.*

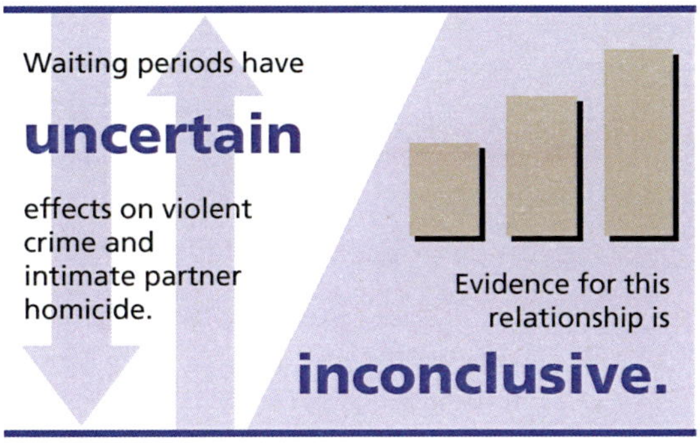

## Effects on Mass Shootings

### Research Synthesis Findings

Neither NRC (2004) nor Hahn et al. (2005) identified research examining the effects of waiting periods on mass shootings in the United States. Our search yielded two studies that met our inclusion criteria.

Lott (2003) used a Poisson regression model to estimate the effect of waiting periods on fatalities, injuries, and the incidence of *multiple-victim public shootings*, which the author defined as events unrelated to other criminal activity in which two or more people were killed or wounded in a public location. The analysis covered 1977 to 1997, and regression models included controls for state and year fixed effects, other state firearm policies, and a broad range of state-level socioeconomic and demographic characteristics. The author characterized waiting-period laws using three variables: a dummy variable for whether state laws required a waiting period before delivery of a firearm, the length of the waiting period in days, and the length of the waiting period in days squared. For all three policy variables, findings showed effects that were small and not statistically significant for total casualties from multiple-victim public shootings and for total number of multiple-victim public shooting incidents (see Figure 14.2). However, these models had an unfavorable ratio of estimated parameters to observations (approximately one to eight), suggesting that the model may have been overfit, and thus the estimated effects of these laws may be poor indicators of their true effects. In addition, the model did not adjust for clustered standard errors. Together, these shortcomings suggest that the model results may not accurately describe the true effects of waiting periods.

Using a two-way fixed-effects linear probability model, Luca, Deepak, and Poliquin (2016) estimated the effects of waiting periods on a binary indicator for whether a mass shooting occurred in a given state-year. The authors included two measures of waiting periods: the number of days that purchasers must wait before accepting delivery of a handgun and the number of days before accepting delivery of a long gun. The authors' regression analysis covered 1989–2014 and included controls for time-invariant state characteristics, national trends, and a host of other state-level gun policies, as well as time-varying state-level demographic, socioeconomic, and political characteristics. Their findings showed uncertain effects that were small in magnitude of both waiting-period measures on the probability of a mass shooting event. However, assessing the effects of gun policies on mass shootings was not the primary focus of Luca, Deepak, and Poliquin (2016), and the authors intended the estimates to serve solely as a robustness check for their main specification (the effects of mass shootings on gun policy). Although the paper provided limited information to use in evaluating the reported statistical models (e.g., on how these policies were coded), it is clear that the analysis used a linear model to predict a dichotomous outcome. Therefore, model assumptions were violated, making CIs unreliable.

Figure 14.2 displays the IRRs and CIs associated with the waiting-period policies examined in these studies.

**Figure 14.2**
**Incidence Rate Ratios Associated with the Effect of Waiting Periods on Mass Shootings**

| Study, by Policy | Outcome Measure | Effect Size (IRR) [95% CI] |
|---|---|---|
| **Handgun waiting period (days)** | **Mass shooting** | |
| Luca, Deepak, & Poliquin (2016) | State-year indicator (political controls) | 1.04 [0.98, 1.11] |
| **Long-gun waiting period (days)** | | |
| Luca, Deepak, & Poliquin (2016) | State-year indicator (political controls) | 0.95 [0.64, 1.26] |
| **Waiting period** | | |
| Lott (2003) | Total deaths and injuries (waiting period dummy) | 0.90 [0.67, 1.21] |
| Lott (2003) | Total deaths and injuries (waiting period in days) | 0.99 [0.97, 1.01] |
| Lott (2003) | Number of shooting incidents (waiting period dummy) | 4.20 [0.66, 26.87] |
| Lott (2003) | Number of shooting incidents (waiting period in days) | 0.67 [0.39, 1.16] |

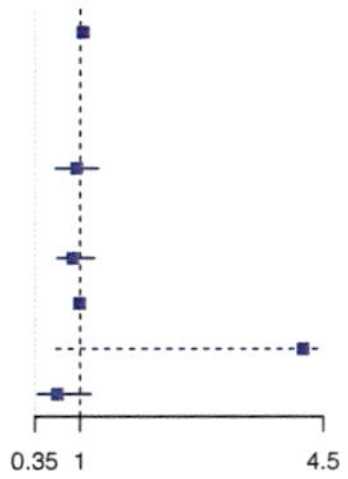


NOTE: IRR values marked with blue squares indicate that methodological concerns are discussed in the text. See Appendix B for details. We abbreviated the full range of the CI for one Lott (2003) outcome measure so that it fit within the scale of the figure; for this CI, we use a dotted line.

## Conclusions

We identified two qualifying studies examining the effect of waiting periods on mass shooting outcomes. Luca, Deepak, and Poliquin (2016) found the length of waiting periods required for handguns and for long guns to have uncertain effects on the likelihood that at least one mass shooting occurred in a state. Lott (2003) found a suggestive effect consistent with the passage of any waiting-period law increasing the incidence of mass shootings. However, estimates in the same model also showed a suggestive effect of waiting-period length on decreasing the incidence of mass shootings, which complicates interpretation of the overall effect of the law. Further, Lott (2003) found uncertain effects of both waiting-period measures on the number of casualties from mass shooting events. Based on these studies, we find *inconclusive evidence for the effect of waiting periods on mass shootings.*

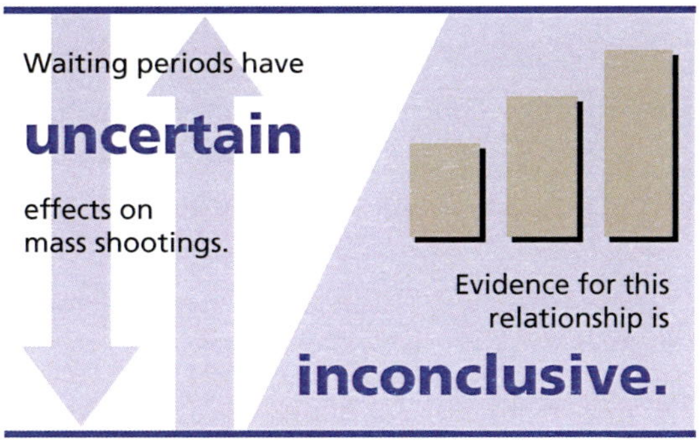

## Outcomes Without Studies Examining the Effects of Waiting Periods

Neither NRC (2004) nor Hahn et al. (2005) identified any research examining the effects of waiting periods on the following outcomes, and we identified no such studies that met our inclusion criteria:

- unintentional injuries and deaths
- officer-involved shootings
- defensive gun use
- hunting and recreation
- gun industry.

## Chapter Fourteen References

Anestis, M. D., "Prior Suicide Attempts Are Less Common in Suicide Decedents Who Died by Firearms Relative to Those Who Died by Other Means," *Journal of Affective Disorders*, Vol. 189, No. 1, 2016, pp. 106–109.

Azrael, Deborah, Lisa Hepburn, David Hemenway, and Matthew Miller, "The Stock and Flow of U.S. Firearms: Results from the 2015 National Firearms Survey," *Russell Sage Foundation Journal of the Social Sciences*, Vol. 3, No. 5, 2017, pp. 38–57.

Braga, Anthony A., Garen J. Wintemute, Glenn L. Pierce, Philip J. Cook, and Greg Ridgeway, "Interpreting the Empirical Evidence on Illegal Gun Market Dynamics," *Journal of Urban Health*, Vol. 89, No. 5, 2012, pp. 779–793.

Buchanan, Larry, Josh Keller, Richard A. Oppel, Jr., and Daniel Victor, "How They Got Their Guns," *New York Times*, June 12, 2016. As of March 16, 2017: https://www.nytimes.com/interactive/2015/10/03/us/how-mass-shooters-got-their-guns.html

Bureau of Alcohol, Tobacco, and Firearms, *Crime Gun Trace Reports (2000): Memphis, Tennessee*, Washington, D.C.: U.S. Department of the Treasury, July 2002.

Cook, P. J., and Jens Ludwig, "The Effect of the Brady Act on Gun Violence," in B. Harcourt, ed., *Guns, Crime, and Punishment in America*, New York: New York University Press, 2003, pp. 283–298.

Criminal Justice Information Services Division, *National Instant Criminal Background Check System (NICS) Operations 2013*, Washington, D.C.: U.S. Department of Justice, Federal Bureau of Investigation, 2014. As of June 29, 2017: https://archives.fbi.gov/archives/about-us/cjis/nics/reports/2013-operations-report

———, *National Instant Criminal Background Check System (NICS) Operations 2014*, Washington, D.C.: U.S. Department of Justice, Federal Bureau of Investigation, 2015. As of March 16, 2017: https://www.fbi.gov/file-repository/2014-nics-ops-report-050115.pdf

Daigle, M. S., "Suicide Prevention Through Means Restriction: Assessing the Risk of Substitution—A Critical Review," *Accident Analysis and Prevention*, Vol. 37, 2005, pp. 625–632.

Giffords Law Center to Prevent Gun Violence, "Waiting Periods," web page, undated-g. As of October 18, 2017: http://lawcenter.giffords.org/gun-laws/policy-areas/gun-sales/waiting-periods/

Glatt, K. M., "Helpline: Suicide Prevention at a Suicide Site," *Suicide and Life-Threatening Behavior*, Vol. 17, 1987, pp. 299–309.

Hahn, Robert A., Oleg Bilukha, Alex Crosby, Mindy T. Fullilove, Akiva Liberman, Eve Moscicki, Susan Snyder, Farris Tuma, and Peter A. Briss, "Firearms Laws and the Reduction of Violence: A Systematic Review," *American Journal of Preventive Medicine*, Vol. 28, No. 2, 2005, pp. 40–71.

Krouse, W. J., *Gun Control: Statutory Disclosure Limitations on ATF Firearms Trace Data and Multiple Handgun Sales Reports*, Washington, D.C.: Congressional Research Service, 7-5700, 2009.

Lewiecki, E. M., and S. A. Miller, "Suicide, Guns, and Public Policy," *American Journal of Public Health*, Vol. 103, No. 1, 2013, pp. 27–31.

Lott, John R., Jr., *The Bias Against Guns: Why Almost Everything You've Heard about Gun Control Is Wrong*, Washington, D.C.: Regnery Publishing, Inc., 2003.

Luca, Michael, Lahotra Deepak, and Christopher Poliquin, *The Impact of Mass Shootings on Gun Policy*, working paper, Boston, Mass.: Harvard Business School, 2016.

Ludwig, J., and P. J. Cook, "Homicide and Suicide Rates Associated with Implementation of the Brady Handgun Violence Prevention Act," *JAMA*, Vol. 284, No. 5, 2000, pp. 585–591.

Miller, M., D. Azrael, and C. Barber, "Suicide Mortality in the United States: The Importance of Attending to Method in Understanding Population-Level Disparities in the Burden of Suicide," *Annual Review of Public Health*, Vol. 33, 2012, pp. 393–408.

National Research Council, *Firearms and Violence: A Critical Review*, Washington, D.C.: National Academies Press, 2004.

NRC—*See* National Research Council.

Office of the Inspector General, U.S. Department of Justice, *Audit of the Handling of Firearms Purchase Denials Through the National Instant Criminal Background Check System,* Washington, D.C., September 2016. As of May 11, 2017:
https://oig.justice.gov/reports/2016/a1632.pdf

Roberts, Darryl W., "Intimate Partner Homicide: Relationships to Alcohol and Firearms," *Journal of Contemporary Criminal Justice*, Vol. 25, No. 1, 2009, pp. 67–88.

Simon, T. R., A. C. Swann, K. E. Powell, L. B. Potter, M. Kresnow, and P. W. O'Carroll, "Characteristics of Impulsive Suicide Attempts and Attempters," *Suicide and Life-Threatening Behavior*, Vol. 32, No. 1, 2002, pp. 49–59.

United States Code, Title 18, Section 922, Unlawful Acts.

Vyrostek, S. B., J. L. Annest, and G. W. Ryan, "Surveillance for Fatal and Nonfatal Injuries—United States, 2001," *MMWR Surveillance Summary*, Vol. 53, 2004, pp. 1–57.

Webster, D.W., and G. J. Wintemute, "Effects of Policies Designed to Keep Firearms from High-Risk Individuals," *Annual Review of Public Health*, Vol. 36, 2015, pp. 21–37.

Wintemute, G. J., C. A. Parham, J. J. Beaumont, M. Wright, and C. Drake, "Mortality Among Recent Purchasers of Handguns," *New England Journal of Medicine*, Vol. 341, No. 21, 1999, pp. 1583–1589.

CHAPTER FIFTEEN

# Gun-Free Zones

Federal and state laws bar most individuals from carrying firearms or other weapons in certain locations. For instance, federal laws prohibit the possession of firearms in federal facilities, other than federal court facilities, except for hunting or other lawful purposes (18 U.S.C. 930). Similarly, firearms are prohibited on property belonging to the U.S. Department of Veterans Affairs (38 C.F.R. 1.218) or the U.S. Postal Service (39 C.F.R. 232.1).

Two federal laws restrict guns in or around schools offering elementary or secondary education. The Gun-Free School Zones Act of 1990 prohibits most firearms within 1,000 feet of a school, but it does not apply to possession by individuals with state licenses (18 U.S.C. 922).[1] In addition, the Gun-Free Schools Act of 1994 applies to schools receiving federal funds and requires the schools to expel for at least one year any student found in possession of a firearm on school property (20 U.S.C. 7961).

Gun-free zones are intended to reduce violent crime, suicides, unintentional firearm injuries and deaths, and mass shootings in specific locations. In theory, the gun-free zone reduces or eliminates the presence of guns in these areas, thereby eliminating the risk of unintentional firearm injuries due to recklessness, escalatory conflicts, or criminal activity. Gun-free zones establish the legal foundation for imposing screening measures, such as bag checks at stadiums or magnetometer screening at some schools or public buildings, that can be used to ensure that fewer or no guns are present in the location.

Alternatively, if the presence or potential presence of armed civilians deters violence, gun-free zones could serve as more-attractive targets to violent criminals or mass shooters because perpetrators will be less likely to encounter armed resistance in these areas. There is debate over the extent to which perpetrators target gun-free zones. One analysis of 133 mass shooting events between 2009 and 2016 found that 10 percent of

[1] The law states, "It shall be unlawful for any individual knowingly to possess a firearm that has moved in or that otherwise affects interstate or foreign commerce at a place that the individual knows, or has reasonable cause to believe, is a school zone." A Supreme Court decision (*United States v. Lopez*, 514 U.S. 549) ruled the act to be an unconstitutional attempt to legislate under the Commerce Clause of the U.S. Constitution, so the law was amended in 1995 to restrict application to firearms that have moved via interstate commerce.

incidents occurred in designated gun-free zones (Everytown for Gun Safety Support Fund, 2017b). However, another analysis focused on public mass shootings between 1998 and 2015 and reported that 96.2 percent of incidents took place in gun-free zones (Crime Prevention Research Center, 2014). While the discrepancy in these estimates is partially due to differences in how mass shootings are defined—the latter study restricts analysis to public mass shootings—there also appears to be some disagreement about how gun-free zones are classified.

To evaluate the effects of gun-free zones, the ideal data would be at fine-enough geographic detail to examine changes in outcomes specifically in areas in which gun-free zones were implemented or removed. However, a nationwide database on gun-free zones does not exist, and different decisions about how to classify these areas can lead to widely differing conclusions. Determining whether a given shooting incident occurred in a gun-free zone requires collecting information on local firearm policies; determining whether the place an incident occurred had a policy of allowing or disallowing firearms; and determining whether it had a means of enforcing that policy, such as bag checks or magnetometer screening.

## State Implementation of Gun-Free Zones

Courts are explicitly exempted from the ban on weapons in federal facilities, but many states have enacted laws banning firearms, or concealed firearms, in state court buildings.[2] Most states prohibit guns in schools for kindergarten through grade 12. In addition, many have more-restrictive laws for gun-free school zones, extending the prohibition to holders of concealed-carry permits (see Chapter Thirteen), prohibiting the open carry of firearms, or making colleges and other postsecondary schools gun-free zones (Giffords Law Center to Prevent Gun Violence, undated-c).

---

[2] Alaska, Arkansas, California, Colorado, Florida, Georgia, Idaho, Illinois, Kansas, Kentucky, Louisiana, Maine, Michigan, Minnesota, Mississippi, Missouri, Nebraska, Nevada, New Hampshire, New Mexico, North Carolina, Ohio, Oklahoma, Oregon, Pennsylvania, Rhode Island, South Carolina, South Dakota, Tennessee, Texas, Utah, Vermont, Virginia, Washington, West Virginia, Wisconsin, and Wyoming. See Alaska Stat. Ann. § 11.61.220; Ark. Code Ann. § 5-73-122; Calif. Penal Code § 171b; Col. Rev. Stat. § 18-12-214; Fla. Stat. Ann. § 790.06; Ga. Stat. Ann. § 16-11-127; Ida. Code Ann. § 18-3302C; 430 Ill. CS 66/65; Kan. Stat. Ann. § 21-6309; Ky. Rev. Stat. Ann. § 237.110; La. Stat. Ann. § 1379.3; 17 Me. Rev. Stat. Ann. § 1058; Administrative Order of the Michigan Supreme Court 2001-1; Minn. Stat. Ann. § 609.66; Miss. Ann. Code § 45-9-101; Mo. Stat. Ann. § 571.030; Neb. Rev. Stat. § 69-2441; Nev. Rev. Stat. Ann. § 202.3673; N.H. Rev. Stat. § 159:19; N.M. Stat. Ann. § 29-19-11; N.C. Gen. Stat. Ann. § 14-269.4; Ohio Rev. Code Ann. § 2923.123; Okla. Stat. Ann. § 1272; Ore. Rev. Stat. Ann. § 166.370; 18 Pa. Cons. Stat. § 91; R.I. Supreme Court Executive Order 2003-6; S.C. Ann. Code § 23-31-215; S.D. Cod. Laws § 22-14-23; Tenn. Code Ann. § 39-17-1306; Tex. Penal Code § 46.03; Utah Code Ann. § 78A-2-203; 18 Vt. Stat. Ann. § 4016; Va. Code Ann. § 18.2-283.1; Wash. Rev. Code Ann. § 9.41.300; W. Va. Code § 61-7-11a; Wisc. Stat. Ann. § 175.60; Wyo. Stat. § 6-5-209.

Recently, some states have passed laws requiring college and university campuses to allow concealed carry,[3] although some of these states still prohibit, or allow schools to prohibit, guns in particular locations on campus.[4] Idaho removed the authority of the governing bodies of colleges or universities to regulate or prohibit gun possession on campus.[5] Tennessee allows nonstudents to carry concealed weapons on campus.[6]

In Colorado, the courts found that only the General Assembly can regulate firearm possession on any college campus, and according to statute, concealed weapons are allowed on campus. Schools may regulate but not ban guns.[7] Similarly, Oregon's Court of Appeals ruled that public colleges and universities may not ban weapons on campus grounds.[8] In contrast, Oklahoma recently granted schools and universities authority to make their own policies concerning guns on campus.[9]

## Outcomes Without Studies Examining the Effects of Gun-Free Zones

Although Hahn et al. (2005) did identify one cross-sectional study on the effect of magnetometers on school violence, neither the National Research Council (2004) nor Hahn et al. (2005) identified any research examining the effects of gun-free zones on the following outcomes, and we identified no such studies that met our inclusion criteria:

- suicide
- violent crime
- unintentional injuries and deaths
- mass shootings
- officer-involved shootings
- defensive gun use
- hunting and recreation
- gun industry.

---

[3] Idaho, Kansas, Mississippi, Texas, Utah, and Wisconsin. See Ida. Code Ann. § 18-3309; Kan. Stat. Ann. § 75-7c20 (concealed weapons shall not be prohibited unless adequate security measures are in place to ensure that no weapons are permitted); Miss. Ann. Code §§ 97-37-7, 45-9-101 (advanced permit required); Tex. Govt. Code § 411.2031; Utah Code Ann. § 53B-3-103; Wisc. Stat. Ann. § 943.13.

[4] For example, Idaho and Texas.

[5] Ida. Code Ann. § 18-3309.

[6] Tenn. Code Ann. § 39-17-1309.

[7] *Regents of the Univ. of Colorado v. Students of Concealed Carry on Campus, LLC*, 271 P.3d 496 (Colo. 2012); Colo. Rev. Stat. Ann. § 18-12-201 et seq.

[8] Ore. Firearms Educ. Found. v. Bd. Of Higher Educ., 264 P.3d 160 (Or. Ct. App. 2011).

[9] Okla. Stat. Ann. tit 21, § 1277.

## Chapter Fifteen References

Code of Federal Regulations, Title 38, Section 1.218, Security and Law Enforcement at VA Facilities.

Code of Federal Regulations, Title 39, Section 232.1, Conduct on Postal Property.

Crime Prevention Research Center, "Updated: More Misleading Information from Bloomberg's Everytown for Gun Safety on Guns: 'Analysis of Recent Mass Shootings,' Showing How Mass Public Shootings Keep Occurring in Gun-Free Zones," September 1, 2014. As of March 13, 2017: http://crimeresearch.org/2014/09/more-misleading-information-from-bloombergs-everytown-for-gun-safety-on-guns-analysis-of-recent-mass-shootings/

Everytown for Gun Safety Support Fund, "Mass Shootings in the United States: 2009–2016," April 11, 2017b. As of May 3, 2017: http://everytownresearch.org/reports/mass-shootings-analysis/

Giffords Law Center to Prevent Gun Violence, "Guns in Schools," web page, undated-c. As of October 18, 2017: http://lawcenter.giffords.org/gun-laws/policy-areas/guns-in-public/guns-in-schools/

Hahn, Robert A., Oleg Bilukha, Alex Crosby, Mindy T. Fullilove, Akiva Liberman, Eve Moscicki, Susan Snyder, Farris Tuma, and Peter A. Briss, "Firearms Laws and the Reduction of Violence: A Systematic Review," *American Journal of Preventive Medicine*, Vol. 28, No. 2, 2005, pp. 40–71.

National Research Council, *Firearms and Violence: A Critical Review*, Washington, D.C.: National Academies Press, 2004.

United States Code, Title 18, Section 922, Unlawful Acts.

United States Code, Title 18, Section 930, Possession of Firearms and Dangerous Weapons in Federal Facilities.

United States Code, Title 20, Section 7961, Gun-Free Schools Act.

PART C

# Supplementary Essays on Gun Policy Mechanisms and Context

## A Note on the Scope of Part C

The 13 policies reviewed in Part B and the scope of the systematic review for the research syntheses were selected a priori and represent the central focus of our research synthesis efforts. Nevertheless, in reviewing evidence on these policies, other important themes emerged that we believed warranted further discussion or review. Therefore, to augment and provide context for Part B's syntheses, Part C includes supplementary essays on what rigorous studies reveal about

- the possible mechanisms by which laws may affect outcomes (Chapters Sixteen and Seventeen on the effects of firearm prevalence on suicide and violent crime)
- how taxes, access to health care, and media campaigns might affect gun violence (Chapters Eighteen through Twenty)
- the effectiveness of laws used to target domestic violence (Chapter Twenty-One)
- methodological challenges in defining and estimating the prevalence of mass shootings and defensive gun use (Chapters Twenty-Two and Twenty-Three)
- how suicide, violent crime, and mass shootings were affected by Australia's implementation of the National Firearms Agreement (Chapter Twenty-Four).

CHAPTER SIXTEEN

# The Relationship Between Firearm Availability and Suicide

In 2004, the National Research Council (NRC) concluded,

> States, regions, and countries with higher rates of household gun ownership have higher rates of gun suicide. There is also cross-sectional, ecological association between gun ownership and *overall* risk of suicide, but this association is more modest than the association between gun ownership and gun suicide; it is less consistently observed across time, place, and persons; and the causal relation remains unclear. . . . The risk of suicide is highest immediately after the purchase of a handgun, suggesting that some firearms are specifically purchased for the purpose of committing suicide.

Suicide attempts involving a firearm are more likely to result in death than attempts using any other means (Azrael and Miller, 2016). If firearms are available to a person who is thinking about taking his or her life, the presence of firearms might be linked with a higher likelihood of suicide and higher regional suicide rates. However, if firearms are not available, a person might either not attempt to take his or her life or might do so using other means. In this chapter, we examine the empirical evidence on the relationship between firearm availability (or prevalence) and suicide.

## Methods

Our literature review strategy was based on the comprehensive search described in Chapter Two of this report. Although the focus of that search was from 2003 forward, we highlight some highly cited articles published prior to 2003. As we did for the policy discussions (Chapters Three through Fifteen), we prioritize the evidence from studies that employ a quasi-experimental approach. However, because this line of scientific inquiry is so much more extensive than most of the other topics reviewed in these syntheses, we take a broader approach referencing noteworthy international studies and cross-sectional studies that were identified in our review.

We categorize these studies as those that examine associations between individual *access* to firearms and suicide rates and those that examine associations between the regional *prevalence* of firearms and suicide rates in census regions, states, and cities.

## Individual Access to Firearms

A primary conclusion of the NRC report was that although there are limitations of studies that examine suicide outcomes among those with access to guns (e.g., gun purchasers) or those that look at firearm ownership among suicide decedents relative to some other group, these research approaches have generally been "underutilized in the literature" (NRC, 2004, p. 183). These studies are broadly defined as "individual-level studies" and, as described in this section, can be categorized into two groups: those that examine suicide risk among gun owners and those that examine firearm access among suicide decedents.

Our review identified eight U.S.-based individual-level studies conducted since 2003, six of which analyzed data from the 1993 National Mortality Followback Survey (Dahlberg, Ikeda, and Kresnow, 2004; Joe, Marcus, and Kaplan, 2007; Kung, Pearson, and Liu, 2003; Kung, Pearson, and Wei, 2005; Shenassa et al., 2004; Wiebe, 2003), one of which examined suicides in the Navy (Stander et al., 2006), and one of which examined suicides in California (Grassel et al., 2003).

### Suicide Risk Among Gun Owners

In 2004, NRC identified that the strongest evidence for the effect of firearm availability on individual suicide rates derived from two studies that examined individual outcomes after the purchase of a firearm; we identified no similar studies that have been conducted since NRC published its findings. Cummings et al. (1997b) used a case-control approach in which they linked health insurance records with firearm licenses in Washington state from 1980 to 1992. During this time, those who died by suicide (using any means) were more likely than living, demographically matched controls to have a history of the decedent or somebody in the family having purchased a handgun (24.6 percent versus 15.1 percent, respectively; incidence rate ratio [IRR] = 1.9; 95-percent confidence interval [CI]: 1.4, 2.5). Compared with the controls, this risk was greatest in the year after the handgun was purchased (3.1 percent versus 0.7 percent; IRR = 5.7; 95-percent CI: 2.4, 13.5); the median interval between the first handgun purchase and any suicide with a firearm was 10.7 years (range: 11 days to 52.5 years). Wintemute et al. (1999) took a prospective study approach in which they linked applications for handgun purchases among California residents in 1991 to death records maintained by the state from 1991 to 1994. Compared with the general mortality trends in the state for the same years and adjusting for age and sex, handgun purchasers had elevated standardized mortality ratios for suicide (4.31) and firearm suicide

(7.12). The elevated firearm suicide rate among purchasers was seen across all six years after purchase, although the effect was greatest in the first week after purchase (644 per 100,000) and diminished over longer intervals—specifically, the first month after purchase (350–375 per 100,000) and the first year after purchase (75–100 per 100,000). This pattern may indicate that a subset of handgun purchasers acquire a firearm for the purpose of killing themselves.

Whether the mere availability of a gun increases the risk of suicide is a complex question to disentangle from observational data because some of the association between gun accessibility and suicide is likely attributable to the fact that those who wish to kill themselves may go out of their way to procure a gun or otherwise ensure that a gun is accessible. Others with access to guns may be at higher risk of suicide because their attempt to kill themselves with an available gun is more likely to be fatal than if they had used a less lethal means, such as poison or drug overdose. Experimental studies that could systematically test the effects of gun availability on suicides are unlikely to be performed, because they would almost certainly be found to be unethical. The next-best source of rigorous evidence, quasi-experimental observational studies, may never be able to adequately control for the myriad, sometimes intersecting, reasons why individuals might want guns available and might also wish to kill themselves. Nevertheless, the results of such studies shed some light on this association, as we discuss next.

#### Firearm Access Among Suicide Decedents

Prior to 2004, a series of U.S.-based studies routinely and consistently found that access to a firearm, particularly a handgun, in one's home was more prevalent among those who died by suicide than among various comparison groups. These studies were generally based on psychological autopsies, in which ascertainment about the presence of firearms was provided by proxy respondents for the decedent after his or her death and compared with the presence of firearms as reported by comparison or control cases who were matched to the decedent in various ways but who typically had not died. A concern with all such studies is the possibility that cases and controls may not be matched on important characteristics that influence both the person's decision to acquire firearms and his or her risk of suicide. Relatedly, while proxy respondents are likely to know and acknowledge that the decedent who died by firearm suicide had access to a firearm, it is less certain that all controls would acknowledge having access to a gun. Either bias could result in firearm access appearing to be more closely associated with suicide risk than it really is. (For more on potential biases in psychological autopsy studies, see NRC, 2004, pp. 171–172.) Only three U.S.-based psychological autopsy studies have been conducted since 2005.

The relationship between firearm access and suicide has been shown in studies comparing suicide decedents with those who have died by other causes (Dahlberg, Ikeda, and Kresnow, 2004; Grassel et al., 2003; Kung, Pearson, and Liu, 2003; Kung, Pearson, and Wei, 2005; Shenassa et al., 2004), those living in the same community

(Bailey et al., 1997; Brent et al., 1993a; Brent et al., 1993b; Brent et al., 1999; Conwell et al., 2002; Kellermann et al., 1992; Wiebe, 2003), and those with histories of mental illness who have not died by suicide (Brent et al., 1991; Brent et al., 1993a; Brent et al., 1994). This relationship has also been seen in suicides among older adolescents and adults in the general population (Dahlberg, Ikeda, and Kresnow, 2004; Grassel et al., 2003; Kellermann et al., 1992; Kung, Pearson, and Liu, 2003; Kung, Pearson, and Wei, 2005; Shenassa et al., 2004; Wiebe, 2003), as well as specifically among older age groups (Conwell et al., 2002), adolescents (Brent et al., 1991; Brent et al., 1993a; Brent et al., 1993b; Brent et al., 1994; Brent et al., 1999; Bukstein et al., 1993), and women (Bailey et al., 1997). In addition, studies with community-based controls often control for demographic characteristics (through either matching or covariate adjustment) and other family and clinical characteristics (e.g., history of mental illness, alcohol misuse, drug use). Furthermore, studies limited to suicide decedents have shown that prevalence of firearms was higher among those who died by suicide using a firearm than those who used other means (Dahlberg, Ikeda, and Kresnow, 2004; Joe, Marcus, and Kaplan, 2007; Shenassa et al., 2004; Stander et al., 2006).

Eight individual-level studies were published in or after 2003 (Dahlberg, Ikeda, and Kresnow, 2004; Grassel et al., 2003; Joe, Marcus, and Kaplan, 2007; Kung, Pearson, and Liu, 2003; Kung, Pearson, and Wei, 2005; Shenassa et al., 2004; Stander et al., 2006; Wiebe, 2003) (see Table 16.1 for details). One of these studies (Grassel et al., 2003) is particularly informative, as it linked California death data with administrative data on handgun purchases. Findings showed that those who died by suicide were more likely to have purchased a handgun in the previous three years, with the relationship even greater between suicide death and purchase of a handgun in the past year, an effect magnified for women. Five studies used the 1993 National Mortality Followback Survey. One compared suicide decedents with living, matched controls from the National Health Interview Survey and found having a gun in the home to be associated with suicide and specifically firearm suicide, but not with nonfirearm suicide (Wiebe, 2003). The other four studies limited their findings to decedents only and found a relationship between having a gun in the home and elevation in the risk of suicide (Kung, Pearson, and Wei, 2005; Shenassa et al., 2004), a relationship generally robust in models that stratify by gender (Dahlberg, Ikeda, and Kresnow, 2004; Kung, Pearson, and Liu, 2003)[1] and race (Kung, Pearson, and Wei, 2005). Two studies limited their analysis of the 1993 National Mortality Followback Survey to suicides and found a relationship between having a gun in the home and firearm suicide (Dahlberg, Ikeda, and Kresnow, 2004; Joe, Marcus, and Kaplan, 2007), an approach similar to that employed by Stander et al. (2006) in analysis of Navy suicides.

---

1 For an exception, see Dahlberg, Ikeda, and Kresnow (2004), who found that among suicides in the home, the relationship for women was only marginally statistically significant, as the lower limit of the CI was the null value, 1.0.

With individual-level studies, any observed differences in gun access between groups can be interpreted in at least two ways: The differences could suggest that gun access increases the risk of suicide, or they could suggest that people who are suicidal may obtain guns at a higher rate because they are considering killing themselves with guns. In other words, these studies are criticized for providing little insight into the relationship between firearm access and suicide because they are generally consistent with a wide range of causal models, including models postulating effects in opposite directions. A recent review by Azrael and Miller (2016) suggests that the evidence in support of the former of these two interpretations (that gun access increases the risk of suicide) is strong based on two findings. First, the authors note that a series of studies find that the relationship between household gun ownership and suicide exists not just for the firearm owner but for all other household members. Second, although covariate adjustment for factors related to suicidality could attenuate the relationship between the presence of a firearm and suicide, a number of studies reveal no difference in past suicide attempts (described in the next section), mental illness, and substance use disorders between households with firearms and those without. In addition, an omitted variable analysis suggests that if there is actually some third risk factor associated with both household firearm ownership and suicide, this third factor would need to be a better predictor of suicide than any currently known risk factor to fully account for the association between household firearms and suicide (Miller, Swanson, and Azrael, 2016). While compelling, this does not entirely refute an argument about reverse causation: An individual feeling suicidal may acquire a firearm as a means to take his or her life and thus make the weapon readily available in the household.

Other work has used different control groups to attempt to address this selection bias (that suicidal people are more likely to acquire guns so that they can kill themselves). For example, firearm access was higher among adolescents who had committed suicide than among adolescents in inpatient mental health treatment who had either previously attempted suicide or never attempted suicide (Brent et al., 1991). Additionally, adolescent suicides with no history of a mental health disorder had higher rates of firearm access relative to adolescent suicides with a mental health disorder (Brent et al., 1994). This pattern of results may indicate that access to firearms was a causal factor in the suicidal adolescent's death or that parents or caretakers removed guns from the homes of adolescents at risk of suicide because of prior attempts or mental health problems, or a combination of the two.

### Firearm Storage Among Suicide Decedents

Individual-level studies have examined not only whether decedents had access to firearms in their households but also how those guns were stored. In general, these studies consistently show that, relative to comparison groups of individuals who die other ways or of living community members, those who die by suicide have guns stored less safely (Conwell et al., 2002; Shenassa et al., 2004; Grossman et al., 2005). These studies suggested to one set of researchers a "dose-response" relationship between firearm accessibility and risk for suicide (Azrael and Miller, 2016). However, the relationship is not seen in all studies. Brent et al. (1991; 1993b) found no differences in storage practices in homes with adolescents who died by suicide and a comparison group of adolescents living in the community. Dahlberg, Ikeda, and Kresnow (2004) found no association between storage practices and firearm suicide (versus suicide by other means).

**Suicidality (Not Death) as an Outcome**

Individual-level studies that conduct postmortem inventories of the presence of firearms may be biased because they rely on proxy respondents who may report incorrect information either purposely or because they do not know the correct information. At times, researchers have used proxy outcomes—most commonly, living individuals' past suicide attempts and *suicide ideation* (thinking about suicide), which they can ascertain directly from the individuals whose behavior and firearm access are being studied. Yet, while suicide attempts and ideation are potentially important markers of anguish or distress, they are not reliable proxies for or predictors of suicide deaths.[2]

Since 2005, one longitudinal study (Watkins and Lizotte, 2013) and a series of cross-sectional studies (described in Table 16.1) examined firearm access among those who have attempted suicide (and survived), who have made plans to kill themselves, or who have thought about suicide (*suicide ideation*). In general, there was not much evidence of a relationship between suicide ideation and firearm access (Ilgen et al., 2008; Miller et al., 2009; Oslin et al., 2004; Simonetti et al., 2015; Smith, Currier, and Drescher, 2015), although Thompson et al. (2006) found that veterans receiving outpatient treatment for opioid dependence and who had suicide ideation were more likely to own a firearm than those in treatment without such thoughts. However, those with a history of suicide attempts are less likely to have access to a firearm in both population-based (Ilgen et al., 2008; Miller et al., 2009; Simonetti et al., 2015) and psychiatric clinical samples (Kolla, O'Connor, and Lineberry, 2011; Smith, Currier, and Drescher, 2015).[3] In another study, firearm access was higher among those who had made a plan to take their lives using a firearm than among those who made a plan involving some other means (Betz, Barber, and Miller, 2011). Although cross-sectional studies examining suicide attempts and ideation are common, they provide little insight into the relationship between firearm access and suicide, because these results are consistent with a wide range of causal models, including ones that postulate effects in opposite directions.

---

[2] A history of self-injurious thoughts and behaviors is a weak predictor of risk for suicide death (Ribeiro et al., 2016).

[3] An exception is Borowsky et al. (1999), which found that knowing where to get a gun was associated with lifetime suicide attempts among American Indian youth, particularly girls.

There are similar studies examining suicide attempts and ideation with respect to firearm storage practices. Studies generally find no difference in storage practices between adults who have thought about or attempted suicide versus those who have not (Betz et al., 2016; Ilgen et al., 2008; Oslin et al., 2004; Smith, Currier, and Drescher, 2015).

Although suicide attempts and ideation are not reliable proxies of suicide risk, these studies do yield insights into the differences in suicidality between those who have access to guns and those who do not. These studies find little evidence that firearm access or storage practices are associated with suicidality among household members, which refutes criticism that associations between access and suicide are due to differences in a propensity to take one's life and whether a person owns or how he or she stores guns. However, other problems in a household might cause poor storage security and increased suicide risk, which could account for their apparent association without storage practice itself contributing to suicide risk. Still, at least one study suggests that such an omitted variable would need to be improbably influential to explain the strong observed association between household firearm access and suicide risk (Miller, Swanson, and Azrael, 2016).

### Weapon-Carrying and Suicide Attempts

A third type of individual-level study examined the association between weapon-carrying and suicide attempts. Three such studies fell within the time frame of our literature review (2003–2016), most of which derived from analyses of the Youth Risk Behavior Survey. Two studies documented positive relationships between past suicide attempts and carrying a gun in the past 30 days (Molina and Duarte, 2006; Ruggles and Rajan, 2014), and one found a positive relationship between past suicide attempts and carrying a weapon (though not necessarily a gun) in the past 30 days (Swahn et al., 2012). Again, these results are consistent with a wide range of causal models, including ones that postulate effects in opposite directions (i.e., that suicidality causes one to carry a weapon).

Table 16.1 details the studies published in or after 2003 that examined the relationship between firearm access and suicide.

**Table 16.1**
**Individual-Level Studies Published in or After 2003 That Examined the Relationship Between Firearm Access and Suicide**

| Study | Sample | Cases | Controls | Results |
|---|---|---|---|---|
| Case status: Suicide deaths | | | | |
| Grassel et al., 2003 | California deaths in 1998 | 2,798 suicides in California | 207,851 noninjury causes of death (with some exclusions) | Those who died by suicide were more likely to have purchased a handgun in the past three years (aOR = 6.8; CI: 5.7, 8.1) and in the past year (aOR = 12.5; CI: 10.0, 15.6). The association for purchase in the past three years was especially pronounced for women (aOR = 33.9; CI: 19.3, 59.3). |
| Kung, Pearson, and Liu, 2003 | 1993 National Mortality Followback Survey | 441 female and 1,022 male suicides | 2,337 female and 5,055 male deaths from natural causes | Both males and females who died by suicide were more likely to have lived in a home with a gun, regardless of whether they lived alone or with others (female, lived with others: aOR = 2.99; CI: 1.58, 5.65; female, lived alone: aOR = 25.83; CI: 8.36, 77.29; male, lived with others: aOR = 3.53; CI: 2.42, 5.15; male, lived alone: aOR = 16.13; CI: 6.97, 37.25). |
| Wiebe, 2003 | 1993 National Mortality Followback Survey | 1,959 suicides | 13,535 respondents from the 1994 National Health Interview Survey | Those who died by suicide were more likely to have lived in a home with a gun (aOR = 3.44; CI: 3.06, 3.86). Having a gun in the home was also associated with firearm suicide (aOR = 16.89; CI: 13.26, 21.52) but inversely associated with nonfirearm suicide (aOR = 0.68; CI: 0.55, 0.84). |
| Dahlberg, Ikeda, and Kresnow, 2004 | 1993 National Mortality Followback Survey | 1,049 suicides in the home and 687 firearm suicides | 535 deaths in the home from other means, excluding suicide, and 362 nonfirearm suicides | Males with guns in the home were at a significantly greater risk of suicide than males without guns in the home (OR = 10.4; CI: 5.8, 18.9); the association for females included the null value (= 1.0) in the CI. Among those who died by suicide, those living with a gun in the home were more likely to take their lives using a gun than other means. There was no evidence of an association between suicide method and type or number of guns in the home or between suicide method and storage practices. |
| Shenassa et al., 2004 | 1993 National Mortality Followback Survey | Firearm suicide | Died from other causes | Those who died by firearm suicide were more likely to have lived in a home with a firearm (no adjustment). |

**Table 16.1—Continued**

| Study | Sample | Cases | Controls | Results |
|---|---|---|---|---|
| Kung, Pearson, and Wei, 2005 | 1993 National Mortality Followback Survey | Suicide death among those aged 15–64 | Death from natural causes among those aged 15–64 | Those who died by suicide were more likely to have lived in a home with a gun in analyses adjusted for race, living arrangements, educational status, marijuana use, excessive alcohol use, depressive symptoms, and past-year use of mental health services. |
| Stander et al., 2006 | 1999–2004 Navy suicides | Firearm suicide | Nonfirearm suicide | Among Navy suicides, 66 percent of those with access to a military weapon used a gun to die, compared with 54 percent of those without access. Furthermore, 65 percent of those with training on military weapons used a gun to die, compared with 54 percent of those without training. |
| Joe, Marcus, and Kaplan, 2007 | 1993 National Mortality Followback Survey | Firearm suicide | Nonfirearm suicide | In models controlling for demographic, socioeconomic, and clinical variables, having a firearm in the home was associated with firearm suicide in the total sample and when stratified by race. |
| Case status: Suicide ideation or attempts | | | | |
| Oslin et al., 2004 | Older adults receiving primary care treatment | Suicide ideation | No suicide ideation | There was no relationship between suicide ideation and having a gun in the home. |
| Thompson et al., 2006 | Veterans receiving outpatient treatment for opiate addiction | Suicide ideation ($n$ = 26) | No suicide ideation ($n$ = 75) | Owning a firearm was associated with suicide ideation in bivariate analyses. |
| Ilgen et al., 2008 | National Comorbidity Survey | Those who report having ever thought about committing suicide, made a plan for committing suicide, or attempted suicide | Those who did not meet case criteria | There was no significant difference in gun access between those who thought about attempting suicide (31 percent) or made a plan to attempt suicide (31 percent) and those who did not (36 percent for both sets of controls), but those who had attempted suicide were less likely to have access (36 percent versus 24 percent; OR = 0.6; CI: 0.5, 0.8). |
| Miller et al., 2009 | National Comorbidity Survey Replication | Past-year suicide ideation, suicide planning, or suicide attempt | No past-year suicide ideation, suicide planning, or suicide attempt | Living in a home with a firearm was not associated with past-year suicide ideation, planning, or attempts in models that accounted for age, sex, race/ethnicity, educational attainment, and poverty. |

**Table 16.1—Continued**

| Study | Sample | Cases | Controls | Results |
|---|---|---|---|---|
| Betz, Barber, and Miller, 2011 | Second Injury Control and Risk Survey | 20 people who, in the past 12 months, had a suicide plan involving a firearm | 155 people who, in the past 12 months, had a suicide plan that did not involve a firearm | Of those who had a suicide plan involving a firearm, 81 percent lived in a home with a firearm, compared with 38 percent of those whose plan did not involve a firearm (OR = 7.4). |
| Kolla, O'Connor, and Lineberry, 2011 | Psychiatric inpatients | Access to a firearm (*N* = 138) | No access to a firearm | Females, those with a past suicide attempt, those with a family history of a suicide attempt, and those aged 65 or older were less likely to report access to a firearm in multiple logistic regression. Patients with bipolar disorder diagnoses were more likely to report access in multiple regression analyses. |
| Simonetti et al., 2015 | National Comorbidity Survey: Adolescent Supplement | Access to a firearm in the home | No access to a firearm in the home | There was no relationship between household access to a firearm and lifetime suicide ideation, planning, or attempts, nor in any stratified analyses or multivariable models. |
| Smith, Currier, and Drescher, 2015 | Veterans entering treatment for posttraumatic stress disorder | Two samples of veterans with suicidal thoughts or attempts:<br>• Sample 1: *N* = 82 ideators, 62 attempters<br>• Sample 2: *N* = 27 ideators, 23 attempters | Veterans without suicidal thoughts or attempts (Sample 1 = 57, Sample 2 = 22) | In Sample 1, attempters were less likely to own a gun at the beginning of treatment (26 percent) relative to ideators (39 percent) or nonattempters/nonideators (32 percent). In Sample 2, there were no significant differences among groups (attempters = 29 percent, ideators = 36 percent, nonattempters/nonideators = 36 percent). |
| Betz et al., 2016 | Seven emergency departments across the United States | 1,358 emergency department patients with suicidal thoughts or an attempt | None | Of patients with suicidal thoughts or an attempt, 11 percent reported having access to a gun at home. Among those with a firearm at home, 58 percent of men and 25 percent of women personally owned at least one gun. |

NOTE: All CIs in this table are at the 95-percent level. aOR = adjusted odds ratio; OR = odds ratio.

## Regional Availability of Firearms

NRC (2004) concluded that there were regional associations between firearm prevalence and firearm suicide but uncertain relationships between firearm availability and total suicides. The report also concluded that results varied by the age group studied, the covariates included in the models, and the measure of firearm availability used (discussed later in this section). Further, the report noted that there was uncertain evidence that firearm prevalence explained changes in total suicide rates over time. Evidence about change over time derived primarily from studies examining suicide rates in the District of Columbia before and after 1976, when the District established a policy that prohibited the purchase, sale, transfer, and possession of handguns. There was a 23-percent reduction in the frequency of firearm-related suicides following the policy change, and no changes in nonfirearm-related suicides or in firearm-related suicides in the surrounding areas (Loftin et al., 1991), although, as NRC pointed out, this study was sensitive to modeling choices (Britt, Kleck, and Bordua, 1996), and its results may have been caused by other changes in the District of Columbia over the same period (Jones, 1981).

In this discussion, we prioritize longitudinal studies conducted since 2003 that applied a quasi-experimental research design. We describe these studies in the following sections, noting that while some studies are longitudinal, only a handful utilize measures of exposure (firearm prevalence, or a proxy for prevalence) and outcome (suicides) that vary over time, conditions necessary to employ a quasi-experimental design. The studies meeting that criteria are Briggs and Tabarrok (2014), Miller et al. (2006), Phillips and Nugent (2013), and Rodriguez Andrés and Hempstead (2011). Each of these four studies employs unique methods to reach empirical and causal estimates of the effects of changes in firearm prevalence on changes in suicides. This is challenging to estimate empirically because firearm prevalence does not change significantly over regions over time (Smith and Son, 2015) and because, in cross-sectional analyses, firearm prevalence is consistently associated with suicide. Thus, methods need to decompose within-region changes over time from cross-region known associations. In the four studies described here, three (Miller et al., 2006; Briggs and Tabarrok, 2014; and Rodriguez Andrés and Hempstead, 2011) did so in a time-series model with regional fixed effects. Phillips and Nugent (2013) employed a decomposition random-effects model approach that estimated separate between- and within-region effects.

### Measures of Firearm Prevalence

One of the biggest challenges to estimating the effects of regional firearm availability (i.e., prevalence) on suicide risk is the lack of valid data on the exposure of interest: household prevalence of firearms or of firearm ownership at the state level. Survey data on firearm ownership collected as part of the Centers for Disease Control and Prevention's Behavioral Risk Factor Surveillance Survey (BRFSS) for all 50 states are available for three years (2001, 2002, and 2004) and for census regions (and large cities) as part of the General Social Survey (GSS) biannually (though for some periods, annually). Thus, while there are studies examining the relationship between regional prevalence rates and suicide outcomes, researchers interested in examining variability in gun prevalence and its association with suicide at the state level must rely on proxy measures. Sometimes they apply the earlier BRFSS estimates to the current period or apply regional measures to the states within the region.

Some studies validate different proxy measures of firearm prevalence (see, for example, Azrael, Cook, and Miller, 2004; Kleck, 2004; Siegel, Ross, and King, 2014). However, evidence for the validity of these proxies as measures of gun prevalence over time is limited (Kleck, 2004), and establishing such evidence in the absence of survey data, particularly at the state level, over time is challenging. Our goal here is not to review all proxy measures; rather, we describe information on the ones found in the quasi-experimental studies described in this chapter, as well as those used in Chapter Seventeen. The proxy measures we discuss are as follows:

- *FS/S*. The most frequently utilized measure of firearm prevalence is the proportion of total suicides that are firearm suicides (FS/S). The correlation between FS/S and BRFSS state-based prevalence estimates is 0.80 (Siegel, Ross, and King, 2014), between FS/S and GSS regional-based prevalence estimates is 0.93 (Azrael, Cook, and Miller, 2004), and between FS/S and estimates from large cities is 0.87 (Kleck, 2004). NRC (2004, p. 169), however, emphasized that FS/S could introduce biases in models examining the effects of gun availability on suicide.
- *Hunting licenses per capita*. Rodriguez Andrés and Hempstead (2011) used hunting licenses per capita. Kleck (2004) provided only a correlation of this proxy with 45 large cities and estimated a weak correlation of 0.37, although Rodriguez Andrés and Hempstead (2011) reported that hunting license per capita has a 0.74 correlation with FS/S.
- *FS/S combined with hunting license rate*. In Chapter Seventeen, we review Siegel, Ross, and King (2014), which used a composite measure that includes both FS/S and the hunting license rate. The authors presented evidence that this measure has a 0.95 correlation with BRFSS estimates, although they suggest that the measure overestimates absolute levels of gun ownership and thus its utility should be restricted to a proxy reflecting proportional differences between states.
- *Google searches for gun-related terms*. Briggs and Tabarrok (2014) used as a proxy of gun ownership Google searches, aggregated to states, for gun-related terms. The correlation between this measure and the three-year average of the BRFSS estimates is greater than 0.80, although the authors did not present the actual correlation estimate.
- *Composite index of FS/S, the rate of background checks for gun purchases, and the rate of* unintentional *death by firearm*. Briggs and Tabarrok (2014) also used this

> composite index to "overcome weaknesses" of the measures individually. The correlation between this composite measure and the three-year average of the BRFSS estimates is 0.84.

For other proxy measures—including firearm homicides divided by homicides, subscriptions to firearm-related publications (e.g., *Guns & Ammo*), membership in the National Rifle Association, percentage of hunters, and carry permits per population—see Azrael, Cook, and Miller (2004) and Kleck (2004).

### Quasi-Experimental Results

In the earliest of the four studies in our review, Miller et al. (2006) used data from the GSS on firearm prevalence in census regions over time. Using generalized estimating equations with region-level fixed effects, the authors concluded that a *regional reduction* in firearms of 10 percent would result in an estimated 4.2-percent reduction in firearm suicides, 2.5-percent reduction in total suicides, and no change in nonfirearm suicides.

Briggs and Tabarrok (2014) used four measures of gun prevalence over time: state-level ownership from the BRFSS in 2001, 2002, and 2004; state-level estimates of searches for gun-related terms on Google from 2004 to 2009; FS/S from 2000 to 2009; and a composite index comprising FS/S, the rate of background checks for gun purchases, and the rate of unintentional death by firearm for 2000 to 2009. In ordinary-least-squares models with time and regional (not state) fixed effects, along with other regional covariate adjustments, all four measures of gun prevalence showed that a 1-percent increase in the prevalence of individuals having firearms in their households in a state is associated with a positive and statistically significant increase in firearm suicides (between 1.3 and 3.1 percent), and three of the four measures found positive and statistically significant increases in total suicides (between 0.7 and 0.9 percent) (Table 16.2). The effect on total suicide was not significant at $p < 0.05$ for the direct measure of gun ownership from the BRFSS.

The foregoing findings were correlational, without additional analyses that attempted to determine whether the correlation should be interpreted as evidence

**Table 16.2**
**Estimated Effects of a 1-Percent Increase in Firearm Prevalence on Firearm and Total Suicides**

| Measure of Gun Prevalence | Increase in Firearm Suicide | Increase in Total Suicide |
|---|---|---|
| Gun ownership (from the BRFSS) | 1.7 percent | 0.5 percent (not significant) |
| Gun-related Google searches | 1.3 percent | 0.7 percent |
| FS/S | 3.1 percent | 0.9 percent |
| Composite index (FS/S, rate of background checks for gun purchases, rate of unintentional death by firearm) | 2.3 percent | 0.8 percent |

NOTE: All effects are significant at $p < 0.01$, except as noted (Briggs and Tabarrok, 2014).

that increases in gun prevalence cause an increased suicide rate. However, Briggs and Tabarrok (2014) also reported results using methods that might better support causal interpretation. In these analyses, gun prevalence measures were modeled using "interest in hunting" (based on hunting magazine subscriptions and Google searches for hunting-related terms). This type of "instrumental variable" method can provide evidence of a causal effect if the chosen instrument has no direct effect on suicide but instead can affect suicide only indirectly through its effect on gun prevalence. These models showed suggestive, but nonsignificant, effects consistent with gun prevalence causing suicide. However, the authors provided no empirical evidence for the validity of their instruments, and the instruments' conceptual validity may also be questioned.

Phillips and Nugent (2013) used a decomposition random-effects model that provided separate estimates for the effect of gun prevalence on suicide between states and on annual suicides within states from 1976 to 2000. The authors measured gun prevalence using GSS data at the regional level (with each state in a region assigned the regional value). They found that gun prevalence was associated with total and firearm suicides across states, but there was no evidence that prevalence explained variation *within* states (for total, firearm, or nonfirearm suicides) over time.

Rodriguez Andrés and Hempstead (2011) was the only study to find no association between changes in firearm prevalence and total or firearm suicides. The authors used a negative binomial model of suicides between 1995 and 2004 with fixed effects for state and year. However this analysis used one of the weakest proxies of gun ownership: hunting licenses per capita (Kleck, 2004).

Table 16.3 details the four longitudinal studies conducted since 2003 that applied a quasi-experimental research design and examined the regional relationship between firearm availability and suicide.

**Table 16.3**
**Quasi-Experimental Studies Published in or After 2003 That Examined the Regional Relationship Between Firearm Prevalence and Suicide**

| Study | Sample | Outcome | Measure of Prevalence | Covariates | Analytic Approach | Results |
|---|---|---|---|---|---|---|
| Miller et al., 2006 | U.S. Census regions | Suicide rates, 1981–2002 | GSS gun ownership data (1982, 1984, 1985, 1987–1991, 1993, 1994, 1996–2002; missing years imputed); for sex-specific and child outcomes, gun availability was estimated using responses from these specific groups | Age, unemployment, per capita alcohol consumption, poverty, and region of the country | Log-log generalized estimating equation regressions with regional fixed effects | Percentage decrease in outcome based on a 10-percent regional decrease in firearm ownership:<br>• Total suicides: 2.5 percent (95% CI: 1.4, 3.6)<br>• Firearm suicides: 4.2 percent (95% CI: 2.3, 6.1)<br>• Nonfirearm suicides: 0.3 percent (95% CI: −1.4, 2.3).<br>Rate of decline did not vary significantly by gender but was greatest for those aged 0–19. |
| Rodriguez Andrés and Hempstead, 2011 | U.S. states | Number of male suicides, 1999–2004 | Hunting licenses per capita | Education, income, alcohol consumption, percentage older than age 65, percentage non-Hispanic white, relevant population size, one index of gun availability (general prohibitions) | Negative binomial with state and year fixed effects | There was no statistically significant association between gun availability and outcome. |
| Phillips and Nugent, 2013 | U.S. states | Suicide rates, 1976–2000 | GSS gun ownership (regional) using the three-year moving average | Percentage aged 15–24; percentage older than age 65; percentage male; percentage white; population size; percentage living in urban areas; percentage foreign-born; unemployment rate; per capita income; percentage divorced; religious adherence rate per 1,000; percentage Catholic, Episcopalian, or other mainline Protestant; annual alcohol consumption | Decomposition model with random effects and regional and year-level fixed effects | Gun ownership rate was associated with increases in total suicide rate across states (0.105 percent, $p < 0.05$) and firearm suicide rate across states (0.129 percent, $p < 0.05$) but not across time for either outcome. Also, neither outcome was related to nonfirearm suicide. |

**Table 16.3—Continued**

| Study | Sample | Outcome | Measure of Prevalence | Covariates | Analytic Approach | Results |
|---|---|---|---|---|---|---|
| Briggs and Tabarrok, 2014 | U.S. states | Suicide rates, 2000–2009 | (1) BRFSS gun ownership from 2001, 2002, and 2004; (2) Google searches for gun-related terms (2004–2009); (3) FS/S; (4) composite index comprising FS/S, the rate of background checks for gun purchases, and the rate of unintentional death by firearm | Baseline model: population, poverty rate, annual average unemployment rate, percentage urban land area, percentage urban population, Gini coefficient of household income inequality, prevalence of drug and/or alcohol abuse or dependence in the population aged 12+, prevalence of frequent mental distress among noninstitutionalized adults, percentage of males aged 65+, and percentage white<br><br>Full model: median household, percentage of children living in a single-mother family, percentage of divorced adults, distance to the nearest hospital emergency room, and a measure of social connectedness | Ordinary-least-squares model with time-specific and regional-specific (not state-specific) fixed effects; standard errors account for clustering at the state level. Minimal model excluded Gini, frequent mental distress, drug/alcohol covariates. Used circulation of *Field & Stream* magazine as an instrumental variable. For Google exposure, the instrumental variable was a Google search for hunting-related terms. | **Ownership (BRFSS):**<br>• Total suicides: $\beta = 0.003$–$0.005$, $p < 0.10$ in baseline and minimal model, not significant in full model<br>• Firearm suicides: $\beta = 0.014$–$0.017$, $p < 0.01$<br>• Nonfirearm suicides: $\beta = -0.008$–$0.01$, $p < 0.01$ in full model, $p < 0.05$ in baseline model, $p < 0.10$ in minimal model<br>**Google searches, baseline model:**<br>• Total suicides: $\beta = 0.007$, $p < 0.01$<br>• Firearm suicides: $\beta = 0.013$, $p < 0.01$<br>• Nonfirearm suicides: $\beta = -0.000$, $p$ = not significant<br>**FS/S, baseline model:**<br>• Total suicides: $\beta = 0.009$, $p < 0.01$<br>• Firearm suicides: $\beta = 0.031$, $p < 0.01$<br>• Nonfirearm suicides: $\beta = -0.012$, $p < 0.01$<br>**Composite index, baseline model:**<br>• Total suicides: $\beta = 0.008$, $p < 0.01$<br>• Firearm suicides: $\beta = 0.023$, $p < 0.01$<br>• Nonfirearm suicides: $\beta = -0.007$, $p < 0.01$<br><br>When adding a quadratic term to the baseline regressions, they found that it was significant and negative (diminishing effect). The instrumental variable results reported qualitatively similar findings. |

### Longitudinal, Non-Quasi-Experimental Results

In addition to the four studies just discussed, our search identified two other U.S.-based longitudinal studies that do not meet our criteria for a quasi-experimental design. Desai, Dausey, and Rosenheck (2008) did not use a measure of gun prevalence that varied over time but found that state-level firearm prevalence (measured prior to hospital discharge) is associated with increased risk that a veteran discharged from an inpatient U.S. Department of Veterans Affairs facility with a psychiatric diagnosis will use a firearm to take his or her life relative to not taking his or her life or doing so using some other means. Wadsworth, Kubrin, and Herting (2014) did not employ a control group but found that the suicide rate increase among black males aged 15–34 between 1982 and 1993 was not associated with changes in gun availability (while also controlling for social and economic disadvantage) but that reductions in gun availability during the 1990s had some association with decreasing suicide rates in that group over the same period.

### Cross-Sectional Results

Cross-sectional studies that examined regional associations provided little or no evidence for the causal effect of gun availability on suicide. Nonetheless, most such studies since 2003 generally found a positive relationship between gun prevalence and total or firearm suicide in the United States (Duggan, 2003; Miller, Azrael, and Hemenway, 2004; Price, Thompson, and Dake, 2004; Miller et al., 2009; Kubrin and Wadsworth, 2009; Price, Mrdjenovich, and Dake, 2009; Kposowa, 2013; Miller et al., 2013; Smith and Kawachi, 2014; Miller et al., 2015; Kposowa, Hamilton, and Wang, 2016), although there were exceptions (e.g., Shenassa, Daskalakis, and Buka, 2006). Details of these studies are presented in Table 16.4.

**Table 16.4**
**Cross-Sectional Studies Published in or After 2003 That Examined the Regional Relationship Between Firearm Availability and Suicide**

| Study | Focal Area | Main Findings |
|---|---|---|
| Duggan, 2003 | U.S. states | Firearm prevalence (FS/S and sales rates for *Guns & Ammo* magazine) was positively correlated with total, firearm, and nonfirearm suicide rates (although there were age groups for which the relationship with nonfirearm suicides was not significant or was negative). Change in firearm prevalence (sales rates for *Guns & Ammo* magazine, 1980–1998) was correlated with change in firearm suicide, but there was no evidence of a statistically significant association with nonfirearm suicide, while the association with total suicide was dependent on model specification. |
| Miller, Azrael, and Hemenway, 2004 | U.S. states | Among seven Northeastern states, prevalence of firearms was positively correlated with suicides (except female suicides) and firearm suicides (but not nonfirearm suicides), as well as suicide attempts (except among those aged 15–64), firearm suicide attempts, and nonfirearm suicide attempts among females. |

**Table 16.4—Continued**

| Study | Focal Area | Main Findings |
|---|---|---|
| Price, Thompson, and Dake, 2004 | U.S. states | Firearm prevalence (FS/S) was positively associated with firearm suicide mortality (1999) in models controlling for number of firearm dealers, race, presence of gun laws, per capita alcohol consumption, level of urbanization, violent crime rate, and socioeconomic status. |
| Shenassa, Daskalakis, and Buka, 2006 | Chicago neighborhoods | Neighborhood levels of gun-carrying and gun availability (based on youth self-report) were not associated with the proportion of suicides by firearm. |
| Kubrin and Wadsworth, 2009 | U.S. cities | Firearm prevalence (combined FS/S and ratio of homicides that are firearm homicides) was associated with a greater number of suicides among both white males and black males aged 35 or younger aggregated between 1998 and 2001, with some suggestion that gun availability mediates the effect of structural disadvantage and suicide among black males. |
| Miller et al., 2009 | U.S. states | Firearm prevalence (2001 BRFSS) was positively associated with 2000–2002 total and firearm suicides in models that controlled for rates of unemployment, urbanization, poverty, serious mental illness, and alcohol and illicit drug dependence and abuse. |
| Price, Mrdjenovich, and Dake, 2009 | U.S. states | Firearm prevalence (2002 BRFSS) was positively associated with firearm suicide mortality (2002) in models controlling for prevalence of serious mental illness, psychotropic medications, access to mental health care, per capita expenditures for mental health services, race/ethnicity, untreated mental health conditions, and educational expenditures and attainment. |
| Kposowa, 2013 | U.S. states | Firearm prevalence (2001 BRFSS) was positively associated with death by suicide relative to other causes of death (2000–2004) in models that controlled for individual-level (marital status, sex, race, place of residence, city size, age, year of death) and state-level (2000 suicide rate, percentage voted for George W. Bush, percentage church adherents, percentage immigrants) variables. |
| Miller et al., 2013 | U.S. states | Firearm prevalence (2004 BRFSS) was positively associated with 2008–2009 total and firearm suicide rates in models that accounted for state-level suicide attempt rates. These relationships held in models stratified by gender and age (18–29, 30+). |
| Smith and Kawachi, 2014 | U.S. states | Firearm prevalence (2001 BRFSS) was positively associated with 1999–2002 total suicides among all men and all women, as well as in stratified analyses for white men and non-Hispanic white men. |
| Miller et al., 2015 | U.S. cities | Firearm prevalence (BRFSS averaged for 2002 and 2004) was positively associated with firearm and total suicides in U.S. cities (data aggregated from 1999 to 2010). |
| Kposowa, Hamilton, and Wang, 2016 | U.S. states | Firearm prevalence (BRFSS) was positively associated with 2011–2013 total and firearm suicide rates in models that controlled for religious adherence, long-term unemployment, percentage of population with a serious mental illness, divorce rate, and percentage rural. |

### International Evidence

Some of the most suggestive evidence that the prevalence of guns in a community may have a causal effect on suicide rates comes from two international studies published since 2003. Reisch et al. (2013) examined suicide rates in Switzerland between 1995 and 2008, following large-scale reforms in the Swiss military in 2004 that reduced the size of the Swiss Army by half; lowered the discharge age from 43 to 33; and adopted new policies that, among other things, increased the cost to service members of purchasing their military guns after separation from the service and introduced a gun license requirement. This study showed that suicide rates among men aged 18–43 were lower immediately after the 2004 Army reforms than would have been expected based on the pre-reform trends. The authors reasonably suggested that the two new firearm policies probably had the effect of reducing firearm ownership in the country and that this reduced gun prevalence caused the observed reductions in suicide rates.

The quasi-experimental Reisch et al. (2013) study relied on data from a single treated unit: Switzerland (i.e., there was no control or comparison country or region). To demonstrate that it was specifically the firearm restrictions imposed in 2004 that led to reductions in suicide by younger men, rather than other aspects of the Army reform or other changes in Swiss society around 2004, the authors noted that the observed reductions among younger men were exclusively found for firearm suicides, not other forms of suicide, and that similar reductions were not found among women after 2004. In addition, they found that the effect was more pronounced for younger men (aged 18–43) who would be more directly affected by the firearm restrictions than older men (aged 44–53).

The strength of these findings rests on the question of whether it is plausible that changes other than a reduction in gun prevalence could account for this pattern. For instance, there were, contemporaneously, large-scale changes to the military and, by extension, to Swiss society and the experience of young men after the military reforms. It is plausible that these large social changes affected suicide rates or attitudes toward firearm suicide. If so, then the effect of the additional cost of acquiring a firearm and any consequent effect on firearm prevalence is not well identified. Moreover, other changes in Swiss society must have been responsible for the substantial declines in suicide rates and firearm suicide rates among younger men in the years immediately preceding the Army reforms. Without understanding the factors driving that change, it is not possible to know whether they also shifted around 2004 in ways that further reduced firearm suicides.

Moreover, the comparison group of older men does not offer a strong demonstration that the effect was specific to those who would have been directly affected by the Army's new gun policies. Specifically, Reisch et al. (2013) found marginally significant reductions in suicide rates after 2004 among older men aged 44–53. Although this effect was no longer significant after Bonferonni corrections, the report did not provide an estimate for whether the reductions found among younger men were significantly different from those found for older men. If the two estimates were not significantly different, then either reducing access to separating soldiers' service weapons had powerful spillover effects that reduced suicides among older men or, conversely, the Army reforms were not the best explanation of reduced suicides among younger men. If the reductions in suicides among younger and older men were significantly different, then (as the authors argued) changes in firearm policies may well have been the Army reforms' key feature that explains why suicides declined among younger men.

In our assessments of quasi-experimental studies of U.S. law, we raised concerns about any study with fewer than four treated units. This is because, as the number of treated units declines, it becomes increasingly difficult to distinguish the effect of interest from the effects of other contemporaneous events affecting the treated unit or units. Given that only one treated unit was available in the Reisch et al. (2013) natural experiment, stronger evidence for the effect of firearm restrictions on suicide reductions among younger men in Switzerland might include evidence that reductions in suicide rates were disproportionately found among younger men who left the Army in 2004 or later, or that reductions in suicides were disproportionately found among those using their service weapon to kill themselves. Similarly, evidence that Army reforms had a meaningful effect on household gun ownership among younger men could bolster the argument that the effects of Army reforms on suicide were likely to have been mediated by significant changes to gun prevalence among younger men.

A second compelling foreign study examined a 2006 policy implemented by the Israel Defense Forces, which required soldiers to leave their firearms on base when they returned home on weekends. The Israeli suicide rate among men aged 18–21 (including men both in service and not in service) following this policy decreased by 40 percent, from 28 per year in 2003–2005 to 16.5 per year in 2007–2008—a change largely resulting from weekend firearm suicide rates (ten per year in 2003–2005 to three per year in 2007–2008) (Lubin et al., 2010).

As with the Swiss study, Lubin et al. (2010) investigated an intervention on a single treatment unit (Israeli soldiers), so it must provide a strong argument that it was the weekend firearm policy that accounted for the observed changes, not any other contemporaneous changes that could have affected suicide rates. Because firearm and nonfirearm suicide rates were falling in Israel over the studied period (World Health Organization, 2017), the fact that firearm suicides among men aged 18–21 declined by 40 percent may not itself be distinguishable from declines in firearm suicides in groups that would be less directly affected by the military policy. For instance, firearm suicides among Israelis aged 25–29 also fell by 40 percent over this same period, from 10.7 per year to 6.3 per year (World Health Organization, 2017). On the other hand, the fact that greater reductions in firearm suicide rates among those aged 18–21 were found among weekend suicides rather than weekday suicides suggests that the policy may well have had an influence on suicidal behavior. Whether that involved shifting suicides from the weekend to the weekday or contributing to the ongoing reductions in suicides cannot be answered with the reported analyses.

Both the Swiss and Israeli studies provide some evidence that gun prevalence may have a causal effect on suicides. Both also suffer from studying a single intervention that occurred once in a particular population. The challenge posed by this design is to show persuasively that other events that occurred at the same time, such as the large-scale reform of the Army in Switzerland, do not provide plausible alternative explanations for observed changes in suicide rates. Other relevant international evidence is reviewed in Chapter Twenty-Four on Australia's experience banning certain firearms through its National Firearms Agreement. However, that law also does not provide strong evidence of a causal effect of gun prevalence on suicide risk. As we conclude later in the report, although there is some evidence that the 1996 agreement reduced firearm suicides in Australia, studies also found significant reductions in nonfirearm suicides at the same time, calling into question whether the reductions in firearm and nonfirearm suicides were caused by the new law or some other concurrent events.

## Conclusions

NRC (2004) concluded that the causal relationship between household gun ownership and suicide is unclear. Since that 2004 report, evidence from U.S.-based studies has substantiated associations that existed then—namely, that

- people who die by suicide are more likely than matched controls to live in a house known by informants to contain a gun
- living in a house known by informants to have a gun stored unsafely is associated with higher risk of firearm suicide than living in a house with a safely secured gun, but unsafe storage has no association with nonfirearm suicide
- changes in firearm prevalence in a region are associated with changes in suicide prevalence in the region.

These observations are all consistent with the conclusion that gun availability increases the risk of suicide. Indeed, there appears to be a consensus among most experts in the public health community that these observed associations, in combination with the results of natural experiments like those in Switzerland and Israel (Reisch et al., 2013; Lubin et al., 2010), provide strong evidence that gun availability has a causal effect on suicide rates. Despite this mounting evidence, quasi-experimental studies providing strong evidence for an effect of gun prevalence on suicide risk have not yet been conducted. Therefore, those who doubt the causal effect can view the observed associations between gun prevalence and suicide rates over time or across regions as indicating that the kinds of people who might consider suicide at some future time may be more likely to purchase a gun (which is a plausible interpretation of, for instance, findings in Wintemute et al., 1999) or that informants in case-control studies may be biased toward describing unsafe storage practices in cases where firearms were used in suicides or may be more likely to incorrectly deny gun availability for control cases in which no firearm injuries occurred.

For example, Kleck (1997) suggests that "one would expect the personality trait of self reliance to encourage both suicide and gun ownership for self-protection, contributing to a spurious correlation between the two" (p. 282). Miller, Swanson, and Azrael (2016) counter this suggestion by noting that any such third-factor explanation (such as a "self-reliance" trait) would have to be as strong a predictor of suicide as are the strongest known predictors (e.g., major depression), as well as "an order of magnitude more imbalanced across households with versus without firearms than is any known risk factor" (p. 1). This, the authors argue correctly, would make explanations of the association based on unmeasured factors highly unlikely. However, their analysis is based on the large gun availability effect sizes produced by the same case-control studies that are subject to methodological concerns about, for instance, whether informants provide unbiased information about gun availability in case versus control homes.

The natural experiments investigated in Switzerland and Israel (Reisch et al., 2013; Lubin et al., 2010) are quite interesting and suggest a possible effect of firearm prevalence on suicide risk but, for reasons described earlier, do not provide especially strong or unambiguous evidence for such an effect. Moreover, even if the studies did provide strong evidence, it is not clear whether similar interventions would have comparable effects in the context of the United States. For these reasons, even though new and important studies have been published since NRC reviewed the case for gun prevalence having a causal effect on suicides, we draw the same conclusion that NRC reached in 2004: Available empirical research does not provide strong causal evidence for the effects of gun prevalence on suicide risk.

Although the empirical research is ambiguous, which suggests that there is more to learn before we can conclude with confidence that gun prevalence has a causal effect of increasing suicide rates, the theoretical or logical arguments for this claim are sufficiently compelling that individuals and policymakers might reasonably choose to assume that gun availability *does* increase the risk of suicide. These logical considerations include that guns are an especially lethal means of attempting suicide and that suicide attempts are impulsive acts that may never be repeated if the first attempt fails. Because those who impulsively attempt suicide with a gun rarely get a chance to reconsider the decision, it is reasonable to suspect that when guns are less available, fewer suicide attempts will result in fatality, more people will have the chance to reconsider their decisions, and suicide rates will therefore decline. We view this as a logical and reasonably persuasive argument but distinguish it from what empirical research can currently demonstrate persuasively about the net effects of gun prevalence on suicide rates.

Stronger study designs may be available to more persuasively establish the causal effects of gun availability or gun prevalence on suicide risk. However, many such study designs are currently hampered by poor information on the prevalence of gun ownership and the consequent reliance on proxy measures of availability and prevalence. For this reason, we recommend in Chapter Twenty-Five that the Centers for Disease Control and Prevention or another federal agency resume routine collection of voluntarily provided survey data on gun ownership and use.

## Chapter Sixteen References

Azrael, Deborah, Philip J. Cook, and Matthew Miller, "State and Local Prevalence of Firearms Ownership Measurement, Structure, and Trends," *Journal of Quantitative Criminology*, Vol. 20, No. 1, March 2004, pp. 43–62.

Azrael, Deborah, and Matthew Miller, "Reducing Suicide Without Affecting Underlying Mental Health: Theoretical Underpinnings and a Review of the Evidence Base Lining the Availability of Lethal Means and Suicide," in Rory C. O'Connor and Jane Pirkis, eds., *The International Handbook of Suicide Prevention*, 2nd ed., Hoboken, N.J.: John Wiley and Sons, 2016.

Bailey, J. E., A. L. Kellermann, G. W. Somes, J. G. Banton, F. P. Rivara, and N. P. Rushforth, "Risk Factors for Violent Death of Women in the Home," *Archives of Internal Medicine*, Vol. 157, No. 7, 1997, pp. 777–782.

Betz, M. E., C. Barber, and M. Miller, "Suicidal Behavior and Firearm Access: Results from the Second Injury Control and Risk Survey," *Suicide and Life-Threatening Behavior*, Vol. 41, No. 4, 2011, pp. 384–391.

Betz, M. E., M. Miller, C. Barber, B. Beaty, I. Miller, C. A. Camargo, Jr., and E. D. Boudreaux, "Lethal Means Access and Assessment Among Suicidal Emergency Department Patients," *Depression and Anxiety*, Vol. 33, No. 6, 2016, pp. 502–511.

Borowsky, I. W., M. D. Resnick, M. Ireland, and R. W. Blum, "Suicide Attempts Among American Indian and Alaska Native Youth: Risk and Protective Factors," *Archives of Pediatrics and Adolescent Medicine*, Vol. 153, No. 6, 1999, pp. 573–580.

Brent, D. A., M. Baugher, J. Bridge, T. H. Chen, and L. Chiappetta, "Suicide in Affectively Ill Adolescents: A Case-Control Study," *Journal of Affective Disorders*, Vol. 31, No. 3, 1994, pp. 193–202.

———, "Age- and Sex-Related Risk Factors for Adolescent Suicide," *Journal of the American Academy of Child and Adolescent Psychiatry*, Vol. 38, No. 12, 1999, pp. 1497–1505.

Brent, D. A., J. A. Perper, C. J. Allman, G. M. Moritz, M. E. Wartella, and J. P. Zelenak, "The Presence and Accessibility of Firearms in the Homes of Adolescent Suicides: A Case-Control Study," *JAMA*, Vol. 266, No. 21, 1991, pp. 2989–2995.

Brent, D. A., J. Perper, G. Moritz, M. Baugher, and C. Allman, "Suicide in Adolescents with No Apparent Psychopathology," *Journal of the American Academy of Child and Adolescent Psychiatry*, Vol. 32, No. 3, 1993a, pp. 494–500.

Brent, D. A., J. A. Perper, G. Moritz, M. Baugher, J. Schweers, and C. Roth, "Firearms and Adolescent Suicide—A Community Case-Control Study," *American Journal of Diseases of Children*, Vol. 147, No. 10, 1993b, pp. 1066–1071.

Briggs, J. T., and A. Tabarrok, "Firearms and Suicides in U.S. States," *International Review of Law and Economics*, Vol. 37, 2014, pp. 180–188.

Britt, Chester L., Gary Kleck, and David J. Bordua, "A Reassessment of the D.C. Gun Law: Some Cautionary Notes on the Use of Interrupted Time Series Designs for Policy Impact Assessment," *Law and Society Review*, Vol. 30, No. 2, 1996, pp. 361–380.

Bukstein, O. G., D. A. Brent, J. A. Perper, G. Moritz, M. Baugher, J. Schweers, C. Roth, and L. Balach, "Risk Factors for Completed Suicide Among Adolescents with a Lifetime History of Substance Abuse: A Case-Control Study," *Acta Psychiatrica Scandinavica*, Vol. 88, No. 6, 1993, pp. 403–408.

Conwell, Y., P. R. Duberstein, K. Connor, S. Eberly, C. Cox, and E. D. Caine, "Access to Firearms and Risk for Suicide in Middle-Aged and Older Adults," *American Journal of Geriatric Psychiatry*, Vol. 10, No. 4, 2002, pp. 407–416.

Cummings, P., T. D. Koepsell, D. C. Grossman, J. Savarino, and R. S. Thompson, "The Association Between the Purchase of a Handgun and Homicide or Suicide," *American Journal of Public Health*, Vol. 87, No. 6, 1997b, pp. 974–978.

Dahlberg, L. L., R. M. Ikeda, and M. J. Kresnow, "Guns in the Home and Risk of a Violent Death in the Home: Findings from a National Study," *American Journal of Epidemiology*, Vol. 160, No. 10, 2004, pp. 929–936.

Desai, R. A., D. Dausey, and R. A. Rosenheck, "Suicide Among Discharged Psychiatric Inpatients in the Department of Veterans Affairs," *Military Medicine*, Vol. 173, No. 8, 2008, pp. 721–728.

Duggan, Mark, "Guns and Suicide," in Jens Ludwig and Philip J. Cook, eds., *Evaluating Gun Policy: Effects on Crime and Violence*, Washington, D.C.: Brookings Institution Press, 2003, pp. 41–73.

Grassel, K. M., G. J. Wintemute, M. A. Wright, and M. P. Romero, "Association Between Handgun Purchase and Mortality from Firearm Injury," *Injury Prevention*, Vol. 9, No. 1, 2003, pp. 48–52.

Grossman, D. C., B. A. Mueller, C. Riedy, M. D. Dowd, A. Villaveces, J. Prodzinski, J. Nakagawara, J. Howard, N. Thiersch, and R. Harruff, "Gun Storage Practices and Risk of Youth Suicide and Unintentional Firearm Injuries," *JAMA*, Vol. 293, No. 6, 2005, pp. 707–714.

Ilgen, M. A., K. Zivin, R. J. McCammon, and M. Valenstein, "Mental Illness, Previous Suicidality, and Access to Guns in the United States," *Psychiatric Services*, Vol. 59, No. 2, 2008, pp. 198–200.

Joe, S., S. C. Marcus, and M. S. Kaplan, "Racial Differences in the Characteristics of Firearm Suicide Decedents in the United States," *American Journal of Orthopsychiatry*, Vol. 77, No. 1, 2007, pp. 124–130.

Jones, Edward D. III, "The District of Columbia's 'Firearms Control Regulations Act of 1975': The Toughest Handgun Control Law in the United States—or Is It?" *Annals of the American Academy of Political and Social Science*, Vol. 455, 1981, pp. 138–149.

Kellermann, A. L., F. P. Rivara, G. Somes, D. T. Reay, J. Francisco, J. G. Banton, J. Prodzinski, C. Fligner, and B. B. Hackman, "Suicide in the Home in Relation to Gun Ownership," *New England Journal of Medicine*, Vol. 327, No. 7, 1992, pp. 467–472.

Kleck, Gary, *Targeting Guns: Firearms and Their Control*, New York: Aldine de Gruyter, 1997.

———, "Measures of Gun Ownership Levels for Macro-Level Crime and Violence Research," *Journal of Research in Crime and Delinquency*, Vol. 41, No. 1, 2004, pp. 3–36.

Kolla, B. P., S. S. O'Connor, and T. W. Lineberry, "The Base Rates and Factors Associated with Reported Access to Firearms in Psychiatric Inpatients," *General Hospital Psychiatry*, Vol. 33, No. 2, 2011, pp. 191–196.

Kposowa, A. J., "Association of Suicide Rates, Gun Ownership, Conservatism and Individual Suicide Risk," *Social Psychiatry and Psychiatric Epidemiology*, Vol. 48, No. 9, 2013, pp. 1467–1479.

Kposowa, A., D. Hamilton, and K. Wang, "Impact of Firearm Availability and Gun Regulation on State Suicide Rates," *Suicide and Life-Threatening Behavior*, Vol. 46, No. 6, 2016, pp. 678–696.

Kubrin, Charis E., and Tim Wadsworth, "Explaining Suicide Among Blacks and Whites: How Socioeconomic Factors and Gun Availability Affect Race-Specific Suicide Rates," *Social Science Quarterly*, Vol. 90, No. 5, 2009, pp. 1203–1227.

Kung, H. C., J. L. Pearson, and X. Liu, "Risk Factors for Male and Female Suicide Decedents Ages 15–64 in the United States—Results from the 1993 National Mortality Followback Survey," *Social Psychiatry and Psychiatric Epidemiology*, Vol. 38, No. 8, 2003, pp. 419–426.

Kung, H. C., J. L. Pearson, and R. Wei, "Substance Use, Firearm Availability, Depressive Symptoms, and Mental Health Service Utilization Among White and African American Suicide Decedents Aged 15 to 64 Years," *Annals of Epidemiology*, Vol. 15, No. 8, 2005, pp. 614–621.

Loftin, C., D. McDowall, B. Wiersema, and T. J. Cottey, "Effects of Restrictive Licensing of Handguns on Homicide and Suicide in the District of Columbia," *New England Journal of Medicine*, Vol. 325, No. 23, 1991, pp. 1615–1620.

Lubin, G., N. Werbeloff, D. Halperin, M. Shmushkevitch, M. Weiser, and H. Y. Knobler, "Decrease in Suicide Rates After a Change of Policy Reducing Access to Firearms in Adolescents: A Naturalistic Epidemiological Study," *Suicide and Life-Threatening Behavior*, Vol. 40, No. 5, 2010, pp. 421–424.

Miller, M., D. Azrael, and D. Hemenway, "The Epidemiology of Case Fatality Rates for Suicide in the Northeast," *Annals of Emergency Medicine*, Vol. 43, No. 6, 2004, pp. 723–730.

Miller, M., D. Azrael, L. Hepburn, D. Hemenway, and S. J. Lippmann, "The Association Between Changes in Household Firearm Ownership and Rates of Suicide in the United States, 1981–2002," *Injury Prevention*, Vol. 12, No. 3, 2006, pp. 178–182.

Miller, M., C. Barber, D. Azrael, D. Hemenway, and B. E. Molnar, "Recent Psychopathology, Suicidal Thoughts and Suicide Attempts in Households With and Without Firearms: Findings from the National Comorbidity Study Replication," *Injury Prevention*, Vol. 15, No. 3, 2009, pp. 183–187.

Miller, M., C. Barber, R. A. White, and D. Azrael, "Firearms and Suicide in the United States: Is Risk Independent of Underlying Suicidal Behavior?" *American Journal of Epidemiology*, Vol. 178, No. 6, 2013, pp. 946–955.

Miller, M., S. A. Swanson, and D. Azrael, "Are We Missing Something Pertinent? A Bias Analysis of Unmeasured Confounding in the Firearm-Suicide Literature," *Epidemiologic Reviews*, Vol. 38, No. 1, 2016, pp. 62–69.

Miller, M., M. Warren, D. Hemenway, and D. Azrael, "Firearms and Suicide in U.S. Cities," *Injury Prevention*, Vol. 21, No. E1, 2015, pp. E116–E119.

Molina, J. A., and R. Duarte, "Risk Determinants of Suicide Attempts Among Adolescents," *American Journal of Economics and Sociology*, Vol. 65, No. 2, 2006, pp. 407–434.

National Research Council, *Firearms and Violence: A Critical Review*, Washington, D.C.: National Academies Press, 2004.

NRC—*See* National Research Council.

Oslin, D. W., C. Zubritsky, G. Brown, M. Mullahy, A. Puliafico, and T. Ten Have, "Managing Suicide Risk in Late Life: Access to Firearms as a Public Health Risk," *American Journal of Geriatric Psychiatry*, Vol. 12, No. 1, 2004, pp. 30–36.

Phillips, J. A., and C. N. Nugent, "Antidepressant Use and Method of Suicide in the United States: Variation by Age and Sex, 1998–2007," *Archives of Suicide Research*, Vol. 17, No. 4, 2013, pp. 360–372.

Price, James H., Adam J. Mrdjenovich, and Joseph A. Dake, "Prevalence of State Firearm Mortality and Mental Health Care Resources," *Journal of Community Health*, Vol. 34, No. 5, 2009, pp. 383–391.

Price, James H., Amy J. Thompson, and Joseph A. Dake, "Factors Associated with State Variations in Homicide, Suicide, and Unintentional Firearm Deaths," *Journal of Community Health*, Vol. 29, No. 4, 2004, pp. 271–283.

Reisch, T., T. Steffen, A. Habenstein, and W. Tschacher, "Change in Suicide Rates in Switzerland Before and After Firearm Restriction Resulting from the 2003 'Army XXI' Reform," *American Journal of Psychiatry*, Vol. 170, No. 9, 2013, pp. 977–984.

Ribeiro, J. D., J. C. Franklin, K. R. Fox, K. H. Bentley, E. M. Kleiman, B. P. Chang, and M. K. Nock, "Self-Injurious Thoughts and Behaviors as Risk Factors for Future Suicide Ideation, Attempts, and Death: A Meta-Analysis of Longitudinal Studies," *Psychological Medicine*, Vol. 46, No. 2, January 2016, pp. 225–236.

Rodriguez Andrés, Antonio, and Katherine Hempstead, "Gun Control and Suicide: The Impact of State Firearm Regulations in the United States, 1995–2004," *Health Policy*, Vol. 101, No. 1, 2011, pp. 95–103.

Ruggles, K. V., and S. Rajan, "Gun Possession Among American Youth: A Discovery-Based Approach to Understand Gun Violence," *PLoS ONE*, Vol. 9, No. 11, 2014.

Shenassa, E. D., C. Daskalakis, and S. L. Buka, "Utility of Indices of Gun Availability in the Community," *Journal of Epidemiology and Community Health*, Vol. 60, No. 1, 2006, pp. 44–49.

Shenassa, E. D., M. L. Rogers, K. L. Spalding, and M. B. Roberts, "Safer Storage of Firearms at Home and Risk of Suicide: A Study of Protective Factors in a Nationally Representative Sample," *Journal of Epidemiology and Community Health*, Vol. 58, No. 10, 2004, pp. 841–848.

Siegel, M., C. S. Ross, and C. King, "Examining the Relationship Between the Prevalence of Guns and Homicide Rates in the USA Using a New and Improved State-Level Gun Ownership Proxy," *Injury Prevention*, Vol. 20, No. 6, 2014, pp. 424–426.

Simonetti, Joseph A., Jessica L. Mackelprang, Ali Rowhani-Rahbar, Douglas Zatzick, and Frederick P. Rivara, "Psychiatric Comorbidity, Suicidality, and in-Home Firearm Access Among a Nationally Representative Sample of Adolescents," *JAMA Psychiatry*, Vol. 72, No. 2, 2015, pp. 152–159.

Smith, N. D., and I. Kawachi, "State-Level Social Capital and Suicide Mortality in the 50 U.S. States," *Social Science and Medicine*, Vol. 120, 2014, pp. 269–277.

Smith, P. N., J. Currier, and K. Drescher, "Firearm Ownership in Veterans Entering Residential PTSD Treatment: Associations with Suicide Ideation, Attempts, and Combat Exposure," *Psychiatry Research*, Vol. 229, No. 1–2, 2015, pp. 220–224.

Smith, T. W., and J. Son, *Trends in Gun Ownership in the United States, 1972–2014,* Chicago, Ill.: NORC at the University of Chicago, March 2015. As of March 9, 2017:
http://www.norc.org/PDFs/GSS%20Reports/
GSS_Trends%20in%20Gun%20Ownership_US_1972-2014.pdf

Stander, V. A., S. M. Hilton, A. P. Doran, A. D. Werbel, and C. J. Thomsen, *Department of the Navy Suicide Incident Report (DONSIR): Summary of 1999–2004 Findings*, San Diego, Calif.: Naval Health Research Center, 2006.

Swahn, M. H., B. Ali, R. M. Bossarte, M. van Dulmen, A. Crosby, A. C. Jones, and K. C. Schinka, "Self-Harm and Suicide Attempts Among High-Risk, Urban Youth in the U.S.: Shared and Unique Risk and Protective Factors," *International Journal of Environmental Research and Public Health,* Vol. 9, No. 1, 2012, pp. 178–191.

Thompson, R., V. Kane, J. M. Cook, R. Greenstein, P. Walker, and G. Woody, "Suicidal Ideation in Veterans Receiving Treatment for Opiate Dependence," *Journal of Psychoactive Drugs*, Vol. 38, No. 2, 2006, pp. 149–156.

Wadsworth, T., C. E. Kubrin, and J. R. Herting, "Investigating the Rise (and Fall) of Young Black Male Suicide in the United States, 1982–2001," *Journal of African American Studies*, Vol. 18, No. 1, 2014, pp. 72–91.

Watkins, Adam M., and Alan J. Lizotte, "Does Household Gun Access Increase the Risk of Attempted Suicide? Evidence from a National Sample of Adolescents," *Youth and Society*, Vol. 45, No. 3, 2013, pp. 324–346.

Wiebe, Douglas J., "Homicide and Suicide Risks Associated with Firearms in the Home: A National Case-Control Study," *Annals of Emergency Medicine*, Vol. 41, No. 6, 2003, pp. 771–782.

Wintemute, G. J., C. A. Parham, J. J. Beaumont, M. Wright, and C. Drake, "Mortality Among Recent Purchasers of Handguns," *New England Journal of Medicine*, Vol. 341, No. 21, 1999, pp. 1583–1589.

World Health Organization, World Health Organization Mortality Database, Geneva, 2017. As of October 13, 2017:
http://www.who.int/healthinfo/mortality_data/en/

CHAPTER SEVENTEEN

# The Relationship Between Firearm Prevalence and Violent Crime

In its 2004 review, the National Research Council (NRC) found that

> existing research studies and data include a wealth of descriptive information on homicide, suicide, and firearms, but, because of the limitations of existing data and methods, do not credibly demonstrate a causal relationship between the ownership of firearms and the causes or prevention of criminal violence or suicide.

Conceptually, the effects of gun prevalence on violent crimes are ambiguous. Firearms could embolden criminals or disputants or make their encounters more lethal, suggesting that as the prevalence of firearms increases, so too would the number of violent crimes. But gun prevalence may also deter would-be criminals, which could have the opposite effect on violent crime (see Chapter Twenty). In this chapter, we examine the empirical evidence on the relationship between firearm prevalence and violent crime, including homicide, domestic violence, aggravated assault, rape, and robbery. Most of the studies we examined used the proportion of suicides that were firearm suicides (FS/S) as a proxy for gun prevalence.

## Methods

Our synthesis focuses on research published after NRC (2004) and takes up where that report left off, reviewing the literature from 2005 to 2016 to assess available new evidence on the relationship between firearm prevalence and violent crime. Our search yielded 25 studies that examined the relationship between gun availability and homicide, other types of violent crime, or domestic violence. We focus our synthesis on U.S.-based studies that met similar methodological criteria for our policy discussions (Chapters Three through Fifteen) in that they attempted to identify a causal effect of prevalence on violent crime. The studies we include here either identify the effect of gun prevalence on violent crime using changes over time in gun prevalence and in violent crime outcomes or use an instrumental-variable approach to cross-sectional data on gun prevalence and violent crime ($N = 11$).

## Firearm Prevalence and Violent Crime

We identified 11 studies that met our criteria. Two were by the same authors: Kleck, Kovandzic, and Schaffer (2005) and Kovandzic, Schaffer, and Kleck (2013). We consider the 2013 study, which used the same basic data and approach as the 2005 study, to supersede the earlier study. One study (Hoskin, 2011) provided insufficient information on its methods for us to evaluate the evidence it provided; in particular, the study used instrumental-variable methods, but the author did not indicate what variable(s) he used to instrument for household gun prevalence and did not provide results of empirical tests for the appropriateness of the instrument(s). We thus excluded this study from consideration in our assessment of the overall weight of the evidence. Three studies (Miller, Azrael, and Hemenway, 2002; Swedler et al., 2015; and Monuteaux et al., 2015) employed longitudinal data but had study designs that limited causal inference, and we thus excluded them from our synthesis results. Specifically, Miller, Azrael, and Hemenway (2002) analyzed data from 2001 to 2003 but aggregated the outcome (homicide rate) over the three-year period, resulting in a cross-sectional analysis. Swedler et al. (2015) pooled data from 1996 to 2010 to create a state-level law enforcement officer homicide rate because these deaths are rare, so the main analyses in that study were cross-sectional as well. The authors reanalyzed their data using three five-year periods but provided few details and no tabled results on this analysis. Additionally, their primary measure of gun prevalence was an average measure from the Behavioral Risk Factor Surveillance Survey for the 2001–2004 period, potentially violating a requirement of causal analysis that causes must be known to precede their effects. Monuteaux et al. (2015) analyzed state-level firearm ownership rates and annual rates of criminal acts from 2001, 2002, and 2004. But the length of the longitudinal panel was limited, and the authors were not primarily using the temporal variation in firearm ownership and outcomes for identification.

The six remaining studies examined a range of homicide outcomes, including total homicides, firearm-related homicides, nonfirearm-related homicides, intimate partner homicides, homicides committed by youth (aged 13–17 or 18–24), and homicides by race (of the decedent). These six studies are summarized in Table 17.1.

Five studies (Cook and Ludwig, 2006; Zeoli and Webster, 2010; Chauhan et al., 2011; Parker et al., 2011; Siegel, Ross, and King, 2014) used longitudinal data to analyze changes over time in gun prevalence and changes over time in homicide outcomes. Cook and Ludwig (2006) identified the effect of gun prevalence on total homicides, firearm homicides, and nonfirearm homicides using data from 200 large U.S. counties from 1980 to 1999. Given the absence of longitudinal information on gun prevalence, the authors used as a proxy of gun prevalence the proportion of suicides committed with a firearm (FS/S), an approach commonly used in the literature. They found statistically significant positive effects of gun prevalence on the total homicide rate and firearm homicide rate and no statistically significant effect of gun prevalence

**Table 17.1**
**Studies Published in or After 2005 That Examined the Relationship Between Firearm Prevalence and Violent Crime**

| Study | Sample | Time Frame | Gun Prevalence Measure | Crime Measure | Result |
|---|---|---|---|---|---|
| Cook and Ludwig, 2006 | 200 largest U.S. counties (in 1990) | 1980–1999 | FS/S in county; sensitivity with FS/S by state | Total, firearm, and nonfirearm homicide rates | Firearm prevalence positively associated with total and firearm homicides |
| Zeoli and Webster, 2010 | 46 large U.S. cities | 1979–2003 | FS/S in the county in which the majority of city residents reside | Intimate partner homicide rate; firearm intimate partner homicide rate | No statistically significant effects |
| Chauhan et al., 2011 | 76 New York City police precincts | 1990–1999 | FS/S by precinct | Firearm homicide rate by race of decedent (black, white, Hispanic) | Firearm prevalence positively associated with firearm homicides of Hispanics |
| Parker et al., 2011 | 91 large U.S. cities | 1984–2006 | FS/S by city; data for 1990 and 2000; interpolated in other years | Homicides committed by youth aged 13–17; homicides committed by youth aged 18–24 | Firearm prevalence positively associated with homicides committed by youth aged 13–17 and youth aged 18–24 |
| Kovandzic, Schaffer, and Kleck, 2013 | U.S. counties with population of 25,000 or more (in 1990) | 1990 | FS/S in county, averaged 1987–1993 | Total, firearm, and nonfirearm homicide rates, averaged for 1987–1993 | Firearm prevalence negatively associated with total and firearm homicides |
| Siegel, Ross, and King, 2014 | 50 U.S. states | 1981–2010 | FS/S; also FS/S combined with hunting license rate | Total, firearm, and nonfirearm homicide rates | Firearm prevalence positively associated with total and firearm homicides |

on the nonfirearm homicide rate. Parker et al. (2011) used data from 91 large U.S. cities spanning 1984–2006 to study the effect of gun prevalence on homicides by two categories of young offenders (aged 13–17 and aged 18–24). The authors used FS/S, measured at the city level, as a proxy for gun prevalence. They found a positive and statistically significant effect of gun prevalence on homicides committed by both those aged 13–17 and those aged 18–24. A methodological limitation was the imputation of FS/S for most observations in the time series (other than 1990 and 2000). Using data from 76 New York City police precincts and FS/S as a proxy for gun prevalence, Chauhan et al. (2011) found a statistically significant positive effect of gun prevalence on the homicide rate of Hispanics. However, sample sizes of suicides by precinct were likely to be relatively small, affecting the precision of the proxy, and the localized nature of the data also limited the generalizability of the findings.

Zeoli and Webster (2010) used data from 46 large U.S. cities spanning 1979–2003 and found no statistically significant effect of county-level gun prevalence (proxied by FS/S) on the city-level intimate partner homicide rate. For this study, measurement of the outcome variable was affected by missing data on the characteristics of the perpetrators of violent crime—either because the perpetrator was not known or the characteristics of the perpetrator were not available (e.g., whether the perpetrator was an intimate partner). This was also true for the Parker et al. (2011) study, but the authors employed a multiple imputation approach to address the issue of missing data on offender age. Siegel, Ross, and King (2014) analyzed state-level data covering 1981–2010. As a proxy for gun prevalence, the authors used FS/S and a measure that incorporated both FS/S and the hunting license rate. They found that higher gun prevalence was associated with more total and firearm homicides. But the authors acknowledged that their methodological approach primarily relied on cross-sectional variation for identification of the effect of gun prevalence on homicide outcomes.

Instead of analyzing changes over time in gun prevalence and changes over time in homicides, Kovandzic, Schaffer, and Kleck (2013) used an instrumental-variable approach to analyzing cross-sectional data from large U.S. counties in 1990. The authors used FS/S as a proxy for gun prevalence and tested the following four instruments, as well as different combinations of these instruments:

- subscriptions per 100,000 people to *Field & Stream, Outdoor Life,* and *Sports Afield*
- percentage of county voting for George H. W. Bush in the 1988 presidential election
- military veterans per 100,000 people
- subscriptions per 100,000 people to *Guns & Ammo.*

The authors analyzed the fourth instrument, in part, because it was used in previous research (Duggan, 2001, 2003), but they suggested that, conceptually, it may be endogenous because "subscribers may include people who have an interest in violence more generally." The authors' preferred specification used a combination of the first three instruments (outdoor magazines, voting, veteran variables), although in the first-stage analysis with this combination of instruments, only the voting and magazine measures were statistically significant predictors of firearm prevalence. In the authors' preferred specification, they found a statistically significant negative relationship between firearm prevalence and firearm homicides and the same for total homicides. In analyses that used the voting, veteran population, and outdoor magazine instruments individually (each of which was statistically significant in the first stage), the authors found no statistically significant effect of firearm prevalence on firearm homicides for two of the instruments (voting, veteran population) and a statistically significant negative relationship between firearm prevalence and firearm homicides for the third (outdoor magazine subscription rate). When the subscription rate to *Guns & Ammo* was used, the direction of the effect changed (became positive), but the effect was not statistically significant, and the authors noted that the instrument failed a statistical test for exogeneity.

With the exception of Siegel, Ross, and King (2014), none of the studies used data from the past decade. For example, Kovandzic, Schaffer, and Kleck (2013) used data from 1990, now more than 25 years old, and Cook and Ludwig (2006) used data from before 2000.

## Conclusions

The NRC (2004) review found insufficient evidence to draw a conclusion about the causal relationship between gun prevalence and violent crime. We examined new evidence from U.S.-based studies since the NRC review (2005–2016) that were designed to estimate the causal effect of gun prevalence on violent crime. The six studies we identified examined total homicides, firearm-related homicides, nonfirearm-related homicides, intimate partner homicides, homicides committed by youth (aged 13–17 or 18–24), and homicides by race (of the decedent).

Four of the six studies found the prevalence of firearms to be significantly and positively associated with homicide rates, and these associations were found across reasonably independent data sets. A fifth study found no significant effect of gun prevalence on the intimate partner homicide rate and the firearm intimate partner homicide rate, and a sixth study found significant negative effects (indicating that gun prevalence reduced violent crime) in the preferred specification. While most of the new studies provide evidence consistent with the hypothesis that gun prevalence increases violent crime, the methodological weaknesses that led NRC (2004) to conclude that the causal effects of gun prevalence were not proven continue to apply. In particular, if people are more likely to acquire guns when crime rates are rising or high (as suggested by, for instance, Bice and Hemley, 2002, and Kleck and Patterson, 1993), then the same pattern of evidence would be expected, but it would be crime rates causing gun prevalence, not the reverse.

A fundamental limitation for all of the studies is the lack of direct measures of gun prevalence. All of the authors use FS/S as a proxy for gun prevalence (with one study combining FS/S with an indicator of the hunting license rate). Moreover, in the new evidence we examined, FS/S was imputed for all but the beginning and end periods of the decade in one study, and in another, the number of suicides for the small catchment area being studied was likely to be relatively limited, affecting the precision of the proxy. Other methodological issues are specific to studies that examine specific types of homicides, such as those committed by youth or by an intimate partner. Because many homicides go unsolved, issues of missing data may be important. Finally, in studies that use an instrumental variable approach, the conceptual and empirical validity of possible instruments has been an issue. One of the six more recent studies took this approach, and the results were sensitive to specification, including which and how many of the instruments of the potential set were included.

Stronger study designs may be available to more persuasively establish the causal effects of gun ownership or gun prevalence on violent crime; however, many such study designs are currently hampered by poor information on the prevalence of gun ownership and the consequent reliance on proxy measures of availability and prevalence. For this reason, we recommend in Chapter Twenty-Five that the Centers for Disease Control and Prevention or another federal agency resume routine collection of voluntarily provided survey data on gun ownership and use.

## Chapter Seventeen References


Bice, Douglas C., and David D. Hemley, "The Market for New Handguns: An Empirical Investigation," *Journal of Law & Economics*, Vol. 45, No. 1, 2002, pp. 251–265.

Chauhan, P., M. Cerda, S. F. Messner, M. Tracy, K. Tardiff, and S. Galea, "Race/Ethnic-Specific Homicide Rates in New York City: Evaluating the Impact of Broken Windows Policing and Crack Cocaine Markets," *Homicide Studies*, Vol. 15, No. 3, 2011, pp. 268–290.

Cook, Philip J., and Jens Ludwig, "The Social Costs of Gun Ownership," *Journal of Public Economics*, Vol. 90, No. 1–2, 2006, pp. 379–391.

Duggan, Mark, "More Guns, More Crime," *Journal of Political Economy*, Vol. 109, No. 5, 2001, pp. 1086–1114.

———, "Guns and Suicide," in Jens Ludwig and Philip J. Cook, eds., *Evaluating Gun Policy: Effects on Crime and Violence*, Washington, D.C.: Brookings Institution Press, 2003, pp. 41–73.

Hoskin, Anthony, "Household Gun Prevalence and Rates of Violent Crime: A Test of Competing Gun Theories," *Criminal Justice Studies*, Vol. 24, No. 1, 2011, pp. 125–136.

Kleck, Gary, Tomislav Kovandzic, and Mark E. Schaffer, *Gun Prevalence, Homicide Rates and Causality: A GMM Approach to Endogeneity Bias,* London: Centre for Economic Policy Research, Discussion Paper No. 5357, 2005.

Kleck, G., and E. B. Patterson, "The Impact of Gun Control and Gun Ownership Levels on Violence Rates," *Journal of Quantitative Criminology*, Vol. 9, No. 3, 1993, pp. 249–287.

Kovandzic, Tomislav, Mark E. Schaffer, and Gary Kleck, "Estimating the Causal Effect of Gun Prevalence on Homicide Rates: A Local Average Treatment Effect Approach," *Journal of Quantitative Criminology*, Vol. 29, No. 4, 2013, pp. 477–541.

Miller, M., D. Azrael, and D. Hemenway, "Household Firearm Ownership and Suicide Rates in the United States," *Epidemiology*, Vol. 13, No. 5, 2002, pp. 517–524.

Monuteaux, M. C., L. K. Lee, D. Hemenway, R. Mannix, and E. W. Fleegler, "Firearm Ownership and Violent Crime in the U.S.: An Ecologic Study," *American Journal of Preventive Medicine*, Vol. 49, No. 2, 2015, pp. 207–214.

National Research Council, *Firearms and Violence: A Critical Review*, Washington, D.C.: National Academies Press, 2004.

NRC—*See* National Research Council.

Parker, R. N., K. R. Williams, K. J. McCaffree, E. K. Acensio, A. Browne, K. J. Strom, and K. Barrick, "Alcohol Availability and Youth Homicide in the 91 Largest U.S. Cities, 1984–2006," *Drug and Alcohol Review*, Vol. 30, No. 5, 2011, pp. 505–514.

Siegel, M., C. S. Ross, and C. King, "Examining the Relationship Between the Prevalence of Guns and Homicide Rates in the USA Using a New and Improved State-Level Gun Ownership Proxy," *Injury Prevention*, Vol. 20, No. 6, 2014, pp. 424–426.

Swedler, D. I., M. M. Simmons, F. Dominici, and D. Hemenway, "Firearm Prevalence and Homicides of Law Enforcement Officers in the United States," *American Journal of Public Health*, Vol. 105, No. 10, 2015, pp. 2042–2048.

Zeoli, A. M., and D. W. Webster, "Effects of Domestic Violence Policies, Alcohol Taxes and Police Staffing Levels on Intimate Partner Homicide in Large U.S. Cities," *Injury Prevention*, Vol. 16, No. 2, 2010, pp. 90–95.

CHAPTER EIGHTEEN

# Firearm and Ammunition Taxes

Taxation is a policy lever frequently used as a means to influence social welfare and well-being. In this chapter, we synthesize the limited research that has been conducted on firearm and ammunition taxes in the United States. The information was collected from a targeted search of the literature separate from that described in Chapter Two of this report.

Taxation has rarely been used as a policy tool to manage risks associated with gun violence. A federal excise tax of 10–11 percent on the import and production of firearms and ammunition has been in place since 1919, but the rate has not been changed since it was first instituted. The National Firearms Act of 1934 imposed a $200 tax on the transfer of certain firearms, but the tax applied to a very narrow set of weapons and has not been changed since initial enactment. Only two states impose special taxes on guns and ammunition over the standard sales tax: Pennsylvania adds a $3 surcharge on firearms subject to the sales tax, and Tennessee has a $0.10 special privilege tax for use, possession, and sales of shotgun shells of metallic cartridges (Pinho and Rappa, 2013).

Local jurisdictions have recently taken action to directly influence the prices of guns and ammunition. In January 2016, Seattle, Washington, began collecting taxes at the point of sale of $25 for each firearm and $0.02 to $0.05 for each round of ammunition sold within city limits. Cook County, Illinois, which passed a $25 tax on firearms in 2013, implemented a similar tax increase on ammunition of $0.01 to $0.05 per cartridge in June 2016. While these local tax increases were primarily intended as revenue-generating mechanisms, larger tax hikes have occasionally been proposed as a preventive mechanism to reduce new purchases of firearms or ammunition and limit gun violence. Most proposed state and local measures to this effect have not passed, but in April 2016, the Northern Mariana Islands (a U.S. territory) passed a provision imposing a $1,000 tax on pistols.

Understanding the potential consequences of higher taxes on guns and ammunition is important both for policy considerations moving forward and for assessing laws that increase the effective price of legal gun purchases, such as permit-to-purchase laws (Cook and Leitzel, 1996). While opponents have voiced concern that increased local taxes will push legal consumers and suppliers to conduct business outside city limits

(Beekman, 2015), to our knowledge, no rigorous evaluations of the causal effects of taxation policy on the gun industry have been reported.

Conceptually, the societal effects of increasing taxes on firearms or ammunition will hinge on how responsive gun purchasers are to changes in price and how this varies for different types of purchasers (i.e., those using firearms for recreational, self-protection, or criminal purposes). Because guns are durable goods, there is also a need to understand price linkages between the formal and informal markets.[1] Just as the "durability" of ammunition may vary across individuals and reasons for use, policies affecting the price of firearms may have very different consequences compared with policies affecting the price of ammunition. While several studies have examined the theoretical consequences of increasing the price of firearms (e.g., McDonald, 1999; Chaudri and Geanakoplos, 1998; Cook and Leitzel, 1996), there exists little empirical evidence to inform whether taxation can be an effective policy measure to limit criminal or violent gun misuse.

Several factors complicate evaluation of the price sensitivity of demand for guns or ammunition. First, because few policy changes have substantially influenced the price of firearms or ammunition, research has faced insufficient variation to empirically estimate the price responsiveness of various participants in gun markets. Second, in the absence of exogenous price shocks, researchers cannot disentangle changes in consumer demand that are driven by changes in price from changes in price that are driven by changes in consumer demand. And third, the market for firearms and ammunition is highly differentiated, and there are no publicly available gun or ammunition price data over a sufficient period to support policy analysis (National Research Council, 2004). A few sources provided information on national average prices of guns and ammunition,[2] but these averages obscured notable price variation across jurisdictions and offered only a rough approximation of the retail prices facing consumers. Thus, these data have generally been used to evaluate how demand shocks influence prices and not to estimate how responsive consumers are to changes in prices (Koper and Roth, 2002).

Furthermore, because these data sources applied solely to the formal market, they provided little insight into linkages between the formal and informal markets, which limited analysis of how taxation in the formal market would affect criminal markets for firearms. Theoretically, price changes in the primary market should affect informal markets, but some evidence suggests that the informal market for firearms operates quite differently from the formal market. For instance, qualitative interviews with adult male detainees in Cook County Jail found that 40 percent of inmate respon-

---

1 The *informal market* is defined here as comprising legal but unrecorded private transactions (i.e., secondary markets), as well as illegal trade in firearms (i.e., black markets), following Cook and Leitzel (1996).

2 See, for example, Fjestad (2017) and *Shotgun News* (renamed *Firearm News Magazine*). AmmoSpy (undated), a relatively new website, provides web-scraped data on ammunition prices.

dents acquired firearms through means other than purchase or trade (Cook, Parker, and Pollack, 2015), most commonly through borrowing or sharing arrangements. The importance of social networks in illegal gun markets has been found in other studies (Cook et al., 2007; Kennedy, Piehl, and Braga, 1996; Sheley and Wright, 1993), but while this provides some evidence about how criminal markets for firearms function, there exist no reliable estimates of the price elasticity of demand for guns or ammunition by violent individuals or criminal organizations (Cook and Pollack, 2016). As research grows in this area and examines underground gun markets across different jurisdictions, we may gain a better understanding of whether taxation can serve as an effective measure to prevent criminal acquisition and use of firearms.

In contrast to violent or criminal offenders, there exists some empirical evidence on how responsive hunters are to changes in price. Several articles that exploited variation in hunting license fees have found hunting demand to be relatively unrelated to changes in license fees (Poudyal, Cho, and Bowker, 2008; Sun, Van Kooten, and Voss, 2005; Teisl, Boyle, and Record, 1999). While this research suggests that moderate tax increases on guns or ammunition would do little to disrupt hunting or recreational gun use, the evidence is based on changes in hunting license fees (which are a very small fraction of the total cost of hunting) and may not be congruent with the actual response to significant increases in the price of firearms or ammunition.

## Conclusions

Overall, we currently have little empirical evidence to indicate how taxation would influence firearm-related outcomes, such as violent crime or suicides. Nor is there evidence establishing how taxing firearms or ammunition would affect the gun industry, defensive gun use, or recreational gun use. Given that taxation has been a standard policy lever for other potentially harmful goods (e.g., cigarettes, alcohol, and soda or sugary beverages), we may be able to derive insights from policy changes in these markets. However, understanding the costs and benefits of taxation in gun markets requires special consideration of the varied purposes for which individuals acquire and retain firearms or ammunition, the relationship between various market sources for guns and ammunition, and the political feasibility of imposing price regulations in a market for which regulations are already highly contentious.

## Chapter Eighteen References


AmmoSpy, "Trending," web page, undated. As of June 29, 2017: http://www.ammospy.net/trending

Beekman, Daniel, "How Gun-Tax Legislation Would Affect Seattle Firearms Stores," *Seattle Times*, July 29, 2015. As of February 20, 2017: http://www.seattletimes.com/seattle-news/politics/how-gun-tax-legislation-would-affect-seattle-firearms-stores/

Chaudri, V., and J. Geanakoplos, "A Note on the Economic Rationalization of Gun Control," *Economics Letters,* Vol. 58, 1998, pp. 51–53.

Cook, P. J., and J. A. Leitzel, "'Perversity, Futility, Jeopardy': An Economic Analysis of the Attack on Gun Control," *Law and Contemporary Problems,* Vol. 59, No. 1, 1996, pp. 91–118.

Cook, P. J., J. Ludwig, S. Venkatesh, and A. A. Braga, "Underground Gun Markets," *Economic Journal*, Vol. 117, 2007, pp. F558–F888.

Cook, P. J., and H. A. Pollack, "Reducing Access to Guns by Violent Offenders," presented at RSF Journal Conference: The Underground Gun Market, April 2016.

Cook, Philip J., Susan T. Parker, and Harold A. Pollack, "Sources of Guns to Dangerous People: What We Learn by Asking Them," *Preventive Medicine,* Vol. 79, 2015, pp. 28–36.

Fjestad, S. P., *Blue Book of Gun Values*, 38th ed., Minneapolis, Minn.: Blue Book Publications, 2017.

Kennedy, D. M., A. M. Piehl, and A. A. Braga, "Youth Violence in Boston: Gun Markets, Serious Youth Offenders, and a Use-Reduction Strategy," *Law and Contemporary Problems*, Vol. 59, No. 1, 1996, pp. 147–196.

Koper, Christopher S., and Jeffrey A. Roth, "The Impact of the 1994 Federal Assault Weapons Ban on Gun Markets: An Assessment of Short-Term Primary and Secondary Market Effects," *Journal of Quantitative Criminology,* Vol. 18, No. 3, 2002, pp. 239–266.

McDonald, J. F., "An Economic Analysis of Guns, Crime, and Gun Control," *Journal of Criminal Justice*, Vol. 27, No. 1, 1999, pp. 11–20.

National Research Council, *Firearms and Violence: A Critical Review*, Washington, D.C.: National Academies Press, 2004.

Pinho, R., and J. Rappa, *Special Taxes on Guns, Ammunition, and Gun Shows*, Hartford, Conn.: Connecticut General Assembly, Office of Legislative Research, OLR Research Report 2013-r-0034, January 10, 2013.

Poudyal, N., S. H. Cho, and J. M. Bowker, "Demand for Resident Hunting in the Southeastern United States," *Human Dimensions of Wildlife*, Vol. 13, No. 3, 2008, pp. 158–174.

Sheley, J. F., and J. D. Wright, *Gun Acquisition and Possession in Selected Juvenile Samples*, Washington, D.C.: National Institute of Justice, 1993.

Sun, L. G., C. Van Kooten, and G. M. Voss, "Demand for Wildlife Hunting in British Columbia," *Canadian Journal of Agricultural Economics,* Vol. 53, 2005, pp. 25–46.

Teisl, M. F., K. J. Boyle, and R. E. Record, Jr., "License-Sales Revenues: Understanding Angler and Hunter Reaction to Changes in License Prices," *Human Dimensions of Wildlife,* Vol. 4, No. 4, 1999, pp. 1–17.

CHAPTER NINETEEN

# Mental Health Care Access and Suicide

Increased access to mental health services is commonly promoted as a strategy to decrease firearm violence and suicide. Indeed, organizations on opposite sides of gun regulation debates often agree that policies designed to improve access to mental health care offer a promising approach to reducing gun violence.[1] Here, we synthesize the evidence on access to mental health care and its effects on suicide; we find that evidence regarding the relationship between the two has been mixed. The information was collected from a targeted search of the literature separate from that described in Chapter Two of this report.

*Access to care* can be defined in many ways. Several studies have defined access as the *availability of health care and mental health services* in a given region. Other studies focus on the *use of health and mental health services* by individuals who have a history of suicide ideation, suicide attempts, or a completed suicide. Still others focus on the *barriers to mental health care* that may preclude an individual from accessing services even when they are available. Finally, a handful of studies has focused on more-foundational *policies that may affect access* to and availability of care (e.g., health insurance laws, mental health expenditures). Our synthesis proceeds by examining the evidence for each of these definitions.

## Availability of Health Care and Mental Health Services

Several studies examining the availability of health care have used state-level data on suicide rates in different regions, as well as the density of health care providers, including general practitioners, psychiatrists, and clinical psychologists. These studies have yielded some evidence that density of mental health providers is associated with lower suicide rates. For instance, one study examined the association between indexes of health care access—including proportion of state residents without health insurance and proportion of psychiatrists and nonpsychiatrist physicians per 100,000 residents—and rates of suicide at the state level. Data were obtained from the U.S. Census Bureau,

[1] See, for example, Lexington (2013) or Robbins (2014).

the Centers for Disease Control and Prevention (CDC), and the American Board of Medical Specialties, with most data collected in the early 2000s. Both the density of psychiatrists and density of nonpsychiatrist physicians were associated with lower suicide rates (Tondo, Albert, and Baldessarini, 2006), controlling for sociodemographic factors (e.g., population density, proportion of men, and proportion of racial/ethnic minorities) and economic indexes (e.g., amount of federal mental health aid received by the state). A second study focused on access to care and suicide rates at the state level using data from the CDC (Thomson Healthcare, 2007). That study found evidence that states with higher proportions of psychiatrists, psychologists, and social workers had lower suicide rates, although these conclusions were based on bivariate analyses. Both of these studies used cross-sectional designs, raising questions about whether the proportion of health care providers accounts for lower suicide rates or whether some other factor associated with both suicide and health care availability causes the observed associations.

However, if access to mental health care is an important predictor of suicide risk, we might expect that the farther individuals have to travel to access care, the higher their risk of suicide might be. McCarthy et al. (2012) examined this relationship in the population of military veterans living at a range of distances from the nearest U.S. Department of Veterans Affairs (VA) mental health provider. Among veterans who accessed outpatient or inpatient services during fiscal years 2003–2004 and 2006–2007, and controlling for sociodemographic factors and mental health diagnoses, the authors found that distance to the nearest provider was not a predictor of suicide, except among the subgroup of veterans living at extreme distances (i.e., more than 800 miles) from the nearest VA provider. However, this study focused on individuals who used VA services at least once, regardless of the distance to the nearest hospital. If distance to the nearest VA provider could discourage an initial visit, as well as follow-up visits, then this study design could fail to observe true effects of health care services on suicide risk.

Price, Mrdjenovich, and Dake (2009) examined state-level variation in firearm suicide rates in relation to state indexes of access to care, including the number of clinically active mental health professionals per 100,000 population (including psychiatrists, psychologists, social workers, and counselors per state), the number of mental health facilities and psychiatric treatment beds, the number of physicians who wrote prescriptions for psychotropic medications, and the proportion of psychiatrists to other physicians who wrote prescriptions for psychotropic medications. In bivariate analyses, states with higher numbers of physicians writing psychotropic medication prescriptions, and those with higher proportions of psychiatrists to other physicians writing these prescriptions, had lower rates of firearm suicide. However, in multivariate models, neither of these factors was associated with firearm suicide rates. Instead, the significant predictors of firearm suicide rates were firearm ownership and state educational expenditures.[2] The authors did not examine total suicide rates.

Fewer studies have focused on the availability of specific services rather than the availability of practitioners. Shumway et al. (2012) examined the effect of psychiatric care capacity reductions in a large city in the United States. The primary provider of inpatient and emergency psychiatric services for the community experienced a reduction in acute inpatient capacity. However, this did not appear to impact rates of suicide among individuals who were engaged in community mental health services in the city. Because there was no comparison group for this study, it was not possible to rule out the possibility that reductions in psychiatric care capacity did affect suicide rates, but this relationship was obscured by other contemporaneous changes to suicide risk with the opposite effect.

These studies suggest that states with more mental health providers have lower rates of suicide. However, the cause of this association is not clear. It may be that mental health providers have a direct protective effect on suicide risk; however, findings that distance to providers is only weakly associated with suicide risk or that the association disappears when controlling for state-level indicators of education level and firearm ownership rates raise questions about this conclusion. Alternatively, it may be that other factors associated with both suicide risk and mental health availability explain the association.

## Use of Health and Mental Health Services

Even when services are available, not all individuals with mental health treatment needs use them. For this reason, several studies have focused on use of health and mental health services by individuals who have expressed suicide ideation, attempted suicide, or completed suicide.

A systematic review conducted in 2002 examined rates of contact with mental health and primary care services among individuals who died by suicide (Luoma, Martin, and Pearson, 2002). The authors included 40 studies from the United States, Australia, and Europe from inception to 2000. On average, 19 percent (95-percent confidence interval [CI]: 7, 28) of decedents made contact with the mental health system in the month before death, and 32 percent (95-percent CI: 16, 46) made contact in the year before death. Older adults and men were generally less likely to make contact with the mental health system. Contact with primary care providers was more common: Across studies, an average of 45 percent made such contact in the month before death, and 77 percent made contact within the year before death. Older adults were more likely to make contact with primary care providers. A more recent study

[2] See Chapter Sixteen for more on the association between suicide and firearm ownership.

used data from 18 U.S. states to examine mental health treatment among suicide decedents (Niederkrotenthaler et al., 2014). Using data from the National Violent Death Reporting System from 2005 to 2010, researchers identified 57,877 suicides. This study found similar results to the previously described review: 38.5 percent of suicide decedents received mental health treatment during the two months before death. Individuals with depressed mood, substance use problems, and a history of suicide attempts were more likely to have accessed treatment, suggesting that individuals with a longer history of mental health problems may be more likely to access services.

Although these studies suggest that a large proportion of individuals who take their lives make contact with the health or mental health system prior to their deaths, the studies do not answer whether the availability and use of mental health care reduce the incidence of suicide that would exist without such care. Moreover, there are unanswered questions about the quality and appropriateness of the care received by those at risk of suicide (e.g., with respect to frequency, service type or setting, or intensity). In addition, given that these studies are generally based on record reviews or psychological autopsies, it is usually not possible to determine whether providers assessed respondents for depression or suicide risk or whether the problems elevating individuals' suicide risk were ever discussed (Simon and Gold, 2016). Moreover, there are still large numbers of individuals who do not make contact with the health care system leading up to their deaths. These factors all make it difficult to interpret the meaning of findings that individuals who take their lives have often accessed health and mental health services leading up to their deaths.

## Barriers to Mental Health Care

Also relevant to these questions is a consideration of barriers to care. Even when mental health care is available, there are numerous reasons why individuals might not access services. In surveys of college students who have thought about suicide or were identified as being at elevated risk for suicide (due to current suicide ideation, history of suicide attempt, current depression, or current alcohol abuse), common barriers included beliefs that they can manage their problems without treatment or that their problems did not warrant treatment (Arria et al., 2011; Czyz et al., 2013). Some students reported preferences to seek help from family or friends, whereas others cited logistical challenges, including a lack of time to seek treatment, long waiting periods for services, and financial barriers. A study in Utah contacted the family (including parents, siblings, and other relatives) and friends of 49 youth (aged 13–21) who took their lives (Moskos et al., 2007). The most commonly endorsed barrier to mental health treatment was a belief that treatment would not help (cited as a barrier by more than 70 percent of parents, siblings, relatives, and friends), stigma toward help-seeking (endorsed by 52–79 percent of interviewees), and reluctance to admit that there was a problem (endorsed by 58–79 percent of interviewees). Substantial proportions of family members and friends reported that the decedent did not know where to go to seek help, could not afford help, or did not have insurance coverage for mental health services. A larger-scale analysis of state-level characteristics also found that rates of suicide were higher in states in which a higher proportion of the population reported that they were unable to obtain health care because of costs (Thomson Healthcare, 2007). However, there is little evidence examining whether removing these barriers increases the likelihood of accessing needed services and what this may mean for reducing suicide risk.

## Policies That May Affect Access to Services

U.S. studies have found that state mental health expenditures per capita are not associated with rates of suicide (Thomson Healthcare, 2007; Price, Mrdjenovich, and Dake, 2009). However, there is some evidence that states receiving more federal mental health aid have lower suicide rates (Tondo, Albert, and Baldessarini, 2006), and in a multivariate model, this was a stronger correlate of suicide rates than the proportion of uninsured individuals in the state, density of psychiatrists or physicians, or sociodemographic variables (specifically, male gender). Because these studies are generally based on cross-sectional state-level data, however, it is difficult to know what type of effect an increase in mental health funding or increase in the number of insured individuals would have on rates of suicide.

A recent study by Lang (2013) analyzed the implementation of mental health parity laws on suicide rates. These laws require health insurance plans to provide comparable coverage for physical and mental health (U.S. Department of Labor, 2010). Between 1990 and 2004, 29 states enacted parity laws, and this study used variation in implementation dates to explore the causal effect of parity laws on suicide. Results demonstrated that in the first year after states enacted parity laws, the suicide rate declined by 5 percent. Moreover, these effects were maintained two or more years after the laws were enacted, although the magnitude of the change decreased somewhat. Subsequent analyses demonstrated that these laws had a particular effect on adults aged 18–64 but did not seem to affect the suicide rate in older adults who were less likely to be affected by the laws. Because this study was able to examine changes in suicide rates before and after the implementation of parity laws, it provided a more rigorous test of the association between access to services and suicide.

## International and Cross-National Studies

International studies provide fairly consistent evidence that the presence of psychiatrists in a region is associated with lower suicide rates. In Japan, municipalities with at least one psychiatrist experienced lower rates of suicide (Kawaguchi and Koike, 2016), and in Slovenia, regions with a higher number of psychiatrists working in outpatient settings had lower suicide rates (Jagodič et al., 2013). In addition, a multinational study found that countries with a higher density of psychiatrists had lower suicide rates (Rajkumar et al., 2013). However, studies in other countries, such as Austria, have found no association between the density of psychiatrists and suicide standardized mortality ratios (Kapusta et al., 2010). Most of these studies were based on cross-sectional data, and when multiyear data were available, the effects of changes over time were not reported. Therefore, it is not clear that the prevalence of psychiatrists caused reductions in suicide rates, because other factors may be associated with both the presence of psychiatrists and lower suicide rates (e.g., urbanicity, gun ownership, education).

The evidence regarding nonphysician mental health providers has been more mixed. An Austrian study focused on the availability of psychotherapists—a broad category that included psychologists, psychiatrists, teachers, and social workers—and found that a larger number of psychotherapists was associated with lower rates of suicide (Kapusta et al., 2009). In contrast, other studies have found no association between the density of nonphysician psychotherapists, clinical psychologists, and general practitioners and suicide (Jagodič et al., 2013; Kapusta et al., 2010). The availability of certain types of services may also make a difference: A study in Finland found that regions with a higher ratio of outpatient to inpatient services had lower rates of suicide (Pirkola et al., 2009).

As in the United States, there have been efforts in other countries to examine suicide decedents' health care utilization prior to death. These studies share many of the same weaknesses as the U.S. studies, including an inability to directly connect use of mental health services to increased or decreased risk of suicide. However, one study in the United Kingdom highlighted the importance of identifying periods of vulnerability for individuals who are engaged with the health care system. Appleby et al. (1999) compared individuals who had inpatient psychiatric care within five years of their suicide with a comparison group of individuals who received inpatient care but did not die by suicide. Comparison participants were identified from hospitals in the same region as decedents, which were selected via block randomization and, to the extent possible, were matched on age (within five years), sex, diagnosis, and date of admission (within six months). This study focused on care received by patients after discharge. The authors found that individuals who died by suicide were more likely to have had their level of care reduced at the final appointment before their deaths. These decreases in care included reduced appointment frequency, transfer to a less supervised care location, or a lowered medication dose. For 56 percent of these cases, the death was within three months of the reduction in care. This study suggests that the period of time following a reduction in care may be particularly risky for suicidal individuals. This is an important consideration, even when a reduction in the intensity or level of care is clinically indicated.

## Conclusions

Correlations have frequently been found between suicide rates and the availability of mental health care, use of mental health care, or barriers to use of care. Typically, these correlations are found in cross-sectional studies, where it is not possible to establish with confidence whether the observed associations are attributable to a causal effect of mental health care or to other factors that might be associated with both suicide risk and the availability or use of mental health care. However, two studies that use methods better designed to establish causal effects suggest that (1) mental health parity laws, which facilitate access to mental health services, may indeed reduce suicide rates and (2) suicidal individuals may be particularly at risk after experiencing reductions in their health care.

## Chapter Nineteen References

Appleby, Louis, John A. Dennehy, Christopher S. Thomas, E. Brian Faragher, and Glyn Lewis, "Aftercare and Clinical Characteristics of People with Mental Illness Who Commit Suicide: A Case-Control Study," *Lancet*, Vol. 353, No. 9162, 1999, pp. 1397–1400.

Arria, Amelia M., Emily R. Winick, Laura M. Garnier-Dykstra, Kathryn B. Vincent, Kimberly M. Caldeira, Holly C. Wilcox, and Kevin E. O'Grady, "Help Seeking and Mental Health Service Utilization Among College Students with a History of Suicide Ideation," *Psychiatric Services*, Vol. 62, No. 12, 2011, pp. 1510–1513.

Czyz, Ewa K., Adam G. Horwitz, Daniel Eisenberg, Anne Kramer, and Cheryl A. King, "Self-Reported Barriers to Professional Help Seeking Among College Students at Elevated Risk for Suicide," *Journal of American College Health*, Vol. 61, No. 7, 2013, pp. 398–406.

Jagodič, Helena Korošec, Tatjana Rokavec, Mark Agius, and Peter Pregelj, "Availability of Mental Health Service Providers and Suicide Rates in Slovenia: A Nationwide Ecological Study," *Croatian Medical Journal*, Vol. 54, No. 5, 2013, pp. 444–452.

Kapusta, Nestor D., Thomas Niederkrotenthaler, Elmar Etzersdorfer, Martin Voracek, Kanita Dervic, Elisabeth Jandl-Jager, and Gernot Sonneck, "Influence of Psychotherapist Density and Antidepressant Sales on Suicide Rates," *Acta Psychiatrica Scandinavica*, Vol. 119, No. 3, 2009, pp. 236–242.

Kapusta, Nestor D., Martin Posch, Thomas Niederkrotenthaler, Melitta Fischer-Kern, Elmar Etzersdorfer, and Gernot Sonneck, "Availability of Mental Health Service Providers and Suicide Rates in Austria: A Nationwide Study," *Psychiatric Services*, Vol. 61, No. 12, 2010, pp. 1198–1203.

Kawaguchi, Hideaki, and Soichi Koike, "Association Between the Density of Physicians and Suicide Rates in Japan: Nationwide Ecological Study Using a Spatial Bayesian Model," *PLoS ONE*, Vol. 11, No. 2, 2016.

Lang, Matthew, "The Impact of Mental Health Insurance Laws on State Suicide Rates," *Health Economics*, Vol. 22, No. 1, 2013, pp. 73–88.

Lexington, "Why the NRA Keeps Talking About Mental Illness, Rather Than Guns," *Economist*, March 13, 2013. As of June 29, 2017: http://www.economist.com/blogs/lexington/2013/03/guns-and-mentally-ill

Luoma, Jason B., Catherine E. Martin, and Jane L. Pearson, "Contact with Mental Health and Primary Care Providers Before Suicide: A Review of the Evidence," *American Journal of Psychiatry*, Vol. 159, No. 6, 2002, pp. 909–916.

McCarthy, John F., Frederic C. Blow, Rosalinda V. Ignacio, Mark A. Ilgen, Karen L. Austin, and Marcia Valenstein, "Suicide Among Patients in the Veterans Affairs Health System: Rural-Urban Differences in Rates, Risks, and Methods," *American Journal of Public Health*, Vol. 102, No. S1, March 2012, pp. S111–S117.

Moskos, Michelle A., Lenora Olson, Sarah R. Halbern, and Doug Gray, "Utah Youth Suicide Study: Barriers to Mental Health Treatment for Adolescents," *Suicide and Life-Threatening Behavior*, Vol. 37, No. 2, 2007, pp. 179–186.

Niederkrotenthaler, Thomas, Joseph E. Logan, Debra L. Karch, and Alex Crosby, "Characteristics of U.S. Suicide Decedents in 2005–2010 Who Had Received Mental Health Treatment," *Psychiatric Services*, Vol. 65, No. 3, 2014, pp. 387–390.

Pirkola, Sami, Reijo Sund, Eila Sailas, and Kristian Wahlbeck, "Community Mental-Health Services and Suicide Rate in Finland: A Nationwide Small-Area Analysis," *Lancet*, Vol. 373, No. 9658, 2009, pp. 147–153.

Price, James H., Adam J. Mrdjenovich, and Joseph A. Dake, “Prevalence of State Firearm Mortality and Mental Health Care Resources,” *Journal of Community Health*, Vol. 34, No. 5, 2009, pp. 383–391.

Rajkumar, A. P., E. M. Brinda, A. S. Duba, P. Thangadurai, and K. S. Jacob, “National Suicide Rates and Mental Health System Indicators: An Ecological Study of 191 Countries,” *International Journal of Law and Psychiatry*, Vol. 36, No. 5, 2013, pp. 339–342.

Robbins, Mel, “The Real Gun Problem Is Mental Health, Not the NRA,” CNN, 2014. As of June 29, 2017:
http://www.cnn.com/2014/06/24/opinion/robbins-mental-health

Shumway, Martha, Jennifer Alvidrez, Mark Leary, Deborah Sherwood, Eric Woodard, Emily K. Lee, Heather Hall, Ralph A. Catalano, and James W. Dilley, “Impact of Capacity Reductions in Acute Public-Sector Inpatient Psychiatric Services,” *Psychiatric Services*, Vol. 63, No. 2, 2012, pp. 135–141.

Simon, Robert I., and Liza H. Gold, “Decreasing Suicide Mortality: Clinical Risk Assessment and Firearm Management,” in Liza H. Gold and Robert I. Simon, eds., *Gun Violence and Mental Illness*, Arlington, Va.: American Psychiatric Association Publishing, 2016, pp. 249–289.

Thomson Healthcare, *Ranking America’s Mental Health: An Analysis of Depression Across the States*, Washington, D.C.: Mental Health America, 2007.

Tondo, Leonardo, Matthew J. Albert, and Ross J. Baldessarini, “Suicide Rates in Relation to Health Care Access in the United States: An Ecological Study,” *Journal of Clinical Psychiatry*, Vol. 67, No. 4, 2006, pp. 517–523.

U.S. Department of Labor, *Fact Sheet: The Mental Health Parity and Addiction Equity Act of 2008 (MHPAEA),* Washington, D.C., January 29, 2010. As of October 18, 2017:
https://www.dol.gov/sites/default/files/ebsa/about-ebsa/our-activities/resource-center/fact-sheets/mhpaea.pdf

CHAPTER TWENTY

# Education Campaigns and Clinical Interventions for Promoting Safe Storage

The safe storage of firearms has been proposed by both gun advocacy groups and violence prevention groups as a means to address suicides and unintentional injuries and deaths associated with guns in the United States. In addition, safe storage is described explicitly in the Surgeon General's 2012 *National Strategy for Suicide Prevention* (Office of the Surgeon General and National Action Alliance for Suicide Prevention, 2012).

In this chapter, we briefly review the evidence on the relationship between firearm storage and both suicides and unintentional injuries and deaths. Then, we review two nonpolicy approaches: education campaigns and clinical interventions. Safe storage policy approaches—specifically, child-access prevention laws—are discussed in Chapter Ten. The information was collected from a targeted search of the literature separate from that described in Chapter Two of this report but relies heavily on a recent systematic review (Rowhani-Rahbar, Simonetti, and Rivara, 2016) that updated an earlier review (McGee, Coyne-Beasley, and Johnson, 2003).

## Evidence on Safe Storage

As discussed in Chapter Sixteen (on the relationship between firearm prevalence and suicide), there is evidence that those who die by suicide have guns stored less safely than various comparison groups (Conwell et al., 2002; Shenassa et al., 2004). A study on adolescent suicides did not yield similar results but may have been underpowered (Brent et al., 1991; Brent et al., 1993b). In addition, Grossman et al. (2005) examined a combined group of fatal and nonfatal youth suicides and unintentional injuries relative to community controls. They found that, relative to controls, guns used in the injuries or deaths were less likely to be stored unloaded or locked, to have the ammunition locked, or to have the ammunition and gun stored separately and were more likely to be stored without using an extrinsic device. Research has also shown a correlation between firearm storage practices among gun owners, measured in 2004, and state-level unintentional firearm deaths aggregated between 1991 and 2000 (Miller et al., 2005).

## Education Campaigns

Public health communication is a common mechanism used to inform or influence audience behaviors to produce positive health benefits to individuals and society. Decades of research on public health campaigns for a range of behaviors reveal that, over time, campaigns can produce long-term, systemic behavioral change. Communication has been a major contributor, for example, to both the increase in tobacco use (caused by advertising and promotion) and the substantial decline of smoking since the 1960s (through public health campaigns) (National Cancer Institute, 2008). Meta-analyses of how media campaigns affect behavior change provide evidence that campaigns can produce short-term effects of approximately 9 percent more people performing a desired behavior after the campaign than before (Snyder and Hamilton, 2002). When combining campaigns with enforcement strategies (for instance, the campaign combines messages designed to change behavior and to advise the public of penalties for noncompliance), effect sizes can jump to 17 percent (Snyder and Hamilton, 2002). Other meta-analyses corroborate significant effect sizes from more-specific types of campaigns. For example, Noar, Benac, and Harris (2007) examined interventions promoting messages about health behavior change and found small but significant average effects.

Gun rights advocacy organizations, violence prevention organizations, and public health advocacy organizations have implemented small- to large-scale educational campaigns to promote safe firearm storage and safe use. For instance, the National Shooting Sports Foundation (2016) promotes Project ChildSafe, a program designed to encourage safe storage of firearms. With funding from the U.S. Department of Justice, the Ad Council and the National Crime Prevention Council developed the "Lock It Up" information campaign in 2013, which included public service announcements delivered to nearly 15,000 radio stations and more than 500 cable networks in 210 markets (U.S. Department of Justice, 2013). Relatedly, the Brady Campaign to Prevent Gun Violence (undated) produces a variety of safety and education materials spanning various media (e.g., digital, print, and social media). The Brady Campaign's approach extends beyond safe storage practices and implements campaigns targeting gun dealers to promote background checks for all gun sales, illegal dealers who supply guns used in crimes, and the general public to educate them about the dangers of guns in the home (for more about the relationship between firearm prevalence and violent crime, see Chapter Seventeen). The Everytown for Gun Safety Support Fund also has a "Be SMART" program, which promotes safely storing firearms, modeling responsible behavior around guns, asking about unsecured guns in other homes, and recognizing the risks of teen suicide (Everytown for Gun Safety Support Fund, 2017a).

There is only one rigorous evaluation of a national-level mass media campaign promoting safe firearm storage. That campaign centered on the slogan "Buy a Box for Your Gun, Not Your Kid" and included television and radio announcements, billboards, community-distributed materials, and discount coupons for lockboxes (Sidman et al., 2005). Campaign materials contained memorable images of an empty, child-sized coffin or an unlocked cabinet containing a handgun. The campaign materials were distributed to physicians, clinics, nursing organizations, churches, schools, parent-teacher conferences, and law enforcement offices (Sidman et al., 2005). The evaluation did not find the campaign to have statistically significant effects on improving safe storage practices.

## Clinical Interventions

The Surgeon General's 2012 *National Strategy for Suicide Prevention* specifically states that one of its objectives is to "encourage providers who interact with individuals at risk for suicide to routinely assess for access to lethal means" (Office of the Surgeon General and National Action Alliance for Suicide Prevention, 2012). The report states that "providers can educate individuals with suicide risk and their loved ones about safe firearm storage and access." There is recent guidance about when and how physicians can counsel their patients on firearms (Wintemute, Betz, and Ranney, 2016), but such counseling is not often performed (Butkus and Weissman, 2014).

Rowhani-Rahbar, Simonetti, and Rivara (2016) identified five randomized controlled trials or quasi-experimental studies that evaluated clinical-based interventions designed to promote safe firearm storage practices. All interventions were conducted at family medicine or pediatric clinics in the United States, in which practitioners generally counseled families with children. Two of the trials, both of which provided a free safe storage device for firearms in addition to counseling, showed that the intervention improved safe storage (Carbone, Clemons, and Ball, 2005; Barkin et al., 2008). One of the trials that did not provide a free storage device also found positive effects (Stevens et al., 2002). On the other hand, there was no evidence that an intervention that provided counseling plus economic incentives (e.g., coupons for discounted locking devices) to encourage safe storage was effective (Grossman et al., 2000).[1]

## Conclusions

Safe storage of firearms may prevent suicide and unintentional injuries and deaths. As described in Chapter Ten, there is comparatively strong evidence that child-access prevention laws, which require safe storage practices, can effectively reduce suicides and unintentional injuries and deaths. Interventions other than laws may also success-

[1] A sixth study was not a clinical intervention per se but installed free long storage cabinets in western Alaska. Households that received a free cabinet installation improved safe storage of guns and ammunition (Grossman et al., 2012).

fully promote safe storage. Although education campaigns have been found to produce behavior change in other domains, evidence that they have successfully promoted safe storage of firearms is limited. On the other hand, there is evidence that clinicians who counsel patients (mostly families with children) can effectively promote safe storage practices, particularly if storage devices (e.g., gun locks) are given away for free.

## Chapter Twenty References

Barkin, Shari L., Stacia A. Finch, Edward H. Ip, Benjamin Scheindlin, Joseph A. Craig, Jennifer Steffes, Victoria Weiley, Eric Slora, David Altman, and Richard C. Wasserman, "Is Office-Based Counseling About Media Use, Timeouts, and Firearm Storage Effective? Results from a Cluster-Randomized, Controlled Trial," *Pediatrics*, Vol. 122, No. 1, 2008, pp. E15–E25.

Brady Campaign to Prevent Gun Violence, "About Brady," web page, undated. As of January 10, 2016:
http://www.bradycampaign.org/about-brady

Brent, D. A., J. A. Perper, C. J. Allman, G. M. Moritz, M. E. Wartella, and J. P. Zelenak, "The Presence and Accessibility of Firearms in the Homes of Adolescent Suicides: A Case-Control Study," *JAMA*, Vol. 266, No. 21, 1991, pp. 2989–2995.

Brent, D. A., J. A. Perper, G. Moritz, M. Baugher, J. Schweers, and C. Roth, "Firearms and Adolescent Suicide—A Community Case-Control Study," *American Journal of Diseases of Children*, Vol. 147, No. 10, 1993b, pp. 1066–1071.

Butkus, Renee, and Arlene Weissman, "Internists' Attitudes Toward Prevention of Firearm Injury," *Annals of Internal Medicine*, Vol. 160, No. 12, 2014, pp. 821–827.

Carbone, Paul S., Conrad J. Clemens, and Thomas M. Ball, "Effectiveness of Gun-Safety Counseling and a Gun Lock Giveaway in a Hispanic Community," *Archives of Pediatrics and Adolescent Medicine*, Vol. 159, No. 11, 2005, pp. 1049–1054.

Conwell, Y., P. R. Duberstein, K. Connor, S. Eberly, C. Cox, and E. D. Caine, "Access to Firearms and Risk for Suicide in Middle-Aged and Older Adults," *American Journal of Geriatric Psychiatry*, Vol. 10, No. 4, 2002, pp. 407–416.

Everytown for Gun Safety Support Fund, "Be SMART," web page, 2017a. As of May 7, 2017:
http://besmartforkids.org/

Grossman, David C., Peter Cummings, Thomas D. Koepsell, Jean Marshall, Luann D'Ambrosio, Robert S. Thompson, and Chris Mack, "Firearm Safety Counseling in Primary Care Pediatrics: A Randomized, Controlled Trial," *Pediatrics*, Vol. 106, No. 1, 2000, pp. 22–26.

Grossman, D. C., B. A. Mueller, C. Riedy, M. D. Dowd, A. Villaveces, J. Prodzinski, J. Nakagawara, J. Howard, N. Thiersch, and R. Harruff, "Gun Storage Practices and Risk of Youth Suicide and Unintentional Firearm Injuries," *JAMA*, Vol. 293, No. 6, 2005, pp. 707–714.

Grossman, David C., Helen A. Stafford, Thomas D. Koepsell, Ryan Hill, Kyla D. Retzer, and Ward Jones, "Improving Firearm Storage in Alaska Native Villages: A Randomized Trial of Household Gun Cabinets," *American Journal of Public Health*, Vol. 102, No. S2, 2012, pp. S291–S297.

McGee, K. S., T. Coyne-Beasley, and R. M. Johnson, "Review of Evaluations of Educational Approaches to Promote Safe Storage of Firearms," *Injury Prevention*, Vol. 9, No. 2, 2003, pp. 108–111.

Miller M., D. Azrael, D. Hemenway, and M. Vriniotis, "Firearm Storage Practices and Rates of Unintentional Firearm Deaths in the United States," *Accident Analysis and Prevention*, Vol. 37, No. 4, 2005, pp. 661–667.

National Cancer Institute, *The Role of the Media in Promoting and Reducing Tobacco Use*, Washington, D.C.: U.S. Department of Health and Human Services, National Institutes of Health, No. 07-6242, 2008.

National Shooting Sports Foundation, "Project ChildSafe," web page, 2016. As of January 10, 2017:
http://www.projectchildsafe.org/

Noar, Seth M., Christina N. Benac, and Melissa S. Harris, "Does Tailoring Matter? Meta-Analytic Review of Tailored Print Health Behavior Change Interventions," *Psychological Bulletin,* Vol. 133, No. 4, 2007, pp. 673–693.

Office of the Surgeon General and National Action Alliance for Suicide Prevention, *National Strategy for Suicide Prevention: Goals and Objectives for Action: A Report of the U.S. Surgeon General and of the National Action Alliance for Suicide Prevention,* Washington, D.C.: U.S. Department of Health and Human Services, 2012.

Rowhani-Rahbar, Ali, Joseph A. Simonetti, and Frederick P. Rivara, "Effectiveness of Interventions to Promote Safe Firearm Storage," *Epidemiologic Reviews*, Vol. 38, No. 1, 2016, pp. 111–124.

Shenassa, E. D., M. L. Rogers, K. L. Spalding, and M. B. Roberts, "Safer Storage of Firearms at Home and Risk of Suicide: A Study of Protective Factors in a Nationally Representative Sample," *Journal of Epidemiology and Community Health*, Vol. 58, No. 10, 2004, pp. 841–848.

Sidman, Elanor A., David C. Grossman, Thomas D. Koepsell, Luann D'Ambrosio, John Britt, Evan S. Simpson, Frederick P. Rivara, and Abraham B. Bergman, "Evaluation of a Community-Based Handgun Safe-Storage Campaign," *Pediatrics*, Vol. 115, No. 6, 2005, pp. E654–E661.

Snyder, L. B., and M. A. Hamilton, "A Meta-Analysis of U.S. Health Campaign Effects on Behavior: Emphasize Enforcement, Exposure, and New Information, and Beware the Secular Trend," in R. C. Hornik, ed., *Public Health Communication: Evidence for Behavior Change*, New York: Lawrence Erlbaum Associates, Inc., 2002, pp. 357–383.

Stevens, Marguerite M., Ardis L. Olson, Cecelia A. Gaffney, Tor D. Tosteson, Leila A. Mott, and Pamela Starr, "A Pediatric, Practice-Based, Randomized Trial of Drinking and Smoking Prevention and Bicycle Helmet, Gun, and Seatbelt Safety Promotion," *Pediatrics*, Vol. 109, No. 3, 2002, pp. 490–497.

U.S. Department of Justice "Department of Justice Awards $1 Million to the National Crime Prevention Council to Support Gun Safety Campaign," press release, March 7, 2013. As of January 10, 2016:
https://www.justice.gov/opa/pr/department-justice-awards-1-million-national-crime-prevention-council-support-gun-safety

Wintemute, Garen J., Marian E. Betz, and Megan L. Ranney, "Yes, You Can: Physicians, Patients, and Firearms," *Annals of Internal Medicine*, Vol. 165, No. 3, 2016, pp. 205–213.

CHAPTER TWENTY-ONE

# Restricting Access to Firearms Among Individuals at Risk for or Convicted of Domestic Violence or Violent Crime

Nearly half of all women murdered in the United States are killed by a current or former intimate partner, often with a firearm (Petrosky et al., 2017). In about 10 percent of these murders, the women had already been victims of violence in the preceding month (Petrosky et al., 2017). Under some definitions of mass shootings, more than half of the mass shootings between 2009 and 2016 involved domestic violence (Everytown for Gun Safety Support Fund, 2017b). Recognizing the potential lethality of domestic violence, many states have implemented laws designed to prevent domestic violence perpetrators from acquiring or retaining firearms. Chapter Three reviews the literature on background checks, and Chapter Eleven reviews the literature on surrender of firearms by prohibited possessors. Both types of policies can be applied to persons convicted of domestic violence offenses. In this chapter, we consolidate findings from research studies of the effects of laws designed to reduce intimate partner violence, several of which were described in Part B. We review five empirical studies identified during our full-text review (described in Chapter Two) that met our review criteria—that is, at a minimum, the study included (1) time-series data that were used to establish that policies preceded their apparent effects and (2) a control group or comparison group.

## The Policy Defined

In 1994, Congress enacted the Violent Crime Control and Law Enforcement Act (Pub. L. 103-322), making it illegal to possess or receive a firearm while subject to a restraining order protecting an intimate partner or the child of an intimate partner. Subsequently, in 1996, the Lautenberg Amendment (Pub. L. 104-208) to the Gun Control Act of 1968 prohibited possession of a firearm by anyone who has been convicted of a misdemeanor crime of domestic violence, although not all domestic violence misdemeanors are covered. Both before and after the 1994 and 1996 federal law changes, many states enacted additional and sometimes more-stringent legislation related to the purchase or possession of guns by those under domestic violence restraining orders or who have been convicted of a misdemeanor domestic violence offense.

These domestic violence–related "prohibited-possessor" restrictions are one form of a broad class of policy levers meant to reduce violent crime by limiting the availability of guns to individuals who are likely to use them criminally. Such requirements may result in prohibited possessors purchasing guns through other (unregulated or illegal) markets or relying more heavily on gun theft (instead of buying guns through the affected markets). On the other hand, restrictions on the legal market for gun purchase may have trickle-down effects on gun supply in illegal markets because many guns cross from legal to illegal markets. In the case of prohibited-possessor regulations related to domestic violence, these restrictions may also reduce violent crime by restricting the availability of guns to individuals who may have no criminal intent at the time of purchase and are unwilling to commit the act of illegally obtaining a gun but for whom access to a firearm may result in impulsive illegal violence.

## Research Synthesis Findings

Vigdor and Mercy (2006) examined the effects on intimate partner homicide of two types of legislation: that which prohibits people under a domestic violence restraining order from purchasing or possessing a firearm and that which prohibits people who have been convicted of a misdemeanor domestic violence offense from possessing a firearm. The authors also examined laws that allow law enforcement officers to confiscate firearms at the scene of alleged domestic violence incidents. Their state-level analysis of intimate partner homicide rates from 1982 to 2002 found no effect of regulations related to domestic violence misdemeanors (or confiscation policies) but a statistically significant reduction in intimate partner violence from restraining order policies. The authors acknowledged that potentially dissimilar laws related to restraining order and misdemeanor convictions were grouped together in the analysis and that further research is needed to understand how differences in these policies and their enforcement influence their effectiveness. They also noted that the effect of federal law provisions (not estimated by Vigdor and Mercy, 2006) might dominate the effects of marginally more-restrictive state laws.

Similarly, Bridges, Tatum, and Kunselman (2008) examined the effects on intimate partner homicide of laws that prohibit people under a domestic violence restraining order from purchasing or possessing a firearm and others that prohibit people who have been convicted of a misdemeanor domestic violence offense from possessing a firearm. The authors used state-level data from 1995 to 1999 and found a reduction in family homicide rates from prohibited-possessor policies related to people under a restraining order, but they found no effect of the state policies related to misdemeanor domestic violence convictions. However, their narrow time frame means that identification of the effect of these policies came from just a handful of states that enacted relevant legislation during this period and that had both pre- and post-policy observations.

In addition to examining the effects of restricted access for those on domestic violence–related restraining orders or those convicted of misdemeanors, Zeoli and Webster (2010) studied the effects of state laws allowing police to confiscate firearms from a domestic violence incident, allowing police to make warrantless arrests for domestic violence restraining order violations, and mandating arrest for domestic violence restraining order violations. The authors analyzed data from 46 cities from 1979 to 2003 and found a reduction in intimate partner homicides from laws that restrict access to firearms for domestic violence–related restraining orders and laws that allow police to arrest restraining order violators.

Rather than estimating the effects of laws related to domestic violence restraining orders and misdemeanors, Sen and Panjamapirom (2012) examined the effect of whether a state, in its background check process, checks on restraining orders and misdemeanors. They found that the existence of these checks was associated with fewer firearm homicides.

Instead of focusing on the effects of state legislation, Raissian (2016) looked at the effect of the federal 1996 Lautenberg Amendment. She identified the effect of the federal law by exploiting variation across states in their assault statues, which affected the applicability of the law. Specifically, at the time of the 1996 amendment, some states had only a general assault statute and others had both a general statute and a domestic violence statute. Defendants convicted under domestic violence statutes were subject to the gun ban and those convicted under a general statute were not—unless a circuit court ruling applied the ban to misdemeanor domestic violence defendants convicted of a general assault statute. This narrow interpretation of the applicability of the gun ban ended in 2009 with the Supreme Court's *United States v. Hayes* decision. Raissian (2016) used this variation in the implementation dates of domestic violence gun bans to identify the effects of the ban on changes in intimate partner violence. The author found that intimate partner homicides and other family homicides declined when the federal law took effect barring firearm possession among those with a domestic violence misdemeanor conviction.

## Conclusions

Policies that make it illegal for particular groups of people to purchase or possess guns are one form of a broad class of policy levers that attempt to reduce the incidence of criminal gun violence. Recent research evidence suggests that such laws targeting domestic violence offenders may reduce homicide rates. There is less-compelling evidence that laws permitting police to confiscate firearms at scenes of domestic violence reduce violence, although the extent to which police have used this authority is unclear.

## Chapter Twenty-One References

Bridges, F. Stephen, Kimberly M. Tatum, and Julie C. Kunselman, "Domestic Violence Statutes and Rates of Intimate Partner and Family Homicide," *Criminal Justice Policy Review*, Vol. 19, No. 1, 2008, pp. 117–130.

Everytown for Gun Safety Support Fund, "Mass Shootings in the United States: 2009–2016," April 11, 2017b. As of May 3, 2017:
http://everytownresearch.org/reports/mass-shootings-analysis/

Petrosky, E., J. M. Blair, C. J. Betz, K. A. Fowler, S. P. Jack, and B. H. Lyons, "Racial and Ethnic Differences in Homicides of Adult Women and the Role of Intimate Partner Violence—United States, 2003–2014," *Morbidity and Mortality Weekly Report*, Vol. 66, No. 28, 2017, pp. 741–746.

Public Law 103-322, Violent Crime Control and Law Enforcement Act of 1994, 1994.

Public Law 104-208, Gun Ban for Individuals Convicted of a Misdemeanor Crime of Domestic Violence, 1996.

Raissian, Kerri M., "Hold Your Fire: Did the 1996 Federal Gun Control Act Expansion Reduce Domestic Homicides?" *Journal of Policy Analysis and Management*, Vol. 35, No. 1, Winter 2016, pp. 67–93.

Sen, B., and A. Panjamapirom, "State Background Checks for Gun Purchase and Firearm Deaths: An Exploratory Study," *Preventive Medicine*, Vol. 55, No. 4, 2012, pp. 346–350.

Vigdor, E. R., and J. A. Mercy, "Do Laws Restricting Access to Firearms by Domestic Violence Offenders Prevent Intimate Partner Homicide?" *Evaluation Review*, Vol. 30, No. 3, 2006, pp. 313–346.

Zeoli, A. M., and D. W. Webster, "Effects of Domestic Violence Policies, Alcohol Taxes and Police Staffing Levels on Intimate Partner Homicide in Large U.S. Cities," *Injury Prevention*, Vol. 16, No. 2, 2010, pp. 90–95.

CHAPTER TWENTY-TWO

# Mass Shootings

In this chapter, we provide an overview of mass shootings, one of the eight outcomes examined in our research syntheses (Chapters Three through Fifteen). We first describe different approaches for defining a mass shooting and then discuss how using different definitions can influence estimates of mass shooting levels and trends. The information was collected from a targeted search of the literature separate from that described in Chapter Two of this report.

## What Is a Mass Shooting?

In the 1980s, the Federal Bureau of Investigation (FBI) defined *mass murderer* as someone who "kills four or more people in a single incident (not including himself), typically in a single location" (Krouse and Richardson, 2015). However, the government has never defined *mass shooting* as a separate category, and there is not yet a universally accepted definition of the term. Thus, media outlets, academic researchers, and law enforcement agencies frequently use different definitions when discussing mass shootings, which can complicate our understanding of mass shooting trends and their relationship to gun policy. Table 22.1 provides examples of the variation in the criteria set by five of the most commonly referenced data sources on mass shootings in the United States.

Although there is no official standard for the casualty threshold that distinguishes a mass shooting from other violent crimes involving a firearm, a common approach in the literature is to adopt the FBI's criteria for a mass murderer and set a casualty threshold of four fatalities by firearm, excluding the offender or offenders (Duwe, Kovandzic, and Moody, 2002; Krouse and Richardson, 2015; Gius, 2015c; Fox and Fridel, 2016). However, this categorization is not without controversy. It does not capture incidents in which fewer than four victims were killed but additional victims were injured, and it does not include multiple-victim homicides in which fewer than four fatalities resulted from gunshots but additional fatalities occurred by other means. Additionally, the FBI classification of mass murderer was established primarily with the aim of clarifying criminal profiling procedures, not for the purpose of data collection or statistical

**Table 22.1**
**Variation in How Mass Shootings Are Defined and Counted**

| Source | Casualty Threshold (for injuries or deaths by firearm) | Location of Incident | Motivation of Shooter | Number of U.S. Mass Shootings in 2015 |
|---|---|---|---|---|
| *Mother Jones* (see Follman, Aronsen, and Pan, 2017) | Three fatal injuries (excluding shooter)[a] | Public | Indiscriminate (excludes crimes of armed robbery, gang violence, or domestic violence) | 7 |
| Gun Violence Archive (undated) | Four fatal or nonfatal injuries (excluding shooter) | Any | Any | 332 |
| Mass Shooting Tracker (undated) | Four fatal or nonfatal injuries (including shooter) | Any | Any | 371 |
| Mass Shootings in America database (Stanford Geospatial Center, undated) | Three fatal or nonfatal injuries (excluding shooter) | Any | Not identifiably related to gangs, drugs, or organized crime | 65 |
| Supplementary Homicide Reports (FBI) (see Puzzanchera, Chamberlin, and Kang, 2017) | The FBI's Supplementary Homicide Reports do not define *mass shooting* but do provide information on the number of victims, and the reports have been used by researchers in conjunction with news reports or other data sources. | | | |

[a] Before January 2013, the casualty threshold for *Mother Jones* was four fatal injuries (excluding the shooter).

analysis (Ressler, Burgess, and Douglas, 1988). Thus, many have chosen alternative definitions of casualty thresholds for mass shootings. For instance, Lott and Landes (2000) adopted the definition of two or more injured victims, the Gun Violence Archive (undated) defined *mass shooting* as an incident in which four or more victims (excluding the shooter) are injured or killed, and Mass Shooting Tracker (undated) set a criterion of four or more people injured or killed (including the shooter).

Another definitional disagreement is whether to include multiple-victim shooting incidents that occur in connection with some other crime or domestic dispute. Because mass shootings that stem from domestic and gang violence are contextually distinct from high-fatality indiscriminate killings in public venues, some have argued that they should be treated separately. In their analyses of "mass public shootings," Lott and Landes (2000) excluded any felony-related shooting, and Duwe, Kovandzic, and Moody (2002) excluded incidents where "both the victims and offender(s) were involved in unlawful activities, such as organized crime, gang activity, and drug deals" (p. 276). Similarly, Gius (2015c) restricted analysis to events that occurred in a relatively public area and in which victims appeared to have been selected randomly. However, others have claimed that this narrow definition ignores a substantial proportion of gun-related violence from family- or felony-related murder (Fox and Levin, 2015). Data collection efforts by Mass Shooting Tracker and the Gun Violence Archive thus counted all incidents that met their designated casualty threshold as mass shootings, regardless of the circumstances that led to the event.

These definitions matter. Depending on which data source is referenced, there were seven, 65, 332, or 371 mass shootings in the United States in 2015 (see Table 22.1), and those are just some examples. More-restrictive definitions (e.g., *Mother Jones*) focus on the prevalence of higher-profile events motivated by mass murder, but they omit more-common incidents occurring in connection with domestic violence or criminal activity, which make up about 80 percent of mass shooting incidents with four or more fatally injured victims (Krouse and Richardson, 2015). Broader definitions (e.g., Mass Shooting Tracker) provide a more comprehensive depiction of the prevalence of gun violence, but they obscure the variety of circumstances in which these incidents take place and their associated policy implications. Furthermore, if the effects of a firearm policy are expected to affect only public mass shooting incidents, then analysis that includes domestic violence mass shootings in the outcome measure could obscure identification of significant effects that would be found in a more targeted analysis of public mass shootings alone. There is thus value in having multiple measurements of mass shootings—but only if their definitions are clearly and precisely explained and they are used by researchers in a manner appropriate to the analysis.

## Are Mass Shootings on the Rise?

In 2014, the FBI released a study showing that "active shooting incidents" had increased at an average annual rate of 16 percent between 2000 and 2013 (Blair and Schweit, 2014). In contrast to the varied definitions for mass shootings, there is an agreed-upon definition among government agencies for *active shooter*: "an individual actively engaged in killing or attempting to kill people in a confined and populated area; in most cases, active shooters use firearm(s) and there is no pattern or method to their selection of victims" (U.S. Department of Homeland Security, 2008, p. 2). Using a modified version of this definition to include incidents that had multiple offenders or occurred in confined spaces, Blair and Schweit (2014) found that active shootings had increased from only one incident in 2000 to 17 in 2013.

The FBI study (Blair and Schweit, 2014) highlighted several key issues in determining trends in mass shootings. First, the absence of a systematic definition of mass shootings can lead to misinterpretation of reported evidence. While the study explicitly stated, "This is not a study of mass killings or mass shootings" (p. 5), extensive media coverage cited the study as evidence of a sharp rise in mass shootings and mass shooting fatalities (Lott, 2015). However, the definition of an *active-shooter incident* is broader than any of the commonly used criteria for mass shootings (see Table 22.1) because it does not set any casualty threshold. Of the 160 active-shooter incidents included in the FBI's analysis, 7 percent resulted in zero casualties, 20 percent resulted in zero fatalities, and 22 percent resulted in a single fatality (Lott, 2015). Setting a threshold of zero victims increases the potential for measurement error, because shooting incidents with no casualties are more difficult to identify from police records and are less likely to receive media coverage (Duwe, Kovandzic, and Moody, 2002). Additionally, because it should be relatively easier to identify more-recent shootings with few fatalities, a low casualty threshold will tend to systematically bias estimates of the number of shootings upward over time. For example, the Stanford Mass Shootings in America database, which relies solely on online media sources to identify mass shooting events, cautions its users, "Data in the [database] spans a time period that includes the transition from traditional media to digital media in reporting. Numbers of incidents per year should at least in part be assumed to reflect this collection methodology and not just changes in incident frequency." Thus, the more than threefold surge in mass shooting incidents from 2014 to 2015 shown in the Stanford data likely reflects increased online reporting and not necessarily a true increase in the rate of mass shootings.

Even when a more restrictive casualty threshold of four or more fatally injured victims (excluding the shooter) is imposed, empirical evidence on trends in these incidents varies depending on whether the motivation of the shooter is included as a criterion for considering an event a mass shooting. In their analysis of mass shooting trends from 1999 to 2013, Krouse and Richardson (2015) distinguished between mass shootings occurring in public locations that are indiscriminate in nature ("mass public shootings"), mass shootings in which the majority of victims are members of the offender's family and that are not attributable to other criminal activity ("familicide mass shootings"), and mass shootings that occur in connection to some other criminal activity ("other felony mass shootings"). Figures 22.1 and 22.2 show trends in these types of mass shooting incidents and fatalities, respectively, using the data provided in Krouse and Richardson (2015). Extending the data back to the 1970s, two studies found evidence of a slight increase in the frequency of mass public shootings over the past three decades (Cohen, Azrael, and Miller, 2014; Krouse and Richardson, 2015). However, using an expanded definition that includes domestic- or felony-related killings, there is little evidence to suggest that mass shooting incidents or fatalities have increased (Cohen, Azrael, and Miller, 2014; Krouse and Richardson, 2015; Fox and Fridel, 2016). Thus, different choices about how to define a mass shooting result in different findings for both the prevalence of these events at a given time and whether their frequency has changed over time.

Definitional issues aside, the relative rarity of mass shooting events makes analysis of trends particularly difficult. Chance variability in the annual number of mass shooting incidents makes it challenging to discern a clear trend, and trend estimates will be sensitive to outliers and to the time frame chosen for analysis. For example, while Krouse and Richardson (2015) found evidence of an upward trend in mass public

**Figure 22.1**
**Trends in Mass Shooting Incidents, by Type of Incident**

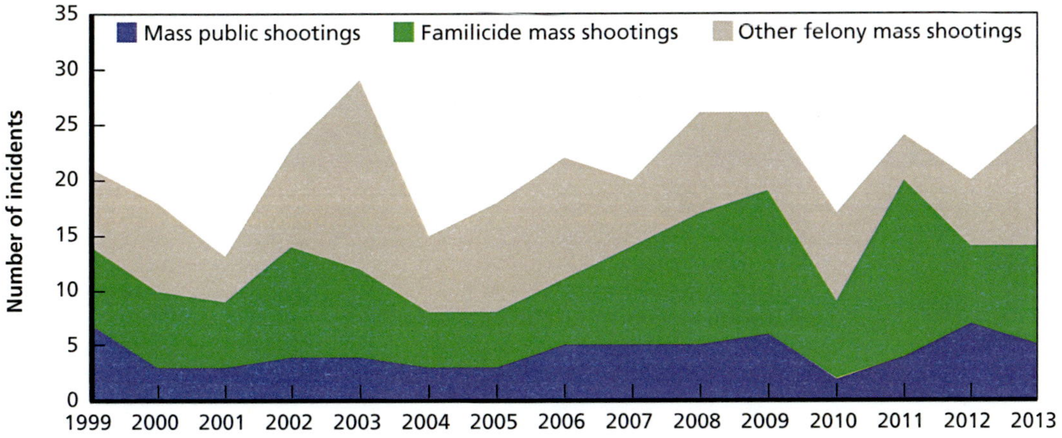


SOURCE: Adapted from data in Krouse and Richardson, 2015.
RAND *RR2088-22.1*

**Figure 22.2**
**Trends in Mass Shooting Fatalities, by Type of Incident**

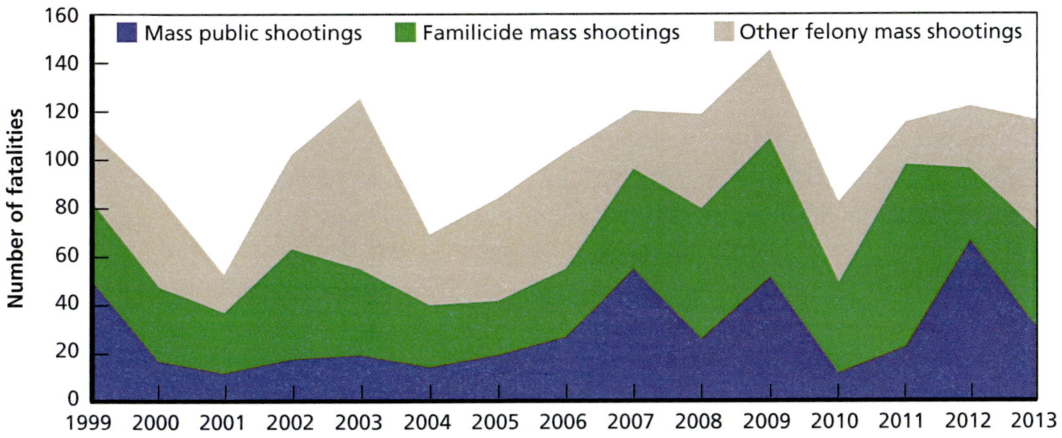


SOURCE: Adapted from data in Krouse and Richardson, 2015.
RAND *RR2088-22.2*

shootings from 1999 to 2013, they noted that the increase was driven largely by 2012, which had an unusually high number of mass public shooting incidents. Additionally, Lott (2015) showed that the FBI study's estimate of a dramatic increase in active-shooter incidents was largely driven by the choice of 2000 as the starting date, because that year had an unusually low number of shooting incidents; extending the analysis to cover 1977 onward and adjusting the data to exclude events with fewer than two fatalities, Lott (2015) found a much smaller and statistically insignificant increase (less than 1 percent annually) in mass shooting fatalities over time.

## Conclusions

While different choices about how to define a mass shooting and the period over which to calculate mass shooting trends have resulted in disagreement about whether the frequency of mass shootings has risen, there is clear evidence that the media's use of the term *mass shooting* has increased significantly over recent decades (Roeder, 2016). Unfortunately, the ambiguity in how mass shootings are defined and counted may result in increased media coverage influencing public perception without better informing our understanding of the prevalence of mass shootings or their determinants, trends, social costs, or policy implications.

## Chapter Twenty-Two References


Blair, J. Pete, and Katherine W. Schweit, *A Study of Active Shooter Incidents, 2000–2013*, Washington, D.C.: Texas State University and Federal Bureau of Investigation, U.S. Department of Justice, 2014.

Cohen, Amy P., Deborah Azrael, and Matthew Miller, "Rate of Mass Shootings Has Tripled Since 2011, Harvard Research Shows," *Mother Jones,* October 15, 2014.

Duwe, Grant, Tomislav Kovandzic, and Carlisle E. Moody, "The Impact of Right-to-Carry Concealed Firearm Laws on Mass Public Shootings," *Homicide Studies*, Vol. 6, No. 4, 2002, pp. 271–296.

Follman, Mark, Gavin Aronsen, and Deanna Pan, "U.S. Mass Shootings, 1982–2017: Data from *Mother Jones*' Investigation," *Mother Jones*, June 14, 2017. As of August 25, 2017: http://www.motherjones.com/politics/2012/12/mass-shootings-mother-jones-full-data/

Fox, James A., and Emma E. Fridel, "The Tenuous Connections Involving Mass Shootings, Mental Illness, and Gun Laws," *Violence and Gender*, Vol. 3, No. 1, 2016, pp. 14–19.

Fox, James A., and Jack Levin, *Extreme Killing: Understanding Serial and Mass Murder*, 3rd ed., Thousand Oaks, Calif.: Sage Publications, 2015.

Gius, Mark, "The Impact of State and Federal Assault Weapons Bans on Public Mass Shootings," *Applied Economics Letters,* Vol. 22, No. 4, 2015c, pp. 281–284.

Gun Violence Archive, homepage, undated. As of October 20, 2016: http://www.gunviolencearchive.org/

Krouse, William J., and Daniel J. Richardson, *Mass Murder with Firearms: Incidents and Victims, 1999–2013*, Washington, D.C.: Congressional Research Service, R44126, 2015.

Lott, John R., Jr., "The FBI's Misinterpretation of the Change in Mass Public Shootings," *ACJS Today*, Vol. 40, No. 2, 2015, pp. 18–29.

Lott, John R., Jr., and William Landes, "Multiple Victim Public Shootings," 2000 (unpublished). As of June 29, 2017: http://www.shack.co.nz/pistoltaupo/SSRN_ID272929_code010610560.pdf

Mass Shooting Tracker, homepage, undated. As of October 20, 2016: https://www.massshootingtracker.org

Puzzanchera, C., G. Chamberlin, and W. Kang, "Easy Access to the FBI's Supplementary Homicide Reports: 1980–2014," Office of Juvenile Justice and Delinquency Prevention, 2017. As of March 22, 2017: https://www.ojjdp.gov/ojstatbb/ezashr/

Ressler, Robert K., Ann W. Burgess, and John E. Douglas, *Sexual Homicide: Patterns and Motives*, New York: Simon and Schuster, 1988.

Roeder, Oliver, "The Phrase 'Mass Shooting' Belongs to the 21st Century," FiveThirtyEight, January 21, 2016. As of January 12, 2017: http://fivethirtyeight.com/features/we-didnt-call-them-mass-shootings-until-the-21st-century/

Stanford Geospatial Center, "Mass Shootings in America," Stanford, Calif.: Stanford University Libraries, undated. As of October 20, 2016: https://library.stanford.edu/projects/mass-shootings-america

U.S. Department of Homeland Security, *Active Shooter: How to Respond,* Washington, D.C., October 2008.

CHAPTER TWENTY-THREE

# Defensive Gun Use

In the United States, self-protection is a predominant reason that many people choose to own a gun (Masters, 2016). For some gun owners, the self-defense utility they derive from ownership is *potential* in nature; that is, gun ownership provides them with comfort in knowing that they will be able to defend themselves in the face of some future possible criminal threat. For others, the self-defense utility is *realized*—they have used their guns defensively in the context of an actual criminal threat. In this chapter, we focus on, and provide an overview of, the latter outcome—the realized utility of gun ownership through defensive gun use (DGU).

Unlike other outcomes that we analyze, such as suicide and homicide, DGU is not itself an outcome of interest. Rather, DGU is important because it is a mechanism through which gun owners hope to reduce harms to themselves or others, such as through a reduction in the probability of victimization; the probability of injury, conditional on a crime being committed; or the severity of injury, conditional on both a crime being committed and an injury occurring.

In this chapter, our focus is on reviewing the literature that examines the effect of DGU on these outcomes of interest. We note that one overarching challenge in this literature is defining the appropriate counterfactual. When we estimate the effect of DGU on the probability of being a victim of a crime or on the probability of injury or severity of injury, are we interested in the estimate of DGU compared with an alternative outcome resulting from *no action* by the intended victim, compared with resistance but without any weapon, or compared with resistance but with a different weapon? Differences in counterfactuals are important for understanding differences in results across studies in the effect of DGU.

A second overarching issue—and one that affects not only the literature examining how DGU affects victimization and injury but also studies on the effect of gun policies on DGU—is determining *what is meant by DGU.* Different conceptualizations of DGU abound. Consequently, measures of DGU vary tremendously, depending on the conceptualization being used. Additionally, as in many cases in the literature on gun policy, measurement is complicated and limited by data availability, even for a given DGU definition.

In this chapter, we summarize the literature and evidence on these issues. First, we describe definitional challenges related to DGU. Second, we describe challenges related to measuring DGU. Third, we examine the literature that estimates the effect of DGU on outcomes, such as victimization and injury. The information in this chapter was collected from a targeted search of the literature separate from that described in Chapter Two of this report.

## What Is Defensive Gun Use?

It is difficult to start a narrative on the prevalence of DGU without first defining the term, but defining DGU is no simple task. The 2004 National Research Council (NRC) report on firearms and violence explains the difficulties:

> Self-defense is an ambiguous term that involves both objective components about ownership and use and subjective features about intent (National Research Council, 1993). Whether one is a defender (of oneself or others) or a perpetrator, for example, may depend on perspective. Some reports of defensive gun use may involve illegal carrying and possession (Kleck and Gertz, 1995; [Kleck, 2001]), and some uses against supposed criminals may legally amount to aggravated assault (Duncan, 2000a, 2000b; [McDowall, Loftin, and Presser, 2000; Hemenway, Azrael, and Miller, 2000]; Hemenway and Azrael, 2000). Likewise, protecting oneself against possible or perceived harm may be different from protecting oneself while being victimized. (NRC, 2004, p. 106)

Understanding the ambiguity is critical because the same factors that complicate defining DGU present difficulties in measuring its prevalence. DGU has primarily been defined in the empirical literature through the use of surveys. Within these surveys, DGUs are often defined as incidents that involve protection against humans (i.e., not animals); gun use by civilians (e.g., not military, police, or security personnel); contact between persons rather than suspicious circumstances only; specific crimes; and actual use of a gun, at least as a visual or verbal threat. There is, of course, some variation even within these parameters. For example, some surveys define DGU only within the context of certain crimes having been committed, while others include a broader set of crimes, as well as suspected and averted crimes. Perceptions about the incident and an individual's role are important because much of the literature relies on self-reports: The respondent must have perceived there to have been a crime (or, in some surveys, a suspected or averted crime) and must consider himself or herself a victim rather than a mutual combatant. Even such stringent definitions, however, may not be sufficient to determine whether the event was lawful, legitimate, or desirable from a social perspective.

## What Are the Challenges in Measuring Defensive Gun Use?

The extensive and conflicting literature on the prevalence of DGU was summarized by the NRC (2004) report:

> Over the past decade, a number of researchers have conducted studies to measure the prevalence of defensive gun use in the population. However, disagreement over the definition of defensive gun use and uncertainty over the accuracy of survey responses to sensitive questions and the methods of data collection have resulted in estimated prevalence rates that differ by a factor of 20 or more. These differences in the estimated prevalence rates indicate either that each survey is measuring something different or that some or most of them are in error. (pp. 6–7)

The NRC report summarized the major methodological challenges to studying DGU, and these challenges have received limited attention since then. Given the preponderance of survey evidence in this literature, we focus on the major methodological concerns regarding survey-based measurement. We highlight differences between the National Crime Victimization Survey (NCVS)—a national survey that is administered twice per year by the Bureau of Justice Statistics and that provides among the most-conservative estimates of DGU—and private gun surveys that have been conducted at only one point in time, such as the National Self Defense Survey (NSDS; Kleck and Gertz, 1995) conducted in 1993 or the National Survey of Private Ownership of Firearms (NSPOF; Cook and Ludwig, 1996) conducted in 1994, which provide among the least-conservative estimates. As NRC (2004) describes, definitional differences and survey differences have resulted in wide-ranging estimates. For example, McDowall, Loftin, and Wiersema (1998) estimated that there were 116,000 DGU incidents annually using the NCVS, while Kleck and Gertz (1995) estimated between 2.2 million and 2.5 million DGUs annually, of which between 1.5 million and 1.9 million involved handguns. In this section, we summarize key factors that underlie these large differences in DGU estimates, including the scope of included incidents, survey sample size and response rates, and challenges related to estimating the prevalence of rare events.

### Scope of Included Incidents

A major difference between the NCVS and private surveys is the scope of included events. In the NCVS, questions about defensive or self-protective actions are asked only of those who first reported that they had been the victims of certain personal contact crimes—even if those crimes had not been completed. These personal contact crimes include rape, assault, burglary, personal and household larceny, and car theft. As a result, respondents in several other categories are not given the opportunity to report defensive action. Among the potentially excluded respondents are those reporting incidents involving other crimes (e.g., trespassing, commercial crimes), victims of crimes in the included categories but who did not report those crimes earlier in the interview,[1] and those reporting incidents that were not completed crimes (e.g., suspected crimes). Also, it is important to note that the NCVS does not ask directly about gun use. Rather, it simply asks the respondents to indicate what, if anything, they did in response to the crime. By not asking directly about gun use, it is possible that some respondents may fail to report a gun-related event, especially one that did not result in harm. Relatedly, there is concern that the NCVS may undercount individuals involved in criminal or other deviant behaviors—a group that may have higher rates of victimization and DGU (McDowall and Wiersema, 1994).

On the other hand, private gun surveys, such as the NSDS and the NSPOF, generally ask all respondents directly about DGU, which allows the respondents to determine which incidents to report regardless of whether the incident involved a crime or not. This approach may allow for a more comprehensive assessment of the prevalence and nature of DGU but also may count as DGU events that are more ambiguous. For example, respondents may include such events as the use of a weapon (1) while investigating a suspicious noise but not actually seeing an individual or (2) to deter someone suspected of thinking about committing a crime. While the former may be eliminated by specifying in the survey question that the incident must involve contact with another person, the latter is based solely on the perception of the survey respondent.

#### Survey Samples and Response Rates

The NCVS provides a large sample of the noninstitutionalized U.S. population aged 12 or older (approximately 50,000 households and 100,000 individuals). Private surveys are typically much smaller. By comparison, the NSDS sample comprised 4,977 individuals aged 18 or older.[2] This is a stark difference considering that the NSDS is among the larger private gun surveys. The private NSPOF included 2,568 respondents.

The representativeness of the samples may also differ. The NCVS typically has a very high response rate—up to 95 percent of eligible households. Private gun surveys tend to have lower response rates. For the NSDS, 61 percent of eligible phone numbers answered by a human completed a survey. Lower response rates may influence the representativeness of the sample and the validity of the findings. Because we often do not know very much about the individuals who did not respond, it is difficult to infer how their absence affects the findings. But the higher the response rate, the fewer individuals for whom there is no information and the less likely that there are differences between those who opted to participate in a survey about gun use and those who did not.

---

[1] There is some evidence that the NCVS underestimates the count of rapes, certain types of assaults, and even gunshot woundings (Cook, 1985; Loftin and MacKenzie, 1990; McDowall and Wiersema, 1994; NRC, 2014).

[2] The NSDS is a random digit–dialing survey and, hence, limited to individuals with phones.

It is important to note that all surveys may miss some components of the population and outcomes of interest. An obvious limitation is that surveys exclude those who suffer fatal injuries and thus cannot participate. Therefore, whether fatally injured persons engaged in a DGU and whether that played a role in their deaths cannot be addressed with survey data. That said, omission of those who died after DGU could result only in underestimates of the true rate of DGU.

#### Inaccuracies in Survey Estimates

There are compelling reasons to suspect that the true number of DGU events are exaggerated in surveys like the NSPOF and the NSDS. There are many implications of the especially high rates of DGU those surveys report that do not appear to be consistent with more-trusted sources of information. For instance, the NSDS estimates suggest that, while using a firearm for self-defense, U.S. residents likely injured or killed an opponent 207,000 times per year, but only about 100,000 people die or are treated for gunshot injuries in hospitals each year, most of whom either shot themselves or were victims of criminal assaults (Hemenway, 1997). Similarly improbable numbers of injuries are implied by self-reports of DGU in the NSPOF survey (Cook, Ludwig, and Hemenway, 1997).

Furthermore, the implied rates of DGU in response to specific crime types appear to be inconsistent with known rates of those crimes. For instance, Hemenway (1997) calculates that the 845,000 DGUs during burglaries implied by the NSDS exceeds the total estimate of burglaries that occurred against victims who owned guns, were home, and were awake when the crime occurred.

Kleck (1999) has defended the high DGU estimates, suggesting that there is greater reason to believe they represent underestimates than overestimates, because of survey respondents' reluctance to discuss their own potentially illegal behavior. He argued that all apparent inconsistencies are illusory. For instance, he suggests that the NSDS was underpowered for reliable estimates of the number of U.S. residents likely killed or injured and that analysis of such a rare subset of the DGU phenomena will naturally be less reliable than the overall DGU estimates. This is a reasonable argument, but the apparently extreme overestimate of DGU injuries raises the question of whether the confidence intervals for the estimate of 207,000 injuries and deaths could span any plausible values. This cannot, however, be calculated from the information provided in the NSDS report. If the confidence interval does not span plausible figures, this would reinforce the view that the NSDS and NSPOF yield overestimates. Kleck (1999) also argues that many gunshot injury victims avoid hospital treatment because they fear it may expose them to legal jeopardy. If, however, the number of such injuries were 207,000 per year, this would entail an implausibly large number and proportion of all injured parties foregoing medical treatment.

In response to the apparently implausible number of crimes of specific types at which DGUs were reported, Kleck (1999) notes that estimates of the number of burglaries, rapes, and other crimes are known to be underestimates—and sometimes large underestimates, as with sexual assaults and domestic violence. Therefore, because we do not know the true number of burglaries and other crimes, "we cannot possibly know if any given DGU estimate is implausibly large relative to these unknown (and possibly unknowable) quantities" (Kleck, 1999, p. 115). Concluding that the estimated number of DGUs in response to burglaries is implausibly high requires, as Kleck notes, some assumptions about the plausible magnitude of underreporting of burglaries. As with the estimate of 207,000 DGU injuries and deaths, the assumptions required to reconcile the apparent inconsistencies are sufficiently extreme that we take such comparisons as evidence that the NSDS and NSPOF produce overestimates of the prevalence of DGU and associated phenomena, although the magnitude of this overestimate is not clear.

DGUs are rare events. In the NSDS sample of 4,977 individuals, which oversampled those most likely to be involved in DGU (e.g., men in southern and western states), 222 respondents reported DGU during the five-year recall and 66 during the past year. When events are rare, small errors in reporting can be problematic. Even a small false positive response rate can substantially influence prevalence measures. Moreover, for relatively rare events, equivalent rates of false negatives do not cancel out the inflationary effect of the false positives. For instance, if the true prevalence is 1 percent, and 1 percent of those who either experienced or did not experience a DGU incorrectly report their DGU experience, the resulting estimate will suggest that DGUs occur with twice the true prevalence.[3] The fact that private gun surveys tend to ask everyone (rather than just crime victims, as in the NCVS) about DGU may cause such errors to be magnified (e.g., Ludwig, 2000). Indeed, some authors caution against extrapolating prevalence estimates from their own survey results because small reporting errors can lead to very large errors in prevalence estimates (e.g., Hemenway, Azrael, and Miller, 2000). Because private gun surveys question respondents only once, they can contribute to false positives due to telescoping—that is, individuals may report incidents that do not fall within the appropriate recall period (e.g., 12 months). Telescoping may substantially inflate the number of events (Andersen, Frankel, and Kasper, 1979; Cantor, 1989; Lehnen and Skogan, 1984). The NCVS, on the other hand, interviews the same individuals every six months, which is a strategy to guard against telescoping because responses are checked against the individuals' previous responses to avoid the same event being reported multiple times.

In response to concerns about false positives, some have argued that false negatives in the NCVS are also a concern. The NCVS is conducted face to face by someone working for a government agency rather than via the anonymous random digit–dialing

---

[3] If true prevalence is $t$ and the error rate is $e$, then the estimated prevalence will be the true prevalence minus the false negatives, plus the false positives: $t - et + e(1-t)$. If $t = 0.01$ and $e = 0.01$, estimated prevalence will be 1.98 times, or approximately twice, the true prevalence.

used by many private survey firms. The NCVS approach could yield more-accurate responses if individuals are less likely to exaggerate events that they believe are socially desirable in a nonanonymous, face-to-face interview (Ludwig, 2000; Hemenway, 1997). On the other hand, this approach may lead to underreporting if respondents are concerned about the legitimacy or legality of their gun use and the lack of anonymity. Indeed, there is evidence that a substantial share of those reporting DGU did not own a legal gun or have one in the household at the time of the incident, and many DGU incidents occurred outside the home, thereby implying gun-carrying. Furthermore, judicial review suggests that many DGU incidents may be illegal or socially undesirable (even if the individual was permitted or licensed and the incident truthfully reported) (see, for example, Kleck and Gertz, 1995; Cook and Ludwig, 1996, 1997, 1998; Hemenway, Azrael, and Miller, 2000).

As noted earlier, however, there are also good reasons to suspect that the NCVS underestimates the true number of DGUs. The NCVS provides an opportunity for respondents to describe DGUs only in the context of certain types of crimes. DGUs resulting from crimes not covered by the NCVS will likely be undercounted. DGUs may occur in the context of suspected crimes that respondents on the NCVS might not judge to qualify as events in which they were a victim of a crime, in which case those DGUs would be undercounted. At the time research on DGUs was being conducted, the NCVS did not explicitly ask crime victims whether they used a firearm to defend themselves. Thus, some DGUs might go uncounted if respondents choose not to volunteer their use of a gun when asked whether they attempted to resist the perpetrator (Kleck, 1999). Finally, NCVS respondents victimized while engaging in illegal activity may not volunteer these experiences, meaning any associated DGUs would not be counted (McDowall and Wiersema, 1994).

NCVS and NSDS estimates of the prevalence of DGU differ by an order of magnitude. In an effort to understand these differences, McDowall, Loftin, and Presser (2000) fielded both surveys in an experimental design to determine whether "survey methods account for the divergent results" or "the questions cover unrelated activities." The goal was to compare across surveys rather than provide prevalence estimates, so the authors selected individuals to contact from commercial gun lists. Half the sample ($n$ = 1,522) responded to the NCVS first and then the NSDS, while the other half ($n$ = 1,484) completed the surveys in reverse order. Certain questions were standardized between surveys (e.g., one-year recall, specific question about gun use, only self-reports versus household reports) to eliminate them as sources of diverging results.

The conclusion was that the NCVS measures a particular dimension of DGU (self-protective behaviors in response to crime) while the NSDS measures a wider array of behaviors, which may include preemptive action in response to what may or may not have been an intended crime. DGU cases were more common in the NSDS even after excluding items that were clearly not self-defense (e.g., practice for self-defense). The NCVS identified 24 cases, and the NSDS identified between 48 and 72 cases (with

24 cases defined as ambiguous[4]). Regression analyses suggested that, even after standardizing some questions across surveys, the differences were not entirely attributable to their different scope but that other methods also contributed. Interviews with individuals who differed in their reports between surveys indicated that questions were not well understood, respondents were not clear on why they did not report an incident, or the incident did not involve serious harm.

### Conclusions

Estimates for the prevalence of DGU span wide ranges and include high-end estimates—for instance, 2.5 million DGUs per year—that are not plausible given other information that is more trustworthy, such as the total number of U.S. residents who are injured or killed by guns each year. At the other extreme, the NCVS estimate of 116,000 DGU incidents per year almost certainly underestimates the true number. There have been few substantive advances in measuring prevalence counts or rates since the NRC (2004) report. The fundamental issues of how to define DGU and what method for obtaining and assessing those measurements is the most unbiased have not been resolved. As a result, there is still considerable uncertainty about the prevalence of DGU. Efforts to resolve the uncertainty provide insight into some, but not all, aspects of DGU measurement, which may drive the large differences in prevalence estimates. The difficulties of defining and measuring DGU have implications for understanding not only the prevalence of DGU but also the relationship between DGU and outcomes of interest, such as the probability of victimization and injury. We turn to the evidence on this question in the next section.

## Does Defensive Gun Use Reduce Harm?

In theory, DGU provides individuals with additional means to protect themselves, their families, their property, and others from crimes. Police officers are issued firearms because society believes that they will be able to use those weapons effectively to produce similar defensive and protective benefits. The extent to which DGU actually reduces harm for individuals or society is controversial. NRC (2004) summarized what was known then about the effects of DGU:

> The results suggest interesting associations: victims who use guns defensively are less likely to be harmed than those using other forms of self-protection. Whether these findings reflect underlying causal relationships or spurious correlations remains uncertain. Much of the existing evidence reports simple bivariate correlations, without controlling for any confounding factors. Kleck and DeLone (1993) rely on multivariate linear regression methods that implicitly assume that firearms

[4] Ambiguous cases included incidents in which the respondent failed to provide sufficient details.

> use, conditional on observed factors, is statistically independent of the unobserved factors influencing the outcomes, as would be the case in a classical randomized experiment. Is this exogenous selection assumption reasonable? Arguably, the decisions to own, carry, and use a firearm for self-defense are very complex, involving both individual and environmental factors that are related to whether a crime is attempted, as well as the outcomes of interest. The ability of a person to defend himself or herself, attitudes toward violence and crime, emotional well-being, and neighborhood characteristics may all influence whether a person uses a firearm and the resulting injury and crime. Thus, in general, it is difficult to be confident that the control variables account for the numerous confounding factors that may result in spurious correlations. Furthermore, the committee is not aware of any research that considers whether the finding is robust to a variety of methodological adjustments. Without an established body of research assessing whether the findings are robust to the choice of covariates, functional form, and other modeling assumptions, it is difficult to assess the credibility of the research to date.

Similar to the literature on the prevalence of DGU (see earlier discussion), there has been little additional work on this question since the NRC (2004) report.

### Methods

When researching this topic, we included studies that provided an empirical estimate of whether DGU reduces harm, which is operationalized as perceptions of whether DGU affected crime completion, injury, level of injury, or property loss.

### Findings

Using multivariate logistic regression with extensive controls to analyze the NCVS, Kleck and DeLone (1993) found that self-defense was associated with a lower probability of robbery completion and victim injury. However, the results were not always statistically significantly different from other forms of resistance. The results also indicated that victim resistance was significantly and negatively associated with the offender's choice of weapon. Offender gun use reduced the likelihood of the victims engaging in resistance (of any kind), which raises concerns that the decision to resist may not be independent. That is, the apparent relationship between DGU and improved outcomes may reflect the fact that DGUs are more likely to occur when offenders are not using guns, rather than because DGUs themselves produce better outcomes.

Examining robberies and assaults in NCVS data from 1992 to 1999, Schnebly (2002) used multinomial logit regression to examine whether DGU influences the likelihood of being injured and the severity of injury. DGU was associated with significantly lower odds of severe injury (odds ratio [OR] = 0.61; $p < 0.05$) and mild injury (OR = 0.49; $p < 0.05$) but not significantly associated with severe versus mild injury. The benefits of DGU were primarily found among men, in urban settings, and among higher-income respondents. However, the analyses did not account for the specifics of other action taken by comparing DGU with no action or any other action combined, did not differentiate whether the injury occurred before or after the DGU, and could not control for other factors that might influence the decision to use a gun defensively. Moreover, assaults might be considered somewhat controversial in that they may involve mutual combat (albeit the respondent may perceive himself or herself to be the victim), whereas robberies have more clearly defined roles.

A later study by Tark and Kleck (2004) examined the association between DGU and property loss and between DGU and injury using NCVS data from 1992 to 2001. Multivariate logistic regression models found that when the victim attacked the offender with a gun, there was a lower risk of property loss for robberies, and when the victim threatened the offender with a gun, there was a lower risk of property loss for all included property crimes. These associations were generally not statistically significantly different from those of some other protective actions, such as the victim attacking or threatening the offender with a nongun weapon.

Tark and Kleck (2004) found that crime victims who resist attackers by any means are rarely injured after they initiate some form of active resistance. Considering just those confrontations in which victims initiate resistance before having been injured, the authors found no statistically significant reduction in injuries among those who threatened or attacked the assailant with a gun compared with those who called the police. Indeed, the only form of resistance that was significantly better than calling the police was running or hiding. There were no significant differences in victim injuries and whether victims threatened with or attacked with a gun.

There may be important differences between crimes in which victims are able to resist or resist before being injured and those in which they are not. Similarly, crimes in which victims are armed may differ systematically from those in which they are not. These differences raise questions about what causal effects of resistance, armed or otherwise, can be drawn from Tark and Kleck (2004)'s models. The authors acknowledged these challenges and responded by including a host of controls describing the offender, victim, and incident,[5] but they acknowledged that the results could not necessarily be interpreted causally because of the lack of clear insight into how the decisions to resist and means of resistance were made, including the decisions on whether to own and to carry a gun.

---

[5] Covariates included 16 self-protective actions, proxies for power differences (number of offenders, male offender, offender aged 15–29 while victim is under age 15 or over age 30, offender weapon [gun, knife, sharp object], and whether offender attacked victim), victim characteristics (owned the house, had a job last week or for two weeks in the past six months, aged 65 or older, married, high school diploma or higher, black, Asian, Hispanic, and number of victimizations in the past six months), offender characteristics (gang member, substance at time of incident, sexual partner of victim, acquaintance of victim, work acquaintance of victim, black, white, and repeat offender), and incident characteristics (urban, home, near home, public place [may have security], and others present).

Most recently, Hemenway and Solnick (2015b) provided additional evidence using NCVS data from 2007 to 2011. Among personal contact crimes, DGU was not uniquely beneficial in reducing injury or property loss, implying that it did not necessarily improve outcomes over other forms of resistance. With respect to injury, cross-tabulations indicated that victims who engaged in DGU were less likely to be injured (10.9 percent) relative to other self-protective action, but injury rates were similar to those who took no self-protective action (11 percent). And multivariate analyses controlling for a host of covariates indicated that DGU did not significantly improve the odds of no injury overall (OR = 0.67; not significant) relative to all incidents. Further, taking advantage of the chronology of results suggests that DGU did not improve the odds of no injury after self-protective action (OR = 1.28; not significant) relative to all incidents involving self-protective action.[6] These findings suggest that DGU incidents may be intrinsically different from incidents that do not involve DGUs; for example, the incidents with DGU may involve escalating violence so that the defender has a greater opportunity to respond with a gun or is more aware or more able to respond quickly. With respect to property loss, individuals who took action were less likely to experience loss.[7] DGU improved the odds of no property loss in robbery, larceny, and personal contact larceny relative to not taking that defensive action (OR range = 0.26 to 0.30; significant) but not necessarily relative to other defensive action.[8] While this work is a recent and substantive contribution to the literature, there remain concerns about relying on self-reports and the difficulty of assessing situational differences between events that involved DGU and those that did not.

An important concern with survey reports is that the assessment of the outcome is provided by the same respondent who decided to engage in a particular action. Another fundamental concern is that the individuals who suffered the most harm are, by definition, excluded; that is, those who were fatally injured cannot self-report, so the extent to which DGU or other actions played a role cannot be explored.

Branas et al. (2009) took an entirely different approach to assessing the perceived benefits of DGU. They considered whether gun possession increased the likelihood that an individual was shot or killed in an assault. They assessed the circumstances surrounding 677 individuals shot in Philadelphia. The police determined that, in 6 percent of these cases, the victims had a gun in their possession at the time they were shot. The authors compared these cases with controls recruited by a survey firm via random digit–dialing and asked about gun possession at the time when matched cases had been shot; about 7 percent of controls had a gun in their possession. Comparing cases and

---

[6] Control variables included defender (age, gender, urban/rural), incident (at home/away), and offender (male, had gun) characteristics.

[7] The chronology of events was not available for property loss.

[8] Some non-DGU protective actions produced similar and significant ORs, suggesting that DGU is not uniquely beneficial.

controls, Branas et al. (2009) found that when victims had a gun in their possession, they had 4.46 times higher odds of being shot compared with victims who had no gun. The authors' second set of results incorporated whether victims had a chance to defend themselves. Among those who had the opportunity to resist, those with a gun were even more likely to be shot than those without a gun. The authors noted, "Case participants with at least some chance to resist were typically either 2-sided, mutual combat situations precipitated by a prior argument or 1-sided attacks where a victim was face-to-face with an offender who had targeted him or her for money, drugs, or property." That is, an opportunity to resist does not necessarily mean that it was not mutual combat (versus defensive only).

The results suggest that gun possession may not be an effective way to ensure safety. But the decision to carry a gun is not random, which raises similar concerns about inferring causality as are present with survey-based studies: Individuals who decide to carry at a particular time or to use a gun within a specific circumstance may have considered themselves at greater risk for reasons that may be unobservable to the researcher.

Hemenway, Azrael, and Miller (2000) broadened the assessment of the benefits of DGU incidents by examining whether they represent legal and socially desirable events. The authors summarized DGU incidents in the Harvard Injury Control Research Center surveys and then sent these descriptions to five criminal court judges from California, Pennsylvania, and Massachusetts. Approximately half of the incidents were deemed potentially illegal and contrary to interests of society, even under the assumptions that the individual had a permit to own and carry and had characterized the situation honestly. Given that survey reports are already one-sided (e.g., incidents may involve mutual combat even though the individual perceives himself or herself as the victim) and that additional DGU incidents could not be summarized and evaluated because respondents refused details, the authors concluded that the majority of reported DGUs were likely illegal and contrary to society's interests.

### Conclusions

There has been little empirical work since the NRC (2004) report, so the serious limitations in the literature remain largely unresolved. At first glance, individuals engaged in DGU appear less likely to lose property and suffer injury and more likely to report that their action helped the outcome. However, several important caveats emerge. First, it is not clear that DGU is uniquely beneficial relative to other actions. Second, given that the literature is largely based on cross-tabulations and relatively basic multivariate analyses, when associations are found between DGU and reduced injury, for instance, it is not clear whether this is due to a causal effect of the DGUs on reduced injury or whether the circumstances that make a DGU possible also make injury less likely. In the latter case, it may not be DGUs that reduce the likelihood of injury but rather unique features of the circumstances in which DGUs occur. For instance, individuals may be more likely to defend themselves with a weapon when they feel that they have a greater opportunity to be successful in that defense, which may bias estimates toward a beneficial impact of gun use. Statistical models designed to identify the causal effect of DGUs on various outcomes have not yet been reported.

Survey-based analyses of the effects of DGU suffer from more-general limitations. For example, individuals reporting the outcomes were also the ones who made the decision to engage in DGU, which may influence their assessment. Furthermore, survey data cannot be used to assess the relationship between DGU and fatalities, because those killed during incidents cannot be included. And more broadly, it is unclear whether this literature, which rests largely on the NCVS, suffers from the limited generalizability of DGU events within its scope. It has been widely noted that DGUs not involving an included crime category are less likely to be captured by the NCVS. To the extent that these incidents have different outcomes or different characteristics, NCVS-based findings may not be generalizable. Efforts to use other sources of data, however, have encountered similar limitations regarding the size and representativeness of samples and the ability to identify the causal effects of DGU.

Finally, even if DGUs have a positive causal effect on such outcomes as injuries and property loss, it may still be the case that DGUs do not provide net societal benefits if many or most involve illegal use of firearms. Whether any net social harms outweigh the benefits to those individuals who succeed with legitimate or just DGU in protecting their own or others' well-being is a value judgment that society must make. Having better data on the frequency of legitimate and illegitimate DGU, and on the magnitude of harms and benefits associated with those events, would assist in making that judgment.

For these reasons, we conclude that the existing evidence for any causal effect of DGU on reducing harm to individuals or society is inconclusive.

## Chapter Twenty-Three References

Andersen, Ronald, Martin R. Frankel, and Judith Kasper, *Total Survey Error: Applications to Improve Health Surveys*, San Francisco, Calif.: Jossey-Bass, 1979.

Branas, C. C., T. S. Richmond, D. P. Culhane, T. R. Ten Have, and D. J. Wiebe, "Investigating the Link Between Gun Possession and Gun Assault," *American Journal of Public Health*, Vol. 99, No. 11, 2009, pp. 2034–2040.

Cantor, D., "Substantive Implications of Longitudinal Design Features: The National Crime Survey as a Case Study," in D. Kasprzyk, G. Duncan, G. Kalton, and M. P. Singh, eds., *Panel Surveys*, New York: John Wiley, 1989, pp. 25–51.

Cook, Philip J., "The Case of the Missing Victims: Gunshot Woundings in the National Crime Survey," *Journal of Quantitative Criminology*, Vol. 1, No. 1, March 1985, pp. 91–102.

Cook, Philip J., and Jens Ludwig, *Guns in America: Results of a Comprehensive National Survey on Firearms Ownership and Use*, Washington, D.C.: Police Foundation, 1996.

———, *Guns in America: National Survey on Private Ownership and Use of Firearms: Research in Brief*, Rockville, Md.: National Institute of Justice, 1997.

———, "Defensive Gun Uses: New Evidence from a National Survey," *Journal of Quantitative Criminology*, Vol. 14, No. 2, 1998, pp. 111–131.

Cook, Philip J., Jens Ludwig, and David Hemenway, "The Gun Debate's New Mythical Number: How Many Defensive Uses Per Year?" *Journal of Policy Analysis and Management*, Vol. 16, No. 3, 1997, pp. 463–469.

Duncan, O. D., *As Compared to What? Offensive and Defensive Gun Use Surveys, 1973–1994*, Rockville, Md.: National Institute of Justice, working paper 185056, 2000a.

———, "Gun Use Surveys: In Numbers We Trust?" *Criminologist,* Vol. 25, No. 1, 2000b, pp. 1–6.

Hemenway, David, "Survey Research and Self-Defense Gun Use: An Explanation of Extreme Overestimates," *Journal of Criminal Law and Criminology*, Vol. 87, No. 4, 1997, pp. 1430–1445.

Hemenway, David, and Deborah Azrael, "The Relative Frequency of Offensive and Defensive Gun Uses: Results from a National Survey," *Violence and Victims,* Vol. 15, No. 3, 2000, pp. 257–272.

Hemenway, David, Deborah Azrael, and Matthew Miller, "Gun Use in the United States: Results from Two National Surveys," *Injury Prevention*, Vol. 6, No. 4, 2000, pp. 263–267.

Hemenway, David, and Sara J. Solnick, "The Epidemiology of Self-Defense Gun Use: Evidence from the National Crime Victimization Surveys 2007–2011," *Preventive Medicine*, Vol. 79, 2015b, pp. 22–27.

Kleck, Gary, "Degrading Scientific Standards to Get the Defensive Gun Use Estimate Down," *Journal on Firearms and Public Policy*, Vol. 11, 1999, pp. 77–138.

———, "The Nature and Effectiveness of Owning, Carrying and Using Guns for Self-Protection," in G. Kleck and D. B. Kates, eds., *Armed: New Perspectives on Gun Control,* New York: Prometheus Books, 2001.

Kleck, G., and M. A. DeLone, "Victim Resistance and Offender Weapon Effects in Robbery," *Journal of Quantitative Criminology*, Vol. 9, No. 1, 1993, pp. 55–81.

Kleck, Gary, and Marc G. Gertz, "Armed Resistance to Crime: The Prevalence and Nature of Self-Defense with a Gun," *Journal of Criminal Law and Criminology*, Vol. 86, No. 1, 1995, pp. 150–187.

Lehnen, R., and W. Skogan, *The National Crime Survey: Working Papers*, Vol. 2: *Methodological Studies*, Washington, D.C.: U.S. Department of Justice, Bureau of Justice Statistics, 1984.

Loftin, Colin, and Ellen J. MacKenzie, "Building National Estimates of Violent Victimization," paper presented at the National Research Council Symposium on the Understanding and Control of Violent Behavior, Destin, Fla., April 1–6, 1990.

Ludwig, Jens, "Gun Self-Defense and Deterrence," *Crime and Justice: A Review of Research*, Vol. 27, 2000, pp. 363–417.

Masters, Kate, "Fear of Other People Is Now the Primary Motivation for American Gun Ownership, a Landmark Survey Finds," *The Trace*, September 19, 2016. As of October 13, 2017: https://www.thetrace.org/2016/09/harvard-gun-ownership-study-self-defense/

McDowall, D., C. Loftin, and S. Presser, "Measuring Civilian Defensive Firearm Use: A Methodological Experiment," *Journal of Quantitative Criminology*, Vol. 16, No. 1, 2000, pp. 1–19.

McDowall, D., C. Loftin, and B. Wiersema, "Estimates of the Frequency of Firearm Self Defense from the National Crime Victimization Survey," Albany, N.Y.: State University of New York, School of Criminal Justice, Violence Research Group Discussion Paper 20, 1998 (unpublished).

McDowall, D., and B. Wiersema, "The Incidence of Defensive Firearm Use by U.S. Crime Victims, 1987 Through 1990," *American Journal of Public Health,* Vol. 84, No. 12, 1994, pp. 1982–1984.

National Research Council, *Understanding and Preventing Violence,* A. J. Reiss and J. Roth, eds., Washington, D.C.: National Academies Press, 1993.

———, *Firearms and Violence: A Critical Review*, Washington, D.C.: National Academies Press, 2004.

———, *Estimating the Incidence of Rape and Sexual Assault*, Washington, D.C.: National Academies Press, 2014.

NRC—*See* National Research Council.

Schnebly, Stephen M., "An Examination of the Impact of Victim, Offender, and Situational Attributes on the Deterrent Effect of Defensive Gun Use: A Research Note," *Justice Quarterly*, Vol. 19, No. 2, 2002, pp. 377–398.

Tark, Jongyeon, and Gary Kleck, "Resisting Crime: The Effects of Victim Action on the Outcomes of Crimes," *Criminology*, Vol. 42, No. 4, 2004, pp. 861–909.

CHAPTER TWENTY-FOUR

# The Effects of the 1996 National Firearms Agreement in Australia on Suicide, Violent Crime, and Mass Shootings

Following a 1996 mass shooting in which 35 people in Tasmania, Australia, were killed, Australian states and territories reached the National Firearms Agreement (NFA) to adopt "a consistent set of firearm management principles into their own legislation and regulation" (McPhedran, 2016, p. 65). The principle features of the agreement, as described in a study on regulatory reform, were as follows:

- Ban on importation, ownership, sale, resale, transfer, possession, manufacture, or use of all self loading centre rifles, all self loading and pump action shotguns, and all self-loading rimfire rifles (some exemptions allowable to primary producers and clay target shooters)
- Compensatory buyback scheme through which firearm owners would be paid the market value for prohibited firearms handed in during a 12-month amnesty
- Registration of all firearms as part of integrated shooter licensing scheme
- Shooter licensing based on requirement to prove "genuine reason" for owning a firearm, including occupational use, demonstrated membership of an authorized target shooting club, or hunting (with proof of permission from a rural landowner)
- Licensing scheme based on five categories of firearms, minimum age of 18 years, and criteria for a "fit and proper person"
- New licence applicant required to undertake accredited training course in firearm safety
- As well as licence to own a firearm, separate permit required for each purchase of a firearm subject to a 28-day waiting period
- Uniform and strict firearm storage requirements
- Firearms sales to be conducted only through licensed firearm dealers and all records of sale to be provided to the police
- Sale of ammunition only for firearms for which purchaser is licensed and limitations on quantities purchased within time period. (Ozanne-Smith et al., 2004, pp. 282–283)

During the 12-month amnesty (the second principle in the list), Australia purchased back 695,940 newly prohibited firearms as of August 2001, and during a second buyback, in 2003, 68,727 handguns were destroyed (Chapman, Alpers, and Jones, 2016).[1]

The 2004 National Research Council (NRC) review of gun policies did not comment extensively on the Australian reform. The report referenced a 2003 study (Reuter and Mouzos, 2003) that estimated that approximately 20 percent of Australia's firearms were retrieved during the buyback but that these weapons did not account for a significant share of the prior homicides or violent crimes. Whereas Reuter and Mouzos (2003) found no evidence of a decline in homicides, violent crime, or total suicides after the buyback, they noted that, during the six post-law years, there "were no mass murders with firearms and fewer mass murders than in the previous period," findings that NRC (2004) called "weak tests given the small numbers of such incidents annually."

## Methods

In our review, the available evidence of the effect of the NFA on mass shootings, homicides, and suicides all derives from the same preliminary source. McPhedran (2016) reviewed the effect of the NFA on homicide. Studies that were included had to meet the following criteria:

- Contain original quantitative data analysis (i.e., the author excluded summaries, representations, or replications of previously published work; letters to the editor; opinion pieces; literature reviews; legal analyses; media analyses; and the like).
- Focus specifically on firearm homicide in Australia.
- Include time-series data.
- Use formal statistical methods to detect legislative impacts or change over time.

Although McPhedran's review was limited to homicide, the five studies that were included in the review also examined suicide. Thus, we use the same five articles to examine these outcomes.

We also include additional studies for mass shootings and suicide identified in our search for U.S. policy effects (described in earlier chapters). Two studies—Chapman, Alpers, and Jones (2016) and Baker and McPhedran (2015)—are also relevant to homicide but were published the same year as or shortly before McPhedran (2016) and thus were not included in her review but are referenced here.

Because NFA principles were applied universally throughout Australia, researchers are generally unable to conduct case-control analyses, such as comparing outcomes

[1] The National Handgun Buyback Bill of 2003 prohibited handguns with (1) a barrel length of less than 100 mm for revolvers and 120 mm for semiautomatics, (2) a caliber in excess of .38 (except for specially accredited events), and (3) a shot capacity in excess of ten rounds.

in one Australian state that enacted a law with outcomes in another state that did not (McPhedran, 2016; Chapman et al., 2006). As a result, most researchers exploited changes over time to assess the effects of the law, although one examined changes in mass shootings in Australia versus New Zealand (McPhedran and Baker, 2011) and two examined regional variation: Ozanne-Smith et al. (2004) examined one Australian state (Victoria), which had firearm legislation in place prior to the NFA, relative to the rest of Australia, and Leigh and Neill (2010) examined variation in the number of guns in each state that were reportedly "bought back" and the association with suicide and homicide rates in those states.

## Research Synthesis Findings

### Suicide

McPhedran (2016) produced an evidence table, and we created a modified version of it that focuses on suicide (Table 24.1). Six of the studies found statistically significant evidence that suicide rates declined more rapidly after implementation of the NFA in 1996 than before. In addition, Leigh and Neill (2010) found that Australian states with the highest per capita rates of turning in banned guns also had greater declines in firearm suicides. These findings are consistent with the claim that the NFA reduced suicides in Australia (Baker and McPhedran, 2007; Baker and McPhedran, 2015; Chapman, Alpers, and Jones, 2016; Chapman et al., 2006; Klieve, Sveticic, and De Leo, 2009; Ozanne-Smith et al., 2004).

Two sets of findings, however, raise questions about whether these observed associations are attributable to a causal effect of the NFA. First, two models (McPhedran and Baker, 2012; Lee and Suardi, 2010) that used similar methods examined changes in suicide rates over time and failed to find evidence of a break at the time of the NFA, with one exception: McPhedran and Baker (2012) examined trends in population subgroups and found some evidence of a break in 1997 in firearm suicide trends among those aged 35–44, but the evidence was not robust across statistical tests.

Perhaps more importantly, three studies that did find reductions in firearm suicides also found statistically significant reductions in nonfirearm suicides (Chapman et al., 2006; Chapman, Alpers, and Jones, 2016; Baker and McPhedran, 2015). McPhedran and Baker (2012) also found significant breaks in the time series of hanging suicides in 1997 among those aged 15–24 and 25–34, and in 1998 among those aged 35–44. Although it is possible that the NFA caused reductions in firearm and nonfirearm suicides, the mechanism by which it may have had an effect on nonfirearm suicides was not obvious, nor would most public health experts predict such an effect. An alternative explanation for these findings is that factors other than the NFA led to changes in nonfirearm suicide rates around 1996, and these factors might also have had an effect on firearm suicide that was independent of the NFA's effects. Another study found only

**Table 24.1**
**Summary of Studies Examining the Effects of the National Firearms Agreement on Suicide in Australia**

| | | | | | Available Statistical Information and Main Findings | | |
|---|---|---|---|---|---|---|---|
| Study | Geographic Coverage | Statistical Method | Research Focus | Period | Firearm Suicide | Nonfirearm Suicide | Total Suicide |
| Ozanne-Smith et al., 2004 | Focus on one Australian state (Victoria); comparisons performed against the rest of Australia | Poisson regression | Did trends differ between the different periods? | 1979–2000 | • –31.7-percent change (a reduction) between 1979–1987 and 1988–1996 ($p = 0.008$)<br>• No statistical information provided for 1988–1996 and 1997–2000 or for 1979–1987 and 1997–2000 | Not available | Not available |
| Chapman et al., 2006 | Whole of Australia | Negative binomial regression | Did trends differ before and after 1997? | 1979–2003 | • Trend before 1997: IRR = 0.970 (95% CI: 0.964, 0.977)<br>• Trend after 1997: IRR = 0.926 (95% CI: 0.892, 0.961)<br>• Ratio of slopes: IRR = 0.954 (95% CI: 0.922, 0.987); $p = 0.007$ (sig.) | • Trend before 1997: IRR = 1.023 (95% CI: 1.018, 1.029)<br>• Trend after 1997: IRR = 0.959 (95% CI: 0.951, 0.968)<br>• Ratio of slopes: IRR = 0.938 (95% CI: 0.920, 0.956); $p < 0.001$ (sig.) | • Trend before 1997: IRR = 1.010 (95% CI: 1.005, 1.015)<br>• Trend after 1997: IRR = 0.956 (95% CI: 0.948, 0.964)<br>• Ratio of slopes: IRR = 0.946 (95% CI: 0.930, 0.963); $p < 0.001$ (sig.) |
| Baker and McPhedran, 2007 | Whole of Australia | Autoregressive integrated moving average (ARIMA), paired sample *t*-tests | Did trends differ before and after 1996? | 1979–2004 | • Mean predicted rate (per 100,000) after 1996: 1.85<br>• Mean observed rate (per 100,000) after 1996: 1.22<br><br>$p < 0.001$ (sig.) | • Mean predicted rate (per 100,000) after 1996: 11.82<br>• Mean observed rate (per 100,000) after 1996: 11.31<br><br>$p = 0.21$ (n.s.) | Not available |

**Table 24.1—Continued**

| Study | Geographic Coverage | Statistical Method | Research Focus | Period | Available Statistical Information and Main Findings: Firearm Suicide | Nonfirearm Suicide | Total Suicide |
|---|---|---|---|---|---|---|---|
| Klieve, Sveticic, and De Leo, 2009 | Queensland | Negative binomial regression | Did trends differ before and after 1996? | 1988–2004 | • Queensland ratio of trends (1990–2004): 1.0072; $p = 0.7794$ (n.s.)<br>• Australia ratio of trends: 0.9672; $p = 0.0102$ (sig.) | Not available | Not available |
| Lee and Suardi, 2010 | Whole of Australia | ARIMA, Quandt (Chow), Bai and Perron | Were there changes in the time-series structure? | 1915–2004 | • Quandt: no sig. break<br>• Bai and Perron:<br>◦ UDmax = 10.45; critical value = 8.88 ($p < 0.05$)<br>◦ WDmax = 10.68; critical value = 9.91 ($p < 0.05$)[a]<br>• Estimated break date: 1987 (90% CI: 1978, 2001) | • Quandt: no sig. break<br>• Bai and Perron:<br>◦ UDmax = 3.97; critical value = 8.88 (n.s.)<br>◦ WDmax = 4.72; critical value = 9.91 (n.s.) | Not available |
| Leigh and Neill, 2010 | Whole of Australia, based on jurisdiction-level data | Linear regression<br><br>Difference between averages for 1990–1995 and 1998–2003 | What was the estimated effect of the number of guns handed in on firearm, nonfirearm, and total suicides? | 1990–2003 | • 1990–1995 average death rate (per million) = 2.55<br>• Implied change in death rate 1998–2003 (per million) = −1.9 (95% CI: −2.9, −0.8); $p = 0.004$ (sig.) | • 1990–1995 average death rate (per million) = 10.2<br>• Implied change in death rate 1998–2003 (per million) = 1.7 (95% CI: −4.7, 8.2); $p = 0.532$ (n.s.) | • 1990–1995 average death rate (per million) = 12.7<br>• Implied change in death rate 1998–2003 (per million) = −0.01 (95% CI: −6.2, 5.9); $p = 0.956$ (n.s.) |

**Table 24.1—Continued**

| Study | Geographic Coverage | Statistical Method | Research Focus | Period | Available Statistical Information and Main Findings: Firearm Suicide | Nonfirearm Suicide | Total Suicide |
|---|---|---|---|---|---|---|---|
| McPhedran and Baker, 2012 | Whole of Australia | Zivot-Andrews, Quandt | Were there changes in the time-series structure? | 1907–2007 | Zivot-Andrews:<br>• Estimated break date, ages 25–34:<br>◦ 1994 (intercept only, 1979–2007; $p < 0.05$)<br>◦ 1994 (intercept and trend, 1979–2007; $p < 0.05$)<br>• Estimated break date, ages 35–44:<br>◦ 1993 (intercept only, 1979–2007; $p < 0.05$)<br>◦ 1997 (intercept and trend, 1979–2007; $p < 0.05$)<br>Quandt:<br>• Estimated break date 1997, ages 35–44 (1979–2007): Max F statistic = 3.90 (n.s.) | Results for suicide by hanging:<br>Zivot-Andrews:<br>• Estimated break date, ages 15–24:<br>◦ 1987 (intercept only, 1907–2007; $p < 0.05$)<br>◦ 1997 (intercept and trend, 1979–2007; $p < 0.10$)<br>• Estimated break date, ages 25–34: 1998 (intercept and trend, 1979–2007; $p < 0.01$)<br>• Estimated break date, ages 35–44: 1998 (intercept and trend, 1979–2007; $p < 0.05$)<br>Quandt:<br>• Estimated break date 1987, ages 15–24 (1979–2007): Max F statistic = 176.38; $p < 0.01$<br>• Estimated break date 1987, ages 15–24 (1979–2007): Max F statistic = 63.20; $p < 0.01$<br>• Estimated break date 1987, ages 25–34 (1979–2007): Max F statistic = 54.90; $p < 0.01$<br>• Estimated break date 1988, ages 25–34 (1979–2007): Max F statistic = 14.20; $p < 0.01$ | Not available |

**Table 24.1—Continued**

| Study | Geographic Coverage | Statistical Method | Research Focus | Period | Available Statistical Information and Main Findings | | |
|---|---|---|---|---|---|---|---|
| | | | | | Firearm Suicide | Nonfirearm Suicide | Total Suicide |
| Baker and McPhedran, 2015 | Whole of Australia | ARIMA | Did trends differ before and after 1996? | 1979–2010 | • Mean predicted rate (per 100,000) after 1996: 1.50<br>• Mean observed rate (per 100,000) after 1996: 1.05<br><br>$p < 0.001$ (sig.) | • Mean predicted rate (per 100,000) after 1996: 12.35<br>• Mean observed rate (per 100,000) after 1996: 10.64<br><br>$p < 0.0.1$ (sig.) | Not available |
| Chapman, Alpers, and Jones, 2016 | Whole of Australia | Negative binomial regression | Did trends differ before and after 1996? | 1979–2013 | • Ratio of trends = 0.981 (95% CI: 0.970, 0.993); $p = 0.001$ (sig.)<br>• Step change = 0.652 (95% CI: 0.582, 0.731); $p < 0.001$ (sig.) | • Ratio of trends = 0.981 (95% CI: 0.958, 0.973); $p < 0.001$ (sig.)<br>• Step change = 1.070 (95% CI: 0.988, 1.159); $p = 0.10$ (n.s.) | • Ratio of trends = 0.975 (95% CI: 0.968, 0.982); $p < 0.001$ (sig.)<br>• Step change = 1.004 (95% CI: 0.931, 1.083); $p = 0.90$ (n.s.) |

NOTE: CI = confidence interval; IRR = incidence rate ratio; sig. = significant; n.s. = not significant.
[a] UDmax and WDmax are test statistics evaluating whether there is evidence that time-series data show a departure from their expected trendline.

nonsignificant declines in nonfirearm suicide rates after passage of the NFA, despite finding significant decreases in firearm suicides associated with the number of banned guns turned in across Australia's provinces and states (Leigh and Neill, 2010). The study did not show, however, that the declines in firearm suicide rates associated with turning in guns were significantly greater than the nonsignificant declines in nonfirearm suicides. Thus, although there is some evidence that the 1996 agreement reduced firearm suicides in Australia, studies also found significant reductions in nonfirearm suicides at the same time, calling into question whether it was the NFA or some other concurrent events that led to reductions in gun and nongun suicides.

### Violent Crime

Australia's homicide rate was decreasing prior to the 1996 NFA. Thus, as reviewed by McPhedran (2016), the research focus has largely investigated whether the rate at which homicides were declining changed after the NFA was implemented (Baker and McPhedran, 2007; Chapman et al., 2006; Ozanne-Smith et al., 2004; Baker and McPhedran, 2015; Chapman, Alpers, and Jones, 2016). Other lines of research have examined the relationship between the number of firearms turned in during the buyback period and firearm homicides (Leigh and Neill, 2010) and for any structural breaks in the rate of firearm homicides between 1915 and 2004 (Lee and Suardi, 2010). No study found statistically significant evidence that trends in firearm homicides changed from before to after implementation of the NFA.[2] However, Chapman, Alpers, and Jones (2016) found that the ratio of pre-law to post-law trends was statistically significant and less than one (suggesting a more rapid decline in the post-law period) for total homicide, nonfirearm homicide, and total firearm deaths (suicide and homicide). The greater declines in nonfirearm homicides led the authors to doubt whether any changes can be attributed to the NFA.

### Mass Shootings

Two studies examined the impact of the NFA on mass shootings. Both studies indicated that there were mass shootings in Australia prior to enactment of the law, but there were none thereafter. Specifically, Chapman, Alpers, and Jones (2016)—which defined *mass shootings* as those in which five or more people, excluding the shooter, were killed by gunshot—found that there were 13 mass shooting incidents in Australia between 1979 and the NFA's implementation in 1996 but none between 1997 and May 2016. Using the broader definition of four or more people killed, McPhedran and Baker (2011) reported that there were 12 such incidents from 1980 to 1996 and none between 1997 and 2009. McPhedran and Baker (2011) also reported that there have been no mass shootings in New Zealand since 1996 (though four between 1980 and

---

[2] The relationship between number of guns returned in Leigh and Neill (2010) was also not statistically significant.

1996), even though New Zealand did not introduce a similar ban on certain firearms. On the basis of this analysis, the authors suggest that reductions in mass shootings in Australia are not likely to be attributable to the NFA, because similar reductions were seen elsewhere without laws like the NFA. However, this analysis may be flawed: At least one mass shooting occurred in New Zealand after 1996 (in 1997, when Stephen Anderson used a shotgun to kill six and wound four; Leask, 2017). Moreover, New Zealand did pass a law in 1992 (though not subsequently) tightening its regulation of guns. In other words, mass shootings in New Zealand declined from four to one, and that reduction occurred shortly after imposing stricter gun legislation. Therefore, we do not view the McPhedran and Baker (2011) results as offering a strong refutation of the possibility that the NFA caused a reduction in mass shootings in Australia.

## Conclusions

Analyses of the effects of Australia's NFA are limited by the lack of a comparison group—the exceptions being Leigh and Neill (2010) and McPhedran and Baker (2011). Attributing reductions in suicide and homicide rates to the NFA is complicated by the fact that these rates were decreasing even before the NFA was enacted. There is more evidence consistent with the claim that the NFA caused reductions in firearm suicides and mass shootings than reductions in violent crime, but there is also evidence that raises questions about whether those changes can be attributed to the NFA or to other factors that influenced suicide and mass shooting rates around the time the NFA was implemented.

## Chapter Twenty-Four References

Baker, Jeanine, and Samara McPhedran, "Gun Laws and Sudden Death: Did the Australian Firearms Legislation of 1996 Make a Difference?" *British Journal of Criminology*, Vol. 47, No. 3, 2007, pp. 455–469.

———, "Australian Firearm Related Deaths: New Findings and Implications for Crime Prevention and Health Policies Following Revisions to Official Death Count Data," *International Journal of Criminal Justice Sciences*, Vol. 10, No. 1, 2015, pp. 1–9.

Chapman, S., P. Alpers, K. Agho, and M. Jones, "Australia's 1996 Gun Law Reforms: Faster Falls in Firearm Deaths, Firearm Suicides, and a Decade Without Mass Shootings," *Injury Prevention*, Vol. 12, No. 6, 2006, pp. 365–372.

Chapman, Simon, Philip Alpers, and Michael Jones, "Association Between Gun Law Reforms and Intentional Firearm Deaths in Australia, 1979–2013," *JAMA*, Vol. 316, No. 3, 2016, pp. 291–299.

Klieve, H., J. Sveticic, and D. De Leo, "Who Uses Firearms as a Means of Suicide? A Population Study Exploring Firearm Accessibility and Method Choice," *BMC Medicine*, Vol. 7, 2009.

Leask, Anna, "Raurimu 20 Years On: The Madman, the Massacre and the Memories," *New Zealand Herald*, February 4, 2017.

Lee, Wang-Sheng, and Sandy Suardi, "The Australian Firearms Buyback and Its Effect on Gun Deaths," *Contemporary Economic Policy*, Vol. 28, No. 1, 2010, pp. 65–79.

Leigh, Andrew, and Christine Neill, "Do Gun Buybacks Save Lives? Evidence from Panel Data," *American Law and Economics Review*, Vol. 12, No. 2, 2010, pp. 462–508.

McPhedran, Samara, "A Systematic Review of Quantitative Evidence About the Impacts of Australian Legislative Reform on Firearm Homicide," *Aggression and Violent Behavior*, Vol. 28, 2016, pp. 64–72.

McPhedran, Samara, and Jeanine Baker, "Mass Shootings in Australia and New Zealand: A Descriptive Study of Incidence," *Justice Policy Journal*, Vol. 8, No. 1, 2011.

———, "Lethal and Non-Lethal Violence Against Women in Australia: Measurement Challenges, Conceptual Frameworks, and Limitations in Knowledge," *Violence Against Women*, Vol. 18, No. 8, 2012, pp. 958–972.

National Research Council, *Firearms and Violence: A Critical Review*, Washington, D.C.: National Academies Press, 2004.

NRC—*See* National Research Council.

Ozanne-Smith, J., K. Ashby, S. Newstead, V. Z. Stathakis, and A. Clapperton, "Firearm Related Deaths: The Impact of Regulatory Reform," *Injury Prevention*, Vol. 10, No. 5, 2004, pp. 280–286.

Reuter, Peter, and Jenny Mouzos, "Australia: A Massive Buyback of Low-Risk Guns," in Jens Ludwig and Philip J. Cook, eds., *Evaluating Gun Policy: Effects on Crime and Violence*, Washington, D.C.: Brookings Institution Press, 2003, pp. 121–156.

PART D

# Summary of Findings and Recommendations

CHAPTER TWENTY-FIVE

# Summary and Conclusions

Although large majorities of Americans agree on the merits of some gun policies, gun policy is divisive in the United States. In this report, we have attempted to provide a rigorous and balanced assessment of what current scientific knowledge can tell the public and policymakers about the true effects of many gun policies that are frequently discussed in state legislatures. The most recent of such comprehensive attempts, conducted more than a dozen years ago, found the research base too thin to draw any conclusions about the effects of gun laws. Specifically, a committee of the National Research Council (NRC) found that the evidence was so weak and contradictory that no causal associations between the laws it examined and crime or violence could be determined (NRC, 2004). Separately, the Community Preventive Services Task Force "found the evidence available from identified studies was insufficient to determine the effectiveness of any of the firearms laws reviewed singly or in combination" (Hahn et al., 2005).

We have thoroughly updated and expanded on the findings in NRC (2004) and Hahn et al. (2005) with studies published between 2003 and spring 2016. We systematically reviewed all empirical research that examined the effects of 13 types of state gun policies on eight outcomes, including outcomes related to public health and safety and outcomes of interest to sport shooters, hunters, and those who work in the gun industry. We restricted our analysis to only those studies using methods designed to identify plausibly causal effects of the policies. After reviewing many thousands of candidate studies, we identified just 62 meeting our inclusion criteria (described in Chapter Two), of which 45 were published since 2003.

There is a need for a factual basis on which to make policy. This does not mean basing decisions just on facts about which policies will reduce homicides or suicides the most; it means basing decisions on an accurate understanding of the trade-offs that policies entail. To make fair and effective gun policies, we need to know more about their implementation challenges, whom they affect most or least, what their unintended consequences might be, how they can be revised for better effect, what they cost society in general and gun owners in particular, and other issues central to the acceptability of any policy. These scientific questions about what is true and knowable do not supersede questions of individual rights or Second Amendment rights. Both should be central considerations in policymaking.

Facts have never dictated policy, but they can inform it. The relevance of research to inform gun policy has been tarnished by deeply held assumptions about "true" policy effects, measurement error associated with key variables (such as gun ownership), skepticism about research methods, and mistrust of researchers' motives when they draw unwelcome conclusions or focus on just one aspect of what is a complex phenomenon affecting multiple stakeholders with diverse interests. We have attempted to address these concerns through the rigor and transparency of our methods and through our organizational commitment to nonpartisan, objective policy analysis. We hope, therefore, that all stakeholders in gun policy debates give our analysis of the available science a fair hearing and our recommendations careful consideration.

In this chapter, we summarize our judgments about the strength of evidence available for the effects of gun policies on outcomes of interest. We then outline our conclusions and recommendations, which are organized into two sections: What can we conclude about the effects of gun policies, and why don't we know more?

## Summarizing the Strength of Evidence

We categorized all policy and outcome pairings as having supportive, moderate, limited, inconclusive, or no evidence. We never conclude that evidence suggests that a policy has no effect. Even when multiple studies fail to find a significant effect, it is not correct that this implies the policy has no effect. Instead, the effects may simply be too small to reliably detect, or the data available to assess the policy's effects may not be sufficiently specific to the intended effects of the law. More generally, it seems reasonable to suspect that every policy has some effect on each outcome, however small or unintended. Therefore, the failure to detect a law's effects reveals more about the weakness of the analytic methods than about the possibility that a policy truly has no effect.

We categorized evidence as *inconclusive* when studies with comparable methodological rigor identified inconsistent evidence for the policy's effect on an outcome or when a single study found only uncertain or suggestive effects. We categorized evidence as *limited* when at least one study meeting our inclusion criteria and not otherwise compromised by serious methodological problems reported a significant effect of the policy on the outcome. Effects for which there is *moderate* evidence are those for which two or more studies found significant effects in the same direction and contradictory evidence was not found in other studies with equivalent or strong methods. Our finding of *supportive* evidence of an effect is limited to cases for which at least three studies found suggestive or significant effects in the same direction, and the effect was found in at least two data sets that were reasonably independent of each other (e.g., firearm suicides and hospital admissions for self-inflicted firearm injuries).

Our ratings, therefore, reflect the relative strength of evidence, not, for instance, whether the evidence is strong enough that we can be highly confident that observed effects would be generalizable to future implementations of a particular law. Rather, evidence for these effects is strong relative to evidence for other gun policy effects and not necessarily strong relative to the quality and quantity of evidence available in other fields of study. For instance, the evidence that cigarette smoking causes cancer is vastly stronger than the evidence concerning any gun policy's effect on any outcome.

Table 25.1 summarizes our judgments for all 13 classes of policies across the eight outcomes. Several outcomes show multiple judgments, and these correspond to different characterizations of the specific policy-outcome association. For instance, we identified limited evidence that background checks reduce *total suicides* and moderate evidence that they reduce *firearm suicides.* Looking down the columns, it is apparent that research into four outcomes is essentially unavailable. It is noteworthy that three of these four outcomes—defensive gun use, hunting and recreation, and the gun industry—are issues of particular concern to gun owners or gun industry stakeholders, including firearm manufacturers, firearm dealers, hunting outfitters, firing ranges, and others. That there is no empirical research examining these outcomes limits the ability for policymakers to use evidence to consider how laws are likely to affect different interests.

**Table 25.1**
**Strength of Evidence Across Gun Policies and Outcomes**

| | Background Checks | Bans on the Sale of Assault Weapons and High-Capacity Magazines | Stand-Your-Ground Laws | Prohibitions Associated with Mental Illness | Lost or Stolen Firearm Reporting Requirements | Licensing and Permitting Requirements | Firearm Sales Reporting and Recording Requirements | Child-Access Prevention Laws | Surrender of Firearms by Prohibited Possessors | Minimum Age Requirements | | Concealed-Carry Laws | | Waiting Periods | Gun-Free Zones |
|---|---|---|---|---|---|---|---|---|---|---|---|---|---|---|---|
| | | | | | | | | | | Purchasing | Possessing | Shall Issue | Permitless Carry | | |
| Suicide | | | | | | | | | | | | | | | |
| Total suicides | ↓ L | | I | ↓ L | | I | | ↓ L | | I | I | I | | | |
| Firearm suicides | ↓ M | | I | ↓ L | | I | | ↓ M | | | I | I | | | |
| Firearm suicides among children | | | | | | | | | | ↓ L | | | | | |
| Firearm self-injuries (nonfatal) | | | | | | | | | | | | I | | | |
| Firearm self-injuries (including suicides) | | | | | | | | ↓ S | | | | | | | |
| Violent crime | ↓ L | | | ↓ M | | | | I | I | | | ↑ L | | I | |
| Total homicides | ↓ L | I | ↑ M | ↓ L | | I | | | | I | I | I | | | |
| Firearm homicides | ↓ M, I[a] | I | ↑ L | I | | I | | I | | I | I | I | | | |
| Intimate partner homicides | | | | | | | | | I | | | | | I | |
| Robberies | | | | | | | | | | | | I | | | |
| Assaults | | | | | | | | | | | | I | | | |
| Rapes | | | | | | | | | | | | I | | | |
| Other violent crime | | | I | | | | | | | | | | | | |

**Table 25.1—Continued**

| | Background Checks | Bans on the Sale of Assault Weapons and High-Capacity Magazines | Stand-Your-Ground Laws | Prohibitions Associated with Mental Illness | Lost or Stolen Firearm Reporting Requirements | Licensing and Permitting Requirements | Firearm Sales Reporting and Recording Requirements | Child-Access Prevention Laws | Surrender of Firearms by Prohibited Possessors | Minimum Age Requirements | | Concealed-Carry Laws | | Waiting Periods | Gun-Free Zones |
|---|---|---|---|---|---|---|---|---|---|---|---|---|---|---|---|
| | | | | | | | | | | Purchasing | Possessing | Shall Issue | Permitless Carry | | |
| Unintentional injuries and deaths | | | | | | | | | | | | | | | |
| Unintentional firearm deaths | | | | | | | | | | | I | | | | |
| Unintentional firearm injuries and deaths among adults | | | | | | | | ↓ L | | | | | | | |
| Unintentional firearm injuries and deaths among children | | | | | | | | ↓ S | | | | | | | |
| Unintentional firearm injuries among adults | | | | | | | | | | | | ↑ L | | | |
| Unintentional firearm injuries among children | | | | | | | | | | | | I | | | |
| Mass shootings | I | I | | | | I | | I | | I | | I | I | I | |
| Officer-involved shootings | | | | | | | | | | | | | | | |
| Defensive gun use | | | I | | | | | | | | | | | | |
| Hunting and recreation | | | | | | | | | | | | | | | |

**Table 25.1—Continued**

| | Background Checks | Bans on the Sale of Assault Weapons and High-Capacity Magazines | Stand-Your-Ground Laws | Prohibitions Associated with Mental Illness | Lost or Stolen Firearm Reporting Requirements | Licensing and Permitting Requirements | Firearm Sales Reporting and Recording Requirements | Child-Access Prevention Laws | Surrender of Firearms by Prohibited Possessors | Minimum Age Requirements | | Concealed-Carry Laws | | Waiting Periods | Gun-Free Zones |
|---|---|---|---|---|---|---|---|---|---|---|---|---|---|---|---|
| | | | | | | | | | | Purchasing | Possessing | Shall Issue | Permitless Carry | | |
| Gun industry | | | | | | | | | | | | | | | |
| Gun ownership | | | | | | | | | | | | I | | | |
| Prices of banned firearms in the short term | | ↑ L | | | | | | | | | | | | | |

NOTE: I = inconclusive; L = limited; M = moderate; S = supportive. When we identified no studies meeting eligibility criteria, cells are blank. ↑ = the policy increases the outcome; ↓ = the policy decreases the outcome.

[a] We concluded that there is moderate evidence that dealer background checks decrease firearm homicides, and there is inconclusive evidence for the effect of private-seller background checks on firearm homicides.

## What Can We Conclude About the Effects of Gun Policies?

Our first set of conclusions and recommendations describes the policy-outcome combinations with the strongest available evidence as identified through our review of the existing literature, as well as recommendations for policy based on this evidence.

**Conclusion 1**. Available evidence supports the conclusion that child-access prevention (CAP) laws, or safe storage laws, reduce self-inflicted fatal or nonfatal firearm injuries among youth. There is moderate evidence that these laws reduce firearm suicides among youth and limited evidence that the laws reduce total (i.e., firearm and nonfirearm) suicides among youth.

**Conclusion 2**. Available evidence supports the conclusion that CAP laws, or safe storage laws, reduce unintentional firearm injuries or unintentional firearm deaths among children. In addition, there is limited evidence that these laws may reduce unintentional firearm injuries among adults.

In the available literature examining CAP laws, self-inflicted injuries represent an ambiguous outcome because not all self-inflicted firearm injuries are the result of a suicide attempt. Some are unintentional injuries. But with case fatality rates for suicide attempts with a firearm at around 82.5 percent (Spicer and Miller, 2000), a substantial number of self-inflicted firearm injuries are likely the result of a suicide attempt. Furthermore, there is a clear pattern of CAP laws appearing to reduce a range of related firearm injuries to youth, ranging from unintentional injuries to suicides. That they also reduce the more ambiguous "self-inflicted injuries" fits squarely within that pattern and contributes to our confidence that the evidence currently supports a conclusion that CAP laws reduce these injuries and fatalities.

Across all of the 13 classes of policies that we studied, only CAP laws had any evidence that we classified as *supportive* for a particular conclusion. CAP laws differ from many of the other policies we considered in this report. Most of the others affect the acquisition of new firearms (e.g., background checks or waiting periods), or they are designed to affect a relatively small proportion of gun owners (e.g., prohibitions that target the mentally ill; firearm surrender laws, which have usually targeted domestic violence offenders). Thus, the other laws generally concern either the small proportion of guns that are newly acquired every year or a small proportion of the gun-owning population. CAP laws, in contrast, are designed to influence how all guns in a state are stored when children could be expected to encounter them. This likely represents a large proportion of all guns because one-third of all households in the country have children under age 18 (Vespa, Lewis, and Kreider, 2013), and many more have children as occasional visitors. With such large numbers of guns potentially affected, even imperfect compliance with CAP laws may have a greater chance than other types of laws of producing observable effects in population-level outcome statistics.

*Recommendation 1.* States without CAP laws should consider adopting them as a strategy to reduce firearm suicides and unintentional firearm injuries and deaths.

> We note, however, that scientific research cannot, at present, address whether these laws might increase or decrease crime or rates of legal defensive gun use.
>
> *Recommendation 2.* When considering adopting or refining CAP laws, states should consider making child access to firearms a felony; there is some evidence that felony laws may have the greatest effects on unintentional firearm deaths.

Gun industry and gun-owner organizations have promoted voluntary and educational programs to promote the safe storage of firearms. Our conclusions and recommendations should not be interpreted to suggest that only CAP laws can reduce firearm deaths. As we discussed in Chapter Twenty, scientific evaluations of education campaigns have found that they can produce behavior change in domains other than gun storage, but rigorous evidence that they have successfully promoted safe storage of firearms is limited. On the other hand, there is evidence that clinicians who counsel patients (mostly families with children) can effectively promote safe storage practices, particularly if storage devices (e.g., gun locks) are provided along with the counseling.

**Conclusion 3**. There is moderate evidence that background checks reduce firearm suicides and firearm homicides, as well as limited evidence that these policies can reduce overall suicide and violent crime rates.

Most available studies have examined the effects of dealer background checks or the combined effects of dealer and private-seller background checks when both are required by a state. Therefore, the evidence base for universal background checks compared with the dealer background checks required under federal law is quite limited. Logically, however, if there is moderate evidence that dealer background checks reduce firearm suicides and homicides, it seems likely that extending those same background checks to private sales of firearms could further reduce firearm suicides and homicides. We emphasize, though, that the available research on this question is limited and inconclusive.

**Conclusion 4**. There is moderate evidence that stand-your-ground laws may increase state homicide rates and limited evidence that the laws increase firearm homicides in particular.

**Conclusion 5**. There is moderate evidence that laws prohibiting the purchase or possession of guns by individuals with some forms of mental illness reduce violent crime, and there is limited evidence that such laws reduce homicides in particular. There is also limited evidence these laws may reduce total suicides and firearm suicides.

Federal law prohibits some people who have been adjudicated as mentally ill from purchasing or possessing firearms, but this prohibition is not uniformly enforced across the nation. States maintain mental health records, but many have been reluctant to share those records for use in the Federal Bureau of Investigation (FBI)'s National Instant Criminal Background Check System (NICS), the federal database used for background checks. Although most states have laws allowing for the voluntary sharing of some mental health records with NICS, there is considerable variation in which classes of individuals prohibited under federal law are shared with NICS. Thus, by the end of 2016, there were large differences in the number of active mental health records in NICS across states; for example, Alaska, Montana, New Hampshire, Rhode Island, and Wyoming had contributed less than 500 records, whereas most other states had tens of thousands or hundreds of thousands of active mental health records in the database (Criminal Justice Information Services Division, 2016).

Our finding that there is limited evidence that some mental health–related background checks can reduce gun violence should be of interest to states that currently share only partial or limited mental health data with NICS and that do not have a comprehensive in-state database that is reliably used for background checks for firearm sales. It is likely that many individuals with mental health histories making them prohibited possessors under federal law can nevertheless purchase firearms in these states. Moreover, states that do check state databases but do not share information on all individuals with disqualifying mental health histories with NICS create opportunities for prohibited possessors to purchase firearms out of state. Establishing procedures to prevent these people from purchasing firearms appears to yield small but appreciable reductions in suicides, homicides, and other violent crimes after implementing mental health checks.

> *Recommendation 3*. States that currently do not require a background check investigating all types of mental health histories that lead to federal prohibitions on firearm purchase or possession should consider implementing robust mental illness checks, which appear to reduce rates of gun violence. The most robust procedures involve sharing data on all prohibited possessors with NICS.

**Conclusion 6**. There is limited evidence that before implementation of a ban on the sale of assault weapons and high-capacity magazines, there is an increase in the sales and prices of the products that the ban will prohibit.

This finding is based on persuasive evidence from a single case, the implementation of the Violent Crime Control and Law Enforcement Act of 1994, which banned the sale of certain semiautomatic weapons designated in the law as assault weapons. Therefore, this finding may not generalize well to other instances of assault weapon bans. For instance, the 1994 law grandfathered banned weapons sold before the law's implementation date. This likely created a market for speculators who drove up sales and prices in the months preceding the ban (Koper, 2004).

**Conclusion 7**. There is limited evidence that a minimum age of 21 for purchasing firearms may reduce firearm suicides among youth.

**Conclusion 8**. No studies meeting our inclusion criteria have examined required reporting of lost or stolen firearms, required reporting and recording of firearm sales, or gun-free zones.

## Why Don't We Know More?

Based on our review of the existing literature on the effects of firearm policy changes, we offer the following conclusions and recommendations for improving the evidence base on the effects of gun laws.

**Conclusion 9**. The modest growth in knowledge about the effects of gun policy over the past dozen years reflects, in part, the reluctance of the U.S. government to sponsor work in this area at levels comparable to its investment in other areas of public safety and health, such as transportation safety.

Of the 54 studies meeting our inclusion criteria that have been published since 2003, just seven (13 percent) reported receiving any federal funding. Two studies listed funding from the National Science Foundation, and one study each listed funding from the National Institute of Justice; National Institute on Drug Abuse; National Institute on Alcohol Abuse and Alcoholism; National Heart, Lung, and Blood Institute; and the Centers for Disease Control and Prevention (CDC). Ten studies received some foundation support, with the Robert Wood Johnson Foundation and the Joyce Foundation each supporting four. Of studies since 2003 that met our inclusion criteria, the large majority (40 studies, or 74 percent) reported no sources of external support.

While most of the 54 studies focused on public safety or health outcomes (e.g., suicide and homicide), the number of high-quality quasi-experimental studies on which to base estimates of the effects of policies was surprisingly small compared with the literatures that evaluate the effects of many other policies, such as those designed to improve traffic safety, a problem that claims about as many lives each year as are lost in firearm suicides and homicides.

Federal funding for research on gun-related mortality is far below the levels for other sources of mortality in the United States. Stark and Shah (2017), for instance, found that federal gun violence research funding is just 1.6 percent the amount predicted based on federal funding for other leading causes of death. With this federal inattention comes a corresponding deficit in research: Stark and Shah (2017) also found that the volume of research publications on gun mortality was just 4.5 percent of what would be expected based on publication volume for other leading causes of mortality.

The federal government previously supported a more robust program of research examining firearm violence and policy. In the 1990s, the CDC was sponsoring millions of dollars of research on firearm violence, until researchers found that having a gun in the home was associated with an elevated risk of firearm homicide for members of the household. This finding was viewed by some as a one-sided attempt to manipulate the gun policy debate.

In an effort led by the National Rifle Association (Cagle and Martinez, 2004), a sufficient proportion of Congress was persuaded to adopt the Dickey Amendment in 1996, cutting $2.6 million of funding from the CDC, an amount equal to what its injury prevention center had been spending on gun violence research. The Dickey

Amendment also introduced new language forbidding the CDC from advocating or promoting gun control. This language did not explicitly prohibit all research on gun violence or gun policy, but concern that any gun research could be viewed as advocacy has led the CDC to avoid supporting gun policy research lest it invite a budget adjustment like that in 1996 (Kellermann and Rivara, 2013).

Congress has included Dickey Amendment language in each CDC appropriations bill since 1996. Moreover, in 2012, similar language was added to an appropriations bill for the National Institutes of Health in the Consolidated Appropriations Act of 2012 (Pub. L. 112-74).

Research on firearm policy and violence prevention has since declined dramatically. According to a report by the advocacy organization Mayors Against Illegal Guns, by 2012, CDC funding of gun violence research had declined 96 percent since the mid-1990s, and academic publishing on gun violence fell 64 percent from 1998 to 2012 (Mayors Against Illegal Guns, 2013; Alcorn, 2016). Although comparable numbers of people die in car crashes and by firearm suicides and homicides, federal investment in traffic safety research funding is more than 270 times greater than in firearm violence research (Mayors Against Illegal Guns, 2013).

As suggested in a 2015 joint statement by Jay Dickey, the sponsor of the Dickey Amendment, and Mark Rosenberg, who ran the CDC's injury center when the amendment first passed, a gun violence research agenda should be developed with the dual goals of protecting citizens' and gun owners' rights and making our homes and communities safer:

> Our nation does not have to choose between reducing gun-violence injuries and safeguarding gun ownership. Indeed, scientific research helped reduce the motor vehicle death rate in the United States and save hundreds of thousands of lives—all without getting rid of cars. For example, research led to the development of simple four-foot barricades dividing oncoming traffic that are preventing injuries and saving many lives. We can do the same with respect to firearm-related deaths, reducing their numbers while preserving the rights of gun owners. (Dickey and Rosenberg, 2015).

The science on which to base gun policy has advanced slowly since 2004, when the NRC panel concluded, "If policy makers are to have a solid empirical and research base for decisions about firearms and violence, the federal government needs to support a systematic program of data collection and research that specifically addresses that issue." Unfortunately, federal support for research that could help states and communities reduce firearm crime, violence, and suicide remains virtually nonexistent, and the state and federal surveys describing gun ownership and use, on which a better understanding of state policies could be built, have not lived up to the optimism expressed in NRC (2004) and Hahn et al. (2005). In some important respects, such federal support has deteriorated since then.

*Recommendation 4.* To improve understanding of the real effects of gun policies, Congress should consider whether to lift current restrictions in appropriations legislation, and the administration should invest in firearm research portfolios at the CDC, the National Institutes of Health, and the National Institute of Justice at levels comparable to its current investment in other threats to public safety and health.

*Recommendation 5.* Given current limitations in the availability of federal support for gun policy research, private foundations should take further steps to help fill this funding gap by supporting efforts to improve and expand data collection and research on gun policies.

**Conclusion 10.** Research examining the effects of gun policies on officer-involved shootings, defensive gun use, hunting and recreation, and the gun industry is virtually nonexistent.

The lack of rigorous studies examining the effects of gun policies on these outcomes is problematic because many stakeholders in gun policy debates are especially concerned about the effects laws could have on these matters. The desire to protect oneself, for instance, is self-reported as one of the primary reasons for gun ownership among 63 percent of all U.S. gun owners and among 76 percent of all U.S. handgun owners (Azrael et al., 2017), yet rigorous studies of the effects of laws on this outcome have rarely been conducted. As we discuss in Chapter Twenty-Three, on defensive gun use, the lack of research in this area stems, to some extent, from difficulties defining and measuring legal defensive gun use. In some—perhaps most—such cases, guns may contribute to an individual's self-defense by deterring crimes that would otherwise occur. For this reason and others, it has proven difficult to estimate the frequency with which guns are used defensively.

Nevertheless, opportunities for understanding how policies affect defensive gun use exist and should be pursued. For instance, it may be possible to examine whether policies change the rate at which gun owners are the victims of crime or are injured during a crime. Similarly, FBI records of justifiable homicides, although imperfect as a proxy for defensive gun use, may nevertheless be useful for examining one aspect of a policy's effects on defensive gun use, as demonstrated by Cheng and Hoekstra (2013). Given the strength of evidence of CAP laws on self-inflicted and unintentional injuries, studying the impact of these policies on defensive gun use can help inform the trade-offs between this outcome and the potential public safety benefits.

The dearth of research examining how policies affect the gun industry is a particularly significant shortcoming in the available scientific literature. Data from the U.S. Bureau of Labor Statistics (2017) suggest that more than 47,000 people in the United States are employed just in the manufacture of small arms and ammunition. The National Sports Shooting Foundation, a gun industry trade association, estimates that an additional 250,000 may be employed in the distribution and sale of firearms and hunting supplies or in ancillary services, such as operating gun ranges or providing supplies or services to manufacturers and retailers (National Sports Shooting Foundation, 2017). The National Survey of Fishing, Hunting, and Wildlife-Associated Recreation Survey in 2011 found that more than 12 million people used firearms for hunting, with total expenditures on firearms exceeding $3 billion and expenditures on ammunition exceeding $1.2 billion (U.S. Fish and Wildlife Service, U.S. Department of the Interior, and U.S. Department of Commerce, 2012). In addition, more than 50 percent of all hunters participated in target shooting, and 22 percent of hunters visited shooting ranges (U.S. Fish and Wildlife Service, U.S. Department of the Interior, and U.S. Department of Commerce, 2012). As important as the concerns of this industry may be to the fate of proposed gun policies, there is, at present, little scientific evidence available to the public on this topic.

> *Recommendation 6.* To improve understanding of outcomes of critical concern to many in gun policy debates, the U.S. government and private research sponsors should support research examining the effects of gun laws on a wider set of outcomes, including crime, defensive gun use, hunting and sport shooting, officer-involved shootings, and the gun industry.

**Conclusion 11**. The lack of data on gun ownership and availability and on guns in legal and illegal markets severely limits the quality of existing research.

There are no regularly collected data series that describe gun ownership or use at the state level since the CDC suspended its collection of this information on the Behavioral Risk Factor Surveillance System more than a decade ago. Most gun laws are designed to specify who can own guns or to change the ways that gun owners store and use their weapons. Therefore, gun ownership and use are the behaviors through which laws may affect such outcomes as suicide, homicide, hunting and recreation, and firearm sales. In the absence of reliable state-level information about gun ownership and use, researchers cannot assess the most-direct intended effects of policies—that is, the effects on gun ownership and use—which may otherwise be easier to detect than the downstream effects of such policies on comparatively rare outcomes, such as suicide and homicide. Is it the case that gun laws cannot have their intended effect because the stock of guns is so great in the United States that anyone who wants a gun can easily obtain one, whether or not they are prohibited? This is a question that cannot easily be answered with available data on gun ownership and use.

> *Recommendation 7.* To make important advances in understanding the effects of gun laws, the CDC or another federal agency should resume collecting voluntarily provided survey data on gun ownership and use.

Additionally, the federal government no longer collects or shares with researchers data on illegal gun markets, which investigators could use to examine how policies change the availability of firearms. This is a problem that has also worsened since NRC (2004) identified it as a critical shortcoming for research on gun policy. Specifically, the Tiahrt Amendments (a series of provisions attached to Bureau of Alcohol, Tobacco, Firearms and Explosives appropriations bills since 2003) block researchers and others from studying gun trace data and gun purchaser data. When trace data were available to researchers prior to 2003, the information provided important insights into how criminals obtain their weapons (Kennedy, Piehl, and Braga, 1996; Bureau of Alcohol, Tobacco, and Firearms, 1997); whether states with more-restrictive gun laws create shortages of guns for those who may be prohibited from purchasing them (Weil and Knox, 1996; Cook and Braga, 2001); how guns move between states with less- and more-restrictive gun laws (Cook and Braga, 2001; Webster, Vernick, and Hepburn, 2001); the characteristics of gun sales likely to be associated with diversion to prohibited possessors (Pierce et al., 2003); and other valuable, actionable, policy-relevant information (for further discussion, see Braga et al., 2012).

Trace data and purchaser data have significant limitations that can make inferences about gun markets and crime difficult or uncertain. That is a caveat that applies to most data used in evaluating gun policies, but it should not be a reason for prohibiting access to trace data for research purposes.

> *Recommendation 8*. To foster a more robust research program on gun policy, Congress should consider whether to eliminate the restrictions it has imposed on the use of gun trace data for research purposes.

**Conclusion 12**. Crime and victimization monitoring systems are incomplete and not yet fulfilling their promise of supporting high-quality gun policy research in the areas we investigated.

NRC (2004) and Hahn et al. (2005) each expressed optimism about new sources of data that had only recently begun and that could, in theory, be used to improve the study of gun policy. These included the National Violent Death Reporting System (NVDRS) and the National Incident-Based Reporting System (NIBRS).

The NVDRS was designed to provide unprecedented detail on the circumstances of violent deaths in participating states, such as information on the victim's life stresses, the relationship between the victim and the offender, and other crimes that were committed at the time of the suicide or homicide. Despite the richness of the information available through the NVDRS, not one of the quasi-experimental studies meeting the inclusion criteria for this report used NVDRS data. It could be that there have not been enough states participating in the NVDRS collection process for long enough to permit the use of strong causal models. State participation in the NVDRS is voluntary and has been growing slowly but steadily. Currently, 42 states participate, but data are available from only 18, and not from some large states, such as California and Texas.

The NIBRS was designed to collect more-detailed information on incidents of crime in the United States than has been available through the FBI's Uniform Crime Reporting system. Whereas the FBI system collects summary or aggregate statistics on serious violent and property crimes reported to law enforcement agencies, NIBRS was designed to collect incident-level information about crimes reported to police. It officially launched in the mid-1980s, but by the time of the NRC review, only 16 percent of the U.S. population was served by a law enforcement agency that reported crime information to NIBRS (NRC, 2004, p. 33). Because the NIBRS program is voluntary and can be costly for law enforcement agencies to adopt, participation rates have not improved as rapidly as the NRC reviewers may have expected. By 2012, the proportion of U.S. residents served by a participating law enforcement agency had risen to just 30 percent (Bureau of Justice Statistics [BJS], 2017a). Perhaps for this reason, none of the studies meeting the inclusion criteria for this report used NIBRS data.

Although the current NIBRS data are of limited use for the kind of research we have reviewed, a new BJS initiative offers hope that this could soon change. The National Crime Statistics Exchange is an attempt to recruit and facilitate the participation of a representative sample of 400 law enforcement agencies to participate in NIBRS. With this sampling approach and data from the more than 6,000 agencies already participating, BJS expects to be able to begin generating reliable national crime trend information based on NIBRS data.

> *Recommendation 9.* To improve the quality of evidence used to evaluate gun policies, the NVDRS should be expanded to include all states with rigorous quality control standards.

> *Recommendation 10.* BJS should examine the cost and feasibility of expanding its existing programs to generate state-level crime data.

Another potentially valuable source of information on crimes is the National Crime Victimization Survey (NCVS), which collects detailed information on crime from a panel of U.S. residents selected to be representative of the nation. This survey provides critically important information about crimes that may never be reported to the police, as well as credible information on how victims and potential crime victims have been able to use guns defensively. But NCVS cannot readily be used to understand the effects of state gun laws on crime because it does not generate state-level estimates. Therefore, the studies meeting our eligibility criteria primarily used data from the Uniform Crime Reporting program (or its Supplemental Homicide Report) when examining crimes, meaning they worked with data that had few details about individual crimes and, thus, could examine only the subset of crimes reported to law enforcement.

Recognizing the need for state-level victimization data, BJS has explored options for generating such estimates through NCVS (BJS, 2017b). BJS is conducting a pilot program that expands the survey panel with the intention of eventually generating reliable estimates for 22 states. In addition, the bureau has published model-based state estimates for some types of crime over three-year periods from 1999 to 2013 (Fay and Diallo, 2015).

> *Recommendation 11.* BJS should continue to pursue its efforts to generate state-level victimization estimates. The current goal of generating such estimates for 22 states is a reasonable compromise between cost and the public's need for more-detailed information. However, the bureau should continue to expand its development of model-based victimization rates for all states and for a wider set of victimization experiences (including, for instance, crimes involving firearm use by an assailant or victim).

**Conclusion 13**. The methodological quality of research on firearms can be significantly improved.

Over the past several decades, studies have offered a great deal of information about how to use what data are available to generate reliable and credible estimates of the effects of gun policies on various outcomes, and the computing power that researchers need to implement the increasingly demanding modeling requirements has more than kept pace with the diffusion of knowledge about appropriate statistical methods. Nevertheless, the scientific literature we reviewed shows that many of the best recent studies suffer from important limitations that should be addressed in future research. These shortcomings concern the following:

- Interpreting effects generated in models that lack the statistical power to have any reasonable chance of detecting the likely effects of policies. This problem can result in a high likelihood that statistically significant effects are in the opposite direction of the true effects or that the statistically significant effects grossly exaggerate the magnitude of the true effects.
- Estimating too many parameters for the number of available observations. This problem can result in statistically significant effects that tell virtually nothing about the true generalizable effects of the policies.
- Poorly calibrated tests for whether the effects of policies are statistically significant. This problem can result in many discoveries of effects that reject the null hypothesis that the policy had no effect when, in fact, under proper inferential procedures, the discoveries would be consistent with the law having no effect (or a small effect in the opposite direction).

- Poorly justified selections of statistical models or covariates. This problem can result in estimates of a policy's effects that are in the wrong direction or that badly misconstrue the magnitude or statistical significance of their effects.
- Presenting the results of exploratory statistical modeling as though they reflect findings from a confirmatory analysis. When dozens of hypothesis tests are conducted, about 5 percent would be expected to achieve statistical significance at the $p < 0.05$ level even if the law had no effect. Failure to acknowledge that findings are the result of exploratory analysis can lead to overconfident interpretations of effect estimates that may not reflect the true effects of a policy.
- Undisclosed categorization of which states had which laws and when they were implemented. Gun policy analysts need reliable and shared databases of state laws. Correct coding of state laws is challenging, and when researchers have disclosed their state law codings, those codings have often been found to contain errors that could affect results.
- Poorly justified models of the time course of a policy's effects. Statistical models of the effects of a policy impose assumptions about the period over which the effects of the policy will build. Often, the implicit assumption is that the full effect of the policy will be observed instantaneously in the first year after the date it is scheduled for implementation. At best, this can lead to underestimates of the effects of policies.
- The use of spline and hybrid models that do not estimate coherent causal effects.
- Inadequate attention to threats of reciprocal causation or simultaneity biases in effect estimation.

These are technical points of interest chiefly to researchers, so we relegate our detailed discussion of each point to Appendix A. However, our final recommendations are for other researchers interested in the analysis of the effects of gun policies.

> *Recommendation 12.* As part of the Gun Policy in America initiative, we have published a database containing a subset of state gun laws from 1979 to 2016 (Cherney, Morral, and Schell, 2018). We ask that others with expertise on state gun laws help us improve the database by notifying us of its errors, proposing more-useful categorizations of laws, or submitting information on laws not yet incorporated into the database. With such help, we hope to make the database a resource beneficial to all analysts.

> *Recommendation 13.* Researchers, reviewers, academics, and science reporters should expect new analyses of the effects of gun policies to improve on earlier studies by persuasively addressing the methodological limitations of earlier studies, including problems with statistical power, model overfitting, covariate selection, poorly calibrated standard errors, multiple testing, undisclosed state varia-

tion in law implementation, and unjustified assumptions about the time course of each policy's effects.

In conclusion, with a few exceptions, there is a surprisingly limited base of rigorous scientific evidence concerning the effects of many commonly discussed gun policies. This does not mean that these policies are ineffective; they might well be quite effective. Instead, it reflects shortcomings in the contributions that scientific study can currently offer to policy debates in these areas. It also reflects, in part, the policies we chose to investigate, all of which have been implemented in some U.S. states and, therefore, have proven to be politically and legally feasible, at least in some states. This decision meant that none of the policies we examined would dramatically increase or decrease the stock of guns or gun ownership rates in ways that would produce more readily detectable effects on public safety, health, and industry outcomes. The United States has a large stock of privately owned guns in circulation—estimated in 2014 to be somewhere between 200 million and 300 million firearms (Cook and Goss, 2014). Laws designed to change who may buy new weapons, what weapons they may buy, or how gun sales occur will predictably have only a small effect on, for example, homicides or participation in sport shooting, which are affected much more by the existing stock of firearms. Although small effects are especially difficult to identify with the statistical methods common in this field, they may be important. Even a 1-percent reduction in homicides corresponds to more than 1,500 fewer deaths over a decade.

By highlighting where scientific evidence is accumulating, we hope to build consensus around a shared set of facts that have been established through a transparent, nonpartisan, and impartial review process. In so doing, we also mean to highlight areas where more and better information could make important contributions to establishing fair and effective gun policies.

## Chapter Twenty-Five References


Alcorn, Ted, "Trends in Research Publications About Gun Violence in the United States, 1960 to 2014," *JAMA Internal Medicine*, Vol. 177, No. 1, 2016, pp. 124–126.

Azrael, Deborah, Lisa Hepburn, David Hemenway, and Matthew Miller, "The Stock and Flow of U.S. Firearms: Results from the 2015 National Firearms Survey," *Russell Sage Foundation Journal of the Social Sciences*, Vol. 3, No. 5, 2017, pp. 38–57.

BJS—*See* Bureau of Justice Statistics.

Braga, Anthony A., Garen J. Wintemute, Glenn L. Pierce, Philip J. Cook, and Greg Ridgeway, "Interpreting the Empirical Evidence on Illegal Gun Market Dynamics," *Journal of Urban Health*, Vol. 89, No. 5, 2012, pp. 779–793.

Bureau of Alcohol, Tobacco, and Firearms, *Crime Gun Trace Analysis Reports: The Illegal Youth Firearms Market in Seventeen Communities*, Washington, D.C.: U.S. Department of the Treasury, 1997.

Bureau of Justice Statistics, "Data Collection: National Incident-Based Reporting System (NIBRS)," web page, 2017a. As of May 12, 2017:
https://www.bjs.gov/index.cfm?ty=dcdetail&iid=301

———, "NCVS Redesign: Subnational," web page, 2017b. As of May 12, 2017:
https://www.bjs.gov/index.cfm?ty=tp&tid=911

Cagle, M. Christine, and J. Michael Martinez, "Have Gun, Will Travel: The Dispute Between the CDC and the NRA on Firearm Violence as a Public Health Problem," *Politics & Policy*, Vol. 32, No. 2, 2004, pp. 278–310.

Cheng, Cheng, and Mark Hoekstra, "Does Strengthening Self-Defense Law Deter Crime or Escalate Violence? Evidence From Expansions to Castle Doctrine," *Journal of Human Resources*, Vol. 48, No. 3, 2013, pp. 821–853.

Cherney, Samantha, Andrew R. Morral, and Terry L. Schell, *RAND State Firearm Law Database*, Santa Monica, Calif.: RAND Corporation, TL-283-RC, 2018. As of March 2, 2018:
https://www.rand.org/pubs/tools/TL283.html

Cook, Philip J., and Anthony A. Braga, "Comprehensive Firearms Tracing: Strategic and Investigative Uses of New Data on Firearms Markets," *Arizona Law Review*, Vol. 43, No. 2, 2001, pp. 277–309.

Cook, Philip J., and Kristin A. Goss, *The Gun Debate: What Everyone Needs to Know*, New York: Oxford University Press, 2014.

Criminal Justice Information Services Division, "National Instant Criminal Background Check System (NICS) Section Active Records in the NICS Index," Washington, D.C.: U.S. Department of Justice, Federal Bureau of Investigation, December 31, 2016. As of March 31, 2017:
https://www.fbi.gov/file-repository/active-records-in-the-nics-index-by-state.pdf/view

Dickey, Jay, and Mark Rosenberg, "How to Protect Gun Rights While Reducing the Toll of Gun Violence," *Washington Post*, December 25, 2015.

Fay, Robert E., and Mamadou S. Diallo, *Developmental Estimates of Subnational Crime Rates Based on the National Crime Victimization Survey*, Washington, D.C.: Westat, 2015. As of May 12, 2017:
https://www.bjs.gov/index.cfm?ty=pbdetail&iid=5499

Hahn, Robert A., Oleg Bilukha, Alex Crosby, Mindy T. Fullilove, Akiva Liberman, Eve Moscicki, Susan Snyder, Farris Tuma, and Peter A. Briss, "Firearms Laws and the Reduction of Violence: A Systematic Review," *American Journal of Preventive Medicine*, Vol. 28, No. 2, 2005, pp. 40–71.

Kellermann, Arthur L., and Frederick P. Rivara, "Silencing the Science on Gun Policy," *JAMA*, Vol. 309, No. 6, 2013, pp. 549–550.

Kennedy, D. M., A. M. Piehl, and A. A. Braga, "Youth Violence in Boston: Gun Markets, Serious Youth Offenders, and a Use-Reduction Strategy," *Law and Contemporary Problems*, Vol. 59, No. 1, 1996, pp. 147–196.

Koper, Christopher S., *Updated Assessment of the Federal Assault Weapons Ban: Impacts on Gun Markets and Gun Violence 1994–2003*, Washington, D.C.: National Institute of Justice, U.S. Department of Justice, 2004.

Mayors Against Illegal Guns, "Access Denied: How the Gun Lobby Is Depriving Police, Policy Makers, and the Public of the Data We Need to Prevent Gun Violence," Everytown for Gun Safety Support Fund, 2013. As of May 12, 2017:
http://everytownresearch.org/reports/access-denied/

National Research Council, *Firearms and Violence: A Critical Review*, Washington, D.C.: National Academies Press, 2004.

National Shooting Sports Foundation, *Firearms and Ammunition Industry Economic Impact Report,* Newtown, Conn., 2017. As of October 18, 2017:
https://d3aya7xwz8momx.cloudfront.net/wp-content/uploads/2017/07/EconomicImpactofIndustry2017.pdf

NRC—*See* National Research Council.

Pierce, Glenn L., Anthony A. Braga, Christopher Koper, Jack McDevitt, David Carlson, Jeffrey Roth, Alan Saiz, Raymond Hyatt, and Roberta E. Griffith, *The Characteristics and Dynamics of Crime Gun Markets: Implications for Supply-Side Focused Enforcement Strategies*, Boston, Mass.: National Institute of Justice, 2003.

Public Law 112-74, Consolidated Appropriations Act, 2012, December 23, 2011.

Spicer, R. S., and T. R. Miller, "Suicide Acts in 8 States: Incidence and Case Fatality Rates by Demographics and Method," *American Journal of Public Health*, Vol. 90, No. 12, 2000, pp. 1885–1891.

Stark, David E., and Nigam H. Shah, "Funding and Publication of Research on Gun Violence and Other Leading Causes of Death," *JAMA*, Vol. 317, No. 1, January 3, 2017, pp. 84–86.

U.S. Bureau of Labor Statistics, "Current Employment Statistics (National)," 2017. As of May 15, 2017:
https://www.bls.gov/web/empsit/ceseeb1a.htm

U.S. Fish and Wildlife Service, U.S. Department of the Interior, and U.S. Department of Commerce, *2011 National Survey of Fishing, Hunting, and Wildlife-Associated Recreation,* Washington, D.C., FH2/11-NAT, 2012.

Vespa, Jonathan, Jamie M. Lewis, and Rose M. Kreider, *America's Families and Living Arrangements: 2012, Current Population Reports*, Washington, D.C.: U.S. Census Bureau, P20-570, 2013.

Webster, Daniel W., Jon S. Vernick, and Lisa M. Hepburn, "Relationship Between Licensing, Registration, and Other Gun Sales Laws and the Source State of Crime Guns," *Injury Prevention*, Vol. 7, 2001, pp. 184–189.

Weil, Douglas S., and Rebecca C. Knox, "Effects of Limiting Handgun Purchase on Interstate Transfer of Firearms," *JAMA*, Vol. 275, No. 22, 1996, pp. 1759–1761.

# Appendixes

APPENDIX A

# Methodological Challenges to Identifying the Effects of Gun Policies

A review by the National Research Council (NRC) (2004) highlighted important problems with the methods used in many studies examining the effects of gun policies. Since then, the literature has grown, often in a series of critiques and counter-critiques of the statistical methods used by different sets of researchers. Having carefully reviewed, discussed, and debated among our own project team the relative merits of different methods used in this literature, we offer here our assessment of the principal methodological challenges that future research on gun policy should seek to overcome.

## Power

Statistical models using variation in state policies to identify causal effects of gun policies sometimes face serious problems with statistical power, meaning that the models may have little chance to detect effects even when they exist, and any statistically significant effects the models detect are likely to have greatly exaggerated magnitudes and may often get the direction of the effect wrong. These serious problems are common when effects of interest are small relative to other sources of variation in the outcomes (Gelman and Carlin, 2014). This is likely the case for the effects of gun policies (like those we examined in this report) that might affect new purchases of firearms but not the much larger stock of firearms available for use or that might have a modest effect on a small number of firearm incidents.

Nevertheless, even small effects may be important. For example, a 3-percent reduction in firearm deaths corresponds to 1,000 fewer deaths per year nationally. But a 3-percent effect, or an incidence rate ratio (IRR) of 0.97, is small relative to the much larger variation in firearm death rates over time or across U.S. states. Many observations (for instance, years of data for each state) may be required before a model has sufficient power to detect such an effect. Moreover, power is diminished as large numbers of covariates are added to the model.

To illustrate, consider the preferred model reported by one set of researchers reviewed here. The reported effect for one policy was an IRR of 0.97 (confidence interval [CI]: 0.72, 1.15). We can infer from these statistics that such a model could detect a realistically small 3-percent reduction in the outcome at the $p < 0.05$ level of significance with a power of just 6 percent, well below the 80-percent level researchers typically seek when designing research.[1] Moreover, there is a nearly one in four chance that any statistically significant effect identified is in the wrong direction, and any statistically significant effect the model identifies will necessarily describe an effect size vastly greater than the true effect size. In the present example in which the true effect has an IRR of 0.97, the model would not identify a statistically significant effect any smaller in magnitude than an IRR of about 0.74. That is, the true 3-percent reduction would be found to be significant only if the model estimates it to actually be a 26-percent reduction in the outcome.

In other words, models like some that we find in the existing literature have almost no chance of detecting realistically small effects of firearm policies, and any significant effects the models do discover are likely to be grossly exaggerated in their magnitude and almost equally likely to be in the wrong direction as the right one. While this problem is by no means universally true in this literature, it is common enough that we present it as a general concern rather than citing by name the article from which we drew our example.

### Overfitting

The problem of poorly powered models is exacerbated when, as is common in this field, investigators include many covariates and fixed effects in their models of the effects of policies. Most guidance on reliable regression modeling emphasizes that models should have at least ten or 15 times as many observations as parameters being estimated (Cavanaugh, 1997; Draper and Smith, 1998; Good and Hardin, 2012). However, with fixed effects for each year in time-series data; fixed effects for each state; and a wide range of demographic, social, and economic covariates, models in this field frequently violate such recommendations, sometimes falling below even five observations per parameter (Schell and Morral, 2016). Such models are likely to be overfit, meaning, among other things, that their estimates are unreliable or unlikely to describe generalizable relationships between covariates of interest (such as policies) and the modeled outcomes.

Although problems with statistical power are common in this literature, they may not be inevitable. Models that do a good job explaining sources of variance across time or among states will have more statistical power than those that explain less of this variance. In a separate line of work, RAND's Gun Policy in America project has examined the performance (power, bias, and error rates) for many gun policy model specifications

---

[1] The inferences about power in this paragraph rely on power calculations and calculations of the probability of an error in the sign of the estimate and the magnitude of the estimate using methods described in Gelman and Carlin (2014). We assume that the standard error of the (unexponentiated) model estimate is (log(IRR) – log(LB))/1.96, where IRR is the reported effect size, and LB is the lower (or higher) bound of the 95-percent CI reported for the estimate.

using simulations for which the true effect of policies is known. This work demonstrates that many statistical models commonly used in gun policy research have quite poor performance in terms of type 1 error, power, and bias but that there are modeling approaches with comparatively good characteristics on these and other criteria.[2]

## Standard Errors

Most of the studies meeting our inclusion criteria identified the effects of policies by examining state-level changes in an outcome (such as homicides) over time. In many such models, there is a strong correlation within states among the error terms over time. Whether this clustering of error components mandates some adjustment to ensure that standard errors and even parameter estimates are unbiased has been a source of contention and confusion in the field. According to NRC (2004), cluster adjustments for fixed-effects models like many we reviewed in this report were unnecessary and produced misleadingly large CIs.

As Aneja, Donohue, and Zhang (2014) have argued, however, NRC did not properly consider how serial correlations in panel data can produce misleading standard errors when no adjustments are made for state-level clustering within the data. The authors provided compelling evidence that, without adjustment, standard errors are so severely underestimated that two-thirds or more of effects known to have no systematic association with the outcome variable appear to be statistically significant, a proportion far higher than the 5 percent expected for significance levels set at the $p < 0.05$ level. They further showed that even a common cluster adjustment procedure does not fully correct the underestimation of standard errors. Although state-level cluster adjustment vastly improves upon unadjusted estimates, standard errors are still inflated, frequently leading to statistically significant null effects at rates between 10 percent and 15 percent where a properly calibrated standard error would produce such errors in only 5 percent of cases.

Longitudinal analyses of state firearm policies that take no steps to address clustering continue to be published, although there is good evidence that the kinds of serial correlation found in state panel data used in gun policy research can result in large biases in estimated standard errors (Aneja, Donohue, and Zhang, 2014). The significance of the effects that these studies report should be regarded with deep skepticism. Similarly, studies frequently use robust standard error corrections or weight the regression models by state or county populations, but neither approach is likely to satisfactorily account for bias resulting from serial correlation, and population weighting could make it worse (Aneja, Donohue, and Zhang, 2014; Durlauf, Navarro, and Rivers, 2016). Further challenges for estimating standard errors arise for studies that

---

[2] A report on this effort is forthcoming and will be available on the Gun Policy in America project website.

use difference-in-differences approaches in which policy effects are identified from only a small number of states (or jurisdictions), because inference based on clustered standard errors has been shown to severely over-reject in these cases (Conley and Taber, 2011; MacKinnon and Webb, 2017).

## Multiple Testing

Among studies examining the effects of firearm policies, it is common to present multiple model specifications, each with multiple effect estimates and sometimes run on multiple subsets of the population (e.g., deaths of those under age 19 or over age 55). In some cases, additional models may have been explored using alternative covariates or design characteristics. This type of exploratory modeling is valuable. It clarifies how robust findings are to different aspects of model specification, and it can detect associations or effects that are important but might otherwise have been overlooked.

In the context of such exploratory modeling, however, conventional interpretations of statistical significance erode. Whereas a significant effect at the $p < 0.05$ level is designed to occur in only one of 20 tests where there is, in fact, no effect, a study that conducts 20 such tests stands a good chance of identifying at least one statistically significant effect, even when no true effects are present. Such accidental statistically significant effects could contribute to the confusing and sometimes contradictory findings reported in the literature.

There are procedures for adjusting levels of statistical significance in the presence of multiple hypotheses testing that could help to reduce erroneous findings (Shaffer, 1995), but these were rarely used in the studies we examined. Moreover, these procedures would not address all sources of questionable findings that can occur in exploratory analysis. Instead, we believe that studies of the effects of state policies should be explicitly treated as exploratory rather than as testing a specific hypothesis. Therefore, strong conclusions about the apparent effects of policies should almost never be made. Instead, effects should be regarded with suspicion until they have been confirmed through independent studies. Because results in this field tend to be sensitive to details of the model specification and covariates, we propose that anyone undertaking such confirmatory analyses preregister the details of their models and data before assembling an analytic data set. Such preregistration does not prevent investigators from making changes to the analytic plan that may become necessary once results become available, but departing from the preregistered plan should signal to the researchers that their analysis should be considered exploratory rather than confirmatory.

## Coding State Laws

Gun policy analysts need a reliable and shared database of state laws. There are many well-known problems associated with the coding of state laws. As noted by NRC (2004) and Hahn et al. (2005), there are frequently inconsistencies across studies in the specification of which states or jurisdictions have which laws and when they took effect. In some cases, researchers have used the year in which bills were passed into law as the year the law was implemented; in others, researchers have used the year the law was designed to take effect or the first full year after the law took effect. Although some researchers (e.g., Aneja, Donohue, and Zhang, 2014; Lott and Mustard, 1997; Rosengart et al., 2005; Vernick and Hepburn, 2003) have published or shared their coding of laws, which allows for debate and improvement of the coding schemes, such coding often is not transparent and cannot be reviewed for accuracy or to understand what assumptions about laws were made. More generally, public databases of gun laws over time are unavailable for many laws. Because of the cost and complexity of constructing such data sets, researchers interested in the effectiveness of gun laws have often favored weak, cross-sectional study designs or have collected proprietary data sets of laws that are not shared.

One important assumption that all such efforts necessarily must make concerns the features of different laws that make them sufficiently similar to be grouped together under a broad class of laws. For instance, as we described in Chapter Ten, on child-access prevention laws, states differ in whether penalties for violating the law result in criminal, misdemeanor, or civil penalties, and there is evidence (albeit inconclusive) that criminal penalties may have different and stronger effects than other approaches. Such variation in laws and their associated effects means that combining them within a particular class of laws, such as child-access prevention laws, may obscure important effects that some variants of the law have (Alcorn and Burris, 2016). On the other hand, distinguishing each variant of a law reduces the number of jurisdictions implementing any particular version of the law, which reduces the statistical power of most models used to identify the causal effects of the law. Therefore, specification of a homogenous set of laws could increase the average effect size, but it also can reduce the statistical power that models have to detect the larger effects. Rarely, however, have published analyses explicitly addressed this conflict or the choices and assumptions made to address it.

We believe that the science of gun policy will be substantially advanced with the public release of comprehensive state law time-series data, and we have made that one of the goals of the Gun Policy in America project. Specifically, we have assembled a state law database for 1979–2016 that codes our 13 broad classes of state gun policies and many subcategories (see Cherney, Morral, and Schell, 2018). As noted, this database is available for use and further improvement by the scientific community.

## Coding the Time Course of a Policy's Effects

Even with a reliable database of state laws, however, investigators of gun policy effects face a further complication in coding the time course over which gun laws exert their effects. Frequently, investigators assume that a policy's full effects occur in the year it is implemented or the first full year after the year of implementation. This coding implies that all of a policy's effect is observed shortly after its implementation, which may be reasonable for some types of policies. Others, however, might accumulate their effects over longer periods. For instance, laws that expand the class of prohibited possessors will primarily affect those members of the class who are seeking to buy new firearms but not those who already own firearms. Indeed, it may be many years before such a law affects firearm ownership of a sizable proportion of the population. The proper coding of this type of effect might involve additive or multiplicative effects over several years.

Similarly, the effects of some policies, such as child-access prevention laws, may not be fully realized until a large proportion of gun owners become aware of them, meaning that the time course of the effect may depend on media campaigns to raise awareness or high-profile prosecutions under the law. Unfortunately, however, unless investigators know when these effects occur, their effect estimates will underestimate the policy's true effects. For this reason, we believe that researchers modeling the effects of policies should carefully consider when effects are likely to appear and should make these assumptions and the corresponding model specifications explicit in their analyses.

## Spline and Hybrid Effect Coding

Several studies investigating the effects of concealed-carry policies (see Chapter Thirteen) and studies of Australia's 1996 National Firearms Agreement (see Chapter Twenty-Four) have used model specifications referred to as *spline* or *hybrid* models within this field. In most models investigating the causal effects of a policy on an outcome, the effect is assumed to produce a shift in the level of the outcome; for example, a policy may result in a lower homicide rate after implementation relative to before. The type of spline models used in this field differ from standard causal effect models because the policy is assumed to modify the trajectory of the outcome over time rather than the level or in addition to a change in the level. More specifically, these models assume that the states or counties that implement the policy will diverge from the national trend at a constant rate for an indefinite period.[3]

---

[3] Typically in gun policy models, a spline will be entered as a predictor in a regression equation that takes on values of zero before the policy was implemented (as well as in states that never implemented) and then takes on values that increase linearly in time for a given state once the policy is implemented in that state. For the models used in this field, these state-specific trends are estimated while controlling for national trends by including year

Although we discuss the reported results of these models, for practical and theoretical reasons, we do not present effect sizes from these spline models (or from spline and dummy hybrid models), even when the authors preferred those models. The practical reason is that the effect size is assumed to vary over time, so there is no single effect size to report. In fact, at a date sufficiently long after implementation, these models often assume that the states that implemented the policy will have extremely large or small effects on the outcome. In such cases, the effect size one presents is based entirely on a relatively arbitrary decision about the length of time over which to compute the effect. Moreover, even if we had arbitrarily selected a specific time interval over which to compute the effect, the research articles do not contain the information necessary to assess the CIs around those estimates.

Furthermore, two features of these spline models make them difficult to interpret as the causal effects of a gun policy. First, the spline coefficient is highly sensitive to the timing of any shifts in the outcome, and it responds to the timing in the opposite way as would standard methods for causal inference. A large increase in crime that does not occur until many years after a policy has been implemented will yield a large positive spline coefficient, suggesting that the policy is harmful. However, a similarly large increase in crime that occurs immediately after the policy is implemented will yield a negative spline coefficient, suggesting that the policy is beneficial even though it was followed immediately by an increase in crime.[4] Standard frameworks for inferring causality from observations (e.g., Mill, 1843) would suggest that an increase in crime immediately after the policy was implemented is the strongest evidence that the policy was harmful, and if a similar increase did not occur until years after implementation, it would constitute weaker evidence of a harmful effect of the policy. However, inferring causation from the spline coefficient leads to the opposite inferences, with an immediate increase in the outcome interpreted as the policy causing a decrease in the outcome but a delayed increase interpreted as evidence that the policy caused the outcome to increase. It is important to note that this interpretational challenge occurs in models that use only the spline to indicate the causal effect, as well as in hybrid models that use both a dummy variable and a spline (i.e., a step and a slope). (For more information, see the box on the next page.)

---

fixed effects in the same model. Thus, the splines are state trends that should be interpreted as deviations from the national trend.

[4] More technically, the spline predictor in the regression equation has a mean value that corresponds to a specific time after implementation. This spline's mean typically falls a few years after implementation, but precisely when it occurs depends on the number of states that implemented the law and how long the study follows the states. Any increase in crime that occurs before this mean spline creates a more negative spline coefficient. An increase in crime, no matter how large, that occurs at that mean has no effect on the spline coefficient. Any increase in crime that occurs after that mean results in a more positive spline coefficient, with progressively greater leverage over the coefficient occurring with greater time.

**The Interpretational Problem with Spline and Hybrid Models**

To illustrate the problem discussed here, consider a hypothetical state that would have shown a constant linear trend in crime (slope = 1) from 1980 to 2001 (see Table A.1). However, a policy went into effect in 1991 that raised the crime rate by 1 point in that year. If one fits a linear trend and standard spline effect to these data, it yields a spline coefficient of –0.04. If one fits a hybrid effect to these data, it yields a spline coefficient of –0.05 and a dummy effect of 0.36. Thus, although everyone who views this data series would conclude that it is inconsistent with the conclusion that the policy caused a decline in crime, the spline coefficient is negative in both models.

**Table A.1. Illustrative Data, with Spline and Dummy-Coded Effect Variables**

| Year | Crime Rate | Spline | Dummy |
|---|---|---|---|
| 1980 | 10 | 0 | 0 |
| 1981 | 11 | 0 | 0 |
| 1982 | 12 | 0 | 0 |
| 1983 | 13 | 0 | 0 |
| 1984 | 14 | 0 | 0 |
| 1985 | 15 | 0 | 0 |
| 1986 | 16 | 0 | 0 |
| 1987 | 17 | 0 | 0 |
| 1988 | 18 | 0 | 0 |
| 1989 | 19 | 0 | 0 |
| 1990 | 20 | 0 | 0 |
| 1991 | 22 | 1 | 1 |
| 1992 | 22 | 2 | 1 |
| 1993 | 23 | 3 | 1 |
| 1994 | 24 | 4 | 1 |
| 1995 | 25 | 5 | 1 |
| 1996 | 26 | 6 | 1 |
| 1997 | 27 | 7 | 1 |
| 1998 | 28 | 8 | 1 |
| 1999 | 29 | 9 | 1 |
| 2000 | 30 | 10 | 1 |
| 2001 | 31 | 11 | 1 |

Stated more generally, the direction and size of the spline coefficient serves as an unbiased estimator of the causal effect if, and only if, the duration of the spline's slope corresponds to the actual period over which the policy's effects are increasing in magnitude. If the true effect phases in earlier than assumed by the chosen spline function, the spline coefficient will be biased away from the true direction of the causal effect, possibly even reversing the sign of the true effect. Thus, researchers should probably avoid using splines that assume that the effect of the policy increases linearly into perpetuity. Such an assumption makes it likely that the true effect of the policy is in the opposite direction of the spline coefficient.

The second challenge in the interpretation of the spline coefficient as a causal effect comes from the null hypothesis that is typically used when testing the spline coefficient. Specifically, the state-specific linear slope in the outcome with respect to time after the implementation of the policy is compared with the state-specific linear slope over the years prior to implementation. The null hypothesis in this case is that a given state's deviation from a national trend in the pre-policy period should be expected to continue in a linear manner, absent any intervention, indefinitely. Thus, the null hypothesis being tested is derived from a time trend that has been extrapolated, often many years into the future. This assumption has not been justified within this field, neither with a theory about an underlying data-generating mechanism for which the assumption is appropriate nor by showing that it is a good fit to the available data. In contrast, our analysis of U.S. crime data suggests that the data do not show the pattern predicted by this assumption.[5] Moreover, making an assumption of constant state-specific trends in crime can result in obvious research artifacts. Many types of data show regression to the mean, which describes a pattern of data generated by a random process in which an extreme observation is more likely to be followed by a less extreme observation than a more extreme observation. Failure to account for regression to the mean can result in spurious research conclusions. For example, if legislators pass gun legislation as a response to rising crime rates, any tendency for crime rates to return toward more-typical levels due to regression to the mean may be misinterpreted as evidence that the legislation lowered crime.

The risk of this type of error is much greater in spline models because the assumption used to generate the null hypothesis is that the data display regression away from the mean. Essentially, these models assume a process in which extreme observations are likely to be followed by observations that become progressively more extreme in the same direction—the opposite of regression to the mean. In contrast, in data showing regression to the mean, the null hypothesis that the trend before a given date equals

[5] Specifically, the assumption predicts that state trends that deviate from the national trend in a positive direction (increasing crime rates relative to the nation) will continue to get progressively higher over time, while those states that deviate negatively (decreasing crime rates relative to the nation) will continue to decrease indefinitely. This predicts a "fan" pattern in crime trends in which the divergence in crime rates across states perpetually increases over time. Actual crime data do not show any consistent divergence of trends across states.

the trend after the date is routinely rejected. That is, the null hypothesis that state-specific deviations from the national crime trend will continue to grow indefinitely can often be rejected in the states that implemented the policy of interest, as well as many of those that did not.[6] Rejecting this implausible null hypothesis is not evidence of a causal effect of any policy.

In spite of clear statistical problems with inferring causal effects of policy on crime data using these methods, some researchers advocate this approach. In our view, their arguments misinterpret conventional effects identified by a shift in the mean (e.g., dummy-coded effects) and spline effects based on changes in slope. For example, Lott, Moody, and Whitley (2016) stated,

> The problems with using the dummy variable can be illustrated using results of 3 other papers. Santaella-Tenorio et al. [2016] reported the dummy model from Table 8b of the article by Ayres and Donohue [2003a]. Had they reported the other specification in Table 8b (or other tables) that showed the trends before and after implementation of the law (specifications that reject the assumptions behind the simple dummy approach), they would have shown the statistically significant downward trend in murder rates that indicated that the longer the right-to-carry laws were in effect, the greater the drop in murder rates was.

That is, the three papers interpret the spline coefficient as a "statistically significant downward trend in murder rates." This is incorrect; the negative spline term indicates that the slope coefficient is of lower value after implementation than before, but it does not imply that rates are actually declining over time either in absolute terms or relative to the other states that did not implement *shall-issue* (or right-to-carry) laws (see Chapter Thirteen). It is quite possible to get a negative spline coefficient even if shall-issue laws cause a large and immediate spike in murder. Similarly, such a negative coefficient could occur even if the law has no effect on murder, because it is not reasonable to extrapolate a pre-implementation trend of increasing murder rates indefinitely into the future. Historically, state-specific increases in murder have been followed by later reversion to more-typical values, even without passage of shall-issue laws. Indeed, if the authors' descriptions of the data as showing progressively larger drops in murder rates over time had been correct, there would have been a lower murder rate after implementation than before. That is, if their descriptions of the data were correct, there

---

[6] For example, imagine that the states that implemented a given policy had an aggregate firearm homicide rate of eight homicides per 100,000 population in the year leading up to implementation and nine homicides per 100,000 in the year prior to that. The null hypothesis based on extrapolating this trend is that the rate of homicides will be seven per 100,000 the year after implementation and will decline to exactly zero homicides within eight years in all of the states that implemented the policy. It is likely that the null hypothesis will be correctly rejected because the states do not actually have zero homicides after eight years, but it would also be rejected because it incorrectly assumed that preexisting trends would continue, unchanged and indefinitely. The null would be rejected for reasons that have nothing to do with any causal effect of firearm policy.

would have been a significant negative coefficient on the dummy variable that they dismissed as unimportant, but there may or may not have been a significant negative spline coefficient.

It is important to note that our critique of how spline models have been used in this field is not, in any way, a critique of the use of splines more generally. Splines are extremely general regression tools to allow variations in slopes across a predictor variable. It is entirely reasonable to assume, for example, that the effects of a policy on crime phase in over several years. In such a case, a simple dummy-coded effect may underestimate the true effect size, while using a spline that is designed for that particular phase-in period would not. In our view, using these types of splines to identify a causal effect of policy on some crime outcome would require the following three things:

1. The model would need to be constructed so that the researchers would not conclude that increases in crime immediately after policy implementation are evidence that the policy lowers crime. This is a typical feature of spline models, particularly when the change in slope is modeled as persisting for a long period. This problem can be limited by using splines whose slopes operate over a narrow time frame, which can be justified as the phase-in period of the policy's effect (e.g., as used in the preferred specifications in Donohue, 2004). Such splines are similar to dummy-coded variables but with a gradual transition between 0 and 1 rather than an abrupt transition. If the phase-in period is hypothesized to last more than a few years, it may be necessary to estimate a more complex function to avoid making the wrong causal inference.
2. The null hypothesis that is interpreted as no causal effect must be something that is reasonably true in the absence of the policy in question. The null should be a hypothesis that would not be routinely rejected if tested within states that never implemented the policy or if tested using randomized implementation dates. In practice, this usually requires a null hypothesis that does not extrapolate pre-policy crime trends indefinitely into the future. Instead, the null should be based on deviations from the pre-policy average crime level or on deviations from a state-specific trend that is identified by both pre-implementation and post-implementation crime rates (i.e., based on deviations from an interpolated rather than extrapolated trend).
3. When regression models contain multiple effects of the policy, such as hybrid models that contain a spline and a dummy variable, the various effects cannot be tested or interpreted independently. The effect size and statistical significance can be assessed only by integrating all of the ways in which the policy influences the outcome within the model. For example, researchers should not claim that a policy is associated with a reduction in crime based on a significant negative spline coefficient when the model includes another effect that simultaneously predicts increased crime following implementation of the policy. Despite the

significant negative spline, the model may still predict that the policy is associated with a subsequent increase in crime in all years represented in the data. Thus, while hybrid models can avoid some of the interpretational problems of spline models, any conclusions about the effect of the policy on crime must reflect all of the modeled effects relating the policy to the outcome within the model. Ideally, this analysis would test the effect at some point after the policy is hypothesized to be fully phased in but well within the period that states were typically followed in the data set. This requirement applies to the direction, size, and statistical significance of the joint effect.

Our view of the existing literature is that none of the available studies presents a spline or hybrid model that meets these three requirements for interpreting the effects. Some of the models in the literature meet some of these requirements, but none is readily interpreted as estimating a causal effect of gun policies. For this reason, we generally present the simple dummy-coded causal effect when it is provided by the authors, although we do discuss the authors' preferred specification in the text.

## Simultaneity and Reciprocal Causation

To obtain an unbiased estimate for the causal effect of firearm policy changes, the ideal research design would be akin to a randomized trial in which policies were randomly assigned across states and over time (Aneja, Donohue, and Zhang, 2014; Donohue, 2003). This type of experimental design is infeasible in the context of gun policies, so researchers have had to rely on quasi-experimental methods in which the implicit assumptions require that state adoption of a given firearm policy is unconfounded by omitted factors that influence both law passage and the outcome of interest (i.e., omitted variables bias) and that changes in firearm policy are not themselves driven by changes in the outcome of interest (i.e., simultaneity bias). These issues are not unique to the study of firearm policies and merit consideration across a broad range of program and policy evaluations.

Potential issues of simultaneity have been discussed primarily in the research on shall-issue laws and crime (for a discussion of shall-issue and other concealed-carry laws, see Chapter Thirteen). Specifically, many studies have noted the potential for reciprocal causation—that is, that state legislatures pass shall-issue laws as a response to high or rising rates of violent crime (Aneja, Donohue, and Zhang, 2014; Grambsch, 2008; Kovandzic, Marvell, and Vieraitis, 2005; Ayres and Donohue, 2003a; Donohue, 2003; Manning, 2003; Kovandzic and Marvell, 2003; Plassman and Whitley, 2003; Lott and Mustard, 1997). Indeed, Grossman and Lee (2008) found that the percentage change in the violent crime rate over the preceding five years had a statistically significant positive effect on the likelihood that states with may-issue laws switch to shall-issue laws; Luca, Deepak, and Poliquin (2016) found that the occurrence of a public mass shooting significantly increased the number of firearm bills introduced within a state one year later. If such reciprocal causation exists, the estimated effects of firearm policies on crime rates from the difference-in-differences strategy employed by most of the qualifying studies we identified may be inconsistent and biased, although the direction of such bias is ambiguous. While some studies have tested for potential reciprocal causation and found little evidence of bias driven by differential pre-trends in law-enacting states (Rosengart et al., 2005; Plassman and Whitley 2003), other studies have found this to be an issue of concern for shall-issue laws (Aneja, Donohue, and Zhang, 2014; Grambsch, 2008; Donohue, 2003).

The presence of reciprocal causation complicates causal identification of the true effects of firearm policy changes and requires alternative approaches to those used most commonly in the literature we identified. Unfortunately, some of the existing methods for handling simultaneity problems may not be feasible or may face other limitations. For instance, Lott and Mustard (1997) and Gius (2015a) employ instrumental variables techniques, but the instruments chosen are questionable and neither study provides sufficient evidence to assess instrument validity (Manning, 2003). Synthetic control methods (Abadie, Diamond, and Hainmueller, 2010) have been used to construct a counterfactual "control state" that matches the pre-trend of the law-passing state (Crifasi et al., 2015; Rudolph et al., 2015), but these methods do not readily accommodate inferential statistics and provide estimated effects that are often identified from a policy change in only one state or one state-year, meaning the observed effect is confounded with many other changes in the state that might equally explain any observed differences between the state and its synthetic controls.

More research and methodological innovation is required to address simultaneity and reciprocal causation challenges to causal inference in this and other fields of research. In particular, it would be useful to understand better the factors leading to state or municipal decisions to pass different types of policies. Studies estimating the effects of laws should explore and report whether states that passed the laws differed systematically from those that did not, in terms of their recent gun use or violence trends. In some cases, explorations of the possible effects of reciprocal causation on effect estimates may provide useful insights.

## Appendix A References

Abadie, Alberto, Alexis Diamond, and Jens Hainmueller, "Synthetic Control Methods for Comparative Case Studies: Estimating the Effect of California's Tobacco Control Program," *Journal of the American Statistical Association*, Vol. 105, No. 490, 2010, pp. 493–505.

Alcorn, Ted, and Scott Burris, "Gun Violence Prevention," *Lancet*, Vol. 388, No. 10041, 2016, p. 233.

Aneja, Abhay, John J. Donohue III, and Alexandria Zhang, *The Impact of Right to Carry Laws and the NRC Report: Lessons for the Empirical Evaluation of Law and Policy*, Stanford, Calif.: Stanford Law School, Olin Working Paper No. 461, December 1, 2014. As of May 21, 2017: https://papers.ssrn.com/sol3/papers.cfm?abstract_id=2443681

Ayres, Ian, and John J. Donohue III, "Shooting Down the More Guns, Less Crime Hypothesis," *Stanford Law Review*, Vol. 55, No. 4, 2003a, pp. 1193–1312.

Cavanaugh, Joseph E., "Unifying the Derivations for the Akaike and Corrected Akaike Information Criteria," *Statistics and Probability Letters*, Vol. 33, No. 2, April 1997, pp. 201–208.

Cherney, Samantha, Andrew R. Morral, and Terry L. Schell, *RAND State Firearm Law Database*, Santa Monica, Calif.: RAND Corporation, TL-283-RC, 2018. As of March 2, 2018: https://www.rand.org/pubs/tools/TL283.html

Conley, Timothy G., and Christopher R. Taber, "Inference with 'Difference in Differences' with a Small Number of Policy Changes," *Review of Economics and Statistics*, Vol. 93, No. 1, 2011, pp. 113–125.

Crifasi, C. K., J. S. Meyers, J. S. Vernick, and D. W. Webster, "Effects of Changes in Permit-to-Purchase Handgun Laws in Connecticut and Missouri on Suicide Rates," *Preventive Medicine*, Vol. 79, 2015, pp. 43–49.

Donohue, John J. "The Impact of Concealed-Carry Laws," in Jens Ludwig and Philip J. Cook, eds., *Evaluating Gun Policy: Effects on Crime and Violence*, Washington D.C.: Brookings Institution Press, 2003, pp. 287–324.

———, "Guns, Crime, and the Impact of State Right-to-Carry Laws," *Fordham Law Review*, Vol. 73, No. 2, 2004, pp. 623–652.

Draper, Norman R., and Harry Smith, *Applied Regression Analysis*, 3rd ed., New York: John Wiley and Sons, 1998.

Durlauf, Steven, Salvador Navarro, and David Rivers, "Model Uncertainty and the Effect of Shall-Issue Right-to-Carry Laws on Crime," *European Economic Review*, Vol. 81, 2016, pp. 32–67.

Gelman, Andrew, and John Carlin, "Power Calculations: Assessing Type S (Sign) and Type M (Magnitude) Errors," *Perspectives on Psychological Science*, Vol. 9, No. 6, 2014, pp. 641–651.

Gius, Mark, "The Effects of State and Federal Background Checks on State-Level Gun-Related Murder Rates," *Applied Economics*, Vol. 47, No. 38, 2015a, pp. 4090–4101.

Good, Phillip I., and James W. Hardin, *Common Errors in Statistics (And How to Avoid Them)*, 4th ed., New York: John Wiley and Sons, 2012.

Grambsch, Patricia, "Regression to the Mean, Murder Rates, and Shall-Issue Laws," *American Statistician*, Vol. 62, No. 4, 2008, pp. 289–295.

Grossman, Richard S., and Stephen A. Lee, "May Issue Versus Shall Issue: Explaining the Pattern of Concealed-Carry Handgun Laws, 1960–2001," *Contemporary Economic Policy*, Vol. 26, No. 2, 2008, pp. 198–206.

Hahn, Robert A., Oleg Bilukha, Alex Crosby, Mindy T. Fullilove, Akiva Liberman, Eve Moscicki, Susan Snyder, Farris Tuma, and Peter A. Briss, "Firearms Laws and the Reduction of Violence: A Systematic Review," *American Journal of Preventive Medicine*, Vol. 28, No. 2, 2005, pp. 40–71.

Kovandzic, Tomislav V., and Thomas B. Marvell, "Right-to-Carry Concealed Handguns and Violent Crime: Crime Control Through Gun Decontrol," *Criminology and Public Policy*, Vol. 2, No. 3, 2003, pp. 363–396.

Kovandzic, Tomislav V., Thomas B. Marvell, and Lynne M. Vieraitis, "The Impact of 'Shall-Issue' Concealed Handgun Laws on Violent Crime Rates," *Homicide Studies*, Vol. 9, No. 4, 2005, pp. 292–323.

Lott, John R., Jr., Carlisle E. Moody, and John E. Whitley, "Re: 'What Do We Know About the Association Between Firearm Legislation and Firearm-Related Injuries?'" *American Journal of Epidemiology*, Vol. 184, No. 1, 2016, pp. 81–82.

Lott, J. R., and D. B. Mustard, "Crime, Deterrence, and Right-to-Carry Concealed Handguns," *Journal of Legal Studies*, Vol. 26, No. 1, 1997, pp. 1–68.

Luca, Michael, Lahotra Deepak, and Christopher Poliquin, *The Impact of Mass Shootings on Gun Policy*, working paper, Boston, Mass.: Harvard Business School, 2016.

MacKinnon, James G., and Matthew D. Webb, "Wild Bootstrap Inference for Wildly Different Cluster Sizes," *Journal of Applied Econometrics*, Vol. 32, No. 2, 2017, pp. 233–254.

Manning, Willard, "Comment: The Impact of Concealed-Carry Laws," in Jens Ludwig and Philip J. Cook, eds., *Evaluating Gun Policy: Effects on Crime and Violence*, Washington, D.C.: Brookings Institution Press, 2003, pp. 331–341.

Mill, John Stuart, *A System of Logic*, London: Parker, 1843.

National Research Council, *Firearms and Violence: A Critical Review*, Washington, D.C.: National Academies Press, 2004.

NRC—*See* National Research Council.

Plassman, Florenz, and John Whitley, "Confirming 'More Guns, Less Crime,'" *Stanford Law Review*, Vol. 55, No. 4, 2003, pp. 1313–1369.

Rosengart, M., P. Cummings, A. Nathens, P. Heagerty, R. Maier, and F. Rivara, "An Evaluation of State Firearm Regulations and Homicide and Suicide Death Rates," *Injury Prevention*, Vol. 11, No. 2, 2005, pp. 77–83.

Rudolph, K. E., E. A. Stuart, J. S. Vernick, and D. W. Webster, "Association Between Connecticut's Permit-to-Purchase Handgun Law and Homicides," *American Journal of Public Health*, Vol. 105, 2015, pp. E49–E54.

Santaella-Tenorio, J., M. Cerdá, A. Villaveces, and S. Galea, "What Do We Know About the Association Between Firearm Legislation and Firearm-Related Injuries?" *Epidemiologic Reviews*, Vol. 38, No. 1, 2016, pp. 140–157.

Schell, Terry L., and Andrew R. Morral, *Evaluating Methods and Findings from a Study of State Gun Policies*, Santa Monica, Calif.: RAND Corporation, RR-1642-RC, 2016. As of January 13, 2017: http://www.rand.org/pubs/research_reports/RR1642.html

Shaffer, J. P., "Multiple Hypothesis Testing," *Annual Review of Psychology*, Vol. 46, 1995, pp. 561–584.

Vernick, J. S., and L. M. Hepburn, "State and Federal Gun Laws: Trends for 1970–1999," in Jens Ludwig and Philip J. Cook, eds., *Evaluating Gun Policy: Effects on Crime and Violence*, Washington, D.C.: Brookings Institution Press, 2003, pp. 345–402.

APPENDIX B

# Source Data Used to Produce the Forest Plot Figures

To construct the figures in this report showing estimated effect sizes (i.e., the forest plots), we used results reported as the preferred models in each study. In some cases, these sources reported incidence rate ratios (IRRs) as the estimated effect of a law and provided confidence intervals (CIs). In such cases, we used these numbers as reported. In other cases, we calculated IRRs from effects estimated in the studies as regression coefficients, and we calculated CIs from standard errors, test statistics, or reported *p*-values. Discussion of these calculations is provided in Chapter Two. Table B.1 provides the source data used in this report to calculate IRRs and CIs as presented in each forest plot figure.

**Table B.1**
**Source Data Used to Estimate Study Effect Sizes in the Forest Plot Figures**

| Report Figure | Study | Specific Policy or Independent Variable | Specific Outcome | Population | Estimate | Standard Error | Lower CI | Upper CI | Test Statistic | *p* | Source Table |
|---|---|---|---|---|---|---|---|---|---|---|---|
| 3.1 | Ludwig and Cook (2000) | Brady Act | Firearm suicide rate | Aged 21+ | 0.98 | | 0.94 | 1.02 | | | Table 1: Col 3 |
| 3.1 | Ludwig and Cook (2000) | Brady Act | Firearm suicide rate | Aged 55+ | 0.94 | | 0.90 | 0.98 | | | Table 1: Col 6 |
| 3.1 | Ludwig and Cook (2000) | Brady Act | Nonfirearm suicide rate | Aged 21+ | 1.01 | | 0.95 | 1.08 | | | Table 1: Col 3 |
| 3.1 | Ludwig and Cook (2000) | Brady Act | Nonfirearm suicide rate | Aged 55+ | 1.03 | | 0.97 | 1.11 | | | Table 1: Col 6 |
| 3.1 | Ludwig and Cook (2000) | Brady Act | Proportion of suicides with firearm | Aged 21+ | 1.17 | | 0.87 | 1.58 | | | Table 1: Col 3 |
| 3.1 | Ludwig and Cook (2000) | Brady Act | Proportion of suicides with firearm | Aged 55+ | 0.97 | | 0.94 | 0.99 | | | Table 1: Col 6 |
| 3.1 | Ludwig and Cook (2000) | Brady Act | Total suicide rate | Aged 21+ | 0.98 | | 0.93 | 1.03 | | | Table 1: Col 3 |
| 3.1 | Ludwig and Cook (2000) | Brady Act | Total suicide rate | Aged 55+ | 0.97 | | 0.93 | 1.01 | | | Table 1: Col 6 |
| 3.1 | Sen and Panjamapirom (2012) | Check on fugitive status | Firearm suicide rate | All ages | 0.95 | | 0.90 | 0.99 | | | Table 2: Col 4 |
| 3.1 | Sen and Panjamapirom (2012) | Check on fugitive status | Total suicide rate | All ages | 0.91 | | 0.87 | 0.95 | | | Table 2: Col 6 |
| 3.1 | Sen and Panjamapirom (2012) | Check on mental illness | Firearm suicide rate | All ages | 0.96 | | 0.92 | 0.99 | | | Table 2: Col 4 |

**Table B.1—Continued**

| Report Figure | Study | Specific Policy or Independent Variable | Specific Outcome | Population | Estimate | Standard Error | Lower CI | Upper CI | Test Statistic | *p* | Source Table |
|---|---|---|---|---|---|---|---|---|---|---|---|
| 3.1 | Sen and Panjamapirom (2012) | Check on mental illness | Total suicide rate | All ages | 0.97 | | 0.95 | 0.99 | | | Table 2: Col 6 |
| 3.1 | Sen and Panjamapirom (2012) | Check on misdemeanor | Firearm suicide rate | All ages | 0.95 | | 0.92 | 1.00 | | | Table 2: Col 4 |
| 3.1 | Sen and Panjamapirom (2012) | Check on misdemeanor | Total suicide rate | All ages | 0.98 | | 0.95 | 1.02 | | | Table 2: Col 6 |
| 3.1 | Sen and Panjamapirom (2012) | Check on "other miscellaneous" records | Firearm suicide rate | All ages | 1.01 | | 0.97 | 1.05 | | | Table 2: Col 4 |
| 3.1 | Sen and Panjamapirom (2012) | Check on "other miscellaneous" records | Total suicide rate | All ages | 1.00 | | 0.97 | 1.03 | | | Table 2: Col 6 |
| 3.1 | Sen and Panjamapirom (2012) | Check on restraining order | Firearm suicide rate | All ages | 1.03 | | 0.98 | 1.09 | | | Table 2: Col 4 |
| 3.1 | Sen and Panjamapirom (2012) | Check on restraining order | Total suicide rate | All ages | 1.02 | | 0.98 | 1.06 | | | Table 2: Col 6 |
| 3.1 | Sen and Panjamapirom (2012) | Background check comprehensiveness | Firearm suicide rate | All ages | 0.98 | | 0.96 | 1.00 | | | Table 2: Col 2 |
| 3.2 | Sen and Panjamapirom (2012) | Check on "other miscellaneous" records | Total homicide rate | All ages | 1.05 | | 0.98 | 1.13 | | | Table 2: Col 5 |

**Table B.1—Continued**

| Report Figure | Study | Specific Policy or Independent Variable | Specific Outcome | Population | Estimate | Standard Error | Lower CI | Upper CI | Test Statistic | *p* | Source Table |
|---|---|---|---|---|---|---|---|---|---|---|---|
| 3.2 | Sen and Panjamapirom (2012) | Check on "other miscellaneous" records | Firearm homicide rate | All ages | 1.12 | | 1.03 | 1.22 | | | Table 2: Col 3 |
| 3.2 | Sen and Panjamapirom (2012) | Background check comprehensiveness | Firearm homicide rate | All ages | 0.93 | | 0.91 | 0.96 | | | Table 2: Col 1 |
| 3.2 | Sen and Panjamapirom (2012) | Check on restraining order | Total homicide rate | All ages | 0.91 | | 0.85 | 0.98 | | | Table 2: Col 5 |
| 3.2 | Sen and Panjamapirom (2012) | Check on restraining order | Firearm homicide rate | All ages | 0.87 | | 0.79 | 0.95 | | | Table 2: Col 3 |
| 3.2 | Sen and Panjamapirom (2012) | Check on mental illness | Total homicide rate | All ages | 0.93 | | 0.86 | 0.99 | | | Table 2: Col 5 |
| 3.2 | Sen and Panjamapirom (2012) | Check on mental illness | Firearm homicide rate | All ages | 0.93 | | 0.87 | 1.01 | | | Table 2: Col 3 |
| 3.2 | Sen and Panjamapirom (2012) | Check on fugitive status | Total homicide rate | All ages | 0.77 | | 0.71 | 0.84 | | | Table 2: Col 5 |
| 3.2 | Sen and Panjamapirom (2012) | Check on fugitive status | Firearm homicide rate | All ages | 0.79 | | 0.72 | 0.88 | | | Table 2: Col 3 |
| 3.2 | Sen and Panjamapirom (2012) | Check on misdemeanor | Total homicide rate | All ages | 1.02 | | 0.95 | 1.1 | | | Table 2: Col 5 |

**Table B.1—Continued**

| Report Figure | Study | Specific Policy or Independent Variable | Specific Outcome | Population | Estimate | Standard Error | Lower CI | Upper CI | Test Statistic | *p* | Source Table |
|---|---|---|---|---|---|---|---|---|---|---|---|
| 3.2 | Sen and Panjamapirom (2012) | Check on misdemeanor | Firearm homicide rate | All ages | 0.99 | | 0.9 | 1.08 | | | Table 2: Col 3 |
| 3.2 | La Valle (2013) | Brady Act | Total homicide rate | All ages | 0.003 | 0.060 | | | | | Table 7 |
| 3.2 | La Valle (2013) | Brady Act | Firearm homicide rate | All ages | 0.022 | 0.071 | | | | | Table 7 |
| 3.2 | Gius (2015a) | State dealer background check | Gun-related murder rate | All ages | –0.683 | | | | –5.34 | | Table 2 |
| 3.2 | Gius (2015a) | State private-seller background check | Gun-related murder rate | All ages | 1.05 | | | | 7.47 | | Table 2 |
| 3.2 | Ludwig and Cook (2000) | Brady Act | Total homicide rate | Aged 21+ | 0.97 | | 0.87 | 1.08 | | | Table 1: Col 3 |
| 3.2 | Ludwig and Cook (2000) | Brady Act | Firearm homicide rate | Aged 21+ | 0.99 | | 0.86 | 1.13 | | | Table 1: Col 3 |
| 3.2 | Ludwig and Cook (2000) | Brady Act | Nonfirearm homicide rate | Aged 21+ | 0.94 | | 0.87 | 1.02 | | | Table 1: Col 3 |
| 3.2 | Ludwig and Cook (2000) | Brady Act | Proportion of homicides with firearm | Aged 21+ | 1.02 | | 0.99 | 1.04 | | | Table 1: Col 3 |
| 3.2 | Ludwig and Cook (2000) | Brady Act | Total homicide rate | Aged 55+ | 1.00 | | 0.90 | 1.12 | | | Table 1: Col 6 |
| 3.2 | Ludwig and Cook (2000) | Brady Act | Firearm homicide rate | Aged 55+ | 1.07 | | 0.97 | 1.16 | | | Table 1: Col 6 |
| 3.2 | Ludwig and Cook (2000) | Brady Act | Nonfirearm homicide rate | Aged 55+ | 0.95 | | 0.81 | 1.12 | | | Table 1: Col 6 |

**Table B.1—Continued**

| Report Figure | Study | Specific Policy or Independent Variable | Specific Outcome | Population | Estimate | Standard Error | Lower CI | Upper CI | Test Statistic | $p$ | Source Table |
|---|---|---|---|---|---|---|---|---|---|---|---|
| 3.2 | Ludwig and Cook (2000) | Brady Act | Proportion of homicides with firearm | Aged 55+ | 1.07 | | 0.98 | 1.18 | | | Table 1: Col 6 |
| 3.2 | Swanson et al. (2016) | NICS reporting (Fla.) | Violent crime arrest | No crim. disqualified | 0.62 | | 0.50 | 0.76 | | | In text (page 1071) |
| 3.2 | Wright, Wintemute, and Rivara (1999) | No felony prohibition/checks | Any offense | Calif. purchasers | 1.05 | | 1.04 | 1.07 | | | Table 1, row 3 |
| 3.2 | Wright, Wintemute, and Rivara (1999) | No felony prohibition/checks | Gun offense | Calif. purchasers | 1.21 | | 1.08 | 1.36 | | | Table 1, row 3 |
| 3.2 | Wright, Wintemute, and Rivara (1999) | No felony prohibition/checks | Violent offense | Calif. purchasers | 1.24 | | 1.11 | 1.39 | | | Table 1, row 3 |
| 3.3 | Luca, Deepak, and Poliquin (2016) | Background check (all handgun sales) | Any mass shooting incident | N/A | –0.112 | 0.089 | | | | | Table C2: Col 1 |
| 3.3 | Luca, Deepak, and Poliquin (2016) | Background check (all handgun sales) | Any mass shooting incident | N/A | –0.124 | 0.098 | | | | | Table C2: Col 2 |
| 3.3 | Luca, Deepak, and Poliquin (2016) | Background check (all firearm sales) | Any mass shooting incident | N/A | 0.011 | 0.131 | | | | | Table C2: Col 1 |
| 3.3 | Luca, Deepak, and Poliquin (2016) | Background check (all firearm sales) | Any mass shooting incident | N/A | –0.032 | 0.142 | | | | | Table C2: Col 2 |
| 4.1 | Lott (2010) | State/federal assault weapon ban | Total homicide | All ages | 0.004 | | | | 0.11 | | Table A6.3 |
| 4.1 | Gius (2014) | State assault weapon ban | Firearm murder rate | All ages | –0.29 | | | | –1.57 | | Table 1 |
| 4.2 | Gius (2015c) | State assault weapon ban | Mass shooting deaths | All ages | –0.59202 | | | | –2.28 | | Table 1: Col 1 |

**Table B.1—Continued**

| Report Figure | Study | Specific Policy or Independent Variable | Specific Outcome | Population | Estimate | Standard Error | Lower CI | Upper CI | Test Statistic | p | Source Table |
|---|---|---|---|---|---|---|---|---|---|---|---|
| 4.2 | Gius (2015c) | State assault weapon ban | Mass shooting injuries | All ages | 0.298 | | | | 1.16 | | Table 1: Col 2 |
| 4.2 | Luca, Deepak, and Poliquin (2016) | State assault weapon ban | Any mass shooting incident | N/A | 0.062 | 0.056 | | | | | Table C2: Col 1 |
| 4.2 | Luca, Deepak, and Poliquin (2016) | State assault weapon ban | Any mass shooting incident | N/A | 0.067 | 0.057 | | | | | Table C2: Col 2 |
| 5.1 | Humphreys, Gasparrini, and Wiebe (2017) | Stand-your-ground law | Total suicide rate | All ages | 0.99, 1.00 | | | | | 0.97 | Table 1 |
| 5.1 | Humphreys, Gasparrini, and Wiebe (2017) | Stand-your-ground law | Firearm suicide rate | All ages | 0.98, 0.95 | | | | | 0.54 | Table 1 |
| 5.2 | Cheng and Hoekstra (2013) | Castle doctrine law | Homicide | All ages | 0.0937 | 0.029 | | | | | Table 5: Col 3 |
| 5.2 | Cheng and Hoekstra (2013) | Castle doctrine law | Burglary | All ages | 0.0223 | 0.0223 | | | | | Table 4: Col 3 |
| 5.2 | Cheng and Hoekstra (2013) | Castle doctrine law | Robbery | All ages | 0.0262 | 0.0229 | | | | | Table 4: Col 3 |
| 5.2 | Cheng and Hoekstra (2013) | Castle doctrine law | Aggravated assault | All ages | 0.0372 | 0.0319 | | | | | Table 4: Col 3 |
| 5.2 | Webster, Crifasi, and Vernick (2014) | Stand-your-ground law | Total homicide rate | All ages | 0.102 | 0.183 | | | | | Corrected Supplement Table 3 |
| 5.2 | Webster, Crifasi, and Vernick (2014) | Stand-your-ground law | Firearm homicide rate | All ages | 0.16 | 0.17 | | | | | Corrected Supplement Table 1 |

**Table B.1—Continued**

| Report Figure | Study | Specific Policy or Independent Variable | Specific Outcome | Population | Estimate | Standard Error | Lower CI | Upper CI | Test Statistic | $p$ | Source Table |
|---|---|---|---|---|---|---|---|---|---|---|---|
| 5.2 | Webster, Crifasi, and Vernick (2014) | Stand-your-ground law | Nonfirearm homicide rate | All ages | 0.01 | 0.1 | | | | | Corrected Supplement Table 2 |
| 5.2 | Humphreys, Gasparrini, and Wiebe (2017) | Stand-your-ground law | Total homicide rate | All ages | 1.24, 1.06 | | | | | 0.001 | Table 1 |
| 5.2 | Humphreys, Gasparrini, and Wiebe (2017) | Stand-your-ground law | Firearm homicide rate | All ages | 1.32, 1.08 | | | | | 0.001 | Table 1 |
| 5.3 | Cheng and Hoekstra (2013) | Castle doctrine law | Justifiable homicide | All ages | 0.283 | 0.235 | | | | | Table 6: Panel E: Col 3 |
| 6.1 | Sen and Panjamapirom (2012) | Check on mental illness | Total suicide rate | All ages | 0.97 | | 0.95 | 0.99 | | | Table 2: Col 6 |
| 6.1 | Sen and Panjamapirom (2012) | Check on mental illness | Firearm suicide rate | All ages | 0.96 | | 0.92 | 0.99 | | | Table 2: Col 4 |
| 6.2 | Sen and Panjamapirom (2012) | Check on mental illness | Total homicide rate | All ages | 0.93 | | 0.86 | 0.99 | | | Table 2: Col 5 |
| 6.2 | Sen and Panjamapirom (2012) | Check on mental illness | Firearm homicide rate | All ages | 0.93 | | 0.87 | 1.01 | | | Table 2: Col 3 |
| 6.2 | Swanson et al. (2016) | NICS reporting (Fla.) | Violent crime arrest | No crim. disqualified | 0.62 | | 0.50 | 0.76 | | | In text (p. 1071) |
| 8.1 | Webster et al. (2004) | Permit-to-purchase law | Total suicide rate | Aged 14–17 | 1.06 | | 0.92 | 1.23 | | | Table 2: Col 1 |

**Table B.1—Continued**

| Report Figure | Study | Specific Policy or Independent Variable | Specific Outcome | Population | Estimate | Standard Error | Lower CI | Upper CI | Test Statistic | *p* | Source Table |
|---|---|---|---|---|---|---|---|---|---|---|---|
| 8.1 | Webster et al. (2004) | Permit-to-purchase law | Total suicide rate | Aged 18–20 | 1.18 | | 1.04 | 1.34 | | | Table 2: Col 2 |
| 8.1 | Webster et al. (2004) | Permit-to-purchase law | Firearm suicide rate | Aged 14–17 | 0.92 | | 0.76 | 1.10 | | | Table 2: Col 1 |
| 8.1 | Webster et al. (2004) | Permit-to-purchase law | Firearm suicide rate | Aged 18–20 | 1.22 | | 1.04 | 1.43 | | | Table 2: Col 2 |
| 8.1 | Webster et al. (2004) | Permit-to-purchase law | Nonfirearm suicide rate | Aged 14–17 | 1.27 | | 1.00 | 1.61 | | | Table 2: Col 1 |
| 8.1 | Webster et al. (2004) | Permit-to-purchase law | Nonfirearm suicide rate | Aged 18–20 | 1.14 | | 0.93 | 1.39 | | | Table 2: Col 2 |
| 8.1 | Crifasi et al. (2015) | Permit-to-purchase law | Total suicide rate | All ages | 1.01 | | 0.95 | 1.08 | | | Appendix Table 2 |
| 8.1 | Crifasi et al. (2015) | Permit-to-purchase law | Firearm suicide rate | All ages | 0.88 | | 0.81 | 0.96 | | | Appendix Table 2 |
| 8.1 | Crifasi et al. (2015) | Permit-to-purchase law | Nonfirearm suicide rate | All ages | 1.14 | | 1.05 | 1.24 | | | Appendix Table 2 |
| 8.1 | Crifasi et al. (2015) | Repeal of Missouri permit-to-purchase | Total suicide rate | All ages | 1.03 | | 0.97 | 1.08 | | | Appendix Table 2 |
| 8.1 | Crifasi et al. (2015) | Repeal of Missouri permit-to-purchase | Firearm suicide rate | All ages | 1.02 | | 0.96 | 1.09 | | | Appendix Table 2 |
| 8.1 | Crifasi et al. (2015) | Repeal of Missouri permit-to-purchase | Nonfirearm suicide rate | All ages | 1.03 | | 0.95 | 1.11 | | | Appendix Table 2 |
| 8.2 | Webster, Crifasi, and Vernick (2014) | Repeal of Missouri permit-to-purchase | Total homicide rate | All ages | 1.08 | 0.16 | | | | | Corrected Table 2 |
| 8.2 | Webster, Crifasi, and Vernick (2014) | Repeal of Missouri permit-to-purchase | Firearm homicide rate | All ages | 1.18 | 0.13 | | | | | Corrected Table 2 |

**Table B.1—Continued**

| Report Figure | Study | Specific Policy or Independent Variable | Specific Outcome | Population | Estimate | Standard Error | Lower CI | Upper CI | Test Statistic | *p* | Source Table |
|---|---|---|---|---|---|---|---|---|---|---|---|
| 8.2 | Webster, Crifasi, and Vernick (2014) | Repeal of Missouri permit-to-purchase | Nonfirearm homicide rate | All ages | −0.08 | 0.1 | | | | | Corrected Table 2 |
| 8.2 | Rudolph et al. (2015) | Connecticut permit-to-purchase | Firearm homicide rate | All ages | 0.60 | | | | | 0.04 | In text (p. e51) and Table 2, "2xMSPE" |
| 8.3 | Luca, Deepak, and Poliquin (2016) | Handgun permit system | Any mass shooting incident (no political controls) | All ages | −0.009 | 0.115 | | | | | Table C2: Col 1 |
| 8.3 | Luca, Deepak, and Poliquin (2016) | Handgun permit system | Any mass shooting incident (political controls) | All ages | 0.004 | 0.117 | | | | | Table C2: Col 2 |
| 10.1 | Cummings et al. (1997a) | CAP law | Firearm suicide rate | Aged 0–14 | 0.81 | | 0.66 | 1.01 | | | In text (p. 1085) |
| 10.1 | Cummings et al. (1997a) | CAP law | Nonfirearm suicide rate | Aged 0–14 | 0.95 | | 0.75 | 1.2 | | | In text (p. 1085) |
| 10.1 | Webster et al. (2004) | CAP law | Total suicide rate | Aged 14–17 | 0.92 | | 0.86 | 0.98 | | | Table 2: Col 1 |
| 10.1 | Webster et al. (2004) | CAP law | Total suicide rate | Aged 18–20 | 0.89 | | 0.85 | 0.93 | | | Table 2: Col 2 |
| 10.1 | Webster et al. (2004) | CAP law | Firearm suicide rate | Aged 14–17 | 0.89 | | 0.83 | 0.96 | | | Table 2: Col 1 |
| 10.1 | Webster et al. (2004) | CAP law | Firearm suicide rate | Aged 18–20 | 0.87 | | 0.82 | 0.92 | | | Table 2: Col 2 |
| 10.1 | Webster et al. (2004) | CAP law | Nonfirearm suicide rate | Aged 14–17 | 1.00 | | 0.91 | 1.10 | | | Table 2: Col 1 |

**Table B.1—Continued**

| Report Figure | Study | Specific Policy or Independent Variable | Specific Outcome | Population | Estimate | Standard Error | Lower CI | Upper CI | Test Statistic | *p* | Source Table |
|---|---|---|---|---|---|---|---|---|---|---|---|
| 10.1 | Webster et al. (2004) | CAP law | Nonfirearm suicide rate | Aged 18–20 | 0.91 | | 0.85 | 0.98 | | | Table 2: Col 2 |
| 10.1 | DeSimone, Markowitz, and Xu (2013) | Negligent storage (11 states) | Firearm self-inflicted injury rate | Aged 0–17 | −1.165 | 0.339 | | | | | Table 3: Col 3 |
| 10.1 | DeSimone, Markowitz, and Xu (2013) | Negligent storage (11 states) | Firearm self-inflicted injury rate | Aged 18+ | −0.003 | 0.228 | | | | | Table 3: Col 4 |
| 10.1 | DeSimone, Markowitz, and Xu (2013) | Negligent storage or reckless provision (11 states) | Firearm self-inflicted injury rate | Aged 0–17 | −1.06 | 0.296 | | | | | Table 3: Col 1 |
| 10.1 | DeSimone, Markowitz, and Xu (2013) | Negligent storage or reckless provision (11 states) | Firearm self-inflicted injury rate | Aged 18+ | 0.161 | 0.227 | | | | | Table 3: Col 2 |
| 10.1 | Gius (2015b) | CAP law | Firearm suicide rate | Aged 0–19 | −0.218 | | | | −4.36 | | Table 4 |
| 10.2 | Cummings et al. (1997a) | CAP law | Firearm homicide rate | Aged 0–14 | 0.89 | | 0.76 | 1.05 | | | In text (p. 1085) |
| 10.2 | Cummings et al. (1997a) | CAP law | Nonfirearm homicide rate | Aged 0–14 | 0.96 | | 0.86 | 1.06 | | | In text (p. 1085) |
| 10.2 | Lott and Whitley (2001) | Safe storage law | Murder rate | All ages | 0.039 | | | | 1.141 | | Table 3: Col 2 |
| 10.2 | Lott and Whitley (2001) | Safe storage law | Rape rate | All ages | 0.092 | | | | 3.357 | | Table 3: Col 3 |
| 10.2 | Lott and Whitley (2001) | Safe storage law | Robbery rate | All ages | 0.1056 | | | | 2.823 | | Table 3: Col 4 |

**Table B.1—Continued**

| Report Figure | Study | Specific Policy or Independent Variable | Specific Outcome | Population | Estimate | Standard Error | Lower CI | Upper CI | Test Statistic | p | Source Table |
|---|---|---|---|---|---|---|---|---|---|---|---|
| 10.2 | Lott and Whitley (2001) | Safe storage law | Assault rate | All ages | −0.041 | | | | 1.493 | | Table 3: Col 5 |
| 10.3 | Cummings et al. (1997a) | CAP law | Unintentional firearm death rate | Aged 0–14 | 0.77 | | 0.63 | 0.94 | | | In text (p. 1085) |
| 10.3 | Cummings et al. (1997a) | CAP law | Unintentional firearm death rate | Aged 15–19 | 0.91 | | 0.77 | 1.08 | | | In text (p. 1085) |
| 10.3 | Cummings et al. (1997a) | CAP law | Unintentional firearm death rate | Aged 20–24 | 0.84 | | 0.68 | 1.03 | | | In text (p. 1085) |
| 10.3 | Webster and Starnes (2000) | CAP law | Unintentional firearm death rate | Aged 0–14 | 0.83 | | 0.71 | 0.97 | | | Table 1 |
| 10.3 | Webster and Starnes (2000) | Felony CAP law | Unintentional firearm death rate | Aged 0–14 | 0.69 | | 0.56 | 0.85 | | | Table 1 |
| 10.3 | Webster and Starnes (2000) | Misdemeanor CAP law | Unintentional firearm death rate | Aged 0–14 | 1.00 | | 0.81 | 1.22 | | | Table 1 |
| 10.3 | Webster and Starnes (2000) | Florida CAP law | Unintentional firearm death rate | Aged 0–14 | 0.49 | | 0.25 | 0.69 | | | Table 1 |
| 10.3 | Webster and Starnes (2000) | Non-Florida CAP law | Unintentional firearm death rate | Aged 0–14 | 0.95 | | 0.80 | 1.12 | | | Table 1 |
| 10.3 | Hepburn et al. (2006) | CAP law | Unintentional firearm death rate | Aged 0–14 | 0.78 | | 0.61 | 0.99 | | | Table 3: Col 1 |

**Table B.1—Continued**

| Report Figure | Study | Specific Policy or Independent Variable | Specific Outcome | Population | Estimate | Standard Error | Lower CI | Upper CI | Test Statistic | *p* | Source Table |
|---|---|---|---|---|---|---|---|---|---|---|---|
| 10.3 | Hepburn et al. (2006) | CAP law | Unintentional firearm death rate | Aged 55–74 | 0.88 | | 0.63 | 1.22 | | | Table 3: Col 2 |
| 10.3 | Hepburn et al. (2006) | Felony CAP law | Unintentional firearm death rate | Aged 0–14 | 0.64 | | 0.46 | 0.89 | | | Table 3: Col 1 |
| 10.3 | Hepburn et al. (2006) | Felony CAP law | Unintentional firearm death rate | Aged 55–74 | 0.90 | | 0.72 | 1.12 | | | Table 3: Col 2 |
| 10.3 | Hepburn et al. (2006) | Misdemeanor CAP law | Unintentional firearm death rate | Aged 0–14 | 0.93 | | 0.76 | 1.13 | | | Table 3: Col 1 |
| 10.3 | Hepburn et al. (2006) | Misdemeanor CAP law | Unintentional firearm death rate | Aged 55–74 | 0.88 | | 0.54 | 1.44 | | | Table 3: Col 2 |
| 10.3 | Hepburn et al. (2006) | CAP law (exclude Fla.) | Unintentional firearm death rate | Aged 0–14 | 0.86 | | 0.72 | 1.03 | | | Table 3: Col 1 |
| 10.3 | Hepburn et al. (2006) | CAP law (exclude Fla.) | Unintentional firearm death rate | Aged 55–74 | 0.87 | | 0.61 | 1.28 | | | Table 3: Col 2 |
| 10.3 | Hepburn et al. (2006) | CAP law (exclude Calif.) | Unintentional firearm death rate | Aged 0–14 | 0.77 | | 0.56 | 1.06 | | | Table 3: Col 1 |
| 10.3 | Hepburn et al. (2006) | CAP law (exclude Calif.) | Unintentional firearm death rate | Aged 55–74 | 0.86 | | 0.45 | 1.27 | | | Table 3: Col 2 |

**Table B.1—Continued**

| Report Figure | Study | Specific Policy or Independent Variable | Specific Outcome | Population | Estimate | Standard Error | Lower CI | Upper CI | Test Statistic | p | Source Table |
|---|---|---|---|---|---|---|---|---|---|---|---|
| 10.3 | Gius (2015b) | CAP law | Unintentional firearm death rate | Aged 0–19 | −0.036 | | | | −0.8 | | Table 5 |
| 10.3 | DeSimone, Markowitz, and Xu (2013) | CAP law, negligent storage (11 states) | Unintentional firearm injury rate | Aged 0–17 | −0.273 | 0.184 | | | | | Table 3: Col 3 |
| 10.3 | DeSimone, Markowitz, and Xu (2013) | CAP law, negligent storage (11 states) | Unintentional firearm injury rate | Aged 18+ | −0.343 | 0.143 | | | | | Table 3: Col 4 |
| 10.3 | DeSimone, Markowitz, and Xu (2013) | Negligent storage or reckless provision (11 states) | Unintentional firearm injury rate | Aged 0–17 | −0.191 | 0.154 | | | | | Table 3: Col 1 |
| 10.3 | DeSimone, Markowitz, and Xu (2013) | Negligent storage or reckless provision (11 states) | Unintentional firearm injury rate | Aged 18+ | −0.283 | 0.121 | | | | | Table 3: Col 2 |
| 10.4 | Lott (2003) | Safe storage law | Shooting fatalities and injuries | All ages | 1.073774 | | | | 0.459 | | Appendix Table 6.2: Col 3 |
| 10.4 | Lott (2003) | Safe storage law | Number of shooting incidents | All ages | 0.8250622 | | | | 0.628 | | Appendix Table 6.2: Col 4 |
| 11.1 | Vigdor and Mercy (2006) | Confiscation law | Total IPH rate | All ages | 0.95 | | 0.87 | 1.04 | | | Table 5: Panel 1 |
| 11.1 | Vigdor and Mercy (2006) | Confiscation law | Firearm IPH rate | All ages | 0.94 | | 0.83 | 1.07 | | | Table 5: Panel 1 |
| 11.1 | Vigdor and Mercy (2006) | Confiscation law | Total IPH rate | Female victims | 0.98 | | 0.89 | 1.09 | | | Table 5: Panel 1 |

**Table B.1—Continued**

| Report Figure | Study | Specific Policy or Independent Variable | Specific Outcome | Population | Estimate | Standard Error | Lower CI | Upper CI | Test Statistic | *p* | Source Table |
|---|---|---|---|---|---|---|---|---|---|---|---|
| 11.1 | Vigdor and Mercy (2006) | Confiscation law | Firearm IPH rate | Female victims | 0.96 | | 0.82 | 1.11 | | | Table 5: Panel 1 |
| 11.1 | Zeoli and Webster (2010) | Confiscation law | Total IPH rate | All ages | 1.10 | | 0.92 | 1.31 | | | Table 1 |
| 11.1 | Zeoli and Webster (2010) | Confiscation law | Firearm IPH rate | All ages | 1.19 | | 0.97 | 1.46 | | | Table 1 |
| 11.1 | Raissian (2016) | Gun Control Act expansion | Firearm IPH rate | All intimate partners | −0.0667 | 0.0309 | | | | | Table 3: Model 3 |
| 11.1 | Raissian (2016) | Gun Control Act expansion | Firearm IPH rate | Female IPH victims | −0.136 | 0.0443 | | | | | Table 3: Model 3 |
| 11.1 | Raissian (2016) | Gun Control Act expansion | Firearm IPH rate | Male IPH victims | 0.0053 | 0.0312 | | | | | Table 3: Model 3 |
| 12.1 | Webster et al. (2004) | State minimum purchase age | Total suicide rate | Aged 14–17 | 1.04 | | 0.90 | 1.21 | | | Table 2: Col 1 |
| 12.1 | Webster et al. (2004) | State minimum purchase age | Total suicide rate | Aged 18–20 | 0.97 | | 0.91 | 1.05 | | | Table 2: Col 2 |
| 12.1 | Webster et al. (2004) | State minimum purchase age | Firearm suicide rate | Aged 14–17 | 1.04 | | 0.87 | 1.16 | | | Table 2: Col 1 |
| 12.1 | Webster et al. (2004) | State minimum purchase age | Firearm suicide rate | Aged 18–20 | 0.91 | | 0.83 | 1.00 | | | Table 2: Col 2 |
| 12.1 | Webster et al. (2004) | State minimum purchase age | Nonfirearm suicide rate | Aged 14–17 | 1.05 | | 0.85 | 1.31 | | | Table 2: Col 1 |
| 12.1 | Webster et al. (2004) | State minimum purchase age | Nonfirearm suicide rate | Aged 18–20 | 1.05 | | 0.94 | 1.17 | | | Table 2: Col 2 |
| 12.1 | Webster et al. (2004) | State minimum possession age | Total suicide rate | Aged 14–17 | 0.97 | | 0.90 | 1.05 | | | Table 2: Col 1 |

**Table B.1—Continued**

| Report Figure | Study | Specific Policy or Independent Variable | Specific Outcome | Population | Estimate | Standard Error | Lower CI | Upper CI | Test Statistic | $p$ | Source Table |
|---|---|---|---|---|---|---|---|---|---|---|---|
| 12.1 | Webster et al. (2004) | State minimum possession age | Total suicide rate | Aged 18–20 | 1.13 | | 1.01 | 1.27 | | | Table 2: Col 2 |
| 12.1 | Webster et al. (2004) | State minimum possession age | Firearm suicide rate | Aged 14–17 | 1.02 | | 0.92 | 1.12 | | | Table 2: Col 1 |
| 12.1 | Webster et al. (2004) | State minimum possession age | Firearm suicide rate | Aged 18–20 | 1.14 | | 0.98 | 1.34 | | | Table 2: Col 2 |
| 12.1 | Webster et al. (2004) | State minimum possession age | Nonfirearm suicide rate | Aged 14–17 | 0.93 | | 0.82 | 1.05 | | | Table 2: Col 1 |
| 12.1 | Webster et al. (2004) | State minimum possession age | Nonfirearm suicide rate | Aged 18–20 | 1.07 | | 0.90 | 1.27 | | | Table 2: Col 2 |
| 12.1 | Webster et al. (2004) | Federal minimum purchase age | Total suicide rate | Aged 14–17 | 1.02 | | 0.91 | 1.14 | | | Table 2: Col 1 |
| 12.1 | Webster et al. (2004) | Federal minimum purchase age | Firearm suicide rate | Aged 14–17 | 1.00 | | 0.87 | 1.16 | | | Table 2: Col 1 |
| 12.1 | Webster et al. (2004) | Federal minimum purchase age | Nonfirearm suicide rate | Aged 14–17 | 1.08 | | 0.91 | 1.28 | | | Table 2: Col 1 |
| 12.1 | Webster et al. (2004) | Federal minimum possession age | Total suicide rate | Aged 14–17 | 0.98 | | 0.90 | 1.08 | | | Table 2: Col 1 |
| 12.1 | Webster et al. (2004) | Federal minimum possession age | Firearm suicide rate | Aged 14–17 | 0.99 | | 0.89 | 1.09 | | | Table 2: Col 1 |
| 12.1 | Webster et al. (2004) | Federal minimum possession age | Nonfirearm suicide rate | Aged 14–17 | 1.12 | | 0.99 | 1.26 | | | Table 2: Col 1 |
| 12.1 | Gius (2015b) | State minimum possession age | Firearm suicide rate | Aged 0–19 | −0.046 | | | | −1.05 | | Table 4 |
| 12.1 | Rosengart et al. (2005) | State minimum purchase age of 21 | Total suicide rate | All ages | 1.02 | | 0.98 | 1.07 | | | Table 4 |

**Table B.1—Continued**

| Report Figure | Study | Specific Policy or Independent Variable | Specific Outcome | Population | Estimate | Standard Error | Lower CI | Upper CI | Test Statistic | *p* | Source Table |
|---|---|---|---|---|---|---|---|---|---|---|---|
| 12.1 | Rosengart et al. (2005) | State minimum purchase age of 21 | Total suicide rate | Aged 0–19 | 1.1 | | 0.94 | 1.29 | | | Table 3 |
| 12.1 | Rosengart et al. (2005) | State minimum purchase age of 21 | Total suicide rate | Aged 20+ | 1.04 | | 0.99 | 1.1 | | | Table 3 |
| 12.1 | Rosengart et al. (2005) | State minimum purchase age of 21 | Firearm suicide rate | All ages | 1 | | 0.94 | 1.06 | | | Table 4 |
| 12.1 | Rosengart et al. (2005) | State minimum purchase age of 21 | Firearm suicide rate | Aged 0–19 | 0.94 | | 0.8 | 1.06 | | | Table 3 |
| 12.1 | Rosengart et al. (2005) | State minimum purchase age of 21 | Firearm suicide rate | Aged 20+ | 1.02 | | 0.96 | 1.08 | | | Table 3 |
| 12.1 | Rosengart et al. (2005) | State minimum possession age of 21 | Total suicide rate | All ages | 1.03 | | 0.96 | 1.11 | | | Table 4 |
| 12.1 | Rosengart et al. (2005) | State minimum possession age of 21 | Total suicide rate | Aged 0–19 | 1.15 | | 0.93 | 1.42 | | | Table 3 |
| 12.1 | Rosengart et al. (2005) | State minimum possession age of 21 | Total suicide rate | Aged 20+ | 1.04 | | 0.95 | 1.13 | | | Table 3 |
| 12.1 | Rosengart et al. (2005) | State minimum possession age of 21 | Firearm suicide rate | All ages | 0.99 | | 0.88 | 1.13 | | | Table 4 |
| 12.1 | Rosengart et al. (2005) | State minimum possession age of 21 | Firearm suicide rate | Aged 0–19 | 0.93 | | 0.77 | 1.12 | | | Table 3 |
| 12.1 | Rosengart et al. (2005) | State minimum possession age of 21 | Firearm suicide rate | Aged 20+ | 0.99 | | 0.88 | 1.13 | | | Table 3 |
| 12.2 | Rosengart et al. (2005) | State minimum purchase age of 21 | Total homicide rate | All ages | 1 | | 0.94 | 1.05 | | | Table 2 |
| 12.2 | Rosengart et al. (2005) | State minimum purchase age of 21 | Total homicide rate | Aged 0–19 | 0.92 | | 0.81 | 1.05 | | | Table 3 |

**Table B.1—Continued**

| Report Figure | Study | Specific Policy or Independent Variable | Specific Outcome | Population | Estimate | Standard Error | Lower CI | Upper CI | Test Statistic | *p* | Source Table |
|---|---|---|---|---|---|---|---|---|---|---|---|
| 12.2 | Rosengart et al. (2005) | State minimum purchase age of 21 | Total homicide rate | Aged 20+ | 1.01 | | 0.95 | 1.06 | | | Table 3 |
| 12.2 | Rosengart et al. (2005) | State minimum purchase age of 21 | Firearm homicide rate | All ages | 0.98 | | 0.91 | 1.06 | | | Table 2 |
| 12.2 | Rosengart et al. (2005) | State minimum purchase age of 21 | Firearm homicide rate | Aged 0–19 | 0.92 | | 0.8 | 1.06 | | | Table 3 |
| 12.2 | Rosengart et al. (2005) | State minimum purchase age of 21 | Firearm homicide rate | Aged 20+ | 0.99 | | 0.93 | 1.06 | | | Table 3 |
| 12.2 | Rosengart et al. (2005) | State minimum possession age of 21 | Total homicide rate | All ages | 1.02 | | 0.89 | 1.18 | | | Table 2 |
| 12.2 | Rosengart et al. (2005) | State minimum possession age of 21 | Total homicide rate | Aged 0–19 | 0.98 | | 0.79 | 1.2 | | | Table 3 |
| 12.2 | Rosengart et al. (2005) | State minimum possession age of 21 | Total homicide rate | Aged 20+ | 1.03 | | 0.88 | 1.2 | | | Table 3 |
| 12.2 | Rosengart et al. (2005) | State minimum possession age of 21 | Firearm homicide rate | All ages | 1.06 | | 0.88 | 1.27 | | | Table 2 |
| 12.2 | Rosengart et al. (2005) | State minimum possession age of 21 | Firearm homicide rate | Aged 0–19 | 0.91 | | 0.72 | 1.15 | | | Table 3 |
| 12.2 | Rosengart et al. (2005) | State minimum possession age of 21 | Firearm homicide rate | Aged 20+ | 1.08 | | 0.89 | 1.31 | | | Table 3 |
| 12.2 | Rudolph et al. (2015) | State minimum purchase age of 21 | Firearm homicide rate | All ages | 0.6 | | | | | 0.04 | In text (p. e51) and Table 2, "2xMSPE" |
| 12.3 | Gius (2015b) | State minimum possession age | Unintentional firearm death rate | Aged 0–19 | –0.0636 | | | | –1.6 | | Table 5 |

**Table B.1—Continued**

| Report Figure | Study | Specific Policy or Independent Variable | Specific Outcome | Population | Estimate | Standard Error | Lower CI | Upper CI | Test Statistic | *p* | Source Table |
|---|---|---|---|---|---|---|---|---|---|---|---|
| 12.4 | Luca, Deepak, and Poliquin (2016) | State minimum purchase age of 18 | Any mass shooting incident | N/A | 0.007 | 0.025 | | | | | Table C2: Col 1 |
| 12.4 | Luca, Deepak, and Poliquin (2016) | State minimum purchase age of 18 | Any mass shooting incident | N/A | 0.01 | 0.026 | | | | | Table C2: Col 2 |
| 12.4 | Luca, Deepak, and Poliquin (2016) | State minimum purchase age of 21 | Any mass shooting incident | N/A | –0.059 | 0.051 | | | | | Table C2: Col 1 |
| 12.4 | Luca, Deepak, and Poliquin (2016) | State minimum purchase age of 21 | Any mass shooting incident | N/A | –0.075 | 0.051 | | | | | Table C2: Col 2 |
| 13.1 | Rosengart et al. (2005) | Shall-issue law | Total suicide rate | All ages | 0.98 | | 0.96 | 1.01 | | | Table 4 |
| 13.1 | Rosengart et al. (2005) | Shall-issue law | Firearm suicide rate | All ages | 1 | | 0.97 | 1.02 | | | Table 4 |
| 13.1 | DeSimone, Markowitz, and Xu (2013) | Shall-issue law | Self-inflicted firearm injury rate | Aged 0–17 | 0.662 | 0.747 | | | | | Table 5 |
| 13.1 | DeSimone, Markowitz, and Xu (2013) | Shall-issue law | Self-inflicted firearm injury rate | Aged 18+ | 0.742 | 0.163 | | | | | Table 6 |
| 13.2 | Rosengart et al. (2005) | Shall-issue law vs. no CC permitted | Total homicide rate | All ages | 1.07 | | 0.98 | 1.17 | | | Table 2 |
| 13.2 | Rosengart et al. (2005) | Shall-issue law vs. no CC permitted | Firearm homicide rate | All ages | 1.11 | | 0.99 | 1.24 | | | Table 2 |
| 13.2 | Grambsch (2008) | Shall-issue vs. no CC (random effects) | Murder rate | All ages | 0.005 | 0.011 | | | | | Table 3 |
| 13.2 | Grambsch (2008) | Shall-issue vs. no CC (fixed effects) | Murder rate | All ages | 0.06 | 0.015 | | | | | Table 3 |

**Table B.1—Continued**

| Report Figure | Study | Specific Policy or Independent Variable | Specific Outcome | Population | Estimate | Standard Error | Lower CI | Upper CI | Test Statistic | *p* | Source Table |
|---|---|---|---|---|---|---|---|---|---|---|---|
| 13.2 | French and Heagerty (2008) | Shall-issue law vs. no CC | Firearm homicide rate | All ages | 1.101 | | 0.993 | 1.22 | | | In text (p. 14) |
| 13.2 | Roberts (2009) | May-issue vs. shall-issue | Total IPH rate | All ages | 1.7128 | 0.216 | | | | | Table 2 |
| 13.2 | Roberts (2009) | No CC vs. shall-issue | Total IPH rate | All ages | 0.9621 | 0.212 | | | | | Table 2 |
| 13.2 | Roberts (2009) | May-issue vs. shall-issue | Firearm IPH rate | All ages | 1.1202 | 0.128 | | | | | Table 3 |
| 13.2 | Roberts (2009) | No CC vs. shall-issue | Firearm IPH rate | All ages | 0.8608 | 0.19 | | | | | Table 3 |
| 13.2 | La Valle and Glover (2012) | May-issue | Total homicide rate | All ages | –0.214 | 0.065 | | | | | Table 8 |
| 13.2 | La Valle and Glover (2012) | Shall-issue | Total homicide rate | All ages | 0.206 | 0.08 | | | | | Table 8 |
| 13.2 | La Valle and Glover (2012) | May-issue | Firearm homicide rate | All ages | –0.263 | 0.08 | | | | | Table 7 |
| 13.2 | La Valle and Glover (2012) | Shall-issue | Firearm homicide rate | All ages | 0.274 | 0.075 | | | | | Table 7 |
| 13.2 | La Valle (2013) | Shall-issue law vs. no CC permitted | Total homicide rate | All ages | –0.137 | 0.062 | | | | | Table 7 |
| 13.2 | La Valle (2013) | Shall-issue law vs. no CC permitted | Firearm homicide rate | All ages | –0.166 | 0.073 | | | | | Table 7 |
| 13.2 | Webster, Crifasi, and Vernick (2014) | Shall-issue law vs. no CC permitted | Total homicide rate | All ages | 0.38 | 0.23 | | | | | Corrected Supplement Table 3 |
| 13.2 | Webster, Crifasi, and Vernick (2014) | Shall-issue law vs. no CC permitted | Firearm homicide rate | All ages | 0.25 | 0.21 | | | | | Corrected Supplement Table 1 |

**Table B.1—Continued**

| Report Figure | Study | Specific Policy or Independent Variable | Specific Outcome | Population | Estimate | Standard Error | Lower CI | Upper CI | Test Statistic | *p* | Source Table |
|---|---|---|---|---|---|---|---|---|---|---|---|
| 13.2 | Webster, Crifasi, and Vernick (2014) | Shall-issue law vs. no CC permitted | Nonfirearm homicide rate | All ages | 0.21 | 0.12 | | | | | Corrected Supplement Table 2 |
| 13.2 | Webster, Crifasi, and Vernick (2014) | Shall-issue law vs. no CC permitted | Murder/ manslaughter rate | All ages | 0.58 | 0.42 | | | | | Corrected Supplement Table 4 |
| 13.2 | Gius (2014) | Restrictive vs. lenient CC laws | Firearm murder rate | All ages | 0.365 | | | | 3.74 | | Table 1 |
| 13.2 | Aneja, Donohue, and Zhang (2014) | Shall-issue vs. any other CC law | Murder rate | All ages | 0.0331 | 0.0651 | | | | | Table 8A |
| 13.2 | Aneja, Donohue, and Zhang (2014) | Shall-issue vs. any other CC law | Rape rate | All ages | 0.1153 | 0.0573 | | | | | Table 8A |
| 13.2 | Aneja, Donohue, and Zhang (2014) | Shall-issue vs. any other CC law | Robbery rate | All ages | 0.1385 | 0.0803 | | | | | Table 8A |
| 13.2 | Aneja, Donohue, and Zhang (2014) | Shall-issue vs. any other CC law | Assault rate | All ages | 0.0803 | 0.0446 | | | | | Table 8A |
| 13.2 | Martin and Legault (2005) | Shall-issue (vs. other CC law) | Violent crime | All ages | –0.0566 | | | | –3.067 | | Table 6: Model V |
| 13.2 | Martin and Legault (2005) | Shall-issue (vs. other CC law) | Murder rate | All ages | –0.0492 | | | | –1.696 | | Table 6: Model V |
| 13.2 | Martin and Legault (2005) | Shall-issue (vs. other CC law) | Rape rate | All ages | –0.0161 | | | | –0.739 | | Table 6: Model V |
| 13.2 | Martin and Legault (2005) | Shall-issue (vs. other CC law) | Aggravated Assault | All ages | –0.0705 | | | | –2.927 | | Table 6: Model V |
| 13.2 | Martin and Legault (2005) | Shall-issue (vs. other CC law) | Robbery rate | All ages | –0.0385 | | | | –1.322 | | Table 6: Model V |

**Table B.1—Continued**

| Report Figure | Study | Specific Policy or Independent Variable | Specific Outcome | Population | Estimate | Standard Error | Lower CI | Upper CI | Test Statistic | *p* | Source Table |
|---|---|---|---|---|---|---|---|---|---|---|---|
| 13.2 | Kendall and Tamura (2010) | Shall-issue (vs. other CC law) | Murder rate | All ages | −0.003 | | | | 1.52 | | Table 3 |
| 13.2 | Kendall and Tamura (2010) | Shall-issue (vs. other CC law) | Rape rate | All ages | −0.002 | | | | 0.99 | | Table 3 |
| 13.2 | Kendall and Tamura (2010) | Shall-issue (vs. other CC law) | Robbery rate | All ages | 0.001 | | | | 0.55 | | Table 3 |
| 13.2 | Kendall and Tamura (2010) | Shall-issue (vs. other CC law) | Assault rate | All ages | 0 | | | | 0.05 | | Table 3 |
| 13.3 | Lott and Mustard (1997) | Shall-issue law | Unintentional handgun death rate | All ages | 0.00478 | | | | 0.096 | | Table 18: Col 1 |
| 13.3 | Lott and Mustard (1997) | Shall-issue law | Unintentional nonhandgun death rate | All ages | 0.098 | | | | 1.706 | | Table 18: Col 2 |
| 13.3 | DeSimone, Markowitz, and Xu (2013) | Shall-issue law | Unintentional firearm injury rate | Aged 0–17 | 0.53 | 0.364 | | | | | Table 5 |
| 13.3 | DeSimone, Markowitz, and Xu (2013) | Shall-issue law | Unintentional firearm injury rate | Aged 18+ | 0.823 | 0.191 | | | | | Table 6 |
| 13.4 | Lott (2003) | Shall-issue law | Multiple-victim gun deaths, injuries | All ages | 0.2151 | | | | 9.609 | | Appendix Table 6.2: Col 3 |
| 13.4 | Lott (2003) | Shall-issue law | No. of multiple-victim gun incidents | All ages | 0.3280486 | | | | 3.82 | | Appendix Table 6.2: Col 4 |
| 13.4 | Luca, Deepak, and Poliquin (2016) | Permitless carry | Any mass shooting incident | All ages | 0.152 | 0.182 | | | | | Table C2: Col 1 |

**Table B.1—Continued**

| Report Figure | Study | Specific Policy or Independent Variable | Specific Outcome | Population | Estimate | Standard Error | Lower CI | Upper CI | Test Statistic | *p* | Source Table |
|---|---|---|---|---|---|---|---|---|---|---|---|
| 13.4 | Luca, Deepak, and Poliquin (2016) | Permitless carry | Any mass shooting incident | All ages | 0.207 | 0.18 | | | | | Table C2: Col 2 |
| 13.4 | Luca, Deepak and Poliquin (2016) | Shall-issue law | Any mass shooting incident | All ages | –0.011 | 0.039 | | | | | Table C2: Col 1 |
| 13.4 | Luca, Deepak and Poliquin (2016) | Shall-issue law | Any mass shooting incident | All ages | –0.009 | 0.038 | | | | | Table C2: Col 2 |
| 13.5 | Duggan (2001) | Right-to-carry laws | Gun ownership | None | 0.0038 | 0.0099 | | | | | Table 10: Col 3 |

NOTE: CAP = child-access prevention; CC = concealed carry; Col = column; IPH = intimate partner homicide; N/A = not applicable; NICS = National Instant Criminal Background Check System.

Table B.2 shows the most-common methodological concerns we identified for analyses included in this report's forest plot figures. When we identified no such concerns for a study, the forest plots show that study's IRR values with green circles (see, for example, Figure 3.1). In Table B.2, we identify five categories of concerns:

- The *Parameter* column identifies with an *X* the analyses we believed to have been performed with fewer than ten observations per parameter estimate. In several cases, models with random effects were conducted, but no estimate of the effective number of parameters was reported. In these cases, we guessed that the effective number of random effect parameters was about half the total number of random effects. This resulted in none of the random effects models having fewer than ten observations per parameter estimate.
- The *Tx Units* column identifies the analyses that we believed identified a causal effect with three or fewer units (states, usually) exposed to the law.
- The *Cluster* column identifies the analyses that appeared to make no adjustments to the standard error to account for either serial correlation in the longitudinal data or heteroscedasticity. We were sparing in assigning this concern to analyses, giving credit for some type of standard error adjustment even when papers reported, for instance, having checked for the presence of serial correlation or performing adjustments of doubtful validity. Studies that made no reference to any type of adjustment or check are identified with this concern.
- The *Model* column identifies the analyses that reported results from models we believe may have been misspecified. We assigned this concern to just two types of models: those using ordinary least squares (OLS) to model dichotomous outcomes and those using OLS to model rates, many of which are close to zero. We did not assign this concern to OLS models of logged rate values, although this too is problematic.
- The *Other* column identifies studies with other methodological features that raised significant concerns for us. It was often the case that studies had multiple idiosyncratic methodological features that concerned us. However, we did not assign the *Other* concern to studies that had already been identified as having one of the other four common concerns. When a study is listed as having an *Other* concern, that concern is described in the text of the report whenever the study is discussed.

**Table B.2**
**Methodological Concerns Identified for Analyses Included in the Report's Forest Plot Figures**

| Report Figure | Study | Specific Policy or Independent Variable | Specific Outcome | Population | Parameter | Tx Units | Cluster | Model | Other |
|---|---|---|---|---|---|---|---|---|---|
| 3.1 | Ludwig and Cook (2000) | Brady Act | Firearm suicide rate | Aged 21+ | X | | | | |
| 3.1 | Ludwig and Cook (2000) | Brady Act | Firearm suicide rate | Aged 55+ | X | | | | |
| 3.1 | Ludwig and Cook (2000) | Brady Act | Nonfirearm suicide rate | Aged 21+ | X | | | | |
| 3.1 | Ludwig and Cook (2000) | Brady Act | Nonfirearm suicide rate | Aged 55+ | X | | | | |
| 3.1 | Ludwig and Cook (2000) | Brady Act | Proportion of suicides with firearm | Aged 21+ | X | | | | |
| 3.1 | Ludwig and Cook (2000) | Brady Act | Proportion of suicides with firearm | Aged 55+ | X | | | | |
| 3.1 | Ludwig and Cook (2000) | Brady Act | Total suicide rate | Aged 21+ | X | | | | |
| 3.1 | Ludwig and Cook (2000) | Brady Act | Total suicide rate | Aged 55+ | X | | | | |
| 3.1 | Sen and Panjamapirom (2012) | Check on fugitive status | Firearm suicide rate | All ages | | X | | | |
| 3.1 | Sen and Panjamapirom (2012) | Check on fugitive status | Total suicide rate | All ages | | X | | | |
| 3.1 | Sen and Panjamapirom (2012) | Check on mental illness | Firearm suicide rate | All ages | | | | | |
| 3.1 | Sen and Panjamapirom (2012) | Check on mental illness | Total suicide rate | All ages | | | | | |
| 3.1 | Sen and Panjamapirom (2012) | Check on misdemeanor | Firearm suicide rate | All ages | | | | | |
| 3.1 | Sen and Panjamapirom (2012) | Check on misdemeanor | Total suicide rate | All ages | | | | | |
| 3.1 | Sen and Panjamapirom (2012) | Check on "other miscellaneous" records | Firearm suicide rate | All ages | | | | | |
| 3.1 | Sen and Panjamapirom (2012) | Check on "other miscellaneous" records | Total suicide rate | All ages | | | | | |

**Table B.2—Continued**

| Report Figure | Study | Specific Policy or Independent Variable | Specific Outcome | Population | Parameter | Tx Units | Cluster | Model | Other |
|---|---|---|---|---|---|---|---|---|---|
| 3.1 | Sen and Panjamapirom (2012) | Check on restraining order | Firearm suicide rate | All ages | | | | | |
| 3.1 | Sen and Panjamapirom (2012) | Check on restraining order | Total suicide rate | All ages | | | | | |
| 3.1 | Sen and Panjamapirom (2012) | Background check comprehensiveness | Firearm suicide rate | All ages | | | | | |
| 3.2 | Sen and Panjamapirom (2012) | Check on "other miscellaneous" records | Total homicide rate | All ages | | | | | |
| 3.2 | Sen and Panjamapirom (2012) | Check on "other miscellaneous" records | Firearm homicide rate | All ages | | | | | |
| 3.2 | Sen and Panjamapirom (2012) | Background check comprehensiveness | Firearm homicide rate | All ages | | | | | |
| 3.2 | Sen and Panjamapirom (2012) | Check on restraining order | Total homicide rate | All ages | | | | | |
| 3.2 | Sen and Panjamapirom (2012) | Check on restraining order | Firearm homicide rate | All ages | | | | | |
| 3.2 | Sen and Panjamapirom (2012) | Check on mental illness | Total homicide rate | All ages | | | | | |
| 3.2 | Sen and Panjamapirom (2012) | Check on mental illness | Firearm homicide rate | All ages | | | | | |
| 3.2 | Sen and Panjamapirom (2012) | Check on fugitive status | Total homicide rate | All ages | | X | | | |
| 3.2 | Sen and Panjamapirom (2012) | Check on fugitive status | Firearm homicide rate | All ages | | X | | | |
| 3.2 | Sen and Panjamapirom (2012) | Check on misdemeanor | Total homicide rate | All ages | | | | | |
| 3.2 | Sen and Panjamapirom (2012) | Check on misdemeanor | Firearm homicide rate | All ages | | | | | |
| 3.2 | La Valle (2013) | Brady Act | Total homicide rate | All ages | | | | | |

**Table B.2—Continued**

| Report Figure | Study | Specific Policy or Independent Variable | Specific Outcome | Population | Parameter | Tx Units | Cluster | Model | Other |
|---|---|---|---|---|---|---|---|---|---|
| 3.2 | La Valle (2013) | Brady Act | Firearm homicide rate | All ages | | | | | |
| 3.2 | Gius (2015a) | State dealer background check | Gun-related murder rate | All ages | | | | X | |
| 3.2 | Gius (2015a) | State private-seller background check | Gun-related murder rate | All ages | | X | | X | |
| 3.2 | Ludwig and Cook (2000) | Brady Act | Total homicide rate | Aged 21+ | X | | | | |
| 3.2 | Ludwig and Cook (2000) | Brady Act | Firearm homicide rate | Aged 21+ | X | | | | |
| 3.2 | Ludwig and Cook (2000) | Brady Act | Nonfirearm homicide rate | Aged 21+ | X | | | | |
| 3.2 | Ludwig and Cook (2000) | Brady Act | Proportion of homicides with a firearm | Aged 21+ | X | | | | |
| 3.2 | Ludwig and Cook (2000) | Brady Act | Total homicide rate | Aged 55+ | X | | | | |
| 3.2 | Ludwig and Cook (2000) | Brady Act | Firearm homicide rate | Aged 55+ | X | | | | |
| 3.2 | Ludwig and Cook (2000) | Brady Act | Nonfirearm homicide rate | Aged 55+ | X | | | | |
| 3.2 | Ludwig and Cook (2000) | Brady Act | Proportion of homicides with a firearm | Aged 55+ | X | | | | |
| 3.2 | Swanson et al. (2016) | NICS reporting (Fla.) | Violent crime arrest | No crim. disqualified | | X | | | |
| 3.2 | Wright, Wintemute, and Rivara (1999) | No felony prohibition/ checks | Any offense | Calif. purchasers | | | | | |
| 3.2 | Wright, Wintemute, and Rivara (1999) | No felony prohibition/ checks | Gun offense | Calif. purchasers | | | | | |
| 3.2 | Wright, Wintemute, and Rivara (1999) | No felony prohibition/ checks | Violent offense | Calif. purchasers | | | | | |

**Table B.2—Continued**

| Report Figure | Study | Specific Policy or Independent Variable | Specific Outcome | Population | Parameter | Tx Units | Cluster | Model | Other |
|---|---|---|---|---|---|---|---|---|---|
| 3.3 | Luca, Deepak, and Poliquin (2016) | Background check (all handgun sales) | Any mass shooting incident | N/A | | | X | X | |
| 3.3 | Luca, Deepak, and Poliquin (2016) | Background check (all handgun sales) | Any mass shooting incident | N/A | | | | X | |
| 3.3 | Luca, Deepak, and Poliquin (2016) | Background check (all firearm sales) | Any mass shooting incident | N/A | | | | X | |
| 3.3 | Luca, Deepak, and Poliquin (2016) | Background check (all firearm sales) | Any mass shooting incident | N/A | | | | X | |
| 4.1 | Lott (2010) | State/federal assault weapon bans | Total homicide | All ages | X | | X | | |
| 4.1 | Gius (2014) | State assault weapons ban | Firearm murder rate | All ages | | | X | X | |
| 4.2 | Gius (2015c) | State assault weapons ban | Mass shooting deaths | All ages | | | X | | |
| 4.2 | Gius (2015c) | State assault weapons ban | Mass shooting injuries | All ages | | | X | | |
| 4.2 | Luca, Deepak, and Poliquin (2016) | State assault weapons ban | Any mass shooting incident | N/A | | | | X | |
| 4.2 | Luca, Deepak, and Poliquin (2016) | State assault weapons ban | Any mass shooting incident | N/A | | | | X | |
| 5.1 | Humphreys, Gasparrini, and Wiebe (2017) | Stand-your-ground law | Total suicide rate | All ages | | X | | | |
| 5.1 | Humphreys, Gasparrini, and Wiebe (2017) | Stand-your-ground law | Firearm suicide rate | All ages | | X | | | |
| 5.2 | Cheng and Hoekstra (2013) | Castle doctrine law | Homicide | All ages | X | | | | |

**Table B.2—Continued**

| Report Figure | Study | Specific Policy or Independent Variable | Specific Outcome | Population | Parameter | Tx Units | Cluster | Model | Other |
|---|---|---|---|---|---|---|---|---|---|
| 5.2 | Cheng and Hoekstra (2013) | Castle doctrine law | Burglary | All ages | X | | | | |
| 5.2 | Cheng and Hoekstra (2013) | Castle doctrine law | Robbery | All ages | X | | | | |
| 5.2 | Cheng and Hoekstra (2013) | Castle doctrine law | Aggravated assault | All ages | X | | | | |
| 5.2 | Webster, Crifasi, and Vernick (2014) | Stand-your-ground law | Total homicide rate | All ages | X | X | | X | |
| 5.2 | Webster, Crifasi, and Vernick (2014) | Stand-your-ground law | Firearm homicide rate | All ages | X | X | | X | |
| 5.2 | Webster, Crifasi, and Vernick (2014) | Stand-your-ground law | Nonfirearm homicide rate | All ages | X | X | | X | |
| 5.2 | Humphreys, Gasparrini, and Wiebe (2017) | Stand-your-ground law | Total homicide rate | All ages | | X | | | |
| 5.2 | Humphreys, Gasparrini, and Wiebe (2017) | Stand-your-ground law | Firearms homicide rate | All ages | | X | | | |
| 5.3 | Cheng and Hoekstra (2013) | Castle doctrine law | Justifiable homicide | All ages | X | | | | |
| 6.1 | Sen and Panjamapirom (2012) | Check on mental illness | Total suicide rate | All ages | | | | | |
| 6.1 | Sen and Panjamapirom (2012) | Check on mental illness | Firearm suicide rate | All ages | | | | | |
| 6.2 | Sen and Panjamapirom (2012) | Check on mental illness | Total homicide rate | All ages | | | | | |
| 6.2 | Sen and Panjamapirom (2012) | Check on mental illness | Firearm homicide rate | All ages | | | | | |
| 6.2 | Swanson et al. (2016) | NICS reporting (Fla.) | Violent crime arrest | No crim. disqualified | | X | | | |
| 8.1 | Webster et al. (2004) | Permit-to-purchase law | Total suicide rate | Aged 14–17 | | X | | | |
| 8.1 | Webster et al. (2004) | Permit-to-purchase law | Total suicide rate | Aged 18–20 | | X | | | |

**Table B.2—Continued**

| Report Figure | Study | Specific Policy or Independent Variable | Specific Outcome | Population | Parameter | Tx Units | Cluster | Model | Other |
|---|---|---|---|---|---|---|---|---|---|
| 8.1 | Webster et al. (2004) | Permit-to-purchase law | Firearm suicide rate | Aged 14–17 | | X | | | |
| 8.1 | Webster et al. (2004) | Permit-to-purchase law | Firearm suicide rate | Aged 18–20 | | X | | | |
| 8.1 | Webster et al. (2004) | Permit-to-purchase law | Nonfirearm suicide rate | Aged 14–17 | | X | | | |
| 8.1 | Webster et al. (2004) | Permit-to-purchase law | Nonfirearm suicide rate | Aged 18–20 | | X | | | |
| 8.1 | Crifasi et al. (2015) | Permit-to-purchase law | Total suicide rate | All ages | | X | | | |
| 8.1 | Crifasi et al. (2015) | Permit-to-purchase law | Firearm suicide rate | All ages | | X | | | |
| 8.1 | Crifasi et al. (2015) | Permit-to-purchase law | Nonfirearm suicide rate | All ages | | X | | | |
| 8.1 | Crifasi et al. (2015) | Repeal of Missouri permit-to-purchase | Total suicide rate | All ages | | X | | | |
| 8.1 | Crifasi et al. (2015) | Repeal of Missouri permit-to-purchase | Firearm suicide rate | All ages | | X | | | |
| 8.1 | Crifasi et al. (2015) | Repeal of Missouri permit-to-purchase | Nonfirearm suicide rate | All ages | | X | | | |
| 8.2 | Webster, Crifasi, and Vernick (2014) | Repeal of Missouri permit-to-purchase | Total homicide rate | All ages | X | X | | X | |
| 8.2 | Webster, Crifasi, and Vernick (2014) | Repeal of Missouri permit-to-purchase | Firearm homicide rate | All ages | X | X | | X | |
| 8.2 | Webster, Crifasi, and Vernick (2014) | Repeal of Missouri permit-to-purchase | Nonfirearm homicide rate | All ages | X | X | | X | |
| 8.2 | Rudolph et al. (2015) | Connecticut permit-to-purchase | Firearm homicide rate | All ages | | X | | | |
| 8.3 | Luca, Deepak, and Poliquin (2016) | Handgun permit system | Any mass shooting incident | All ages | | | | X | |

**Table B.2—Continued**

| Report Figure | Study | Specific Policy or Independent Variable | Specific Outcome | Population | Parameter | Tx Units | Cluster | Model | Other |
|---|---|---|---|---|---|---|---|---|---|
| 8.3 | Luca, Deepak, and Poliquin (2016) | Handgun permit system | Any mass shooting incident | All ages | | | | X | |
| 10.1 | Cummings et al. (1997a) | CAP law | Firearm suicide rate | Aged 0–14 | | | | | |
| 10.1 | Cummings et al. (1997a) | CAP law | Nonfirearm suicide rate | Aged 0–14 | | | | | |
| 10.1 | Webster et al. (2004) | CAP law | Total suicide rate | Aged 14–17 | | | | | |
| 10.1 | Webster et al. (2004) | CAP law | Total suicide rate | Aged 18–20 | | | | | |
| 10.1 | Webster et al. (2004) | CAP law | Firearm suicide rate | Aged 14–17 | | | | | |
| 10.1 | Webster et al. (2004) | CAP law | Firearm suicide rate | Aged 18–20 | | | | | |
| 10.1 | Webster et al. (2004) | CAP law | Nonfirearm suicide rate | Aged 14–17 | | | | | |
| 10.1 | Webster et al. (2004) | CAP law | Nonfirearm suicide rate | Aged 18–20 | | | | | |
| 10.1 | DeSimone, Markowitz, and Xu (2013) | Negligent storage (11 states) | Firearm self-inflicted injury rate | Aged 0–17 | | | | | X |
| 10.1 | DeSimone, Markowitz, and Xu (2013) | Negligent storage (11 states) | Firearm self-inflicted injury rate | Aged 18+ | | | | | X |
| 10.1 | DeSimone, Markowitz, and Xu (2013) | Negligent storage or reckless provision (11 states) | Firearm self-inflicted injury rate | Aged 0–17 | | | | | X |
| 10.1 | DeSimone, Markowitz, and Xu (2013) | Negligent storage or reckless provision (11 states) | Firearm self-inflicted injury rate | Aged 18+ | | | | | X |
| 10.1 | Gius (2015b) | CAP law | Firearm suicide rate | Aged 0–19 | | | | X | |
| 10.2 | Cummings et al. (1997a) | CAP law | Firearm homicide rate | Aged 0–14 | | | | | |
| 10.2 | Cummings et al. (1997a) | CAP law | Nonfirearm homicide rate | Aged 0–14 | | | | | |

**Table B.2—Continued**

| Report Figure | Study | Specific Policy or Independent Variable | Specific Outcome | Population | Parameter | Tx Units | Cluster | Model | Other |
|---|---|---|---|---|---|---|---|---|---|
| 10.2 | Lott and Whitley (2001) | Safe storage law | Murder rate | All ages | X | | X | X | |
| 10.2 | Lott and Whitley (2001) | Safe storage law | Rape rate | All ages | X | | X | X | |
| 10.2 | Lott and Whitley (2001) | Safe storage law | Robbery rate | All ages | X | | X | X | |
| 10.2 | Lott and Whitley (2001) | Safe storage law | Assault rate | All ages | X | | X | X | |
| 10.3 | Cummings et al. (1997a) | CAP law | Unintentional firearm death rate | Aged 0–14 | | | | | |
| 10.3 | Cummings et al. (1997a) | CAP law | Unintentional firearm death rate | Aged 15–19 | | | | | |
| 10.3 | Cummings et al. (1997a) | CAP law | Unintentional firearm death rate | Aged 20–24 | | | | | |
| 10.3 | Webster and Starnes (2000) | CAP law | Unintentional firearm death rate | Aged 0–14 | | | | | |
| 10.3 | Webster and Starnes (2000) | Felony CAP law | Unintentional firearm death rate | Aged 0–14 | | X | | | |
| 10.3 | Webster and Starnes (2000) | Misdemeanor CAP law | Unintentional firearm death rate | Aged 0–14 | | | | | |
| 10.3 | Webster and Starnes (2000) | Florida CAP law | Unintentional firearm death rate | Aged 0–14 | | X | | | |
| 10.3 | Webster and Starnes (2000) | Non-Florida CAP law | Unintentional firearm death rate | Aged 0–14 | | | | | |
| 10.3 | Hepburn et al. (2006) | CAP law | Unintentional firearm death rate | Aged 0–14 | | | | | X |
| 10.3 | Hepburn et al. (2006) | CAP law | Unintentional firearm death rate | Aged 55–74 | | | | | X |

**Table B.2—Continued**

| Report Figure | Study | Specific Policy or Independent Variable | Specific Outcome | Population | Parameter | Tx Units | Cluster | Model | Other |
|---|---|---|---|---|---|---|---|---|---|
| 10.3 | Hepburn et al. (2006) | Felony CAP law | Unintentional firearm death rate | Aged 0–14 | | X | | | X |
| 10.3 | Hepburn et al. (2006) | Felony CAP law | Unintentional firearm death rate | Aged 55–74 | | X | | | X |
| 10.3 | Hepburn et al. (2006) | Misdemeanor CAP law | Unintentional firearm death rate | Aged 0–14 | | | | | X |
| 10.3 | Hepburn et al. (2006) | Misdemeanor CAP law | Unintentional firearm death rate | Aged 55–74 | | | | | X |
| 10.3 | Hepburn et al. (2006) | CAP law (exclude Fla.) | Unintentional firearm death rate | Aged 0–14 | | | | | X |
| 10.3 | Hepburn et al. (2006) | CAP law (exclude Fla.) | Unintentional firearm death rate | Aged 55–74 | | | | | X |
| 10.3 | Hepburn et al. (2006) | CAP law (exclude Calif.) | Unintentional firearm death rate | Aged 0–14 | | | | | X |
| 10.3 | Hepburn et al. (2006) | CAP law (exclude Calif.) | Unintentional firearm death rate | Aged 55–74 | | | | | X |
| 10.3 | Gius (2015b) | CAP law | Unintentional firearm death rate | Aged 0–19 | | | | X | |
| 10.3 | DeSimone, Markowitz, and Xu (2013) | CAP law, negligent storage (11 states) | Unintentional firearm injury rate | Aged 0–17 | | | | | X |
| 10.3 | DeSimone, Markowitz, and Xu (2013) | CAP law, negligent storage (11 states) | Unintentional firearm injury rate | Aged 18+ | | | | | X |
| 10.3 | DeSimone, Markowitz, and Xu (2013) | Negligent storage or reckless provision (11 states) | Unintentional firearm injury rate | Aged 0–17 | | | | | X |

**Table B.2—Continued**

| Report Figure | Study | Specific Policy or Independent Variable | Specific Outcome | Population | Parameter | Tx Units | Cluster | Model | Other |
|---|---|---|---|---|---|---|---|---|---|
| 10.3 | DeSimone, Markowitz, and Xu (2013) | Negligent storage or reckless provision (11 states) | Unintentional firearm injury rate | Aged 18+ | | | | | X |
| 10.4 | Lott (2003) | Safe storage law | Shooting fatalities + injuries | All ages | X | | X | | |
| 10.4 | Lott (2003) | Safe storage law | Number of shooting incidents | All ages | X | | X | | |
| 11.1 | Vigdor and Mercy (2006) | Confiscation law | Total IPH rate | All ages | | | | | |
| 11.1 | Vigdor and Mercy (2006) | Confiscation law | Firearm IPH rate | All ages | | | | | |
| 11.1 | Vigdor and Mercy (2006) | Confiscation law | Total IPH rate | Female victims | | | | | |
| 11.1 | Vigdor and Mercy (2006) | Confiscation law | Firearm IPH rate | Female victims | | | | | |
| 11.1 | Zeoli and Webster (2010) | Confiscation law | Total IPH rate | All ages | | | | | |
| 11.1 | Zeoli and Webster (2010) | Confiscation law | Firearm IPH rate | All ages | | | | | |
| 11.1 | Raissian (2016) | Gun Control Act expansion | Firearm IPH rate | All intimate partners | | | | X | |
| 11.1 | Raissian (2016) | Gun Control Act expansion | Firearm IPH rate | Female IPH victims | | | | X | |
| 11.1 | Raissian (2016) | Gun Control Act expansion | Firearm IPH rate | Male IPH victims | | | | X | |
| 12.1 | Webster et al. (2004) | State minimum purchase age | Total suicide rate | Aged 14–17 | | | | | |
| 12.1 | Webster et al. (2004) | State minimum purchase age | Total suicide rate | Aged 18–20 | | | | | |

**Table B.2—Continued**

| Report Figure | Study | Specific Policy or Independent Variable | Specific Outcome | Population | Parameter | Tx Units | Cluster | Model | Other |
|---|---|---|---|---|---|---|---|---|---|
| 12.1 | Webster et al. (2004) | State minimum purchase age | Firearm suicide rate | Aged 14–17 | | | | | |
| 12.1 | Webster et al. (2004) | State minimum purchase age | Firearm suicide rate | Aged 18–20 | | | | | |
| 12.1 | Webster et al. (2004) | State minimum purchase age | Nonfirearm suicide rate | Aged 14–17 | | | | | |
| 12.1 | Webster et al. (2004) | State minimum purchase age | Nonfirearm suicide rate | Aged 18–20 | | | | | |
| 12.1 | Webster et al. (2004) | State minimum possession age | Total suicide rate | Aged 14–17 | | X | | | |
| 12.1 | Webster et al. (2004) | State minimum possession age | Total suicide rate | Aged 18–20 | | X | | | |
| 12.1 | Webster et al. (2004) | State minimum possession age | Firearm suicide rate | Aged 14–17 | | X | | | |
| 12.1 | Webster et al. (2004) | State minimum possession age | Firearm suicide rate | Aged 18–20 | | X | | | |
| 12.1 | Webster et al. (2004) | State minimum possession age | Nonfirearm suicide rate | Aged 14–17 | | X | | | |
| 12.1 | Webster et al. (2004) | State minimum possession age | Nonfirearm suicide rate | Aged 18–20 | | X | | | |
| 12.1 | Webster et al. (2004) | Federal minimum purchase age | Total suicide rate | Aged 14–17 | | | | | |
| 12.1 | Webster et al. (2004) | Federal minimum purchase age | Firearm suicide rate | Aged 14–17 | | | | | |
| 12.1 | Webster et al. (2004) | Federal minimum purchase age | Nonfirearm suicide rate | Aged 14–17 | | | | | |

**Table B.2—Continued**

| Report Figure | Study | Specific Policy or Independent Variable | Specific Outcome | Population | Parameter | Tx Units | Cluster | Model | Other |
|---|---|---|---|---|---|---|---|---|---|
| 12.1 | Webster et al. (2004) | Federal minimum possession age | Total suicide rate | Aged 14–17 | | | | | |
| 12.1 | Webster et al. (2004) | Federal minimum possession age | Firearm suicide rate | Aged 14–17 | | | | | |
| 12.1 | Webster et al. (2004) | Federal minimum possession age | Nonfirearm suicide rate | Aged 14–17 | | | | | |
| 12.1 | Gius (2015b) | State minimum possession age | Firearm suicide rate | Aged 0–19 | | | | X | |
| 12.1 | Rosengart et al. (2005) | State minimum purchase age of 21 | Total suicide rate | All ages | X | | | | |
| 12.1 | Rosengart et al. (2005) | State minimum purchase age of 21 | Total suicide rate | Aged 0–19 | X | | | | |
| 12.1 | Rosengart et al. (2005) | State minimum purchase age of 21 | Total suicide rate | Aged 20+ | X | | | | |
| 12.1 | Rosengart et al. (2005) | State minimum purchase age of 21 | Firearm suicide rate | All ages | X | | | | |
| 12.1 | Rosengart et al. (2005) | State minimum purchase age of 21 | Firearm suicide rate | Aged 0–19 | X | | | | |
| 12.1 | Rosengart et al. (2005) | State minimum purchase age of 21 | Firearm suicide rate | Aged 20+ | X | | | | |
| 12.1 | Rosengart et al. (2005) | State minimum possession age of 21 | Total suicide rate | All ages | X | | | | |
| 12.1 | Rosengart et al. (2005) | State minimum possession age of 21 | Total suicide rate | Aged 0–19 | X | | | | |
| 12.1 | Rosengart et al. (2005) | State minimum possession age of 21 | Total suicide rate | Aged 20+ | X | | | | |

Table B.2—Continued

| Report Figure | Study | Specific Policy or Independent Variable | Specific Outcome | Population | Parameter | Tx Units | Cluster | Model | Other |
|---|---|---|---|---|---|---|---|---|---|
| 12.1 | Rosengart et al. (2005) | State minimum possession age of 21 | Firearm suicide rate | All ages | X | | | | |
| 12.1 | Rosengart et al. (2005) | State minimum possession age of 21 | Firearm suicide rate | Aged 0–19 | X | | | | |
| 12.1 | Rosengart et al. (2005) | State minimum possession age of 21 | Firearm suicide rate | Aged 20+ | X | | | | |
| 12.2 | Rosengart et al. (2005) | State minimum purchase age of 21 | Total homicide rate | All ages | X | | | | |
| 12.2 | Rosengart et al. (2005) | State minimum purchase age of 21 | Total homicide rate | Aged 0–19 | X | | | | |
| 12.2 | Rosengart et al. (2005) | State minimum purchase age of 21 | Total homicide rate | Aged 20+ | X | | | | |
| 12.2 | Rosengart et al. (2005) | State minimum purchase age of 21 | Firearm homicide rate | All ages | X | | | | |
| 12.2 | Rosengart et al. (2005) | State minimum purchase age of 21 | Firearm homicide rate | Aged 0–19 | X | | | | |
| 12.2 | Rosengart et al. (2005) | State minimum purchase age of 21 | Firearm homicide rate | Aged 20+ | X | | | | |
| 12.2 | Rosengart et al. (2005) | State minimum possession age of 21 | Total homicide rate | All ages | X | | | | |
| 12.2 | Rosengart et al. (2005) | State minimum possession age of 21 | Total homicide rate | Aged 0–19 | X | | | | |
| 12.2 | Rosengart et al. (2005) | State minimum possession age of 21 | Total homicide rate | Aged 20+ | X | | | | |
| 12.2 | Rosengart et al. (2005) | State minimum possession age of 21 | Firearm homicide rate | All ages | X | | | | |

**Table B.2—Continued**

| Report Figure | Study | Specific Policy or Independent Variable | Specific Outcome | Population | Parameter | Tx Units | Cluster | Model | Other |
|---|---|---|---|---|---|---|---|---|---|
| 12.2 | Rosengart et al. (2005) | State minimum possession age of 21 | Firearm homicide rate | Aged 0–19 | X | | | | |
| 12.2 | Rosengart et al. (2005) | State minimum possession age of 21 | Firearm homicide rate | Aged 20+ | X | | | | |
| 12.2 | Rudolph et al. (2015) | State minimum purchase age of 21 | Firearm homicide rate | All ages | | X | | | |
| 12.3 | Gius (2015b) | State minimum possession age | Unintentional firearm death rate | Aged 0–19 | | | | X | |
| 12.4 | Luca, Deepak, and Poliquin (2016) | State minimum purchase age of 18 | Any mass shooting incident | N/A | | | | X | |
| 12.4 | Luca, Deepak, and Poliquin (2016) | State minimum purchase age of 18 | Any mass shooting incident | N/A | | | | X | |
| 12.4 | Luca, Deepak, and Poliquin (2016) | State minimum purchase age of 21 | Any mass shooting incident | N/A | | | | X | |
| 12.4 | Luca, Deepak, and Poliquin (2016) | State minimum purchase age of 21 | Any mass shooting incident | N/A | | | | X | |
| 13.1 | Rosengart et al. (2005) | Shall-issue law | Total suicide rate | All ages | X | | | | |
| 13.1 | Rosengart et al. (2005) | Shall-issue law | Firearm suicide rate | All ages | X | | | | |
| 13.1 | DeSimone, Markowitz, and Xu (2013) | Shall-issue law | Self-inflicted firearm injury rate | Aged 0–17 | | X | | | |
| 13.1 | DeSimone, Markowitz, and Xu (2013) | Shall-issue law | Self-inflicted firearm injury rate | Aged 18+ | | X | | | |
| 13.2 | Rosengart et al. (2005) | Shall-issue law vs. no CC permitted | Total homicide rate | All ages | X | | | | |

**Table B.2—Continued**

| Report Figure | Study | Specific Policy or Independent Variable | Specific Outcome | Population | Parameter | Tx Units | Cluster | Model | Other |
|---|---|---|---|---|---|---|---|---|---|
| 13.2 | Rosengart et al. (2005) | Shall-issue law vs. no CC permitted | Firearm homicide rate | All ages | X | | | | |
| 13.2 | Grambsch (2008) | Shall-issue vs. no CC (random effects) | Murder rate | All ages | | | X | | |
| 13.2 | Grambsch (2008) | Shall-issue vs. no CC (fixed effects) | Murder rate | All ages | X | | X | | |
| 13.2 | French and Heagerty (2008) | Shall-issue law vs. no CC | Firearm homicide rate | All ages | | | | | |
| 13.2 | Roberts (2009) | May-issue vs. shall-issue | Total IPH rate | All ages | | | X | | |
| 13.2 | Roberts (2009) | No CC vs. shall-issue | Total IPH rate | All ages | | | X | | |
| 13.2 | Roberts (2009) | May-issue vs. shall-issue | Firearm IPH rate | All ages | | | X | | |
| 13.2 | Roberts (2009) | No CC vs. shall-issue | Firearm IPH rate | All ages | | | X | | |
| 13.2 | La Valle and Glover (2012) | May-issue | Total homicide rate | All ages | | | | | |
| 13.2 | La Valle and Glover (2012) | Shall-issue | Total homicide rate | All ages | | | | | |
| 13.2 | La Valle and Glover (2012) | May-issue | Firearm homicide rate | All ages | | | | | |
| 13.2 | La Valle and Glover (2012) | Shall-issue | Firearm homicide rate | All ages | | | | | |
| 13.2 | La Valle (2013) | Shall-issue law vs. no CC permitted | Total homicide rate | All ages | | | | | |
| 13.2 | La Valle (2013) | Shall-issue law vs. no CC permitted | Firearm homicide rate | All ages | | | | | |
| 13.2 | Webster, Crifasi, and Vernick (2014) | Shall-issue law vs. no CC permitted | Total homicide rate | All ages | X | | | X | |
| 13.2 | Webster, Crifasi, and Vernick (2014) | Shall-issue law vs. no CC permitted | Firearm homicide rate | All ages | X | | | X | |

**Table B.2—Continued**

| Report Figure | Study | Specific Policy or Independent Variable | Specific Outcome | Population | Parameter | Tx Units | Cluster | Model | Other |
|---|---|---|---|---|---|---|---|---|---|
| 13.2 | Webster, Crifasi, and Vernick (2014) | Shall-issue law vs. no CC permitted | Nonfirearm homicide rate | All ages | X | | | X | |
| 13.2 | Webster, Crifasi, and Vernick (2014) | Shall-issue law vs. no CC permitted | Murder/manslaughter rate | All ages | X | | | X | |
| 13.2 | Gius (2014) | Restrictive vs. lenient CC laws | Firearm murder rate | All ages | | | X | X | |
| 13.2 | Aneja, Donohue, and Zhang (2014) | Shall-issue vs. any other CC law | Murder rate | All ages | | | | | |
| 13.2 | Aneja, Donohue, and Zhang (2014) | Shall-issue vs. any other CC law | Rape rate | All ages | | | | | |
| 13.2 | Aneja, Donohue, and Zhang (2014) | Shall-issue vs. any other CC law | Robbery rate | All ages | | | | | |
| 13.2 | Aneja, Donohue, and Zhang (2014) | Shall-issue vs. any other CC law | Assault rate | All ages | | | | | |
| 13.2 | Martin and Legault (2005) | Shall-issue (vs. other CC law) | Violent crime | All ages | X | | X | X | |
| 13.2 | Martin and Legault (2005) | Shall-issue (vs. other CC law) | Murder rate | All ages | X | | X | X | |
| 13.2 | Martin and Legault (2005) | Shall-issue (vs. other CC law) | Rape rate | All ages | X | | X | X | |
| 13.2 | Martin and Legault (2005) | Shall-issue (vs. other CC law) | Aggravated assault | All ages | X | | X | X | |
| 13.2 | Martin and Legault (2005) | Shall-issue (vs. other CC law) | Robbery rate | All ages | X | | X | X | |

**Table B.2—Continued**

| Report Figure | Study | Specific Policy or Independent Variable | Specific Outcome | Population | Parameter | Tx Units | Cluster | Model | Other |
|---|---|---|---|---|---|---|---|---|---|
| 13.2 | Kendall and Tamura (2010) | Shall-issue (vs. other CC law) | Murder rate | All ages | | | | | |
| 13.2 | Kendall and Tamura (2010) | Shall-issue (vs. other CC law) | Rape rate | All ages | | | | | |
| 13.2 | Kendall and Tamura (2010) | Shall-issue (vs. other CC law) | Robbery rate | All ages | | | | | |
| 13.2 | Kendall and Tamura (2010) | Shall-issue (vs. other CC law) | Assault rate | All ages | | | | | |
| 13.3 | Lott and Mustard (1997) | Shall-issue law | Unintentional handgun death rate | All ages | X | | X | | |
| 13.3 | Lott and Mustard (1997) | Shall-issue law | Unintentional nonhandgun death rate | All ages | X | | X | | |
| 13.3 | DeSimone, Markowitz, and Xu (2013) | Shall-issue law | Unintentional firearm injury rate | Aged 0–17 | | X | | | |
| 13.3 | DeSimone, Markowitz, and Xu (2013) | Shall-issue law | Unintentional firearm injury rate | Aged 18+ | | X | | | |
| 13.4 | Lott (2003) | Shall-issue law | Multiple-victim gun deaths, injuries | All ages | X | | X | | |
| 13.4 | Lott (2003) | Shall-issue law | No. of multiple-victim gun incidents | All ages | X | | X | | |
| 13.4 | Luca, Deepak, and Poliquin (2016) | Permitless carry | Any mass shooting incident | All ages | | | | X | |
| 13.4 | Luca, Deepak, and Poliquin (2016) | Permitless carry | Any mass shooting incident | All ages | | | | X | |

**Table B.2—Continued**

| Report Figure | Study | Specific Policy or Independent Variable | Specific Outcome | Population | Parameter | Tx Units | Cluster | Model | Other |
|---|---|---|---|---|---|---|---|---|---|
| 13.4 | Luca, Deepak, and Poliquin (2016) | Shall-issue law | Any mass shooting incident | All ages | | | | X | |
| 13.4 | Luca, Deepak, and Poliquin (2016) | Shall-issue law | Any mass shooting incident | All ages | | | | X | |
| 13.5 | Duggan (2001) | Right-to-carry laws | Gun ownership | None | X | | | | |

NOTE: CAP = child-access prevention; CC = concealed carry; IPH = intimate partner homicide; N/A = not applicable; NICS = National Instant Criminal Background Check System.